HONG KONG COMPETITION LAW

Hong Kong Competition Law

Conor Quigley QC
Suzanne Rab
and Contributors

·H A R T·
PUBLISHING
OXFORD AND PORTLAND, OREGON
2017

Hart Publishing

An imprint of Bloomsbury Publishing Plc

Hart Publishing Ltd	Bloomsbury Publishing Plc
Kemp House	50 Bedford Square
Chawley Park	London
Cumnor Hill	WC1B 3DP
Oxford OX2 9PH	UK
UK	

www.hartpub.co.uk
www.bloomsbury.com

Published in North America (US and Canada) by
Hart Publishing
c/o International Specialized Book Services
920 NE 58th Avenue, Suite 300
Portland, OR 97213-3786
USA

www.isbs.com

**HART PUBLISHING, the Hart/Stag logo, BLOOMSBURY and the
Diana logo are trademarks of Bloomsbury Publishing Plc**

First published 2017

British Library Cataloguing-in-Publication Data
A catalogue record for this book is available from the British Library.

ISBN:	HBK:	978-1-50990-642-0
	ePDF:	978-1-50990-640-6
	ePub:	978-1-50990-641-3

Printed and bound in Great Britain by CPI Group (UK) Ltd, Croydon CR0 4YY

To find out more about our authors and books visit www.hartpublishing.co.uk. Here you will find
extracts, author information, details of forthcoming events and the option to sign up for our newsletters.

Foreword

By the President of the Hong Kong Competition Tribunal

Enacted in June 2012 and made fully operative in December 2015, the Competition Ordinance has finally brought about a cross-sector competition law in Hong Kong. With 190 sections and nine schedules, laying down three competition rules and setting up a Commission and a Tribunal, it is a major piece of legislation that has far-reaching implications for businesses and residents alike in Hong Kong. No case however has yet been filed in the Competition Tribunal and it will be many years before a body of local case-law can be built up. It is therefore particularly gratifying for me to welcome the publication of *Hong Kong Competition Law*. In this splendid volume, in addition to a comprehensive exposition of competition law in Hong Kong, the authors have also offered a piece on the rule against exploitative conduct in the telecommunications industry, an insightful discussion of the application of competition law in specific segments of the Hong Kong economy as well as a comparative overview with reference to Mainland China, Japan and South Korea. The discussions in the text have sensibly drawn on EU and UK jurisprudence and practice which may be expected to provide considerable assistance in the interpretation and application of the Competition Ordinance in Hong Kong. The authors are to be heartily congratulated for producing a work of this quality. I warmly recommend it not only to legal practitioners but also to anyone who desires a serious understanding of competition law in Hong Kong.

Godfrey Lam
Hong Kong

September 2016

Preface

On the coming into effect of the full provisions of the Competition Ordinance in December 2015, Hong Kong has joined with over 130 other jurisdictions throughout the world in having a comprehensive competition law to regulate agreements which may harm competition (the First Conduct Rule) as well as abuse of substantial market power (the Second Conduct Rule) across the Hong Kong economy. In addition, merger control (the Merger Rule) is introduced for the telecommunications sector and an additional specific rule (the Telco Rule) is established prohibiting exploitative conduct by dominant telecoms operators. Many of these new rules are mirrored in the competition laws of other countries, notably, though far from exclusively, those of the European Union. The precise formulation of the provisions of the Competition Ordinance reflects, however, specific choices of the Hong Kong legislature. For instance, whereas EU competition law prohibits the abuse of a dominant position, in Hong Kong the prohibition of abuse applies to an undertaking that has a substantial degree of market power in a market, which may not necessarily be precisely the same notion as that applying in EU law. The enforcement of the competition rules also differs in Hong Kong, with the Competition Commission having the primary role in assessing whether conduct constitutes an infringement of the rules, whilst reserving for the Competition Tribunal the power to enforce the rules against undertakings. The role of complainants is to provide the Commission with information allowing it to investigate and bring infringement proceedings. Unlike in EU law, complainants have no ability to commence court proceedings of their own accord, although they may, once a decision has been made by the Tribunal finding an infringement has been established, bring follow-on proceedings for damages.

The Competition Commission (together with the Communications Authority which regulates the telecommunications and broadcasting sectors) has issued Guidelines on the application of the competition rules and the procedures it will follow in order to give full effect to the Competition Ordinance. We have endeavoured to set out the full provisions of the Ordinance as supplemented by the Guidelines, with illustrative case law on the application of the applicable principles in EU law as well as other jurisdictions, such as Malaysia, Singapore and the United Kingdom. We have deliberately kept the EU case law to a minimum, since there are many books giving a detailed exposition of EU competition law, and the purpose of including EU references is primarily to show how the law might develop in Hong Kong. Whilst this case law is not binding on the Hong Kong authorities, it will be a most useful starting point for analysing the application of competition law in Hong Kong and enable the Commission and the Tribunal, as well as all those affected by the new rules, to understand the wider implications of the Competition Ordinance. In addition, we have included detailed discussion of existing structures of competition in the main sectors of the Hong Kong economy (construction, energy, financial services, retail, telecommunications and transport) and how these will be affected by the Ordinance. Finally, we include a comparative summary of competition law in mainland China, Japan and South Korea.

We have written the chapters on the substantive content of the competition rules are most grateful to our colleagues who have contributed to the other chapters as follows: Richard Khaw SC, Queenie Lau and Theresa Chow, Temple Chambers, Hong Kong (Chapter 5, Enforcement Procedures); Neil Carabine, Edmund Wan and James Wilkinson, King & Wood Mallesons (Chapter 7, Construction); Duncan Gillespie, consultant solicitor, New Media Law (Chapter 7, Energy); Oliver Bretz and Sarah Long (with research by Joe Ming San Lee), Euclid Law (Chapter 7, Financial Services); Adam Ferguson and Abigail Green, Eversheds (Chapter 7, Retail); Nicolas J Taylor and Alan P Davis (with research by Talia Calgaro), Jones Day (Chapter 7, Telecommunications); Anthony Woolich and Caroline Thomas, Holman Fenwick Willan [Caroline Thomas is now at Laracy & Co.], together with Jonathan Beard and Mark Peacock, ICF International (Chapter 7, Transport); Jet Deng and Ken Dai, Dentons (Chapter 8, China); Kentaro Hirayama, Morrison & Foerster (Chapter 8, Japan); and Sanghoon Shin, Bae, Kim & Lee (Chapter 8, South Korea).

CONOR QUIGLEY Q.C.
SUZANNE RAB
Serle Court, Lincoln's Inn
London

1 October 2016

CONTENTS

TABLE OF CASES

COURT OF JUSTICE OF THE EUROPEAN UNION

GENERAL COURT OF THE EUROPEAN UNION

ENGLISH COURTS

HONG KONG COURTS

UNITED STATES COURTS

TABLE OF COMPETITION ORDINANCE REFERENCES

Chapter One

THE COMPETITION ORDINANCE

1.1 A NEW COMPETITION LAW FOR HONG KONG

Hong Kong's Competition Ordinance 2012   The Competition Ordinance[1] 2012, which fully entered into force as of 14 December 2015, has implemented a new comprehensive competition law in Hong Kong. Despite the fact that competition law already applies in over 130 different jurisdictions throughout the world, this is first time that an economy-wide competition law has been adopted in Hong Kong, superseding the previous regime that regulated solely the telecommunications and broadcasting sectors. The adoption of a generally applicable competition law in Hong Kong is, therefore, consistent with the global trend in competition law compliance. Hong Kong's businesses and consumers are much like anywhere else, with differences in nature, conduct and needs arising from the particular characteristics that make Hong Kong different. Among the matters that appear important in considering the appropriate structure of competition law in Hong Kong are the relative small size of the economy, the limited number of players in some industries, the prospects for trade with other countries and the relationship with other trade partners, particularly the People's Republic of China. These features do not mean that competition law cannot be of benefit to Hong Kong's already vibrant economy. Rather, the law needs to be developed and applied as part of a consistent policy that is coherent with Hong Kong's legal, economic and policy context.

In assessing and analysing the likely development of Hong Kong's competition law, it is appropriate to take an international comparative perspective, whilst at the same time recognising the relevance and limitations of international comparisons. The Competition Ordinance is most closely based on the main elements of European Union competition law. In addition, the United Kingdom, the United States, Australia and some South and East Asian countries, notably Japan, Malaysia, Singapore and South Korea, have a number of interesting features, differences and complementarities in terms of their economic, political and legal frameworks which make a comparison between their respective competition regimes particularly useful in seeking to answer the most important question of what will or should happen in Hong Kong and where might international insights and experience be relevant.

---

[1]   Cap 619.

Development of competition law in Hong Kong　Hong Kong may be regarded as a relatively late adopter of competition law. Despite the introduction of competition law in other prominent Asian economies much earlier, including in China in 2007, it was not until 2012 with the passage of the Competition Ordinance that Hong Kong put competition law on a legislative footing across all economic sectors. The enactment of the Competition Ordinance itself followed years of consultation and resistance among industry and government and for a time Hong Kong defended its pre-existing sector-specific model of competition control in the telecommunications and broadcasting sectors as responsive to the needs of its economy. Indeed, for some time, it was questioned whether there was a need for a general competition law in Hong Kong at all. The Hong Kong government was for some time an opponent of competition law on the international stage such as at the World Trade Organisation.[2] When the Hong Kong government issued its competition policy in May 1998, through a formal policy statement[3] and establishment of the Competition Policy Advisory Group (COMPAG) it stated that instead of introducing a general competition law, it would adopt a sector-specific competition policy framework for the telecommunications and broadcasting sectors. This was based on a view that an economy-wide competition law would not be able to take into account the specific requirements of the individual sectors and that having such a law would amount to overkill. It was also contended that setting up a cross-sector competition authority would be too expensive and would duplicate the functions of existing regulatory bodies. Moreover, Hong Kong was a small and externally-oriented economy that was already highly competitive, so that there was no need for an all-encompassing competition law. This initially resistant approach nevertheless made way for a government announcement in 2007 that Hong Kong should follow its neighbours, notably Singapore which had enacted cross-sector competition law in 2004.

The Competition Ordinance itself came into effect only in part in 2012 with its full entry into force over three years after its initial enactment. In the interim, important steps were taken to pave the way for full implementation. The Competition Tribunal was established as a superior court of record with its primary jurisdiction to hear and adjudicate upon competition cases. The Competition Commission progressed with preparatory work to prepare guidance for business. On 26 May 2014 the Commission consulted with stakeholders on their trade practices to inform its drafting of practical guidelines.[4] It asked stakeholders to provide feedback on a number of issues

---

2　World Trade Organisation Working Group on the Interaction between Trade and Competition Policy, Report on the Meeting of Feb. 20-21 2003, WT/WGTCP/M/21.

3　Competition Policy Advisory Group, Statement on Competition Policy, May 1998.

4　Competition Commission paper, Getting Prepared for the Full Implementation of the Competition Ordinance, 26 May 2014.

including: common trade practices in Hong Kong which may prevent anti-competitive risk; experiences of vertical agreements, in particular resale price maintenance and their efficiencies and risks; views on how to analyse market power and factors to take into account; experiences of information sharing and joint purchasing agreements; experiences of tying and bundling practices; and concerns on the application of the merger rule in the telecommunications sector. The Commission also provided an indication of the areas in which it was likely to prioritise its enforcement activities, at least in the early stage of implementation.

On 27 July 2015 the Competition Commission issued six Guidelines which provide guidance on how it intends to interpret and apply the provisions of the Competition Ordinance in relation to the First Conduct Rule, the Second Conduct Rule, the Merger Rule, Applications for a Decision under Sections 9 and 24 (Exclusions and Exemptions) and Section 15 Block Exemption Orders, Complaints and Investigations. The Guidelines do not have legislative force although they may influence the Competition Tribunal and the courts in interpreting the Competition Ordinance. The Commission also launched a consultation on its leniency policy in September 2015, proposing that it may make a leniency agreement with a person to the effect that it will not bring or continue proceedings in the Competition Tribunal for a financial penalty in exchange for that person's cooperation in an investigation or in proceedings under the Competition Ordinance. The policy resembles many of the features of other leniency regimes internationally and applies only to Serious Anti-Competitive Conduct under the Ordinance (i.e. price fixing, market sharing, output limitation and bid rigging). The final guidance was published in November 2015.[5]

As a final step before the full implementation of the Competition Ordinance in November 2015 the Commission published a policy document on its enforcement policy. This provides guidance on how the Commission intends to exercise its enforcement function in investigating possible contraventions of the competition rules. In particular, it prioritises the use of the Commission's operational resources to investigate conduct that may contravene the Conduct Rules in an efficient and timely manner and identifies an enforcement response that is suitable and proportionate where a contravention of the competition Ordinance has occurred.

Pre-existing competition law for telecoms and broadcasting Prior to the adoption of the Competition Ordinance, Hong Kong had a sector-specific competition law in specific provisions of the Telecommunications Ordinance and the Broadcasting Ordinance applicable to the telecommunications and broadcasting sectors and enforced by the Communications Authority through the Office of Telecommunications Authority. Regulation was introduced in the

---

[5] Leniency Policy for Undertakings Engaged in Cartel Conduct, November 2015.

telecoms sector in 1995 when it was liberalised through the introduction of three new telecoms operators to compete with Hong Kong Telecom (HKT) in the local fixed line telephone service market. Each of the four operators was granted a Fixed Telecommunications Network Services (FTNS) licence which contained competition law prohibitions as General Conditions (GCs). The regulation of the telecoms sector imposed both *ex ante* and *ex post* controls on dominant companies. Under the *ex ante* regime, a dominant company is subject to specific restrictions on conduct. Under the *ex post* regime the dominant company's conduct is regulated after the event. Over the years, Hong Kong made significant progress towards liberalisation in the telecoms sector. Hong Kong Telecom (which later became PCCW-HKT) was treated as dominant in every market in which it operated when it was granted its FTNS licence in 1995. PCCW-HKT progressively applied for declassification as dominant on a market-by-market basis and by 2005 was no longer classified as dominant in any relevant market.

The limited sector-specific approach suffered from defects, notably that the rules under the Telecommunications Ordinance and the Broadcasting Ordinance applied only to relevant licensees so that the Communications Authority had no jurisdiction over non-licensees. This presented an obvious gap where the regulator was unable to address competition problems in the sector where the undertaking responsible was not a relevant licensee. It was also powerless to address competition concerns in other markets.[6] With the passage of the Competition Ordinance and following a transitional period some of the competition provisions of the Telecommunications Ordinance and all of the competition provisions of the Broadcasting Ordinance were repealed.

Despite the move to economy-wide competition law enforcement by the Competition Commission, some of the vestiges of the old regime remain. First, while the Commission is the principal competition authority responsible for enforcing the Competition Ordinance, it has concurrent jurisdiction with the Communications Authority to apply the First Conduct Rule, the Second Conduct Rule and the Merger Rule to the conduct of certain undertakings operating in the telecommunications and broadcasting sectors. Second, the Competition Ordinance creates, through an amendment to the Telecommunications Ordinance, a new prohibition on exploitative conduct that applies only to telecoms licensees holding a dominant position and which is enforced by the Communications Authority.

International influences on Hong Kong's competition law The structure and content of Hong Kong's competition law is heavily influenced by the

---

[6] This was demonstrated by the *Banyan Garden* case where the Communications Authority was forced to adopt a convoluted analysis due to the limitations of the sector-specific regulation. Case T 261/03, *Telephone and Internet Access Services at Banyan Garden Estate* [2003].

competition laws adopted in other jurisdictions, principally the European Union. Specific influences can also be inferred from the competition and anti-trust laws applicable in Australia, Malaysia and Singapore, the United Kingdom, the United States and other jurisdictions.

The European Union is currently a group of 28 individual Member States. One of its core aims is the creation of a single or internal market, with the elimination of barriers to inter-state trade, balanced economic growth and price stability, and a highly competitive social market economy.[7] The internal market includes a system ensuring that competition is not distorted.[8] The main behavioural provisions of Hong Kong's competition law, i.e. the First Conduct Rule and the Second Conduct Rule in section 6 and section 21 of the Competition Ordinance contain identical wording in material respects to Articles 101 and 102 of the Treaty on the Functioning of the European Union (TFEU), dealing with anti-competitive agreements and abuse of a dominant position, respectively. These provisions are implemented and enforced principally by the European Commission, subject to review by the Court of Justice and the General Court of the European Union. Articles 101 and 102 TFEU are also enforced by national competition authorities of the Member States and may be invoked before national courts. The Member States also have national competition laws, based principally on the provisions of Articles 101 and 102 TFEU.

The United Kingdom has a long tradition of regulating anti-competitive practices, including through the restraint of trade doctrine at common law and historically the Restrictive Trade Practices Act 1976. The Chapter I and Chapter II prohibitions contained in the Competition Act 1998, which are effectively the UK domestic equivalent to the EU provisions on anti-competitive and abusive practices, apply where the relevant practices may have an effect on trade in the UK. The UK competition authorities and courts also have powers to apply Articles 101 and 102 TFEU. Hong Kong, which has been a special administrative region of China since 1997, is a former British colony and is, accordingly, the only Chinese region whose legal system has English common law characteristics, albeit supplemented by local law. It is well placed to take account of the legal norms and best practices from the UK.

Where the Competition Ordinance has departed from the approach under EU law, it has adopted some approaches that have counterparts in the UK. For example, Hong Kong has adopted a voluntary merger control system whereby an undertaking must not, directly or indirectly, carry out a merger that has, or is likely to have, the effect of substantially lessening competition in Hong Kong. The test of substantial lessening of competition is also used under the UK's voluntary merger control system. This may be contrasted with the approach

---

[7]   Treaty on European Union (TEU), Article 3.
[8]   TEU, Protocol No 27.

under the EU Merger Regulation[9] which imposes a mandatory pre-notification and suspensory requirement where a transaction is assessed according to whether it gives rise to a significant impediment to effective competition. The system whereby the Competition Commission is the principal competition authority responsible for enforcing the Competition Ordinance, but has concurrent jurisdiction with the Communications Authority in respect of the anti-competitive conduct of certain undertakings operating in the telecommunications and broadcasting sectors is also mirrored in the UK.[10]

The United States has had a free market economy from inception. One of the greatest challenges was curbing anti-competitive practices by monopoly business. This led to the enactment of legislation designed to regulate anti-competitive agreements (cartels) and monopoly power in the late 19th and 20th centuries, including the Sherman Act 1890, the Clayton Act 1914, the Federal Trade Commission Act 1914 and, most recently, dealing with merger control, the Hart-Scott-Rodino Antitrust Improvements Act 1976. The US Federal Government, via both the Antitrust Division of the US Department of Justice (DoJ) and the Federal Trade Commission (FTC), can bring civil lawsuits enforcing the antitrust laws. State attorneys general may file suits to enforce both state and federal antitrust laws. The DoJ alone may bring criminal antitrust suits under federal antitrust laws. As provided by the Hart-Scott-Rodino Antitrust Improvements Act 1976, larger companies attempting to merge must first notify, as appropriate, the FTC/DoJ's Antitrust Division prior to consummating a merger where the relevant commerce test, size of parties test and size of transaction test are met. Although the substantive content of the Competition Ordinance is closer to the TFEU and the UK Competition Act 1998, features of the prosecutorial system under the Competition Ordinance resemble the institutional framework in the US. In particular, the Competition Commission does not have the power to make a final infringement decision in respect of the competition rules but must instead apply to the Competition Tribunal for such a ruling. Similarly, in criminal cartel cases, while the DoJ may issue an indictment, this is not a conclusion that a crime has been committed but merely a finding that there is enough evidence to have a trial. Indicted companies and individuals have the right to trial by jury.

Competition law across the Asia-Pacific region Most countries across the Asia-Pacific region have had legislation on competition law in place before Hong Kong and new laws are in the pipeline. The end of 2015 marked the coming into force of economy-wide competition law in Hong Kong and also

---

[9]   Council Regulation (EC) 139/2004, OJ 2004 L24/1.
[10] The Competition and Markets Authority, as the principal UK competition authority, has powers of investigation and enforcement in relation to Article 101 and 102 TFEU in addition to the Chapter I and II prohibitions of the UK Competition Act 1998. The sector regulators have concurrent powers in relation to their respective industries.

the target date for the ten member states of the Association of South East Asian Nations (ASEAN) to have competition law in place. Against an increasingly globalised antitrust enforcement environment, many of these newer competition laws draw inspiration from the more established regimes, notably those of the EU and the US. The progression of competition law across Asia has created a complex regulatory environment for international businesses seeking to navigate the different systems, often with their local idiosyncrasies. There are calls for greater harmonisation and consistency in the rules and enforcement policies. Yet in a region that is characterised by economic, political and cultural diversity, it may be asked whether greater rationalisation is possible, or even desirable.

Important differentiators include culture, the relatively small size of the economy, the limited number of players in some industries, the prospects for trade with other countries, and the role of the State in the economy. To illustrate the contrasts, some of the ASEAN countries, such as Cambodia and Laos, have very low standards of living compared with the more vibrant economies in Japan, Hong Kong, Singapore or South Korea. Both India and China face a consumer revolution where addressing consumer demands requires supplying more of the right quality goods, improving services and enhancing value for money. But there are differences in size, trade policies and the pace of economic and social development. India is a constitutional or parliamentary democracy, with a population density of 360 inhabitants per square km, a literacy rate of 66% and infant mortality at 55/1000 live births. Contrast this with China, a communist republic with a population density of 129 per square km, a literacy rate of 93% and infant mortality at 23/1000 live births. This does not mean, however, that competition law cannot be of benefit to economies at different stages of development. Rather, the law needs to be formulated and applied as part of a consistent policy that is coherent with the relevant legal, economic and policy context.

There are thus similarities and differences in the approaches that have been adopted to key competition law issues under other competition regimes in South East Asia. Whereas Hong Kong allows for sectoral competition enforcement for telecommunications and broadcasting, India, Indonesia, Japan, Malaysia, Singapore, South Korea, Taiwan, Thailand and Vietnam each have a single dedicated competition authority responsible for economy-wide competition law enforcement. In China, responsibility for enforcing competition law is split between the Ministry of Commerce (MOFCOM), the State Administration for Industry and Commerce (SAIC) and the National Development and Reform Commission (NDRC).

The basic prohibitions of restrictive agreements and abuse of substantial market power or dominance form the central planks of competition law across Asia. The third plank, merger control, is not present in all regimes. While the basic legal tools are similar, there are differences in the enforcement policy and framework. In China, for example, in addition to the stated goals of restraining monopolies and protecting fair market competition, the AML seeks to promote the healthy development of a socialist market economy. In Indonesia, Malaysia and Thailand the competition authority has emphasised that its role includes the protection of smaller companies from more powerful rivals. The regimes can differ in the extent to which they afford exclusions or exemptions from the basic competition law prohibitions. Hong Kong's new competition law provides specific turnover-based exemptions for small and medium sized enterprises and envisages a procedure for individual and block exemptions, whereas in China there are currently no block exemptions of the type existing under EU competition law. Another area that has prompted intense debate relates to the relationship between competition law and intellectual property rights. In India there is a limited exception to the prohibition of anti-competitive agreements which allows reasonable conditions to protect any rights conferred under specific intellectual property legislation.[11] This is restricted to a limited set of rights granted under Indian law and does not apply to cases of abuse of dominance. China's AML contains a similar provision.[12]

Asian countries have adopted different models of merger control. The mandatory premerger filing plus suspension model applies, for example, in China, India, Japan, South Korea, Taiwan and Vietnam. Singapore and Hong Kong have followed the approach in Australia, New Zealand and the UK with voluntary merger control. However, there is no sector-wide merger control in Hong Kong, which limits merger control to the telecommunications sector. The voluntary model has its supporters and has generally worked well in the more established jurisdictions, partly aided by the predictability afforded by a history of decisional practice and guidance. Indonesia's system is a hybrid mandatory post-merger notification system, carrying the risk that a transaction could be unwound after completion if found to be problematic. Malaysia is an outlier with no merger control system in force and no exception from the conduct prohibitions for concentrations.

Challenges of a new competition law for Hong Kong The implementation of a new competition law requires a long-term investment in building awareness of the role of competition law and a tough approach to anti-competitive practices. The complexities of competition law and the introduction of unfamiliar technical concepts mean that the authorities and courts need to be equipped with the necessary legal, financial and economics skills to apply the law intelligently and effectively. It is clear that other competition authorities in Asia and internationally have provided support to the Competition Commission as it has built up capacity in its inception and launch period and some have seconded staff to assist the new authority in its early stages. The new authority is likely to have regard to the experience in other

---

[11]　Competition Act 2002, section 3(5)(i).
[12]　AML, Article 55.

common law jurisdictions and the EU when considering how similar issues have been treated in similar contexts. Moreover, various guidelines adopted by these competition authorities form a useful source of information and inspiration in determining the meaning and effect of the competition rules and enforcement procedures in the Competition Ordinance. It is essential, however, to appreciate the limits of international comparisons due to the different economic, physical and regulatory contexts. International comparisons need to be understood in context so as to inform the basic questions as to what would happen in Hong Kong, taking account of what happened elsewhere and whether any relevant lessons can be learned. The following examples may serve to illustrate the limitations of international comparisons.

Different policy objectives may apply. The First Conduct Rule and the Second Conduct Rule contain substantively equivalent provisions to Articles 101 and 102 TFEU and it can be expected that the Competition Commission and the Competition Tribunal will frequently look to EU precedents for guidance on how similar concepts and issues have been approached by the European Commission and the EU Courts. Nevertheless, it is important to bear in mind that EU competition cases are often decided with internal market integration objectives in mind and that this EU policy does not have an equivalent in Hong Kong. On the other hand, it is likely that the question of the correct geographic scope of reference is going to be increasingly important when evaluating competition cases in Hong Kong. Although Hong Kong is a compact territorial unit, that should not necessarily lead to a geographical market being confined to that territory.

Procedural rules may be assessed in their historical context. For example, Hong Kong has adopted a procedure whereby a party may apply to the Competition Commission for a decision as to whether or not the conduct in question is excluded or exempt from the First Conduct Rule. This resembles the former EU procedure whereby parties to an agreement could notify any agreement, decision or practice, to the European Commission with an application for negative clearance, that is to say, a ruling that, on the basis of the facts in its possession, there were no grounds under Article 101(1) TFEU for action on its part in respect of the agreement, decision or practice. This possibility ceased, as a matter of EU law in 2004, and was replaced by a self-assessment procedure.

Finally, if the conclusion reached by relevant decision makers in Hong Kong is that the international practice is inappropriate for Hong Kong and that it should be reviewed in the light of legal and market developments, it would of course be appropriate to develop an approach that is different for Hong Kong. It should not be overlooked, however, that the practices in the EU, the UK and the US have been developed after lengthy experience and drawing on insights from established competition regimes. In some circumstances, however, it may be more appropriate to seek guidance from the smaller South East Asian economies, such as Malaysia and Singapore, or Australia, where economic or legal conditions may be closer to those in Hong Kong.

1.2 THE COMPETITION RULES

Competition rules in the Competition Ordinance   The Competition Ordinance applies a comprehensive system of competition rules covering anti-competitive agreements, abuse of market power and merger control. Following its enactment in 2012, it came into effect in stages, with an institutional framework becoming operational in 2013, guidelines concerning the competition rules and their enforcement being published in July 2015, and the entry into force of its substantive provisions on 14 December 2015. The substantive competition rules of the Competition Ordinance comprise the First Conduct Rule, the Second Conduct Rule and the Merger Rule.   The Competition Commission and the Competition Tribunal are the main institutional bodies, providing for separate administrative and judicial enforcement functions.

The First Conduct Rule prohibits agreements between undertakings, decisions by associations of undertakings and concerted practices that have as their object or effect the prevention, restriction or distortion of competition in Hong Kong.[13]   The Second Conduct Rule prohibits an undertaking with substantial market power from abusing that power by engaging in conduct that has as its object or effect the prevention, restriction or distortion of competition in Hong Kong.[14] The Merger Rule prohibits an undertaking from carrying out, directly or indirectly, a merger that has, or is likely to have, the effect of substantially lessening competition in Hong Kong.[15] Together these three rules are known as the competition rules.[16]   In addition, the Competition Ordinance amends the Telecommunications Ordinance[17] by introducing the Telco Rule which prohibits a licensee in a dominant position in the telecommunications market from engaging in conduct that is exploitative.[18]

Competition Commission and Communications Authority   The Competition Commission, established pursuant to section 129 of the Competition Ordinance,[19] is the principal competition authority responsible for

---

[13]   Competition Ordinance, section 6(1).

[14]   Competition Ordinance, section 21(1).

[15]   Competition Ordinance, Schedule 7, section 3(1).

[16]   Competition Ordinance, section 2(1).

[17]   Cap 106.

[18]   Competition Ordinance, Schedule 8, section 13, adding section 7Q to the Telecommunications Ordinance.

[19]   Competition Ordinance, section 129(2) provides that the Competition Commission is a body corporate and may:

applying and enforcing the Competition Ordinance. It has 14 members, including the Chairperson, who are appointed by the Chief Executive of the Hong Kong Special Administrative Region. The Commission members are drawn from different fields, including those who have relevant expertise and experience in industry, commerce, economics, law, small and medium enterprises, accounting, finance and consumer protection. In so far as they relate to the conduct of undertakings in the telecommunications and broadcasting sectors, the Communications Authority may perform the functions of the Commission under the Competition Ordinance.[20] References to the Competition Commission are to be read as including the Communications Authority.[21] The Commission has entered into a Memorandum of Understanding with the Communications Authority to coordinate the performance of their functions under the Competition Ordinance.[22]

The Competition Commission is tasked with the following functions:[23]

- to investigate conduct that may contravene the competition rules of the Competition Ordinance and enforce the provisions of the Ordinance;
- to promote public understanding of the value of competition and how the Competition Ordinance promotes competition;
- to promote the adoption by undertakings carrying on business in Hong Kong of appropriate internal controls and risk management systems and to ensure their compliance with the Competition Ordinance;
- to advise the Government on competition matters in Hong Kong and outside Hong Kong;
- to conduct market studies into matters affecting competition in markets in Hong Kong; and

---

(a) acquire, hold and dispose of movable and immovable property;

(b) sue and be sued in its own name; and

(c) so far as is possible for a body corporate, exercise all the rights and powers, enjoy all the privileges and incur all the liabilities of a natural person of full age and capacity.

Schedule 5 contains constitutional, administrative and financial provisions with respect to the Commission.

20 Competition Ordinance, section 159(1). The Communications Authority may perform the functions of the Competition Commission under the Competition Ordinance, in so far as they relate to the conduct of undertakings that are:

(a) licensees under the Telecommunications Ordinance or the Broadcasting Ordinance;

(b) persons who, although not such licensees, are persons whose activities require them to be licensed under the Telecommunications Ordinance or the Broadcasting Ordinance; or

(c) persons who have been exempted from the Telecommunications Ordinance or from specified provisions of that Ordinance under section 39 of that Ordinance.

21 Competition Ordinance, section 159(2).

22 Competition Ordinance, section 161 and Schedule 6. The text of the MoU is at: https://www.compcomm.hk/en/about/inter_agency/files/MoU_e_final_signed.pdf

23 Competition Ordinance, section 130.

- to promote research into and the development of skills in relation to the legal, economic and policy aspects of competition law in Hong Kong.

The Commission may do all such things as appear to it to be necessary, advantageous or expedient for it to do for, or in connection with, the performance of its functions.[24] It is not a servant or agent of the Hong Kong Government and does not enjoy any status, immunity or privilege of the Government.[25]   Members of the Commission, as well as officers and employees of the Commission, enjoy immunity for anything done or omitted to be done in the performance of its functions.[26]

Guidelines issued by the Competition Commission   Various provisions in the Competition Ordinance require the adoption of guidelines by the Competition Commission. In particular, it has issued a series of guidelines pursuant to section 35(1) of the Competition Ordinance in relation to the First and Second Conduct Rules and section 17 of Schedule 7 of the Competition Ordinance in relation to the Merger Rule.[27] The guidelines set out how the Commission intends to interpret and give effect to the competition rules and how it expects to exercise its power to make decisions and grant block exemptions, providing several hypothetical examples.[28] The guidelines may be amended by the Commission.[29] Before issuing any guidelines or amendments,

---

[24] Competition Ordinance, section 131. The Commission may:
  (a) make, give effect to, assign or accept the assignment of, vary or rescind any agreement;
  (b) receive and spend money;
  (c) with the approval of the Financial Secretary, borrow money;
  (d) invest funds of the Commission that are not immediately required, in a manner approved by the Financial Secretary;
  (e) with the approval of the Chief Executive, become a member or affiliate of any international body, whose functions or objects include the promotion of competition or competition law.
[25] Competition Ordinance, section 132.
[26] Competition Ordinance, section 133. This does not affect any liability of the Commission itself for the act or omission.
[27] These guidelines are issued jointly with the Communications Authority which has concurrent jurisdiction with the Competition Commission in respect of the anti-competitive conduct of certain undertakings operating in the telecommunications and broadcasting sectors: Competition Ordinance, section 159(1).
[28] Competition Ordinance, section 35(1) and Schedule 7, section 17(1).
[29] Competition Ordinance, section 35(2) Schedule 7, section 17(2). The Guidelines, and any amendments made to them, may be published in any manner the Competition Commission considers appropriate and must be made available at the Commission's offices, on the internet and in any other manner the Commission considers appropriate: Competition Ordinance, section 35(3) and (5) and Schedule 7, section 17(3) and (5).

the Commission must consult the Legislative Council and any persons it considers appropriate.[30]

The guidelines describe the general approach which the Commission intends to apply, subject to the need to adapt, as appropriate, to the facts and circumstances of the individual matter under consideration. The Competition Tribunal and other courts, however, are responsible ultimately for interpreting the Competition Ordinance, and the Commission's interpretation does not bind them. The application of the guidelines may, therefore, need to be modified in light of the case law of the courts. The guidelines are not a substitute for the Competition Ordinance and do not have binding legal effect.[31] In particular, a person does not incur any civil or criminal liability only because he has contravened any guidelines.[32] Nevertheless, if, in any legal proceedings, the Competition Tribunal or any other court is satisfied that a guideline is relevant to determining a matter that is in issue, the guideline is permissible in evidence in the proceedings and proof that a person contravened or did not contravene the guideline may be relied on by any party to the proceedings as tending to establish or negate the matter.[33] Guidelines are also required to be, and have been, issued by the Commission in relation to its powers concerning complaints[34] and investigations.[35] These guidelines are subject to the same criteria as regards their legal effects.[36]

Competition Tribunal   The Competition Ordinance establishes a dual administrative and judicial system with separate judicial enforcement of the competition rules, whereby the administrative Competition Commission investigates and brings proceedings before the judicial Competition Tribunal which decides if there is a breach of the relevant rules. This is in contra-distinction to models adopted by some other jurisdictions, e.g. the European Union, where the European Commission not only conducts investigations but also imposes sanctions subject only to judicial review in the EU courts. Hong Kong has adopted a judicial enforcement model, whereby the Competition Commission is responsible for handling complaints, conducting investigations and bringing public enforcement action before the Competition Tribunal, whereas the Competition Tribunal adjudicates on competition cases brought by the Commission, reviews of determinations of the Commission and private follow-on actions for damages. In fact, it was the original intention of the Hong Kong government to adopt the administrative model, and in the first draft

---

[30]   Competition Ordinance, section 35(4) and Schedule 7, section 17(4).

[31]   Moreover, the Guidelines do not have the status of subsidiary legislation: Competition Ordinance, section 35(8) and Schedule 7, section 17(8).

[32]   Competition Ordinance, section 35(6) and Schedule 7, section 17(6).

[33]   Competition Ordinance, section 35(7) and Schedule 7, section 17(7).

[34]   Competition Ordinance, section 38.

[35]   Competition Ordinance, section 40.

[36]   Competition Ordinance, section 59.

of the Competition Bill, the Commission was given the power to impose fines.[37]   However, during the drafting process, the Court of Final Appeal decided *Koon Wing Yee v. Insider Dealing Tribunal*,[38] in which it was held that if a fine of a punitive nature is to be imposed in an administrative proceeding, there must be procedural safeguards of a criminal standard provided to the defendants. As the Commission cannot provide criminal procedural safeguards in its internal process, this effectively precludes the adoption of the administrative model in Hong Kong.[39]

The Competition Tribunal is a specialised tribunal established under section 134 of the Competition Ordinance as a superior court of record.[40]   It consists of all Judges of the Court of First Instance, excluding Deputy High Court Judges and Recorders.[41]   It has a President, Deputy President, registrar and bailiff.[42] The President of the Competition Tribunal may sit alone or with more members.   Assessors may also be appointed to assist and advise on technicalities.[43]   The Competition Tribunal has extensive power to grant remedies as in the Court of First Instance.[44]   It hears the following:

(a) cases brought by the Competition Commission for sanctions/redress;[45]
(b) appeals in respect of the Competition Commission's decisions relating to exemptions, exclusions, commitments and leniency;[46]
(c) appeals from decisions of the Tribunal registrar;[47] and
(d) private follow-on damages actions for infringement of the Conduct Rules.[48]

The First Conduct Rule The First Conduct Rule, which is set out in section 6(1) of the Competition Ordinance, prohibits agreements and arrangements that harm competition. It provides that an undertaking must not:[49]

(a) make or give effect to an agreement,
(b) engage in a concerted practice, or

---

[37] See the Report of the Bills Committee on Competition Bill (CB(1)1919/11-12), para 7.
[38] *Koon Wing Yee v. Insider Dealing Tribunal* (2008) 11 HKCFAR 170.
[39] See Ready for Action: Looking Ahead to the Implementation of Hong Kong's Competition Ordinance, Journal of European Competition Law & Practice, 2014, Vol. 5, No. 2, p. 88, Thomas Cheng at p. 91.
[40] Rules of the Tribunal can be found at Cap. 619D (Competition Tribunal Rules). Practice Directions relate to proceedings before the Tribunal (CTPD 1) and confidential information (CTPD 2) respectively.
[41] Competition Ordinance, section 135.
[42] Competition Ordinance, sections 136-138, 156.
[43] Competition Ordinance, section 141.
[44] Competition Ordinance section 142.
[45] Competition Ordinance, sections 92-105.
[46] Competition Ordinance, sections 83-89.
[47] Competition Tribunal Rules, Rule 42.
[48] Competition Ordinance, sections 110-112.
[49] Competition Ordinance, section 6(1).

(c) as a member of an association of undertakings, make or give effect to a decision of the association,

if the object or effect of the agreement, concerted practice or decision is to prevent, restrict or distort competition in Hong Kong.

The First Conduct Rule does not apply to any agreement that:[50]

    (a) contributes to the following objectives:

        (i) improving production or distribution; or

        (ii) promoting technical or economic progress,

        while allowing consumers a fair share of the resulting benefit;

    (b) does not impose on the undertakings concerned restrictions that are not indispensable to the attainment of those objectives; and

    (c) does not afford the undertakings concerned the possibility of eliminating competition in respect of a substantial part of the goods or services in question.

Except in cases involving Serious Anti-Competitive Conduct, the First Conduct Rule does not apply to agreements, practices or decisions of lesser significance, i.e. where the combined turnover of the undertakings involved does not exceed HK$200 million.[51]

The Competition Commission may issue block exemption orders in respect of a particular category of agreements.[52] On application by an undertaking, the Commission may also issue individual decisions as to whether or not an agreement is excluded from the application of the First Conduct Rule or covered by a block exemption.[53] However, in general, it is for undertakings to determine, on the basis of legal advice, whether their agreements comply with the First Conduct Rule.[54]

The Competition Commission has issued a Guideline on the First Conduct Rule[55] which sets out how it intends to interpret and give effect to the First Conduct Rule. In addition, a separate Guideline on Applications for decisions concerning exclusions and exemptions from the First Conduct Rule has been published.[56]

The Second Conduct Rule   The Second Conduct Rule, which is set out in section 21(1) of the Competition Ordinance, provides that an undertaking that has a substantial degree of market power in a market must not abuse that power by engaging in conduct that has as its object or effect the prevention, restriction or distortion of competition in Hong Kong.[57]

---

[50]   Competition Ordinance, Schedule 1, section 1.
[51]   Competition Ordinance, Schedule 1, section 5(1)-(2).
[52]   Competition Ordinance, section 15(1).
[53]   Competition Ordinance, section 9(1).
[54]   Guideline on the First Conduct Rule, Annex, para 1.2.
[55]   Guideline on the First Conduct Rule, 27 July 2015.
[56]   Guideline on Applications, 27 July 2015.
[57]   Competition Ordinance, section 21(1).

The Second Conduct Rule does not apply to conduct of lesser significance, i.e. conduct engaged in by an undertaking the turnover of which does not exceed HK$40 million.[58] There is no general exception that conduct falling within the scope of the Second Conduct Rule may be exempt on grounds of economic efficiency or other objective justification. On application by an undertaking, the Commission may issue individual decisions as to whether or not conduct is excluded or exempted from the application of the Second Conduct Rule.[59] In general, it is for undertakings to determine, on the basis of legal advice, whether their conduct complies with the Second Conduct Rule.[60]

The Competition Commission has issued a Guideline on the Second Conduct Rule.[61] The Guideline sets out how they intend to interpret and give effect to the Second Conduct Rule. In addition, the Guideline on Applications also deals with decisions concerning exclusions and exemptions from the Second Conduct Rule.[62]

Compliance with legal requirements excludes Conduct Rules The First Conduct Rule does not apply to an agreement to the extent that it is made for the purposes of complying with a legal requirement imposed by or under any enactment[63] in force in Hong Kong or imposed by any national law applying in Hong Kong pursuant to Article 18 of the Basic Law.[64] Similarly, the Second Conduct Rule does not apply to any conduct to the extent that it is engaged in for the purpose of complying with such a legal requirement.[65] Similar provisions may be found in UK, Malaysian and Singaporean competition legislation. Although there is no equivalent in EU legislation, the EU courts have recognised that the competition rules do not apply if anti-competitive conduct is required of undertakings by legislation or if the applicable legal framework itself eliminates any possibility of competitive activity on their part,[66] except that, where the legislative framework leaves scope for competitive conduct by allowing some autonomy on the part of the undertakings concerned, they must seek to avoid compromising the remaining competition.[67] The exemption applies only in respect of legal obligations

---

[58] Competition Ordinance, Schedule 1, section 6(1).
[59] Competition Ordinance, section 24(1).
[60] Guideline on the Second Conduct Rule, Annex, para 1.2.
[61] Guideline on the Second Conduct Rule, 27 July 2015.
[62] Guideline on Applications, 27 July 2015.
[63] Competition Ordinance, Schedule 1, section 2(3). An enactment means any Ordinance, any subsidiary legislation made under any Ordinance and any provision or provisions of any Ordinance or subsidiary legislation: Interpretation and General Clauses Ordinance, section 3.
[64] Competition Ordinance, Schedule 1, section 2(1).
[65] Competition Ordinance, Schedule 1, section 2(2).
[66] Cases 40/73 etc., *Suiker Unie v Commission* [1975] ECR 1663; Cases C-359/95P & C-379/95P, *Commission and France v Ladbroke Racing* [1997] ECR I-6265.
[67] Case C-280/08P, *Deutsche Telekom AG v Commission* [2010] ECR I-9555.

imposed by Hong Kong legislation and does not extend to foreign legal requirements, although it might be expected that the Competition Commission and the Competition Tribunal will take such obligations into account in determining whether agreements or conduct have an anti-competitive object or effect.

In order for this exclusion to apply, the relevant legal requirement must eliminate any margin of autonomy on the part of the undertakings concerned compelling them to enter into or engage in the agreement or conduct in question.[68] Where an undertaking has some scope to exercise its independent judgment on whether it will enter into an agreement, the exclusion for complying with legal requirements is not available. Accordingly, if the relevant agreement is merely facilitated or encouraged by an enactment in force in Hong Kong or national law applying in Hong Kong, the exclusion does not apply. Equally, approval or encouragement on the part of the public authorities does not suffice for this general exclusion to apply.[69]

Public policy and international obligation exemptions Agreements and conduct may be exempted from the Conduct Rules where there are compelling reasons of public policy or where it is appropriate in order to avoid a conflict between the Competition Ordinance and an international obligation that directly relates to Hong Kong. Accordingly, the Chief Executive in Council may, by order, exempt a specified agreement or conduct or a specified class of agreement or conduct from the application of the First or Second Conduct Rules, respectively, if he is satisfied that there are exceptional and compelling reasons of public policy for so doing[70] or that it is appropriate to do so in order to avoid a conflict.[71] Such orders may be subject to any conditions or limitations that the Chief Executive in Council considers appropriate.[72] They may provide that the Conduct Rule in question never applied to any agreement or conduct specified in the order.[73] Sole responsibility for making these orders rests with the Chief Executive in Council, the Competition Commission's role, if any, being confined to determining whether the exemption under an order applies in a particular case where a decision has been requested of it, pursuant to section 9 or 24 of the Competition Ordinance, that an agreement or conduct

---

[68] Guideline on the First Conduct Rule, Annex para 3.2; Guidance on the Second Conduct Rule, Annex, para 2.2.
[69] Guideline on the First Conduct Rule, Annex para 3.3; Guidance on the Second Conduct Rule, Annex, para 2.3.
[70] Competition Ordinance, section 31(1).
[71] Competition Ordinance, section 32(1).
[72] Competition Ordinance, sections 31(2) and 32(2). Any such orders must be published in the Gazette and placed before the Legislative Council: section 33.
[73] Competition Ordinance, sections 31(5) and 32(6).

is excluded or exempt from the application of the First or Second Conduct Rule.[74]

Competition Commission's enforcement policy for the Conduct Rules The Competition Commission set out its policy for enforcement of the Conduct Rules in a statement published in November 2015.[75] This policy supplements the Competition Ordinance and the Commission's guidelines. It prioritises the use of the Commission's operational resources to investigate conduct that may contravene the Conduct Rules in an efficient and timely manner and identifies an enforcement response that is suitable and proportionate where a contravention of the Competition Ordinance has occurred.[76] During the initial years of its operations, the Commission intends to focus its resources on encouraging compliance with the Conduct Rules in the Hong Kong economy as a whole, rather than focussing on specific sectors. It will target anti-competitive conduct that is clearly harmful to competition and consumers in Hong Kong and commence proceedings in the Competition Tribunal in appropriate cases in order, over time, to obtain judicial interpretation of the Competition Ordinance. When considering whether to investigate a particular case, the Commission will accord priority to those cases that involve cartels, other agreements causing significant harm to competition in Hong Kong and abuses of substantial market power involving exclusionary behaviour by incumbents.[77] In addition, the Commission will take into account whether the conduct involves one or more of the following severity factors:[78]

  (a) the conduct demonstrates a blatant disregard for the law;
  (b) the deliberateness of the conduct, including whether the person engaging in the conduct took deliberate steps to avoid detection;
  (c) the conduct was engaged in by or under the senior management of an undertaking;
  (d) the person engaged or involved in the conduct has previously been:
    (i) advised by the Commission that it has concerns about the conduct, given a reasonable opportunity to alter its conduct, but has not done so;
    (ii) issued a warning notice or infringement notice, or has previously given a commitment to the Commission regarding similar conduct; or
    (iii) found by the Competition Tribunal to have contravened the Competition Ordinance.

---

[74] Guideline on the First Conduct Rule, Annex, para 8.3; Guideline on the Second Conduct Rule, Annex, para 6.3.
[75] Enforcement Policy, November 2015.
[76] The enforcement policy does not cover the Commission's approach in assessing cases under the Merger Rule.
[77] Enforcement Policy, paras 3.3-3.4.
[78] Enforcement Policy, para 3.12.

The Commission has a range of enforcement options at its disposal under the Competition Ordinance. In exercising its discretion in relation to which option to choose in an individual case, the Commission will generally favour remedies that will stop the unlawful conduct speedily, undo the harm caused by the conduct and impose sufficient economic sanction to encourage compliance with the Conduct Rules. The remedy chosen should be proportionate to the harm caused by the conduct and consistent with remedies that have been applied in matters involving similar conduct, reflecting the culpability of the respective parties, and setting an appropriate standard for future similar case.[79]

Persons may wish at any time to cooperate with the Commission in its investigations. The Commission will take such cooperation into account in considering the proportionate enforcement response in relation to that person. Approaches to the Commission to discuss settlement may be made on a without prejudice basis. Settlement may take various forms, such as the Commission agreeing not to take action against the persons providing assistance, the person concerned entering into a commitment not to engage in anti-competitive conduct again, or the person agreeing to resolve proceedings before the Competition Tribunal on the basis of a consent order. The Commission has also adopted a leniency policy for undertakings engaged in cartel conduct.[80]

At any stage in its consideration of a matter, the Commission may reassess its priorities to make the best use of its limited resources. In this context, it may take account of additional factors including other matters currently under consideration by the Commission, the Competition Tribunal or other courts, as well as whether the resource requirements of further investigation are proportionate to the expected public benefits.[81]

The Merger Rule The provisions governing mergers are set out in Schedule 7 of the Competition Ordinance. The Merger Rule provides that an undertaking must not, directly or indirectly, carry out a merger that has, or is likely to have, the effect of substantially lessening competition in Hong Kong.[82] Agreements or conduct, which result in, or if engaged in would result in, a merger are excluded from the First and Second Conduct Rules.[83] Whereas the First and Second Conduct Rules are generally applicable across the Hong Kong economy, the Merger Rule is sector specific, in that it only applies where an undertaking that directly or indirectly holds a carrier licence within the

---

[79] Enforcement Policy, paras 3.13-3.14.
[80] Enforcement Policy, paras 4.1-4.4.
[81] Enforcement Policy, para 4.8.
[82] Competition Ordinance, Schedule 7, section 3(1).
[83] Competition Ordinance, Schedule 1, section 4. This applies to all mergers, not just those involving holders of a carrier licence that are subject to the Merger Rule: cf Competition Ordinance, section 2(1) and Schedule 7, sections 3 and 5.

meaning of the Telecommunications Ordinance is involved in a merger.[84] A merger takes place where:[85]

(a) two or more undertakings previously independent of each other cease to be independent of each other; or

(b) one or more persons or other undertakings acquire direct or indirect control of the whole or part of one or more other undertakings, including where a joint venture is created to perform, on a lasting basis, all the functions of an autonomous economic entity; or

(c) there is an acquisition by one undertaking of the whole or part of the assets (including goodwill) of another undertaking which results in the acquiring undertaking being in a position to replace, or to substantially replace, the acquired undertaking, in the business or in part of the business concerned in which the acquired undertaking was engaged immediately before the acquisition.

The Merger Rule does not apply to a merger if the economic efficiencies that arise or may arise from the merger outweigh the adverse effects caused by any lessening of competition in Hong Kong.[86] An undertaking that has carried put, or is proposing to carry out, a merger may apply to the Competition Commission for a decision that the merger is excluded from the application of the Merger Rule.[87] The Chief Executive in Council may by order, subject to any conditions or limitations that he considers appropriate, exempt a specified merger or proposed merger from the application of the Merger Rule if he or she is satisfied that there are exceptional and compelling reasons of public policy for doing so.[88]

If the Commission, after carrying out an investigation, has reasonable cause to believe that a merger contravenes the Merger Rule, it may, within six months after the day on which the merger was completed or it became aware of the merger (whichever is the later), bring proceedings in the Competition Tribunal seeking orders to unwind the merger in relation to a completed merger.[89] In relation to an anticipated merger, the Competition Commission may also bring proceedings in the Competition Tribunal seeking to stop the merger.[90]

The Competition Commission has issued a Guideline on the Merger Rule[91] which sets out how it intends to interpret and give effect to the Merger Rule.

---

[84]   Competition Ordinance, Schedule 7, section 4.
[85]   Competition Ordinance, Schedule 7, section 3(2)-(4).
[86]   Competition Ordinance, Schedule 7, section 8(1).
[87]   Competition Ordinance, Schedule 7, section 11(1)-(2).
[88]   Competition Ordinance, Schedule 7, section 9(1)-(2).
[89]   Competition Ordinance, sections 99 and 100.
[90]   Competition Ordinance, section 97.
[91]   Guideline on the Merger Rule, 27 July 2015.

Consideration of applications for exemption or exclusion In considering applications for individual decisions on exemption or exclusion from the Conduct Rules and the Merger Rule, the Competition Commission, which is not required to deal with hypothetical questions, is only required to consider an application if:[92]

    (a) the application poses novel or unresolved questions of wider importance or public interest in relation to the application of exclusions or exemptions under the Competition Ordinance;

    (b) the application raises a question of an exclusion or exemption for which there is no clarification in existing case law or decisions of the Commission; and

    (c) it is possible to make a decision on the basis of the information provided.

The Telco Rule The Telco Rule, as part of the control and supervision of the telecommunications sector under the Telecommunications Ordinance, prohibits exploitative conduct by a dominant telecommunications licensee.[93] A licensee is in a dominant position if, in the opinion of the Communications Authority, it is able to act without significant competitive restraint from its competitors and customers.[94] In considering whether a licensee is dominant, the Authority must take into account relevant matters including, but not limited to:[95]

    (a) the market share of the licensee;

    (b) the licensee's power to make pricing and other decisions;

    (c) any barriers to entry to competitors into the relevant telecommunications market;

    (d) the degree of product differentiation and sales promotion;

    (e) any other relevant matters to be specified in guidelines.[96]

Without limiting the scope of the Telco Rule, the Communications Authority may consider the following conduct to be exploitative:[97]

    (a) fixing and maintaining prices or charges at an excessively high level; and

    (b) setting unfair trading terms and conditions.

Although the Telco Rule shares some of its features and broad aims with the Second Conduct Rule in that it applies to unilateral conduct on the part of an undertaking that has a position of market power, there are some important distinctions. In particular, whereas the Competition Commission and the Communications Authority have concurrent jurisdiction in enforcing the

---

[92] Competition Ordinance, sections 9(2)-(3), 24(2)-(3) and Schedule 7, section 11(3)-(4).

[93] Telecommunications Ordinance, section 7Q(1), as inserted by the Competition Ordinance, Schedule 8, section 13.

[94] Telecommunications Ordinance, section 7Q(2).

[95] Telecommunications Ordinance, section 7Q(3).

[96] No such guidelines have yet been published.

[97] Telecommunications Ordinance, section 7Q(4).

competition rules, the Telco Rule is enforced by the Communications
Authority alone. The enforcement regime for the Telco Rule also departs from
the Competition Ordinance in that the Communications Authority has decision-
making power in respect of a breach of the Telco Rule, whereas, in respect of
the Conduct Rules and the Merger Rule, the Competition Commission must
bring proceedings before the Competition Tribunal which adjudicates on
whether or not there has been an infringement.

1.3 UNDERTAKINGS AND THE COMPETITION ORDINANCE

1.3.1 Undertakings subject to the competition rules

Undertakings The competition rules under the Competition Ordinance apply
to undertakings. The term undertaking refers to any entity, regardless of its
legal status or the way in which it is financed, which is engaged in an
economic activity.[98] This reflects the notion of undertaking found in EU
competition law.[99] Examples of undertakings, which may include natural as
well as legal persons, are individual companies, groups of companies,
partnerships, individuals operating as sole traders or subcontractors,
cooperatives, societies, business chambers, trade associations and non-profit
organisations.[100] An individual acting as a final consumer, since he is not
carrying on an economic activity, is not an undertaking under the Competition
Ordinance.[101]

Economic activity Central to the concept of an undertaking is whether the
relevant entity is engaged in economic activity.[102] The term economic activity
is not itself defined in the Competition Ordinance, but is, nevertheless,
generally understood to refer to any activity consisting of offering products in a
market regardless of whether the activity is intended to earn a profit.[103] An
entity may be treated as an undertaking for certain of its activities but not for
other activities. Where the relevant activities are economic, the entity is an
undertaking with respect to those activities for the purposes of the Competition
Ordinance.[104] EU competition law recognises that an entity carrying on an
activity that has an exclusively social function and is based on the principle of

---

[98]   Competition Ordinance, section 2(1); Guideline on the First Conduct Rule, para 1.7.
[99]   Case C-41/90, *Höfner and Elser v Macrotron GmbH* [1991] ECR I-1979.
[100] Guideline on the First Conduct Rule, para 2.2.
[101] Guideline on the First Conduct Rule, para 2.5.
[102] Guideline on the First Conduct Rule, para 2.2.
[103] Guideline on the First Conduct Rule, para 2.3; cf. Case C-244/94, *FFSA* [1995] ECR I-
       4013; Case C-180/98, *Pavlov v Stichting Pensioenfonds Medische Specialsten* [2000]
       ECR I-6451.
[104] Guideline on the First Conduct Rule, para 2.4.

solidarity is not likely to be treated as carrying on an economic activity such as to qualify it as an undertaking.[105]

Single economic unit The First Conduct Rule, which applies to agreements between undertakings, does not apply to conduct involving two or more entities if the relevant entities are part of the same undertaking. For this purpose, the Competition Commission will assess whether the relevant entities constitute a single economic unit.[106] Determining whether two or more entities should be considered a single economic unit is not limited to the notion of a corporate or company group within the meaning of the Companies Ordinance[107] or other laws but depends on the facts of the individual case. Generally, if one entity exercises decisive influence over the commercial policy of another entity, whether through legal or *de facto* control, the Commission will consider both entities as a single economic unit and part of the same undertaking.[108] The fact that a subsidiary has separate legal personality is not necessarily of itself sufficient to exclude the possibility of imputing its conduct to its parent.[109] A number of factors may be relied on to establish decisive influence including veto rights over key strategic decisions, the exercise of management power by the parent and the extent of the parent's shareholding over the subsidiary. An agreement between a parent company and its subsidiary, or between two companies under the control of a third, will not be subject to the First Conduct Rule if the relevant controlling companies exercise decisive influence over their respective subsidiaries notwithstanding that these various entities might have separate legal personalities.[110] Whether a joint venture entity forms a single undertaking with any one of its parents depends on the facts of the case. Generally, if two or more parent entities have power to block actions which determine the strategic commercial behaviour of the joint venture, i.e. if there is joint control including *de facto* control, the joint venture is not part of the same economic unit as any of its parents.[111]

Independent distributors and distribution agents Suppliers commonly use third parties to distribute their products. Whether the First Conduct Rule applies to the relationship with such third parties depends on whether or not the

---

[105] Cases C-159/91 & C-160/91 *Poucet and Pistre* [1993] ECR I-637.
[106] Guideline on the First Conduct Rule, para 2.6. This determination may also be used to decide whether a parent company should be held liable for the unlawful conduct of a subsidiary.
[107] Cap 622.
[108] Guideline on the First Conduct Rule, paras 2.7- 2.8; Case 22/71, *Béguelin Import Co. v GL Import Export SA* [1971] ECR 949; Case C-73/95P, *Viho Europe v Commission* [1996] ECR I-5457.
[109] Case 48/69, *Imperial Chemical Industries Ltd* [1972] ECR 619.
[110] Guideline on the First Conduct Rule, para 2.9.
[111] Guideline on the First Conduct Rule, para 2.10.

third party is a separate undertaking from the supplier. Where a supplier enters into a distribution agreement with an independent third party distributor the agreement will in principle be subject to the First Conduct Rule. In certain cases, however, a supplier may appoint a third party to negotiate or conclude contracts on behalf of the supplier for the sale of the supplier's products. In that case, the third party acts as a distribution agent for the supplier.[112]

Whether a third party acts as a true distribution agent does not depend on whether that party is labelled an agent or the agreement is labelled an agency agreement. Rather, the relevant factors are the level of control which the supplier exercises over the third party and the level of financial or commercial risk borne by the third party in relation to the activities for which it has been appointed as a distribution agent by the supplier. In particular, a distributor may be considered to act as a true distribution agent of the suppler if it does not bear any, or bears only insignificant, risks in relation to the contracts concluded on behalf of the supplier. This might be the case where title to the contract goods is not transferred to the distributor or the third party does not itself supply the contract services and the distributor does not bear any of the following non-exhaustive types of risks and costs:[113]

- costs linked to the distribution if the contract products, including transport costs;
- costs or risks associated with the maintenance of stocks of the contract products, including costs relating to loss of stocks or where the distributor bears the costs of unsold stock;
- responsibility for damage caused by contact products sold to third parties;
- costs or risks associated with non-performance by customer, such as late payment by the customer;
- costs associated with advertising or sales promotion for the contract products;
- costs associated with market-specific investments in equipment, premises or the training of personnel;
- costs associated with other activities in the same product market as the contract products where these activities are required by the supplier.

Where a distributor is a true distribution agent, the selling function of the distributor with respect to the contract products forms part of the same undertaking as the supplier. The Competition Commission considers that the First Conduct Rule does not apply, therefore, to restrictions imposed in the distribution agreement on the distributor in so far as they relate to the contracts

---

[112] Guideline on the First Conduct Rule, paras 2.11-2.13. The European Commission's Guidelines on Vertical Restraints, paras 12-21, set out the principles in EU competition law as to what constitutes a genuine agent for the purposes of Article 101 TFEU (OJ 2010 C130/01).

[113] Guideline on the First Conduct Rule, paras 2.14-2.15.

concluded on behalf of the supplier. This includes restrictions imposed on the distributor which limit the customers with whom the distributor can deal, the territories where the distributor can sell or the prices and conditions at which the distributor can sell or the prices and conditions at which it can sell the contract goods.[114] The First Conduct Rule may however, continue to apply to other aspects of the relationship with the distributor which do not relate to the sale of the contract products or services but which govern the relationship between the distributor and the supplier more generally.[115]

Employees and trade unions Normally, an employee of an undertaking is not considered to be an undertaking. It follows that discussions or arrangements in relation to salary or other working conditions between one or more employees and their employer take place within the framework of a single economic unit and are outside of scope of the First Conduct Rule.[116] Similarly, where a trade union acts as on behalf of its members in collective bargaining with an employer on terms and conditions of work, the trade union is not an undertaking since it is not engaged in economic activity.[117] In general, self-employed persons will be treated as undertakings provided that they are engaged in economic activity. However, the Competition Commission considers that in some limited circumstances a self-employed person may not be considered an undertaking, for example, where they are regarded as a *de facto* employee of another undertaking.[118]

1.3.2 Statutory bodies, specified persons and activities excluded

Statutory bodies excluded Section 3(1) of the Competition Ordinance provides that statutory bodies are excluded from the First Conduct Rule, the Second Conduct Rule and the Merger Rule, as well as the enforcement powers of the Competition Commission (other than powers relating to complaints and investigations) and the Competition Tribunal, unless they are specifically brought within the scope of those rules by a regulation made by the Chief Executive in Council.[119] A statutory body means a body of persons, corporate or unincorporate, established or constituted by or under an Ordinance or appointed under an Ordinance.[120] It does not include a company, a corporation

---

[114] Guideline on the First Conduct Rule, para 2.16.
[115] Guideline on the First Conduct Rule, para 2.17.
[116] Guideline on the First Conduct Rule, para 2.18.
[117] Guideline on the First Conduct Rule, para 2.19.
[118] Guideline on the First Conduct Rule, paras 2.20-2.21.
[119] Competition Ordinance, section 3(1); Guideline on the First Conduct Rule, Annex, para 9.1; Guideline on the Second Conduct Rule, Annex, para 7.1; Guideline on the Merger Rule, para 4.13.
[120] Competition Ordinance, section 2(1).

of trustees incorporated under the Registered Trustees Incorporation Ordinance,[121] a society registered under the Societies Ordinance,[122] a co-operative society registered under the Co-operative Societies Ordinance[123] or a trade union registered under the Trade Unions Ordinance.[124] By excluding companies from the definition of a statutory body, the exclusion from the competition rules does not extend to legal entities owned or controlled by a statutory body unless those entities are also statutory bodies.[125] A statutory body includes any employee or agent of the statutory body acting in that capacity.[126]

This exclusion of statutory bodies reflects a similar provision in the Singapore Competition Act. It is, however, broader than that applicable in EU competition law, which generally only provides that the exercise of public authority does not constitute an economic activity, while extending the application of the competition law rules to economic activities carried on by a statutory body.

Exclusion inapplicable to specified statutory bodies The exclusion from the competition rules provided for in section 3(1) of the Competition Ordinance does not, however, apply to a specified statutory body or to a statutory body to the extent that it is engaged in a specified activity.[127] For a statutory body or a particular activity to be specified for these purposes, a regulation must be made pursuant to section 5 of the Competition Ordinance by the Chief Executive in Council.[128]

The Chief Executive may only make the regulation with respect to a statutory body if he is satisfied that:[129]

    (a) the statutory body is engaging in an economic activity in direct competition with another undertaking;

    (b) the economic activity of the statutory body is affecting the economic efficiency of a specific market;

    (c) the economic activity of the statutory body is not directly related to the provision of an essential public service or the implementation of public policy;

    (d) there are no other exceptional and compelling reasons of public policy against making such a regulation.

---

[121] Cap 306.
[122] Cap 151.
[123] Cap 33.
[124] Cap 332.
[125] Guideline on the First Conduct Rule, Annex, para 9.2; Guideline on the Second Conduct Rule, Annex, para 7.2.
[126] Competition Ordinance, section 3(1)(3)(b).
[127] Competition Ordinance, section 3(2).
[128] Competition Ordinance, section 3(3).
[129] Competition Ordinance, section 5(3).

Pursuant to this power, the Competition (Application of Provisions) Regulation[130] listed six statutory bodies to whom the exclusion from the competition rules does not apply, leaving the exclusion applicable to all remaining statutory bodies, 581 in total. The statutory bodies in respect of whom the exclusion from the competition rules is inapplicable are as follows:

- Ocean Park Corporation,
- Matilda and War Memorial Hospital,
- Kadoorie Farm and Botanic Garden Corporation,
- The Helena May,
- Federation of Hong Kong Industries,
- The general committee of the Federation of Hong Kong Industries.

Competition rules inapplicable to specified persons and activities Section 4 of the Competition Ordinance provides that the First Conduct Rule, the Second Conduct Rule and the Merger Rule do not apply to specified natural or legal persons, i.e. undertakings, or to persons to the extent that they are engaged in specified activities.[131] For a person or a particular activity to be specified for these purposes, a regulation must be made pursuant to section 5 of the Competition Ordinance by the Chief Executive in Council.[132]

Pursuant to this power, the Competition (Disapplication of Provisions) Regulation[133] lists seven specified persons to whom the competition rules do not apply as follows:

- The Stock Exchange of Hong Kong Limited,
- Hong Kong Futures Exchange Limited,
- Hong Kong Securities Clearing Company Limited,
- HKFE Clearing Corporation Limited,
- The SEHK Options Clearing House Limited,
- OTC Clearing Hong Kong Limited,
- Hong Kong Exchanges and Clearing Limited.

All of these persons are regulated under the Securities and Futures Ordinance[134] and it appears that there were concerns over legal certainty if they were also to be subject to the Competition Ordinance.

---

[130] Cap 619A.
[131] Competition Ordinance, section 4; Guideline on the First Conduct Rule, Annex, para 9.3; Guideline on the Second Conduct Rule, Annex, para 7.3; Guideline on the Merger Rule, para 4.14.
[132] Competition Ordinance, section 3(3).
[133] Cap 619B.
[134] Cap 571.

1.3.3 Undertakings providing services of general economic interest

Services of general economic interest exclusion Section 3 of Schedule 1 of the Competition Ordinance provides that neither the First Conduct Rule nor the Second Conduct Rule applies to an undertaking entrusted by the Government of the Hong Kong Special Administrative Region with the operation of services of general economic interest (SGEI) in so far as the conduct rule would obstruct the performance, in law or in fact, of the particular tasks assigned to the undertaking.[135] The Competition Commission intends to interpret this exclusion strictly, with the onus being on the undertaking seeking the benefit of the exclusion to demonstrate that all the conditions for application of the exclusion are met.[136] Similar provisions apply in Article 106(2) TFEU, as well as in the competition legislation in the Malaysia, Singapore and the UK.[137]

Entrustment The undertaking needs to demonstrate that it has been expressly entrusted by the Government with the service in question. An act of entrustment may be made by way of legislative measure or regulation, through the grant of a concession or licence governed by public law or through some other act of the Government. Mere approval by the Government of the activities carried out by the relevant undertaking does not suffice.[138] In this context, entrustment presupposes that the undertaking in question must perform the services which have been entrusted to it pursuant to the Government measure. The measure in question may be adopted by any branch of the Hong Kong Government in the exercise of its functions as a public authority.[139] The obligation to perform the SGEI may be accepted by the undertaking to whom it is entrusted entering into contractual relations with the Government.

The exclusion applies only to the particular entrusted tasks and not to the undertaking or its activities generally.[140] For obligations imposed on an

---

[135] Competition Ordinance, Schedule I, section 3; Guideline on the First Conduct Rule, Annex, para 4.1; Guideline on the Second Conduct Rule, Annex, para 3.1.

[136] Guideline on the First Conduct Rule, Annex, para 4.2; Guideline on the Second Conduct Rule, Annex, para 3.2.

[137] In the UK, the competition authorities have adopted guidelines on services of general economic interest: OFT 421 (2004), readopted by the CMA (2014). See also, the European Commission's framework on State aid in the form of public service compensation, OJ 2012 C8/15.

[138] Guideline on the First Conduct Rule, Annex, para 4.3; Guideline on the Second Conduct Rule, Annex, para 3.3.

[139] The definition of Government in Competition Ordinance, section 2(1) specifically excludes any company that is wholly or partly owned by the Government.

[140] Guideline on the First Conduct Rule, Annex, para 4.4; Guideline on the Second Conduct Rule, Annex, para 3.4.

undertaking entrusted with the operation of an SGEI to fall within the particular tasks entrusted to it, they must be linked to the subject matter of the SGEI in question and contribute directly to achieving that interest.[141]

Services of general economic interest Whilst it is for the Government to designate SGEIs, the notion of SGEIs is not itself defined in the Competition Ordinance.[142] The Competition Commission states that SGEIs are services, loosely corresponding to the concept of public services, that the public authorities believe should be provided to the public whether or not the private sector would supply the relevant services. SGEIs entail services of an economic nature, which may include activities in the cultural, social and public health fields where their aim is to make a profit.[143] To be considered a service of general economic interest, the service must typically be widely available and not restricted to a certain class, or classes, of buyers. In any event, however, services aimed at a particular group or a particular locality, for example, a disadvantaged group or a remote locality, might qualify in so far as such services are in the general interest.[144] In EU law, SGEIs have been recognised in the case, for example, of transport routes that are not commercially viable,[145] public telephone networks,[146] universal postal services[147] and public national electricity supply.[148]

Obstruction of the performance of the assigned tasks To benefit from the SGEI exclusion, it is not sufficient for an undertaking merely to provide evidence that it has been entrusted with a particular SGEI. The undertaking must also demonstrate that the application of the First Conduct Rule would obstruct the performance of the relevant entrusted tasks.[149] In this respect, the Competition Commission requires that the undertaking must show with supporting evidence that the application of the rule would require it to perform the entrusted tasks under economically unacceptable conditions. It will also

---

[141] Guideline on the First Conduct Rule, Annex, para 4.5; Guideline on the Second Conduct Rule, Annex, para 3.5.

[142] The reference to services includes the distribution of goods and not only the provision of services as such: Guideline on the First Conduct Rule, Annex, para 4.6; Guideline on the Second Conduct Rule, Annex, para 3.6.

[143] Guideline on the First Conduct Rule, Annex, para 4.7; Guideline on the Second Conduct Rule, Annex, para 3.7.

[144] Guideline on the First Conduct Rule, Annex, para 4.8; Guideline on the Second Conduct Rule, Annex, para 3.8.

[145] Case 66/86, *Ahmed Saeed* [1989] ECR 803.

[146] Case C-18/88, *GB-Immo-BM* [1991] ECR I-5941.

[147] Case C-320/91, *Corbeau* [1993] ECR I-2533.

[148] Case C-393/92, *Almelo v Energiebedrijf Ijsselmij NV* [1994] ECR I-1477.

[149] Guideline on the First Conduct Rule, Annex, para 4.9; Guideline on the Second Conduct Rule, Annex, para 3.9.

generally need to show that the entrusted tasks could not be discharged in other ways, which would cause less harm to competition.[150]

1.4 MARKET DEFINITION IN THE COMPETITION RULES

Defining the relevant market   When conducting a competition assessment under the Competition Ordinance, the Competition Commission uses an analytical framework which involves defining the relevant market.   The definition of the relevant market is central to the application of the First Conduct Rule, the Second Conduct Rule and the Merger Rule.[151]   Although there is no reference to markets in the First Conduct Rule[152] or the Merger Rule[153] which refer only to competition in Hong Kong, it is clear that this refers to competition in the market, so that it is necessary to define the relevant market in which competition is affected.   By contrast, the Second Conduct Rule specifically applies to an undertaking having power in a market.[154]   The CJEU has held that the concept of the relevant market implies that there can be an effective competition between the products which form part of it and this presupposes that there is a sufficient degree of interchangeability between all the products forming part of the same market in so far as specific use of such products is concerned.[155]   The purpose of defining the relevant market is to assist with identifying in a systematic way the competitive constraints that undertakings face when operating in a market.   This is the case in particular for determining if undertakings are competitors or potential competitors and when assessing the anti-competitive effects of conduct in a market.   The exercise of defining the relevant market is, however, no more than an analytical tool and not an end in itself.[156]   Guidelines on the market definition have been issued by inter alia the European Commission,[157] the UK Competition and Markets Authority[158] and the competition authorities in Malaysia and Singapore.

When defining the relevant market the Commission will look at evidence that is available and relevant to the case at hand.   The Commission will define

---

[150] Guideline on the First Conduct Rule, Annex, para 4.10; Guideline on the Second Conduct Rule, Annex, para 3.10.

[151] The Competition Commission's guidance on market definition is set out in the Guideline on the Second Conduct Rule, paras 2.1-2.35 but applies generally across the competition rules.

[152] Competition Ordinance, section 6(1).

[153] Competition Ordinance, Schedule 7, section 3(1).

[154] Competition Ordinance, section 21(1).

[155] Case 85/76, *Hoffmann-La Roche & Co v Commission* [1979] ECR 461; Case 322/81, *Michelin NV v Commission* [1983] ECR 3461.

[156] Guideline on the Second Conduct Rule, paras 2.1-2.2.

[157] OJ 1997 C372/5.

[158] OFT 403 (2004), re-adopted by the CMA in 2014.

the boundaries of the relevant market as precisely as required by the circumstances of the case. Where appropriate, it may conduct its competition assessment on the basis of alternative market definitions. Where it is apparent that the investigated conduct is unlikely to have an adverse effect on competition or that the undertaking under investigation does not possess a substantial degree of market power on the basis of any reasonable market definition, the question of the most appropriate market definition can be left open.[159]

The relevant market within which to analyse market power or assess a given competition concern has both a product dimension and a geographic dimension. In this context, the relevant product market comprises all those products which are considered interchangeable or substitutable by buyers because of the products' characteristics, prices and intended use. The relevant geographic market comprises all those regions or areas where buyers would be able or willing to find substitutes for the products in question. The relevant product and geographic market for a particular product may vary depending on the nature of the buyers and suppliers concerned by the conduct under examination and their position in the supply chain. For example, if conduct at the wholesale level is concerned, the relevant market is defined from the perspective of the wholesale buyers. If the concern is conduct at the retail level, the relevant market is defined from the perspective of buyers of retail products.[160]

When defining the relevant market, the Commission will generally have regard to its previous cases. Undertakings may, therefore, wish to use relevant markets defined in past cases as a guide to the Commission's likely approach when assessing the impact of their conduct on competition and/or when assessing whether they might have a substantial degree of market power. That said, the way in which the relevant market for a particular product is defined depends on the specific facts of the case, and may vary from one case to the next based on the structure of the market, the preferences of buyers at the point in time under consideration and the particular competition concern for which the analysis is undertaken. For this reason, a defined relevant market in one case will not bind the Commission in another.[161]

Product market Substitutability from the perspective of the buyer (demand-side substitution) is a central factor for the purposes of market definition. The process of defining the relevant product market will often start by looking at a

---

[159] Guideline on the Second Conduct Rule, paras 2.3-2.4; Guideline on the Merger Rule, para 3.11. The Commission will follow the general analytical framework explained in the Guideline on the Second Conduct Rule, paras 2.1 et seq., but would not expect to follow mechanically each and every step in each and every case.
[160] Guideline on the Second Conduct Rule, paras 2.6-2.7.
[161] Guideline on the Second Conduct Rule, paras 2.8-2.9.

relatively narrow potential product market definition. This would normally be
one (or more) of the products which are the subject of an investigation or, in
the case of a merger, offered by the merging parties. The potential product
market is then expanded to include those substitute products to which buyers
would turn in the face of a price increase above the competitive price. In this
regard, a frequently used method of assessment involves postulating a
candidate product market and considering whether a hypothetical firm with a
monopoly in that market would be able profitably to impose an increase in
price that is small but significant (typically between 5% and 10%) and non-
transitory. Such a small but significant non-transitory increase in price is
referred to as a SSNIP. If enough buyers would switch to substitute products
in the face of a SSNIP to make the attempted price increase unprofitable, the
candidate product market is too narrow. The candidate market is then
expanded to include the substitute products to which buyers would turn, and
the same analysis is performed on this broader candidate product market. The
relevant product market will be that group of products over which a
hypothetical monopolist can profitably impose a SSNIP.[162]

When applying the hypothetical monopolist test in the context of a given
case, the Commission will consider both quantitative and qualitative evidence
of demand-side substitution using appropriate analytical techniques. In
particular, the Commission may undertake an analysis of whether a SSNIP
would be profitable and consider evidence of patterns in price changes. It will
also consider the characteristics of the product in question and the product's
intended use, evidence from undertakings active in the market and their
commercial strategies and evidence regarding the past behaviour of buyers
(relating to, for example, their tendency to switch between products in response
to a price increase).[163]

Geographic market The relevant geographic market can be defined using the
same general process as that used to define the relevant product market. The
geographic market may cover a global or regional area, or be limited to Hong
Kong or a part of Hong Kong. For example, depending on the market in
question, there may be cases where parts of mainland China (such as the Pearl
River Delta area) could be included in the relevant geographic market.[164]

The relevant geographic market can be defined using the same general
process as that used to define the relevant product market. A number of factors
will determine the extent of the relevant geographic market. As in the case of
product market definition, buyers' views of reasonably available substitutes
will drive the Commission's analysis of the relevant geographic market. The
objective of this analysis will therefore be to identify all those areas where

---

[162] Guideline on the Second Conduct Rule, paras 2.10-2.11.
[163] Guideline on the Second Conduct Rule, paras 2.13-2.14.
[164] Guideline on the Second Conduct Rule, para 2.16.

buyers would be able or willing to find substitutes for the products under examination. To determine the relevant geographic market, the Commission will typically begin by looking at a relatively narrow geographic area (the candidate geographic market). The hypothetical monopolist test may then be applied to this area with a view to establishing whether a hypothetical monopolist of the product at issue in the area could profitably sustain a price increase above the competitive level. If not, the test is repeated over wider geographic areas as appropriate until the hypothetical monopolist would find it profitable to sustain a price increase. Accordingly, when defining the relevant geographic market, the Commission may employ a SSNIP analysis to assess the extent to which customers of a product would switch to suppliers located in other areas in response to a hypothetical SSNIP of the relevant product. If, in response to a SSNIP, enough buyers would switch to substitutes in other areas to make the attempted price increase unprofitable, the candidate geographic market is too narrow. The candidate geographic market is then expanded to include the other areas to which buyers would turn, and the same analysis is performed on this broader potential geographic market. [165]

The extent to which buyers are willing and able to purchase the product from different areas may vary with the circumstances and the nature of the buyer. For example, in the case of consumer products, geographic markets may be quite narrow if a significant number of buyers are unlikely to purchase products sold in neighbouring areas. For wholesale or manufacturing markets in which transport costs are low, buyers may be in a better position to switch between suppliers in different regions. Thus, the scope of the geographic market for a particular product might vary depending on whether the buyer is at the end consumer level (in which case the geographic market may be relatively narrow) or the wholesale level (in which case the geographic market may be relatively broad). [166]

When applying the hypothetical monopolist test in the context of defining the relevant geographic market, the Commission will consider both quantitative and qualitative evidence using appropriate analytical techniques. In particular, the Commission may consider evidence of the switching of orders to other areas, prices in the different areas, the geographic pattern of purchases for buyers, trade flows, barriers to switching and switching costs that might be associated with diverting to suppliers in other areas, transport costs relative to the value of the products concerned and cultural factors. [167]

Price discrimination markets Where suppliers are able to differentiate between types of buyers in terms of price, it may be appropriate to assess these types of buyers as being in separate markets. Undertakings might be able to

---

[165] Guideline on the Second Conduct Rule, paras 2.15, 2.17-2.18.
[166] Guideline on the Second Conduct Rule, para 2.19.
[167] Guideline on the Second Conduct Rule, paras 2.20-2.21.

discriminate between buyers for a variety of reasons including, for example, because buyers meet different user profiles (e.g. business users might be charged a different price for a software product than individual users) or because some buyers face such high switching costs that they are locked in to purchasing a particular product.[168]

Aftermarkets An aftermarket is a market for a secondary product, namely a product which is purchased only as a result of buying a primary product. The primary product and the secondary product can be considered to be complementary. For example, a customer might purchase spare parts (the secondary products) for use with a particular machine (the primary product). The appropriate market definition in the case of aftermarkets will depend on the facts of the case. It might be appropriate to define, for example, a single market system or dual or multiple markets. A single system market comprises both the primary product and the secondary product, whereas dual or multiple markets arise where there is a market for the primary product and either a separate market comprising all secondary products or separate secondary markets for each primary product.[169] Thus, certificates of conformity which were required by importers of motor cars and were available only from the manufacturer constituted a distinct market in which the manufacturer was dominant by virtue of its legal monopoly.[170]

Captive production Where a particular market includes vertically integrated firms, the question sometimes arises as to whether production of a product consumed internally by a vertically integrated firm (captive production) should be considered in the product market or only production sold externally to the merchant market should be included. Generally, the Commission will not consider captive production to be within the relevant product market but will assess whether captive production imposes a competitive constraint in terms of potential competition.[171]

Two-sided markets A two-sided market is a market where undertakings compete simultaneously for two groups of customers whose demands are inter-related. In this context the undertakings use a two-sided platform to sell to the two different groups of buyer. An example of a two-sided market is an online auction platform, where the platform provider must attract both parties wishing to sell products through the platform and parties wishing to buy those products. In this circumstance, an increase in the fees charged to the sellers could result in a loss of customers on both sides of the market (if fewer sellers use the

---

[168] Guideline on the Second Conduct Rule, para 2.23.
[169] Guideline on the Second Conduct Rule, para 2.24.
[170] Case 26/75, *General Motors v Commission* [1975] ECR 1367.
[171] Guideline on the Second Conduct Rule, para 2.25.

platform, a smaller range of products will be available on the platform, making it less attractive to buyers). Other examples include video game markets, where the video game manufacturer must attract demand from both video game developers and video game buyers, or newspapers which must attract both readers and advertisers. Because of the two sides of the market and the interaction between the two different groups of buyers, market definition can be more complex than in most traditional one-sided markets. When assessing market power in a two-sided market, competitive constraints on both sides of the market must be considered.[172] An example of a two-sided market is the credit card market constituting an upstream network market and downstream issuing and acquiring markets.[173]

Bidding markets A bidding market is one in which firms typically compete by submitting bids in response to tenders organised by buyers. To identify the competitive constraints a particular undertaking faces, more weight must be placed on identifying the (potential) market participants, i.e. those suppliers that have the capacity to compete for the contract and participate in future bidding competitions. In bidding markets, the relevant market will include all undertakings that can be viewed as credible bidders for the product at issue in the geographic area where they can place a credible bid.[174]

Temporal markets A factor that may be relevant in some markets is time. Examples of how time might be relevant for market definition purposes include peak and off-peak services which some buyers may not view as substitutable and seasonal markets.[175]

Markets characterised by frequent innovation Some industries are characterised by rapid technological change. For example, new products may be developed, formerly separate functionalities may be integrated in a new product and process innovations may lead to the entry of undertakings into the market increasing the competitive pressure on incumbent undertakings. These developments are often unpredictable, leading to the emergence of new

---

[172] Guideline on the Second Conduct Rule, paras 2.26-2.27.

[173] Case AT.39398 – *VISA MIF* in which the European Commission identified: (1) the upstream network inter-system market where payment card scheme operators compete to persuade financial institutions to join their payment card schemes and on which they provide services to such institutions in return for scheme fees; and (2) the downstream intra-system markets in which financial institutions compete with respect to card-related activities, i.e. issuing cards and acquiring merchants for card payment acceptance. It considered that the services provided on the acquiring and issuing markets were complementary in nature but that they had distinct features and were provided to two different customer groups (merchants and cardholders).

[174] Guideline on the Second Conduct Rule, para 2.28.

[175] Guideline on the Second Conduct Rule, para 2.29.

markets or the convergence of formerly separate markets. As a result, market boundaries may shift rapidly and this can pose particular challenges when defining the relevant market in the context of a particular investigation. Equally, market shares at a given point in time might be less indicative of market power depending on the facts of the case.[176]

Supply-side substitution and potential competition Products might be regarded as being subject to three main sources of competitive constraint: substitutability from the perspective of the buyer (demand-side substitutability); supply-side substitutability; and potential competition. The assessment of demand-side substitutability involves a consideration of the range of products viewed as substitutes by buyers and the areas where buyers would be able and willing to find substitutes for the products concerned. Supply-side substitutability refers to the ability of undertakings to switch production to the product under consideration or to begin supplying the product to the geographic area under consideration, in the event of an increase in the price of the product concerned. Potential competition refers to the competitive constraint imposed in the market from the potential entry of new undertakings and the potential expansion of existing ones. Where suppliers cannot switch production in the short term with ease, they are considered as a source of potential competition rather than supply-side substitution.[177]

The Commission will not generally consider supply-side substitutability or potential competition when defining the relevant market. Rather, they will be considered at a later stage in the Commission's analysis where relevant.[178]

---

[176] Guideline on the Second Conduct Rule, para 2.30.
[177] Guideline on the Second Conduct Rule, paras 2.31-2.33
[178] Guideline on the Second Conduct Rule, paras 2.31-2.34.

Chapter Two

THE FIRST CONDUCT RULE
AGREEMENTS THAT HARM COMPETITION

2.1 THE FIRST CONDUCT RULE

The First Conduct Rule The First Conduct Rule, which is set out in section 6(1) of the Competition Ordinance, prohibits agreements and arrangements that harm competition. It provides that an undertaking must not make or give effect to an agreement, engage in a concerted practice or, as a member of an association of undertakings, make or give effect to a decision of the association, if the object or effect of the agreement, concerted practice or decision is to prevent, restrict or distort competition in Hong Kong.[1]

There are four separate criteria that must be fulfilled for the First Conduct Rule to apply:

- there is an agreement, concerted practice or decision of an association of undertakings;
- the agreement or conduct is between undertakings engaged in economic activity;[2]
- the object or effect of the conduct is to prevent, restrict or distort competition in Hong Kong;
- the conduct is not excluded or exempted from the application of the First Conduct Rule.

The First Conduct Rule in Hong Kong competition law is equivalent to Article 101(1) TFEU in European Union competition law and the Chapter I prohibition in the UK Competition Act 1998. Other jurisdictions apply similar legislation, including the Australian Competition and Consumer Act 2010, the New Zealand Commerce Act 1986, the Singapore Competition Act 2004 and the Malaysian Competition Act 2010.

Guideline on the First Conduct Rule In order to help undertakings determine whether their conduct complies with the First Conduct Rule, the Competition Commission has issued a Guideline which sets out a framework of how it intends to interpret and give effect to the Rule and provides

---

[1] Competition Ordinance, section 6(1).
[2] For the definition of undertaking, see Chapter 1, pp. 22-25; Guideline on the First Conduct Rule, paras 2.2-2.21.

hypothetical examples of how it intends to treat particular scenarios.[3] Reference may also be usefully made to the equivalent guidelines issued by competition authorities in other jurisdictions, in particular, the EU guidelines on the applicability of Article 101 TFEU to horizontal cooperation agreements[4] and on vertical restraints[5] and the UK CMA's guidelines on agreements and concerted practices[6] and vertical agreements.[7] The following considerations arise in relation to the application of the First Conduct Rule:

- Consumers, including businesses acting as customers, benefit from competitive rivalry in the marketplace. Hong Kong's free market economy depends on a healthy competitive environment which incentivises businesses to offer a wider variety of better quality products at lower prices.[8]

- Most agreements and arrangements between market participants benefit consumers and the Hong Kong economy. Cooperating between businesses can often stimulate more efficient, cost-effective and innovative business practices. However, the benefits of a competitive market are undermined when market participants collude with their competitors on key parameters such as price, output, product quality, product variety and innovation.[9]

- The First Conduct Rule embodies the proposition that competitors should make decisions on competitive parameters independently.[10]

- The First Conduct Rule applies not only to agreements and arrangements between business that compete with one another (horizontal agreements), but also to other agreements and arrangements between parties who are not competitors (vertical agreements) if they are anti-competitive.[11]

- Certain conduct is classified as Serious Anti-Competitive Conduct and is subject to more rigorous application of the First Conduct Rule than other anti-competitive conduct.[12]

- Agreements, even where they harm competition, might sometimes generate efficiencies which compensate for the harm to competition

---

[3]　Guideline on the First Conduct Rule, 27 July 2015.
[4]　OJ 2011 C11/1.
[5]　OJ 2010 C130/1.
[6]　OFT 410 (2004) re-adopted by the CMA (2014).
[7]　OFT 419 (2004) re-adopted by the CMA (2014).
[8]　Guideline on the First Conduct Rule, para 1.2.
[9]　Guideline on the First Conduct Rule, para 1.3.
[10]　Guideline on the First Conduct Rule, para 1.4.
[11]　Guideline on the First Conduct Rule, para 1.5
[12]　Competition Ordinance, section 2(1)-(2); Guideline on the First Conduct Rule, para 5.1.

and thereby may benefit from exemption from the First Conduct Rule as an agreement enhancing overall economic efficiency.[13]

- Certain conduct engaged in by small and medium-sized enterprises (SMEs) is excluded from the application of the First Conduct Rule under the general exclusion for agreements of lesser significance.[14]
- The application of the First Conduct Rule does not preclude the parallel application of the Second Conduct Rule to the same conduct where the agreement involves an abuse of a substantial degree of market power.[15]
- The First Conduct Rule applies to conduct which causes harm to competition in Hong Kong. Conduct taking place outside Hong Kong may infringe the First Conduct Rule if its object or effect is to prevent, restrict or distort competition in Hong Kong.[16]

Effect of prohibition under the First Conduct Rule Although section 6(1) of the Competition Ordinance does not itself contain the word prohibition, section 6 is headed "Prohibition of anti-competitive agreements, concerted practices and decisions" and section 6(3) states that the prohibition imposed by section 6(1) is to be referred to as the First Conduct Rule. In relation to the equivalent prohibition in Article 101(1) TFEU and Chapter I of the UK Competition Act 1998, Article 101(2) TFEU and section 2(4) of the UK Competition Act 1998 declare that any prohibited agreements or decisions are void. The CJEU held, in *Eco Swiss Time Ltd. v Benetton*, that this followed from the fundamental nature of the prohibition in EU competition law.[17] In English law, the Court of Appeal has held that a prohibited agreement is not only void but also illegal.[18] Provisions of an agreement that are prohibited may, however, be severed from the rest of the agreement where that is permitted under the applicable contract law.[19]

No equivalent declaration applies under the Competition Ordinance, so that it cannot be presumed automatically that agreements and decisions that contravene the First Conduct Rule are void. Moreover, different procedures apply depending on whether the conduct in question constitutes Serious Anti-Competitive Conduct. Where the Competition Commission has reasonable cause to believe that a contravention of the First Conduct Rule has occurred and the contravention does not involve Serious Anti-Competitive Conduct, it

---

[13] Guideline on the First Conduct Rule, para 1.10; cf. Competition Ordinance, Schedule 1, section 1.

[14] Guideline on the First Conduct Rule, para 1.11; cf. Competition Ordinance, Schedule 1, section 5.

[15] Guideline on the First Conduct Rule, para 1.12.

[16] Competition Ordinance, section 8; Guideline on the First Conduct Rule, para 1.13.

[17] Case C-126/97, *Eco Swiss Time Ltd. v Benetton* [1999] ECR I-3055.

[18] *Gibbs Mew v Gemmell* [1998] EuLR 588.

[19] Case 56/65, *Société Technique Minière v Maschinenbau Ulm GmbH* [1966] ECR 235.

must, before bringing proceedings in the Competition Tribunal against the undertaking whose conduct is alleged to constitute the contravention, issue a warning notice under section 82 of the Competition Ordinance to the undertaking or undertakings concerned. The warning notice procedure affords the undertakings an opportunity to cease or alter the investigated conduct within a specified warning period.[20] In cases of Serious Anti-Competitive Conduct, on the other hand, the Commission may institute proceedings before the Tribunal without following the warning procedure.[21] The Tribunal may make an order declaring an agreement that breaches the First Conduct Rule (or any competition rule) void or voidable to extent specified in the order.[22]

Horizontal and vertical agreements Agreements and practices which may contravene the First Conduct Rule fall into two broad categories: horizontal agreements and vertical agreements.[23] A horizontal agreement is an agreement made by two or more actual or potential competitors, each operating at the same level of the production or distribution chain.[24] The First Conduct Rule prohibits certain horizontal agreements that may be particularly liable to harm competition such as price fixing cartels. The Competition Commission accepts, however, that horizontal agreements can also lead to economically beneficial outcomes, in particular if they combine complementary activities, skills or assets. Horizontal agreements of this kind allow parties to share risk, save costs, increase investments, pool know-how, enhance product quality and variety and stimulate innovation. Even if such agreements do harm competition to an extent, they may have sufficient pro-competitive efficiencies to qualify for exemption or may be otherwise excluded from the prohibition.[25]

A vertical agreement is an agreement between undertakings that operate, for the purposes of the agreement, at different levels of the production or distribution chain. This includes, for instance, an agreement between a producer of raw material and a manufacturer of finished products or an agreement between a manufacturer and a distributor.[26] The CJEU has held that vertical agreements, while generally less damaging to competition than horizontal agreements, may sometimes have a particularly significant restrictive potential.[27] The Competition Commission also considers that vertical agreements as compared with horizontal agreements are generally less harmful to competition, but that some vertical agreements may, nonetheless,

---

[20] Competition Ordinance, section 82(1); Guideline on the First Conduct Rule, para 5.1.

[21] Guideline on the First Conduct Rule, para 5.2.

[22] Competition Ordinance, Schedule 3, section 1(i).

[23] Guideline on the First Conduct Rule, para 6.1.

[24] Guideline on the First Conduct Rule, para 6.2.

[25] Guideline on the First Conduct Rule, para 6.4; cf. Competition Ordinance, Schedule 1, section 1.

[26] Guideline on the First Conduct Rule, para 6.5.

[27] Case C-32/11, *Allianz Hungariá Biztosíto v Gazdasági Versenyhivatal* EU:C:2013:160.

cause harm to competition. This may be the case where vertical agreements include restrictions which foreclose existing competition or limit the scope for market entry or expansion. In certain cases, vertical restrictions of competition may also serve to facilitate horizontal coordination between competing suppliers and/or downstream distributors.[28]　However, vertical agreements also frequently improve economic efficiency within a chain of production or distribution by facilitating better cooperation between the participating undertakings. In particular, vertical agreements can lead to a reduction in transaction and distribution costs and/or an optimisation of the parties' sales and investment levels.[29]　The fact that vertical agreements are generally less harmful to competition while offering greater scope for efficiencies will be reflected in the Commission's approach to these arrangements when applying the First Conduct Rule. As a general matter, competition concerns will only arise where there is some degree of market power at the level of the supplier and/or the buyer. The Commission's view is that vertical agreements between SMEs will rarely be capable of harming competition.[30]

Territorial application of the First Conduct Rule　The First Conduct Rule applies, pursuant to section 8 of the Competition Ordinance, to an agreement, concerted practice or decision that has the object or effect of preventing, restricting or distorting competition in Hong Kong even if:[31]

(a) the agreement or decision is made or given effect to outside Hong Kong;

(b) the concerted practice is engaged in outside Hong Kong;

(c) any party to the agreement or concerted practice is outside Hong Kong; or

(d) any undertaking or association of undertakings giving effect to a decision is outside Hong Kong.

This issue concerns subject-matter jurisdiction (i.e. whether the particular conduct is within the scope of the prohibition)[32] and not enforcement jurisdiction (i.e. whether a relevant authority or tribunal has the ability to enforce the prohibition against the infringing undertaking through sanctions such as the imposition of penalties or orders to stop the relevant practices). Unlike EU and UK competition law, which prohibit agreements restricting competition in so far as they may affect trade between EU Member States and trade within the UK, respectively, there is no requirement that trade within Hong Kong be affected. The Competition Commission provides no additional

---

[28]　Guideline on the First Conduct Rule, paras 6.6- 6.7.
[29]　Guideline on the First Conduct Rule, para 6.8.
[30]　Guideline on the First Conduct Rule, para 6.9.
[31]　Competition Ordinance, section 8.
[32]　*Aberdeen Journals Ltd v OFT* [2003] CAT 11.

guidance on how it will interpret or apply the First Conduct Rule to a party or conduct outside of Hong Kong.[33]

2.2 AGREEMENTS, CONCERTED PRACTICES AND DECISIONS OF ASSOCIATIONS

Agreements As defined in section 2(1) of the Competition Ordinance, the notion of an agreement is very broad, including any agreement, arrangement, understanding, promise or undertaking, whether express or implied, written or oral, and whether or not enforceable or intended to be enforceable by legal proceedings.[34] This notion centres around the existence of a concurrence of wills between at least two parties, the form in which it is manifested being unimportant so long as it constitutes the faithful expression of the parties' intention.[35] Any kind of dealing or contact, or a meeting of minds between parties could potentially be counted as an agreement within the scope of the First Conduct Rule. An agreement may exist whether or not there has been a physical meeting of the parties and may be formed, for example, through an exchange of letters, emails, SMS or telephone calls.[36] An undertaking may be found to be party to an agreement if it attends a meeting at which an anti-competitive agreement is reached and it failed to sufficiently object to, and publicly distance itself from, the agreement or the discussions leading to the agreement. This may be the case regardless of whether it played an active part in the meeting or intended subsequently to implement the agreement.[37]

EU case law on the notion of an agreement provides that a gentleman's agreement will fall within the scope of competition law where it amounts to the faithful expression of the joint intention of the parties to the agreement.[38] Unilateral action by one undertaking may constitute an agreement where it forms part of the contractual relations between that undertaking and other undertakings, in particular where it reflects the acceptance, tacit or express, by the latter of a policy pursued by the former.[39] The prohibition on anti-competitive agreements continues to apply to an agreement which is no longer in force as long as it continues to produce anti-competitive effects, in particular where, from the behaviour of the persons concerned there may be inferred the existence of elements of coordination peculiar to the agreement and producing the same result as that envisaged by the agreement.[40] Moreover, the fact that a

---

[33]   Guideline on the First Conduct Rule, para 1.13.
[34]   Competition Ordinance, section 2(1); Guideline on the First Conduct Rule, para 1.6.
[35]   Case T-41/96, *Bayer v Commission* [2000] ECR II-3383.
[36]   Guideline on the First Conduct Rule, para 2.23.
[37]   Guideline on the First Conduct Rule, para 2.24.
[38]   Case 41/69, *ACF Chemiefarma NV v Commission* [1970] ECR 661.
[39]   Case 107/82, *AEG-Telefunken AG v Commission* [1983] ECR 3151.
[40]   Case 51/75, *EMI Records Ltd. v CBS United Kingdom Ltd.* [1976] ECR 811.

clause in an agreement intended to restrict competition has not been implemented by the contracting parties is not sufficient to remove it from the prohibition.[41]

Single overarching agreement   An anti-competitive arrangement might comprise a series of sub-agreements concluded as part of a series of activities undertaken by the undertakings in pursuit of a common objective of harming competition. Where this is the case, the various sub-agreements are considered to form part of a single overarching agreement for the purposes of the First Conduct Rule.[42]   It follows that each participating undertaking will be responsible for the prohibited agreement as a whole.[43]   It is not necessary to show that an undertaking participated in or agreed to each and every aspect of an anti-competitive agreement for the undertaking to be held responsible for the agreement as a whole, if it can be shown that the undertaking knew, or should have known, that the collusion in which it participated was part of an overall plan intended to harm competition. For example, it is not necessary to show that an undertaking attended every meeting of a cartel arrangement if it can be shown that it knew, or should have known, that this was part of a plan intended to harm competition.[44]

The EU General Court held, in *Team Relocations v Commission*, that three conditions must be met in order to establish participation in a single and continuous infringement, namely the existence of an overall plan pursuing a common objective, the intentional contribution of the undertaking to that plan and its awareness, proved or presumed, of the offending conduct of the other participants.[45]   In *Amann & Söhne GmbH v Commission*, the GC stated that where there are numerous bilateral and multilateral contacts between a large number of parties, it cannot be presumed that they all form part of a single continuous infringement, especially where such parties operate on different relevant markets. For the purposes of characterising various instances of conduct as a single and continuous infringement, it is necessary to establish whether they display a link of complementarity in that each of them is intended to deal with one or more consequences of the normal pattern of competition and whether, through interaction, they contribute to the attainment of the set of anti-competitive effects desired by those responsible, within the framework of a global plan having a single objective. It is also necessary to prove that the overall plan included all the constituent elements of the cartel. It is not

---

41   Cases C-89/85 etc., *Åhlström Osakeyhtiö v Commission* [1993] ECR I-5193.
42   Guideline on the First Conduct Rule, para 2.25. This might also be referred to as a single and continuous infringement.
43   Case T-68/04, *SGL Carbon v Commission* [2008] ECR II-2511; Cases T-373/10 etc., *Villeroy & Boch Austria GmbH v Commission* EU:T:2013:445.
44   Guideline on the First Conduct Rule, para 2.26; Case C-49/92, *Commission v Anic Partecipazioi SpA* [1999] ECR I-4162.
45   Case T-204/08, *Team Relocations v Commission* [2011] ECR II-3569.

sufficient to prove that an undertaking participated in one element of the infringement, such as price coordination, for it to be held liable for other elements of the infringement, such as production limitation. Moreover, it is not sufficient to prove that there is a general common objective by reference to a general restriction or distortion of competition in the relevant market. For example, the object of price distortion is inherent in any price cartel and cannot, of itself, prove the existence of a common subjective element.[46]

Concerted practice　The First Conduct Rule covers, in addition to explicit agreements, other looser forms of cooperation known as concerted practices. A concerted practice is a form of cooperation, falling short of an agreement, where undertakings knowingly substitute practical cooperation for the risks of competition.[47]　By its very nature a concerted practice does not have all the elements of a contract but arises out of coordination which becomes apparent from the behaviour of the participants.[48]　Since both agreements and concerted practices fall within the scope of the First Conduct Rule, it should not be necessary for the Competition Commission explicitly to draw a dividing line between the two concepts.[49]　In EU competition law, conduct may amount to a concerted practice even where the parties have not explicitly adhered to a common plan defining their action in the market but knowingly adopt collusive actions which facilitate the co-ordination of their commercial behaviour.[50] Nevertheless, parallel behaviour by competitors in the market does not necessarily mean that the competitors are involved in a concerted practice or have made an agreement. If a market is highly competitive, it is to be expected that competitors will respond almost immediately to each other's pricing in the market.[51]　Thus, the fact that a vendor aligns its price with the highest price charged by a competitor is not necessarily evidence of a concerted practice but may be explained by a need to obtain the maximum profit.[52]　Equally, if one competitor lowers its prices, others may be likely to respond accordingly in order to avoid losing customers. The Competition Commission considers that this is the very essence of competition and is not a concerted practice.[53]

---

[46]　Case T-446/05, *Amann & Söhne GmbH & Co. KG v Commission.* [2010] ECR II-1255.

[47]　Guideline on the First Conduct Rule, para 2.27. The Competition Ordinance does not itself specify a definition of concerted practice.

[48]　Case 48/69, *Imperial Chemicals Industries Ltd. v Commission* [1972] ECR 619; Case C-79/95P, *John Deere v Commission* [1998] ECR I-3111.

[49]　Case C-49/92P, *Commission v Anic Partecipazioni* [1999] ECR I-4125; Case T-305/94, *Limburgse Vinyl Maatschappij v Commission* [1999] ECR II-931.

[50]　Cases 40/73 etc., *Coöperatieve Vereniging Suiker Unie UA v Commission* [1975] ECR 1663; Case T-7/89, *Hercules v Commission* [1991] ECR II-1711.

[51]　Cases C-89/85 etc., *Åhlström Osakeyhtiö v Commission* [1993] ECR I-5193.

[52]　Cases 40/73 etc., *Coöperatieve Vereniging Suiker Unie UA v Commission* [1975] ECR 1663.

[53]　Guideline on the First Conduct Rule, para 2.31.

In order to show that there has been a concerted practice, there must be sufficiently precise and coherent proof to justify the view that the parallel behaviour of the undertakings in question is the result of a concerted action by them.[54] Whether there is a concerted practice can only be correctly determined if the evidence is considered, not in isolation, but as a whole, account being taken of the specific features of the market in question.[55] The Competition Commission, in the Guideline on the First Conduct Rule, states that a concerted practice typically involves an exchange of competitively sensitive information between competitors. Whilst recognising that whether an exchange of such information is made as part of a concerted practice depends on the circumstances of the case, it declares that it will likely conclude that there exists a concerted practice with the object of harming competition where competitively sensitive information such as an undertaking's planned prices or planned pricing strategy is exchanged between competitors where (a) the information is given with the expectation or intention that the recipient will act on the information when determining its conduct in the market and (b) the recipient does act or intends to act on the information. In the absence of a legitimate business reason, it will likely be inferred from an information exchange of this kind that the party providing the information had the requisite expectation or intention to influence a competitor's conduct in the market. Similarly, in the absence of a legitimate business reason for taking receipt of the information or other evidence showing that the recipient did not act or intend to act on the information when determining its conduct in the market, it will likely be inferred that the recipient undertaking acted or intended to act on the information.[56]

This approach has been described in UK competition law variously as A-B-C information exchange or hub and spoke collusion. A, B and C can be seen as parties to a single infringement as opposed to independent vertical agreements if: (a) retailer A discloses to supplier B its future pricing intentions in circumstances where A may be taken to intend that B will make use of that information to influence market conditions by passing that information to other retailers (of whom C is or may be one); (b) B does, in fact, pass that information to C in circumstances where C may be taken to know the circumstances in which the information was disclosed by A to B; and (iii) C does, in fact, use the information in determining its own future pricing intentions.[57]

---

[54] Cases 29-30/83, *Compagnie Royale Asturienne des Mines v Commission* [1984] ECR 1679.

[55] Case 48/69, *Imperial Chemicals Industries v Commission* [1972] ECR 619.

[56] Guideline on the First Conduct Rule, paras 2.28-2.29; Case C-286/13P, *Dole Food Company Inc. v Commission* EU:C:2015:184.

[57] *JJB Sports plc v Office of Fair Trading* [2004] CAT 17.

Decisions of association of undertakings The First Conduct Rule applies where an undertaking, as a member of an association of undertakings, makes or gives effect to a decision of the association which has the object or effect of harming competition.[58] This is intended to prohibit indirect anti-competitive cooperation between undertakings through an association.[59] Examples of associations of undertakings include trade associations, cooperatives, professional associations or bodies, societies, associations without legal personality, and associations of associations. The mere fact that a professional association has statutory or regulatory functions does not mean that it is not an association of undertakings or that its decisions do not have the object or effect of harming competition.[60] It may be noted that agreements between associations of undertakings are treated as agreements between undertakings.[61]

Decisions of an association of undertakings include, without limitation, the constitution of the association, rules of the association, resolutions, rulings, decisions, guidelines or recommendations, whether made by the board, a member, a committee or an employee of the association.[62] A decision of an association will fall within the scope of the First Conduct Rule even if it is non-binding, such as recommended prices, including recommended fee scales of professional bodies.[63] For example, in *IAZ International Belgium NV v Commission*, a non-binding recommendation of a trade association was held to restrict competition where it urged its members not to deal with certain products.[64] In this respect, a recommendation made by an association of undertakings will fall within the scope of the prohibition where it constitutes a faithful expression of the members' intention to conduct themselves on the market in conformity with the terms of the recommendation.[65] Where undertakings, as members of an association of undertakings, make or give effect to a decision of the association of undertakings which has the object or effect of harming competition, the undertakings and the association may both incur liability under the Competition Ordinance.[66]

---

[58]   Competition Ordinance, section 6(1); Guideline on the First Conduct Rule, para 1.8.
[59]   Guideline on the First Conduct Rule, paras 2.32-2.33.
[60]   Guideline on the First Conduct Rule, para 2.34.
[61]   Case 71/74, *FRUBO v Commission* [1975] ECR 563.
[62]   Guideline on the First Conduct Rule, para 2.35.
[63]   Guideline on the First Conduct Rule, para 2.26.
[64]   Cases 96/82 etc., *IAZ International Belgium NV v Commission* [1983] ECR 3369. See also, Case T-90/11, *ONP v Commission* EU:T:2014:1049.
[65]   Cases 209/78 etc., *Heintz van Landewyck sarl v Commission* [1980] ECR 3125.
[66]   Guideline on the First Conduct Rule, paras 2.37 and 6.54. See, for example, Cases T-25/95, etc., *Cimenteries CBR SA v Commission* [2000] ECR II-491; Cases T-217/03 & T-245/03, *FNCBV v Commission* [2006] ECR I-4987.

2.3 OBJECT OR EFFECT OF HARMING COMPETITION

Prevention, restriction or distortion of competition The First Conduct Rule applies where the object or effect of an agreement or conduct is to prevent, restrict or distort competition in Hong Kong.[67] Each of these consequences is regarded as harming competition and the Competition Commission prefers to use the shorthand notion of harming competition throughout its Guideline on the First Conduct Rule.[68] In order to arrive at a true representation of the contractual position, the contract must be placed in the economic and legal context in the light of which it was concluded by the parties.[69] It should be borne in mind that restrictive contractual terms do not necessarily have as either their object or effect a restriction of competition. Such restrictions are not, therefore, within the scope of the First Conduct Rule. Thus, for instance, ancillary restraints that are necessary for the agreement to be workable are excluded.[70]

Object or effect of harming competition For the First Conduct Rule to apply, it is for the Commission to demonstrate that the agreement has either an anti-competitive object or an anti-competitive effect. These are, accordingly, two alternative ways of showing that the agreement harms competition: by object or by effect. Where an agreement has an anti-competitive object, it is not necessary to demonstrate that the agreement also has an anti-competitive effect.[71] The distinction between object and effect is important since once a commercial practice is found to restrict competition by object it will typically be very difficult for the parties to defend their arrangements on the basis that they satisfy the conditions for exclusion or exemption (whether on a self-assessment or in support of their arguments for a decision on their individual case).[72]

2.3.1 Object of harming competition

Object of harming competition Certain types of agreement between undertakings can be regarded by their very nature to be so harmful to the proper functioning of normal competition in the market that there is no need to

---

[67] Competition Ordinance, section 6(1); Guideline on the First Conduct Rule, para 3.1.
[68] Guideline on the First Conduct Rule, para 1.5 and footnote 5.
[69] Cases 142 & 156/84, *British American Tobacco Ltd. v Commission* [1987] ECR 4487.
[70] Guideline on the First Conduct Rule, para 3.28.
[71] Guideline on the First Conduct Rule, para 3.2; Cases 56 & 58/64, *Consten & Grundig v Commission* [1966] ECR 299; Case C-209/07, *Competition Authority v Beef Industry Development Society Ltd.* [2008] ECR I-8637.
[72] Case T-65/98, *Van den Bergh Foods Ltd. v Commission* [2003] ECR II-4662.

examine their effects. These agreements are considered to have the object of harming competition.[73] In *T-Mobile Netherlands*, the CJEU laid down a potentially very broad interpretation of the notion of anti-competitive object, holding that it is sufficient that an agreement has the potential to have a negative impact on competition.[74] However, following the later judgment in *Groupement des Cartes Bancaires v Commission*, it appears that anti-competitive object is to be more restrictively interpreted and limited to coordination which reveals a sufficient degree of harm to competition such that there is no need to examine its anti-competitive effects.[75] It may be noted, nevertheless, that parties to an agreement with the object of harming competition may not argue that their agreement does not contravene the First Conduct Rule merely because they happen to have a very small part of the market.[76]

The CJEU has held that the fact that a restriction is objectively justified on other grounds not related to competition, such as public health, may permit that restriction to be regarded as not having the object of harming competition.[77] In any event, if an agreement has more than one object, it will be capable of contravening the First Conduct Rule if any one of its objects is to harm competition.[78] Efficiencies such as improvements in production or distribution, factors tending to promote technical or economic progress, are not relevant for determining whether an agreement has the object of harming competition.[79]

An agreement may be considered to have an anti-competitive object even if it is not implemented by the parties.[80]

Determining the object of an agreement In order to determine whether an agreement has the object of harming competition, it is necessary to consider the content of the agreement, the way it is implemented and its context, including both the economic and legal context.[81] The CJEU held, in *Groupement des Cartes Bancaires v Commission*, that, when determining that context, it is also

---

[73] Guideline on the First Conduct Rule, para 3.3; Cases 56/64 & 58/64, *Consten & Grundig v Commission* [1966] ECR 299.

[74] Case C-8/08, *T-Mobile Netherlands BV v Raad van Bestuur van de Nederlandse Mededingingsautoriteit* [2009] ECR I-4529.

[75] Case C-67/13P, *Groupment des Cartes Bancaires v Commission* EU:C:2014:2204.

[76] Guideline on the First Conduct Rule, footnote 20; Case C-226/11, *Expedia Inc. v Authorité de la Concurrence* EU:C:2012:795.

[77] Case C-403/04P, *Sumitomo Metal Industries Ltd. v Commission* [2007] ECR I-729.

[78] Competition Ordinance, section 7(1); Guideline on the First Conduct Rule, para 3.12.

[79] Guideline on the First Conduct Rule, para 3.13. These are taken into account instead under the efficiencies assessment under Schedule 1, section 1 of the Competition Ordinance.

[80] Guideline on the First Conduct Rule, para 3.15.

[81] Guideline on the First Conduct Rule, para 3.4; Cases 29-30/83, *Compagnie Royale Asturienne des Mines SA v Commission* [1984] ECR 1679.

necessary to take into consideration the nature of the goods or services affected, as well as the real conditions of the functioning and structure of the market.[82] In *Allianz Hungária Biztosíto*, it held that it was necessary to take into account the structure of the market, the existence of alternative distribution channels and the respective importance and market power of the undertakings concerned.[83] This approach, however, if requiring too much analysis of the facts, risks blurring the distinction between object and effect.

Determining the object of an agreement requires an objective assessment of its aims, i.e. the purpose or aim of the agreement viewed in light of the way it is implemented, and not merely the subjective intention of the parties. Nonetheless, there is nothing to prevent the parties' intention from being taken into account when determining whether or not an agreement has the object of harming competition.[84] Although the category of agreements which have the object of harming competition cannot be reduced to an exhaustive list, the concept of an anti-competitive object can only be applied to conduct which is by its very nature harmful to competition.[85]

Agreements between competitors to fix prices, to share markets, to restrict output or to rig bids are agreements which are considered by the Competition Commission to have the object of harming competition. Agreements of this kind, commonly referred to as cartels, are inherently harmful to competition.[86] Each of these categories is also classified in the Competition Ordinance as Serious Anti-Competitive Conduct.[87] In EU competition law, price fixing, which is prohibited by Article 101(1)(a) TFEU, is considered to be capable of being anti-competitive by object.[88] In its Guidelines on Horizontal Cooperation Agreements, the European Commission also considers that exchange of information regarding future pricing policy is restrictive of competition by object. Agreements to limit output, which are prohibited by Article 101(1)(b) TFEU, and market sharing agreements, prohibited by Article 101(1)(c) TFEU, are also capable of being anti-competitive by object.[89]

In relation to vertical agreements between parties at different levels of the supply chain, the Competition Commission considers that resale price maintenance agreements may also be considered as having the object of

---

[82] Case C-67/13P, *Groupment des Cartes Bancaires v Commission* EU:C:2014:2204.
[83] Case C-32/11, *Allianz Hungariá Biztosíto Zrt. v Gazdasági Versenyhivatal* EU:C:2013:160.
[84] Guideline on the First Conduct Rule, para 3.5.
[85] Guideline on the First Conduct Rule, para 3.6; Case C-209/07, *Competition Authority v Beef Industry Development Society Ltd.* [2008] ECR I-8637.
[86] Guideline on the First Conduct Rule, para 3.7.
[87] Competition Ordinance, section 2(1).
[88] Case C-8/08, *T-Mobile Netherlands BV v Raad van Bestuur van de Nederlandse Mededingingsautoriteit* [2009] ECR I-4529.
[89] Case C-209/07, *Competition Authority v Beef Industry Development Society Ltd.* [2008] ECR I-8637.

harming competition.[90] The imposition of fixed minimum resale prices on distributors is regarded as restrictive of competition by object in EU competition law.[91]

Assessment of agreements having anti-competitive object   Where an agreement has an anti-competitive object, it is not necessary also to show that it has an anti-competitive effect. It follows that an examination of the context of an agreement for the purposes of determining whether it has the object of harming competition does not require or involve an analysis of the effects of the agreement in the market.   It is therefore sufficient to show that the agreement has the potential to harm or is capable of harming competition in the relevant context.[92]   The CJEU confirmed, in *Dole Food Company Inc v Commission*, that the sharing of commercially sensitive information between competitors amounts to an infringement of competition law by its very object. The fact that the undertakings in question routinely discussed and disclosed to each other their pricing plans before implementing them amounted to an anti-competitive concerted practice, without it being necessary to show that there was any connection between the companies' interactions and prices paid by consumers.[93]

Where it is established that an agreement has the object of harming competition, the agreement cannot be defended by the parties showing that the agreement does not in fact have any anti-competitive effects or that such effects are not likely to flow from the agreement.[94] In examining the relevant context for an agreement, the following factors may show that an agreement does not have the object of harming competition:[95]

- in the case of an agreement between parties at the same level of the supply chain, an examination of the relevant context reveals that the parties are neither competitors nor potential competitors;
- an examination of the relevant context reveals that at the relevant time there is in fact no competition in the market to be harmed;
- if the primary objective pursued by the agreement does not contravene the First Conduct Rule, any restrictions which are necessary and proportionate to achieving that primary objective do not have the object of harming competition and will also not contravene the First Conduct Rule.

An undertaking may be taken to have made or given effect to an agreement or decision or to have engaged in a concerted practice that has as its object the

---

[90]   Guideline on the First Conduct Rule, para 3.8.
[91]   Case 161/84, *Pronuptia de Paris GmbH v Schillgalis* [1986] ECR 353.
[92]   Guideline on the First Conduct Rule, para 3.9.
[93]   Case C-286/13 P, *Dole Food Company Inc v Commission* EU:C:2015:184.
[94]   Guideline on the First Conduct Rule, para 3.10.
[95]   Guideline on the First Conduct Rule, para 3.11.

prevention, restriction or distortion of competition even if that object can be ascertained only by inference.[96] In practice, it will often be necessary to infer an anti-competitive object from the facts underlying the agreement and the specific circumstances in which it operates or will operate.[97]

2.3.2 Effect of harming competition

Effect of harming competition   An agreement will contravene the First Conduct Rule where it has as its effect the prevention, restriction or distortion of competition.[98] In determining whether an agreement has anti-competitive effects, an assessment must be made of the agreement as a whole.[99] It is necessary to take into consideration the entire factual, legal and economic context in which the agreement operates.[100]

When demonstrating that an agreement has an anti-competitive effect, consideration is had not only of any actual effects but also effects that are likely to flow from the agreement.[101] Account must be taken not only of the immediate effects of the agreement but also of its potential effects and of the possibility that the agreement may be part of a long term plan.[102] For an agreement to have an anti-competitive effect it must have, or be likely to have, an adverse impact on one or more of the parameters of competition in the market, such as price, output, product quality, product variety or innovation. Agreements can have such an effect by reducing competition between the parties to the agreement or by reducing competition between any one of them and third parties.[103] If an agreement has more than one effect, it is considered to have an anti-competitive effect if one of those effects is anti-competitive.[104]

Determining effects on competition   Anti-competitive effects on competition within a relevant market are likely to occur where it can be expected that, due to the agreement, one or more of the parties would be able profitably to raise prices or reduce output, product quality and variety or innovation. This will depend on several factors such as: the nature and content of the agreement; the extent to which the parties individually or jointly have or obtain some degree of market power; and the extent to which the agreement contributes to the creation, maintenance or strengthening of that market power or allows the

---

[96]   Competition Ordinance, section 7(2).
[97]   Guideline on the First Conduct Rule, para 3.14.
[98]   Competition Ordinance, section 6(1).
[99]   Cases 142 & 156/84, *British American Tobacco Ltd. v Commission* [1987] ECR 4487.
[100]   Case C-234/89, *Delimitis v Heninger Bräu* [1991] ECR I-935.
[101]   Guideline on the First Conduct Rule, para 3.17.
[102]   Cases 142 & 156/84, *British American Tobacco Ltd. v Commission* [1987] ECR 4487.
[103]   Guideline on the First Conduct Rule, para 3.18.
[104]   Competition Ordinance, section 7(3); Guideline on the First Conduct Rule, para 3.19.

parties to exploit market power.[105]   The existence of similar contracts may be taken into consideration in determining whether contracts of this type are capable of restricting competition.[106]   Account should also be taken of the possibility that the agreement might affect potential competition in the market, at least where there this is a real, concrete possibility.[107]

Assessment of agreements having anti-competitive effect   When assessing the actual or likely anti-competitive effects of an agreement, it is necessary to consider the extent to which the undertakings concerned have market power in the relevant market.   The exercise of defining the relevant market assists in identifying in a systematic way the competitive constraints that undertakings face when operating in a market.[108]   Market power can be thought of as the ability to profitably maintain prices above competitive levels for a period of time or to profitably maintain output in terms of product quality, quantity and variety or innovation below competitive levels for a period of time.   Market power is, however, a matter of degree.   The degree of market power for concerns to arise under the First Conduct Rule is not the same as the degree of market power required for concerns to arise under the Second Conduct Rule and is typically less.[109]   The assessment of market power of the parties to an agreement does not rely solely on any single factor and includes, for example, an assessment of the combined market shares of the parties, market concentration, barriers to entry or expansion in the market, the competitive advantages of the parties and the existence of any countervailing power on the part of buyers/suppliers.[110]

In assessing whether an agreement or concerted practice has the actual or likely effect of harming competition, the Competition Commission may assess what the market conditions would have been in the absence of the conduct, commonly referred to as establishing the counter-factual situation.   It will then compare these counter-factual market conditions with the conditions resulting where the conduct is present.[111]

Insignificant anti-competitive effect   Where the effect of an agreement on the competitive process is insignificant, the agreement will be considered as not

---

[105] Guideline on the First Conduct Rule, para 3.20; Case 99/79, *Lancôme SA v Etos BV* [1980] ECR 2511.

[106] Case 23/67, *Brasserie de Haecht v Wilkin* [1967] ECR 407.

[107] Case T-504/93, *Tiercé-Ladbroke v Commission* [1997] ECR II-923; Case T-374/93, *European Night Services v Commission* [1998] ECR II-3141.

[108] Guideline on the First Conduct Rule, para 3.21.

[109] Guideline on the First Conduct Rule, para 3.22-3.23.

[110] Guideline on the First Conduct Rule, para 3.24.

[111] Guideline on the First Conduct Rule, para 3.25. Cf. Case 56/65, *Société Technique Minière v Maschinenbau Ulm GmbH* [1966] ECR 235.

infringing the First Conduct Rule on the basis of its effects.[112]   When considering whether an agreement has an effect on competition that is more than minimal, account may be taken of the cumulative effect on competition of similar agreements in the relevant market and the contribution which the particular agreement under examination makes on the cumulative effect.[113]   In EU law, only appreciable restrictions on competition are held to infringe Article 101 TFEU[114] and the European Commission has adopted *de minimis* rules whereby agreements between undertakings having less than a 10% combined market share and 15% individual market share in horizontal agreements are generally regarded as not having an appreciable effect on competition.[115]   Although similar provisions apply in the UK, as well as Singapore and Malaysia, no such thresholds have been adopted in Hong Kong by the Competition Commission.

Restrictions necessary for a legitimate commercial purpose   Where the main arrangement covered by an agreement is not in itself harmful to competition, the Competition Commission considers that restrictions contained in the agreement which are necessary for the agreement to be workable, referred to as ancillary restraints, fall outside the prohibition in the First Conduct Rule.[116]   A restriction of competition will be ancillary when it is directly related to and necessary for the implementation of a separate, main (non-restrictive) agreement and proportionate to it.   To be considered directly related to the main agreement, the restriction must be subordinate to the implementation of the main agreement and be inseparably linked to it.[117]   For example, in certain circumstances, a restriction may be necessary for the protection of investment in a business which would not have taken place in the absence of the protection from competition.[118]   For a restriction to be truly ancillary, it must also be objectively necessary for the implementation of the main arrangement and proportionate to it.   If, without the restriction, the main agreement would be difficult or impossible to implement, the restriction may be regarded as objectively necessary and proportionate.[119]   This principle may be particularly relevant, for example, in the context of an assessment of a distribution agreement or a joint venture.   For example, in *Société Technique Minière v Maschinenbau Ulm*, an exclusive distributor license was regarded as

---

[112]   Guideline on the First Conduct Rule, para 3.26.   This does not apply to agreements having the object of harming competition.

[113]   Guideline on the First Conduct Rule, para 3.27.

[114]   Case 5/69, *Volk v Vervaecke* [1969] ECR 295.

[115]   EU notice on agreements of minor importance, OJ 2014 C291/1.

[116]   Guideline on the First Conduct Rule, paras 3.28-3.29.

[117]   Guideline on the First Conduct Rule, paras 3.30-3.31.

[118]   Case 258/78, *Nungesser KG v Commission* [1982] ECR 2015.

[119]   Guideline on the First Conduct Rule, para 3.32.

necessary for the penetration of a new sales area.[120]   In the case of a joint venture which is not itself harmful to competition, a non-compete clause between the parent entities and the joint venture might be regarded as ancillary to the joint venture or necessary for the joint venture agreement to be workable for the lifetime of the joint venture.[121]

2.4 AGREEMENTS THAT MAY CONTRAVENE THE FIRST CONDUCT RULE

2.4.1 Serious Anti-Competitive Conduct

Serious anti-competitive conduct   The Competition Commission recognises that most agreements between undertakings are unlikely to be anti-competitive and will not raise concerns under the First Conduct Rule.[122]   Unlike Article 101(1) TFEU and Chapter I of the UK Competition Act 1998,[123] section 6(1) of the Competition Ordinance does not itself provide an indicative list of agreements that are to be regarded as harming competition. The Competition Ordinance instead lists certain types of agreements that will be regarded as Serious Anti-Competitive Conduct.[124]   This is defined in the Competition Ordinance as any conduct that consists of any of the following or any combination of the following:

(a) fixing, maintaining, increasing or controlling the price for the supply of goods or services;

(b) allocating sales, territories, customers or markets for the production or supply of goods or services;

---

[120] Case 56/65, *Société Technique Minière v Maschinenbau Ulm GmbH* [1966] ECR 235.

[121] Guideline on the First Conduct Rule, paras 3.29 and 3.33.

[122] Guideline on the First Conduct Rule, para 3.1.

[123] These provide that agreements within the scope of the respective prohibitions are, in particular, those which:

(a) directly or indirectly fix purchase or selling prices or any other trading conditions;

(b) limit or control production, markets, technical development or investment;

(c) share markets or sources of supply;

(d) apply dissimilar conditions to equivalent transactions with other trading partners, thereby placing them at a competitive disadvantage;

(e) make the conclusion of contracts subject to acceptance by the other parties of supplementary obligations which, by their nature or according to commercial usage, have no connection with the subject of such contracts.

[124] Competition Ordinance, section 2(1). The issue of whether the conduct is considered serious anti-competitive conduct only arises after the Competition Commission forms the view that the conduct contravenes the First Conduct Rule. Thus, whether conduct is considered serious anti-competitive conduct is not part of the determination of whether the conduct contravenes the First Conduct Rule (i.e. because it has the object or effect of harming competition): Guideline on the First Conduct Rule, para 5.7.

(c) fixing, maintaining, controlling, preventing, limiting or eliminating the production or supply of goods or services;

(d) bid-rigging.

The Competition Commission considers that horizontal cartel arrangements between competitors that seek to fix prices, share markets, restrict output or rig bids are forms of Serious Anti-Competitive Conduct.[125] Vertical arrangements are, as a general matter, unlikely to be considered Serious Anti-Competitive Conduct, although they may amount to such conduct in certain cases, such as resale price maintenance.[126]

Whether or not conduct amounts to Serious Anti-Competitive Conduct has important procedural implications. In such cases, the Competition Commission may institute proceedings before the Tribunal without following the Warning Notice procedure.[127] In addition, the general exclusion for agreements of lesser significance does not apply.[128]

Price fixing   Horizontal price fixing agreements, i.e., agreements between competitors with the aim of fixing, maintaining, increasing or otherwise controlling prices, are probably the most egregious form of anti-competitive behaviour since price competition is a fundamental tenet of the market economy. Such agreements are regarded as entailing Serious Anti-Competitive Conduct.[129] They are treated by the Competition Commission as generally having the object of harming competition.[130] Thus, it is not open to a party to argue that the effect of a price fixing agreement is not appreciably to restrict competition.[131] Horizontal price fixing may take a number of forms, such as directly agreeing upon a specified price, the amount or percentage by which prices are to be increased or a price range. Price in this context includes any price element including any discount, rebate, allowance, price concession or other advantage in relation to the supply of products.[132] Price fixing may also be achieved by indirect means, including where, for example, undertakings agree not to quote a price without consulting competitors or not to charge less than any other price in the market.[133] Similarly, the exchange of information

---

[125]   Guideline on the First Conduct Rule, para 5.4.

[126]   Guideline on the First Conduct Rule, paras 5.5-5.6.

[127]   Guideline on the First Conduct Rule, paras 5.1. The warning notice procedure under section 82 of the Competition Ordinance affords an undertaking an opportunity to cease or alter the investigated conduct within a specified warning period.

[128]   Competition Ordinance, Schedule 1, section 5(2).

[129]   Competition Ordinance, section 2(1); Guideline on the First Conduct Rule, para 6.15.

[130]   Guideline on the First Conduct Rule, para 6.10.

[131]   Case C-226/11, *Expedia Inc v Autorité de la concurrence* EU:C:2012:795.

[132]   Guideline on the First Conduct Rule, para 6.11. See, for example, Case T-213/00, *CMA CGM v Commission* [2003] ECR II-913.

[133]   Guideline on the First Conduct Rule, para 6.12. See, for example, Case T-587/08, *Fresh Del Monte Produce v Commission* EU:T:2013:130.

on future price intentions may be assessed as price fixing.[134]   Price fixing may
also arise through the activities of a trade association or professional body such
as where the association issues a recommendation to members on prices and/or
publishes (possibly non-binding) fee scales.[135]   Price fixing may also be
engaged by agreements between buyers fixing the prices at which they will buy
products or services.[136]

An agreement regarding price may still amount to price fixing even if it
does not entirely eliminate all price competition.   Competition may, for
example, be harmed despite the ability to grant discounts up to a certain agreed
level on a published price list or notwithstanding that parties only fix one price
component while competing on other.[137]   In markets where competition is
already constrained by other factors, such as sectoral regulation, restrictions on
price competition will call for particular examination in order to ensure that
competition is not further limited.[138]

The Competition Commission notes that certain legitimate commercial
arrangements may involve parties agreeing on pricing within the context of the
relevant arrangements.   For example, although joint selling arrangements are
likely to have the object of restricting competition since the pricing policy of
competitors is coordinated, where parties to a production joint venture agree
that the joint venture will sell its jointly produced products at a particular price
and joint sales are necessary for the joint production to be implemented, the
Competition Commission takes the view that the joint setting of the price of the
products will not be considered as having the object of harming competition.[139]

Market sharing   Market sharing agreements are agreements between
competitors that seek to allocate sales, territories, customers or markets for the
production or supply of particular products.   Market sharing entails competing
undertakings agreeing to divide up a market so that the undertakings are
sheltered from competition in their allotted portion of the market.[140]

Agreements between competitors with the aim of sharing markets are
treated by the Competition Commission as having the object of harming
competition.[141]   The Commission considers that horizontal market sharing

---

[134] Guideline on the First Conduct Rule, para 6.12.
[135] Guideline on the First Conduct Rule, para 6.14. Non-binding price recommendations or
       fee scales will likely be assessed as having the object of harming competition, as
       ultimately these arrangements might not differ in substance to a direct agreement or
       concerted practice between the members of the association.
[136] See, for example, Case C-578/11P, *Deltafina spa v Commission* EU:C:2014:1742.
[137] Guideline on the First Conduct Rule, para 6.13.
[138] Case 209/78, etc., *Heintz van Landewyck sarl v Commission* [1980] ECR 3125.
[139] Guideline on the First Conduct Rule, para 6.16.
[140] Guideline on the First Conduct Rule, para 6.17.
[141] Guideline on the First Conduct Rule, para 6.18. Cf. Case C-239/11P, *Seimens AG v
       Commission* EU:C:2013:866.

agreements constitute Serious Anti-Competitive Conduct.[142] It notes, however, that certain legitimate commercial arrangements may involve parties agreeing to share markets. For example, competitors might agree to cease production of certain products so that they can specialise in the production of other products which they can then supply to each other on a reciprocal basis. An objective assessment of the nature of such an arrangement viewed in its context may lead to the conclusion that the arrangement does not have the object of harming competition.[143]

The European Commission's approach to a variety of commonly occurring cooperation arrangements under its Horizontal Cooperation Guidelines may be instructive in seeking to draw the line between harmful and beneficial market sharing. Of particular relevance is its approach to joint production including specialisation. Joint production occurs where the parties agree to produce certain products jointly. Specialisation occurs where the parties agree that one or both of them will withdraw from the production of a product and purchase it from the other party. For those agreements that are not covered by the Specialisation Block Exemption,[144] the parties have to demonstrate improvements in production or other efficiencies. The European Commission recognises that specialisation may give rise to economic benefits in the form of economies of scale or scope or better production technologies, unless they are an instrument for price fixing, output restriction or market or customer allocation.

Output limitation   Output limitation agreements are those agreements between competitors which fix, maintain, control, prevent, limit or eliminate the production or supply of products. Output limitation agreements can take the form of production or sales quota arrangements involving undertakings limiting the volume or type of products available in the market. They may also include agreements that limit or coordinate investment plans or control capacity.[145] Horizontal output limitation agreements constitute Serious Anti-Competitive Conduct.[146] The Competition Commission considers that output limitation agreements between competitors have the object of harming competition.[147] Agreements which reduce or control the level of output of a product by their very nature result in price increases. They may also have other anti-competitive effects, for example by aligning product quality and/or facilitating collusion between suppliers on price.[148] The fact that an industry might be perceived to be in crisis by industry participants as a result of

---

[142] Competition Ordinance, section 2(1); Guideline on the First Conduct Rule, para 6.19.
[143] Guideline on the First Conduct Rule, para 6.20.
[144] Commission Regulation (EC) No 267/2010, OJ 2010 L83/1.
[145] Guideline on the First Conduct Rule, para 6.21.
[146] Competition Ordinance, section 2(1); Guideline on the First Conduct Rule, para 6.24.
[147] Guideline on the First Conduct Rule, para 6.22.
[148] Guideline on the First Conduct Rule, para 6.22.

structural over-capacity is not a defence to an agreement on output limitation being anti-competitive and no special treatment is accorded to such crisis cartels under the Competition Ordinance.[149]

Certain legitimate commercial arrangements may involve parties agreeing on output which will not, viewed in context, be regarded as having the object of harming competition, such as where parties to a joint venture agree to a particular level of output for the joint venture.[150]

Bid-rigging   It is a key feature of competitive tendering procedures that bidders should prepare and submit bids independently or as part of a legitimate consortium. Bid-rigging generally involves two or more undertakings agreeing that they will not compete with one another for particular projects.   For example, they might agree amongst themselves which bidder will be the winner, so that the outcome of an ostensibly competitive process is rigged.[151] Bid-rigging can take a number of forms, including undertakings agreeing:[152]

- that certain parties will not submit a bid or will withdraw a bid previously submitted (bid suppression);
- to take turns at being the bid winner;
- that certain bidders will submit higher bid prices or less attractive terms than the suppler chosen by the parties to win the tender (cover bidding); or
- to take other actions that reduce the competitive tension in the bidding process, such as by agreeing minimum bidding prices or agreeing that the winning bidder will reimburse other bidders' costs.

The Competition Commission considers that bid-rigging is inherently anti-competitive and has the object of harming competition.[153]   Bid-rigging constitutes Serious Anti-Competitive Conduct.[154]   Section 2(2) of the Competition Ordinance provides a specific definition of bid rigging for the purposes of determining whether there is Serious Anti-Competitive Conduct. This applies to an agreement made between two or more undertakings whereby at least one of them agrees not to submit a bid or to withdraw a bid, or a submission of bids that are arrived at by agreement between two or more undertakings, where the fact of the agreement is not made known to the person calling for the bids or tenders.[155]   However, the Commission considers that bid-rigging for the purposes of the First Conduct Rule is not limited to the definition in section 2(2). For example, if the bid-rigging is made known to the

---

[149] Guideline on the First Conduct Rule, para 6.23.
[150] Guideline on the First Conduct Rule, para 6.25.
[151] Guideline on the First Conduct Rule, para 6.26. See, for example, Case T-9/99, *HFB Holding v Commission* [2002] ECR II-1487.
[152] Guideline on the First Conduct Rule, para 6.28.
[153] Guideline on the First Conduct Rule, para 6.29.
[154] Competition Ordinance, section 2(1).
[155] Competition Ordinance, section 2(2).

person calling for or requesting bids at or before the time when a bid is submitted or withdrawn by a party, it will not amount to Serious Anti-Competitive Conduct in the form of bid rigging but it may still contravene the First Conduct Rule if it has the object or effect of harming competition.[156]

Bid-rigging should be distinguished from legitimate forms of joint tendering which will generally be assessed by reference to their actual or likely effects on competition.[157]

2.4.2 Joint action

Joint buying A joint or group buying agreement arises when undertakings agree to jointly purchase products including inputs used for the production of other products.[158] Joint buying can be carried out in a number of ways, for example through a jointly controlled legal entity, through an association, by a contractual arrangement between undertakings, or some looser form of cooperation.[159] Joint buying frequently allows SME undertakings to achieve purchasing efficiencies similar to their larger competitors. This may result in lower prices in the market where the joint buying takes place, lower transaction costs and/or distribution efficiencies for the SMEs. Joint buying of this type seldom gives rise to competition concerns.[160]

A joint buying arrangement would typically not be considered by the Competition Commission to have the object of harming competition unless it is a disguised buyers' cartel, such as where buyers collude in secret on the prices they will pay for purchases made individually. Joint buying arrangements, including any agreement by members of the buying group of the prices to pay suppliers, will, however, be analysed as to whether the effects, actual or likely, of the arrangements are harmful to competition.[161] An analysis of the effects on competition will consider the effects on both the upstream buying and the downstream selling markets, i.e. the relevant markets where the jointly purchased products are subsequently sold or where other products produced using jointly purchased inputs are sold. Harmful effects on competition in the downstream market may occur, if, for example, the joint buying results in competitors in the downstream market achieving a high degree of commonality of costs or where there is some sharing of competitively sensitive information beyond what is necessary for the purposes of the buying arrangement. As regards the upstream buying market, concerns may arise if, for example, the

---

[156] Guideline on the First Conduct Rule, para 6.27.
[157] Guideline on the First Conduct Rule, para 6.30.
[158] Guideline on the First Conduct Rule, para 6.31.
[159] Guideline on the First Conduct Rule, para 6.32.
[160] Guideline on the First Conduct Rule, para 6.33.
[161] Guideline on the First Conduct Rule, para 6.34.

joint buying results in the buying market being foreclosed to competing purchasers.[162] In general, joint buying is unlikely to give rise to concerns under the First Conduct Rule if the parties do not have market power in the relevant downstream markets.[163]

Illustrative of this benevolent stance towards joint purchasing is the CJEU judgment in *Gøttrup-Klim* that a provision in the rules of a cooperative purchasing organisation which forbade its members from participating in other forms of organised cooperation in direct competition with it did not restrict competition. This was the case so long as the provision was restricted to what was necessary to ensure that the cooperative functioned properly and maintained its contractual power in relation to producers. The Court considered that the rules in question were necessary to enable individual farmers to combine their limited purchasing power in the face of very powerful world suppliers of fertilisers and plant protection products.[164] The European Commission, in its Horizontal Cooperation Guidelines, considers that joint purchasing arrangements can cause competition issues where the purchasers have market power in either the purchasing market (where the inputs are purchased), as rivals may be excluded from access to a key input, or the selling market (where the products incorporating the inputs are sold), since reduced costs may not be passed on to consumers as a result of effective competition. It considers that if the parties to the agreement have a combined market share below 15% on both the purchasing and the selling market the agreement is unlikely to restrict competition. The absence of any market share safe harbours in the Competition Commission's Guideline on the First Conduct Rule is a notable point of comparison with the approach of the European Commission.

Exchange of information   In general, the more informed consumers are the more effective competition is likely to be. In the normal course of business, undertakings exchange information on a variety of matters with no risk to the competitive process. Indeed, competition is often enhanced through the sharing of information, for example in relation to best practices or exchanges of information which allow firms to better predict how demand is likely to evolve. Similarly, information exchange may facilitate price comparisons by consumers or reduce consumer search costs.[165] However, the Competition Commission may have concerns where competitors exchange information, in particular where they exchange competitively sensitive information. Competitively sensitive information includes information relating to price,

---

[162] Guideline on the First Conduct Rule, paras 6.35- 6.36.
[163] Guideline on the First Conduct Rule, para 6.37.
[164] Case C-250/90, *Gøttrup-Klim e.a. Grovvareforeninger v Dansk Landbrugs Grovvare-selskab AmbA* [1994] ECR I-5641.
[165] Guideline on the First Conduct Rule, para 6.38; Case C-7/95, *John Deere v Commission* [1998] ECR I-3111.

elements of price or price strategies, customers, production costs, quantities, turnover, sales, capacity, product quality, marketing plans, risks, investments, technologies and innovations.[166]

If competitors share information in private on their future individual intentions or plans with respect to price, the Competition Commission will likely consider that the agreement to exchange such information, or concerted practice giving rise to such an exchange of information, has the object of harming competition.[167] The exchange of competitively sensitive information may occur directly between competitors or indirectly through a third party such as a trade association. In addition, competitors may seek to use a third party supplier or distributor as a conduit for the indirect exchange of, for example, future pricing information.[168] The Competition Commission's intention is that, if undertakings agree with each other to exchange information on their proposed future intentions with respect to price indirectly through a third party conduit, it will likely be considered a form of price fixing with the object of harming competition.[169] Equally, such an information exchange may occur as a result of a concerted practice, for example if: (i) an undertaking exchanges information via a third party functioning as a conduit intending that the third party will make use of the information to influence market conditions by passing it to a competitor of the undertaking; (ii) the third party in fact transmits the information to the competitor; and (iii) the competitor uses the information to determine its conduct in the market.[170]

Where an agreement to exchange information does not have the object of harming competition, the Competition Commission may consider whether it might have anti-competitive effects, depending on the circumstances. It will consider the following, and other relevant, factors when determining when an exchange of information has the effect of harming competition.[171] The smaller the number of undertakings operating in the market (i.e. the more concentrated the market), the more frequent the exchange of information between the undertakings concerned, the more competitively sensitive the information, the more current it is, the more detailed the information exchanged, the more individualised or company specific the information, the more access to the information is limited to the undertakings participating in the information exchange, the more likely it is that the agreement will give rise to concerns under the First Conduct Rule.[172] The type of information exchanged and the structure of the market in which the information exchange occurs are important factors. For example, the exchange of historical, aggregated and anonymised

---

[166] Guideline on the First Conduct Rule, para 6.39.
[167] Guideline on the First Conduct Rule, para 6.40.
[168] Guideline on the First Conduct Rule, para 6.41.
[169] Guideline on the First Conduct Rule, para 6.42.
[170] Guideline on the First Conduct Rule, para 6.43.
[171] Guideline on the First Conduct Rule, paras 6.44-6.45.
[172] Guideline on the First Conduct Rule, para 6.46.

data is less likely to harm competition, since the exchange of such information is unlikely to reduce independent decision-making by undertakings with regard to their actions in the market.[173] In general, the exchange of publicly available information is unlikely to involve a contravention of the First Conduct Rule. Publicly available information in this sense is information that is equally accessible in terms of the cost of access to all competitors and customers. Information which is more costly to obtain for parties not affiliated with the information exchange is unlikely to be considered truly public.[174] Where information is exchanged in public so that all parties have access to the information (including customers), harmful effects are less likely. Exchanges which take place in public are also more likely to generate efficiencies.[175]

The European Commission has provided guidance on information exchange between competitors in its Horizontal Cooperation Guidelines. However, the guidance is far from comprehensive in covering the increasingly diverse situations in which information exchange has attracted the attention of the competition authorities. In seeking to distinguish between acceptable and impermissible information exchange, the focus should be on why the information is being exchanged and the effects, including spill over risks to other markets, evidence of another infringement or another commercial justification. In assessing information exchange as being anti-competitive, market characteristics are important, particularly concentrated markets and markets where the products are not overly complex. A useful approach is to ask whether the information that is being exchanged would not ordinarily be shared with a competitor or is such as to reduce a party's incentives to compete aggressively. Exchanging information on current or future prices, costs, promotions, capacity, margins or quantity is likely to give rise to a presumption of anti-competitive effects.

Group boycotts As a general principle, an undertaking is free to choose with whom it will or will not do business. However, an agreement or concerted practice amongst competitors not to do business with targeted individuals or undertakings may be an anti-competitive group boycott. A group boycott is considered to have the object of harming competition when, in particular, a group of competitors agrees to exclude an actual or potential competitor.[176] Where a boycott is intended to facilitate a wider cartel agreement, the boycott is simply part of the cartel and will be assessed accordingly.[177]

---

[173] Guideline on the First Conduct Rule, para 6.47.
[174] Guideline on the First Conduct Rule, para 6.48. The fact that information could have been gathered from a customer does not mean that the information is publicly available.
[175] Guideline on the First Conduct Rule, para 6.49.
[176] Guideline on the First Conduct Rule, para 6.50-6.51.
[177] Guideline on the First Conduct Rule, para 6.52.

Activities of trade associations and industry bodies   The Competition Commission recognises that trade associations and similar bodies play a valuable role in the economy in terms of furthering the collective interests of members. Such organisations may represent industry players in dealings with Government or help promote the members' interests in the media. They can assist with collecting and disseminating statistical information to members or serve as a forum for agreeing industry standards or standard terms and may offer a range of advisory services for members or training. The Competition Commission acknowledges that many of their activities have a positive impact in the economy and often do not give cause for competition concerns.[178] In the Guideline on the First Conduct Rule, the Competition Commission provides guidance on a number of issues of special relevance for trade associations and similar organisations.[179] The focus of the Competition Commission on the activities of trade associations, while recognising their legitimate aims and functions, reflects the concern that, in bringing competitors together, one element of a potential infringement of competition law will be present – a combination of competitors.

Membership of an association can, in some cases, be an essential pre-condition for competing in a market. In such circumstances, exclusion from membership can significantly impact an undertaking's effectiveness as a competitor and might be equivalent in terms of effect to an anti-competitive boycott.[180] To minimise competition concerns of this kind, the rules of admission to membership of the relevant association should be transparent, proportionate, non-discriminatory, based on objective standards and provide for an appeal procedure in the event of a refusal to admit a party to membership. Rules of admission to membership which do not satisfy these requirements may be viewed by the Competition Commission as having either the object or effect of harming competition.[181] Procedures for members wishing to leave an association and/or join a competing association, or expelling the members of an association, may harm competition where they are not based on reasonable and objective standards or where there is no proper appeals procedure in the event of expulsion from membership.[182]

Certification practices and minimum industry standards   A trade association may certify or award quality labels to members to recognise that they have met certain minimum industry standards. Such practices are often valuable to consumers, for example where they offer a quality assurance or

---

[178] Guideline on the First Conduct Rule, para 6.53.
[179] Guideline on the First Conduct Rule, para 6.55.
[180] Guideline on the First Conduct Rule, para 6.56.
[181] Guideline on the First Conduct Rule, para 6.57.
[182] Guideline on the First Conduct Rule, para 6.58. In this context, the effect of a restriction on leaving an association may prevent undertakings from developing alternative business opportunities thus harming the competitive process.

promote interoperability between products.[183] Where certification is available to all suppliers that meet objective and reasonable quality requirements, this is unlikely to raise concerns under the First Conduct Rule.[184] The Competition Commission may, however, consider certification practices as having the object or effect of harming competition when additional obligations are imposed on members as regards the products they can buy or sell, such as an obligation only to sell the certified products, or where restrictions are imposed on members' pricing or marketing conduct.[185]

Standard terms for the supply of products In certain industries, market participants may agree on standard terms relating to the supply of products.[186] The Competition Commission recognises that the use of standard terms makes it easier for consumers to compare conditions offered and may facilitate switching between alternative suppliers. Standard terms might also result in reduced transaction costs, facilitate market entry and increase legal certainty.[187] However, where standard terms define the nature of, or relate to the scope of, the product, their use may limit product variety and innovation. Similarly, standard terms relating to price can harm price competition. If a standard term becomes an accepted industry standard, restricting access to the standard term makes market entry more difficult.[188]   Moreover, if a trade association prohibits new entrants from accessing its standard terms and the use of those terms is vital for successful entry into the market, the Commission will likely consider such conduct as having the object of harming competition. Standard terms affecting prices charged to consumers, including terms which recommend particular prices, will also be considered as having the object of harming competition.[189]

In general, standard terms which do not affect price are unlikely to raise concerns under the First Conduct Rule if participation in the process for adopting the terms is open and the standard terms are non-binding and accessible to all market participants. However, this may not apply in all cases including where the standard terms define the scope or nature of the product sold as the use of such terms may entail a risk of reduced innovation and product variety. In this case, an assessment of the effects of the arrangements will be required to determine whether they are anti-competitive.[190]

---

[183] Guideline on the First Conduct Rule, para 6.59.
[184] Guideline on the First Conduct Rule, para 6.60.
[185] Guideline on the First Comduct Rule, para 6.61.
[186] Guideline on the First Conduct Rule, para 6.62. The use of such terms is common, for instance, the insurance and banking sectors.
[187] Guideline on the First Conduct Rule, para 6.63.
[188] Guideline on the First Conduct Rule, para 6.64.
[189] Guideline on the First Conduct Rule, para 6.65.
[190] Guideline on the First Conduct Rule, para 6.66.

In some markets, businesses may enter into agreements on the definition of technical or quality requirements with which, for example, current or future products must comply. Such agreements often increase competition, lower production and sales costs, increase interoperability and enhance product quality.[191] Agreements that use a standard as part of a broader restrictive agreement, however, will likely be considered by the Competition Commission as having the object of harming competition, whereas other standardisation agreements will need to be analysed based on their actual or likely effects.[192]

The European Commission has given detailed consideration to standardisation. Its Horizontal Cooperation Guidelines identify two forms of standards which may invite antitrust scrutiny.

- Standardisation: Standardisation agreements are agreements whose primary objective is the definition of technical or quality requirements with which current or future products, production processes, services or methods may comply. The Horizontal Cooperation Guidelines apply to standard setting in the form of product certification as well as to technology standard setting.

- Standard terms: Some industries use standard terms and conditions of sale or purchase developed by a trade association, or directly by competing companies. The Horizontal Cooperation Guidelines cover such standard terms to the extent that they establish standard conditions of sale or purchase of goods or services between competitors and consumers for substitute products.

The Horizontal Cooperation Guidelines may therefore provide a point of reference for determining when standardisation raises competition concerns. An agreement on standards will be compliant with EU competition law provided that (a) manufacturers are free to produce other new products which do not meet the new standard (b) participation in the standard is unrestricted and transparent and (c) the standardisation agreement does not impose an obligation to comply with the standard. If the parties agreed only to produce machinery which conforms to the new standard, the agreement would limit technical development and prevent the parties from selling different products not meeting the standard. This would infringe EU competition law unless the parties are able to satisfy the conditions of Article 101(3), in particular by demonstrating efficiencies that outweigh the restrictive effects on competition.

2.4.3 Vertical price restrictions

Vertical price restrictions Vertical price restrictions are restrictions imposed or recommended by an undertaking which affect the prices at which another

---

[191] Guideline on the First Conduct Rule, para 6.67.
[192] Guideline on the First Conduct Rule, para 6.68.

undertaking operating at a different level of the production or distribution chain sells products.[193] The most common example of vertical price restriction is resale price restriction, where a supplier imposes or recommends prices at which another undertaking sells the products it purchases from the supplier. Vertical price restrictions are not limited, however, to resale prices. While the Competition Commission refers to resale price restrictions in its Guideline on the First Conduct Rule, it states that the principles it outlines should be understood to apply to vertical price restrictions generally and nothing turns on whether there is or is not a resale as such. The key consideration is whether the vertical price is fixed, whether there is a minimum or maximum price level or whether the price level is merely recommended.[194]

Resale price maintenance Resale price maintenance (RPM) occurs whenever a supplier establishes a fixed or minimum resale price to be observed by the distributor when it resells the product affected by the RPM obligation.[195] The Guideline on the First Conduct Rule sets out a number of ways in which RPM can restrict competition:[196]

- RPM facilitates coordination between competing suppliers through enhanced price transparency in the market. In this context, particular concerns may arise where RPM is employed by multiple suppliers in the market or RPM is otherwise common in the market.
- RPM undermines suppliers' incentives to lower prices to distributors and distributors' incentives to negotiate lower wholesale prices.
- RPM limits intra-brand price competition by restricting the ability of distributors to offer lower sales prices for the affected brand as compared with prices offered by competing distributors of the same brand. This is of particular concern where there are strong or well-organised distributors operating in a market. RPM facilitates coordination between distributors on the downstream market affected by the RPM. In this context, concerns arise particularly where there is evidence that the RPM conduct is distributor driven.
- RPM prevents the emergence of new market participants at the distributor level and generally hinders the expansion of distribution models based on low prices, such as the emergence of discounter distributors.
- Where RPM is implemented by a supplier with market power, this may have the effect of excluding smaller suppliers from the market. Distributors are incentivised to promote only the product affected by the RPM causing harm to consumers.

---

[193] Guideline on the First Conduct Rule, para 6.69.
[194] Guideline on the First Conduct Rule, para 6.70.
[195] Guideline on the First Conduct Rule, para 6.71.
[196] Guideline on the First Conduct Rule, para 6.72.

RPM may also be achieved indirectly by, for instance, fixing the distributor's margin or the maximum level of discount the distributor can grant from a prescribed price level. The supplier might also make the grant of rebates or the reimbursement of promotional costs subject to the observance of a given price level by the distributor, or link the prescribed resale price to the resale price of competitors. The supplier might equally use threats, intimidation, warnings, penalties, delays in, or the outright suspension of, deliveries to achieve RPM.[197]

Where an agreement involves direct or indirect RPM, the Competition Commission takes the view that the arrangement may have the object of harming competition. Whether this is in fact the case turns on a consideration of the content of the agreement establishing the RPM, the way the agreement is implemented by the parties and the relevant context.[198] For example, RPM will be considered as having the object of harming competition if there is evidence that the RPM was implemented by a supplier in response to pressure from a distributor seeking to limit competition from competitors of the distributor at the resale level. Similarly, RPM may be considered as having the object of harming competition if it is implemented by a supplier solely to foreclose competing suppliers.[199]

If RPM does not have the object of harming competition, the Competition Commission will assess whether the RPM causes harm by way of its effects.[200] For example, RPM may be required in a franchise distribution system (or other distribution system which entails a uniform model of distribution) for the purposes of organising a coordinated price campaign. In this scenario, the Competition Commission would consider that the RPM does not have the object of harming competition but would assess whether the arrangement had any harmful effects on competition.[201]

The European Commission has long maintained its hostility towards vertical resale price maintenance, as confirmed in the Vertical Restraints Block Exemption[202] and the Guidelines on Vertical Restraints.[203] The latter state that agreements or concerted practices having as their direct or indirect object the establishment of a fixed or minimum resale price or a fixed or minimum price level to be observed by the buyer are treated as having a hardcore restriction. Where an agreement includes RPM, that agreement is presumed to restrict competition and thus to fall within Article 101(1) TFEU. It is acknowledged, however, that RPM may lead to efficiencies in three narrow contexts:

---

[197] Guideline on the First Conduct Rule, para 6.73.
[198] Guideline on the First Conduct Rule, para 6.74.
[199] Guideline on the First Conduct Rule, para 6.75.
[200] Guideline on the First Conduct Rule, para 6.76.
[201] Guideline on the First Conduct Rule, para 6.77.
[202] Commission Regulation (EC) No 330/2010, OJ 2010 L102/1.
[203] EU Guidelines on Vertical Restraints, OJ 2010 C130/1.

- first, where a manufacturer introduces a new product, RPM may be helpful during the introductory period of expanding demand to induce distributors to better take into account the manufacturer's interest to promote the product;
- second, fixed resale prices, and not just maximum resale prices, may be necessary to organise a franchise system or similar distribution system applying a uniform distribution format, so that, for example, a coordinated short term low price campaign (2 to 6 weeks in most cases) will also benefit consumers;
- third, RPM may limit the effects of free-riding on services investments by retailers. The extra margin provided by RPM may allow retailers to provide (additional) pre-sales services, in particular in case of experience or complex products.

Although the European Commission has rarely brought RPM cases, national competition authorities have been bolder in challenging such practices.[204] In practice, the EU authorities have tended to treat the practice as restrictive by object, which raises the evidential burden on the parties to substantiate any efficiencies flowing from RPM. It appears that the authorities would need to be convinced at the very least that there were no less restrictive means of achieving the claimed benefits of RPM.

Recommended or maximum prices Where a supplier merely recommends a resale price to a distributor or requires a reseller to respect a maximum resale price, the agreement will not be considered by the Competition Commission to have the object of harming competition. Instead, agreements that entail recommended or maximum resale prices will be subject to an analysis of their competitive effects.[205] Such agreements may give rise to a concern where they serve to establish a focal point for distributor pricing[206] and/or where they soften competition between suppliers or otherwise facilitate coordination between suppliers. An important factor in the analysis is the market position of the supplier. The more the supplier has market power, the more likely it is that the conduct will have the effect of harming competition.[207]

Where recommended or maximum resale arrangements are combined with measures that make them work in reality as fixed or minimum prices, the Competition Commission will assess them in the same manner as RPM.[208] This could include:

- the use of a price monitoring system;

---

[204] The German Federal Cartel Office for example fined WALA, a maker of herbal therapies and beauty products, €6.5 million in 2013 for putting pressure on retailers and using contractual provisions to enforce its recommended resale prices.
[205] Guideline on the First Conduct Rule, para 6.78.
[206] That is, where the distributors generally follow the recommended or maximum price.
[207] Guideline on the First Conduct Rule, para 6.80.
[208] Guideline on the First Conduct Rule, para 6.81.

- an obligation on distributors to report other members of a distribution network that deviate from the recommended or maximum price level; or
- other measures which reduce the distributor's incentive to lower the resale price.[209]

Where a firm retaliates or threatens to retaliate when its recommended resale price is not followed, the Competition Commission will assess the conduct as a form of RPM.[210]

2.4.4 Distribution agreements

Exclusive distribution and exclusive customer allocation In considering exclusive distribution, the Competition Commission distinguishes between:

- exclusive distribution agreements where a supplier assigns exclusivity for the resale of its products in a particular territory to a single distributor or reseller; and
- exclusive customer allocation agreements where the supplier assigns exclusivity to a single distributor for resale to a particular group of customers.

The possible risks to competition from such agreements are reduced competition between distributors for the same products or brands, potential market sharing and a reduction in competition through limiting market access to potentially competing distributors.[211] Exclusive distribution and exclusive customer allocation agreements will not generally be considered by the Commission to have the object of harming competition.[212] The assessment of these types of provision will generally depend on their effects or likely effects on competition in the relevant market, including an assessment of how intra-brand or inter-brand competition is affected, the extent of the territorial and/or customer sales limitations, and whether exclusive distributorships are common generally in the markets impacted by the agreements under consideration.[213]

Whilst no market share safe harbours are set out in the Guideline on the First Conduct Rule, it may be noted that, under the European Commission's Vertical Restraints Block Exemption, where the relevant market shares of the parties do not exceed 30% a wide variety of exclusivity provisions in

---

[209] Guideline on the First Conduct Rule, para 6.82. Where the presence of these practices or similar mechanisms may support a conclusion that ostensibly recommended or maximum resale price arrangements function in reality as RPM, this is not inevitably the case and the position must be assessed in light of all available facts.

[210] Guideline on the First Conduct Rule, para 6.83.

[211] Guideline on the First Conduct Rule, para 6.85.

[212] Guideline on the First Conduct Rule, para 6.86

[213] Intra-brand competition is competition between products of the same brand. Inter-brand competition is competition between products of differing brands.

distribution agreements are treated as compatible with Article 101 TFEU, provided that no hardcore restrictions are included. A distinction may be drawn between restrictions on active and passive sales. The European Commission cites the following as examples of what it regards as hardcore restrictions of passive sales which, if included in a distribution agreement, would result in the unavailability of exemption under the block exemption:

- agreeing that the (exclusive) distributor shall prevent customers located in another (exclusive) territory from viewing its website or shall put on its website automatic rerouting of customers to the manufacturer's or other (exclusive) distributors' websites;
- agreeing that the (exclusive) distributor shall terminate consumers' transactions over the internet once their credit card data reveals an address that is not within the distributor's (exclusive) territory;
- agreeing that the distributor shall limit a proportion of overall sales made over the internet;
- agreeing that the distributor shall pay a higher price for products intended to be sold by the distributor online than for products intended to be sold offline.

Franchise agreements   A franchise is an arrangement where independent businesses agree that the franchisee will sell the product and use the brand name, know-how, client care and marketing of the franchisor. Franchise arrangements are a common business model for the production and distribution of products in Hong Kong.[214] With limited investment and risk, franchise agreements permit franchisors to quickly establish a network of entities with a uniform brand image and consistent product offering. Franchise agreements also allow franchisees with limited resources to benefit from the reputation and support services of a more widely known brand.[215] Measures necessary for maintaining the identity and reputation of a franchise network and/or provisions of a franchise agreement which are essential to protect the franchisor's branding, trademarks and know-how do not raise concerns under the First Conduct Rule. Other restrictions in a franchise agreement may contravene the First Conduct Rule where they have the object or effect of harming competition.[216]

Restrictions with the object of maintaining the identity and reputation of a franchise network, whilst limiting a franchisee's commercial freedom, do not raise concerns under the First Conduct Rule where they relate directly to and

---

[214] Guideline on the First Conduct Rule, para 6.115.
[215] Guideline on the First Conduct Rule, para 6.116.
[216] Guideline on the First Conduct Rule, para 6.117.

are necessary for the implementation of the franchise agreement.[217] These may include the following obligations on the franchisee:[218]

- to apply the business method developed by the franchisor;
- not to use the franchisor's trademarks, trade names or other marks anywhere other than at the agreed franchise location;
- to exploit the franchise from the agreed location and not to change location without the consent of the franchisor;
- in certain circumstances, not to sell competing goods apart from those supplied by or selected by the franchisor;
- to sell products only in a manner consistent with instructions of the franchisor, e.g. following a particular recipe, using particular technology, sales methods or promotional material; or
- to decorate the franchise premises in a manner specified by the franchisor.

Certain provisions that legitimately protect the franchisor's know-how and expertise are inherent in the nature of franchising and, as such, typically raise no concerns under the First Conduct Rule. Such provisions may include, for example, a restriction on the transfer of the franchise, requirements on the use of the franchisor's intellectual property or obligations in relation to protecting confidential information and know-how, a prohibition during the term of the franchising contract on opening the same kind of shop in an area where it might compete with another franchisee or on carrying on any kind of competing business, or a prohibition for a reasonable period after the termination of the franchise on opening the same kind of shop in an area where it might compete with another franchisee.[219]

Selective distribution agreements   Selective distribution systems are a common feature of the market in Hong Kong, particularly as regards the sale of branded final products. Selective distribution is an arrangement whereby a business sells products to end consumers through a network of authorised retailers chosen on the basis of particular criteria. Generally the suppliers will prevent the authorised retailers from reselling the products concerned to non-authorised retailers. Selective distribution is very often economically beneficial and an effective way of furthering inter-brand competition. In particular, it may assist in establishing a quality reputation for a new product, incentivise retailers to increase marketing efforts and serve to maintain brand image and quality standards.[220] In determining the application of competition law to selective distribution systems, a distinction needs to be drawn between qualitative and quantitative criteria.

---

[217] Guideline on the First Conduct Rule, para 6.118.
[218] Guideline on the First Conduct Rule, para 6.119.
[219] Guideline on the First Conduct Rule, para 6.120.
[220] Guideline on the First Conduct Rule, paras 6.121-6.122.

Qualitative criteria include: criteria relating to the training or qualifications required of staff; criteria relating to the type of equipment available on the premises of the retail outlet; a stipulation that the products be sold in a specialist shop or that there be a separate display for the products; criteria requiring sales outlets to have a certain appearance; a stipulation requiring particular opening hours; a stipulation requiring the provision of after sales services. Generally, where a supplier selects retailers on the basis of purely qualitative criteria, the arrangement will not give rise to concerns under the First Conduct Rule where the following conditions apply:[221]

- the nature of the product is such as to require a selective distribution network in order to preserve its quality and ensure its proper use;
- authorised retailers are selected on the basis of non-discriminatory qualitative criteria relating to their technical ability to handle the product or the suitability of their premises to protect the brand image of the product; and
- the relevant criteria do not go beyond what is necessary for the particular product concerned.

Where the selective distribution system does not meet these conditions the Competition Commission may need to assess the effects of the arrangement on competition. In this context, it may consider, for example, whether the arrangement leads to anti-competitive foreclosure at the distributor/retailer level and/or serves to facilitate collusion between suppliers or distributors/retailers.[222] Risks to competition may be more likely when the supplier has market power, where the number of authorised retailers is small and/or all major competing suppliers in the market have similar selective distribution methods.[223]

Some selective distribution systems select retailers on quantitative criteria, e.g. sales targets or a pre-defined of number of retailers in a particular locality. In addition, they may contains restrictions that do not relate to the qualitative needs of the supplier, for example, where retailers are prevented from making cross sales to other members of the system or sales to customers outside a prescribed class of customers. Such arrangements may give rise to concerns under the First Conduct Rule on the basis of their effects on competition.[224] In assessing the effects of such arrangements, the Commission will consider the market power of the supplier. Selective distribution systems are more likely to cause concern where inter-brand competition is limited and the supplier's market position is particularly strong. In addition, where there is widescale use of selective distribution in the relevant market, the risks of foreclosing certain types of retailer, such as more efficient retailers or price discounters, and

---

[221] Guideline on the First Conduct Rule, para 6.123.
[222] Guideline on the First Conduct Rule, para 6.124.
[223] Guideline on the First Conduct Rule, para 6.125.
[224] Guideline on the First Conduct Rule, para 6.126.

collusion between the major suppliers, i.e. competing brands, are more likely to arise.[225]

2.4.5 Joint venture agreements

Joint ventures The notion of a joint venture may be used to describe various types of cooperative arrangements including joint production arrangements, joint buying arrangements, joint selling, distribution and marketing arrangements, and joint R&D ventures. The activities of a joint venture may be carried out through a legal entity separate from the parties to the joint venture or by some or all parties to the joint venture.[226] Where a joint venture amounts to a merger, the joint venture is excluded from scope of the First Conduct Rule.[227] The creation of a joint venture to perform, on a lasting basis, all the functions of an autonomous economic entity[228] constitutes a merger for these purposes. The Competition Commission considers that the following non-exhaustive factors provide an indication that a joint venture does not perform on a lasting basis all the functions of an autonomous economic entity and is therefore within the scope of the First Conduct Rule:[229]

- the joint venture does not have a management dedicated to its day-to-day operations or access to sufficient resources including finance, staff, and assets, in order to conduct on a lasting basis its business activities;
- the joint venture merely takes over a specific function within the parent companies' business activities, as is the case with joint ventures limited to production or R&D or where the joint venture effectively acts as a distribution arm for the parent entities;
- the joint venture sells a significant proportion of its output to its parents; and/or
- the joint venture is created for a short period of time.

Where a joint venture falls within the scope of the First Conduct Rule, the Commission will consider whether it has the object or effect of harming competition in Hong Kong. However, if the joint venture, viewed as a whole, does not have the object or effect of harming competition, restrictions which are directly related to and necessary for implementing the joint venture will also fall outside of the First Conduct Rule. For example, a non-compete clause between the parent entities and their joint venture might be regarded as directly related to and necessary for implementing the joint venture for the lifetime of

---

[225] Guideline on the First Conduct Rule, para 6.127.
[226] Guideline on the First Conduct Rule, para 6.90.
[227] Competition Ordinance, Schedule 1, section 4.
[228] Competition Ordinance, Schedule 7, section 3(4).
[229] Guideline on the First Conduct Rule, para 6.92.

the joint venture.[230] Common types of joint ventures involve joint production agreements, joint tendering and joint selling, distribution and marketing arrangements.

Joint production agreements Joint production agreements may take a number of forms. Thus, they provide that production is carried out by one party or by two or more parties or the parties may establish a separate legal entity for the purposes of the joint production.[231] Although agreements which involve price-fixing or output limitation are generally considered as having the object of harming competition, the Competition Commission will not consider joint venture agreements that agree to a particular level of output for the joint venture as having the object of harming competition but will instead assess such arrangements based on whether the production joint venture as a whole has the effect of harming competition.[232] Similarly, if the parties agree that the joint venture will sell the jointly produced products, the joint setting of the price of those products will not be considered as having the object of harming competition where joint sales are necessary for the joint production to be implemented in the first place, i.e. if, absent the joint selling, the parents would not otherwise enter into the joint production. Again, in these circumstances, the Commission will consider the actual or likely effects of the joint venture as a whole on competition.[233] Where a joint production agreement allows parties to produce a product that they would not, objectively, be able to produce alone, the Commission considers that the agreement will not likely have the object or effect of harming competition.[234]

Joint production agreements may sometimes have the effect of harming competition, for example, where:[235]

- producing jointly leads to reduced product variety in the markets where the joint venture partners competed prior to forming the joint venture;
- producing jointly results in higher prices for customers;
- producing jointly results in an increase in the parties' commonality of costs with the result that the parties can more easily coordinate market prices; or
- the agreement leads to an exchange of competitively sensitive information beyond that which is strictly necessary for producing jointly.

---

[230] Guideline on the First Conduct Rule, para 6.93-6.94.
[231] Guideline on the First Conduct Rule, para 6.95.
[232] Guideline on the First Conduct Rule, para 6.96.
[233] Guideline on the First Conduct Rule, para 6.97.
[234] Guideline on the First Conduct Rule, para 6.98.
[235] Guideline on the First Conduct Rule, para 6.99.

The European Commission, in its Guidelines on Horizontal Cooperation Agreements, accepts that joint production between non-competitors does not generally give rise to competition issues. However, if there are indications that a potential competitor would have entered the market independently without incurring a significant cost, the cooperation will need to be examined more closely. It further considers that joint production agreements between competitors do not necessarily give rise to competition issues if the cooperation is the only commercially feasible way to enter a new market, to launch a new product or service, or to carry out a specific project, or if significant cost reductions are realised. Efficiencies may be generated, for example, where joint production follows joint R&D. The main source of competition issues arising in joint production is the coordination of the parties' behaviour as suppliers.

Joint tendering Joint tendering generally involves undertakings cooperating openly with a view to making a joint bid.[236] If the aim or effect of the agreements is to artificially inflate the bid price it may fall foul of the First Conduct Rule. The Competition Commission accepts that where the joint tendering activity is carried out in the open and the arrangement is known to the party organising the tender, competition concerns may not arise at all.[237] In particular, the submission of a joint tender can be of benefit to competition where it allows participation by companies which would not have been able to make a stand-alone bid, thereby resulting in additional bids. Equally, joint tendering may enable companies to submit more competitive bids, e.g. through a consortium arrangement.[238] Moreover, joint tendering is less likely to give rise to competition concerns where the undertakings involved pool their complementary skills or different specialities. For example, the undertakings may have access to different and complementary technologies or the cooperation may facilitate access to raw materials, the workforce necessary for the project, or finance.[239]

Joint tendering will not generally be considered by the Commission to have the object of harming competition, and such arrangements will be assessed based on their actual or likely effects.[240] For example, where the parties could have made independent bids, joint tendering which leads to a reduction in the number of potential bidders is more likely to have harmful effects where there is already a limited number of potential bidders in a concentrated market.[241]

---

[236] Guideline on the First Conduct Rule, para 6.101. Joint tendering may be contrasted with bid-rigging which more often involves collusion by competing bidders which nonetheless submit separate bids.

[237] Guideline on the First Conduct Rule, para 6.102.

[238] Guideline on the First Conduct Rule, para 6.103.

[239] Guideline on the First Conduct Rule, para 6.104.

[240] Guideline on the First Conduct Rule, para 6.106.

[241] Guideline on the First Conduct Rule, para 6.105.

Moreover, even where the party commissioning the bids is aware of joint bidding arrangements which are ostensibly transparent, questions can arise over, for example, side arrangements which might involve agreement on allocations or subcontracting of the main agreement in the event that the joint bid is successful.

Joint selling, distribution and marketing   Agreements where undertakings agree to jointly sell, distribute or market particular products, known as sales-related joint ventures, provide a wide range of possible joint ventures.   Such arrangements range from collaboration in respect of advertising only or the joint provision of after-sales service through to joint selling involving the joint determination of key commercial parameters including price.[242]   A sales-related joint venture can be an effective way of facilitating market entry for a new product, particularly where SMEs collaborate with a view to selling a new product which they could not market individually.   The Competition Commission accepts that a sales related joint venture does not give rise to competition concerns where the joint venture is objectively necessary for a party to enter a market it could not have entered on its own or with a smaller number of parties than those actually involved in the collaboration.[243]

Sales-related joint ventures can give rise to concerns under the First Conduct Rule, however, where they lead to price fixing, output restriction, market sharing or the exchange of competitively sensitive information.[244]   For example, agreements between competitors which are limited to the joint selling of products can serve as a vehicle for price fixing and may also entail restricting the output of the parties concerned.   Equally, competing undertakings might enter into a reciprocal distribution arrangement with a view to limiting competition between them by allocating markets.   In such cases, the agreements are likely to have the object of harming competition and may also be considered Serious Anti-Competitive Conduct.[245]

Where sales-related joint ventures between competitors do not have the object of harming competition, they might, nonetheless, give rise to concerns under the First Conduct Rule where the relevant arrangements result in anti-competitive effects.[246]   The Guideline on the First Conduct Rule provides three examples of possible anti-competitive effects.   These might arise (a) if the relevant arrangements increase the parties' commonality of variable costs, (b) if the arrangements involve the exchange of competitively sensitive information which goes beyond what might be necessary for the purposes of implementing the collaboration or (c) in the case of reciprocal and non-

---

[242]   Guideline on the First Conduct Rule, para 6.107.
[243]   Guideline on the First Conduct Rule, para 6.108.
[244]   Guideline on the First Conduct Rule, para 6.109.
[245]   Guideline on the First Conduct Rule, paras 6.110-6.111.
[246]   Guideline on the First Conduct Rule, para 6.112.

reciprocal distribution agreements between competitors, if the arrangement serves to undermine the incentive of one party to enter the market of another.[247]

It may be helpful to distinguish different practices by the degree of risk presented. At one end of the spectrum there is joint selling that leads to joint determination of all commercial aspects related to the sale of the product including price. Joint selling between competitors that involves coordination on price needs to be examined carefully given the risk that it will lead to an overall coordination of the parties' pricing. Care also needs to be taken since joint commercialisation provides an opportunity for the exchange of commercially sensitive information between competitors and this can increase the risk of restricting competition. At the other end of the spectrum more limited agreements that only address one specific marketing function such as advertising, distribution, service or after-sales tend to present less of a risk of an unlawful restriction of competition.

The European Commission stated in its Guidelines on Horizontal Cooperation Agreements that commercialisation agreements and joint selling between competitors can only have a restrictive effect on competition if the parties have some degree of market power. If the combined market share of the parties does not exceed 15% on a relevant market, it is likely that the agreement will not be regarded as anti-competitive. If the parties' combined market share is greater than 15%, a closer examination is required taking account of the parties' market power and the characteristics of the relevant market. It is notable that there is no reference to any market share safe harbours in the Competition Commission's Guideline on the First Conduct Rule. The CJEU accepted that joint commercialisation was compatible with Article 101 TFEU where the creation of agricultural cooperatives as a means of encouraging modernisation and rationalisation did not generally have an anti-competitive object and was justified by the existence of large numbers of small producers who are inherently subject to market failure.[248]

2.5 EXCLUSIONS AND EXEMPTIONS FROM THE FIRST CONDUCT RULE

2.5.1 Exclusions and exemptions from the First Conduct Rule

Exclusions and exemptions from the First Conduct Rule Section 30 of the Competition Ordinance provides that the First Conduct Rule does not apply

---

[247] Guideline on the First Conduct Rule, para 6.113.
[248] Case C-399/93, *H.G. Oude Luttikhuis v. Verenigde Coöperatieve Melkindustrie Coberco* [1995] ECR I-4515.

where the agreement, decision or concerted practice falls within the scope of the following categories of exclusions specified in Schedule 1:[249]

- agreements enhancing overall economic efficiency;
- compliance with legal requirements;[250]
- services of general economic interest;[251]
- mergers; and
- agreements of lesser significance.

In addition, the First Conduct Rule will not apply where the conduct in question is covered by a Block Exemption Order issued by the Competition Commission pursuant to section 15 or where the conduct is exempted by section 31 (public policy) or section 32 (international obligations) of the Competition Ordinance,[252] or where the Conduct Rules are disapplied in the case of statutory bodies, specified persons and persons engaged in specified activities as provided for in sections 3 and 4 of the Competition Ordinance.[253]

Mergers To the extent that an agreement results in, or if carried out would result in, a merger, the First Conduct Rule does not apply to the agreement.[254]

Agreements of lesser significance The Competition Ordinance provides a general exclusion from the First Conduct Rule for agreements of lesser significance. Accordingly, Schedule 1, section 5 provides that the First Conduct Rule does not apply to:[255]

(a) an agreement between undertakings in any calendar year if the combined turnover of the undertakings for the turnover period does not exceed HK$200 million;

(b) a concerted practice engaged in by undertakings in any calendar year if the combined turnover of the undertakings for the turnover period does not exceed HK$200 million; or

(c) a decision of an association of undertakings in any calendar year if the turnover of the association for the turnover period does not exceed HK$200 million.

Turnover for the purposes of this general exclusion means the total gross revenues of an undertaking whether obtained in Hong Kong or outside Hong

---

[249] Competition Ordinance, section 30 and Schedule 1; Guideline on the First Conduct Rule, Annex, para 1.6. Section 36 provides that the Chief Executive in Council may by order, subject to the approval of the Legislative Council, amend Schedule 1.

[250] See Chapter One, pp. 16-17

[251] See Chapter One, pp. 28-30.

[252] See Chapter One, pp. 17-18.

[253] See Chapter One, pp. 25-27.

[254] Competition Ordinance, Schedule 1, section 4(1); Guideline on the First Conduct Rule, Annex, para 5.1.

[255] Competition Ordinance, Schedule 1, section 5(1). Section 5(3)-(4) lays down rules for determining the turnover period.

Kong. In the case of an association of undertakings, turnover means the total gross revenues of all the members of the association whether obtained in Hong Kong or outside Hong Kong.[256]

The general exclusion for agreements of lesser significance is not available if the agreement, concerted practice or decision involves Serious Anti-Competitive Conduct.[257]

This exclusion may be contrasted with the more generous *de minimis* rules in other competition law regimes, such as the EU, which exclude the application of the prohibition on restrictive agreements, other than in the case of hard-core restrictions, where the undertakings concerned have a combined market share below 10% in the case of horizontal restrictions and up to 30% in the case of vertical restrictions.

Commission decision confirming exclusion or exemption Undertakings to whom an exclusion or exemption applies will not contravene the First Conduct Rule.[258] This is so even where their conduct has the object or effect of harming competition. There is no requirement to apply to the Competition Commission in order to secure the benefit of a particular exemption or exclusion. Undertakings may assess for themselves whether their conduct falls within the terms of a particular exclusion or exemption. Equally, undertakings may assert the benefit of an exclusion or exemption as a defence in any proceedings before the Competition Tribunal or other courts.[259] However, undertakings seeking greater legal certainty may elect to apply, pursuant to section 9 of the Competition Ordinance, to the Commission for a decision as to whether or not the agreement in question is excluded or exempt from the First Conduct Rule on any of the grounds listed above.[260] The Commission, after considering any representations made by interested parties, may make a decision pursuant to section 11 of the Competition Ordinance as to whether or not the agreement is excluded or exempt from the application of the First Conduct Rule.[261] Where the Commission issues a decision that an agreement is excluded or exempt from the application of the First Conduct Rule, each undertaking specified in the decision is immune from any action under the Competition Ordinance with

---

[256] Competition Ordinance, Schedule 1, section 5(5). Additional rules in respect of the calculation of relevant turnover for the purposes of this particular general exclusion are contained in regulations made by the Secretary for Commerce and Economic Development under section 163(2) of the Competition Ordinance: Guideline on the First Conduct Rule, Annex, para 6.4.

[257] Competition Ordinance, Schedule 1, section 5(2); Guideline on the First Conduct Rule, Annex, para 6.3.

[258] Guideline on the First Conduct Rules, Annex, para 1.2.

[259] Guideline on the First Conduct Rule, Annex, para 1.2.

[260] Competition Ordinance, section 9. See Chapter Five, pp. 3-11 for the procedures in applying for a decision.

[261] Competition Ordinance, section 11(1).

regard to that agreement in so far as the undertaking complies with every condition and limitation imposed by the decision.[262]

2.5.2 Agreements enhancing overall economic efficiency

Agreements enhancing overall economic efficiency   The Competition Ordinance provides for a general exclusion from the First Conduct Rule on the ground that an agreement enhances overall economic efficiency.[263]   This exclusion is available whether the agreement has the object or the effect of harming competition.[264]   Schedule 1, section 1 provides that the economic efficiency exclusion applies where the following cumulative conditions are met, namely where the relevant agreement:

    (a) contributes to–
         (i) improving production or distribution; or
         (ii) promoting technical or economic progress,
        while allowing consumers a fair share of the resulting benefit;
    (b) does not impose on the undertakings concerned restrictions that are not indispensable to the attainment of these objectives; and
    (c) does not afford the undertakings concerned the possibility of eliminating competition in respect of a substantial part of the goods or services in question.

Since the conditions are cumulative, failure to comply with any one of them renders the exclusion inapplicable. Whereas the burden of proving that an agreement restricts competition is on the Competition Commission, the burden of proving that each of the cumulative conditions of the efficiency exclusion is satisfied rests with the undertaking seeking the benefit of the exclusion.[265] Undertakings, therefore, need to substantiate economic efficiencies and may not merely assert them.[266] However, where the Commission has issued an individual decision under section 11 of the Competition Ordinance, or a block exemption under section 15, the undertakings only need to show that their agreement satisfies the terms of the decision.

It is necessary to carry out an economics-based analysis of the agreement and its effects on the relevant market in order to establish whether the economic benefits of the agreement outweigh the anti-competitive effects. The efficiency exclusion uses the same wording as Article 101(3) TFEU which provides for a similar exemption from the prohibition on restrictive agreements

---

[262] Competition Ordinance, section 12.
[263] Competition Ordinance, Schedule 1, section 1.
[264] Guideline on the First Conduct Rule, Annex, para 2.3; Case C-439/09, *Pierre Fabre Dermo-Cosméthique sas v Président de l'Authorité de la Concurrence* [2011] ECR I-9419.
[265] Guideline on the First Conduct Rule, Annex, para 2.4.
[266] Guideline on the First Conduct Rule, footnote 39.

contained in Article 101(1) TFEU. The European Commission has published Guidelines on the Application of Article 101(3) TFEU which offer a comparative basis for applying the efficiency exclusion under Schedule 1, section 1.[267]

Improving production or distribution or promoting technical or economic progress The application of the efficiency exclusion requires an assessment of the contribution of the agreement to improving production or distribution or promoting technical or economic progress.[268] The Competition Commission requires that an undertaking relying on the efficiency exclusion must provide convincing evidence of each of the following:[269]

    (a) the efficiencies, which must be objective in nature;

    (b) a direct causal link between the efficiencies and the agreement;

    (c) the likelihood and magnitude of each efficiency;

    (d) how each efficiency will be achieved; and

    (e) when the efficiencies will be achieved.

For these purposes, efficiencies include all objective economic efficiencies, including cost efficiencies and qualitative efficiencies.[270] Cost efficiencies, i.e. cost savings, can originate from a number of sources. The development of new production technologies, for example, may give rise to cost savings, as may the synergies brought about by an integration of particular assets. Cost efficiencies may also result from economies of scale or scope, such as where producers of different products improve distribution by sharing distribution costs.[271] Qualitative efficiencies arise when agreements between undertakings generate efficiencies in the form of quality improvements, innovation or similar product improvements. This type of efficiency can include technical or technological advances brought about when undertakings cooperate on research and development leading to improved or new products.[272]

Examples of improvements in production or distribution include lower costs arising from longer production or delivery runs or from changes in methods of production or distribution, improvements in product quality, or increases in the range of products produced.[273]

Efficiencies resulting from the promotion of technical progress may include efficiency gains from economies of scale and increased effectiveness in

---

[267] OJ 2004 C101/97. Similar guidelines apply in the UK, Malaysia and Singapore.

[268] Competition Ordinance, Schedule 1, section 1(a); Guideline on the First Conduct Rule, Annex, para 2.6.

[269] Guideline on the First Conduct Rule, Annex, para 2.7.

[270] Guideline on the First Conduct Rule, Annex, para 2.8.

[271] Guideline on the First Conduct Rule, Annex, para 2.9.

[272] Guideline on the First Conduct Rule, Annex, para 2.10.

[273] Guideline on the First Conduct Rule, Annex, para 2.11.

research and development. These efficiencies may be categorised as cost efficiencies or qualitative efficiencies depending on the facts of the case.[274]

Allowing consumers a fair share of the efficiencies   For the efficiency exclusion to apply, it must be demonstrated that the agreement allows consumers to receive a fair share of the efficiencies claimed by the parties and generated by the agreement.[275]   Consumers in this context means all direct and indirect purchasers of the relevant products including businesses acting as purchasers (e.g. manufacturers purchasing inputs, retailers etc.) and final consumers.[276]

The Competition Commission considers that the notion of a fair share means that the benefits accruing to consumers must at a minimum compensate them for the actual or likely harm to competition associated with the relevant restrictive agreement.   While the parties need not demonstrate that consumers receive a share of every efficiency gain, the overall impact for consumers must at least be neutral.   The key consideration is the overall impact on consumers of the products within the relevant market as a whole and not the impact on individual consumers or individual consumer groups within that market.[277] This raises the issue of whether the efficiencies have to give rise to benefits in the relevant market in which the restriction has been identified.   From a practical, legal and economic point of view, it may be artificial to segment an overall arrangement into separate markets and take efficiencies into account only if they are specifically linked to or allocated to an individual market.

An agreement may enhance competition by allowing the parties to compete more effectively in a much wider market than where the actual restriction is imposed or across a number of relevant markets.   Both the Competition Commission and the European Commission, however, appear to take a strict starting point approach of requiring that the relevant benefits arise within the relevant market in which the restriction is imposed.   The EU Guidelines on Article 101(3) TFEU state that the assessment of benefits flowing from restrictive agreements is in principle made within the confines of each relevant market to which the agreement relates and that negative effects on consumers in one geographic market or product market cannot normally be balanced against and compensated by positive effects for consumers in another unrelated geographic market or product market.   Where two markets are related, however, efficiencies achieved on separate markets can be taken into account provided that the group of consumers affected by the restriction and benefiting from the efficiency gains are substantially the same.   Nevertheless, there is

---

[274]   Guideline on the First Conduct Rule, Annex, para 2.12.
[275]   Competition Ordinance, Schedule 1, section 1(a); Guideline on the First Conduct Rule, Annex, para 2.14.
[276]   Guideline on the First Conduct Rule, Annex, para 2.13.
[277]   Guideline on the First Conduct Rule, Annex, para 2.15.

nothing in the wording of Article 101(3) TFEU which requires efficiencies arising on markets other than the markets where the relevant restriction occurs to be disregarded and various judgments of the European Courts suggest that, in appropriate cases, all the benefits generated by an agreement should be taken into account. In the case of network industries which include several related markets, benefits on one market might be taken into account even though the restrictions in question apply on other related markets, as long as the consumers affected by the restrictions and the benefits are the same.[278] For example, in a case involving intermodal transport services covering several markets, the EU General Court held that regard should be had to the advantages arising from the agreement in question, not only for the relevant market, namely that for inland transport services provided as part of intermodal transport, but also in appropriate cases for every other market on which the agreement in question might have beneficial effects and, and even in a more general sense, for any service the quality or efficiency of which might be improved by the existence of that agreement.[279]

In considering the notion of a fair share to consumers, the EU Guidelines emphasise that consumers encompasses both intermediate and end consumers. This includes all direct or indirect users of the products covered by the agreement, including producers that use the products as an input, wholesalers, retailers and final consumers, i.e. natural persons who are acting for purposes which can be regarded as outside their trade or profession. In other words, consumers are the customers of the parties to the agreement and subsequent purchasers. These customers can be undertakings as in the case of buyers of industrial machinery or an input for further processing or final consumers as for instance in the case of buyers of impulse ice-cream or bicycles.

The General Court has also noted the importance of the welfare of the final consumer of the product.[280] In general, the European Commission accepts that cost efficiencies may lead to increased output and lower prices for consumers. If, due to cost efficiencies, the undertakings in question may increase profits by expanding output, consumer pass-on may occur. Consumer pass-on can also take the form of new and improved products, creating value for consumers to compensate for the restrictive effects of the agreement, including a price increase. Any such assessment necessarily involves a value judgment, which focuses attention on qualitative efficiencies. The EU Guidelines provide comparatively more detail on the issue of consumer pass-on than does the Guideline on the First Conduct Rule. In particular, the following factors may be taken into account: characteristics and structure of the market; nature and magnitude of efficiency gains; elasticity of demand; and magnitude of the restriction of competition.

---

[278] Case T-111/08, *Mastercard Inc. v Commission* EU:T:2012:260.
[279] Case T-86/95, *Compagnie Generale Maritime v Commission* [2002] ECR II-1011.
[280] Case T-186/01, *GlaxoSmithKline v Commission* [2006] ECR II-2969.

Non-indispensable restrictions   The agreement must not impose on the undertakings concerned restrictions that are not indispensable to the attainment of the relevant efficiencies.[281]   In practice it may be advisable to address the issue of indispensability of restrictions on competition before assessing the issue of pass-on of benefits to the consumer.   This latter test requires a balancing of the negative and positive effects of an agreement on consumers, which should not include the effects of any restriction that already satisfies the indispensability test.

For the purposes of satisfying this test, the parties must demonstrate that the agreement itself, and each of the individual restrictions contained in the agreement, are reasonably necessary to attain the efficiencies.   The determinative factor in this context is whether the restrictive agreement and the individual restrictions in it make it possible to perform the activity in question more efficiently than would likely have been the case in the absence of the agreement or the restrictions.[282]   This condition implies that, as regards the agreement, taking account of market conditions and business realities facing the parties, there are no other economically practicable and less restrictive means of achieving the efficiencies.   If the parties can show that the agreement is reasonably necessary to achieve the efficiencies in this sense, they must then demonstrate that the individual restrictions in the agreement are also reasonably necessary in order to produce the efficiencies.   An individual restriction can be considered indispensable or reasonably necessary if its absence would eliminate or significantly reduce the relevant efficiencies or make it significantly less likely that they will materialise.[283]   This entails an assessment of the effects of alternative options on competition, taking into account any actual and potential improvement in the area of competition through the removal of a restriction or the application of a less restrictive solution.

Some additional matters arising from the EU Guidelines on Article 101(3) TFEU may also be taken into account.   For example, although the Guideline on the First Conduct Rule does not specifically addressed any temporal dimension in this respect, the EU Guidelines provide that it is relevant to consider over what time period the parties could have achieved the efficiencies through another less restrictive agreement.   In addition, it is appropriate to consider the severity of the restriction arising from the agreement, such that the more restrictive the effect on competition, the stricter the evidential burden of satisfying the test of indispensability.[284]

---

[281] Competition Ordinance, Schedule 1, section 1(b).
[282] Guideline on the First Conduct Rule, Annex, para 2.16.
[283] Guideline on the First Conduct Rule, Annex, para 2.17.
[284] Case T-86/95, *Compagnie Generale Maritime v Commission* [2002] ECR II-1011.

Possibility of elimination of competition The agreement must not afford the undertakings concerned the possibility of eliminating competition in respect of a substantial part of the goods or services in questions.[285] The Competition Commission takes the view that this recognises that protecting the competitive process takes priority over the potential efficiency gains which might result from a particular agreement, such that ultimately the competitive process is the best guarantor of efficiency in the longer term.[286] Whether there is a possibility of competition being eliminated depends on the reduction in competition that the agreement brings about and the state of competition in the market. The weaker the state of existing competition in the market, the smaller any further reduction in competition would need to be for competition to be eliminated. Similarly, the more the relevant agreement causes harm to competition, the greater the likelihood that the undertakings concerned are afforded the possibility of eliminating competition.[287] A similar approach applies under the efficiency exclusion in the EU Guidelines on Article 101(3) TFEU which state that the application of this test requires a realistic analysis of the various sources of competition in the market, the level of competitive constraint that they impose on the parties to the agreement and the impact of the agreement on this competitive constraint. In practice there tends to be less focus on this condition. This might be because the agreement has already failed to meet another condition or because the agreement has sufficient benefits for this condition not to be an issue.

  An evaluation of whether there is a possibility of competition being eliminated requires consideration of the various sources of competition in the relevant market and the impact of the agreement on those various sources of competitive restraint. While sources of actual competition will generally be more important in this assessment, potential competition must also be considered. In this context, the parties will need to do more than merely assert that barriers to entry are low.[288] Moreover, the notion of eliminating competition means the possibility of eliminating effective competition in respect of a substantial part of the goods or services in question. A risk of elimination of one of the most important expressions of effective competition will suffice for the purposes of fulfilling this criterion. This will be particularly the case if the agreement affords the parties the possibility of eliminating effective price competition in respect of a substantial part of the goods or services concerned.[289] In the Guideline on the First Conduct Rule, the Commission gives a hypothetical example of a situation where reliance on the efficiency exclusion would be misplaced on the grounds that in light of the

---

[285] Competition Ordinance, Schedule 1, section 1(c).
[286] Guideline on the First Conduct Rule, Annex, para 2.18.
[287] Guideline on the First Conduct Rule, Annex, para 2.19.
[288] Guideline on the First Conduct Rule, Annex, para 2.20
[289] Guideline on the First Conduct Rule, Annex, para 2.21.

market positions of the parties and the absence of a competitive response to their joint conduct, it might reasonably be concluded that the parties to the agreement are not subject to any significant competitive pressures.[290]

Pricing restrictions Horizontal price fixing agreements, being the essence of cartel agreements involving Serious Anti-Competitive Conduct, are unlikely to be regarded as allowing for economic efficiencies. The Competition Commission recognises, however, that vertical price restrictions, including resale price maintenance, may sometimes lead to efficiencies of the type that would qualify the arrangements for exclusion from the First Conduct Rule as arrangements enhancing overall economic efficiency.[291] While efficiencies must be assessed on a case by case basis, the Commission refers to possible efficiencies in two specific circumstances.[292]

First, RPM may help address so-called free rider problems at the distribution level where the extra margin guaranteed by the RPM structure encourages parties to provide certain sales for the benefit of consumers. This efficiency may have some relevance in the case of experience or complex products, although the Commission expects to see compelling evidence of an actual free rider problem.[293]

Secondly, in the case of maximum resale prices, the resale price restriction may help to ensure that the brand in question competes more effectively with other brands, notably where it avoids double-marginalisation. Double marginalisation occurs where the supplier and buyer both have market power and both apply a high margin when selling the product, with the result that the end price is higher than the price that would have been charged by a vertically integrated monopolist. A maximum resale price may, therefore, have the effect of reducing the end price and increasing output.[294]

Exclusive distribution and exclusive customer allocation Exclusive distribution or exclusive customer allocation may sometimes lead to efficiencies of the type that would qualify the arrangements for exclusion from the First Conduct Rule as arrangements enhancing overall economic efficiency. The Competition Commissions warns, however, that, generally, in the case of exclusive distribution and exclusive customer allocation, arguments raised and

---

[290] The hypothetical scenario relates to coordination of passenger traffic schedules and tariffs in the context of a codeshare between airlines who have together more than 70% of the passenger traffic on the route between a foreign destination and Hong Kong, leading to price rises of 30-50%.

[291] Competition Ordinance, Schedule 1, section 1.

[292] Guideline on the First Conduct Rule, para 6.84.

[293] Guideline on the First Conduct Rule, para 6.84(a).

[294] Guideline on the First Conduct Rule, para 6.84(b) and footnote 40.

supported by evidence that the agreements in question entail economic efficiencies will require careful consideration.[295]

Economic efficiencies may arise, for example, where investments by distributors are required to protect or build up the brand image or where specific equipment, skills or experience are required for a particular group of customers. The Commission refers to possible efficiencies of exclusivity provisions in terms of incentivising distributors to invest in marketing and customer service, thereby making the concerned product more competitive as against other branded products. This, in turn, ensures a wider range of product choices for final consumers. Exclusive distribution agreements may also lead to savings in logistics costs due to economies of scale in transport and distribution.[296]

The level of trade affected by the exclusivity might also be relevant in this context. For example, a manufacturer might choose a particular wholesaler to be its exclusive distributor for the whole of Hong Kong. Assuming there are no resale restrictions on the wholesaler, the Commission considers that the loss of intra-brand competition at the wholesale level might be justified by reference to efficiencies in terms of logistics considerations.[297]

Selective distribution agreements   In the Guideline on the First Conduct Rule, the Competition Commission analyses selective distribution agreements from the perspective of whether they restrict competition, acknowledging that selective distribution is very often economically beneficial and an effective way of furthering inter-brand competition.[298] The Commission does not give any guidance on whether selective distribution agreements that restrict competition might benefit from the exclusion in Schedule 1, section 1 on grounds of enhancing economic efficiencies.   In EU law, however, one area that continues to attract interest relates to the differentiation between luxury and other goods. While selective distribution falls within the Block Exemption on Vertical Agreements regardless of the nature of the product concerned, the Guidelines on Vertical Restraints state that, where the characteristics of the product do not require selective distribution, or do not require the applied criteria, such as for instance the requirement for distributors to have one or more brick and mortar shops or to provide specific services, such a system does not generally bring about efficiency effects to offset a significant reduction in intra-brand competition.

Joint production agreements   Joint production agreements may sometimes lead to efficiencies of the type that would qualify the arrangements for

---

[295]   Guideline on the First Conduct Rule, para 6.89.
[296]   Guideline on the First Conduct Rule, para 6.87.
[297]   Guideline on the First Conduct Rule, para 6.88.
[298]   Guideline on the First Conduct Rule, para 6.122.

exclusion from the First Conduct Rule as arrangements enhancing overall economic efficiency. The Competition Commission considers that this might particularly be the case where the joint production results in significant cost savings and synergies and/or economies of scale or scope, or improvements in product range or quality.[299]

The European Commission issued a block exemption[300] in the area of joint production[301] and specialisation.[302] Joint production/specialisation is exempted provided that this is concluded between competitors with a combined market share not exceeding 20% and the other conditions of the block exemption are met. For those agreements that are not covered by the block exemption, the parties have to demonstrate improvements in production or other efficiencies. Efficiencies that benefit only the parties or cost savings that are caused by output reduction or market allocation cannot be taken into account.

Sales-related joint ventures Sales-related joint ventures may sometimes lead to efficiencies of the type that would qualify the arrangements for exclusion from the First Conduct Rule as arrangements enhancing overall economic efficiency. The Competition Commission refers to possible efficiencies in terms of significant cost savings and synergies and/or economies of scale or scope, or improvements in product range or quality.[303]

2.5.3 Block Exemption Orders

Block Exemption Orders If the Competition Commission is satisfied that a particular category of agreement is excluded from the application of the First Conduct Rule by or as a result of the efficiency exclusion contained in section 1 of Schedule 1 to the Competition Ordinance, it may issue a Block Exemption Order in respect of that category of agreement.[304] The Commission may issue a Block Exemption Order either of its own volition or on application by an undertaking or an association of undertakings.[305] A Block Exemption Order may impose conditions or limitations subject to which it is to have effect and specify a date from which the order is to cease to have effect.[306] Where an agreement falls within scope of a Block Exemption Order issued by the

---

[299] Guideline on the First Conduct Rule, para 6.100.
[300] Commission Regulation (EC) No 1218/2010, OJ 2010 L 335/43.
[301] Joint production occurs where the parties agree to produce certain products jointly.
[302] Specialisation is where the parties agree that one or both of them will withdraw from the production of a product and to purchase it from the other party.
[303] Guideline on the First Conduct Rule, para 6.114.
[304] Competition Ordinance, section 15(1).
[305] Competition Ordinance, section 15(2).
[306] Competition Ordinance, section 15(3).

Commission, the agreement is exempt from application of the First Conduct Rule.[307]

Whereas the Competition Commission has yet to adopt any Block Exemption Orders,[308] an indication of the type of measures that might be adopted in the future may be gleaned from the various measures adopted by the European Commission, which has issued several block exemptions and guidance notices to assist parties to assess compliance of both horizontal and vertical agreements with EU competition law. In the area of horizontal agreements, it has recognised that changing markets have generated an increasing variety and use of cooperation agreements ranging from R&D cooperation, specialisation or sub-contracting to agreements on standards. Vertical agreements, which are generally treated more flexibly in EU competition law than agreements with competitors, may be covered by the Vertical Restraints Block Exemption.[309] Other EU block exemptions include:

- Technology Transfer Block Exemption, covering technology transfer agreements including patent, know-how and software copyright licences;[310]
- Sector-specific block exemptions, including the Motor Vehicles Block Exemption[311] and the Insurance Block Exemption;[312]
- R&D Block Exemption, covering agreements whereby two or more undertakings agree to jointly carry out research and development and to jointly exploit the results;[313]
- Specialisation Block Exemption, covering joint production agreements by virtue of which two or more parties agree to produce certain products jointly.[314]

---

[307] Competition Ordinance, section 17.
[308] A proposal for a block exemption for shipping liner conferences was published by the Competition Commission in September 2016.
[309] Commission Regulation (EC) No 330/2010, OJ 2010 L102/1.
[310] Commission Regulation (EU) No 316/2014, OJ 2014 L93/17.
[311] Commission Regulation (EC) No 461/2010, OJ 2010 L129/52.
[312] Commission Regulation (EC) No 267/2010, OJ 2010 L83/1.
[313] Commission Regulation (EC) No 1217/2010, OJ 2010 L335/36.
[314] Commission Regulation (EC) No 1218/2010, OJ 2010 L335/43.

Chapter Three

THE SECOND CONDUCT RULE
ABUSE OF SUBSTANTIAL MARKET POWER

3.1 THE SECOND CONDUCT RULE

The Second Conduct Rule The Second Conduct Rule, which is set out in section 21(1) of the Competition Ordinance, provides that an undertaking that has a substantial degree of market power in a market must not abuse that power by engaging in conduct that has as its object or effect the prevention, restriction or distortion of competition in Hong Kong.[1] The Second Conduct Rule therefore applies where the following elements are present:[2]

- the entity engaged in the relevant conduct is an undertaking;[3]
- the undertaking has a substantial degree of market power in a market;[4]
- the undertaking abuses its market power by engaging in conduct that has as its object or effect the prevention, restriction or distortion of competition in Hong Kong;
- the conduct is not excluded or exempted from the application of the Second Conduct Rule.

The Second Conduct Rule in Hong Kong competition law is equivalent, though not identical, to Article 102 TFEU in EU law and Chapter II of the UK Competition Act 1998. Other jurisdictions apply similar legislation, including the Australian Competition and Consumer Act 2010, the New Zealand Commerce Act 1986, the Singapore Competition Act 2004 and the Malaysian Competition Act 2010.

Guideline for applying the Second Conduct Rule The Competition Commission has issued a Guideline on the Second Conduct Rule[5] which provides a framework for the Commission's analysis of conduct under the Second Conduct Rule and which also helps undertakings to determine whether their conduct complies with the Second Conduct Rule.[6] The Guideline also

---

[1] Competition Ordinance, section 21(1).
[2] Guideline on the Second Conduct Rule, para 1.3.
[3] For the definition of undertaking, see Chapter One, pp. 22-25; Guideline on the First Conduct Rule, paras 2.2-2.21; Guideline on the Second Conduct Rule, para 1.4.
[4] For market definition, see Chapter One, pp. 30-36; Guideline on the Second Conduct Rule, paras 2.1-2.35.
[5] Guideline on the Second Conduct Rule, 27 July 2015.
[6] Guideline on the Second Conduct Rule, para 1.1.

provides hypothetical examples of how the Commission intends to interpret and treat particular scenarios under the Second Conduct Rule. Reference may also be usefully made to the equivalent guidelines issued by competition authorities in other jurisdictions, in particular, the EU guidance on the European Commission's enforcement priorities in applying Article 102 TFEU to abusive exclusionary conduct by dominant undertakings[7] and the UK CMA's guidance on abuse of dominance[8] and assessment of market power.[9]

The following considerations arise in relation to the application of the Second Conduct Rule:

- The expressions substantial degree of market power and dominance[10] may to some extent be used interchangeably when describing the position of a party that is able to act independently in the market. For practical purposes, this usually means that an undertaking is able to raise prices profitably without sufficient competitive constraint. Nevertheless, the choice in the Competition Ordinance not to refer to dominance was deliberate, reflective of the fact that several economic sectors in Hong Kong are oligopolistic, and the notion of a substantial degree of market power may imply a lower threshold than is required to establish dominance.

- The Second Conduct Rule is not concerned with preventing firms from gaining market power or being able to exercise it to increase their profits for a time, since the pursuit of market power and higher profits through innovation and competition is key to a prosperous free market economy. To remove this profit motive would risk dampening rather than invigorating competition.[11]

- The most obvious manifestation of market power is the ability of an undertaking to raise prices above the competitive level for a sustained period. Market power may, however, be manifested in other ways.[12] For example, an undertaking with market power may be able to:

  (a) reduce the quality of its products below competitive levels for a sustained period

  (b) reduce the range or variety of its products below competitive levels for a sustained period;

  (c) lower customer service standards below competitive levels for a sustained period;

  (d) impair, relative to competitive levels and for a sustained period, innovation or any other parameter of competition in the market.

---

[7]   OJ 2009 C45/7.
[8]   OFT 402 (2004) readopted by the CMA (2014).
[9]   OFT 415 (2004) readopted by the CMA (2014).
[10] Article 102 TFEU and Chapter II of the UK Competition Act 1998 prohibit any abuse by one or more undertakings of a dominant position.
[11] Guideline on the Second Conduct Rule, para 1.9.
[12] Guideline on the Second Conduct Rule, para 1.7.

- The Second Conduct Rule relates to the abuse of a substantial degree of market power by an undertaking occupying that position.[13] Stringent competition law requirements apply to undertakings who enjoy a substantial degree of market power so that certain behaviour that would be acceptable for an undertaking that does not enjoy such a position is unlawful for one that does.[14]

- Potentially any conduct which has the object or effect of preventing, restricting or distorting competition in Hong Kong may constitute abusive conduct where the conduct is attributable to an undertaking with a substantial degree of market power. Abusive conduct is an open category, so that abusive conduct under the Second Conduct Rule includes but is not limited to the types of conduct discussed in the Guideline.[15] Although section 21(2) of the Competition Ordinance lists predatory behaviour towards competitors and limiting production, markets or technical development to the prejudice of consumers as particular illustrative examples of abuse, this is not an exhaustive list of unlawful abusive behaviours that are prohibited under the Second Conduct Rule.[16]

- The pursuit of profit may lead some undertakings with a substantial degree of market power to abuse that power with a view to protecting or increasing their position of power and profits. For example, a powerful undertaking may:[17]

  (a) seek to maintain its substantial degree of market power by abusing it to prevent challenges to its position by existing or new competitors; or

  (b) leverage its substantial degree of market power in one market to harm competition in a second market instead of competing on the merits for customers in that second market.

  When undertakings with a substantial degree of market power abuse it in this way, the negative effects of that power for the economy and consumers (including businesses acting as customers) become entrenched. Instead of the profits of market power rewarding competition and innovation, they become a reward for causing harm to economically beneficial outcomes.[18]

- Smaller undertakings are unlikely to have a substantial degree of market power, so that the commercial conduct of SMEs is unlikely to

---

[13] Guideline on the Second Conduct Rule, para 1.8.

[14] Guideline on the Second Conduct Rule, para 1.13. The CJEU has held that undertakings occupying a dominant position in the market have a special responsibility not to harm competition: Case 322/81, *Michelin v Commission* [1983] ECR 3461.

[15] Guideline on the Second Conduct Rule, para 1.8.

[16] Guideline on the Second Conduct Rule, para 1.12.

[17] Guideline on the Second Conduct Rule, para 1.10.

[18] Guideline on the Second Conduct Rule, para 1.11.

contravene the Second Conduct Rule.[19]   The commercial conduct of smaller undertakings with an annual turnover under HK$40 million will fall within the exclusion for conduct of lesser significance.[20]
- The application of the Second Conduct Rule does not preclude the parallel application of the First Conduct Rule to the same conduct.[21]

Territorial application of the Second Conduct Rule   The Second Conduct Rule applies to conduct that has as its object or effect of preventing, restricting or distorting competition in Hong Kong even if the undertaking engaging in the conduct is outside Hong Kong or the conduct is engaged in outside Hong Kong.[22]   This allows potentially for a wide scope of application of the Second Conduct Rule by reference to the effects of the conduct in question regardless of the place where the conduct was engaged in.   Unlike EU and UK competition law, which prohibit abuse of dominance in so far as it may affect trade between EU Member States and trade within the UK, respectively, section 21(1) of the Competition Ordinance makes no reference to trade in Hong Kong, but is concerned solely with conduct that may harm competition in Hong Kong.

3.2 ASSESSMENT OF SUBSTANTIAL MARKET POWER

Substantial degree of market power   Section 21(3) of the Competition Ordinance sets out certain matters that may be taken into consideration in determining whether an undertaking has a substantial degree of market power. The matters that may be taken into account, however, are not limited to these listed matters.[23]   The listed matters are:
- (a) the market share of the undertaking;
- (b) the undertaking's power to make pricing and other decisions;
- (c) any barriers to entry to competitors into the relevant market; and
- (d) any other relevant matters specified in the Guideline on the Second Conduct Rule.

An assessment of market power thus comprises an analysis of several factors including market share, countervailing buyer power, barriers to entry or expansion and market-specific characteristics. These factors are not exhaustive and there may be other considerations to be taken into account in an

---

[19]   Guideline on the Second Conduct Rule, para 1.5.
[20]   Guideline on the Second Conduct Rule, para 1.6.   This threshold does not imply, however, that undertakings with an annual turnover above HK$40 million would automatically be considered to have a substantial degree of market power or be more likely to contravene the Second Conduct Rule.
[21]   Guideline on the Second Conduct Rule, para 1.15.
[22]   Competition Ordinance, section 23; Guideline on the Second Conduct Rule, para 1.16.
[23]   Competition Ordinance, section 21(3).

assessment of market power in a given case.[24]   Examples of markets having specific characteristics which may give rise to particular issues in any assessment of substantial market power include bidding markets and markets subject to vertical integration and or capacity constraints.[25]

Market power is a matter of degree to be assessed based on the circumstances of the case. An undertaking does not need to be a monopolist to have a substantial degree of market power. When assessing whether an undertaking has a substantial degree of market power, the Commission will consider the extent to which that undertaking faces constraints on its ability profitably to sustain prices above competitive levels.[26]   This definition of a substantial degree of market power does not preclude the possibility of more than one undertaking having a substantial degree of market power in a relevant market, particularly if the market is highly concentrated with only a few large market participants.[27]   It may be noted, however, that, whereas section 21(1) of the Competition Ordinance applies to abuse by an undertaking, Article 102 TFEU, in prohibiting abuse by one or more undertakings, clearly allows for the notion of joint dominance which tends to occur where there are a small number of undertakings in a market who make strategic decisions by taking into account the prospective conduct of their rivals. The result is that where a collective dominant position exists that position can, in principle, be abused by one of the relevant undertakings, or by the undertakings together.[28]

Market power might equally arise on the buyer side of the market (known as monopsony power). In that case, a substantial degree of market power may exist where the buyer has the ability to obtain purchase prices below the competitive level for a sustained period of time.[29]   A buyer who has a substantial degree of market power in the market where it purchases particular products is therefore subject to the Second Conduct Rule. Should such a buyer in its capacity as buyer engage in conduct which has the object or effect of harming competition, the buyer may be found to have contravened the Second Conduct Rule.[30]   For example, British Airways was found to have held a dominant position on the UK market for purchasing travel agency services since its position on the market for air transport made it an obligatory trading partner for travel agents.[31]

---

[24]   Guideline on the Second Conduct Rule, para 3.8. Cf. The UK CMA's guidance on assessment of market power for additional factors that might be considered.

[25]   Guideline on the Second Conduct Rule, para 3.33.

[26]   Guideline on the Second Conduct Rule, para 3.6.

[27]   Guideline on the Second Conduct Rule, para 3.3. It may be noted, however, that Article 102 TFEU, in prohibiting abuse by one or more undertakings, allows for the notion of joint dominance.

[28]   Case C-7/95P, *John Deere v Commission* [1993] ECR I-1375.

[29]   Guideline on the Second Conduct Rule, para 3.5.

[30]   Guideline on the Second Conduct Rule, para 3.32.

[31]   Case T-219/99, *British Airways plc v Commission* [2003] ECR II-5917.

Assessment of substantial market power In a competitive market, there is generally an ongoing rivalry between undertakings in terms of price, service, innovation and quality to which each undertaking must react if its products are to remain attractive to consumers. As a result, undertakings, both big and small, will usually be mutually constrained in their pricing, output and related commercial decisions by the activity or anticipated activity of other undertakings that compete in, or may compete in, that market. A substantial degree of market power arises where an undertaking does not face sufficiently effective competitive constraints in the relevant market. Substantial market power can be thought of as the ability profitably to charge prices above competitive levels, or to restrict output or quality below competitive levels, for a sustained period of time, which the Competition Commission, following generally accepted international practice, considers to be two years. This period may, however, be shorter or longer depending on the facts, in particular with regard to the product and the circumstances of the market in question.[32] This definition resembles the classic definition of dominance in EU competition law cases where the test for establishing dominance is a position of economic strength enjoyed by an undertaking which enables it to prevent effective competition being maintained on the relevant market by giving it the power to behave to an appreciable extent independently of its competitors, customers and ultimately of its consumers.[33]

An undertaking in a competitive market may be able temporarily to raise its price above the competitive level, but it will be unable to sustain such a price increase because customers will switch to cheaper suppliers or additional suppliers will enter the market. Hence, if an undertaking can profitably charge prices above competitive levels over a sustained period, it can be considered to have a substantial degree of market power. An undertaking with a substantial degree of market power might also have the ability and incentive to harm the process of competition by, for example, weakening existing competition, raising entry barriers or slowing innovation.[34]

Market share and market concentration In general, an analysis of market shares may be useful as an initial screening device in the assessment of substantial market power.[35] Undertakings are more likely to have a substantial degree of market power where they have high market shares. However, a high market share does not necessarily imply a substantial degree of market power. For example, where undertakings compete to improve the quality of their products, a persistently high market share might simply reflect the fact that an undertaking is a particularly effective innovator. A determination of the

---

[32] Guideline on the Second Conduct Rule, paras 3.1-3.2.
[33] Case 27/76, *United Brands v Commission* [1978] ECR 207.
[34] Guideline on the Second Conduct Rule, para 3.4.
[35] Guideline on the Second Conduct Rule, para 3.9.

presence or absence of a substantial degree of market power will, therefore, be made on the facts of the particular case, taking into account all relevant factors, in particular the characteristics of the industry involved, the nature of competition in the relevant markets and not merely the market shares of the market participants.[36]

The Competition Commission stresses that it is important to consider the evolution of the market shares of the undertakings in the relevant market, as this will often be more informative than a snapshot picture of market shares at a single point in time. This will be particularly relevant, for example, where the market under consideration is dynamic, characterised by frequent innovation or highly competitive, in which case market shares might be volatile. Frequent changes in market shares may also indicate that barriers to entry or expansion in a market are low and this would tend to suggest an absence of market power. In contrast, an undertaking is more likely to have a substantial degree of market power if it has a high market share which it has either maintained or grown over time, while its competitors have relatively weak positions. Relative market share can therefore be an important factor in the analysis. The evolution of shares over a period of years might be particularly relevant for bidding markets, where demand may be lumpy and market share may vary dramatically from one year to the next.[37]

How market shares are calculated depends on the case at hand. The following data may be used:[38]

- turnover or sales value data;
- sales volume data, particularly when products are homogenous in nature;
- capacity, particularly where capacity is an important feature of an undertaking's ability to compete, such as in an industry operating at, or close to, full capacity;
- other indicators, for example, product reserves held, customer base or share of new customers.

In some cases, the indications provided by measuring market shares may be supplemented by measuring the level of concentration in the market. Market concentration in this context refers to the number and size of undertakings in the market. A concentrated market is one with a small number of leading undertakings with a large combined market share. Market concentration can provide useful information about the market structure and can be used to assess the relative positions of the undertakings in the market as part of an assessment of market power.[39]

---

[36] Guideline on the Second Conduct Rule, para 3.10.
[37] Guideline on the Second Conduct Rule, para 3.11.
[38] Guideline on the Second Conduct Rule, para 3.12.
[39] Guideline on the Second Conduct Rule, paras 3.13-3.14.

Market shares evidencing substantial market power The Guideline on the Second Conduct Rule does not provide any indicative market share thresholds.[40] EU competition law recognises that although a company's market share may be a good indicator of dominance, it is important to understand that a high market share does not necessarily mean that a company is dominant. Nevertheless, in *Hoffmann-La Roche*,[41] the CJEU noted in relation to market shares that, although the importance of the market shares may vary from one market to another, the view may legitimately be taken that very large shares are in themselves, and save in exceptional circumstances, evidence of the existence of a dominant position. An undertaking which has a very large market share and holds it for some time, by means of the volume of production and the scale of the supply which it stands for – without those having much smaller market shares being able to meet rapidly the demand from those who would like to break away from the under-taking which has the largest market share – is by virtue of that share in a position of strength which makes it an unavoidable trading partner and which, already because of this secures for it, at the very least during relatively long periods, that freedom of action which is the special feature of a dominant position. Based on European Commission practice, a market share of less than 25% is unlikely to give rise to dominance. Market share of 25-40% is unlikely to give rise to dominance except where the rest of the market is fragmented or there are other significant factors. A share greater than 40% may evidence dominance, where this is supported by other factors. A share of 50% is strong evidence of dominance, unless this can be explained by other exceptional factors.[42] A 75% market share is indicative of dominance and a share of 85% or more is typically conclusive.

Potential entry or expansion Barriers to entry are factors that prevent or hinder a prospective new entrant from entering the market or otherwise place it at a significant competitive disadvantage relative to incumbents. Barriers to entry may arise from a variety of sources, including regulatory or legal restrictions, economic or structural factors or the conduct of the undertaking under assessment (so-called strategic barriers). When evaluating whether an undertaking has a substantial degree of market power, the Commission will consider whether entry by potential competitors or expansion by existing market participants (or the threat of entry or expansion) would deter or defeat the exercise of such market power. The relevant question is whether entry or expansion, or the threat of it, pose a credible competitive constraint on the

---

[40] This may be contrasted with the Guideline on the Merger Rule, para 3.15, where a market share of the merged firm of 40% is likely to raise concerns of a substantial lessening of competition.

[41] Case 85/76, *Hoffmann La Roche v Commission* [1979] ECR 461.

[42] Case C-62/86, *AKZO Chemie BV v Commission* [1991] ECR I-3359.

undertaking concerned.   Where that is the case, the undertaking under examination will likely not have a substantial degree of market power.   The lower the barriers to entry or expansion, the more likely it will be that potential competition will prevent an undertaking from profitably sustaining prices above competitive levels.   Persistently high market shares may be an indicator of the presence of barriers to entry or expansion.   Moreover, an undertaking with a large market share in a market protected by significant entry barriers is likely to have a substantial degree of market power.   By contrast, even an undertaking with a very large market share would be unlikely to have a substantial degree of market power in a market where there are very low entry barriers.[43]

For entry or expansion (or the threat thereof) to be considered an effective competitive constraint, the entry or expansion must be likely, timely and sufficient. In this respect, timely means that entry or expansion will occur within such period as will serve to deter or defeat the exercise of market power, likely refers to the expectation that entry will occur and be profitable and sufficient means that entry will occur on an adequate scale to prevent or deter undertakings from exercising market power.[44]   Examples of barriers to entry or expansion include:[45]

(a)   regulatory and legal barriers (such as licensing requirements);
(b)   structural barriers (such as significant economies of scale and/or scope, or network effects); and
(c)   strategic barriers intentionally created or enhanced by incumbent undertakings in the market.

Regulatory and legal barriers   Regulation by a government or an industry sector regulator may give rise to barriers to entry or expansion.   For example, regulation may limit the number of undertakings which can operate in a market through a requirement that parties obtain a licence.   In this case the licence can be thought of as a necessary input before production can take place.   Similarly, planning and licensing laws that impose limits on the number of retail outlets limit expansion and entry possibilities at the retail level and in turn may make it more difficult for suppliers to gain access to efficient distribution.[46]

Intellectual property rights (IPRs) may also amount to legal barriers when they prevent or make more difficult entry or expansion by (potential) competitors.   In principle, IPRs are indicative of a substantial degree of market power only when the product or technology protected by the IPR corresponds to a relevant product or technology market.   While an IPR might confer a legal monopoly, it does not follow that this legal monopoly confers market power in

---

[43]   Guideline on the Second Conduct Rule, paras 3.15-3.17.
[44]   Guideline on the Second Conduct Rule, para 3.18.
[45]   Guideline on the Second Conduct Rule, para 3.19.
[46]   Guideline on the Second Conduct Rule, para 3.20.

an economic sense, so that IPRs do not automatically give rise to barriers and do not necessarily imply substantial market power as firms might well be able to invent around the relevant IPR.[47]

Structural barriers   Structural barriers to entry may prevent potential competitors from competing in a market.[48] Sunk costs of entry or expansion are an example of structural barriers. Sunk costs, which create entry risks which may in turn create barriers to entry, are costs that are incurred on entering or remaining active in a market, cannot be economically recouped within a short period of time, and are not recoverable on exit. Examples of sunk costs include investments in product research and development, the construction of a specialised production facility, start-up marketing and on-going advertising expenditures. When considering whether sunk costs give rise to entry barriers, it may be useful to consider the extent to which sunk costs give an incumbent an advantage over potential new entrants. The mere existence of sunk costs in a particular industry is not, however, proof of the existence of a barrier to entry or expansion. The relevant question is whether an undertaking seeking to enter or expand must incur the sunk costs to be an effective competitor.[49]

Structural entry barriers may also arise where important inputs or distribution channels are scarce. If an incumbent undertaking has privileged access to these inputs or channels, they may obtain an advantage over a potential entrant, making entry more difficult.[50]

Economies of scale may give rise to barriers to entry or expansion. Such economies exist where average cost falls as output increases. Where a market is characterised by large economies of scale, a potential entrant may need to enter the market on a large scale (in relation to the size of the market) in order to compete effectively. A barrier to entry could arise where such entry or expansion requires relatively large sunk costs to be incurred. Similarly, where a potential entrant would be able to reach a viable scale of production only after a significant period of time, this may deter entry or expansion. Even where entry or expansion is not deterred by economies of scale, the incumbent may retain a substantial degree of market power for a significant period of time if new entrants would take time to establish a sufficient operation to be able to compete effectively.[51] Closely related to economies of scale are network effects. Network effects arise when the value a consumer places on connecting to a network (such as payment card schemes or online classifieds) depends on

[47] Guideline on the Second Conduct Rule, para 3.21.
[48] Case 27/76, *United Brands v Commission* [1978] ECR 207; Case 85/76, *Hoffmann -La Roche v Commission* [1979] ECR 461.
[49] Guideline on the Second Conduct Rule, paras 3.22-3.23.
[50] Guideline on the Second Conduct Rule, para 3.24.
[51] Guideline on the Second Conduct Rule, para 3.25.

the number of others already connected to the network. Network effects may act as a barrier to entry or expansion because an incumbent may have the advantage of significant network effects, which an entrant would lack unless it can displace the incumbent's network.[52]

The costs of entry or expansion may also be affected by economies of scope. Such economies arise where the production or distribution of multiple products leads to a reduction in long-run average costs. If economies of scope are significant, an undertaking intending to produce only one product may be at a cost disadvantage relative to the incumbent and therefore a less effective competitor. The existence of scope economies raises the cost of successful entry or expansion as a result.[53]

Strategic barriers   Strategic barriers are barriers which are created or enhanced by incumbents in a particular market, possibly with a view to deterring potential entry or expansion. Strategic barriers can be distinguished from structural barriers, which arise from the characteristics of the market itself. An example of a strategic barrier is strategic brand proliferation practices engaged in by the incumbent which may crowd out product space and result in only limited opportunities to enter or expand. Other examples include long term contracts concluded by incumbents, or where an incumbent decides to build excess capacity to send a signal to potential new entrants that it could push prices down to levels which, while still profitable for the incumbent, would not permit new entrants to earn sufficient revenue to cover their sunk costs.[54]

Countervailing buyer power   The strength of buyers and the structure of the buyers' side of the market may prevent a supplier from having a substantial degree of market power. Buyer power is not so much a matter of the size of the buyer but more a matter of bargaining strength and whether buyers have a choice between alternative suppliers. Generally speaking, buyer power implies the existence of a credible threat to bypass the supplier if no acceptable deal can be reached. A buyer will be more likely to have this kind of buyer power where one or more of the following factors apply:[55]

(a) the buyer is well informed about alternative sources of supply and could readily, at little cost to itself, and within a reasonable period, switch substantial purchases (although not necessarily all of its purchases) from a given supplier (i.e. any threat to switch must be credible);

---

[52]   Guideline on the Second Conduct Rule, para 3.27.
[53]   Guideline on the Second Conduct Rule, para 3.26.
[54]   Guideline on the Second Conduct Rule, para 3.28.
[55]   Guideline on the Second Conduct Rule, para 3.29.

(b) the buyer could commence production itself (e.g. by vertically integrating) or sponsor new entry or expansion by another supplier relatively quickly and without substantial sunk costs;

(c) the buyer is an important customer for the supplier (so that the supplier is willing to offer better terms to keep the buyer as a customer); and/or

(d) the buyer can intensify competition among suppliers by purchasing through a competitive tender.

To prevent a substantial degree of market power from arising, buyer power must be countervailing, such that it is a sufficiently effective competitive constraint which operates to protect the market as a whole. Buyer power will not be considered a sufficiently effective competitive constraint if it only ensures that a particular or limited segment of customers is shielded from the exercise of market power. For example, an undertaking may still be able to exercise a substantial degree of market power even though certain of its larger customers can secure preferable terms. Countervailing buyer power should be reasonably foreseeable for some future period, and not merely temporary or transient.[56]

Bidding markets　　Sometimes buyers choose their suppliers through procurement auctions or tenders. The main feature of bidding markets is that there is competition for the market as opposed to competition in the market. In these circumstances, even if there are only a few suppliers, competition might be intense. This is more likely to be the case where tenders are infrequent (so that suppliers are more likely to bid), and where suppliers are not subject to capacity constraints (so that all suppliers are in a position to place competitive bids). If competition at the bidding stage is effective, a high market share at a given point in time would not necessarily reflect long term market power. For this reason, it may be more appropriate to assess market power over an extended period.[57]

Vertical integration　　Vertically integrated firms may be able to prevent an undertaking from having a substantial degree of market power. For example, suppose a supplier produces an input A which is a necessary input for the manufacture of a product B. Suppose also that a vertically integrated supplier that does not supply a substitute for input A on the merchant market supplies a product C which is a substitute for B. The ability of customers to substitute product C may constrain the ability of the non-vertically integrated producer of input A to raise its price, thereby precluding the supplier of input A from having a substantial degree of market power in relation to input A.[58]

---

[56]　Guideline on the Second Conduct Rule, paras 3.30-3.31.
[57]　Guideline on the Second Conduct Rule, para 3.34.
[58]　Guideline on the Second Conduct Rule, para 3.35.

Capacity constraints Sometimes an undertaking's competitors will not be in a position to respond to the exercise of market power by increasing output in response to higher prices in the relevant market. For example, an undertaking operating in an industry with limited capacity would be in a stronger position to increase prices above competitive levels than an undertaking with a similar market share operating in an industry with substantial excess capacity. Moreover, even existing excess capacity may be so expensive to employ that it will not in practice constitute a competitive constraint. For example, the costs of introducing another shift in a factory with excess capacity might be so high as to hinder a competitor from responding to the exercise of market power.[59]

3.3 ABUSE OF SUBSTANTIAL MARKET POWER

Abuse of substantial market power An undertaking that has a substantial degree of market power in a market must not abuse that power by engaging in conduct that has as its object or effect the prevention, restriction or distortion of competition in Hong Kong.[60] Section 21(2) of the Competition Ordinance specifies that conduct may, in particular, constitute such an abuse if it involves:
   (a) predatory behaviour towards competitors; or
   (b) limiting production, markets or technical development to the prejudice of consumers.
The Competition Commission, however, stresses that abusive conduct is potentially any conduct which has the object or effect of harming competition in Hong Kong and that the category of abusive conduct is open.[61] Moreover, it is possible for an undertaking with a substantial degree of market power in one market to commit an abuse in a different market. In this regard, the relevant undertaking might leverage its market power in the first market to harm competition in the second.[62]

Anti-competitive foreclosure Abusive conduct may in particular result in harm to competition through anti-competitive foreclosure.[63] Where competitors are foreclosed from access to buyers or sources of supply simply as a result of the business efficacy of, and/or the provision of better products or services by, the undertaking with a substantial degree of market power, this will not be regarded as anti-competitive foreclosure. Anti-competitive foreclosure occurs, however, when competitors, actual or potential, are denied access to buyers of their products or to suppliers as a result of the conduct of

---

[59] Guideline on the Second Conduct Rule, para 3.36.
[60] Competition Ordinance, section 21(1).
[61] Guideline on the Second Conduct Rule, para 4.1.
[62] Guideline on the Second Conduct Rule, para 4.2.
[63] Case T-155/06, *Tomra Systems v Commission* [2010] ECR II-4361.

the undertaking with a substantial degree of market power. Anti-competitive foreclosure can result in the undertaking with a substantial degree of market power being able to charge higher prices or in reduced product quality or choice, to the detriment of consumers. For anti-competitive foreclosure to occur access to buyers or suppliers does not need to be entirely eliminated. Degraded or diminished access can be sufficient.[64]

Economic efficiencies arising out of the conduct Unlike in the case of the general exclusion from the First Conduct Rule for agreements enhancing overall economic efficiency, there is no comparable efficiency-based exclusion for conduct within scope of the Second Conduct Rule. Undertakings may, however, wish to argue that conduct does not in fact contravene the Second Conduct Rule because it entails efficiencies sufficient to guarantee no net harm to consumers. A key consideration will be whether, notwithstanding the market power of the undertaking concerned, the claimed efficiencies are in fact passed on to consumers and whether the undertaking with a substantial degree of market power can demonstrate in fact no net harm to consumers.[65]

Objective justification Abusive conduct cannot itself be objectively justified, although the Competition Commission recognises that an undertaking may decide not to enter into a trading relationship with another party for a variety of legitimate commercial reasons.[66] An undertaking may, in particular, be able to demonstrate that the conduct concerned is not abusive where it is indispensable and proportionate to the pursuit of some legitimate objective unconnected with the tendency of the conduct to harm competition. For example, a refusal to deal may not be abusive under the Second Conduct Rule where an undertaking with a substantial degree of market power refuses to supply a particular input to a customer because the customer is, as an objective matter, insufficiently creditworthy. Similarly, below cost pricing may not be abusive where the pricing policy is a genuine promotional offer of limited duration relating to the launch of a new product or entry into a new market. Below cost pricing is also unlikely to be abusive if the practice is genuinely intended to minimise losses in respect of obsolescent or deteriorating products.[67] The existence of technical requirements relating to the product in question that the other party is unable to fulfil may also objectively justify a refusal to deal.[68]

---

[64] Guideline on the Second Conduct Rule, para 4.3.
[65] Guideline on the Second Conduct Rule, para 4.5. Cf. Case C-209/10, *Post Danmark A/S v Konkurrenceradet* EU:C:2012:172.
[66] Guideline on the Second Conduct Rule, para 5.16.
[67] Guideline on the Second Conduct Rule, para 4.4.
[68] Case 31/84, *CBEM v Compagnie Luxembourgeoise de télédiffusion* [1985] ECR 3261.

Object of harming competition Certain types of conduct by undertakings with a substantial degree of market power can be regarded, by their very nature, to be so harmful to the proper functioning of normal competition in the market that there is no need to examine their effects. Such conduct is considered to have the object of harming competition contrary to the Second Conduct Rule.[69] The category of conduct which has the object of harming competition cannot be reduced to an exhaustive list.[70] In order to determine whether conduct has the object of harming competition, regard must be had to the nature of the conduct (including, if the conduct is contained in an agreement, the content of the agreement and the way it is implemented) and its context (including both the economic and legal context).[71] If conduct has more than one object, it has the object of harming competition if one of its objects is to prevent, restrict or distort competition.[72] Moreover, an anti-competitive object may be ascertained by inference.[73] In practice, it will often be necessary to infer an anti-competitive object from the facts underlying the conduct and the surrounding circumstances.[74]

Determining the object of particular conduct requires an objective assessment of its aims. That is, the object of conduct refers to the purpose or aim of the conduct, viewed in its context and in light of the way it is implemented, and not merely the subjective intentions of the undertaking concerned. Nonetheless, there is nothing to prevent the Commission from taking the relevant undertaking's subjective intention into account when determining whether or not particular conduct has the object of harming competition. This is not to say that a subjective intention to harm competition can suffice to show an anti-competitive object. Evidence of subjective intent is merely a factor to which the Commission can have regard in its objective assessment of the aims of the conduct.[75]

An examination of the context of particular conduct for the purposes of determining whether it has the object of harming competition does not require or involve an analysis of the effects of the conduct in the market. Where it is shown that conduct has the object of harming competition, the Commission does not need to demonstrate that the conduct has anti-competitive effects or is likely to have such effects, for example, a foreclosure effect. It is sufficient for the Commission to show that the conduct has the potential to harm or is capable of harming competition in the relevant context.[76] Where it is

---

[69] Competition Ordinance, section 21(1); Guideline on the Second Conduct Rule, para 4.6.
[70] Guideline on the Second Conduct Rule, para 4.12.
[71] Guideline on the Second Conduct Rule, para 4.7.
[72] Competition Ordinance, section 22(1); Guideline on the Second Conduct Rule, para 4.11.
[73] Competition Ordinance, section 22(2).
[74] Guideline on the Second Conduct Rule, para 4.11.
[75] Guideline on the Second Conduct Rule, para 4.8.
[76] Guideline on the Second Conduct Rule, para 4.9.

established that particular conduct has the object of harming competition, the conduct cannot be defended by the relevant undertaking showing that the conduct does not in fact have any anti-competitive effects or that such effects are not likely to flow from the conduct.[77]

An example of conduct which may have the object of harming competition is predatory pricing, where an undertaking with a substantial degree of market power sets prices below its average variable costs.[78] Certain exclusive dealing arrangements by an undertaking with a substantial degree of market power might also be considered to have the object of harming competition when viewed in their context. Similarly, should it be established that an undertaking with a substantial degree of market power paid a distributor or customer to delay the introduction of a competitor's product, such conduct might be assessed as having the object of harming competition.[79]

Effect of harming competition   If conduct does not have the object of harming competition, it will contravene the Second Conduct Rule if it nevertheless has the effect of harming competition.[80] When demonstrating that conduct has an anti-competitive effect, the Commission may consider not only any actual effects but also effects that are likely to flow from the conduct.[81] In assessing whether conduct has the actual or likely effect of harming competition, the Commission may assess what the market conditions would have been in the absence of the conduct (i.e. the counter-factual) and compare these counter-factual market conditions with the conditions resulting where the conduct is present. However, this is not a necessary step. For example, it may not be possible to determine the counter-factual in some cases (such as where an undertaking has held a substantial degree of market power for many years).[82] If conduct has more than one effect, it will be capable of contravening the Second Conduct Rule if any one of its effects is to prevent, restrict or distort competition.[83]

Conduct might have the actual or likely effect of harming competition where it results in or is likely to result in:[84]

(a) higher prices;

---

[77] Guideline on the Second Conduct Rule, para 4.10.

[78] Guideline on the Second Conduct Rule, para 4.13; Case C-62/86, *AKZO Chemie BV v Commission* [1991] ECR I-3359.

[79] Guideline on the Second Conduct Rule, para 4.14; Case T-286/09, *Intel Corp. v Commission* EU:T:2014:547.

[80] Competition Ordinance, section 21(1); Guideline on the Second Conduct Rule, para 4.15.

[81] Guideline on the Second Conduct Rule, para 4.16.

[82] Guideline on the Second Conduct Rule, para 4.17.

[83] Competition Ordinance, section 22(3); Guideline on the Second Conduct Rule, para 4.20.

[84] Guideline on the Second Conduct Rule, para 4.18.

(b) a restriction in output;

(c) a reduction in product quality or variety; and/or

(d) anti-competitive foreclosure.

For conduct to have the actual or likely effect of harming competition, it must harm the process of competition causing harm to consumers, and not simply harm an individual competitor. Consumers benefit when competitors have strong incentives to win the competitive battle against one another. In a highly competitive market some competitors will leave the market over time while new ones will enter. The Competition Ordinance is concerned with protecting competition in the market and not the commercial interests of particular market participants.[85]

Competition authorities internationally are increasingly adopting an effects-based approach to enforcement of the prohibition on abuse of substantial market power/dominance. The reference to effect focuses attention on the economic impact of the practices rather than their legal form. As the Competition Commission's decisional practice and approach develops it may be useful to refer to the practice of the European Commission in approaching effects based assessment in abuse of dominance cases under EU competition law. In particular, the European Commission's guidance on its enforcement priorities in applying Article 102 TFEU to exclusionary abuses of dominance is intended to reflect a more effects-based approach.[86]

3.4 CONDUCT THAT CONSTITUTES AN ABUSE OF MARKET POWER

Examples of abuse of substantial market power   Section 21(2) of the Competition Ordinance states that conduct may constitute an abuse if it involves, in particular, predatory behaviour towards competitors or limiting production, markets or technical development to the prejudice of consumers.[87] The Competition Commission, in its Guideline on the Second Conduct Rule sets out the following specific non-exhaustive examples of types of conduct

---

[85]   Guideline on the Second Conduct Rule, para 4.19.

[86]   OJ 2009 C45/2. The purpose of the European Commission's guidance is to outline a more effects-based approach by looking at the merits of competition, whether there is a benefit to the consumer or if there is foreclosure on the market and likely harm to the consumer. However, it is important to note that despite the evolving approach there are remnants of a form-based approach in both the decided case law and practice of the European Commission and the EU Courts in the period post-dating the Article 102 Guidance. The Article 102 guidance deals only with exclusionary abuses (i.e. practices that exclude competition such as refusal to supply) as opposed to exploitative abuses (e.g. rent seeking practices such as excessive pricing which more directly benefit the dominant company).

[87]   Competition Ordinance, section 21(2).

that it may, in appropriate circumstances, consider an abuse of a substantial degree of market power:

(a) predatory pricing;

(b) tying and bundling;

(c) margin squeeze conduct;

(d) refusal to deal; and

(e) exclusive dealing.

The Commission notes that the specific conduct under examination in a given case may involve more than one type of abuse.[88] Moreover, since the list is non-exhaustive, it follows that there are other types of conduct that might constitute an abuse.[89] In EU law, for example, abusive litigation has been considered as falling within the scope of Article 102 TFEU.[90] The Competition Commission has emphasised that it will be concerned with exclusionary conduct and it does not state that it will challenge exploitative conduct.[91] Nevertheless, exploitative conduct, in particular excessive pricing, might well attract the Commission's attention.[92]

It may also be noted that the whether or not conduct amounts to abuse may be linked to the degree of market power held by the undertaking in question, so that the higher the degree of market power the more likely that certain conduct may be regarded as exclusionary.[93]

Predatory pricing Whereas offering low prices to consumers is the epitome of competitive conduct, lower prices resulting from competition on the merits must be distinguished from alleged predatory pricing conduct. An undertaking with a substantial degree of market power may be engaging in predatory pricing where it sets prices so low that it deliberately foregoes profits in an attempt to force one or more other undertakings out of the market and/or in an attempt to otherwise discipline competitors. In this context, the undertaking may incur losses in the short run in the expectation that it will be able to charge higher prices in the longer term (for example, following the exit of relevant competitors from the market). Consumers will ultimately be worse off if competition is weakened in this way, leading to higher prices and reduced product quality and choice.[94]

---

[88] Guideline on the Second Conduct Rule, paras 5.1-5.2.

[89] Article 102 TFEU, for example, lists as possible abuses the imposition of discriminatory conditions or making the conclusion of contracts subject to supplementary obligations having no connection with the subject of the contracts.

[90] Case T-111/96, *ITT Promedia NV v Commission* [1998] ECR II-2937.

[91] The Telco Rule, by contrast, is concerned with exploitative abuse of dominance.

[92] Article 102 TFEU specifically prohibits abuse entailing the imposition of unfair purchase or selling prices.

[93] Cases C-395/96P & C-396/95P, *Compagnie Maritime Belge Transports v Commission* [2000] ECR I-1365.

[94] Guideline on the Second Conduct Rule, paras 5.3-5.4.

Generally speaking, an adverse effect on competition will arise where there is or is likely to be anti-competitive foreclosure of existing competitors or new entrants. Where reliable data is available, the Commission will seek to demonstrate anti-competitive foreclosure when assessing predatory pricing conduct. It will not, however, be necessary for the Commission to demonstrate that competitors have actually exited the market in order to show a foreclosure effect. An undertaking with a substantial degree of market power may prefer merely to undermine the ability of competitors to compete effectively rather than to force them from the market. Such conduct may also amount to anti-competitive foreclosure.[95]

When assessing whether predation is taking (or has taken) place, the Commission will typically consider whether the undertaking is pricing below an appropriate measure of cost. Abusive predatory pricing can be distinguished from below cost pricing pursuant to some legitimate commercial objective unconnected with the tendency of the conduct to harm competition. For example, where the pricing practice is a genuine promotional offer of limited duration or genuinely intended to minimise losses in respect of obsolescent or deteriorating products the practice is unlikely to be abusive. Although different cost benchmarks may be used to identify predatory behaviour depending on the facts of the case, the Commission makes the following general remarks, distinguishing between pricing below average variable cost and pricing below average total cost.[96]

Pricing below average variable cost (AVC) is unlikely to be economically rational, because an undertaking that does so is making losses on each unit of output it produces even with respect only to the costs that it must immediately and unavoidably incur in producing those units of output (i.e. its variable costs). For this reason, where an undertaking with a substantial degree of market power sets prices below AVC, the Commission may consider that this is undertaken for a predatory purpose. Moreover, in the absence of evidence to the contrary, the Commission is likely to infer that the conduct has the object of harming competition. In such a scenario, the Commission need not demonstrate actual or likely anti-competitive foreclosure.[97]

---

[95] Guideline on the Second Conduct Rule, para 5.5.

[96] Guideline on the Second Conduct Rule, para 5.6.

[97] Guideline on the Second Conduct Rule, para 5.6(a). Long run average incremental cost (LRAIC) is another benchmark that may be used as an alternative to AVC. LRAIC is sometimes considered a more appropriate cost measure than AVC when the alleged predatory conduct involves products that have large fixed costs and low marginal costs of production. Pricing below average avoidable cost (AAC) is a further benchmark that can be used as an alternative to AVC depending on the facts of the case. AAC is sometimes considered a more appropriate cost measure than AVC when analysing profit sacrificed and avoidable losses. AAC focuses on the costs incurred to generate increased output weighed against the revenues received.

Where an undertaking prices above its AVC (or a comparable measure) but below its average total cost (ATC), the conduct may be entirely rational commercial behaviour because the immediately unavoidable costs of production (the variable costs) are more than met, even if not all costs in the longer term (i.e. fixed costs) are covered. When analysing this type of conduct, evidence of actual or likely anti-competitive effects may be considered or there may be documentary evidence of a predatory strategy. The Commission may also investigate whether the allegedly predatory conduct resulted in losses that could have been avoided or whether the undertaking's pricing strategy makes commercial sense only because of its tendency to harm competition.[98]

When considering whether below-cost pricing constitutes predatory conduct, the Commission may also consider the extent to which the predating undertaking is in the longer term able to recoup its short term losses stemming from the below-cost pricing by subsequently charging supra-competitive prices as a result of increased market power.[99] It may be noted that there is no requirement in EU competition law for recoupment to be proved in order to establish predatory pricing.[100]

Tying and bundling Tying occurs when a supplier makes the sale of one product (the tying product) conditional upon the purchase of another (the tied product) from the supplier (i.e. the tying product is not sold separately). A distinction may be made between technical tying and contractual tying.[101] Bundling refers to situations where a package of two or more products is offered at a discount. Tying and bundling are common commercial arrangements that generally do not harm competition and often promote competition. Many undertakings, whether or not they have a substantial degree of market power, engage in tying and bundling and such arrangements often result in lower production costs, reduced transaction and information costs, and increased convenience and variety for consumers.[102]

An undertaking with a substantial degree of market power in the tying market, however, can use tying to harm competitors in the tied market. In this circumstance, the undertaking leverages its substantial degree of market power from the tying market into the tied market. By tying, it may be able to reduce the number of potential buyers that are available for its competitors in the tied market – that is, the tied market is foreclosed. This may in turn cause those

---

[98] Guideline on the Second Conduct Rule, para 5.6(b).

[99] Guideline on the Second Conduct Rule, para 5.7.

[100] Case T-93/91, *Tetra Pak International v Commission* [1994] ECR II-755; EU guidance on Article 102 TFEU, para 71.

[101] Technical tying occurs when the tying product is designed in such a way that it only works properly with the tied product, and not with alternatives offered by competitors. Contractual tying occurs when the customer who purchases the tying product undertakes also to purchase the tied product.

[102] Guideline on the Second Conduct Rule, paras 5.8-5.9.

competitors to be less effective as competitors or to exit the tied market, with the result that the undertaking with a substantial degree of market power can raise prices to the detriment of consumers.   Similarly, in the context of bundling, an undertaking with a substantial degree of market power in the market for one of the products that forms part of the bundle may use bundling to harm competitors in the markets for the other products that are part of the same bundle. This may give rise to foreclosure in the latter markets, leading potentially to higher prices for consumers.[103]

When assessing tying and bundling conduct, the Commission will consider whether the tying and tied products (or products in the bundle) are distinct products and, if so, whether the conduct has an anti-competitive effect. An anti-competitive effect may arise in particular when the conduct results in anti-competitive foreclosure.[104]

Margin squeeze A margin squeeze may arise where a vertically integrated undertaking with a substantial degree of market power supplies an important input to undertakings operating on a downstream market where it also operates. A margin squeeze occurs where the undertaking with a substantial degree of market power reduces or squeezes the margin between the price it charges for the input to its competitors on the downstream market and the price its downstream operations charge to its own customers, such that the downstream competitor is unable to compete effectively. A margin squeeze requires that the undertaking supplying the relevant input has a substantial degree of market power in the market where it sells the input – that is, the upstream market.[105]

When assessing whether conduct amounts to an abusive margin squeeze, the Commission may consider the nature of the upstream input concerned and the level of the margin squeeze. An anti-competitive effect is more likely if the upstream product is an indispensable input from the perspective of the participants in the downstream market.   Nonetheless, an abusive margin squeeze cannot be excluded even if there are alternatives available for the upstream input. A margin squeeze arises where the difference between the downstream prices charged by the firm with substantial market power and the upstream prices it charges its competitors in the downstream market for the relevant input is: (i) negative (that is, if the upstream price is higher than the downstream price charged by the undertaking with a substantial degree of market power); or (ii) at least insufficient to cover the downstream product-specific costs of the firm with substantial market power. In this respect, the Commission will consider whether a downstream competitor with the same

---

[103] Guideline on the Second Conduct Rule, paras 5.10-5.11.
[104] Guideline on the Second Conduct Rule, para 5.12.
[105] Guideline on the Second Conduct Rule, paras 5.13-5.14. See, for example, Case C-280/08P, *Deutsche Telekom AG v Commission* [2010] ECR II-9555.

product-specific costs as the downstream operations of the vertically integrated undertaking with a substantial degree of market power would be profitable in light of the upstream and downstream prices levied by that undertaking.[106]

Refusal to deal As a general matter, an undertaking, whether or not it has a substantial degree of market power, is free to decide with whom it will or will not do business. An undertaking might not wish to enter into a trading relationship with another party for a variety of legitimate commercial reasons, for example because it has objectively justified concerns about the creditworthiness of the other party. A refusal to deal by an undertaking with a substantial degree of market power is likely to be abusive in very limited or exceptional circumstances. Refusal to deal is a situation where an undertaking with a substantial degree of market power refuses to supply an input to another undertaking, or is willing to supply that input only on objectively unreasonable terms, known as a constructive refusal to deal. Constructive refusal could, for example, consist of unduly delaying or otherwise degrading the supply of the relevant input, or imposing a price for the input that is excessive.[107]

A refusal to deal may harm competition in the downstream market by preventing the undertaking seeking access to the relevant input either from operating in that market or from operating in that market as an effective competitive constraint. Competition concerns are more likely to arise when the undertaking with a substantial degree of market power competes in the downstream market with the party with whom it refuses to deal (that is, where the undertaking with a substantial degree of market power is vertically integrated). Concerns may arise in particular when the refusal relates to an input that is indispensable for undertakings operating in the downstream market. In this context, the Competition Commission will consider whether undertakings operating in the downstream market are able to duplicate the relevant input or whether they would be able to duplicate it only at unreasonable cost (i.e. where the cost is so high that it would not make commercial sense to incur it).[108]

In assessing whether a refusal to deal is a contravention of the Second Conduct Rule, the Commission may consider as appropriate:[109]

(a) whether or not it is technically and economically feasible for the undertaking with a substantial degree of market power to provide the input in question;

(b) the past history of dealing between the undertakings (the termination of an existing supply arrangement might more readily be characterised as abusive); and/or

---

[106] Guideline on the Second Conduct Rule, para 5.15.
[107] Guideline on the Second Conduct Rule, paras 5.16-5.17.
[108] Guideline on the Second Conduct Rule, paras 5.18-5.19.
[109] Guideline on the Second Conduct Rule, para 5.20.

(c) the terms and conditions at which the products in question are generally supplied or are supplied in other contexts.

Given the importance of intellectual property rights (IPRs) in encouraging innovation, the Commission will consider an undertaking's refusal to license an IPR as a contravention of the Second Conduct Rule only in exceptional circumstances. It may assess whether a refusal to licence prevents the development of a secondary market or new product or otherwise limits technical development resulting in consumer harm.[110] Where an undertaking with a substantial degree of market power holds an IPR which is essential to an industry standard, and the undertaking gave a commitment at the time when the standard was adopted by the industry that it would license the IPR on fair, reasonable and non-discriminatory (FRAND) terms, a subsequent refusal to honour the FRAND commitment may be an abuse. Equally, it may also be an abuse for the holder of a standard essential patent with a FRAND commitment to seek injunctive relief against a willing licensee in certain circumstances.[111]

Exclusive dealing   Exclusive dealing is commonly used in commercial arrangements and in most cases will not harm competition. Where exclusive dealing is pursued by an undertaking with a substantial degree of market power, however, the exclusive dealing conduct may amount to an abuse if it has the object or effect of harming competition. An undertaking with substantial market power may seek to foreclose competitors by preventing them from selling to customers though exclusive dealing arrangements. Exclusive dealing in this context includes arrangements requiring a customer to purchase, directly or indirectly, all or a substantial proportion of its requirements of a particular product from a particular undertaking. This may take the form of either an exclusive purchasing obligation or a conditional rebate. Exclusive dealing is a broad category of conduct which also covers exclusive supply obligations or incentive arrangements with a similar effect. Where an undertaking with a substantial degree of market power uses such arrangements to foreclose competitors by preventing them from accessing particular inputs, this may amount to an abuse if the exclusive supply or relevant incentive arrangement locks up most of the efficient input suppliers in the market and competitors of the undertaking with a substantial degree of market power are unable to secure the inputs concerned from alternative suppliers.[112]

---

[110]   Cf. Case T-201/04, *Microsoft Corp. v Commission* [2007] ECR II-3601.
[111]   Guideline on the Second Conduct Rule, paras 5.21-5.22. A failure to honour a FRAND commitment might equally raise issues of excessive pricing or discriminatory pricing. Where the holder of a FRAND obligated standard essential patent seeks injunctive relief against a willing licensee, that may be assessed as a refusal to deal but equally it might be appropriate to assess such conduct as an abusive use of litigation.
[112]   Guideline on the Second Conduct Rule, paras 5.23-5.26. Other exclusive dealing practices or similar structures which may give rise to concern under the Second Conduct

An exclusive purchasing obligation requires a customer to purchase its requirements of a particular product exclusively or to a large extent only from the undertaking with a substantial degree of market power. Other obligations, such as stocking requirements, may have the same effect as exclusive purchasing even though they do not, strictly speaking, entail exclusivity. The Commission will have particular concerns where:

(a) the undertaking with a substantial degree of market power has imposed exclusive purchasing obligations on many customers;

(b) it is likely that consumers as a whole will not derive a benefit; and

(c) the relevant obligations, as a whole, have the effect of preventing the entry or expansion of competing undertakings because, for example, the exclusive purchasing locks up a significant part of the relevant market, that is, where there is anti-competitive foreclosure.[113]

In cases where competitors can compete on equal terms for the entirety of each individual customer's demand, exclusive dealing is unlikely to harm competition unless the duration of the exclusivity gives rise or is likely to give rise to a foreclosure effect. In the case of bidding markets for example, where there is competition for the market, exclusivity might merely be the result of a highly competitive market.[114]

Conditional rebates, in particular loyalty or fidelity rebates, involve the grant of a rebate to customers as a reward for particular purchasing behaviour. Typically, a loyalty rebate scheme involves offering a financial incentive to encourage the buyer to commit to purchasing more from the supplier. As a general matter, rebates of this kind are normal commercial arrangements intended to stimulate demand to the benefit of consumers. However, rebates which are granted by an undertaking with a substantial degree of market power can have foreclosure effects similar in nature to those caused by exclusive purchasing obligations. Usually a loyalty rebate involves the customer being awarded the rebate if the customer's purchases over a defined period exceed a defined threshold. Loyalty rebates may be granted either on all purchases from the undertaking with a substantial degree of market power (retroactive rebates) or only on purchases above the relevant threshold (incremental rebates). Retroactive rebates have the potential to foreclose the market significantly since buyers switching portions of their demand to an alternative supplier

---

Rule, depending on the facts of the case, include arrangements in supply agreements to match more favourable terms offered by competing suppliers (known as "English clauses"), slotting allowances paid by suppliers to retailers, incentives in the form of storage or other equipment provided free of charge in return for an exclusive stocking commitment or, in certain limited circumstances, category management arrangements.

[113] The undertaking with a substantial degree of market power might of course simply choose to target customers who are particularly important for competitors in terms of possibilities to enter or expand, thereby increasing the risk of anti-competitive foreclosure. Such conduct could equally amount to an abuse.

[114] Guideline on the Second Conduct Rule, paras 5.27-5.29.

would lose the rebate in respect of all products purchased and not only the incremental amount for which the buyer is considering alternative suppliers. Rebates may be individualised in nature (where the relevant thresholds are tailored to each customer according to its particular requirements) or standardised (where the same thresholds apply for all customers). Generally, an individualised threshold allows the undertaking with a substantial degree of market power to set the threshold at such a level as will maximise its foreclosure effect, while a standardised rebate may be too high for some buyers and/or too low for others to have a sufficient loyalty enhancing effect. Standardised rebates are therefore less likely to raise competition concerns. General quantity rebates, conditional on the size of a particular order, are also unlikely to raise competition concerns unless they are predatory in nature.[115]

3.5 EXCLUSIONS AND EXEMPTIONS FROM THE SECOND CONDUCT RULE

Exclusions and exemptions from the Second Conduct Rule Section 30 of the Competition Ordinance provides that the Second Conduct Rule does not apply where the conduct falls within the scope of the following categories of exclusions specified in Schedule 1:[116]

- compliance with legal requirements;[117]
- services of general economic interest;[118]
- mergers;
- conduct of lesser significance.

In addition, the Second Conduct Rule will not apply where the conduct in question in exempted by section 31 (public policy) or section 32 (international obligations) of the Competition Ordinance,[119] or where it is disapplied in the case of statutory bodies, specified persons and persons engaged in specified activities as provided for in sections 3 and 4 of the Competition Ordinance.[120]

Mergers To the extent that conduct results in, or if engaged in would result in, a merger, the Second Conduct Rule does not apply to the conduct.[121]

---

[115] Guideline on the Second Conduct Rule, paras 5.30-5.32.
[116] Competition Ordinance, section 30 and Schedule 1; Guideline on the Second Conduct Rule, Annex, para 1.1. Section 36 provides that the Chief Executive in Council may by order, subject to the approval of the Legislative Council, amend Schedule 1.
[117] See Chapter One, pp. 16-17.
[118] See Chapter One, pp. 28-30.
[119] See Chapter One, pp. 17-18.
[120] See Chapter One, pp. 25-27.
[121] Competition Ordinance, Schedule 1, section 4(2); Guideline on the Second Conduct Rule, Annex, para 4.1.

Conduct of lesser significance The Second Conduct Rule does not apply to conduct engaged in by an undertaking the turnover of which does not exceed HK$40 million for the turnover period.[122] It is thought that this will exclude nearly 95% of all SMEs in Hong Kong from the application of the Second Conduct Rule. Turnover for the purposes of this general exclusion means the total gross revenues of an undertaking whether obtained in Hong Kong or outside Hong Kong.[123] Additional rules in respect of the general exclusion for conduct of lesser significance are to be contained in regulations that may be made by the Secretary for Commerce and Economic Development under section 163(2) of the Competition Ordinance.[124]

Commission decision confirming exclusion or exemption Undertakings to whom exclusions and exemptions apply will not contravene the Second Conduct Rule. There is no requirement for undertakings to apply to the Competition Commission in order to secure the benefit of a particular exclusion or exemption. Undertakings can assess for themselves whether their conduct falls within the terms of a particular exclusion or exemption. Equally, undertakings may assert the benefit of any exclusion or exemption as a defence in any proceedings before the Competition Tribunal or other courts.[125]

Undertakings seeking greater legal certainty may, however, pursuant to section 24 of the Competition Ordinance, apply to the Commission for a decision as to whether or not the conduct is excluded or exempted.[126] The Commission, after considering any representations made by interested parties, may make a decision pursuant to section 26 of the Competition Ordinance as to whether or not the conduct in question is excluded or exempt from the application of the Second Conduct Rule.[127] Where the Commission issues a decision that conduct is excluded or exempt from the application of the Second Conduct Rule, each undertaking specified in the decision is immune from any action under the Competition Ordinance with regard to that conduct in so far as the undertaking complies with every condition and limitation imposed by the decision.[128]

---

[122] Competition Ordinance, Schedule 1, section 6(1); Guideline on the Second Conduct Rule, Annex, para 5.1. Section 6(2)-(3) lays down rules for determining the turnover period. See also the Competition Commission's guidance "How to assess turnover for exclusions from the Competition Ordinance Conduct Rules".

[123] Competition Ordinance, Schedule 1, section 6(4).

[124] Guideline on the Second Conduct Rule, Annex, para 5.2.

[125] Guideline on the Second Conduct Rule, Annex, para 1.2.

[126] Competition Ordinance, section 24(1); Guideline on the Second Conduct Rule, Annex, para 1.3. See Chapter Five, pp. 3-11 for the procedures in applying for a decision.

[127] Competition Ordinance, section 26(1).

[128] Competition Ordinance, section 27.

Chapter Four

THE MERGER RULE

4.1 SCOPE OF THE MERGER RULE

The Merger Rule The Merger Rule is established by Schedule 7, and takes effect pursuant to section 162, of the Competition Ordinance. It provides that an undertaking must not, directly or indirectly, carry out a merger that has, or is likely to have, the effect of substantially lessening competition in Hong Kong.[1] Hong Kong has a sector-specific merger control system that applies only to certain mergers in the telecommunications sector in that the Merger Rule only applies where an undertaking that directly or indirectly holds a carrier licence[2] within the meaning of the Telecommunications Ordinance[3] is involved in a merger.[4] Nevertheless, apart from this limitation, the provisions governing the Merger Rule are drafted in general rather than sector-specific terms, with a view to their possible general extension in the future. The Competition

---

[1] Competition Ordinance, Schedule 7, section 3(1).

[2] Carrier licence is defined in section 2(1) of the Telecommunications Ordinance (Cap 106) as a licence issued for the establishment or maintenance of a telecommunications network for carrying communications to or from the public between fixed locations, between moving locations or between fixed locations and moving locations, within Hong Kong, or between Hong Kong and places outside Hong Kong, on a point-to-point, point-to-multipoint or broadcasting basis, such locations within Hong Kong being separated by unleased Government land, but does not include the licences listed in Schedule 1 [of the Telecommunications Ordinance]. The licences listed in Schedule 1 are:

- Public Radiocommnications Service Licence for radio paging services;
- Public Radiocommnications Service Licence for trunked radio services;
- Public Radiocommnications Service Licence for radiolocation services;
- Broadcast Relay Station Licence;
- Broadcast Radio Relay Station Licence;
- Closed Circuit Television Licence;
- Satellite Master Antenna Television Licence;
- Hotel Television Services Licence.

A list of the holders of carrier licences is available on the Communications Authority website: www.coms-auth.hk.

[3] Competition Ordinance, Schedule 7, section 1.

[4] Competition Ordinance, Schedule 7, section 4; Guideline on the Merger Rule, para 2.15.

Commission[5] has issued a Guideline on the Merger Rule[6] which sets out how it intends to interpret and give effect to the Merger Rule.[7]

Merger control in Hong Kong is voluntary in the sense that there is no requirement under the Merger Rule to notify the Commission of a merger or a proposed merger.[8]   The Commission may, however, use its powers to investigate a merger and take the necessary action to ensure compliance with the Merger Rule. As such, it may be in the interest of the parties to a proposed merger that would fall within the scope of the Merger Rule to approach the Commission to discuss the transaction and seek informal advice on the transaction on a confidential basis. Parties to a merger or proposed merger may propose commitments to the Commission to address any concerns it may have about a possible contravention of the Merger Rule.[9] Where applicable, parties to a merger or proposed merger may also apply to the Commission for a decision whether the merger or proposed merger is excluded from the application of the Merger Rule.[10]

Territorial application of the Merger Rule The Merger Rule applies to a merger even if:[11]

(a) the arrangements for the creation of the merger take place outside Hong Kong;

(b) the merger takes place outside Hong Kong; or

(c) any party to the arrangements for the creation of the merger, or any party involved in the merger is outside Hong Kong.

A similar provision on territorial application is found in the Singapore Competition Act, but not in EU merger legislation.[12]

Relevant transactions In general, transactions that involve the merging of two or more undertakings into one, the acquisition of one (or part of an) undertaking by another, the forming of a joint venture and the acquisition of assets by one undertaking from another may potentially give rise to a merger

---

5   While the Competition Commission is the principal competition authority responsible for enforcing the Competition Ordinance, it has concurrent jurisdiction with the Communications Authority in respect of the anti-competitive conduct of certain undertakings operating in the telecommunications and broadcasting sectors.

6   Guideline on the Merger Rule, 27 July 2015, pursuant to Competition Ordinance, Schedule 7, section 17.

7   Guideline on the Merger Rule, para 1.2.

8   Guideline on the Merger Rule, para 1.3.

9   Competition Ordinance, section 60.

10   Competition Ordinance, Schedule 7, section 11.

11   Competition Ordinance, Schedule 7, section 2.

12   Nevertheless, EU merger control may be applied to mergers outside the EU having foreseeable, immediate and substantial effects within the EU: Case T-102/96, *Gencor Ltd. v Commission* [1999] ECR II-753.

which needs to be examined under the Merger Rule.[13] This is mirrored on the Singapore Competition Act.[14] A number of key concepts that are central to the assessment of what constitutes a merger under the Merger Rule are also mirrored in the EU Merger Regulation (EUMR).[15] These include the concepts of control, decisive influence and full function joint ventures. The European Commission has issued extensive guidance on its approach to what constitutes a merger under the EUMR. In particular, it has adopted a Consolidated Jurisdictional Notice[16] which may provide assistance for assessing similar concepts under the Merger Rule.

The Merger Rule applies to mergers where one of the undertakings concerned is a holder of a carrier licence. This has potentially wide application. For example, a conglomerate, including a subsidiary which is a holder of a carrier licence, may merge with another undertaking which is not a holder, directly or indirectly, of a carrier licence. Nevertheless, as long as one of the undertakings concerned holds a carrier licence, the Merger Rule appears to apply even though there may be no immediate effect on telecommunications markets as such.

Mergers between previously independent undertakings A merger within the scope of the Merger Rule takes place if two or more undertakings previously independent of each other cease to be independent of each other,[17] where one or more of the undertakings holds a carrier licence or, directly or indirectly, controls an undertaking that holds a carrier licence.[18] A merger takes place when, for example, two or more previously independent undertakings amalgamate into a new undertaking and cease to exist as separate legal entities. A merger may also occur where, in the absence of a legal merger, there is a *de facto* amalgamation of the undertakings concerned into a single economic unit, by establishing a permanent, single economic management. Other relevant factors for the determination of a *de facto* merger may include internal profit and loss compensation or a revenue distribution between the various entities within the group, and their joint liability or external risk sharing. The *de facto* amalgamation may be solely based on contractual arrangements, but it can also be reinforced by cross-shareholdings between the undertakings forming the economic unit. A merger may take place where there is *de facto* amalgamation of undertakings concerned into a single economic unit, by establishing a permanent, single economic

---

[13] Guideline on the Merger Rule, para 2.1.
[14] The Competition Commission of Singapore has issued guidelines on the substantive assessment of mergers (2007).
[15] Council Regulation (EC) 139/2004 on the control of concentrations between undertakings, OJ 2004 L24/1.
[16] Consolidated Jurisdictional Notice under the EUMR, OJ 2008 C95/1.
[17] Competition Ordinance, Schedule 7, section 3(2)(a).
[18] Competition Ordinance, Schedule 7, section 4(a).

management.[19]   The requirement that the merger involves two or more independent undertakings means that intra-group mergers are excluded from the scope of the Merger Rule.

Acquisition of control A merger within the scope of the Merger Rule takes place when one or more persons or other undertakings acquire direct or indirect control of the whole or part of one or more other undertakings,[20] where the undertaking or the person or persons acquiring control or the undertaking in which control is acquired holds a carrier licence or, directly or indirectly, controls an undertaking that holds a carrier licence.[21]   Control may be exercised by one party on its own or jointly with one or more other parties.[22] Direct control is acquired where it is exercisable by the persons which are the holders of the rights conferring control.   Indirect control arises where third parties have the power to exercise those rights, such as in the case of a fund manager having control over decisions of an investment fund.

Control, whether solely or jointly, in relation to an undertaking, is to be regarded as existing if, by reason of rights, contracts or any other means, or any combination of rights, contracts or other means, decisive influence is capable of being exercised with regard to the activities of the undertaking and, in particular, by:[23]

(a) ownership of, or the right to use all or part of, the assets of an undertaking; or

(b) rights or contracts which enable decisive influence to be exercised with regard to the composition, voting or decisions of any governing body of an undertaking.

Control is acquired by any person or other undertaking if the person or undertaking:[24]

(a) becomes a holder of the rights or contracts, or entitled to use the other means; or

(b) although not becoming such a holder or entitled to use those other means, acquires the power to exercise the rights derived from them.

Given that control is deemed to exist where decisive influence is capable of being exercised, the ability to exercise control is an objective notion independent of whether control is actually exercised or not.   In determining whether decisive influence is capable of being exercised, regard must be had to all the circumstances of the case and not solely to the legal effect of any instrument, deed, transfer, assignment or other act done or made.[25]   Decisive

---

[19]   Guideline on the Merger Rule, para 2.4.
[20]   Competition Ordinance, Schedule 7, section 3(2)(b).
[21]   Competition Ordinance, Schedule 7, section 4(b).
[22]   Guideline on the Merger Rule, para 2.5.
[23]   Competition Ordinance, Schedule 7, section 5(1).
[24]   Competition Ordinance, Schedule 7, section 5(2).
[25]   Competition Ordinance, Schedule 7, section 5(3)

influence refers to the power to determine decisions (including the making or vetoing of such decisions) relating to the strategic commercial behaviour of an undertaking, such as the budget, the business plan, major investments or the appointment of senior management. Control may therefore occur on a legal or *de facto* basis.[26]

Joint ventures The creation of a joint venture to perform, on a lasting basis, all the functions of an autonomous economic entity constitutes a merger in the same way as acquisition of control.[27] Joint ventures which satisfy these requirements bring about a lasting change in the structure of the undertakings concerned and the relevant market.[28]

Performing all the functions of an autonomous economic entity means that a joint venture must operate on a market and perform the functions normally carried out by an undertaking operating on that market. In order to do so, the Competition Commission considers that the joint venture must have a management dedicated to its day-to-day operations and access to sufficient resources, including finance, staff and assets (tangible and intangible), in order to conduct on a lasting basis its business activities within the area provided for in the joint venture agreement.[29]

A joint venture does not perform all the functions of an autonomous economic entity if it only takes over one specific function within the parent companies' business activities, such as research and development or production, without access to or presence on the market. Such joint ventures are auxiliary to their parent companies' business activities. This is also the case where a joint venture is essentially limited to the distribution or sales of its parent companies' products and, therefore, acts principally as a sales agency. However, the fact that a joint venture makes use of the distribution network or outlet of one or more of its parent companies normally will not disqualify it from being considered as performing all the functions of an autonomous economic entity, as long as the parent companies are acting only as agents of the joint venture.[30]

The joint venture must be intended to operate for a sufficiently long period to bring about a lasting change in the structure of the undertakings concerned.[31] The fact that the parent companies commit to the joint venture the resources to carry out all the functions of an autonomous economic entity normally demonstrates that this is the case. However, joint ventures for a short finite

---

[26] Guideline on the Merger Rule, para 2.7.
[27] Competition Ordinance, Schedule 7, section 3(4).
[28] Guideline on the Merger Rule, para 2.8.
[29] Guideline on the Merger Rule, para 2.9.
[30] Guideline on the Merger Rule, para 2.10.
[31] The European Commission has usually considered at least 5 years to be a sufficiently long period when considering whether a joint venture is to be treated as full function under the EUMR.

duration are unlikely to be considered as creating such a lasting change. For example, a joint venture established for a specific project which does not include ongoing operational activities is unlikely to be viewed as a merger. In addition, where a joint venture's core activities depend on a third party's decision which at the time of establishment remains outstanding (e.g. a tender award, the grant of a licence, etc.), it remains unclear whether the joint venture would become operational at all. Thus, at that stage the joint venture cannot be considered to perform autonomous economic functions on a lasting basis.[32]

The Commission will also take into account the presence of the joint venture's parent companies in upstream or downstream markets. Where a substantial proportion of sales or purchases between the parents and the joint venture are likely for a lengthy period and are not on an arm's length basis, the joint venture is likely to be viewed as lacking sufficient economic autonomy in its operational activities.[33]

Asset acquisition A merger within the scope of the Merger Rule may also take place by way of an acquisition by one undertaking of the whole or part of the assets, including goodwill, of another undertaking[34] which results in the acquiring undertaking being in a position to replace the acquired undertaking, or to substantially replace the acquired undertaking, in the business or in part of the business concerned in which the acquired undertaking was engaged immediately before the acquisition.[35] The assets acquired in a merger may include both tangible assets (such as a network, equipment, customer base, etc.) and intangible assets (such as licences, rights, permissions, etc.).[36] In order to fall within the scope of the Merger Rule, the acquiring undertaking or the acquired undertaking must hold a carrier licence or, directly or indirectly, control an undertaking that holds a carrier licence, and the relevant business conducted by the acquired undertaking immediately before the acquisition must have been conducted under a carrier licence.[37]

Changes in control of a short-term nature Unlike EU merger control, the Competition Ordinance does not include a requirement, other than in the case of joint ventures, that the change in control must be on a lasting basis. It is possible, therefore, that some mergers that would not fall under the EUMR would be subject to the Merger Rule in Hong Kong. Nevertheless, the Competition Commission has stated in the Guideline on the Merger Rule that, in general, it will not be concerned about changes in the control of

---

[32] Guideline on the Merger Rule, para 2.11.
[33] Guideline on the Merger Rule, para 2.12.
[34] Competition Ordinance, Schedule 7, section 3(2)(c).
[35] Competition Ordinance, Schedule 7, section 3(3).
[36] Guideline on the Merger Rule, para 2.13.
[37] Competition Ordinance, Schedule 7, section 4(c).

undertakings which are not of a lasting nature. Changes in control which are purely transitory in nature, such as a transaction that is short-term and is only an intermediate step among several operations occurring in succession, are unlikely to have any effect on competition in the relevant market.[38] Subject to the specific facts of the case, the Commission will normally take the view that the following transactions are unlikely to give rise to competition concerns:[39]

- the acquisition of securities in a carrier licensee or in an undertaking which directly or indirectly controls a carrier licensee on a temporary basis by financial institutions satisfying certain specified conditions where the securities are acquired with a view to reselling them;[40]

- the acquisition of control of a carrier licensee or an undertaking which directly or indirectly controls a carrier licensee by the liquidators and receivers of the carrier licensee or the undertaking which directly or indirectly controls a carrier licensee (as the case may be) by virtue of their offices;

- the acquisition of holdings in a carrier licensee or in an undertaking which directly or indirectly controls a carrier licensee by a financial holding company, i.e. a company whose sole object is to acquire and manage holdings in other undertakings and to turn them into profit without involving itself directly or indirectly in the management of those undertakings; or

- a charge over securities in a carrier licensee or an undertaking which directly or indirectly controls a carrier licensee to an authorized institution within the meaning of the Banking Ordinance if:

    (i) the securities are charged pursuant to a deed or instrument with a view to securing a loan to the chargor, the carrier licensee or the

---

[38] Guideline on the Merger Rule, para 2.17.

[39] Guideline on the Merger Rule, para 2.16.

[40] The specified conditions are: (1) the acquisition of securities must be by (i) an authorized institution within the meaning of the Banking Ordinance (Cap. 155), (ii) an insurer who is authorized within the meaning of the Insurance Companies Ordinance (Cap. 41), or (iii) an exchange participant within the meaning of the Securities and Futures Ordinance (Cap. 571), or a person licensed or exempt to carry on a business in dealing in securities or securities margin financing under Part V of that Ordinance; (2) the authorized institution, insurer, or exchange participant, registered institution or licensed corporation (as the case may be) does not exercise voting rights in the securities; or (3) it exercises the voting rights in the securities only with a view to preparing the disposal of all or part of the securities of the carrier licensee or the undertaking which directly or indirectly controls a carrier licensee (as the case may be), or of the assets of the carrier licensee or the undertaking which directly or indirectly controls a carrier licensee (as the case may be), and the disposal takes place within one year of the date of the acquisition or, where the Commission is satisfied that the disposal is not reasonably possible within one year of the date of the acquisition, within such further period as the Commission considers appropriate.

undertaking which directly or indirectly controls a carrier licensee or otherwise; and

(ii) the authorized institution either does not exercise voting rights in the securities or has not given notice in writing to the chargor under the charge of an intention to exercise the right to vote attaching to such voting shares or, having given notice in writing to the chargor under the charge of an intention to exercise the right to vote attaching to such voting shares, exercises the right to vote only to maintain the full value of the security and without directly or indirectly affecting or influencing the competitive conduct of the carrier licensee or the undertaking which directly or indirectly controls a carrier licensee.

Ancillary restrictions The Competition Commission recognises that a merger can involve the acceptance of restrictions which go beyond the merger agreement itself, including non-compete covenants, licences for intellectual property or purchase and supply agreements.[41] The Commission considers that, where the restrictions are directly related and necessary to the implementation of the merger agreement, they will be treated as ancillary restrictions and will be assessed as part of the merger transaction under the Merger Rule. Where the restrictions are not directly related and necessary in this sense, they will fall to be assessed under the First and/or Second Conduct Rules.[42]

Although the Commission does not provide guidance in the Guideline on the Merger Rule on the factors it will take into account when considering ancillary restraints, the concept of ancillary restraints is required to be considered in EU merger control.[43] The European Commission has issued guidance[44] on restrictions directly related and necessary to concentration, pursuant to which, in order for a restriction to be treated as ancillary, it must:

- have a direct link to the establishment of the concentration;
- be necessary to the implementation of the concentration so that without the restriction the concentration could not be implemented or could only be implemented under more uncertain conditions, or at a substantially higher cost, over an appreciably longer period or with considerably less probability of success;
- be proportionate (in terms of duration, subject matter and geographic application).

---

[41] Guideline on the Merger Rule, para 2.18.
[42] Guideline on the Merger Rule, para 2.19.
[43] Case T-251/00, *Lagardère and Canal+ v Commission* [2002] ECR II-4825.
[44] OJ 2005 C56/24.

Public policy exemption   The Chief Executive in Council may, by order published in the Gazette, exempt a specified merger or proposed merger from the application of the Merger Rule if he or she is satisfied that there are exceptional and compelling reasons of public policy for doing so. Any such order may be subject to any conditions or limitation that the Chief Executive in Council considers appropriate.[45] This provision only applies to the specified merger and does not give rise to wider exemption or exclusion on grounds of public policy. It follows that parties to a merger may not self-assess public policy matters so as to exclude the application of the Merger Rule.

4.2 COMPETITION ASSESSMENT

General overview   The Merger Rule seeks to prevent any merger that has, or is likely to have, the effect of substantially lessening competition in Hong Kong.[46] The Competition Commission recognises that merger and acquisition activities do not necessarily raise competition concerns under the Merger Rule. Indeed, mergers can be normal business activities without competition consequences that perform an important function in the efficient operation of the economy. They may allow firms to achieve efficiencies such as economies of scale or scope, synergies and risk spreading. Although some mergers may lessen competition to an extent, concerns under the Merger Rule are unlikely to arise where there are sufficient competitive constraints on the merged entity that will discipline its post-merger commercial behaviour.[47] However, the Commission considers that some mergers may have the effect of changing the structure of the market in such a way that this diminishes market participants' incentives to compete and where such an effect is likely to substantially lessen competition, the transaction will contravene the Merger Rule.[48] It sets out in the Guideline on the Merger Rule the considerations that it will take into account when considering whether a merger transaction is likely to substantially lessen competition.

The promotion of competition in the context of the Competition Ordinance has an economic objective to increase economic efficiencies and, ultimately, consumer welfare (typically in the form of lower prices, higher output, wider choice, better quality or more innovation). Given that economic objective, the Commission requires a meaningful economic framework of analysis for the assessment of a merger.[49] It follows that an assessment of the competitive

---

[45]   Competition Ordinance, Schedule 7, section 9. Detailed procedural rules in relation to such orders are set out in section 10.

[46]   Competition Ordinance, Schedule 7, section 3(1).

[47]   Guideline on the Merger Rule, para 3.1.

[48]   Guideline on the Merger Rule, para 3.2.

[49]   Guideline on the Merger Rule, para 3.3.

effects of a merger generally entails an identification of the relevant market(s) and an assessment of whether the transaction has, or is likely to have, the effect of substantially lessening competition in the identified market(s). However, these two issues are not distinct and separate aspects of the analysis since many of the factors affecting the identification of the relevant market(s) will also be relevant to the assessment of the state of competition within the identified market(s).[50]

4.2.1 Market definition

Market definition   The Competition Commission stresses that a proper examination of the competitive effects of a merger rests on a sound understanding of the competitive constraints under which the merged entity will operate. The scope of those constraints, if any, is identified through a market definition analysis which offers an insight into the sources of competition to the merging parties and the alternatives available to customers. Market definition, however, is not an end in itself but is a framework for analysing the direct competitive pressures faced by the merged entity.[51]

While the basic principles of market definition are similar to those applicable under the First and Second Conduct Rules, it should not be overlooked that the approach to assessment of competitive constraints, as identified through the framework of market definition may be different in merger analysis relative to assessment in other contexts, for example when analysing unilateral conduct under the Second Conduct Rule. Nevertheless, the Commission takes the view that the definition of a relevant market for the practical enforcement of the Merger Rule involves the same basic approach as that employed in defining relevant markets in other contexts.[52]   Accordingly, the delimitation of relevant markets has two basic dimensions: product scope and geographic scope.[53]   In general, when assessing the potential competitive impact of a merger, the main competitive concern is whether the merger has resulted or is likely to result after the merger in an increase in prices above the prevailing level or an adverse impact on other parameters of competition in the market such as output, product quality, product variety, and innovation.[54]   This inquiry is essentially prospective (i.e. whether post-merger prices will increase) as opposed to the more backward-looking approach in unilateral conduct cases (i.e. whether an abuse of substantial market power has occurred).

---

[50]   Guideline on the Merger Rule, paras 3.4-3.5.
[51]   Guideline on the Merger Rule, para 3.6.
[52]   Guideline on the Merger Rule, para 3.7.
[53]   Guideline on the Merger Rule, para 3.8.
[54]   Guideline on the Merger Rule, para 3.9.

For the purpose of merger analysis, the Commission's market definition focuses attention on the areas of overlap in the merging parties' activities. This is particularly the case in differentiated product markets, where the merging parties' products or services may not be identical, but may still be substitutes for each other.[55] The Commission will look at the evidence which is relevant to the case in question, although it admits that, to an extent, it will be constrained by the evidence and time available to review the evidence. In particular it may be clear in certain cases that, although there is potentially more than one market definition, the merger would not give rise to a substantial lessening of competition based on any sensible market definition. In such cases, it will not normally be necessary to establish a final position on which of the potential market definitions is correct. It may for example be possible to conclude that even on the narrowest plausible market definition no substantial lessening of competition would result from the merger.[56]

A common theme in markets that are subject to innovation and technical change is the difficulty of formulating an accurate market definition that takes account of new and prospective entry and even displacement of market power by new products and services. This issue has particular prominence in telecommunications markets which are characteristically subject to evolution. The Commission acknowledges that, in relation to telecommunications, markets may be characterised by dynamic and rapid technological change so that market boundaries are not likely to remain constant.[57]

In the EU, the phenomenon of convergence has acquired a particular impetus when considering competition in the telecommunications sector. There is wide recognition of the need to take account of market evolution in the telecommunications sector and a variety of decisions purport to address convergence when approaching relevant markets and analysis. For example, Microsoft's acquisition of Skype illustrates how telecommunications companies expanding globally are often driven by a search for complementarity and opportunities to enter new markets. The European Commission identified minimal overlaps at the horizontal level and did not identify any adverse competition effects. However, this was after an extensive inquiry covering multiple product markets and indicating a readiness to grapple with the realities of converging telecommunications and related markets. Moreover, the analysis focused heavily on supply-side factors when assessing the different technologies that may be used to deliver products and services to the consumer and provided a contrast to conventional approaches to market definition based on demand-side factors.[58]

---

[55] Guideline on the Merger Rule, para 3.10.
[56] Guideline on the Merger Rule, para 3.11.
[57] Guideline on the Merger Rule, para 3.12.
[58] Case COMP/M.6291, *Microsoft/ Skype*, 7 October 2011.

Indicative safe harbours The Competition Commission specifies safe harbours to give guidance as to which mergers are unlikely to substantially lessen competition. Safe harbours provide a screening device and are not intended as a replacement for a case-by-case analysis. Thus, if a merger falls outside the safe harbour thresholds, it is not necessarily an indication that the transaction would substantially lessen competition in a market for the purposes of the Merger Rule but merely indicates that further inquiry may be made by the Commission to assess the extent of any potential anti-competitive effects. In general, for a horizontal merger where the post-merger combined market share of the parties to the transaction is 40% or more, it is likely that the merger will raise competition concerns and the Commission is likely to make a detailed investigation of the transaction.[59]

The Commission has identified two safe harbour measures that it intends to apply concurrently, thereby expanding the effective coverage of the indicative safe harbour mechanism beyond a single measure. A merger that meets either one of the safe harbour measures will fall within the safe harbour. The application of these safe harbour measures requires identification of the relevant market and the respective market shares of the players in the relevant market.[60] These two safe harbours are indicative in nature. While the Commission is unlikely to further assess any mergers which fall below these thresholds, it does not categorically rule out intervention. Occasionally, such a merger may still raise competition concerns, for example where it involves a vertically integrated firm with market power in a related upstream or downstream market.[61]

The first safe harbour measure is based on concentration ratios. These ratios measure aggregate market shares of the leading firms in the relevant market. The Commission intends to apply a test based on a four-firm concentration ratio. If the post-merger combined market share of the four (or fewer) largest firms (CR4) in the relevant market is less than 75%, and the merged firm has a market share of less than 40%, the Commission takes the view that it is unlikely that there will be a need to carry out a detailed investigation or to intervene. Where the CR4 is 75% or more, the Commission is unlikely to investigate the transaction if the combined market share of the merged entity is less than 15%.[62]

The second safe harbour measure is based on the Herfindahl-Hirschman Index (HHI). The HHI measures market concentration and is calculated by adding together the squares of the market shares of all the firms operating in the market. The increase in the HHI resulting from the merger is calculated by subtracting the pre-merger index from the expected value of the HHI following

---

[59] Guideline on the Merger Rule, para 3.13.
[60] Guideline on the Merger Rule, para 3.14.
[61] Guideline on the Merger Rule, para 3.20.
[62] Guideline on the Merger Rule, para 3.15.

the merger, the difference being known as the delta. Both the absolute level of the HHI and the expected change resulting from the merger can provide an indication of whether a merger is likely to raise competition concerns.[63] In respect of the application of HHI, any market with a post-merger HHI of less than 1,000 will be regarded as unconcentrated. Mergers resulting in unconcentrated markets are unlikely to result in a substantial lessening of competition and normally require no further investigation.[64]

Markets with a post-merger HHI of between 1,000 and 1,800 will be regarded as moderately concentrated. Mergers producing an increase in the HHI of less than 100 in these markets are unlikely to result in a substantial lessening of competition and normally require no further investigation. However, mergers producing an increase in the HHI of more than 100 potentially raise competition concerns and will normally require further investigation.[65] Markets with a post-merger HHI of more than 1,800 will be regarded as highly concentrated. Mergers producing an increase in the HHI of less than 50 are unlikely to substantially lessen competition, even in a highly concentrated market. Mergers producing an increase of more than 50 in the HHI will potentially raise competitive concerns and will normally require further investigation.[66]

The Commission is not unusual in taking into account market shares and concentration when assessing the level of competition after a merger. However, its approach may be contrasted with that under the EUMR where a combined market share of less than 25 per cent would generally be presumed compatible with the internal market and therefore approved. In addition to taking account of market shares, the European Commission also considers other concentration measures such as the HHI as an initial indicator of competition concerns. As a general rule, however, the European Commission appears to take a more relaxed attitude to changes in post-merger HHI than the Competition Commission.[67] This is perhaps explained by the relative size of markets in Hong Kong relative to the EU and their relative degree of existing concentration.

---

[63] Guideline on the Merger Rule, para 3.16.

[64] Guideline on the Merger Rule, para 3.17.

[65] Guideline on the Merger Rule, para 3.18.

[66] Guideline on the Merger Rule, para 3.19.

[67] The European Commission is unlikely to identify horizontal competition concerns in a market with a post-merger HHI below 1,000. It is also unlikely to identify horizontal competition concerns in a merger with a post-merger HHI between 1,000 and 2,000 and a delta below 250, or a merger with a post-merger HHI above 2,000 and a delta below 150, except where there are special circumstances.

4.2.2 Assessment of level of competition after a merger

Assessment of competition after a merger   Where the safe harbour thresholds are not satisfied, or the Competition Commission otherwise considers that a detailed investigation into the merger is necessary, the next issue is to assess the level of competition following the merger.   Market structure comprises those factors that influence the level of competition in a market.   Competition in a market is influenced by the structural features of the market such as market shares, market concentration, barriers to entry, vertical integration, buying power and import competition.   A merger, by its nature, will change the market structure.   For non-structural factors, one that may be particularly relevant is the strategic behaviour of firms.   Such strategic behaviour is directed at altering the market structure itself, for example, by raising barriers to entry, and in this sense goes beyond the normal competitive rivalry between firms.   Accordingly, the Commission will take into account structural factors and non-structural factors such as strategic behaviour, when assessing the level of competition in a market and the likely effect the merger would have on that level of competition.   In this way, the Merger Rule is intended to ensure that market structures which are likely to harm competition are not created.[68]   In the Guideline on the Merger Rule, the Commission discusses several analytical issues that it considers relevant to any merger analysis concerning the protection of the competitive process, enhancement and exercise of market power, counterfactual analysis, market share and concentration, and prices and profit margins.[69]

Protection of the process, not the competitor   The Competition Commission emphasises that its merger review jurisdiction is limited to protecting the process of competition and not individual competitors.   Competition in a market is essentially a dynamic process rather than a static situation where particular conduct may competitively disadvantage a particular competitor at a particular time.   By its very nature competition is a deliberate and at times ruthless process as competitors jockey for position.   That a particular competitor may be injured or competitively disadvantaged at a particular time does not necessarily lessen competition in a market, let alone substantially.   Indeed, it may be the epitome of the competitive process.   As part of the process, disadvantaged competitors would be expected to respond to any competitive initiatives in the market.   It is only when they are unable to respond as a direct consequence of the merger in question that concerns arise about the effects on the competitive process in a market.[70]

---

[68]   Guideline on the Merger Rule, paras 3.21-3.24.
[69]   Guideline on the Merger Rule, para 3.25.
[70]   Guideline on the Merger Rule, paras 3.26-3.27.

Substantiality test Since the relevant test to be applied for the Merger Rule is whether the merger has, or is likely to have, the effect of substantially lessening competition (SLC) in Hong Kong, the focus of the Competition Commission's assessment is the likely competitive effects of the merger on the relevant market(s) in Hong Kong. The requirement that the effect on competition be substantial avoids application of the regime to situations where there are limited effects on the competitive process, such as may occur when there is day-to-day injury to individual competitors but the competitive process within the relevant market remains strong.[71] The Commission will generally interpret a substantial lessening of competition by reference to the creation or enhancement of market power. A merger creates or enhances market power if it is likely to encourage one or more firms to raise price, reduce output, limit innovation, or otherwise harm consumers as a result of diminished competitive constraints or incentives.[72] Accordingly, in assessing a merger, the Commission will consider whether it creates or enhances market power. If there is a reasonable likelihood that prices in the relevant market will be maintained at a significantly greater level than would be the case in the absence of the merger, or where competitive outcomes would otherwise be distorted, such as by a reduction in consumer choice, product quality or innovation in a relevant market, the Commission will consider that the merger substantially lessens competition in contravention of the Merger Rule.[73]

It is apparent that the substantive test under the Merger Rule is a competition-based rather than wider public interest test. The SLC test is used in other jurisdictions, for example in the UK where the Competition Appeal Tribunal has ruled that a significant lessening of competition will be sufficient without having regard to whether the lessening of competition is large in an absolute sense.[74] By contrast, a different formulation of the substantive test applies in EU merger control law under the EUMR, which provides that a concentration which would significantly impede effective competition (SIEC) in the internal market or in a substantial part of it, in particular as a result of the creation or strengthening of a dominant position, shall be declared incompatible with the internal market. It is suggested that the EUMR needs to be understood in its historic context and that the EU case law under the current substantive test is informative for the Competition Commission's assessment under the SLC test. The current substantive test under the EUMR is based on a single concept: whether the concentration would significantly impede effective competition. This test refers to dominance as an example of a situation where a SIEC may arise, although this is not the sole determinant of compatibility. As a matter of practice, a SIEC will generally arise from the creation or

---

[71] Guideline on the Merger Rule, paras 3.28-3.29.
[72] Guideline on the Merger Rule, para 3.30.
[73] Guideline on the Merger Rule, para 3.31.
[74] *Global Radio Holdings Limited v Competition Commission* [2013] CAT 26.

strengthening of a dominant position. The facts that the European Commission must take into account when determining the issue of compatibility under the EUMR are very similar to those which the Competition Commission takes into account in the Guideline on the Merger Rule. The reformulation of the substantive test as embodied in the current version of the EUMR was designed to confirm that the substantive test covers all forms of harmful scenarios, whether arising as a result of dominance enjoyed by a single firm or a situation of oligopoly.[75]

Exercise of market power: unilateral and coordinated effects   The Competition Commission explains in its Guideline on the Merger Rule that a horizontal merger may lessen competition in two ways, in terms of creating unilateral effects and coordinated effects. A single merger may raise both types of effects.[76]

Unilateral effects may arise in a merger when one firm merges with a competitor that previously provided a competitive constraint, allowing the merged firm profitably to raise prices or to reduce output or otherwise exercise market power it has gained, even given the expected responses of other market participants to the resulting change in market conditions.[77]

Coordinated effects take place where the merger increases, enables or encourages post-merger coordinated interaction among the firms in the market. Coordinated interaction involves conduct by multiple firms that is profitable for each of them only as a result of the accommodating reactions of others. These reactions can blunt a firm's incentive to offer customers better deals by undercutting the extent to which such a move would win business away from rivals. They also can enhance a firm's incentive to raise prices, by assuaging the fear that such a move would lose customers to rivals. Coordinated interaction can involve the explicit negotiation of a common understanding of how firms will compete or refrain from competing. Coordinated interaction alternatively can involve parallel accommodating conduct not pursuant to any prior understanding, which can still have the effect of dampening competition.

---

[75] The evolving decisional practice of the European Commission reflected an apparent extension of the concept of dominance to cover the situation where two or more firms occupy a dominant position although this was limited to a situation where the merger increases the possibility of tacit collusion between them (co-ordinated effects). There was some doubt, however, as to whether the traditional dominance test would address a situation where competitive constraints were reduced as a result of the merger but in the absence of evidence that co-ordination would be increased (non-coordinated effects). The revised test was therefore designed to address this apparent gap by emphasising the effects of the merger as opposed to issues of market structure.

[76] Guideline on the Merger Rule, para 3.32.

[77] Guideline on the Merger Rule, para 3.33.

Conditions conducive to coordination typically include concentrated markets, product homogeneity and transparent pricing.[78]

The Competition Commission notes that coordinated effects can be disrupted by the presence of a maverick firm, which has the economic incentive not to follow coordinated action. A firm is more likely to be a maverick if it has excess capacity (a feature of some telecommunications markets) and low incremental costs (thus making it profitable to charge low prices). It is a feature of network industries, including telecommunications, that services which are provided over networks tend to have low incremental costs. However, excess capacity amongst the remaining coordinated firms may be used as an effective weapon to punish a maverick firm.[79]

This maverick theory has been deployed by the European Commission in a variety of telecommunications merger contexts, as in *T-Mobile Austria/tele.ring* where there were concerns that the transaction would eliminate a firm which, pre-merger, had been a source of competitive constraint on the pricing of T-Mobile Austria and Mobilkom.[80] The concern to preserve the competitive pressure exerted by a maverick also arises, as in *T-Mobile/ Orange*, where the transaction presents a risk of harm to the competitive position of a disruptive third party player who may be dependent on a merging party.[81] At the European national level in *Belgacom/Scarlet*[82] the Belgian competition authority found that Belgacom's acquisition of DSL provider Scarlet would deprive the Belgian market of an innovative competitor with a developed optical glass fibre network, quite apart from its small market share. This case may be contrasted with *Iliad/Liberty Surf*,[83] a merger between two telephone and internet providers, where the French competition authority found that rather than eliminating a maverick player the merger would likely strengthen a vibrant competitor.

Counterfactual: with and without test In assessing whether competition is likely to be substantially lessened by a merger, the Competition Commission will usually employ an analytical tool that it labels the with-and-without test. The level of competition that is likely to exist in a market with the merger is assessed and compared with the level of competition that is likely to exist in the market without the merger. The situation without the merger is commonly referred to as the counterfactual. This analysis will be applied prospectively,

---

[78]   Guideline on the Merger Rule, para 3.34.
[79]   Guideline on the Merger Rule, para 3.35.
[80]   Case COMP/M.3916, *T-Mobile Austria/tele.ring,* 26 April 2006.
[81]   Case COMP/M.5650, *T-Mobile/ Orange*, 1 March 2010.
[82]   E-Competitions, The Belgian Competition Council approves upon remedies the takeover of alternative DSL-provider by the incumbent, 7 November 2008, no 23527.
[83]   E-Competitions, The French Minister of economics clears telecom merger without remedies after investigating possible coordinated effects and elimination of a maverick, 22 August 2008, no 23603.

that is, future competition will be assessed with and without the merger.[84] In most cases, the best guide to the appropriate counterfactual will be the prevailing conditions of competition as this may provide a reliable indicator of future competition without the merger. However, the Commission may need to take into account likely and imminent changes in the structure of competition in order to reflect as accurately as possible the nature of rivalry without the merger. For example, in cases where one of the parties is failing, pre-merger conditions of competition might not prevail even if the merger were prohibited. The Commission will not, however, apply the with-and-without test relying on agreements or conduct that would contravene the Competition Ordinance, since only lawful prospective options are relevant.[85]

The counterfactual is an analytical tool which other competition authorities including the CMA and the European Commission use to compare the prospects for competition with the merger situation against the competitive position without the merger. By way of example, the CMA tends to adopt the prevailing conditions of competition as the relevant counterfactual (or the situation prevailing pre-merger in the case of a completed merger). The CMA adopts an alternative approach to the counterfactual based on the available evidence where there is a realistic prospect of a counterfactual that is more competitive than the prevailing conditions or where the prospect of continuation of the prevailing conditions is not realistic. At Phase II the CMA may examine multiple scenarios and chooses that which it considers is most likely based on the extent to which their consequences are foreseeable. The principal situations in which the CMA will use an alternative counterfactual to the prevailing competitive conditions are when the merger involves a failing or exiting firm or where there are competing bids.[86]

Market share and market concentration The Competition Commission refers to market shares as part of its assessment framework. Market share refers to the share of a market that a particular firm has. It is usually measured in terms of sales volume or revenue. The latter is a particularly useful indicator of market shares in markets characterised by product differentiation and brand loyalty. In telecommunications markets, the number of subscribers, call minutes, data volume, etc. are obvious measures of sales volume. Transmission capacity or bandwidth may be a relevant form of volume measurement when the transmission service is largely commoditised or undifferentiated. Capacity or reserves may also be useful as a measure of

---

[84] Guideline on the Merger Rule, para 3.36.

[85] Guideline on the Merger Rule, para 3.37.

[86] Merger assessment guidelines, CC2 (Revised)/OFT1254, section 4.3. In particular, if the CMA concludes that there is no realistic prospect of a substantially less anti-competitive alternative to the merger it will conclude that there is no realistic prospect of an SLC. If it cannot reach a sufficient level of confidence in that regard the CMA will use the pre-merger situation as the relevant counterfactual.

market share in markets where there is volatility in market shares measured in terms of sales volume or revenue.[87] Market concentration refers to the degree to which a market is composed of a small number of large firms or made up of many small firms. In general, an unconcentrated market may be more competitive than a concentrated market. A merger which results in the merged entity holding large market share and increases the level of market concentration may lessen the level of competition.[88] High market shares and concentration levels as a result of a merger are generally necessary but not sufficient conditions for the creation or enhancement of market power that may lead to a contravention of the Merger Rule. On the other hand, a merged firm with only small market share in a relatively unconcentrated market would not normally be able to exercise market power and thus is not likely to contravene the Merger Rule.[89]

As information on market shares and concentration levels is more readily obtainable for a pre-merger situation, thresholds on market shares and concentration levels are simple means of screening-out mergers that are not likely to lessen competition. Post-merger information by its nature is prospective and may be based on a number of assumptions on future market structure. As a starting point, post-merger market shares and concentration ratios will be estimated on the basis of historic sales patterns and trends. This is likely to be more informative than considering market shares at a single point in time, which might hide the dynamic nature of the market. The Commission will then consider any submissions as to how these trends may vary, such as through the introduction of new, innovative services or technology. The actual volume or revenue measure used for market share calculation will depend on the characteristics of the product in question. The choice of measure may also be constrained by the availability of reliable data. For example, in telecommunications, retail revenues, call minutes or numbers of subscribers are possible measures for measuring market share of telecommunications operators.[90] In its decision in April 2014 on the proposed acquisition of New World Mobility Limited by HKT Limited, the Communications Authority looked at market shares in the retail mobile telecommunications services market from different perspectives, including market share by subscribers (which was further subdivided into market share of all subscribers and market share of 3G/4G subscribers), and market share by revenue (which was further subdivided into voice revenue, non-voice revenue, total revenue minus handsets, and total retail revenue).[91]

---

[87]   Guideline on the Merger Rule, para 3.38.
[88]   Guideline on the Merger Rule, para 3.39.
[89]   Guideline on the Merger Rule, para 3.40.
[90]   Guideline on the Merger Rule, paras 3.41-4.42.
[91]   www.comsauth.hk/filemanager/statement/en/upload/270/decision_20140502_e.pdf

Price and profit margins The Competition Commission will consider the likelihood of a merger resulting in the merged firm being able to significantly and sustainably increase prices or profit margins.[92] It takes the view that sustained price increases above competitive levels are the most visible sign that the merged firm has increased its market power and there is a substantial lessening of competition in the market. The price increase may be used to protect inefficient operations rather than to accumulate excess profits. Another possibility is that a merger, instead of increasing prices, may prevent prices from falling to the competitive level by forestalling entry such that profit margins are preserved or even increased. Cost reductions which are claimed to result from the merger may not result in lower prices to consumers because the savings may accrue as increased profits.[93]

4.2.3 Determining whether competition is substantially lessened

Non-exhaustive list of relevant matters Section 6 of Schedule 7 of the Competition Ordinance sets out the following non-exhaustive list of relevant matters[94] that may be taken into account in determining whether a merger has, or is likely to have, the effect of substantially lessening competition in Hong Kong:

(a) the extent of competition from competitors outside Hong Kong;

(b) whether the acquired undertaking, or part of the acquired undertaking, has failed or is likely to fail in the near future;

(c) the extent to which substitutes are available or are likely to be available in the market;

(d) the existence and height of any barriers to entry into the market;

(e) whether the merger would result in the removal of an effective and vigorous competitor;

(f) the degree of countervailing power in the market; and

(g) the nature and extent of change and innovation in the market.

As this list is non-exhaustive, other factors might be taken into account by the Competition Commission in its assessment, such as the degree of market concentration or the extent of market regulation.

Extent of competition from competitors outside Hong Kong In an open economy such as Hong Kong, import competition, i.e. competition from competitors outside Hong Kong, can play an important role in restraining the exercise of market power. An example of import competition in the

---

[92] Guideline on the Merger Rule, para 3.43.

[93] Guideline on the Merger Rule, paras 3.44-3.45.

[94] This draws on similar provisions in Australian, Canadian, Singaporean and EU merger legislation.

telecommunications sector is the provision of international telephone services to Hong Kong users by service providers operating outside Hong Kong. In considering the effectiveness of import competition as a restraint to the exercise of market power, the capacity of supply of overseas suppliers and speed of entry into the domestic market have to be considered.[95] However, the Competition Commission considers that in most segments of the telecommunications industry where physical presence in Hong Kong is necessary for the supply of services, the threat of import competition may not be relevant.[96]

Failing firms   The Competition Commission considers that, while, at first glance, one would expect that the acquisition of a failing or failed firm would be unlikely to substantially lessen competition, there may be circumstances where the acquisition of a failing firm may substantially lessen competition.[97] It considers that the acquisition of a failing or failed firm would be unlikely to substantially lessen competition in cases where:[98]

    (a) the firm is likely to experience commercial failure, if the firm has not already failed;

    (b) without the acquisition, the assets of the firm will exit the market; and

    (c) the firm has made unsuccessful, good-faith efforts to elicit reasonable alternative offers to acquire its assets that would keep those assets in the market and would pose a less severe danger to competition.

If all three conditions are satisfied, the competitive effects of the firm being acquired by the acquirer are likely to be no worse than if the assets were allowed to exit the market, consistent with the with and without test.   A competitive influence that would otherwise have been removed by failure is to be removed by acquisition.   Thus, in the absence of other considerations, the acquisition would be unlikely to cause concerns under the Merger Rule.   One issue that may arise in this scenario, however, is the distribution of the failing firm's customer base if this base is significant in terms of market share.   If the assets exited the market, the distribution of the failing firm's customer base among the remaining market participants would be determined by market forces, whereas an acquisition would tend to deliver those customers to the acquiring firm thus increasing its market share.[99]

Other competition authorities have accepted a similar failing firm defence. For example, the European Commission accepts that a concentration is not incompatible with the internal market if one of the parties is a failing company which would be forced out of the market if the concentration were not

---

[95]   Guideline on the Merger Rule, para 3.47

[96]   Guideline on the Merger Rule, para 3.48.

[97]   Guideline on the Merger Rule, para 3.49.

[98]   Guideline on the Merger Rule, para 3.50.

[99]   Guideline on the Merger Rule, paras 3.51-3.52.

implemented, and if there are no other solutions which are less anti-competitive than the concentration. However, it has accepted the failing firm defence in a very limited number of cases.[100] The failing firm defence has been used twice recently by the European Commission to clear mergers that would otherwise have raised competition issues, in *Aegean Airlines/Olympic Air II*[101] and *Nynas/Shell/Harburg Refinery*[102] (where it was a specific asset that was failing rather than an entire company). The principle was accepted in UK merger control proceedings in *Optimax Clinics/Ultralase*[103] and *Alliance Medical/IBA Molecular*,[104] but was rejected in *Royal Bournemouth and Christchurch Hospitals/Poole Hospital.*[105]

Extent to which substitutes are available In considering the extent to which substitutes are available in the market, the Competition Commission will include both existing and potential substitutes from the supply side and the demand side. In considering the extent to which substitutes are available, the Commission may also consider the price elasticity of supply of the firms in the market post-merger. Unless the producers of the substitutes are able to increase supply to meet the demand of customers of the merged firm who intend to switch suppliers in response to a material price increase of the merged firm, the existence of substitutes in the market would not be an effective restraint to the exercise of market power by the merged firm. It may therefore be necessary to consider the relative supply capacity of the firms in the market after the merger, as well as the costs of capacity expansion. If the merged firm ends up controlling a majority of the capacity in the market, other firms in the market may not be able to provide much competitive restraint.[106]

Barriers to entry or expansion An important factor influencing the level of competition in a market is the height of barriers to entry or expansion for rivals, as the threat of entry or expansion of rivals is often viewed as the ultimate regulator of competitive conduct even if the merged firm currently has a high market share.[107] Barriers to entry or expansion of rivals are essentially any market features that prevent an efficient prospective new entrant from entering the market or an existing player in the market from expanding in the market, or otherwise place them at a significant competitive disadvantage to incumbents. They may arise from a variety of sources, from regulatory

---

[100] See, for example, Case COMP/M.2314, *BASF/ Pantochim/ Eurodial.*
[101] Case No COMP/M.6796, *Aegean/ Olympic II*, 9 October 2013.
[102] Case No COMP/M.6360, *Nynas/Shell/Harburg Refinery*, 2 September 2013.
[103] *Optimax Clinics Limited and Ultralase Limited*, 20 November 2013.
[104] *Alliance Medical and IBA Molecular*, 15 August 2014.
[105] *The Royal Bournemouth and Christchurch Hospitals NHS Foundation Trust and Poole Hospital NHS Foundation Trust*, 17 October 2013.
[106] Guideline on the Merger Rule, para 3.53.
[107] Guideline on the Merger Rule, para 3.54.

restrictions to economic factors or from the conduct of the merging parties to the behaviour of third parties. Barriers to entry or expansion of rivals can reduce the prospects of competitive entry by new entrants or expansion of rivals, with the consequence that incumbents are less constrained by the threat of new entry or expansion of rivals to behaving competitively.[108] Recognised barriers to entry that are discussed by the Competition Commission in the Guideline on Merger Rule include sunk costs, economies of scale and scope, network effects, strategic behaviour, product differentiation and brand loyalty, essential facilities and regulatory or legal barriers. Sunk costs and economies of scale and scope are particular features of telecommunications markets and other network-based markets.[109]

Structural barriers to entry Sunk costs are the costs of acquiring capital and other assets that:

(a) are uniquely incurred in entering the market and supplying the services in question;

(b) cannot be economically recouped within a short period of time; and

(c) once incurred, cannot easily be physically recovered and redeployed in another market.

Because of their nature, sunk costs create entry risks which increase with the significance of the costs. In turn, significant risks can create significant barriers to entry. The extent of sunk costs depends on a number of factors such as the proportion of capital involved, the requirements for advertising and promotion to create brand awareness, etc. An example of significant sunk costs typically incurred in telecommunications is the cost of network roll-out (e.g. installing radio base stations, core network equipment, antennae, etc.), a cost which cannot be recovered or easily recouped if the new entrant decides to exit the market within a short period. Accordingly, firms considering entry into the market with significant sunk costs must assess the profitability of entry on the basis of long-term participation in the market until the sunk capital and assets are economically depreciated. In certain circumstances, the cost of providing a new service may also involve costs which cannot be recovered or easily recouped.[110]

With economies of scale and scope, average costs fall as the supply of services or range of services supplied increases respectively. Falling costs are likely to increase barriers to entry where there are minimum efficient scales for entry. When combined with sunk costs and excess capacity, the effect of economies of scale in particular can create significant barriers to entry. Having

---

[108] Guideline on the Merger Rule, para 3.55.

[109] Guideline on the Merger Rule, para 3.56. Additional guidance on barriers to entry is provided in the Guideline on the Second Conduct Rule in the context of assessing substantial market power.

[110] Guideline on the Merger Rule, paras 3.57-3.59.

sunk the infrastructure costs, there are incentives for incumbents in situations of excess capacity to reap the economies of scale by dropping prices in order to gain necessary revenue flows. Even without any strategic purpose, such action can significantly deter new entrants.[111]

Closely related to economies of scale are network effects. By its nature, telecommunications is a network industry and a feature of networks is that they generate network effects (or externalities). Network effects arise when the value a consumer places on connecting to a network (as measured by the price it is willing to pay) depends on the number of others already connected to it. Such network effects are a form of economies of scale, but on the demand side. Network effects generate positive feedback or advantages for incumbents whereby the bigger networks get bigger (and, on the negative side, the weak get weaker). Unrestrained positive feedback can result in the market tipping in favour of one competitor and a winner-takes-all market outcome. Particularly when combined with economies of scale on the supply side, network effects can create significant barriers to entry.[112]

Reputational barriers established by brand loyalty to incumbents (which may in themselves be a strategic barrier to entry) may add to the sunk costs faced by a new entrant in the form of advertising and promotion costs. The ongoing investment in advertising and promotion that is required to maintain a differentiated product will accentuate sunk costs. The nature and extent of the barriers created by brand loyalty and product differentiation can be conceptualised as an investment in sunk costs that is required to shift demand to an unknown brand and create a new differentiated market niche.[113]

In some cases, entry to a market might require the use of an essential facility, an asset or infrastructure where: (1) access to it is indispensable in order to compete in the market; and (2) duplication of the facility is impossible or extremely difficult owing to physical, economic or legal constraints, or is highly undesirable for reasons of public policy. Denial of access to essential facilities is thus capable of constituting a significant barrier to entry, particularly in the telecommunications industry where access to customers in certain situations has to go through a bottleneck or essential facility. However, the potential for essential facilities to act as a barrier to entry can be alleviated by effective regulatory regimes for the interconnection and sharing of bottleneck facilities.[114]

Strategic behaviour as a barrier to entry   The Competition Commission considers that the most important non-structural factor, when assessing barriers to entry, is what is generally referred to as strategic behaviour. This is broadly

---

[111]   Guideline on the Merger Rule, paras 3.60-3.61.
[112]   Guideline on the Merger Rule, paras 3.62-3.63.
[113]   Guideline on the Merger Rule, para 3.64.
[114]   Guideline on the Merger Rule, paras 3.65-3.66.

defined as any actions by a firm to alter the market structure, and so alter the conditions and levels of competition (for example, by raising barriers to entry). As such, it goes beyond the normal competitive rivalry between firms.[115] An incumbent firm can act strategically to create barriers to entry which can be as effective as any traditional structural barriers to entry. These are sometimes described as strategically erected barriers to entry.[116]

Strategic advantages can arise where incumbent firms have advantages over new entrants because of their established position. This is known as the first-mover advantage. Strategic (first-mover) advantages are available to incumbent firms because they are already established in the market and therefore might enjoy advantages over recent or potential new entrants. These advantages could be used by incumbents to raise the barriers to entry, and can involve strategic behaviour designed to deter entry to the market. An example of strategic behaviour which would raise the barriers to entry is where an incumbent firm decides to build excess capacity so as to send credible signals to potential entrants that it could profitably (with economies of scale and low marginal costs) push prices down to levels such that new entrants would not earn sufficient revenue to cover their sunk costs.[117]

Removal of a close competitor By its nature, a horizontal merger will usually remove a competitor from the market. The resulting higher market shares of the merged entity and increased concentration levels are generally necessary, but not sufficient, conditions for the creation or enhancement of market power that may lead to a contravention of the Merger Rule. A factor which may provide guidance on whether market power is created or enhanced is whether the merger results in the removal of a close competitor. The higher the degree of substitutability between the merging firms' products, the higher the degree of closeness of competition between them, and the more likely it is that the merging firms will raise prices significantly. For example, a merger between two undertakings offering products which a substantial number of customers regard as their first and second choices could generate a significant price increase.[118] This approach reflects that of the European Commission in its Horizontal Merger Guidelines that the higher the degree of substitutability between the merging firms' products, the more likely it is that the merging firms will raise prices significantly.[119]

Beyond removing a close competitor, a merger may create a market structure which is conducive to coordinated action or tacit collusion. Effective and vigorous competitors, otherwise known in this context as maverick firms,

---

[115] Guideline on the Merger Rule, para 3.67.
[116] Guideline on the Merger Rule, para 3.70.
[117] Guideline on the Merger Rule, paras 3.68-3.69.
[118] Guideline on the Merger Rule, para 3.71.
[119] See, for example, Case COMP/M.2817, *Barilla/BPS/Kamps*, 18 May 2002.

serve to undermine attempts to coordinate conduct in a market. The role of mavericks has been discussed above in respect of the unilateral and coordinated exercise of market power.[120]

Buying power or countervailing power Market power can be exercised on the demand-side by monopsonists or groups of buyers acting together to depress prices below their competitive levels. The effects are comparable to those associated with the exercise of market power on the supply-side. Market power on the buying side is relevant under the Merger Rule in two principal ways. First, it may make a finding of substantial lessening of competition less likely if customers can use their negotiating strength to limit price rises. Second, the existence of buyer power may contribute to a finding of a substantial lessening of competition where the merging firms purchase similar products and the merger would create or strengthen post-merger buyer power.[121]

Generally, such market power (sometimes referred to as buying or bargaining power) must be supported by a credible threat to bypass the supplier if no acceptable deal can be bargained. The Competition Commission takes the view that this may not always be the case in telecommunications when the existence of alternative suppliers may be constrained by the presence of bottleneck or essential facilities, particularly the network to which the originating or terminating customers are directly connected. While it may not be common in telecommunications, should it occur, the Commission will assess the effects of any demand-side market power in an analogous fashion to assessing supply-side market power.[122]

Other competition authorities have considered buyer power in merger control proceedings, although the most prominent cases have not been in the telecommunications sector. The ability of buyers to constrain any market power that would otherwise be exercised by the merged entity may avert a SIEC for EUMR purposes, particularly where those buyers are large and sophisticated and account for a large proportion of the sales of the merged entity's products.[123] The UK Competition Commission conducted an in-depth merger investigation into a long-term facilities management agreement in the entertainment sector and ruled out competition concerns based on a number of factors including countervailing buyer power.[124]

---

[120] Guideline on the Merger Rule, para 3.72.

[121] Guideline on the Merger Rule, paras 3.73-3.74.

[122] Guideline on the Merger Rule, para 3.75.

[123] Case IV/M.1225, *Enso/Stora*, 25 November 1998, concerned a merger of paper and board companies and reduced the number of liquid packaging suppliers in the EEA to three. However, the Commission found that the merged entity would face significant countervailing power from its customers, principally Tetra Pak.

[124] *AEG Facilities (UK) Limited and Wembley Arena*, 2 September 2013. The Competition Commission found that as a result of the arrangements AEG would operate two of the

Nature and extent of change and innovation in the market The nature and extent of change and innovation in the market may be a relevant factor when determining whether a merger has or is likely to have the effect of substantially lessening competition. The Competition Commission considers that reductions in innovation levels may be a source of legitimate concern. In general, its analysis of innovation issues involves the application of the with-and-without test comparing pre and post-merger innovation levels and, if there is any material change, assessing the effect on competition of the posited reduction in innovation.[125]

The European Commission has been faced with merger cases under the EUMR which reflect ongoing consolidation in the telecommunications and related markets, often spurred on by innovation. The case of *Cisco/Tandberg* provides a useful illustration of its approach to innovation markets. The merging parties overlapped in the markets for video call conferencing. Cisco was active worldwide in the development and sale of network products and video communications systems, while Tandberg was a supplier of video communications systems. The transaction was found to give rise to both vertical and conglomerate effects due to Tandberg's presence in upstream and adjacent markets. Significant competition problems were identified in the market for high-end video conferencing formats known as telepresence. The merger was approved as the parties gave a series of commitments including divestiture of a proprietary protocol to an independent trade body, allowing third party vendors to participate in upgrades and development of the protocol, and commitments on interoperability.[126]

4.2.4 Additional relevant matters for vertical mergers

Vertical mergers A vertical merger is the integration of two functional levels in the supply chain. Vertical mergers can often be pro-competitive as they allow firms to generate efficiencies, particularly through savings on transaction costs and the achievement of economies of scale.[127] In industries with high sunk costs such as telecommunications, vertical mergers can also help reduce the risk of investment. For example, a provider of telecommunications services carried over someone else's network may wish to integrate with the upstream network operator in order to reduce the risk of being held captive by the network owner. More fundamentally, a vertical merger is less likely to be

---

 largest venues in London. However, it did not consider that as a result of the merger AEG would be in a position to increase prices for promoters. It took into account limited pre-merger competition, the buyer power of promoters and the need to safeguard other sources of revenue and contractual incentives for promoters to use the venue.

[125] Guideline on the Merger Rule, para 3.76.
[126] Case COMP/M.5669, *Cisco/ Tandberg*, 29 March 2010.
[127] Guideline on the Merger Rule, para 3.77.

anti-competitive than a horizontal merger because in a vertical merger, the two merging firms will generally supply complementary products whereas in a horizontal merger the parties will supply substitute products in the same market.[128] In assessing a vertical merger for its likely anti-competitive effects, the Competition Commission will particularly inquire as to whether:[129]

(a) there is market power at one or more of the functional levels involved in the merger;

(b) there are incentives to leverage that market power into the upstream or downstream market with the purpose of lessening or foreclosing competition in that market (i.e. where the merged firm operates in a competitive upstream or downstream market);

(c) the market power is likely to be leveraged (for example, where raising rivals costs in downstream markets through discriminatory access pricing would be profitable and would lessen competition); and

(d) the effect is likely to substantially lessen competition in that market.

A vertical merger may also bring about coordinated effects. For example, a vertical merger may increase the degree of symmetry between firms active in the market. This may enhance the likelihood of coordination by making it easier for the firms in the market to achieve a common understanding on the terms of coordination.[130]

Theories of harm The Competition Commission considers that there are two main possible theories of harm for unilateral effects under a vertical merger. First, competitors at the downstream functional level (e.g. retail telecommunications service providers) may have to rely on the supply of an input at an upstream level (e.g. reliance on an upstream network provider to carry their downstream services). Where a vertical merger takes place, the merged entity may have the ability and incentive to foreclose downstream non-integrated rivals' access to the supply of such an input. This is known as input foreclosure theory of harm. Second, customer foreclosure may result from a vertical merger when a supplier integrates with an important customer in the downstream market. Such downstream presence of the merged entity may enable it to foreclose access to a sufficient customer base by its actual or potential rivals in the upstream market (the input market) thereby reducing their ability or incentive to compete.[131]

Leveraging into vertically-related markets Where there is market power at one functional level, there may be incentives to leverage that market power into the vertically-related market for anti-competitive purposes. The leverage,

---

[128] Guideline on the Merger Rule, paras 3.78-3.79.
[129] Guideline on the Merger Rule, para 3.84.
[130] Guideline on the Merger Rule, para 3.85.
[131] Guideline on the Merger Rule, para 3.80.

for example, may take the form of refusing access to an essential facility that the merged firm has recently acquired control of through the merger so as to foreclose competition in a downstream market where it faces competition. Alternatively, access may be supplied only on discriminatory or competitively disadvantageous terms, thus raising its downstream rivals' costs.[132]

To profitably engage in a foreclosure strategy, one must have market power in the relevant market from which to leverage the strategy. Otherwise downstream competitors relying on the upstream facilities of the merged entity would simply bypass the facilities and seek better terms elsewhere in the upstream market (unless the market power is exercised through coordinated action). It may also be relevant to ask in this connection whether the input in question represents a material proportion of the total costs of the final product and whether cost increases are likely to be passed on in whole or in part to purchasers of the final product. Anti-competitive foreclosure concerns are more likely to arise if the answer to one or both of these questions is affirmative.[133]

Approach of other competition authorities The Competition Commission's approach to vertical mergers shares some elements with that of other competition authorities. The European Commission sets out its approach to assessing non-horizontal mergers in its Guidelines on the assessment of non-horizontal mergers.[134] The Commission draws a broad distinction between vertical mergers and conglomerate mergers.[135] The Competition Commission does not provide specific guidance on conglomerate mergers in the Guideline on the Merger Rule.

The European Commission states that non-horizontal mergers are typically less likely to present competition problems than horizontal mergers since they do not involve the loss of a direct competitor in the same relevant market. The European Commission also accepts that vertical (and conglomerate) mergers provide substantial scope for efficiencies. When explaining the potential benefits of vertical and conglomerate mergers, the European Commission accepts the potential efficiency benefits arising through the combination of complementary products and services. It states that in vertical relationships, as a result of complementarity, a decrease in mark-ups downstream will lead to higher demand also up-stream with a part of the benefit of this increase in demand accruing to the upstream suppliers. However, it states that non-horizontal mergers may give rise to a significant impediment on effective

---

[132] Guideline on the Merger Rule, paras 3.81-3.82.
[133] Guideline on the Merger Rule, para 3.83.
[134] OJ 2008 C265/6.
[135] These are mergers between parties who are not in a purely horizontal or vertical relationship but are active in closely related markets such as a merger between suppliers of complementary products.

competition, in particular by changing the ability and incentives of the merged entity and competitors and to the detriment of consumers, including intermediate purchasers. As an initial indicator, the European Commission will be unlikely to raise competition concerns in non-horizontal mergers where the post-merger market share of the merged company is below 30% and the HHI is below 2000 in each relevant market. It is likely to subject such mergers to extensive investigation where there are special features such as (1) a merger involving a company that is likely to expand in the near future; (2) there are significant cross-shareholdings or cross-directorships; or (3) there are indicators of previous or continuing coordination between the merging companies or their competitors.

4.3 EXCLUSION BASED ON ECONOMIC EFFICIENCIES

Economic efficiencies outweighing adverse effects Pursuant to section 8(1) of Schedule 7 to the Competition Ordinance, the Merger Rule does not apply to a merger if the economic efficiencies that arise or may arise from the merger outweigh the adverse effects caused by any lessening of competition in Hong Kong.[136] Any undertaking claiming the benefit of this exclusion has the burden of proving the claim.[137] The Competition Commission explains the scope of this exclusion in its Guideline on the Merger Rule.[138] Parties to a merger may apply for a decision of the Commission as to whether the merger is excluded from the Merger Rule on the basis that the economic efficiencies that arise or may arise from the merger outweigh the adverse effects caused by any lessening of competition.[139]

Analysing whether the economic efficiencies that arise or may arise from the merger outweigh the adverse effects involves a net economic benefit analysis. The aim of the analysis is to isolate and ascertain the objective benefits created by the merger and the economic importance of such efficiencies. The efficiencies are not assessed from the subjective viewpoint of the parties.[140] The Commission recognises three types of economic efficiencies:[141]

> (a) productive efficiency, which is achieved where a firm produces the goods and services that it offers to consumers at the lowest cost;

---

[136] Competition Ordinance, Schedule 7, section 8(1).

[137] Competition Ordinance, Schedule 7, section 8(2)

[138] Guideline on the Merger Rule, para 4.1. This exclusion mirrors a similar provision in the Singapore Competition Act. There is no equivalent in the EUMR, although the European Commission recognises the application of the principle.

[139] Competition Ordinance, Schedule 7, section 11(1); Guideline on the Merger Rule, para 4.11.

[140] Guideline on the Merger Rule, para 4.3.

[141] Guideline on the Merger Rule, para 4.4.

(b) allocative efficiency, which is achieved where resources in the economy are allocated to their highest valued uses (i.e. those that provide the greatest benefit relative to costs); and

(c) dynamic efficiency, which is achieved through an ongoing process of introducing new technologies and products in response to changes in consumer preferences and production techniques.

In relation to productive and dynamic efficiencies, competition seeks to achieve these efficiencies organically or internally within a firm. However, mergers also have a potential to generate significant efficiencies by permitting a better utilisation of existing assets and the realisation of economies of scale and scope which would not have been available (or available to the same extent) to either firm without the merger.[142] Efficiencies generated through a merger can enhance the merged firm's ability and incentive to compete. For example, merger generated efficiencies may enhance competition by permitting two ineffective high-cost competitors to become one effective low-cost competitor. If the efficiency gains attributable to a merger would transform the merged entity into a more vigorous competitor, competition in the market as a whole would be increased rather than lessened by the merger.[143] Furthermore, in markets with conditions conducive to coordinated conduct, an efficiency-enhancing merger can undermine those conditions by increasing the incentive for a maverick to break from the pack or, indeed, by creating a new maverick firm.[144]

Evidence substantiating economic efficiency exclusion   Any undertaking claiming the benefit of the economic efficiency exclusion must show that the efficiency gains occur as a direct result of the merger. The efficiencies must be clearly identified and verified and it must be demonstrated that they will be achieved (or achieved to a similar extent) by the merger and would be unlikely to have been achieved (or achieved to a similar extent) without the merger (for example, internal re-organisation) or by another means having less significant anticompetitive effects. In this analysis, the less restrictive alternative must be something that is likely to be practical for firms in the market and not merely a theoretical possibility.[145]

Efficiencies are often difficult to verify and quantify, in part because much of the information relating to efficiencies is uniquely in the possession of the merging firms. Moreover, efficiencies projected reasonably and in good faith by the merging firms may not be realised. Therefore, the Competition Commission requires undertakings not only to assert the claimed efficiencies but to demonstrate that the efficiencies are timely, likely and sufficient to

---

[142]   Guideline on the Merger Rule, para 4.5.
[143]   Guideline on the Merger Rule, para 4.6.
[144]   Guideline on the Merger Rule, para 4.7.
[145]   Guideline on the Merger Rule, para 4.8.

outweigh the adverse effects caused by any lessening of competition. Efficiency claims must be substantiated by the merging parties so that the Commission can verify by reasonable means:[146]

(a) the likelihood and magnitude of each claimed efficiency;

(b) how and when each efficiency would be achieved;

(c) how each efficiency would enhance the merged firm's ability and incentive to compete;

(d) why each efficiency would be merger-specific; and

(e) how the efficiencies would outweigh the adverse effects caused by any lessening of competition.

Certain types of efficiencies are more likely to be identifiable and more substantial than others. In general, cost reductions ought to be capable of verification without excessive difficulty. For example, efficiencies resulting from the shifting of telecommunications traffic from formerly separately owned networks onto the one network may result in a reduction in marginal costs which are merger-specific, identifiable and quantifiably substantial. Other efficiencies, such as those relating to research and development, are potentially substantial but are generally less verifiable. Others, such as those relating to procurement, management, or capital cost, are less likely to be merger-specific or substantial, or may not be as identifiable.[147]

Economic efficiency exclusion in EU and UK merger control In EU merger control proceedings the European Commission has rarely accepted efficiency claims. The EUMR merger notification form contains a specific section for merger efficiencies although it is not mandatory to complete this. In its Horizontal Merger Guidelines the Commission articulates its approach to taking into account efficiencies in the merger assessment. The parties must establish that the efficiencies directly benefit censers, that they are merger-specific, substantial, timely and verifiable and thereby counterbalance the adverse effects of the merger on competition. An example which illustrates the European Commission's approach is *Tom Tom/Tele Atlas*.[148] The European Commission has not cleared a merger that would otherwise give rise to an SIEC purely on the basis of efficiencies.

In the United Kingdom, in considering whether a merger may be expected to result in an SLC the CMA may consider whether efficiencies are created by the merger and whether such gains would have a positive effect on rivalry such that there would be no SLC as a result.[149] When considering whether claimed

---

[146] Guideline on the Merger Rule, para 4.9.

[147] Guideline on the Merger Rule, para 4.10.

[148] COMP/M.4854, *Tom Tom/Tele Atlas*, 14 May 2008.

[149] The CMA may also take into account efficiencies where they do not exclude an SLC but where they are passed on in the form of customer benefits. This may mean that the exception to the duty to refer the merger for a full (Phase II) investigation applies. In

efficiencies promote rivalry the CMA must be satisfied that the efficiencies are sufficient in terms of their likelihood, timelines and scale to avert an SLC that they are merger-specific in that they are a direct consequence of the merger. Global Radio's acquisition of GCap Media is an example of a case where efficiencies were considered by the OFT to make a material difference to the outcome of this case.[150]

Phase II the CMA may also take account of efficiencies when determining the issue of remedies.

[150] OFT press release, Global/GCap radio merger, 8 August 2008.

Chapter Five

ENFORCEMENT PROCEDURES FOR THE COMPETITION RULES

5.1 ENFORCEMENT PROCEDURES

Enforcement of the competition rules The Competition Ordinance establishes a dual administrative and judicial system with separate administrative and judicial functions for applying and enforcing the competition rules. The Competition Commission is the principal competition authority responsible for applying, and ensuring conformity with, the Competition Ordinance,[1] sharing competence in cases concerning telecommunications and broadcasting with the Communications Authority.[2] The Commission has administrative duties concerning the application of the rules, complaints, investigations and settlements. Judicial enforcement of the competition rules, i.e. the First and Second Conduct Rules and the Merger Rule, is effected by the Competition Tribunal on application by the Commission.

Enforcement functions of the Competition Commission The principal functions of the Competition Commission are to investigate conduct that may contravene the competition rules of the Competition Ordinance and enforce the provisions of the Competition Ordinance.[3] The Commission is provided with specific powers to consider applications from undertakings for decisions on exclusions and exemptions from the Conduct Rules as well as applications from undertakings and associations of undertakings for block exemption orders.[4] The Commission has the power to consider complaints from interested parties[5] and to conduct investigations.[6] It may accept commitments from undertakings to take any action or refrain from taking action that the Commission considers appropriate to address its concerns about a possible contravention of a competition rule.[7] Alternatively, where it has reasonable

---

[1] Competition Ordinance, section 130.
[2] Competition Ordinance, section 159(1).
[3] Competition Ordinance, section 130(a).
[4] Competition Ordinance, sections 9, 15 and 24.
[5] Competition Ordinance, section 37.
[6] Competition Ordinance, section 39.
[7] Competition Ordinance, section 60.

cause to believe that an infringement of the First Conduct Rule involving Serious Anti-Competitive Conduct or an infringement of the Second Conduct Rule has occurred, it may issue an infringement notice to the undertaking concerned, offering not to bring proceedings in the Competition Tribunal on condition that the undertaking makes a commitment to comply with the requirements of the notice.[8] In enforcing the Conduct Rules, the Commission may enter into leniency agreements in order to encourage parties to cartel agreements to come forward with information, whereby the party to the leniency agreement will not face proceedings in the Competition Tribunal in respect of its participation in the cartel.[9] Decisions of the Commission may be the subject of judicial review proceedings before the Competition Tribunal at the instigation of any person with sufficient standing.[10]

Where the Commission has carried out an investigation, it is not itself empowered to take a decision that there has been an infringement of the competition rules. Instead, it must bring proceedings before the Competition Tribunal. Before bringing such proceedings, it must, other than in cases involving Serious Anti-Competitive Conduct, issue the parties concerned with a warning notice.[11]

Enforcement functions of the Competition Tribunal Where the Competition Commission decides to pursue infringement proceedings, it must apply to the Competition Tribunal for a fine to be imposed on the undertakings concerned.[12] It may also request the Competition Tribunal to impose other orders, in particular in cases involving infringement of the Merger Rule.[13] The Competition Tribunal may also make a disqualification order preventing an individual from being *inter alia* a director or liquidator of a company.[14]

Where an infringement of a Conduct Rule has been found to have taken place, any person who has suffered loss or damage as a result of the infringement may bring proceedings in the Competition Tribunal for damages.[15]

Appeals from decisions of the Competition Tribunal may lie to the Court of Appeal.

---

[8] Competition Ordinance, section 67.
[9] Competition Ordinance, section 80.
[10] Competition Ordinance, sections 83-87.
[11] Competition Ordinance, section 82.
[12] Competition Ordinance, section 92.
[13] Competition Ordinance, section 94.
[14] Competition Ordinance, section 101.
[15] Competition Ordinance, sections 110-112.

5.2 APPLICATIONS FOR COMMISSION DECISIONS ON EXCLUSIONS AND EXEMPTIONS AND BLOCK EXEMPTIONS ORDERS FROM THE CONDUCT RULES

Applications concerning exclusions or exemptions The Competition Ordinance allows for various exclusions and exemptions from the scope of the Conduct Rules. General exclusions are listed in Schedule 1 covering agreements enhancing overall economic efficiency, compliance with legal requirements, services of general economic interest, mergers, and agreements and conduct of lesser significance, which, if applicable, means that the Conduct Rules do not apply.[16] Statutory bodies and specified persons and activities are excluded by sections 3-5 and exemptions on grounds of public policy and avoidance of conflict with international obligations are provided in sections 31 and 32, respectively. There is no requirement for undertakings to apply to the Competition Commission in order to secure the benefit of a particular exclusion or exemption.[17] Moreover, there is no requirement that there be a decision or block exemption order in place for undertakings to rely on applicable exclusions or exemptions. It is, therefore, up to undertakings to assess for themselves whether their agreements and conduct comply with the Conduct Rules. Moreover, undertakings may assert the benefit of any exclusion or exemption as a defence to any proceedings before the Competition Tribunal or other courts.[18]

Undertakings may elect, however, to apply to the Competition Commission under section 9 and/or section 24 of for a decision under section 11 and/or section 26, as to whether or not an agreement or conduct is excluded or exempt from the First or Second Conduct Rules, respectively. Undertakings may take this route if they wish to seek greater legal certainty.[19] In addition, pursuant to section 15 of the Competition Ordinance, the Commission may issue block exemption orders exempting categories of agreements that enhance overall economic efficiency from the First Conduct Rule.[20] The Commission may issue a block exemption order in response to an application or on its own initiative.[21] The Commission has issued a Guideline on Applications for a decision on exclusions and exemptions and block exemption orders.[22] The Guideline on Applications provides guidance on the procedure for

---

[16] Competition Ordinance, section 30.
[17] Guideline on Applications, para 1.5.
[18] Guideline on Applications, paras 5.5-5.6.
[19] Guideline on Applications, paras 1.6 and 5.7.
[20] Competition Ordinance, section 15(1) and (5).
[21] Guideline on Applications, paras 1.7 and 5.7.
[22] Guideline on Applications for a Decision under Sections 9 and 24 (Exclusions and Exemptions) and Section 15 Block Exemption Orders, 27 July 2015.

undertakings to follow in applying for a decision or a block exemption order and the process that the Commission will follow.[23]

Confidentiality and disclosure   Certain minimum information must be provided to the Competition Commission by applicants for decisions and block exemption orders.[24] Undertakings may not refrain from providing the required information solely on the basis that the information is confidential. Instead, the Commission is required to treat such information as confidential.[25] Where an applicant wishes to make a claim for confidentiality in respect of information provided to the Commission in the context of an application, it should identify the relevant information and provide a statement in writing setting out the reasons why the identified information is, in its opinion, confidential.[26] Unnecessarily broad claims to confidentiality may impede the Commission's ability to assess and rely on the information provided and/or increase the risk that information a party does not want to disclose is disclosed. Applicants should consider the scope of any confidentiality claim with this in mind. In the case of an application for a decision, applicants should submit both confidential and non-confidential versions of the application. The non-confidential version of the application will be published by the Commission on its website with a view to consulting interested parties and/or otherwise released to relevant third parties for the purposes of seeking their views on the application.[27]

Absent an express agreement with the Commission, information provided voluntarily to it by applicants or other parties, including information protected by legal professional privilege, will not be accepted on a without prejudice basis or otherwise on terms that its use is limited for the sole purpose of the Commission making a decision or issuing a block exemption order.[28] The Commission can use any information received in the context of an application, with or without notice to interested parties, for other purposes, including considering whether a contravention of the Competition Ordinance has occurred and/or with a view to enforcement where there has been a contravention. Applicants are encouraged, therefore, to seek legal advice before approaching the Commission about an application for a decision or block exemption order.[29]

---

[23] Guideline on Applications, para 1.18.
[24] Guideline on Applications, paras 6.16 and 11.14.
[25] Competition Ordinance, section 125(1).
[26] Guideline on Applications, paras 3.4-3.5.
[27] Guideline on Applications, paras 3.6-3.10.
[28] Guideline on Applications, paras 4.1, 6.13 and 11.12.
[29] Guideline on Applications, paras 4.1- 4.2.

Whether a decision or block exemption is appropriate Any undertaking may apply to the Competition Commission for a decision or block exemption order.[30] Associations of undertakings may also apply for a block exemption order.[31] There is no obligation on every undertaking involved in an agreement or conduct which is the subject of an application to be a party to the application or to make their own application. However, the Commission expects the cooperation of all undertakings that are parties to the agreements in question to provide information which might assist it in its consideration of the application.[32]

Where similar agreements enhancing overall economic efficiency are commonly used by undertakings throughout a market, it may be more appropriate for undertakings or associations to consider seeking a block exemption order for such agreements rather than apply separately for a decision regarding an individual agreement. This should be discussed with the Commission prior to making any application.[33] An applicant for a block exemption must demonstrate that the category of agreements proposed to be the subject of a block exemption is representative of agreements in wider use in one or more industries.[34] For sector specific block exemption applications, applicants are encouraged to provide evidence showing there is a greater need for cooperation between undertakings in the relevant sector as compared with other sectors in the economy.[35]

Immunity from enforcement action The Competition Ordinance does not afford the undertakings concerned any immunity from enforcement action during its review of an application. The Competition Commission may, in its discretion, initiate enforcement action in respect of any existing agreement or conduct (including proceedings before the Competition Tribunal) if it declines to consider an application, make a decision, or issue a block exemption order. Moreover, the Commission may use information provided by the applicant in the relevant enforcement action.[36] Applicants are therefore encouraged to seek legal advice before making an application.[37]

---

[30] Competition Ordinance, sections 9(1), 15(2) and 24(1).
[31] Competition Ordinance, section 15(2); Guideline on Applications, para 5.1.
[32] Guideline on Applications, para 5.2.
[33] Guideline on Applications, para 5.9.
[34] Guideline on Applications, para 5.3.
[35] Guideline on Applications, para 5.4.
[36] Guideline on Applications, para 5.16.
[37] Guideline on Applications, para 5.17.

5.2.1 Applications for a decision on exclusion or exemption

Timeframe for reviewing application The Competition Ordinance does not provide any timeframe for the Competition Commission's review of an application for a decision on exclusion or exemption or prescribe any deadline for making a decision. The timing of a particular review or the time required to make a decision will vary depending on, for example, the complexity of the case and the availability of Commission resources. The Commission will, however, endeavour to process applications expeditiously.[38] It expects applications to be complete and accurate. Applicants should respond in a timely manner to any requests for additional information.[39]

Factors to be considered The Competition Commission is only required to consider an application for a decision if:[40]

(a) the application poses novel or unresolved questions of wider importance or public interest in relation to the application of exclusion or exemptions under the Competition Ordinance;

(b) the application raises a question of an exclusion or exemption under the Competition Ordinance for which there is no clarification in existing case law or decisions of the Commission;[41] and

(c) it is possible to make a decision on the basis of the information provided.[42]

The Commission will generally only consider applications that fulfil all these criteria.[43] In deciding whether an application poses a novel or unresolved question of wider importance or public interest, it may consider the economic importance, from the point of view of the consumer, of the products or services concerned by the agreement or conduct and/or the extent to which the agreement or conduct or similar agreements or similar conduct is in widespread usage in the marketplace.[44]

The Commission is not required to consider an application if it concerns hypothetical questions or conduct.[45] In this respect, it will not generally consider an application regarding agreements or conduct which have ceased,

---

[38] Guideline on Applications, para 6.2.
[39] Guideline on Applications, para 6.3.
[40] Competition Ordinance, sections 9(2) and 24(2).
[41] Before submitting an application, an applicant should verify that there is no existing clarification in the case law of the Competition Tribunal or other Hong Kong courts, or decisions of the Commission: Guideline on Applications, para 6.7.
[42] Accordingly, the applicant should provide sufficient evidence to support its application: Guideline on Applications, para 6.8.
[43] Guideline on Applications, para 6.5.
[44] Guideline on Applications, para 6.6.
[45] Competition Ordinance, section 24(3).

although undertakings may apply for a decision in relation to a future agreement or conduct in which they intend to engage.[46]

Initial consultation prior to making an application Although there is no obligation to do so, potential applicants are strongly encouraged to approach the Competition Commission for an initial consultation prior to submitting an application for a decision.[47] An initial consultation affords the Commission and the applicant an opportunity to discuss jurisdictional and other matters. In particular, it may allow them to prepare for the process of making an application by identifying key issues and possible competition concerns at an early stage and the evidence that the Commission would need to assess these concerns.[48] During the initial consultation, the Commission may highlight to a potential applicant that an alternative procedural route under the Competition Ordinance may be more appropriate depending on the nature of the specific conduct in question. It may also indicate to the applicant whether the application appears likely to satisfy the criteria required for it to be considered by the Commission.[49]

Preparing an application for a decision An application, accompanied by the appropriate fee,[50] should be made to the Competition Commission by submitting a completed Form AD.[51] Form AD requires, among other things:[52]

   (a) information relating to the applicant and the other parties to the agreement or conduct (including contact information, a description of key business activities, information on controlling shareholders and turnover data);

   (b) a detailed description of the relevant agreement or conduct (including copies of any relevant documents such as agreements or draft agreements);

   (c) information on the provisions or elements of the agreement/conduct which might give rise to competition concerns and an explanation of the nature of those concerns including possible theories of harm;

---

[46] Guideline on Applications, para 6.11.
[47] Guideline on Applications, paragraph 6.12.
[48] Guideline on Applications, paragraph 6.14.
[49] Guideline on Applications, paragraph 6.15.
[50] Cf. Schedule to the Competition (Fees) Regulation, though fees may be waived or reduced with the prior agreement of the Competition Commission. See also the Commission's guidance entitled "Fees Payable for Making an Application to the Commission" dated November 2015.
[51] See https://www.compcomm.hk/en/applications/apply_decision/decision.html for Form AD, the Annex to Form AD and the Commission's Explanatory Note on Form AD. The Commission publishes the most up-to-date requirements for applications on its website: Guideline on Applications, para 5.14.
[52] Guideline on Applications, para 6.16.

(d) an explanation of the applicant's view of the relevant markets involved together with market share data (including for competitors) and other information on the competitive situation in such markets;

(e) information on affected suppliers and customers and their contact details;

(f) an explanation (including supporting evidence) as to why the applicant believes the relevant agreement/conduct satisfies the terms of a particular exclusion or exemption; and

(g) where submissions/applications have been made to competition authorities in other jurisdictions with respect to the same agreement or conduct, a list of the relevant jurisdictions, information on when the submissions/applications were made, and an indication of the status of the various submissions/applications in the jurisdictions concerned.

If an applicant wishes to make a claim for confidentiality in respect of information provided to the Commission, it should submit a non-confidential version, as well as confidential version, of the application.[53]

Preliminary assessment of application　The Competition Commission will conduct a preliminary assessment based on the information provided by the applicant, the purpose of which is to determine whether the criteria requiring it to consider the application are satisfied, and decide whether it will consider the application.[54]　If it declines to consider the application, it will provide a written explanation. This does not indicate the Commission's position on whether the relevant agreement or conduct raises a concern under the conduct rules or is or is not excluded or exempt from them.[55]　If the Commission elects to consider the application, it will inform the applicant. The timeframe for preliminary assessment will depend on the nature and complexity of each matter, although where the applicant has engaged in an initial consultation and provides an application consistent with the issues discussed during that consultation, the timeframe for preliminary assessment may be shorter than otherwise.[56]

Consideration of application　Before making a decision, the Competition Commission will publicise the application and engage with parties likely to be affected by a decision.[57]　Publication of notice of the application, together with a non-confidential version of the application on the Commission's website, is required in order to bring the application to the attention of those the

---

[53]　Guideline on Applications, para 6.17.
[54]　Guideline on Applications, paras 7.1-7.2.
[55]　Guideline on Applications, para 7.3. This does not constitute a decision under section 11 and/or section 26 of the Competition Ordinance.
[56]　Guideline on Applications, paras 7.4-7.5.
[57]　Guideline on Applications, para 8.1.

Commission considers likely to be affected by it.[58] The Commission must also consider any representations about the application that are made to it, such as by competitors, suppliers or customers.[59] The notice must specify a period of at least thirty days within which interested parties may make representations.[60]

During this process, the Commission may meet with the applicant and other parties as appropriate, and in particular, it may invite the applicant to provide additional written representations or information or to attend meetings. The Commission may also seek the views of trade associations, sectoral regulators or industry representative bodies.[61] The applicant may be invited to respond to representations received from other parties. It may also meet with the Commission to discuss such matters as concerns raised by the application, preliminary views on the merits and other questions raised by the applicant or third parties.[62] Moreover, after completion of the review of the application and before making a decision, the Commission may meet with the applicant to convey its views on the merits of the application and any conditions and limitations being considered.[63]

Generally, the Commission will not publish its proposed decision for public comment. However, it may choose in certain cases to publish a proposed decision in non-confidential form or to release a proposed decision in non-confidential form to parties likely to be affected by the decision where the proposed decision is likely to be of wider relevance for the market. The Commission may also choose to consult third parties if it considers that the views of parties likely to be affected by the proposed decision would assist it in its assessment of the application.[64]

Making a decision   The Competition Commission's decision, pursuant to section 11 and/or 26 of the Competition Ordinance, may be that the agreement or conduct:[65]

- is not excluded or exempt from the conduct rules;
- is excluded or exempt from one or more of the conduct rules; or

---

[58]   Competition Ordinance, sections 10(1)(a) and 25(1)(a).

[59]   Competition Ordinance, sections 10(1)(b) and 25(1)(b); Guideline on Applications, para 8.3.

[60]   Competition Ordinance, sections 10(1)(b), 10(2)-(3), 25(1)(b) and 25(2)-(3).

[61]   With a view to transparency in its decision making, the Commission will generally publish any written representations on its website. It thus requires the applicant and other parties to provide non-confidential versions of their written representations: Guideline on Applications, para 8.5.

[62]   Guideline on Applications, paras 8.6-8.7.

[63]   Guideline on Applications, para 8.9. The applicant will be given an opportunity to comment at the meeting or in a timely manner after the meeting.

[64]   Guideline on Applications, para 8.10.

[65]   Competition Ordinance, sections 11(1)-(2) and 26(1)-(2); Guideline on Applications, para 9.1.

- is excluded or exempt from one or more of the conduct rules, subject to conditions or limitations.

The Commission must inform the applicant in writing of the decision, the date of the decision and the reasons for it.[66] A non-confidential version of the decision and the Commission's reasons for it will be published on the Commission's website.[67]

Effect of decisions Where the Competition Commission makes a decision that an agreement or conduct is excluded or exempt, the undertaking specified in the decision is immune from action under the Competition Ordinance with respect to that agreement or conduct.[68] A decision may have effect subject to conditions or limitations, the need for which will be considered on a case by case basis.[69] However, the Commission will likely limit the duration of a decision's effect if the decision confirms the applicability of an exclusion or exemption.[70]

A decision that the agreement or conduct is not excluded or exempt from the conduct rules does not necessarily mean that the Commission has formed a view on whether it has reasonable cause to believe that a contravention of the conduct rules has occurred in connection with that agreement or conduct.[71]

Compliance with conditions or limitations Where the Competition Commission has made its decision subject to conditions or limitations it will monitor compliance with those conditions or limitations.[72] If an undertaking fails or ceases to comply with a condition, the immunity pursuant the decision ceases to apply with effect from the date on which the non-compliance begins.[73] However, if the undertaking starts to comply or resumes compliance with the condition or limitation, the immunity applies with effect from the date on which the compliance begins or resumes.[74] Where an undertaking loses its immunity because of a failure to comply with a condition or limitation, the Commission is entitled to take enforcement action under the Competition

---

[66] Competition Ordinance, sections 11(3) and 26(3); Guideline on Applications, para 9.2.

[67] Guideline on Applications, para 9.3. The Competition Commission will also make an entry in its register of decisions and block exemption orders.

[68] Competition Ordinance, sections 12(1) and 27(1).

[69] Competition Ordinance, sections 12(2) and 27(2).

[70] Guideline on Applications, para 9.5. A limitation of duration will be particularly likely where an agreement is exempt from the First Conduct Rule on the ground of enhancing overall economic efficiency.

[71] Guideline on Applications, para 9.6.

[72] Guideline on Applications, para 10.8.

[73] Competition Ordinance, sections 13(1) and 28(1); Guideline on Applications, para 10.9.

[74] Competition Ordinance, sections 13(2) and 28(2).

Ordinance in relation to a contravention of the First or Second Conduct Rule by that undertaking.[75]

Rescission of decisions The Competition Commission may rescind a decision where it has reason to believe that there has been a material change of circumstances since the decision was made or the information on which it based the decision was incomplete, false or misleading in a material particular.[76] Where the Commission proposes to rescind a decision:

- it will advise the undertaking specified in the decision of its intention and publicise the proposed rescission;[77]
- persons making representations will be given at least 30 days to make representations on the proposed rescission beginning the which the notice published;[78]
- it will engage with, and consider representations from, the persons likely to be affected by the proposed rescission.[79]

Following consideration of any representations, the Commission may then proceed to issue a notice of rescission.[80] Undertakings for which the decision provided immunity from action under the Competition Ordinance lose their immunity from the date the rescission takes effect with regard to anything done after that date.[81] A rescission of a decision may be made with regard to all of the undertakings for which the decision provides immunity or with regard to only one or more of them.[82]

5.2.2. Applications for block exemption order

Whether to issue a block exemption order The Competition Commission, pursuant to section 15 of the Competition Ordinance, may, either of its own volition or on application by an undertaking or association of undertakings, issue a block exemption order where it is satisfied that a particular category of agreement is excluded from the application of the First Conduct Rule on the

---

[75] Competition Ordinance, sections 13(3) and 28(3); Guideline on Applications, para 10.10.

[76] Competition Ordinance, sections 14(1) and 29(1).

[77] Competition Ordinance, sections 14(2) and 29(2).

[78] Competition Ordinance, sections 14(4) and 29(4).

[79] Competition Ordinance, sections 14(2)(b) and 29(2)(b). Since the Commission will generally publish any written representations on its website, it requires the applicant and/or other parties to provide non-confidential versions of their written representations: Guideline on Applications, paras 10.4-10.5.

[80] Competition Ordinance, sections 14(6), 29(6) and 34. An entry will be made in the Commission's register of decisions and block exemption orders.

[81] Competition Ordinance, sections 14(8) and 29(8).

[82] Competition Ordinance, sections 14(9) and 29(9).

ground of enhancing overall economic efficiency.[83]   The Commission may impose conditions or limitations subject to which the block exemption order is to have effect and specify a date from which it will cease to have effect.[84] There is no requirement that the Commission issue a block exemption order in order for undertakings or associations to rely on the exclusion for agreements enhancing overall economic efficiency. Undertakings or associations may self-assess the legality of their conduct having regard to the First Conduct Rule and the applicable exclusions and exemptions from those rules.[85] Undertakings and associations considering making block exemption applications are strongly encouraged to approach the Commission for an initial consultation before making any such application.[86]

The Commission considers that the issue of a sector specific block exemption order should be seen as an exceptional measure. Before starting to consider whether to issue such a block exemption order, the Commission will take into account whether the resources required for such consideration are likely to be proportionate to the expected public benefit of issuing the order.[87] Moreover, since block exemption orders may be relevant to a substantial portion of the Hong Kong economy, developing a thorough understanding of the markets and potential impact of the order may require extensive consultation with multiple stakeholders, which might take a considerable period of time.[88]

Timeframe for reviewing application The Competition Ordinance does not provide any timeframe for the Competition Commission's review of a block exemption application or prescribe any deadline for making a block exemption order. The timing of a particular review will vary depending on, for example, the complexity of the case and the availability of Commission resources. A review of a block exemption application is likely to take considerably more time than an application for an individual decision.[89]

Initial consultation prior to making an application Potential applicants are strongly encouraged to approach the Competition Commission for an initial consultation prior to submitting a block exemption application.[90] The initial consultation is to identify:[91]

---

[83]   Competition Ordinance, section 15(1)-(2); Guideline on Applications, paras 11.1-11.2.
[84]   Competition Ordinance, section 15(3).
[85]   Guideline on Applications, para 11.4.
[86]   Guideline on Applications, para 11.6.
[87]   Guideline on Applications, para 11.3.
[88]   Guideline on Applications, para 11.5.
[89]   Guideline on Applications, paras 11.8-11.9.
[90]   Guideline on Applications, para 11.10.
[91]   Guideline on Applications, para 11.11.

- whether it is possible that the relevant category of agreements may be excluded agreements on the ground of enhancing overall economic efficiency;
- whether a block exemption application is the appropriate procedure under the Competition Ordinance;
- whether there is likely to be sufficient evidence available for the Commission to consider issuing a block exemption order; and
- the resources that might be required to consider the application and issue an eventual block exemption order;
- whether in all the circumstances of the case, including the wider regulatory context and the overall competition regime in Hong Kong, a block exemption order would be appropriate.

Preparing an application A block exemption application, accompanied by the prescribed fee,[92] should be made to the Competition Commission by submitting the following information:[93]

(a) information relating to the applicant and the parties to the agreements concerned (including, to the extent available to the applicant, contact information, a description of key business activities for the parties concerned);

(b) details of the category of agreement concerned (including copies of a sufficiently representative sample of agreements falling within the relevant category);

(c) information on the provisions or elements of the agreements falling within the relevant category of agreement which might give rise to competition concerns and an explanation of the nature of those concerns including possible theories of harm;

(d) an explanation of the view of the applicant on the definition of the relevant markets affected together with market share data (including for competitors) and other information on the competitive situation in such markets;

(e) information on affected suppliers and customers and their contact details to the extent available to the applicant;

(f) an explanation (including supporting evidence) as to why the applicant believes the relevant category of agreement satisfies the terms of section 1 of Schedule 1 to the Competition Ordinance (agreements enhancing overall economic efficiency);

---

[92] Presently, HK$500,000, see paragraph 3 of the Schedule to the Competition (Fees) Regulation. See also the Competition Commission's guidance entitled "Fees Payable for Making an Application to the Commission" dated November 2015.

[93] Guideline on Applications, para 11.13.   The Commission publishes the current requirements for applications on its website: Guideline on Applications, para 11.14.

(g) if relevant, an explanation of factors in support of the applicant's claim that the category of agreements that are the subject of the application are representative of agreements in wider use in one or more industries; and

(h) in the case of a sector specific block exemption application, although this is not a mandatory requirement, evidence showing a greater need for cooperation between undertakings in the relevant sector as compared with other sectors in the economy.

Applicants will generally be required to provide further information during the course of the Commission's review, and will be expected to provide timely responses to any such information requests.[94]

Consideration of application   The Competition Commission will acknowledge receipt of any block exemption application it receives.[95]   It will publicise on its website that the Commission has either initiated a process or received an application and engage with persons likely to be affected by a block exemption order.[96]   The Commission will assess whether the relevant category of agreement is excluded from the First Conduct Rule.[97]   Having regard to the views of persons likely to be affected, it will then elect whether or not to propose to issue a block exemption order or to propose an order subject to conditions or limitations.[98]   If the process was initiated by an application, the Commission will provide an explanation of this outcome to the applicant in writing.[99]

Issuing a block exemption order   Where the Competition Commission proposes to issue a block exemption order, section 16 of the Competition Ordinance prescribes a process that must be undertaken before issuing the order. The Commission must publish notice of the proposed block exemption order in order to bring it to the attention of those the Commission considers likely to be affected. Interested persons will be given at least thirty days to make representations and the Commission must consider those representations. The Commission may also invite relevant parties to provide additional written representations or further information in response to representations received and will seek additional information from parties as necessary.[100]   It will generally publish any written representations on its website, and therefore

---

[94] Guideline on Applications, paras 5.12 and 5.13.
[95] Guideline on Applications, para 11.15.
[96] Guideline on Applications, para 12.1.
[97] Guideline on Applications, para 12.2.
[98] Guideline on Applications, paras 12.3-12.5. The timeframe for the Commission's assessment will depend on the nature and complexity of the matter as well as the resources available to the Commission at the time.
[99] Guideline on Applications, para 12.6.
[100] Competition Ordinance, section 16(1)-(3); Guideline on Applications, paras 13.1-13.4.

requires non-confidential versions of written representations from the applicant and other parties.[101]

Following this process, the Commission will decide whether or not to issue a block exemption order or to issue an order subject to conditions or limitations.[102] If it decides not to issue a block exemption order, it will provide an explanation of this outcome to the applicant in writing if the process was initiated by an application. A decision not to issue a block exemption order, however, does not necessarily mean that the Commission has formed a view on whether it has reasonable cause to believe that a contravention of the First Conduct Rule has occurred in connection with the category of agreements that are the subject of the application.[103]

Where the Commission decides to issue a block exemption order, it will proceed to issue the order.[104] Conditions or limitations may be included on a case by case basis.[105] The Commission may specify a date on which the order will cease to have effect.[106] The order and the Commission's reasons for issuing it will be published on its website.[107]

Effect of a block exemption order   Where the Competition Commission issues a block exemption order, an agreement that falls within the category of agreement specified in the order is exempt from the First Conduct Rule.[108] This immunity applies to an undertaking only if it complies with every condition and limitation to which the order is subject.[109]

Compliance with conditions or limitations   The Competition Commission will monitor the compliance with any conditions or limitations subject to which a block exemption order has effect.[110] If an undertaking fails or ceases to comply with a condition or limitation, the order ceases to apply with respect to that undertaking with effect from the date on which the non-compliance begins.[111] If an undertaking starts to comply or resumes compliance with the condition or limitation, the block exemption order applies to that undertaking

---

[101]   Guideline on Applications, para 13.5.
[102]   Guideline on Applications, para 13.6.
[103]   Guideline on Applications, para 13.7.
[104]   Competition Ordinance, section 15(1)-(2).
[105]   Competition Ordinance, section 15(3)(a); Guideline on Applications, para 13.10.
[106]   Competition Ordinance, section 15(3)(b).
[107]   Guideline on Applications, para 13.8. An entry will be made in the Commission's register of decisions and block exemption orders.
[108]   Competition Ordinance, section 17(1); Guideline on Applications, para 13.9. However, the block exemption does not provide any exemption from the operation of the Second Conduct Rule.
[109]   Competition Ordinance, section 17(2).
[110]   Guideline on Applications, para 14.9.
[111]   Competition Ordinance, section 18(1).

with effect from the date on which the compliance begins or resumes.[112] Enforcement action may be taken under the Competition Ordinance against any undertaking relating to a contravention of the First Conduct Rule by that undertaking that occurs during any period in which the block exemption order does not apply to it.[113]

Review of block exemption orders The Competition Commission must specify in a block exemption order a date, which must be not more than five years from the date of the order, upon which it will commence a review of the order.[114] It must commence the review on the date specified in the order, although it may also review the order at any time prior to that date if it considers it appropriate to do so.[115] When deciding whether or not to review a block exemption order prior to the specified review date, the Commission may consider any number of factors but must consider the following:

- the desirability of maintaining a stable and predictable regulatory environment in relation to competition;
- any developments that have taken place in the economy of Hong Kong or in the economy of any place outside Hong Kong that affect the category of agreement that is the subject of the order; and
- whether any significant new information relating to the particular category of agreement has come to the knowledge of the Commission since the order was first issued.[116]

After its review, the Commission may vary or revoke the block exemption order.[117] If the Commission proposes to vary or revoke a block exemption order it must publicise the proposed variation or revocation with reasons, invite representations from interested parties and consider any representations that are made to it.[118] Following a consideration of any representations received, the Commission may proceed to issue a notice of variation or revocation with reasons, specifying the date on which the variation or revocation is to have effect and setting out any transitional and savings provisions the Commission considers necessary or expedient.[119]

---

[112] Competition Ordinance, section 18(2).

[113] Competition Ordinance, section 18(3).

[114] Competition Ordinance, section 15(4).

[115] Competition Ordinance, sections 19(1)-(2); Guideline on Applications, para 14.1.

[116] Competition Ordinance, section 19(3); Guideline on Applications, para 14.2.

[117] Competition Ordinance, section 20(1); Guideline on Applications, para 14.3.

[118] Competition Ordinance, section 20(2)-(4); Guideline on Applications, paras 14.4-14.7. Interested parties must be given at least 30 days to make representations. The Commission will generally publish any written representations on its website, and it therefore requires parties to provide non-confidential versions of their written representations.

[119] Competition Ordinance, section 20(5); Guideline on Applications para 14.8.

Following a consideration of any representations received within the period identified in the notice of proposed variation and revocation, the Commission may proceed to issue a notice of variation or revocation.[120]

5.3 COMPLAINTS TO THE COMPETITION COMMISSION

Complaints from interested parties In the exercise of its enforcement functions under the Competition Ordinance, the Competition Commission encourages input from the public. In particular, it values any input drawing its attention to suspected contraventions of the competition rules, such as the submission of well-informed complaints.[121] Any persons who suspects that an undertaking has contravened, is contravening, or is about to contravene a competition rule may, pursuant to section 37(1) of the Competition Ordinance, contact the Commission to express their concerns and to make a complaint. The Commission also welcomes queries from the public regarding matters which may be within the scope of the Competition Ordinance.[122] The Commission does not, however, act on behalf of complainants and will consider, in its discretion, what matters to pursue having regard to the public interest in having a competitive marketplace, rather than the complainant's interest.[123]

The Commission has published a Guideline on Complaints which describes the manner and form in which complaints may be made to the Commission.[124] It also sets out information on the processes the Commission will use for determining what action to take in relation to a complaint or query.[125]

Making a complaint to the Competition Commission The Competition Commission relies on complaints and queries from the public as an important means of identifying possible contraventions of the Competition Ordinance. The Commission accepts complaints in any form, including those provided to it directly, anonymously or through an intermediary (such as a legal adviser).[126] A complaint or query may be made by telephone, e-mail, post, by completing an online form on the Commission's website or in person at the Commission's offices (by appointment only).[127] Where the complainant has provided relevant

---

[120] Competition Ordinance, section 20(1).
[121] Guideline on Complaints, para 1.2.
[122] Guideline on Complaints, para 1.3.
[123] Competition Ordinance, section 37(2); Guideline on Complaints, para 1.4.
[124] Guideline on Complaints, 27 July 2015, pursuant to Competition Ordinance, section 38.
[125] Guideline on Complaints, para 1.5.
[126] Guideline on Complaints, para 2.1.
[127] Guideline on Complaints, para 2.2. A complaint may be submitted on behalf of more than one person or party.

contact details, the Commission will usually acknowledge receipt of the complaint promptly.[128]

At the time of making a complaint, it is not necessary to provide all details of the relevant conduct. However, to assist the Commission in assessing the matter, a complainant should submit any information that it has or has access to and is encouraged to provide as much of the following information as possible:[129]

- a description of the relevant facts regarding the conduct the complainant is concerned about;
- information on any documents that relate to the conduct including copies of those documents where possible;
- information about the party or parties involved in the conduct, including their contact information where known;
- if applicable, information concerning the impact of the conduct on the complainant;
- if applicable, information about other parties affected by the conduct, including information on how those parties are affected and contact information where known; and
- other information about the complainant, including name, job title, address, telephone and email address.

The Commission expects complainants to respond in a timely manner to any particular requests for information that the Commission may make.[130]

Confidentiality The Competition Commission will not normally comment on what matters it is considering or investigating.[131] The Commission's ability to effectively investigate a complaint may be impeded where the complaint is publicised or otherwise widely known. To support its ability to conduct effective investigations, the Commission requests that complainants keep their complaints confidential. If a complainant elects to disclose the complaint publicly, it should inform the Commission in advance of any such disclosure.[132]

The Commission is subject to a general obligation to preserve the confidentiality of any confidential information provided to or obtained by it, including information that relates to the identity of any person who has given information to it.[133] The disclosure of confidential information by the Commission is permitted, however, in certain circumstances.[134] Thus,

---

[128] Guideline on Complaints, para 2.3.
[129] Guideline on Complaints, para 2.4.
[130] Guideline on Complaints, para 2.6.
[131] Guideline on Complaints, para 3.1.
[132] Guideline on Complaints, para 3.2.
[133] Competition Ordinance, sections 124 and 125(1).
[134] Competition Ordinance, section 125(2); Guideline on Complaints, para 3.3.

although the Commission will not normally disclose the complainant's identity without its consent, in some exceptional cases it may be necessary to do so. This includes where disclosure is ordered by the Competition Tribunal or the courts or where the Commission considers it necessary to make a disclosure in the performance of its functions or in carrying into effect or doing anything authorised by the Competition Ordinance.[135] When deciding whether or not to disclose confidential information (including a complainant's identity), the Commission must consider the extent to which the disclosure is necessary for the purpose sought to be achieved by the disclosure and the need to exclude, as far as is practical, the following categories of information from such disclosure:[136]

- information, the disclosure of which would, in the Commission's opinion, be contrary to the public interest;
- commercial information the disclosure of which would or might be likely to, in the Commission's opinion, significantly harm the legitimate business interests of person to whom it relates;
- information relating to the private affairs of a natural person, the disclosure of which might, in the Commission's opinion, significantly harm the interests of that person.

Where confidential information is disclosed, the party receiving the confidential information from the Commission must maintain the confidentiality of that information. This includes keeping the identity of a complainant confidential if it is included in such a disclosure.[137]

Assessment of complaints by the Competition Commission Section 37(2) of the Competition Ordinance provides the Competition Commission with a discretion as regards the investigation of complaints. Thus, the Commission will consider any complaint it receives regarding anti-competitive behaviour, although it will not pursue all such complaints.[138] In particular, it is not required to investigate a complaint if it does not consider it reasonable to do so.[139] Without limiting what is considered reasonable for these purposes, the Commission may, in particular, not investigate a complaint if it is trivial, frivolous or vexatious, or misconceived or lacking in substance.[140] As to the meaning of trivial, frivolous or vexatious, reference can be made to case law on striking out pleadings on grounds that they are scandalous, frivolous or vexatious pursuant to O.18 r.19 of the Rules of High Court, and restriction of

---

[135] Competition Ordinance, section 126(1)(b); Guideline on Complaints, para 3.4.
[136] Competition Ordinance, section 126(3)(a); Guideline on Complaints, para 3.5.
[137] Competition Ordinance, sections 127-128; Guideline on Complaints, para 3.6.
[138] Guideline on Complaints, para 4.1.
[139] Competition Ordinance, section 37(2); Guideline on Complaints, para 4.2. Moreover, it may investigate a complaint even where the complainant no longer wishes to cooperate with the Commission.
[140] Competition Ordinance, section 37(2); Guideline on Complaints, para 4.3.

vexatious legal proceedings under section 27 of the High Court Ordinance and O.32A of the Rules of High Court.[141] When considering whether a complaint is misconceived or lacking in substance, the Commission will have regard to factors including:[142]

- the subject matter of the complaint and the scope of the Ordinance;
- any applicable exclusions and exemptions under the Ordinance; and
- the likely veracity of the complaint, including any supporting information provided with it.

In every case the Commission will exercise its discretion having regard to the specific facts of the complaint.[143]

Preliminary review of a complaint   After a preliminary review of a complaint, the Competition Commission will do one of the following:[144]

- take no further action;
- take no action while recommending the complainant refer the complaint to another agency; or
- review the matter further by conducting an Initial Assessment.

If the Commission proposes to take no further action or recommends the complainant refer their concerns to another agency, it will provide an explanation of this outcome to the complainant in writing.[145] Even where it initially decides to take no further action, the Commission may later reconsider the issues raised in a complaint or query. This may occur where additional evidence has been obtained, where a pattern of conduct arises which warrants further consideration or where the Commission has increased capacity to investigate an issue.[146]

If the Commission reviews a complaint further, it will endeavour to keep the complainant generally informed as the matter progresses. This will always be subject to any overriding considerations, including the Commission's ability to conduct effective investigations and the need to preserve confidentiality. The Commission is therefore unlikely to advise a complainant of internal procedural steps taken, such as whether a matter is in the Initial Assessment Phase or Investigation Phase.[147]

---

[141] Generally speaking, a complaint would be considered frivolous or vexatious where it constitutes an abuse of process, is not capable of reasoned argument, is without foundation, where it cannot possibly succeed, or if it is oppressive and/or lacks *bona fides.*

[142] Guideline on Complaints, para 4.4.

[143] Guideline on Complaints, para 4.5.

[144] Guideline on Complaints, para 5.1.

[145] Guideline on Complaints, para 5.2.

[146] Guideline on Complaints, para 5.3.

[147] Guideline on Complaints, para 5.4.

5.4 INVESTIGATIONS BY THE COMPETITION COMMISSION

Introduction   Section 39 of the Competition Ordinance provides the Competition Commission with powers of investigation. The Commission has issued a Guideline on Investigations providing details on procedures to be adopted in deciding whether to conduct an investigation and in conducting an investigation.[148] The Commission may only conduct an investigation where it has reasonable cause to suspect that a contravention of a competition rule has occurred.[149] Where the Commission investigates an alleged contravention of a competition rule, whether initiated by a complaint or otherwise, it will generally do so in two phases: first, an Initial Assessment Phase and secondly, if appropriate, an Investigation Phase.[150]

5.4.1 Initial Assessment Phase

Sources of investigation   The Competition Commission may launch an investigation on its own initiative or where information about a possible contravention is provided by another party. It may conduct an investigation into any conduct that constitutes or may constitute a contravention of a competition rule:[151]

- of its own volition, for example on the basis of its own research and market intelligence gathering or other Commission processes and investigations;
- where it has received a complaint or query made by the public; or
- where any conduct has been referred to it by the Government, the Competition Tribunal or the courts[152] or other statutory bodies or authorities of potentially anti-competitive conduct for investigation.

Initial Assessment Phase   The Initial Assessment Phase is used by the Competition Commission to determine whether it is reasonable to conduct an investigation and whether there is sufficient evidence to establish a reasonable cause to suspect that a contravention of a competition rule has occurred.[153] The Commission may seek information on a voluntary basis, such as by:[154]

- contacting parties by telephone or in writing;

---

[148] Guideline on Investigations, 27 July 2015; cf. Competition Ordinance, section 40.
[149] Competition Ordinance, section 39(2); Guideline on Investigations, para 1.2.
[150] Guideline on Investigations, para 1.3.
[151] Competition Ordinance, section 39(1); Guideline on Investigations, paras 2.1-2.2.
[152] The courts include the Court of First Instance, the Court of Appeal and the Court of Final Appeal.
[153] Guideline on Investigations, para 3.1.
[154] Guideline on Investigations, paras 3.3.

- meeting and interviewing persons who may have knowledge of the conduct;
- reviewing publicly available information including market surveys and industry reports; and
- conducting surveys.

Depending on the circumstances, the Commission may contact undertakings who are the subject of an Initial Assessment to request information relevant to its consideration of the matter. Once they have been made aware that they are the subject of an investigation, the Commission will keep them informed of the progress of investigation subject to overriding operational or confidentiality considerations.[155]

When exercising its discretion under the Competition Ordinance whether or not to pursue or continue pursuing a particular matter, the Commission, having regard to the specific facts of the matter, will take a range of factors into account including:[156]

- whether the available evidence indicates that the Competition Ordinance may have been contravened;
- the potential impact of the alleged conduct on competition and consumers;
- the Commission's current enforcement strategy, priorities and objectives;
- other matters currently under consideration by the Commission and the courts;
- the likelihood of a successful outcome resulting from further investigation; and
- whether the resource requirements of further investigation are proportionate to the expected public benefit.

When deciding whether or not to investigate a matter beyond the Initial Assessment Phase, a consideration of the specific facts of the case and other relevant factors may mean that the Commission decides not to pursue a matter further even if it is possible that further investigation would uncover some evidence that there may be a contravention of the competition rules.[157]

The duration of the Initial Assessment Phase will vary depending on the nature and complexity of each matter, as well as the resources available to the Commission. Where the Commission already has sufficient evidence to form a view, the timeframe may be very short.[158]

---

[155] Guideline on Investigations, paras 3.4-3.5.
[156] Guideline on Investigations, paras 3.6-3.7.
[157] Guideline on Investigations, para 3.8.
[158] Guideline on Investigations, para 3.2.

Possible outcomes of Initial Assessment Phase   The Competition Commission may come to four possible outcomes of the Initial Assessment Phase:[159]

- it takes no further action;[160]
- it commences the Investigation Phase;
- it uses alternative means of addressing the issue, such as referring the matter to another agency or conducting a market study;[161] or
- it accepts a voluntary resolution of the matter, such as accepting a person's commitment[162] to take any action or refrain from taking any action that the Commission considers appropriate to address its concerns about a possible contravention of a competition rule.

5.4.2 Investigation Phase

Investigation Phase   The Competition Commission may only conduct an investigation if it has reasonable cause to suspect that a contravention of a competition rule has taken place, is taking place or is about to take place.[163]   It considers that the test for using its information gathering powers only requires that it is satisfied, at least beyond mere speculation, that there may have been a contravention of a competition rule. It does not require evidence to a standard that, on balance, tends to suggest that a contravention has occurred.[164]   The Investigation Phase may involve the use of the Commission's powers under sections 41, 42 and 48 of the Competition Ordinance to obtain documents and information, to require a person to attend before the Commission and answer questions and to apply for a warrant to enter and search premises from the Court of First Instance respectively. The Commission may, however, seek evidence without relying on its investigation powers during the Investigation Phase. This may include inviting parties to make voluntary submissions relevant to the investigation, such as providing relevant facts and legal and economic arguments, with evidence in support of those arguments.[165]

---

[159] Guideline on Investigations, para 4.1.

[160] The Commission will notify any complainant of the outcome: Guideline on Investigations, para 4.2.

[161] Cf. Competition Ordinance, section 130(e).

[162] Cf. Competition Ordinance section 60(1).

[163] Competition Ordinance, section 39(2); Guideline on Investigations, para 5.2.

[164] Guideline on Investigations, para 5.1.

[165] Guideline on Investigations, paras 5.3-5.4. Although this lower threshold may apply to section 41 notices, it is not obvious that it is equally applicable to section 42 where the Commission is given power for the purpose of conducting an investigation to require a person to attend before the Commission to answer relevant questions relating to any matter it reasonably believes to be relevant to the investigation. The wording rather suggests that an investigation has to be on foot already, and as such the stricter test under section 39 that there need be conduct that constitutes or may constitute a

The duration of an Investigation Phase will largely depend on the nature and complexity of each matter and the level of cooperation, if any, by the parties under investigation.[166]

Powers to obtain documents and information (Section 41)   Where the Competition Commission has reasonable cause to suspect that a person has or may have possession or control of documents or information or may otherwise be able to assist it in relation to a matter that constitutes or may constitute a contravention of a competition rule, it may issue written notices pursuant to section 41 of the Competition Ordinance (section 41 notices). The Commission, accordingly, may use section 41 notices to obtain documents or specified information which relates to any matter it reasonably believes to be relevant to an investigation from any person, such as the person under investigation, their competitors, suppliers and customers or any other parties.[167] A section 41 notice will, amongst other matters:[168]

- indicate the subject matter and purpose of the investigation;
- specify or describe the documents and/or information that the Commission requires;
- provide details of time, place, manner and form in which documents and/or information must be produced; and
- set out the offences[169] that may apply if the recipient of the notice does not comply.

Documents that might be sought under section 41 notices include information recorded in any form.[170] For example, the Commission may request material such as:[171]

- draft documents;
- original documents;
- records in electronic format (and their metadata);
- correspondence; and

---

contravention of a competition rule may need to be satisfied. Similarly, a warrant to enter and search premises under section 48 would only be granted if the judge is satisfied that there are reasonable grounds to suspect that there are or are likely to be, on the premises, documents that may be relevant to an investigation by the Commission. It would appear that an investigation has to be in place in order that a warrant might be issued.

[166] Guideline on Investigations, para 5.46.
[167] Competition Ordinance, section 41(1)-(2); Guideline on Investigations, para 5.7.
[168] Competition Ordinance, section 41(3)-(4); Guideline on Investigations, para 5.8.
[169] Cf. Competition Ordinance, section 52 (failure to comply with requirement or prohibition), section 53 (destroying or falsifying information) and section 55 (providing false or misleading documents or information).
[170] Competition Ordinance, section 2(1).
[171] Guideline on Investigations, para 5.9.

- databases and the means of accessing the information contained in those databases.

Section 41 notices will often include questions or other requests to provide the Commission with information in a particular format. This may involve the creation of new documents, such as:[172]

- written responses to Commission questions set out in the section 41 notice;
- lists of customers and suppliers;
- contact details of relevant persons;
- organisational diagrams and charts; and
- data extracted in various formats.

Section 41 notices may be used at any stage of the Investigation Phase and may be issued to the same person more than once. For example, the Commission may decide to seek further information from the same person to clarify information or documents submitted under an earlier section 41 notice.[173] The Commission can also make copies of or take extracts from documents, require an explanation of the document, or question where a particular document can be found if it is not produced to the Commission.[174] The Commission's power to require the provision of information includes the power, in relation to information recorded otherwise than in legible form, to require the production of a copy of the information in a visible and legible form.[175] The Commission may also require the provision of instruction on the operation of equipment containing information stored electronically.[176] The Commission will consider any representations made by the recipient in a timely manner regarding the scope of section 41 notices.[177]

The Commission will endeavour to provide reasonable timeframes for persons to comply with a section 41 notice having regard to the nature and volume of information and documents requested. In limited circumstances, it will consider requests to extend the deadline for responding. In considering such requests, the Commission will have particular regard to evidence of efforts already made by the recipient to comply with the section 41 notice and whether providing an extension will impede the investigation.[178]

---

[172] Guideline on Investigations, para 5.10. The power accorded to the Competition Commission appears to be wider than what has been accorded to the Securities and Futures Commission (SFC) under section 183(1) of the Securities and Futures Ordinance (Cap. 571), which does not expressly permit the SFC to compel a person to provide assistance in organising data sought.

[173] Guideline on Investigations, para 5.11.

[174] Competition Ordinance, section 41(5); Guideline on Investigations, para 5.12.

[175] Competition Ordinance, section 41(6)(a).

[176] Competition Ordinance, section 41(6)(b).

[177] Guideline on Investigations, para 5.15.

[178] Guideline on Investigations, para 5.14.

Request for attendance before Competition Commission (Section 42)
Under section 42(1) of the Competition Ordinance, the Competition
Commission may require any person, by notice in writing, to appear before it,
at a specified time and place, to answer questions relating to any matter the
Commission reasonably believes to be relevant to an investigation (section 42
notices).[179] Persons with relevant evidence may include: current or former
employees, competitors, customers, distributors or suppliers of the parties
under investigation; representatives of relevant trade associations; or
complainants.[180] A section 42 notice must indicate the subject matter and
purpose of the investigation and set out the offences[181] that may apply if the
recipient of the notice does not comply.[182] Section 42 notices may be used at
any stage of the Investigation Phase and may be issued to the same person
more than once.[183]

When setting the time and place for appearance before it, the Commission
may consider a range of factors including the resources available to the person
and the urgency of the matter.[184] Any person required by the Commission to
appear may be accompanied and represented by a legal adviser admitted to
practise law in Hong Kong and, to the extent required by relevant professional
regulations or rules of conduct, holding a current Hong Kong practising
certificate.[185] If necessary, an appearance before the Commission may be
adjourned after commencement to be continued at a later date if necessary.[186]

Recordings and any transcripts made of the interview will be provided to
the person interviewed upon request when practicable. These recordings and
transcripts will be subject to the person's confidentiality obligations under the
Competition Ordinance.[187]

Warrant to enter and search premises (Section 48) The Competition
Ordinance provides the Competition Commission with search and seizure
powers. Any employee of the Commission may be appointed as an authorised
officer for these purposes.[188] Under section 48(1) of the Competition

---

[179] Competition Ordinance, section 42(1).
[180] Guideline on Investigations, para 5.16.
[181] Cf. Competition Ordinance, section 52 (failure to comply with requirement or
prohibition), section 53 (destroying or falsifying information) and section 55 (providing
false or misleading documents or information).
[182] Competition Ordinance, section 42(2).
[183] Guideline on Investigations, para 5.17. For example, the Commission may require a
person to appear before it after considering responses provided in a previous appearance
before the Commission or to ask about information obtained from other sources.
[184] Guideline on Investigations, para 5.18.
[185] Guideline on Investigations, para 5.19.
[186] Guideline on Investigations, para 5.20.
[187] Guideline on Investigations, para 5.21.
[188] Competition Ordinance, section 47.

Ordinance, a judge of the Court of First Instance may issue a warrant (section 48 warrant) authorising a person specified in the warrant, and any other persons who may be necessary to assist in the execution of the warrant, to enter and search any premises if the judge is satisfied, on application on oath by an authorised officer, that there are reasonable grounds to suspect that there are or are likely to be, on the premises, documents that may be relevant to an investigation by the Commission.[189] The premises specified in the section 48 warrant need not relate to the party under investigation. For example, the premises may belong to the investigated party's supplier or customer.[190] A section 48 warrant may further be subject to any conditions specified in it.[191] The Competition Ordinance does not require the Commission to have first used one of its other investigation powers before applying for a section 48 warrant.[192] An authorised officer executing a section 48 warrant must produce for inspection, upon request, documentary evidence of his identity and of his authorisation and the warrant.[193]

The Commission expects the types of situations where it may seek a section 48 warrant to include, without limitation, matters which involve:[194]

- secretive conduct;
- instances where it considers that documents or information relevant to its investigation may be destroyed or interfered with should the Commission seek them through other means; and/or
- circumstances where the Commission has been unsuccessful in obtaining specific or categories of documents or information (the existence of which the Commission may already be aware of through other sources) or suspects non-compliance with an earlier request for such documents and information, whether the request was voluntary or pursuant to a section 41 notice.

Powers conferred by a section 48 warrant A section 48 warrant authorizes the persons specified in it:[195]

(a) to enter and search the premises specified in the warrant;

(b) to use such force for gaining entry to the premises and for breaking open any article or thing found on the premises as is reasonable in the circumstances;

(c) to make use of such equipment as is reasonable in the circumstances;

(d) to remove by force any person or thing obstructing the execution of the warrant;

---

[189] Competition Ordinance, section 48(1); Guideline on Investigations, paras 5.22-5.23.
[190] Guideline on Investigations, para 5.24.
[191] Competition Ordinance, section 48(2).
[192] Guideline on Investigations, paras 5.26.
[193] Competition Ordinance, section 49; Guideline on Investigations, para 5.28.
[194] Guideline on Investigations, para 5.25.
[195] Competition Ordinance, section 50.

(e) to require any person on the premises to produce any document that appears to be a relevant document, in the possession or under the control of that person;

(f) to make copies of or take extracts from any document that appears to be a relevant document found on the premises or produced to a person executing the warrant;

(g) to prohibit any person found on the premises from—

    (i) altering or otherwise interfering with any document that appears to be a relevant document; or

    (ii) removing any such document from the premises or causing or permitting any other person to remove such document from the premises;

(h) to take possession of any documents found on the premises that appear to be relevant documents if—

    (i) such action appears to be necessary for preserving the documents or preventing interference with them; or

    (ii) it is not reasonably practicable to take copies of the documents on the premises;

(i) to take any other steps that appear to be necessary for the purpose mentioned in (h)(i);

(j) to take possession of any computer or other thing found on the premises that the person executing the warrant has reasonable grounds for believing will, on examination, afford evidence of a contravention of a competition rule;

(k) to require any person on the premises to give an explanation of any document appearing to be a relevant document or to state, to the best of his or her knowledge and belief, where such an explanation may be found or obtained;

(l) to require any information which is stored in electronic form and is accessible from the premises and which the person executing the warrant considers relates to any matter relevant to the investigation, to be produced in a form—

    (i) in which it is visible and legible or from which it can readily be produced in a visible and legible form; and

    (ii) in which it can be taken away.

Competition Commission practice in relation to searches Although a section 48 warrant provides authorised Competition Commission's officers with broad powers to enter specified premises, without providing any prior notice to the occupier, the officers will normally, subject to operational considerations, arrive at the specified premises during usual office hours.[196] If

---

[196] Guideline on Investigations, para 5.27.

there is no one at the premises when the authorised officers arrive, the authorised officers will take reasonable steps to inform the occupier of the intended entry and afford the occupier, or the occupier's representative, a reasonable opportunity to be present when the warrant is executed.[197]   The Commission is not required to wait for a person's legal advisers to attend the premises before commencing its search, unless specified as a condition of the warrant.   However, where parties have requested that their legal advisers be present during a search, and there is no in-house lawyer already on the premises, Commission officers will wait a reasonable time for external legal advisers to arrive.   During such time, the officers may take necessary measures to prevent tampering with evidence, such as instructing employees and other persons at the premises to move away from their workspaces, requesting that computer/IT system access or email accounts be blocked, stopping external communications and sealing offices and/or filing cabinets.   The Commission will immediately commence its search where compliance with such directions or requirements cannot be assured, or where the officers otherwise believe waiting for a legal adviser to arrive will adversely impact the efficacy of the search, or the relevant legal advisers are unable to commit to a timely arrival at the premises.[198]

During the search of the premises, the officers will search, copy and/or confiscate relevant documents and equipment and seek explanations from individuals present at the premises about any documents which may appear to be relevant.[199]   To facilitate an efficient execution of the section 48 warrant, they will request that the person in charge at the premises designate an appropriate person to be a point of contact for the officers during the search.[200] The officers may search any part of the specified premises for relevant documents and other evidence including desks, bookshelves and cabinets, and take away anything which might be or contain relevant evidence (including electronic equipment and devices such as hard drives, servers and mobile phones).   Following a review of the collected evidence, the Commission will return documents and/or equipment if it considers that these are outside the scope of the investigation, or clearly duplicate other relevant documents.[201] Evidence found during the search will be retained by the Commission for as long as necessary for the purposes of the investigation and/or any ensuing legal proceedings.   Upon request, the Commission must provide certified true copies of documents so retained to a person otherwise entitled to possession.[202]

---

[197] Guideline on Investigations, para 5.29.
[198] Guideline on Investigations, para 5.31.
[199] Guideline on Investigations, para 5.32.
[200] Guideline on Investigations, para 5.33.
[201] Guideline on Investigations, para 5.34.
[202] Competition Ordinance, sections 56-57; Guideline on Investigations, para 5.35.

Statutory declarations regarding evidence The Competition Commission will normally require persons to verify, by statutory declaration, the truth of any explanation, further particulars, answer or statement provided it.[203] If a person fails to comply with any requirement to give such a statement, the Commission may require him to state, by statutory declaration, the reasons for the failure.[204]

Legal professional privileged communications None of the Competition Commission's investigative powers under the Competition Ordinance affect any claims, rights or entitlements that may arise on the ground of legal professional privilege, save as to any requirement to disclose the name and address of a counsel's or solicitor's client.[205] The Commission has published guidance on its investigation powers and legal professional privilege.[206] This recognises that persons are not required to provide information to the Commission under section 41 or section 42 where that information is protected by a valid claim to legal professional privilege.[207] In relation to section 48 warrants, disputes may arise as to whether documents or information which Commission officials might wish to seize or copy contain information subject to privilege. Similarly, the investigated parties may assert that computers, other electronic devices or digital material which Commission staff might wish to inspect or take possession of contain privileged information. It is the Commission's policy to ensure that privilege issues arising in the context of a search will be dealt with as fairly and as expeditiously as possible, taking into account the circumstances of the case, by:

- minimising the risk of privileged material being inadvertently read by Commission staff involved in the investigation;
- ensuring that any disputed material seized during a search is properly identified, isolated and securely stored pending resolution of the dispute;
- endeavouring to ensure that disputes relating to privilege are resolved by agreement between the Commission and the investigated parties to the extent possible; and
- ensuring the prompt return of any material or information to its rightful owner as soon as it is determined that the material or information is protected by legal professional privilege.[208]

---

[203] Competition Ordinance, section 43(1); Guideline on Investigations, paras 5.36-5.37.
[204] Competition Ordinance, section 43(3).
[205] Competition Ordinance, section 58; Guideline on Investigations, para 5.38.
[206] Investigation Powers of the Competition Commission and Legal Professional Privilege, December 2015; cf. Guideline on Investigations, para 5.39.
[207] Investigation Powers and LPP, para 1.4.
[208] Investigation Powers and LPP, paras 2.1-2.3.

Where a privileged document can be separated from non-privileged material, it will not be copied. However, where there is a dispute as to the privileged status of a document or where only a part of a document is subject to privilege, the document as a whole will be placed in a container and removed.[209] The person claiming privilege must, with seven days (subject to extension where justified on grounds of voluminous documents), specify in writing its reasons for claiming legal advice privilege or litigation privilege. The Commission will then give its ruling on whether its accepts the claim to privilege, and will return any documents that it accepts are covered by privilege.[210] If a dispute remains as to whether material is subject to privilege, the Commission will confer with the claimant on the best approach to dealing with the matter with a view to resolving all outstanding privilege claims expeditiously. In this context, a process involving an independent third party lawyer may be agreed. Where the Commission and the investigated party fail to agree on resolving this dispute, the parties may apply to the court for determination of the matter.[211] These steps are designed to narrow and expedite the resolution of any disputes over privilege. However, for operational reasons, the Commission will not tolerate undue delays in resolving such disputes. In the event that a party does not substantiate its privilege claim under the procedure in a timely manner, the Commission reserves the right to give the it seven days' written notice of its intention to inspect the materials that are subject to the claim. If, upon the expiry of the seven days' notice, the party has still not substantiated its claim, the privilege claim will be deemed waived and the Commission will proceed to inspect the materials.[212]

Obligations of confidence   A person is not excused from providing any information or producing any document to the Competition Commission under its investigation powers in respect of which an obligation of confidence is owed to any other person.[213] A person who, when required to do so, provides such information or documents, in respect of which an obligation of confidence is owed to any other person, is not personally liable for that act.[214]

Self-incrimination   A person is not excused from giving any explanation or further particulars about a document, or from answering any question from the Competition Commission, on the grounds that to do so might expose the individual to certain proceedings in which the Commission may seek a pecuniary or financial penalty[215] or criminal proceedings.[216] No statement

---

[209] Investigation Powers and LPP, paras 3.1-3.3.
[210] Investigation Powers and LPP, paras 4.1-4.5.
[211] Investigation Powers and LLP, paras 5.1-5.2.
[212] Investigation Powers and LLP, paras 6.1-6.3.
[213] Competition Ordinance, section 46(1).
[214] Competition Ordinance, section 46(2); Guideline on Investigations, para 5.40.
[215] Proceedings pursuant to sections 93 and 169 of the Competition Ordinance respectively.

made under compulsion by a person in giving any explanation or further particulars about a document or in answering any question to the Commission is admissible against that individual in such proceedings unless evidence relating to the statement is adduced, or a question relating to it is asked, by that person or on that person's behalf.[217] This would suggest that derivative use of information obtained under compulsion is available, which has been held to be constitutional in *A v. The Commissioner of the Independent Commission Against Corruption.*[218]

Immunity A person who gives evidence to the Competition Commission, and any counsel, solicitor or other person who appears before the Commission, has the same privileges and immunities as the person would have if the investigation were a civil proceeding in the Court of First Instance.[219]

Sanctions for non-compliance A person who, without reasonable excuse, fails to comply with any requirement or prohibition imposed under section 41 (powers to obtain documents and information), section 42 (persons required to attend before the Commission), section 43 (statutory declaration regarding evidence) and section 50 (powers conferred by warrant) of the Competition Ordinance commits a criminal offence punishable by fines of up to HK$200,000 and imprisonment for 1 year.[220] The Competition Ordinance also creates criminal offences punishable by fines of up to HK$1 million and imprisonment for 2 years under section 53 (destroying, falsifying or concealing documents), section 54 (obstructing a search under a section 48 warrant), section 55 (providing false or misleading information) or section 128(3) (disclosing confidential information received from the Commission).[221]

5.4.3 Confidentiality and disclosure

Investigations conducted in confidence The Competition Commission will generally investigate in private to protect the interests of all persons involved and will not make disclosures except where appropriate. To this end, it will

---

[216] Any criminal proceedings, other than an offence under section 55 of the Competition Ordinance (providing false or misleading documents or information), an offence under Part V (Perjury) of the Crimes Ordinance (Cap 200) or an offence of perjury.

[217] Competition Ordinance, section 45(1)-(2); Guidelines on Investigations, paras 5.41-5.42.

[218] *A v. The Commissioner of the Independent Commission Against Corruption* (2012) 15 HKCFAR 362.

[219] Competition Ordinance, section 44(1)-(2); Guideline on Investigations, para 5.43. This includes producing any document, making any statement, giving any information, explanation or further particulars and answering any question.

[220] Competition Ordinance, section 52(1)-(2); Guideline on Investigations, para 5.44.

[221] Guideline on Investigations, para 5.45.

not normally comment on matters it is considering or investigating. The Commission's ability to investigate a matter may be impeded where the investigation is publicised or otherwise widely known. In appropriate cases, such as where an investigation is made public by another party, the Commission may acknowledge that it is reviewing a matter. To support its ability to conduct effective investigations, it will typically ask that complainants keep their complaint confidential.[222]

Handling confidential information   The Competition Ordinance, section 125, imposes a general obligation on the Competition Commission to preserve, and aid in preserving, the confidentiality of any confidential information provided to or obtained by the Commission and not to permit any other person to have access to confidential information.[223] Confidential information is:[224]

  (a) information that has been provided to or obtained by the Commission in the course of, or in connection with, the performance of its functions under the Competition Ordinance, that relates to:
    (i)   the private affairs of a natural person;
    (ii)   the commercial activities of any person that are of a confidential nature; or
    (iii) the identity of any person who has given information to the Commission;
  (b) information that has been given to the Commission on terms or in circumstances that require it to be held in confidence; or
  (c) information given to the Commission that has been identified by the person providing the information as confidential.

Disclosure of confidential information is to be regarded as made with lawful authority if made in the following circumstances:[225]

  (a) with the required consent;[226]
  (b) in the performance of any function of the Commission or in carrying into effect or doing anything authorised by the Competition Ordinance;[227]
  (c) in accordance with an order of the Competition Tribunal or any other court or in accordance with a law or a requirement made by or under a law;[228]

---

[222] Guideline on Investigations, paras 6.1-6.2.
[223] Competition Ordinance, section 125(1).
[224] Competition Ordinance, section 123(1); Guideline on Investigations, para 6.3.
[225] Competition Ordinance, section 126(1).
[226] The consent required is specified in Competition Ordinance, section 126(2).
[227] Subject to Competition Ordinance, section 126(3).
[228] The Commission will endeavour to notify and consult the person who provided the confidential information prior to making such a disclosure: Guideline on Investigations, para 6.13.

(d) in connection with judicial proceedings arising under the Competition Ordinance;

(e) for the purpose of obtaining legal advice;

(f) with a view to the bringing of, or otherwise for the purposes of, any criminal proceedings, or any investigation carried out under the laws of Hong Kong, in Hong Kong;

(g) with respect to information that has already been lawfully disclosed to the public on an earlier occasion; or

(h) by one competition authority to another.

Such disclosure is not limited to where the Competition Ordinance expressly requires the Commission to publish information, so that the Commission asserts that it may in certain circumstances disclose confidential information without the consent of relevant parties.[229]

Claiming confidentiality   Where a person wishes to identify information given to the Competition Commission as confidential information, its claims to confidentiality should be in writing, setting out the reasons why the identified information is, in the person's opinion, confidential.[230]   Where a document contains a mix of non-confidential and confidential information, persons submitting information to the Commission should identify within the document which parts of the document are confidential.   It is in the parties' interests to clearly specify the reasons for claiming confidentiality.[231]

Disclosure in performance of Competition Commission's functions   Disclosure is permitted in the performance of any function of the Competition Commission or in carrying into effect or doing anything authorised by the Competition Ordinance.[232]   For example, the Commission may need to disclose confidential information to other persons to the extent that is necessary to seek clarifications on existing evidence or to seek relevant evidence.   In deciding whether or not to disclose confidential information, the Commission, having regard to the extent to which the disclosure is necessary for the purpose sought to be achieved by the disclosure, has to pay regard to the need to exclude from disclosure as far as is practicable:[233]

- information the disclosure of which would be contrary to public interest;
- commercial information which would significantly harm the legitimate business interests of the person to whom it relates; and

---

[229]   Guideline on Investigations, para 6.4.

[230]   Competition Ordinance, section 123(2).

[231]   Guideline on Investigations, paras 6.6-6.7.

[232]   Competition Ordinance, section 126(1)(b).

[233]   Competition Ordinance, section 126(3); Guideline on Investigations, paras 6.10-6.11.

- information relating to a natural person's private affairs which may significantly harm that person.

In conducting this assessment, the Commission will usually be in a better position to evaluate the interests of the person to whom the confidential information relates where the person providing the information has, in its reasons, clearly articulated the basis for identifying the relevant information as confidential.[234]

Obligation of other parties to maintain confidentiality Where a person has received confidential information from the Competition Commission or otherwise, directly or indirectly received such information, that person is obliged to maintain the confidentiality of that information. That person must not disclose the information to any other person or permit any other person to have access to the information.[235] Failure to maintain confidentiality is an offence under section 128(3) of the Competition Ordinance. Exceptions to this obligation include where:[236]

- the Commission has consented to a disclosure;
- the information has already been lawfully disclosed to the public;
- disclosure is for the purpose of obtaining professional advice in connection with a matter arising under the Competition Ordinance;
- disclosure is made in connection with any judicial proceedings arising under the Competition Ordinance; or
- disclosure is required by, or in accordance with, any law or court order.

Use of information by the Competition Commission Subject to legal requirements to the contrary, information obtained by the Competition Commission in one matter may be used by the Competition Commission in another matter. The Commission will not normally accept information or documents provided voluntarily on any condition that seeks to limit its use of the information. Accordingly, it will not accept any such information or documents on a without prejudice or limited waiver basis unless it expressly agrees to do so in a specific circumstance.[237]

---

[234] Guideline on Investigations, para 6.12.
[235] Competition Ordinance, section 128(1); Guideline on Investigations, para 6.15.
[236] Competition Ordinance, section 128(2); Guideline on Investigations, para 6.16.
[237] Guideline on Investigations, para 6.17.

5.4.4 Outcomes of the Investigation Phase

Possible outcomes of Investigation Phase   Possible outcomes of the Investigation Phase include the following options for the Competition Commission:

- it takes no further action;
- it uses alternative means of addressing the issue, such as referring the matter to another agency or conducting a market study; or
- it accepts a voluntary resolution of the matter, such as accepting a person's commitment to take any action or refrain from taking any action that the Commission considers appropriate to address its concerns about a possible contravention of a competition rule;
- it issues a warning notice;
- it issues an infringement notice;
- it commences proceedings in the Competition Tribunal;
- it applies for a consent order before the Competition Tribunal.

No further action   Where the Competition Commission considers it unlikely that a contravention of a competition rule has occurred, it will take no further action regarding the matter.[238]   The Commission may, having regard to its resources and priorities, determine at any point of the Investigation Phase that no further action by the Commission is warranted. Where parties swiftly alter any conduct of concern in response to the Commission's enquiries, this will increase the likelihood of the Commission taking no further action. Where a complainant is involved, the Commission will notify the complainant of this outcome.[239]   A decision to take no further action at a point in time does not prevent the Commission from revisiting the issue at a later date. For example, additional evidence or a pattern of conduct may arise warranting further investigation.[240]

Section 60 commitments   At any stage the Competition Commission, pursuant to section 60 of the Competition Ordinance, may accept a commitment[241] from parties under investigation to take any action[242] or refrain from taking any action that the Commission considers appropriate to address its concerns about

---

[238] Guideline on Investigations, para 7.1.
[239] Guideline on Investigations, paras 7.5-7.6.
[240] Guideline on Investigations, para 7.7.
[241] The Commission must give notice in writing to the person who made the commitment of its decision to accept it as soon as practicable and publish the commitment in the register of commitments: Competition Ordinance, section 60(6); Guidelines on Investigations, para 7.12.
[242] This does not include making payment to the Hong Kong Government: Competition Ordinance, section 60(2).

a possible contravention of a competition rule.[243]   The commitment process may be initiated by the Commission or parties subject to a Commission investigation at any time.[244]   Procedural requirements in relation to commitments are set out in Schedule 2 to the Competition Ordinance.[245] Before accepting a commitment, the Commission must give notice of the proposed commitment in order to bring it to the attention of interested parties and it must consider any representations made to it.[246]   If the Commission accepts a commitment, it may agree not to commence an investigation and not to bring proceedings in the Competition Tribunal (or terminate the investigation or proceedings, if already commenced).[247]   Furthermore, the Commission may not commence an investigation or proceedings in relation to any alleged contravention of a competition rule in so far as the investigation or proceedings relate to matters that are addressed by the commitment.[248]   To avoid doubt, the Commission may still commence an investigation or bring or continue proceedings in the Competition Tribunal after accepting a commitment in relation to matters that are not addressed by, or persons who are not subject to, the commitment.[249]   A register of commitments is maintained by the Commission.[250]

The Commission may withdraw its acceptance of a commitment,[251] with effect from the date specified in a written notice[252] to the person making the commitment, if it has reasonable grounds:[253]

- for believing that there has been a material change of circumstances since the commitment was accepted;
- for suspecting a failure to comply with the commitment; or
- for suspecting that the commitment was based on information that was incomplete, false or misleading in a material particular.

In the event that the Commission withdraws an acceptance of a commitment, it may conduct a new investigation or, no more than two years later, begin

---

[243] Competition Ordinance, section 60(1).

[244] Guidelines on Investigations, para 7.8.

[245] Competition Ordinance, section 65.

[246] Competition Ordinance, Schedule 2, section 2.

[247] Competition Ordinance, section 60(3); Guidelines on Investigations, para 7.9.

[248] Competition Ordinance, section 60(4).

[249] Competition Ordinance, section 60(5).

[250] Competition Ordinance, section 64.

[251] Before withdrawing its acceptance of a commitment, the Commission must give notice of the proposed withdrawal so as to allow representations to be made by those likely to be affected by the withdrawal: Competition Ordinance, Schedule 2, section 7.

[252] Where the commitment had been accepted by the Commission on the basis of incomplete, false or misleading information, withdrawal may take effect from an earlier date: Competition Ordinance, section 61(2).

[253] Competition Ordinance, section 61(1); Guidelines on Investigations, para 7.10.

proceedings in the Competition Tribunal and the person who gave the commitment is no longer bound by it.[254]

At any time after the Commission has accepted a commitment, it may accept a variation of the commitment or a new commitment in substitute for it if it is satisfied that the variation or new commitment addresses its concerns about a possible contravention of a competition rule.[255] The Commission may release any person from a commitment if it requested to do so[256] by that person or it has reasonable grounds for believing that its concerns about a possible contravention of the competition rule no longer arises.[257]

If a person fails to comply with a commitment, the Commission may seek to enforce the commitment in the Tribunal under section 63 of the Competition Ordinance, which may ensue in an order that the person take such action or refrain from taking such action as specified in the Commitment, disgorgement of profit made or loss avoided by non-compliance to the Government, compensation of damages to any person and any other order the Tribunal considers appropriate.

Issuance of a warning notice Where the Competition Commission has reasonable cause to believe that there has been a contravention of the First Conduct Rule which does not involve Serious Anti-Competitive Conduct, section 82(1) of the Competition Ordinance provides that it must issue a Warning Notice before commencing proceedings in the Competition Tribunal. The Warning Notice provides parties under investigation with an opportunity to cease the conduct within a specified period.[258] A Warning Notice must set out the alleged contravening conduct, the undertaking(s) involved, the evidence relied upon by the Commission and indicate the manner in which the contravening undertaking may cease the contravening conduct.[259] In determining the warning period, the Commission must have regard to the amount of time which the undertaking is likely to require to cease the contravening conduct.[260] If parties continue to engage or repeat the contravening conduct after the expiry of the warning period, the Commission may without further notice commence proceedings in the Tribunal.[261] Such proceedings may not be brought in respect of any period that precedes the

---

[254] Competition Ordinance, section 61(3)-(4); Guideline on Investigations, para 7.11.
[255] Competition Ordinance, section 62(1) and Schedule 7, section 2..
[256] Before releasing a person from a commitment, the Commission must give notice of the proposed withdrawal so as to allow representations to be made by those likely to be affected by the proposed release: Competition Ordinance, Schedule 2, section 12.
[257] Competition Ordinance, section 62(2).
[258] Competition Ordinance, section 82(1); Guideline on Investigations, para 7.14.
[259] Competition Ordinance, section 82(2); Guideline on Investigations, para 7.15.
[260] Competition Ordinance, section 82(3).
[261] Competition Ordinance, section 82(4); Guideline on Investigations, para 7.15.

warning period.[262] Warning Notices will be published on the Commission's website.[263]

Issuance of an infringement notice Where the Competition Commission has reasonable cause to believe that there has been a contravention of the First Conduct Rule involving Serious Anti-Competitive Conduct or the Second Conduct Rule and it has not yet brought proceedings in the Competition Tribunal, it may issue an Infringement Notice instead of bringing proceedings in the Competition Tribunal, on condition that the person makes a commitment (Infringement Notice Commitment) to comply with the requirements of the Infringement Notice.[264] The Commission is not required, however, to issue an Infringement Notice before commencing proceedings in the Competition Tribunal or accepting a section 60 commitment.[265]

An Infringement Notice must:[266]

(a) identify the conduct rule alleged to have been contravened;

(b) describe the conduct that is alleged to contravene that conduct rule;

(c) identify the person whose conduct is alleged to constitute the contravention;

(d) identify the evidence or other materials that the Commission relies on in support of its allegations;

(e) specify the requirements to be complied with by the person to whom the notice is addressed;

(f) specify both the notification period and the compliance period;

(g) inform the person that it is not obliged to make the commitment.

The requirements of an Infringement Notice may include, but are not limited to, requirements to refrain from any specified conduct, or to take specified action, that the Commission considers appropriate and to admit to a contravention of the relevant conduct rule.[267] A person is not obliged to make a commitment to comply with the requirements of an Infringement Notice. However, if the person does not make the commitment within the compliance period, the Commission may bring proceedings against that person in the Tribunal in relation to the alleged contravention of the conduct rule.[268]

Before issuing an Infringement Notice, the Commission must give the person concerned a pre-notice setting out a draft of the intended Infringement Notice and giving the person an opportunity to make representations, which the Commission must consider.[269] If a person makes a representation, evidence or

---

[262] Competition Ordinance, section 82(5).
[263] Guideline on Investigations, para 7.16.
[264] Competition Ordinance, section 67(1)-(2); Guideline on Investigations, para 7.17.
[265] Guideline on Investigations, para 7.19.
[266] Competition Ordinance, section 69.
[267] Competition Ordinance, section 67(3).
[268] Competition Ordinance, section 68.
[269] Competition Ordinance, section 70(1)-(2).

information provided to the Commission in the representation may not be used against that person. Moreover, no person may obtain discovery of that information or evidence against the Commission in any proceedings, other than proceedings against that person for an offence of providing false information.[270] If, after considering the representation, the Commission decides not to proceed to issue an Infringement Notice, it must inform the person concerned.[271]

If an Infringement Notice has been issued to any person, no proceedings may be brought by the Commission against that person in respect of the alleged contravention if the compliance period has not expired and the Infringement Notice has not been withdrawn. Moreover, the Commission may not publish the Infringement Notice before the expiry of its compliance period, or if no commitment is to comply with the requirements of the notice is received within the compliance period or if the Infringement Notice has been withdrawn by the Commission.[272] The Commission may at any time before the expiry of the compliance period withdraw the Infringement Notice with effect from a specified date.[273] It may also extend the compliance period if it considers there is a good reason for doing so.[274] Once an Infringement Notice Commitment has been accepted, the Commission may publish the Infringement Notice.[275]

Where an Infringement Notice Commitment is made within the compliance period, the Commission may not bring proceedings in the Tribunal in respect of the alleged contravention specified in the Infringement Notice.[276] However, where the Commission has reasonable grounds for suspecting that a person has failed to comply with one or more requirements of an Infringement Notice, the Commission may bring proceedings in the Tribunal.[277]

Commencement of proceedings in the Competition Tribunal Where the Competition Commission has reasonable cause to believe that a person has contravened a competition rule, or been involved in such a contravention, the Commission may initiate proceedings before the Competition Tribunal under sections 92, 94, 99 and/or 101 of the Competition Ordinance to seek appropriate orders and sanctions[278] including, where relevant, interim orders

---

[270] Competition Ordinance, section 70(3).
[271] Competition Ordinance, section 71.
[272] Competition Ordinance, section 72.
[273] Competition Ordinance, section 73.
[274] Competition Ordinance, section 74.
[275] Competition Ordinance, section 78.
[276] Competition Ordinance, section 75. Commitments must be registered by the Commission in the Register of Commitments: section 77.
[277] Competition Ordinance, section 76; Guideline on Investigations, para 7.18.
[278] Sections 93, 96 and 101 and Schedules 3 and 4 of the Competition Ordinance set down the orders that may be made by the Tribunal in relation to contraventions of the Competition Rules.

under sections 95 and 98. Proceedings may be taken against persons who aided and abetted, counselled or procured any other person to contravene a competition rule, induced or attempted to induce another person to contravene a competition rule, were in any way knowingly concerned in or party to a contravention or conspired with another to contravene a competition rule.[279]

The Commission must issue a Warning Notice before applying to the Tribunal where there is suspected contravention of the First Conduct Rule that does not involve Serious Anti-Competitive Conduct. In all other cases prior to commencing proceedings in the Competition Tribunal, the Commission will usually contact parties to advise them of its concerns and/or to provide parties with an opportunity to address those concerns.[280] If proceedings are commenced in the Competition Tribunal, the Commission will issue a press release as soon as practicable after commencing proceedings.[281]

Applying for consent order Even where parties wish to resolve the Competition Commission's concerns, these may in some cases only be satisfactorily addressed by an order made by the Competition Tribunal upon the consent of the Commission and the parties. Subject to the Tribunal's determination, a consent order may provide for a declaration that a person has contravened a Competition Rule, the imposition of a pecuniary penalty, a disqualification order or any other order that may be made by the Tribunal under the Competition Ordinance.[282]

Referral to a Government agency At any stage, the Competition Commission may consider it appropriate to refer a complaint to a Government agency. In such cases, it will provide an explanation of this outcome to the complainant in writing.[283]

Conducting a market study In addition to investigating suspected contraventions of the Competition Rules, the Competition Commission may conduct market studies into cases that affect competition in markets in Hong Kong.[284] Although an investigation is not a necessary precursor for the Commission to conduct a market study, evidence gathered by the Commission during the Initial Assessment or Investigation Phase into particular conduct may lead to a market study being conducted into particular practices or certain industries.[285]

---

[279] Competition Ordinance, section 91; Guideline on Investigations, para 7.20.
[280] Guideline on Investigations, para 7.21.
[281] Guideline on Investigations, para 7.22.
[282] Guideline on Investigations, para 7.23.
[283] Guideline on Investigations, para 7.24.
[284] Competition Ordinance, section 130(e).
[285] Guideline on Investigations, para 7.25.

5.5 LENIENCY

Introduction   Section 80 of the Competition Ordinance provides that the Competition Commission may make a leniency agreement with a person that it will not bring or continue proceedings in the Competition Tribunal for pecuniary penalty in respect of an alleged contravention of a conduct rule in exchange for that person's cooperation in an investigation or in proceedings under the Ordinance. The Commission considers that, given that cartels are economically harmful and difficult to detect, it is in the public interest that leniency should be accorded to an undertaking which is willing to terminate its participation in cartel conduct, report that conduct to the Commission and cooperate, at that undertaking's own cost, in the bringing of proceedings against other parties to the cartel.[286]   In November 2015, the Commission issued its Leniency Policy[287] for undertaking engaged in cartel conduct. This policy is designed to provide a strong and transparent incentive for a cartel member to stop its cartel conduct and to report the cartel to the Commission. Since this policy provides that leniency is available only for the first cartel member who reports the cartel conduct to the Commission and meets all the requirements for receiving leniency, there is a strong incentive for a cartel member to be the first undertaking to apply for leniency. By increasing the risk and cost of participating in a cartel, the policy is intended to deter the formation of cartels that would otherwise harm competition in Hong Kong.[288] The Leniency Policy does not preclude the Commission from entering into a leniency agreement with an undertaking with respect to an alleged contravention of a Conduct Rule which is not covered by the policy.[289]

---

[286] Leniency Policy, paras 1.1-1.2.

[287] Leniency Policy for Undertakings Engaged in Cartel Conduct, November 2015. A template for a leniency agreement for cartel conduct is attached to the Leniency Policy as Annex A.

[288] Leniency Policy, paras 1.3-1.5.

[289] The Leniency Policy does not apply to leniency agreements between the Commission and persons who are not undertakings. The Commission will consider case by case whether it is appropriate to exercise its enforcement discretion towards such persons. Where, however, an undertaking enters into a leniency agreement under the Leniency Policy, the leniency ordinarily extends to any current officer or employee of the undertaking where the relevant individuals provide complete, truthful and continuous cooperation with the Commission throughout its investigation and any ensuing proceedings. The leniency will also extend under the same conditions to any former officer or employee and any current or former agents of the undertaking specifically named in the leniency agreement. Where the undertaking is a partnership, leniency will ordinarily extend to any partner in the partnership and any employee of the partnership: Leniency Policy, para 2.2.

Cartel conduct under the Leniency Policy For the purposes of the Leniency Policy, cartel conduct refers to agreements and concerted practices among undertakings that are, or otherwise would be if not for the cartel conduct, in competition with each other, that seek to do one or any combination of the following activities, which have as their object preventing, restricting or distorting competition in Hong Kong:[290]

- price fixing;
- market sharing;
- output restriction; or
- bid rigging.

Application for leniency Since, under the Leniency Policy, the Competition Commission provides leniency only to the first successful applicant, it uses a marker system to establish a queue in order of the date and time the Commission is contacted with respect to the cartel conduct for which leniency is sought. A potential applicant for leniency, or its legal representative, may contact the Commission to ascertain if a marker is available for particular cartel conduct.[291] To obtain a marker, a caller must provide sufficient information to identify the conduct for which leniency is sought in order to enable the Commission to assess the applicant's place in the queue in relation to that specific cartel. This information includes, as a minimum, the identity of the undertaking applying for the marker; information on the nature of the cartel (such as the product(s) and/or service(s) involved), the main participants in the cartel conduct and the caller's contact details. If these conditions are satisfied, a marker which identifies the time and date of the call will be given to applicant.[292]

On the basis of the information provided when applying for a marker, the Commission will make a preliminary determination whether the reported conduct is cartel conduct and whether leniency is available. Leniency may be available even if the Commission has already begun an investigation, although, absent exceptional circumstances, leniency will not be available under this policy if the Commission has already decided to issue an Infringement Notice or to make an application to the Competition Tribunal in respect of the cartel conduct reported by the undertaking. If the Commission determines that leniency is available, it will notify the undertaking with the highest ranking

---

[290] Leniency Policy, para 2.4.

[291] Leniency Policy, paras 2.6-2.7. A request for a marker may only be made by using the Leniency Hotline at +852 3996 8010. Such enquiries may be made on an anonymous basis. A marker will not, however, be granted on the basis of anonymous enquiries.

[292] Leniency Policy, paras 2.8-2.11. The Commission may issue one or more markers with respect to a specific cartel. In this context, all markers are ranked in descending order of the time and date of the call where the information was provided to the Commission enabling it to grant a marker. As a result, a marker queue is created for each reported cartel.

marker that it may make an application for leniency by a specified date and time.[293] Before the applicant submits its application, it will be asked to agree to a non-disclosure agreement with the Commission which provides that the applicant will keep confidential the fact that it is submitting an application for leniency and the information provided or that will be provided, except as required by law or otherwise agreed by the Commission. This shall not restrict applicants from disclosing information to competition authorities in other jurisdictions or for the purposes of obtaining legal advice.

Undertakings who are not invited to apply for leniency will be informed that they are not currently eligible to apply for leniency under this policy.[294]

Making the leniency application through a proffer The undertaking invited to apply for leniency is asked to provide a detailed description of the cartel, the entities involved, the role of the applicant, a timeline of the conduct and the evidence the leniency applicant can provide in respect of the cartel conduct. This is commonly referred to as a proffer. The proffer may be made in hypothetical terms and through a legal representative on a without prejudice basis. The proffer should include an explanation of how the cartel conduct affects or relates to competition in Hong Kong to establish a jurisdictional nexus and provide an estimate of the value/volume of sales affected by the cartel in Hong Kong.[295] It may be made in hypothetical terms and through a legal representative on a without prejudice basis. It can be made orally or in writing.[296]

The Commission will invite the undertaking to submit an application by completing its proffer within a specified period, ordinarily within thirty calendar days. Should the undertaking fail to complete its proffer within this timeframe, or any extension to it as might be agreed by the Commission, its marker will automatically lapse.[297] In that event, the next undertaking in the marker queue will be invited by the Commission to make an application for leniency.[298] After considering the proffer, the Commission may ask the applicant to provide access to some evidence in support of the proffer such as documentary evidence (including pre-existing documents relating to the cartel)

---

[293] Leniency Policy, paras 2.12-2.14.

[294] Leniency Policy, para 2.17. Such undertakings may, however, consider cooperating with the Commission.

[295] Leniency Policy, para 2.18.

[296] Leniency Policy, para 2.22.

[297] The Commission will consider requests for a time extension, by taking into account evidence of efforts already made by the applicant to meet the original deadline and the impact of the extension, if granted, on the investigation.

[298] Leniency Policy, para 2.19.

or making available witnesses to be interviewed by the Commission.[299] Based on the proffer and any additional information requested and provided by the applicant, the Commission will determine whether to make an offer to enter into a leniency agreement. Such an offer will be made where the Commission concludes that the applicant has demonstrated its capacity to provide full and truthful cooperation and the requirements of this policy are fully satisfied.[300]

Information provided by a party at the proffer stage will be returned to the party concerned where a leniency agreement is not entered into. The Competition Commission reserves its ability to subsequently request for the same information pursuant to section 41 of the Competition Ordinance or to otherwise use its powers under the Ordinance to obtain the information.[301]

Offer to enter into a leniency agreement If the applicant meets the conditions for leniency under the Leniency Policy, it will be asked by the Competition Commission to sign a leniency agreement. The leniency agreement submitted to the applicant will require the applicant to confirm that:[302]

(a) it has provided and will continue to provide full and truthful disclosure to the Commission;

(b) it has not coerced other parties to engage in the cartel conduct;

(c) it has, absent a consent from the Commission, taken prompt and effective action to terminate its involvement in the cartel;

(d) it will keep confidential all aspects of the leniency application and the leniency process unless the Commission's prior consent has been given or the disclosure of information is required by law;

(e) it will provide continuing cooperation, at its own cost, to the Commission including in proceedings against other undertakings that engaged in the cartel conduct or against other persons involved in the cartel conduct;

(f) it will, to the satisfaction of the Commission, agree to and sign a statement of agreed facts admitting to its participation in the cartel on the basis of which the Competition Tribunal may be asked jointly by the Commission and the applicant to make an order under section 94 of the Competition Ordinance declaring that the applicant has contravened the First Conduct Rule by engaging in the cartel; and

---

[299] Leniency Policy, para 2.20. Information of this kind provided to the Commission during the proffer stage will not be used as evidence in proceedings for a finding of a contravention of the First Conduct Rule against the applicant or any other person.

[300] Leniency Policy, para 2.21.

[301] Leniency Policy, para 2.24.

[302] Leniency Policy, para 2.26.

(g) it is prepared to continue with, or adopt and implement, at its own cost, an effective corporate compliance programme to the satisfaction of the Commission.

Leniency agreement The leniency agreement must be executed by an officer of the undertaking. Execution of the agreement by an external legal advisor on behalf of the undertaking will not be accepted.[303] Once an undertaking has entered into a leniency agreement with the Commission, it is required to provide the Commission with all non-privileged information and evidence in respect of the cartel conduct without delay.[304] The Commission is not permitted to commence proceedings in the Competition Tribunal for a pecuniary penalty against the undertaking that has contravened the First Conduct Rule or other persons covered by the agreement. The Commission will also commit not to commence any other proceedings against the undertaking other than proceedings for an order under section 94 of the Competition Ordinance declaring that, as a member of the cartel, it has contravened the First Conduct Rule.[305]

Terminating the leniency agreement Under section 81 of the Competition Ordinance, the Competition Commission may terminate a leniency agreement *inter alia* where it has reasonable grounds to suspect that the information on which it based its decision to make the agreement was incomplete, false or misleading in a material particular or where the Commission is satisfied that the other party to the agreement has failed to comply with the terms of the agreement. Where the Commission is of the view that it may terminate a leniency agreement, it will orally inform the party to the agreement of its concerns and give a period of seven days for the party to take the necessary steps to remedy the situation. If the Commission's concerns remain after that period, it will proceed to give notice in writing as to the date and reasons for termination, and to consider representation about the proposed termination to be made to it.[306]

Where a leniency agreement is terminated, the Commission may at its discretion commence proceedings against the undertaking and/or any persons previously covered by the leniency agreement, including proceedings in the Competition Tribunal seeking a pecuniary penalty. Information provided by an undertaking to the Commission pursuant to a leniency agreement which has been terminated may be retained by the Commission and used as evidence

---

[303] Leniency Policy, para 2.29.
[304] Witnesses will also be interviewed by the Commission and can be called upon to provide evidence before the Competition Tribunal in due course.
[305] Leniency Policy, paras 2.27-2.28.
[306] Leniency Policy, paras 3.1-3.2. Cf. Competition Ordinance, section 81(2)-(5).

against that undertaking and other persons involved in the cartel.[307] However, the Commission may also exercise its enforcement discretion not to commence proceedings in the Tribunal against officers, employees and agents of the undertaking whom previously benefited from the protection of the leniency agreement in return for the on-going cooperation of those persons with the Commission.[308] The Commission will consider offering the next qualifying highest marker holder the option of making a leniency application to enter a leniency agreement.[309]

Undertakings which do not qualify for leniency Undertakings holding a marker but which currently which do not qualify for leniency will be informed of that status. Undertakings which do not qualify for leniency, but which have engaged in cartel conduct, may wish nonetheless to cooperate, at their own cost, with the Commission in its investigation and proceedings before the Competition Tribunal. The Commission will rely on its enforcement discretion regarding undertakings which cooperate with it. The exercise of the Commission's enforcement discretion towards undertakings which have engaged in or been involved in cartel conduct but which do not qualify for leniency may take various forms. In particular, to the extent permitted by law, the Commission will consider a lower level of enforcement action in respect of these undertakings, including recommending to the Competition Tribunal a reduced pecuniary penalty or the making of an appropriate order. The Commission may consider making joint submissions to the Competition Tribunal with the cooperating undertaking on the pecuniary penalty that might be imposed.[310] The Commission will consider a range of factors in assessing the extent and value of the cooperation provided by an undertaking who has engaged in cartel conduct, including whether the undertaking:[311]

(a) approached the Commission in a timely manner seeking to cooperate;
(b) provided significant evidence regarding the cartel conduct;
(c) provided full and truthful disclosure, and cooperated fully and expeditiously on a continuing basis throughout the Commission's investigation and any related court proceedings;
(d) coerced any other person to participate in the cartel; and
(e) acted in good faith in dealings with the Commission.

---

[307] Leniency Policy, paras 3.3-3.4.
[308] Leniency Policy, para 3.6.
[309] Leniency Policy, para 3.5.
[310] Leniency Policy, paras 4.2-4.3.
[311] Leniency Policy, paras 4.4-4.5. Notwithstanding the penalty sought or recommended by the Commission, it is ultimately for the Competition Tribunal or other courts to decide whether a pecuniary penalty is appropriate in the circumstances, and if so, the level of such penalty to be imposed.

Confidentiality and non-disclosure To support the Commission's ability to conduct effective investigations, the leniency applicant is required to keep confidential the fact of the investigation, its application for leniency (including any non-public information received by the applicant from the Commission in that context) and the terms of any leniency agreement entered into with the Commission, unless the Commission's prior consent has been given or the disclosure of the information is required by law. The confidentiality and non-disclosure commitment is on-going throughout an investigation and in any subsequent Tribunal or other court proceedings. If a leniency applicant breaches its confidentiality and non-disclosure commitments, the applicant will cease to be eligible for leniency under the Leniency Policy.[312]

Sections 125 and 126 of the Competition Ordinance impose a general obligation on the Commission to preserve the confidentiality of any confidential information provided to it, subject to specified exceptions where the Commission may disclose confidential information with lawful authority. The Competition Commission will use its best endeavours to protect leniency material, i.e.[313]

(a) any confidential information provided to the Commission by a leniency applicant for the purpose of making a leniency application and/or pursuant to a leniency agreement; and

(b) the Commission's records of the leniency application process, including the leniency agreement.

Subject to the use of information by the Commission in Competition Tribunal or other court proceedings, it is the Competition Commission's policy not to release leniency material and to firmly resist, on public interest or other applicable grounds, requests for leniency material, including the fact that leniency has been sought or is being sought, where such requests are made, for example, in connection with private civil proceedings in Hong Kong or in other jurisdictions unless:[314]

(a) it is compelled to make a disclosure by an order of the Competition Tribunal or any other court, by law or any requirement made by or under a law;

(b) it has the consent of the leniency applicant to disclose the material;

(c) the relevant information or document is already in the public domain; or

(d) the Commission, after entering a leniency agreement, has terminated the leniency agreement under section 81 of the Competition Ordinance.

If a third party makes an application in whatever form seeking to compel the Commission to disclose leniency material, the Commission will advise the

---

[312] Leniency Policy, paras 5.1-5.4.
[313] Leniency Policy, para 5.6.
[314] Leniency Policy, para 5.7.

leniency applicant of that application as soon as practicable, and vice versa if the request was made of the leniency applicant.[315]

Cooperation in cross-border cartel investigations Where a cartel operates in multiple jurisdictions, authorities in these jurisdictions may cooperate with each other when conducting their respective cartel investigations. Undertakings who are cooperating with the Commission, either as a party to a leniency agreement or otherwise, will be expected to provide the Commission with details of the other jurisdictions where they have sought immunity/leniency and an indication of the on-going status of their application in those jurisdictions. In appropriate cases, the Commission may require a leniency applicant to authorise it to exchange confidential information with authorities in another jurisdiction. Undertakings who are cooperating with the Competition Commission will be expected to provide the Commission with details of the other jurisdictions where they have sought immunity/leniency and an indication of the on-going status of their application in those jurisdictions.[316]

No further action taken in respect of a cartel investigation If the Commission decides not to pursue further a matter which is the subject of a marker or leniency application, it will advise the leniency applicant of this outcome.[317]

5.6 PROCEDURES AND ENFORCEMENT IN MERGER CASES

Investigations into mergers by the Competition Commission There is no requirement to notify the Competition Commission of a merger falling within the Merger Rule.[318] Nevertheless, the Commission will keep itself informed about merger activities for example by monitoring the media and/or through information or complaints from third parties, such as competitors, to bring transactions to its attention.[319] Pursuant to section 39 of the Competition Ordinance, the Commission may conduct an investigation into any conduct that constitutes or may constitute a contravention of a competition rule, including the Merger Rule.[320] However, the Commission may only commence an investigation of a completed merger within thirty days after the day on which it first became aware, or ought to have become aware, that the merger has taken

---

[315] Leniency Policy, para 5.8.
[316] Leniency Policy, paras 6.1-6.3.
[317] Leniency Policy, para 7.1.
[318] Guideline on the Merger Rule, para 1.3.
[319] Guideline on the Merger Rule, para 5.1.
[320] Competition Ordinance, section 39(1).

place.[321] If the Commission, after carrying out an investigation, has reasonable cause to believe that a merger contravenes the Merger Rule, it may, within six months after the day on which the merger was completed or it became aware of the merger (whichever is the later), bring proceedings in the Competition Tribunal seeking orders to unwind the merger in relation to a completed merger.[322] In relation to an anticipated merger, the Competition Commission may also bring proceedings in the Competition Tribunal seeking to stop the merger.[323]

It may be in the interest of the parties to a merger to contact the Commission at an early stage to understand whether it has any concerns about a proposed transaction. Such contacts in advance may enable the parties to identify any potential competition concerns and to address the issues in good time, as well as to minimise the risk that proceedings are brought by the Commission before the Tribunal. Parties are therefore encouraged to contact the Commission at the earliest opportunity to discuss a proposed merger that falls within the Merger Rule, where they may seek the Commission's informal advice on the transaction. Parties will proceed at their own risk where they choose not to notify the Commission of a proposed merger in advance.[324]

During an investigation, the Commission may in appropriate circumstances make use of the investigation powers conferred under the Ordinance to obtain evidence from the relevant parties. The Commission may also seek representations from the parties to a merger or an anticipated merger, and/or from relevant third parties, conduct market inquiries which could include consulting competitors of the merging parties, suppliers, customers, industry associations and consumer groups and consider their views in so far as they are relevant, and carry out independent research, for example to help assess the degree of competition in the relevant market.[325] If, after investigation, the Commission considers that there is no reasonable cause to believe that the merger or anticipated merger contravenes or is likely to contravene the Merger Rule, no proceedings will be brought and the Commission will take no further action. The Commission will in general follow the Guideline on Investigations, to the extent it is applicable, in conducting investigations.[326]

Voluntary notification of a proposed merger for informal advice   The Competition Commission is willing to provide informal advice on a proposed merger on a confidential basis. Such informal advice, obtained without the

---

[321] Competition Ordinance, Schedule 7, section 7(1); Guideline on the Merger Rule, para 5.25. The Commission is to be taken to have become aware that a merger has taken place if it has been notified of that fact by one of the parties to the merger: section 7(2).
[322] Competition Ordinance, sections 99 and 100.
[323] Competition Ordinance, section 97.
[324] Guideline on the Merger Rule, para 5.3.
[325] Guideline on the Merger Rule, para 5.26.
[326] Guideline on the Merger Rule, paras 5.27-5.28.

benefit of third party views, would simply be a preliminary view of the Commission, which is not binding on it in any way, as to whether the proposed merger is likely to raise competition concerns. The advice is confidential to the party requesting it and the Commission requests the party concerned (and its advisers) to agree not to publish the advice or to disclose it in any other way without the Commission's prior consent, whether or not the proposed merger has been made public or is completed.[327]

There is no timetable for providing informal advice, although the Commission states that it will try to deal with requests in an efficient and timely manner and within the parties' requested time frame where that is possible.[328] Even where the parties consider that a merger transaction may fall within a safe harbour threshold, the Commission emphasises that meeting one or both of the safe harbour thresholds does not necessarily mean that the proposed transaction does not give rise to competition concerns, so that it may still commence an investigation in appropriate circumstances.[329] Parties considering making an application for informal advice are encouraged to contact the Commission at an early opportunity to discuss the content, timing and scope of information that they may be required to provide. While the Commission does not wish to be entirely prescriptive as to what information it would require in this regard, it would expect parties to provide some evidence that either the heads of agreement, term sheet, or sale and purchase agreement are in place. Parties may make reference to the type of information listed in Form M[330] to the extent applicable although the Commission may require additional information as necessary to enable it to conduct a review of the proposed merger.[331]

After reviewing the information provided, the Commission will advise the parties requesting the advice whether the proposed merger is likely to give rise to concerns under the Merger Rule, on a non-binding and confidential basis. In the event that the Commission is of the view that the proposed merger may be likely to give rise to concerns under the Merger Rule, the Commission may commence an investigation if the parties intend to proceed with the merger nonetheless. The parties may wish to explore possibilities of offering Commitments to the Commission in return for the Commission not taking enforcement actions or assess whether there are justifiable circumstances for them to apply for a decision from the Commission that the merger is excluded from the Merger Rule.[332]

---

[327] Guideline on the Merger Rule, para 5.4.
[328] Guideline on the Merger Rule, para 5.5.
[329] Guideline on the Merger Rule, para 5.6.
[330] Available on the Communications Authority's website (www.coms-auth.hk).
[331] Guideline on the Merger Rule, paras 5.6-5.7.
[332] Guideline on the Merger Rule, para 5.8.

Use of information provided to the Commission   Information provided voluntarily to the Commission by parties seeking informal advice on a proposed merger or approaching the Commission for other purposes (such as for exploring possibilities of commitments or applying for a decision from the Commission that the merger is excluded from the Merger Rule), including information protected by legal professional privilege, will not be accepted by the Commission on a without prejudice basis or otherwise on terms that its use is limited for the sole purpose of seeking an informal advice (or such other purposes as specified by the parties).   The Commission stipulates that it can use any information so received, with or without notice to interested parties, for other purposes under the Competition Ordinance.   This includes for the purposes of considering whether a contravention under the Ordinance has occurred and/or with a view to enforcement where there has been a contravention.   As a general matter, parties to a merger are encouraged by the Commission to seek legal advice before approaching the Commission seeking an informal advice on a proposed merger or for other purposes.[333]

Acceptance of commitments   Pursuant to section 60 of the Competition Ordinance, the Competition Commission may accept from a person a commitment to take any action or refrain from taking action that it considers appropriate to address its concerns about a possible contravention of, inter alia, the Merger Rule, in return for the Commission's agreement not to commence an investigation or bring proceedings in the Competition Tribunal, or to terminate any investigation or proceedings that has been commenced.[334]   This provides an opportunity to the parties to a merger to offer remedies to address the competition concerns that the Commission may identify in relation to it, in return for the Commission not taking, or ceasing, enforcement actions against them.   Such circumstances may arise, for example, where parties to a proposed merger have notified the transaction to the Commission for an informal advice and the Commission is of the view that the proposed merger raises certain competition concerns and intends to take further action were the proposed merger to proceed.[335]

The remedies offered by the parties to a merger or proposed merger as commitments should be able to eliminate or avoid the effect of substantially lessening competition in a relevant market that is, or is likely to be, brought about by the merger or proposed merger.   The Commission will consider accepting both structural and behavioural remedies.   In general, structural remedies will be preferred by the Commission as they are more able to deal with the competition concerns identified at source, by re-establishing the structure of the market expected in the absence of the merger and therefore to

---

[333] Guideline on the Merger Rule, paras 5.32-5.33.
[334] Competition Ordinance, section 60; Guideline on the Merger Rule, para 5.9.
[335] Guideline on the Merger Rule, para 5.10.

restore the process of rivalry. In addition, structural remedies do not generally require ongoing monitoring activity. Structural remedies could include divestment of part of the merged business through the disposal of assets or shares. Typically this might involve an overlapping business. The Commission would require the disposal to be made within a specified time limit. Behavioural remedies are less likely to address competition concerns arising from a merger or a proposed merger as comprehensively as structural remedies. In appropriate cases, behavioural remedies may be accepted where the Commission wishes to ensure that the merged entity does not behave in an anti-competitive way after the merger. For example, the parties may be required not to undertake a particular course of conduct made possible by the merger.[336]

Before accepting a commitment, the Commission must give notice of the proposed commitment to those that are likely to be affected by the merger and the commitment, allow at least a period of 15 days for representations to be submitted, and consider any representations that are made.[337]

Decision that a merger is excluded Parties to a merger or proposed merger may apply to the Competition Commission for a decision, subject to payment of a fee, as to whether or not the merger is, or the proposed merger would if completed be:[338]

(a) excluded from the application of the Merger Rule by or as a result of section 8 of Schedule 7, (i.e. if the economic efficiencies that arise or may arise from the merger outweigh the adverse effects caused by any lessening of competition); or

(b) excluded from the application of Schedule 7 by virtue of section 3 (application to statutory bodies) or section 4 (application to specified persons and persons engaged in specified activities) of the Competition Ordinance.

The Commission is only required to consider such an application if:[339]

(a) the application poses novel or unresolved questions of wider importance or public interest in relation to the application of exclusions under the Ordinance;

(b) the application raises a question of an exclusion under the Ordinance for which there is no clarification in existing case law or decisions of the Commission; and

(c) it is possible to make a decision on the basis of the information provided.

---

[336] Guideline on the Merger Rule, paras 5.11-5.14.
[337] Competition Ordinance, Schedule 2; Guideline on the Merger Rule, para 5.15.
[338] Competition Ordinance, Schedule 7, section 11(1)-(2). Any party who would like to apply for a decision should complete Form M: Guideline on the Merger Rule, para 5.20.
[339] Competition Ordinance, Schedule 7, section 11(3).

The Commission is not required to consider an application for a decision if the application concerns hypothetical questions or conduct.[340]

Before deciding on an application for a decision the Commission, in order to bring the application to the attention of those the Commission considers likely to be affected by the decision, must publish a notice of the application and consider any representations about the application that are made to the Commission. The Commission must allow a period of at least 30 days for representations to be submitted.[341] Where the application involves a proposed merger which is not yet in the public domain, the applicant must give consent to the Commission to publicise the proposed merger for inviting representations from the relevant parties, otherwise the application will not be processed.[342]

The time taken by the Commission to make a decision on the application depends very much on the nature and complexity of the transaction in question (including the volume of data required to be processed and the timeliness of their availability), and the resources available to the Commission. The Commission states, however, that it will endeavour to process applications in an efficient and timely manner with due regard being paid to the circumstances of the case.[343]

If the Commission makes a decision that a merger or proposed merger is or would be excluded from the application of the Merger Rule, then it may not take any action under the Ordinance with respect to the merger or proposed merger unless it rescinds its decision or the merger as implemented is materially different from the proposed merger to which the decision relates.[344]

Rescission of decision that a merger is excluded   The Commission may rescind a decision that a merger is excluded from the Merger Rule if it has reason to believe:[345]

    (a) if the merger has not been carried into effect, that there has been a material change of circumstances since the decision was made; or

    (b) whether or not the merger has been carried into effect:

        (i) that the information provided by a person involved in the merger, on which it based its decision was incomplete, false or misleading in a material particular; or

        (ii) that an undertaking has failed to observe any condition or limitation subject to which the decision has effect.

---

[340] Competition Ordinance, Schedule 7, section 11(4).
[341] Competition Ordinance, Schedule 7, section 12.
[342] Guideline on the Merger Rule, para 5.20.
[343] Guideline on the Merger Rule, para 5.21.
[344] Competition Ordinance, Schedule 7, section 14.
[345] Competition Ordinance, Schedule 7, section 15(1).

Before rescinding the decision, the Commission is required to publish a notice of the proposed rescission in order to bring the proposed rescission to the attention of those the Commission considers likely to be affected by the proposed rescission, allow a period of at least 30 days for representations to be submitted, and consider any representations about the proposed rescission that are made to the Commission. If a Decision is rescinded, a notice of rescission will be issued to each undertaking specified in the decision, informing them of the rescission and the reasons for it, the date on which the determination to rescind the decision was made, and the date from which the rescission takes effect.[346]

Register of merger decisions The Commission must establish and maintain a register of all decisions made in respect of applications for exclusion from the Merger Rule and all notices of rescissions of such decisions. The Commission may omit confidential information from any entry made in the register. Where confidential information has been omitted, that fact must be disclosed on the register.[347]

Enforcement proceedings in the Competition Tribunal If the Competition Commission, after carrying out an investigation, has reasonable cause to believe that an anticipated merger or a merger contravenes, or is likely to contravene the Merger Rule, it may bring proceedings in the Competition Tribunal pursuant to sections 97 and 99, respectively, of the Competition Ordinance seeking orders to stop the contravention. This will, effectively, stop the process in relation to an anticipated merger or unwind a completed merger.[348]

5.7 PROCEEDINGS BEFORE THE COMPETITION TRIBUNAL

Pecuniary penalties The power to impose penalties for contravention, or involvement in a contravention, of a competition rule lies, pursuant to sections 92-93 of the Competition Ordinance, with the Competition Tribunal, on application by the Competition Commission.[349] If the Competition Tribunal is satisfied that a person has contravened or been involved in a contravention of a competition rule, it may order that person to pay to the Hong Kong

---

[346] Competition Ordinance, Schedule 7, section 15(2)-(6); Guideline on the Merger Rule, para 5.23. Pursuant to section 15(7), each undertaking specified in the notice of rescission loses its immunity from action under the Competition Ordinance, as from the date the rescission takes effect, with regard to anything done after that date.

[347] Competition Ordinance, Schedule 7, section 16.

[348] Guideline on the Merger Rule, para 5.29.

[349] Competition Ordinance, section 92.

Government a pecuniary penalty of any amount it considers appropriate.[350] Without limiting the matters to be taken into account, in determining the amount of the pecuniary penalty, the Competition Tribunal must have regard to the following matters:[351]

(a) the nature and extent of the conduct that constitutes the contravention;
(b) the loss or damage, if any, caused by the conduct;
(c) the circumstance in which the conduct took place; and
(d) whether the person has previously been found by the Competition Tribunal to have contravened the Competition Ordinance.

A penalty in respect of a single contravention may be up to 10% of an undertaking's annual turnover in Hong Kong for a maximum of three years.[352] Indemnities of officers, employees or agents of an undertaking against liability for paying pecuniary penalties are void, though there is an exception where an indemnity is on the terms that the funds for defending proceedings are to be repaid in the event of the officer, employee or agent being required by the Tribunal to pay the pecuniary penalty, and the funds are to be repaid not later than the date when the decision of the Tribunal becomes final.[353] There is a five-year limitation period for an application by the Commission for contravention of the Conduct Rules, and a limitation period of six months for contravention of the Merger Rule.[354]

Orders other than pecuniary orders In addition to imposing pecuniary penalties, the Competition Tribunal may, pursuant to section 94 of the Competition Ordinance, make any other order it considers appropriate,[355] including:

- making an injunction against a person from engaging in any conduct that constitutes the contravention or the person's involvement in the contravention;[356]
- ordering that a person be prohibited from making or giving effect to an agreement, or ordering the parties to an agreement to modify or terminate that agreement;[357]
- declaring an agreement to be void or voidable;[358]
- ordering a defendant to pay damages or disgorge profits;[359] and

---

[350] Competition Ordinance, section 93(1).
[351] Competition Ordinance, section 93(2).
[352] Competition Ordinance, section 93(3) and (4).
[353] Competition Ordinance, sections 168 and 169.
[354] Competition Ordinance, section 92(2).
[355] Competition Ordinance, section 94 and Schedule 3; see also Competition Ordinance, section 142(2).
[356] Competition Ordinance, Schedule 3, section 1(b).
[357] Competition Ordinance, Schedule 3, sections 1(g) and 1(h).
[358] Competition Ordinance, Schedule 3, section 1(i).
[359] Competition Ordinance, Schedule 3, sections 1(k) and (p).

- making a disqualification order.[360]

The limitation periods in respect of pecuniary penalties also apply to the other orders that the Competition Tribunal may make under section 94 of the Competition Ordinance, though it may, on application made before the expiry of the six-month limitation period for contraventions of the Merger Rule, extend the period within which an application for other orders may be made in respect of the Merger Rule if it considers it reasonable to do so.[361]

Disqualification orders The Competition Tribunal may, pursuant to section 101 of the Competition Ordinance, make a disqualification order barring an individual from serving as the director of a company for a maximum of five years if two conditions are satisfied:[362]

- a company of which the person is a director has contravened a competition rule; and
- the Competition Tribunal considers that the person's conduct as a director makes the person unfit to be concerned in the management of a company.

The second condition is satisfied where the director's conduct contributed to the contravention of the Competition Ordinance, or if the director had reasonable grounds to suspect that the company was violating the Competition Ordinance but took no steps to prevent it, or the director did not know but ought to have known that the company's conduct constituted a contravention.[363]

Orders by consent One of the underlying objectives of the procedures of the Competition Tribunal is to facilitate the settlement of disputes. In particular, in respect of proceedings concerning applications for enforcement, rule 39 of the Competition Tribunal Rules provides power for the Competition Tribunal to make orders by consent, including any findings, determinations or decisions and orders that are within its power. Where the Competition Ordinance provides that the Competition Tribunal may, upon being satisfied of certain facts, exercise a power, such as the imposition of a pecuniary penalty under section 93 or other orders under section 94, an application for such an order by

---

[360] Competition Ordinance, section 101. An application for a disqualification order may be made only by the Competition Commission: Competition Ordinance, section 104.

[361] Competition Ordinance, section 94(3). An application for an extension of time must be made *ex parte* and supported by an affidavit. An application to set aside an order for extension of time must be made by filing a summons in Form 2 in the Schedule to the Competition Tribunal Rules and within 14 days after the day on which the order is served: Competition Tribunal Rules, rule 80.

[362] Competition Ordinance, section 102.

[363] Competition Ordinance, section 103.

consent should be accompanied by a statement of agreed facts on the basis of which the Competition Tribunal is asked to make the order in question.[364]

Interim orders in merger cases Where proceedings are brought in relation to an anticipated merger and the Competition Tribunal has not finally determined the matter, it may, either of its own motion or on application by the Commission, make an interim order pursuant to section 98 of the Competition Ordinance for the purpose of preventing pre-emptive action that might prejudice the hearing or any final order that might be made on the hearing of the application. Interim orders may:[365]

(a) prohibit or restrict the doing of things that the Competition Tribunal considers would constitute pre-emptive action;

(b) impose on any person concerned obligations as to the carrying on of any activities or the safeguarding of any assets;

(c) provide for the carrying on of any activities or the safeguarding of any assets either by the appointment of a person to conduct or supervise the conduct of any activities (on any terms and with any powers that may be specified or described in the order) or in any other manner.

Final orders in merger cases If the Competition Tribunal is satisfied that an anticipated merger is likely to infringe the Merger Rule, it may, pursuant to section 97(2) of the Competition Ordinance, make an order ordering the person against whom the order is directed not to proceed with the merger or part of the merger and/or not to do anything that would result in the merger.[366] If, on the other hand, the Tribunal is not satisfied that an arrangement, if carried into effect, will result in a merger that is likely to contravene the Merger Rule, it may, pursuant to section 97(3), make a declaration to that effect.[367]

In relation to a completed merger, proceedings must be brought within the period of six months from the day on which the merger was completed or the Competition Commission became aware of the merger, whichever is the later.[368] This period may be extended by the Competition Tribunal on the application of the Commission prior to expiry of the six months if the Competition Tribunal considers it reasonable to do so.[369] If the Competition Tribunal is satisfied that a merger contravenes the Merger Rule, it may make any order it considers appropriate pursuant to section 100(1) for the purpose of bringing the contravention to an end.[370]

---

[364] See paragraph 72 of the Competition Tribunal Practice Direction No.1.
[365] Competition Ordinance, section 98(1)-(2); Guideline on the Merger Rule, para 5.30.
[366] Competition Ordinance, section 97(2).
[367] Competition Ordinance, section 97(3).
[368] Competition Ordinance, section 99(2).
[369] Competition Ordinance, section 99(3).
[370] Competition Ordinance, section 100(1).

An order made by the Competition Tribunal in relation to an anticipated merger or a merger may contain anything permitted by Schedule 4 to the Competition Ordinance.[371]   Schedule 4 provides that such an order may provide for:[372]

(a) the division of any business (whether by the sale of any part of its assets or otherwise); or

(b) the division of any undertaking or association of undertakings.

Such an order may contain any provisions that the Competition Tribunal considers appropriate to effect or take account of the division including, in particular, provision as to:[373]

(a) the transfer or creation of property, rights, liabilities or obligations;

(b) the number of persons to whom the property, rights, liabilities or obligations are to be transferred or in whom they are to be vested;

(c) the time within which the property, rights, liabilities or obligations are to be transferred or vested;

(d) the adjustment of contracts (whether by discharge or reduction of any liability or obligation or otherwise);

(e) the creation, allotment, surrender or cancellation of any shares, stock or securities;

(f) the formation or winding up of any company or other body of persons corporate or unincorporate;

(g) the amendment of the memorandum and articles or other instruments regulating any such company or other body of persons;

(h) the extent to which, and the circumstances in which, provisions of the order affecting a company or other body of persons corporate or unincorporate in its share capital, constitution or other matters may be altered by the company or other body of persons concerned;

(i) the registration of the order under any enactment by a company or other body of persons corporate or unincorporate which is affected by it as mentioned in (h);

(j) the continuation, with any necessary change of parties, of any legal proceedings;

(k) the approval by any person of anything required by virtue of the order to be done or of any person to whom anything is to be transferred, or in whom anything is to be vested, by virtue of the order; or

(l) the appointment of trustees or other persons to do anything on behalf of another person which is required of that person by virtue of the order or to monitor the doing by that person of any such thing.

An order may prohibit or restrict the acquisition by any person of the whole or part of another person's business or the doing of anything that will or may

---

[371] Competition Ordinance, sections 97(4) and 100(2).
[372] Competition Ordinance, Schedule 4, section 1.
[373] Competition Ordinance, Schedule 4, section 2.

result in a merger.[374] If such an acquisition is made or anything is done that results in a merger, an order may require that the persons concerned (or any of them) must observe any prohibitions or restrictions imposed by or under the order.[375]

Enforcement by the Competition Tribunal With respect to the enforcement of its orders and all other matters necessary for the exercise of its jurisdiction, the Competition Tribunal has all the powers, rights and privileges of the Court of First Instance.[376] In particular, the Tribunal may enforce the payment of pecuniary penalties and fines in the same manner in which a judgment of the Court of First Instance for the payment of money may be enforced.[377] An application for enforcement before the Tribunal must be made by filing an originating notice of application[378] which sets out the grounds for the application, the material facts relating to the application, and the relief sought by the applicant.[379] The respondent must file and serve a response within 28 days of his being served with the originating notice of application, otherwise the applicant may apply to the Tribunal for an order granting the relief sought in the application against the respondent.[380] The applicant may file and serve a reply within 28 days on which he is served with a response.[381] The Tribunal may at any stage give directions, including the filing of affidavits, witness statements, expert evidence and other evidence or documents.[382]

Transfer of cases The Competition Tribunal has jurisdiction to hear and determine:[383]

- applications made by the Competition Commission with regard to alleged contraventions, or alleged involvements in contraventions, of the Competition Rules;
- applications for the review of reviewable determinations;
- private actions in respect of contraventions, or involvements in contraventions, of the Conduct Rules;
- allegations of contraventions, or involvements in contraventions, of the Conduct Rules raised as a defence;
- applications for the disposal of property;
- applications for the enforcement of commitments; and

---

[374] Competition Ordinance, Schedule 4, section 3.
[375] Competition Ordinance, Schedule 4, section 4.
[376] Competition Ordinance, section 143(1)(c) and (d) of the Ordinance.
[377] Competition Ordinance, section 155A.
[378] See Form 1 in the Schedule to the Competition Tribunal Rules.
[379] Competition Tribunal Rules, rule 74.
[380] Competition Tribunal Rules, rules 75 and 76.
[381] Competition Tribunal Rules, rule 77.
[382] Competition Tribunal Rules, rule 78.
[383] Competition Ordinance, section 142(1).

- any matter related to a matter referred to in the above sub-paragraphs if the matters arise out of the same or substantially the same facts.

The Court of First Instance must transfer to the Competition Tribunal so much of the proceedings before it that are within the jurisdiction of the Competition Tribunal, except where a matter arises out of the same or substantially the same facts as matters referred to above and the Court of First Instance considers that such transfer would not be in the interests of justice.[384]

If, in any proceedings before the Court of First Instance, a contravention, or involvement in a contravention, of a Conduct Rule is alleged as a defence, the Court must, in respect of the allegation, transfer to the Competition Tribunal so much of those proceedings that are within the latter's jurisdiction. However, the Competition Tribunal may transfer back to the Court so much of those proceedings that it considers should, in the interests of justice, be transferred back.[385]   In a similar way, the Tribunal must transfer to the Court of First Instance so much of the proceedings brought before it that are within the jurisdiction of the Court but are not within the jurisdiction of the Competition Tribunal.[386]

Any person who intends to apply for proceedings in the Competition Tribunal to be transferred to the Court of First Instance should make the application as soon as circumstances have arisen rendering it in the interests of justice for the proceedings or part of them to be transferred. Failure to do so may attract adverse costs consequences.[387]   An application for transfer should be made by a summons taken out in the Competition Tribunal.[388]   An affidavit may or may not be necessary depending on the basis of the application. Where appropriate, the application may be dealt with on paper without a hearing.[389]

Case management   The Competition Tribunal Rules and Competition Tribunal Practice Directions No.1 and No.2 govern the practice and procedure in the Competition Tribunal.   Where the Competition Ordinance and Competition Tribunal Rules make no provision for a matter, the Rules of the High Court (RHC) apply to all proceedings, so far as they may be applicable to that matter.[390]   The Competition Tribunal may decide its own procedures, and

---

[384] Competition Ordinance, section 113. For the practice and procedure after the transfer of proceedings from the Court of First Instance to the Tribunal, see rule 99 of the Competition Tribunal Rules and the Competition Tribunal Practice Direction No.1, paragraphs 109 to 114.

[385] Competition Ordinance, sections 113(3), 114(3) and 115(1); see also sections 116-117.

[386] Competition Ordinance, section 114(1). The Tribunal or the Court of First Instance may refer the alleged contravention to the Commission for investigation: section 118.

[387] Competition Tribunal Practice Direction No.1, para 70.

[388] See Form 2 in the Schedule to the Competition Tribunal Rules.

[389] Competition Tribunal Practice Direction No.1, para 71.

[390] Competition Tribunal Rules, rule 4(1); Competition Tribunal Practice Direction No.1, paras 24 to 26.

may also follow the practice and procedure of the Court of First Instance.[391] The general principles and concepts of the civil procedure of the Court of First Instance are therefore relevant in proceedings before the Tribunal.[392] The Tribunal may, in a particular case, dispense with the application of the RHC if it considers that doing so:[393]

(a) will enable the Competition Tribunal to conduct its proceedings expeditiously with as much informality as is consistent with attaining justice;

(b) will save costs and is consistent with attaining justice; or

(c) is otherwise in the interests of justice.

5.8 APPEALS FROM THE COMPETITION TRIBUNAL

Competition Ordinance An appeal lies as of right to the Court of Appeal against any decision (including a decision as to the amount of any compensatory sanction or pecuniary penalty), determination or order of the Competition Tribunal made under the Competition Ordinance except:[394]

- against an order of the Tribunal allowing an extension of time for appealing against a decision, determination or order of the Tribunal;[395]
- against a decision, determination or order of the Tribunal if it is provided by the Competition Ordinance or by the Tribunal Rules that the decision, determination or order is final;[396]
- without the leave of the Court of Appeal or the Tribunal, against an order of the Tribunal made with the consent of the parties or relating only to costs that are left to the discretion of the Tribunal;[397]
- a decision of the Court of Appeal as to whether a decision, determination or order of the Tribunal is, for any purpose connected with an appeal to the Court, final or interlocutory;[398]
- without the leave of the Court of Appeal or the Tribunal, an interlocutory decision, determination or order of the Tribunal.[399]

The Court of Appeal can:[400]

- confirm, set aside or vary a decision, determination or order of the Tribunal;

---

[391] Competition Ordinance, section 144(1).
[392] See Competition Tribunal Practice Direction No.1, para 21.
[393] Competition Ordinance, section 144(3) and Competition Tribunal Rules, rules 4(2)-(3).
[394] Competition Ordinance, section 154(1).
[395] Competition Ordinance, section 154(2)(a).
[396] Competition Ordinance, section 154(2)(b).
[397] Competition Ordinance, section 154(2)(c).
[398] Competition Ordinance, section 154(4).
[399] Competition Ordinance, section 155; Competition Tribunal Rules, rule 44.
[400] Competition Ordinance, section 154(5).

- where the decision, determination or order of the Tribunal is set aside, substitute any other decision, determination or order it considers appropriate; or
- remit the matter in question to the Tribunal for reconsideration in the light of the decision of the Court.

Except in the case of an appeal against the imposition, or the amount, of a pecuniary penalty, the making of an appeal does not act as an automatic stay of the decision, determination or order to which the appeal relates.[401]

As well as appeals to the Court of Appeal, appeals against decisions of the Tribunal may further be made to the Court of Final Appeal.[402]

Competition Tribunal Rules   A party may appeal against any interlocutory decision, determination or order of the Registrar of the Competition Tribunal given or made in relation to the proceedings concerned to a member of the Tribunal within 14 days after the day on which the interlocutory decision, determination or order was given or made.[403]   Unless the Tribunal otherwise directs, the appeal does not operate as a stay of the proceedings in which the appeal is brought.[404]

An appeal lies to the Court of Appeal against any decision, determination or order (other than an interlocutory decision, determination or order) of the Registrar given or made:

- on the hearing or determination of any cause, matter, question or issue tried before the Registrar under Order 14, rule 6(2) and Order 36, rule 1 of the RHC;
- on an assessment of damages under Order 37 of the RHC or otherwise;
- on the hearing or determination of an application under Order 49B of the RHC (on execution and enforcement of a judgment for money by imprisonment); or
- on the hearing or determination of a disqualification application mentioned in rule 78(2)(b) or an application for leave to participate in a company's affairs under rules 83 or 84 of the Competition Tribunal Rules.[405]

Applications for leave in respect of interlocutory appeals must be made to the Competition Tribunal in the first instance within 14 days of the decision, determination or order, unless the Court of Appeal allows the application for leave to be made direct to the Court of Appeal under Order 59, rule 2BA(2) of the RHC.[406]

---

[401]   Competition Ordinance, section 154(6).
[402]   Competition Ordinance, sections 110(3)(d), 111(1)(c), 119(4)(b).
[403]   The appeal must be made by Form 6 in the Schedule of the Competition Tribunal Rules.
[404]   Competition Tribunal Rules, rule 42.
[405]   Competition Tribunal Rules, rule 43.
[406]   Competition Tribunal Rules, rule 45.   The application must be made inter *partes* if the relevant proceedings are *inter partes*.

5.9 FOLLOW ON ACTIONS

No right of standalone action   The Competition Ordinance does not allow standalone actions where the cause of action is a contravention of a Conduct Rule.[407]   Instead, a person who has suffered loss or damage as a result of any act that has been determined to be a contravention of a Conduct Rule can, pursuant to section 110 of the Competition Ordinance, bring a follow-on action in the Competition Tribunal against any person who has contravened or is contravening the rule, and also any person who is, or has been involved in that contravention.[408]   The limitation period for follow-on actions is three years.[409]   The general rule is that follow-on actions may not be brought before the expiry of the period of appeal for the relevant decision of the Competition Tribunal or Court, though the Court of First Instance or the Tribunal may accede to an application by the party seeking to bring the proceedings even before the expiry of the appeal period.[410]   There is no statutory limit on the level of damages that may be awarded in a follow-on action.

Procedure   A follow-on action must be brought by filing an originating notice of claim[411] and a statement of claim.   The statement of claim may be indorsed on the originating notice of claim.   Alternatively, the statement of claim and the originating notice of claim may be filed separately, but must be filed on the same day unless the Competition Tribunal otherwise directs.[412]

The originating notice of claim:

- must specify the decision of the Tribunal or Court or admission in a commitment on which the plaintiff relies to establish a contravention of a conduct rule; and
- must specify the estimated amount of damages (both general and special damages) claimed as well as the estimated aggregate amount claimed.[413]

The statement of claim:

---

[407] Competition Ordinance, sections 108 and 109.   Where proceedings may be brought, the Commission is entitled to apply to intervene: sections 120-121.

[408] Competition Ordinance, section 110.   Section 107 specifies the persons who may be regarded as involved in a contravention.

[409] Competition Ordinance, section 111(3).

[410] Competition Ordinance, sections 111(1) and (2).   For applications under section 111(2) of the Competition Ordinance, see rule 94 of the Competition Tribunal Rules.

[411] Form 8 in the Schedule of the Competition Tribunal Rules.

[412] Competition Tribunal Rules, rule 93(1), (2) and (3).

[413] Competition Tribunal Rules, rule 93(4); Competition Tribunal Practice Direction No.1, para 97.

- must specify the particular part of the decision or commitment which determines or admits that a relevant act is a contravention of a conduct rule;
- should in general follow the relevant requirements of RHC Order 18;
- must set out full particulars the loss and damage suffered under each head of loss and the respective amounts of damages claimed as well as the aggregate amount claimed; and
- where the plaintiff includes causes of action other than section 110 of the Competition Ordinance, this should be made clear in the statement of claim. The facts in support of each cause of action should be clearly identified so as to make it readily ascertainable whether each claim lies within the jurisdiction of the Competition Tribunal.[414]

The defendant must file and serve his defence within 28 days after the day on which he is served with the originating notice of claim, and must plead specifically with as full particulars as possible to each item of loss and damage allegedly suffered by the plaintiff under each head of loss and to the amount of damages claimed.[415] The plaintiff may file and serve a reply 28 days thereafter.[416]

After filing a reply, or after expiry of the 28 day period for the filing of a reply, the plaintiff must take out a case management summons. If he fails to do so, the defendant may take out a case management summons or apply for an order to dismiss the follow-on action.[417] The form of timetabling questionnaire, which should be filed by each party at least 7 days before the hearing of the case management summons, is annexed to the Competition Tribunal Practice Direction No.1.[418] A hearing bundle should be lodged at least 7 days before the hearing. A copy of the relevant decision of the contravention of a conduct rule or the relevant commitment, as well as a copy of the timetabling questionnaires, should be included in the hearing bundle.[419]

Parties to follow-on actions are particularly encouraged to consider and, where appropriate, adopt alternative methods of dispute resolution, such as mediation. Parties should note that RHC Order 22 (Offers to Settle and Payments into Courts) applies with necessary modification to the Tribunal.[420]

---

[414] Competition Tribunal Rules, rule 93(5) of the Rules; Competition Tribunal Practice Direction No.1, paras 98 to 101.

[415] Competition Tribunal Rules, rule 95; Competition Tribunal Practice Direction No.1, para 103.

[416] Competition Tribunal Rules, rule 96.

[417] Competition Tribunal Rules, rule 97.

[418] Competition Tribunal Practice Direction No.1, para 105.

[419] Competition Tribunal Practice Direction No.1, para 106.

[420] Competition Tribunal Practice Direction No.1, para 107 and 108; Practice Direction 31 (Mediation).

Leniency and follow-on actions The Competition Commission's leniency policy for undertakings engaged in cartel conduct does not preclude the possibility of a follow-on action against cartel members, including a party to a Leniency Agreement, by persons who can prove they have suffered loss or damage as a result of the cartel.[421] Thus, a successful leniency application may expose the applicant to follow-on actions. This is because the applicant may be required to sign a statement admitting its involvement in the cartel, which may lead to the Competition Tribunal making an order declaring that the applicant has contravened the Competition Ordinance. A follow-on action may then be brought in respect of that admission.

---

[421] Leniency Policy, para 1.7.

Chapter Six

THE TELCO RULE: THE PROHIBITION ON EXPLOITATIVE CONDUCT BY A DOMINANT TELECOMMUNICATIONS LICENSEE

6.1 THE TELCO RULE

The Telco Rule   The Telco Rule, pursuant to section 7Q of the Telecommunications Ordinance,[1] provides that a licensee in a dominant position in a telecommunications market must not engage in conduct that in the opinion of the Communications Authority is exploitative.[2]   The Telco Rule applies, therefore, where the following elements are present:

- the entity engaged in the relevant conduct is a telecommunications licensee;
- the licensee has a dominant position in a telecommunications market; and
- the licensee engages in conduct that in the opinion of the Communications Authority is exploitative.

Relationship with Second Conduct Rule   Although the Telco Rule shares some of its features and broad aims with the Second Conduct Rule in that it applies to unilateral conduct on the part of an undertaking that has a position of market power, there are some important distinctions:

- The Telco Rule applies only to a relevant telecommunications licensee as defined in the Telecommunications Ordinance.[3]   The Second Conduct Rule applies across the economy including in relation to a relevant telecommunications licensee that could, in principle, also be subject to the Telco Rule.

---

[1]   The Competition Ordinance, Schedule 8, section 13 amends the Telecommunications Ordinance (Cap.106) to include a new section 7Q.

[2]   Telecommunications Ordinance, section 7Q(1).

[3]   A licensee under the Telecommunications Ordinance, section 2(1):
  (a) means the holder of a licence under the Telecommunications Ordinance;
  (b) includes the holder of a licence (other than a programme service licence)-
    (i) granted under the Ordinance repealed by section 44(1) of the Broadcasting Ordinance;
    (ii) in force immediately before that repeal; and
    (iii) deemed to be a licence granted under the Telecommunications Ordinance by virtue of Schedule 8 to the Broadcasting Ordinance.

- The Telco Rule applies to a licensee in a dominant position in a telecommunications market, whereas the Second Conduct Rule applies to an undertaking that has a substantial degree of market power in a market. In common to both, there is no prohibition on the mere holding of such a dominant position/substantial market power.
- The Telco Rule is enforced by the Communications Authority alone. In contrast, while the Competition Commission is the principal competition authority responsible for enforcing the Competition Ordinance, it has concurrent jurisdiction with the Communications Authority in respect of the anti-competitive conduct of relevant undertakings operating in the telecommunications and broadcasting sectors, including a telecommunications licensee that could be subject to the Telco Rule.
- The enforcement regime for the Telco Rule differs from that of the competition rules in the Competition Ordinance in that the Communications Authority has decision-making power in respect of a breach of the Telco Rule. In contrast, in respect of the competition rules, the Competition Commission must bring proceedings before the Competition Tribunal.
- The Telco Rule is added to the pre-existing sector-specific competition regulation, as amended, which applies in the telecommunications and broadcasting sectors in Hong Kong before the Competition Ordinance came into force and which continues to have independent significance.
- The Competition Commission and the Communications Authority have published a Guideline on the Second Conduct Rule. There is no equivalent guidance on the substantive application of the Telco Rule.[4] The Communications Authority has, however, published a Guide on the Telco Rule detailing how complaints relating to conduct prohibited under sections 7K, 7L, 7N and 7Q of the Telecommunications Ordinance are handled.

Competition and regulation in telecommunications sector In order to set the Telco Rule in context, it is important to examine its historic antecedents and the development of regulation and competition law under the sector-specific regime.   The Telco Rule is bolted on to the existing telecommunications sector regulatory regime which is enforced by the Communications Authority through the Office of Telecommunications Authority, its executive arm. A form of competition law was introduced to the telecommunications sector in 1995 when the sector was liberalised through the

---

[4] Prior to adopting any guidelines in respect of the notion of dominance, the Communications Authority should consult holders of carrier licences: Telecomunications Ordinance, section 6D(4)(a) (as amended by Competition Ordinance, Schedule 8, section 8).

introduction of three new telecommunications operators to compete with Hong Kong Telecom (HKT) in the local fixed line telephone service market. The four operators were granted a Fixed Telecommunications Network Services (FTNS) licence which contained competition law prohibitions as General Conditions (GCs). The sector-specific regulation of the telecommunications sector imposes both *ex ante* and *ex post* controls on dominant companies. Under the *ex ante* regime, a company is declared to be dominant in advance and is subject to specific restrictions on conduct by virtue of that classification. Under the *ex post* regime the dominant company's conduct is regulated after the event. Of particular relevance were the following:

- *Ex post* competition law prohibitions: GC 15 (anti-competitive conduct by a non-dominant licensee) and GC 16 (abuse of a dominant position).
- *Ex ante* regulatory obligations: GC 17 (accounting practices of a dominant licensee); and GCs 20 to 22 (tariff approval system for a dominant licensee).

Of particular note GC 44 allowed a licensee that was previously classified as dominant to apply for review of its dominant status. Once a licensee was de-classified as dominant the previous tariff control and other *ex ante* obligations were no longer applicable. In 2000 these competition law provisions were incorporated with some changes in the Telecommunications Ordinance as sections 7F to H, 7K, 7L and 7N. In addition, in 2003 a new section 7P was incorporated in the Telecommunications Ordinance empowering the Communications Authority to review mergers and acquisitions between licensees.

Hong Kong made significant progress towards liberalisation of the telecommunications sector. HKT (which later became PCCW-HKT) was treated as dominant in every market in which it operated when it was granted its FTNS licence in 1995. PCCW-HKT progressively applied for declassification as dominant on a market-by-market basis and by 2005 was no longer classified as dominant in any relevant market.[5]

The Competition Ordinance brings about some streamlining of the sector-specific regime by repealing the following sections of the Telecommunications Ordinance:

- section 7K (*ex post* prohibition of anti-competitive practices);[6]
- section 7L (*ex post* prohibition of abuse of a dominant position);[7]

---

[5] See, further, Cheng T.K., A tale of Two Competition Law regimes – The Telecom-Sector Competition Regulation in Hong King and Singapore *World Competition* 30(3): 501-526, 2007 in particular at page 515.

[6] Competition Ordinance, Schedule 8, section 9.

[7] Competition Ordinance, Schedule 8, section 10.

- section 7N (duty of a dominant telecommunications licensee not to discriminate in its dealings with other telecommunications operators);[8] and

- section 7P (review of mergers and acquisitions in relation to carrier licensees by the Communications Authority).[9]

6.2 MARKET DEFINITION

Telecommunications market The Telco Rule applies to a licensee in a dominant position in a telecommunications market.[10] As with the Second Conduct Rule, the starting point in any abuse of dominance/market power case is the definition of the relevant market. The Guideline on the Second Conduct Rule provides general guidance on the relevance of market definition for that purpose. It does not make explicit reference to market definition for the purposes of the Telco Rule. The following observations may be made, however, as to the significance and role of the definition of the relevant market for the assessment of conduct in the telecommunications sector based on first principles and drawing on experience in other regulatory contexts, notably the European Union experience.

Fast-moving telecommunications markets The telecommunications sector is characterised by innovation and technical change which can present a difficulty of formulating an accurate market definition that takes account of new and prospective entry and even displacement of market power by new products and services. This issue has particular prominence in telecommunications markets which evolve over time. Competition and regulatory authorities are faced with the challenge of anticipating the likely reactions of consumers, suppliers and competitors over time. The fast-moving nature of telecommunications markets means that regulators must be mindful that today's market share or position may not always correlate with tomorrow's market power, particularly where the boundaries of the relevant market are subject to flux.

Limitations of the hypothetical monopolist test The application of the hypothetical monopolist test, conveniently labelled as the SSNIP test (Small but Significant Non-Transitory Increase in Price) is often used as a tool to inform market definition.[11] This can present challenges when applied to newer

---

[8]   Competition Ordinance, Schedule 8, section 11.
[9]   Competition Ordinance, Schedule 8, section 12. This was substantially recast as the Merger Rule (Competition Ordinance, Schedule 7, section 3).
[10] Telecommunications Ordinance, section 7Q(1).
[11] This test seeks to assess the reactions of consumers in response to an undertaking increasing its prices by, say, 5 – 10% over a period of time of about a year.

markets. The practical application of the SSNIP test gives raise to some thorny issues in telecommunications markets in particular. It is a familiar criticism of the SSNIP test that it is predicated on the assumption that the initial price is competitive. Determining the competitive level may itself require substantial information (if available) and analysis. A switch to another product or service may simply reflect the fact that the existing price is far above the competitive level and not merely by the small but significant 5-10% level which underpins the SSNIP test. This phenomenon may actually lead to perverse outcomes which do not reflect genuine substitution. This is the so-called cellophane fallacy, a concept derived from the reasoning in the *Du Pont* Supreme Court case in the United States.[12]

The difficulties are compounded when one is assessing the effect of a price increase in markets which may be concerned with infrastructure access, e.g. access to a telecommunications network. The determination of the competitive price or the impact of a price increase may be even more delicate and uncertain in such situations which do not involve the consumption of a physical product such as telecommunications services. The determination of a competitive price may for example be rendered more complex in relation to network upgrades, the cost of which will need to be recouped over time and reflected in the price. Further, the SSNIP test does not take account of other benchmarks of competition on which telecommunications players differentiate themselves: innovation, coverage, service levels etc. Thus, the hypothetical reaction of consumers to a hypothetical price increase may tell little about genuine competitive constraints. For this purpose, when approaching market definition in the telecommunications sector a more detailed examination is needed of the relevant economic agents and their horizontal and vertical relationships across the supply chain and the extent to which they exert a genuine competitive constraint on the conduct of the subject.

The challenge of convergence The concept of convergence has acquired a particular impetus when considering competition and regulation in the telecommunications sector. Technical convergence blurs the lines between traditional audiovisual and telecommunications services, networks and devices. In respect of its economic effects, there are a number of practical implications of convergence. They include a transition from scarcity in distribution to abundance, increased use of distribution networks and the emergence of new (and potentially complex) industry structures. There is wide recognition of the need to take account of market evolution in the telecommunications sector and a variety of decisions purport to address convergence when approaching relevant markets and analysis. For example, in the Microsoft/Skype decision, the European Commission observed that as a consequence of the ongoing convergence in the relevant markets, the traditional distinctions between data

---

12 *U.S. v. E. I. du Pont de Nemours* reported at 351 U.S. 377, 76 S.Ct. 994, 100 L.Ed.1264.

and voice, between hardware and software, and between the various distinct products and services that are offered by enterprise communications companies are blurring.[13]　While this statement was made in relation to a merger investigation, the economic effects of convergence in the telecommunications sector are at least as relevant when defining markets in conduct cases.

6.3 DOMINANT POSITION

Definition　Section 7Q(2)-(3) of the Telecommunications Ordinance provides the legal basis for determining dominance under the Telco Rule.　Section 7Q(2) defines a dominant position as the ability of a licensee to act without significant competitive constraint from its competitors and customers.[14]　In determining whether a licensee is in a dominant position for the purposes of the Telco Rule, the Communications Authority, pursuant to Section 7Q(3), must take into account the matters in the following non-exhaustive list:[15]

(a) the market share of the licensee;

(b) the licensee's power to make pricing and other decisions;

(c) any barriers to entry to competitors into the relevant telecommunications market;

(d) the degree of product differentiation and sales promotion;

(e) any other relevant matters specified in guidelines issued by the Communications Authority.

The definition of dominance is the same as that adopted by competition authorities and regulators in other jurisdictions, such as EU law where the test for establishing dominance has been set out by the Court of Justice as a position of economic strength enjoyed by an undertaking which enables it to prevent effective competition being maintained on the relevant market by giving it the power to behave to an appreciable extent independently of its competitors, customers and ultimately of its consumers.[16]　In contrast, whilst the Second Conduct Rule contains no legislative definition of substantial market power, the Competition Commission states that a substantial degree of market power arises where an undertaking does not face sufficiently effective competitive constraints in the relevant market.[17]

The list of factors to be taken into account resembles the factors typically considered by authorities in other jurisdictions when determining dominance. The first three factors (although specific to the telecommunications sector) are

---

[13]　Case COMP/M.6291 – *Microsoft/ Skype*, 7 October 2011.

[14]　Telecommunications Ordinance, section 7Q(2).

[15]　Telecommunications Ordinance, section 7Q(3).

[16]　Case C-27/76, *United Brands v Commission* [1978] ECR 207, para 65.

[17]　Guideline on the Second Conduct Rule, para 3.2.　Reference might also be made to the Communication Authority's guidelines on the competition provisions under the Telecommunications Ordinance (2013) and the Broadcasting Ordinance (2012).

identical to those set out in the Second Conduct Rule as relevant factors to be taken into account when assessing substantial market power under the Second Conduct Rule. The degree of product differentiation and sales promotion does not, however, appear on the face of the Second Conduct Rule nor is this matter referred to specifically in the Guideline on the Second Conduct Rule as a matter relevant in the assessment of substantial market power. However, in principle, there seems no reason why such a factor should not be relevant to an assessment of substantial market power under the Second Conduct Rule. Further, when considering substantial market power under the Second Conduct Rule the Competition Commission cites, as an example of a strategic barrier, brand proliferation practices engaged in by the incumbent which may crowd out product space and result in only limited opportunities to enter or expand[18] which resembles the degree of product differentiation and sales promotion factor referred to in section 7Q(3).

Dominant position: *ex ante* and *ex post* approaches contrasted A note of caution should be made as to the continuing relevance or otherwise of the approach to classification or declassification as dominant for the purposes of *ex ante* regulation when considering dominance in cases under the (*ex post*) Telco Rule. Under the telecommunications sector regulatory regime *ex ante* dominance classification is conducted on a market-by-market basis. It should be noted that nowhere in the Telecommunications Ordinance is there provision for the Communications Authority to grant exemptions from section 7Q on the basis that the licensee is not to be treated as dominant. Nor for that matter was there any procedure for granting exemption from its predecessor section 7L of the Telecommunications Ordinance on (*ex post*) abuse of a dominant position.

It must be noted that the Communications Authority has expressed the view that once a firm has been deemed non-dominant for the purposes of *ex ante* regulation, section 7L was no longer applicable. Consulting on PCCW-HK's application for a declaration of non-dominance in the residential fixed line telephone service market, the Communications Authority was mindful of the implications of rendering the prohibition of certain strategic behaviour under section 7L or GC 16 of the licence inapplicable.[19] Nevertheless, previous cases under the sector-regulatory regime which concerned the *ex ante* identification of dominance may not necessarily be reliable indicators of dominance for the purposes of the Telco Rule. While it is understandable to remove *ex ante* obligations from a firm that has already been declared non-dominant, it is not evident that a prior finding of non-dominance for sector regulatory purposes should exclude the application of *ex post* competition law, including under the

---

18   Guideline on the Second Conduct Rule, para 3.28.
19   Office of Telecommunications Authority, Application for a Declaration of Non-Dominance for PCCW-HKT Telephone Limited in the Market for Residential Direct Exchange Line Services – Industry Consultation Paper.

Telco Rule and the Second Conduct Rule. Declaring a firm to be non-dominant simply means that the firm does not possess dominance/substantial market power to abuse at the time that the assessment is conducted. This does not mean that it may not acquire such power at a future date and that it may not abuse it. In fact, the rationale of *ex post* regulation is to provide the system to control such abuses after they have occurred, with the safeguard for the defendant that it must first be established that it occupies a dominant position at the relevant time.   Nothing in the Competition Ordinance or the Telecommunications Ordinance, however, regarding the previous declarations of the Communications Authority as to the dominant status or otherwise of a licensee, provides that such statements are binding for the application of *ex post* competition law.   If they did, this would insulate a previously declared non-dominant licensee from the full application of *ex post* competition law and, effectively, give it exemption to conduct market abuses at a later stage at a time when it might have gained a position of dominance, subject only to the Communications Authority withdrawing such declaration.

Furthermore, there are important differences in the analytical frameworks for assessment of dominance and the legal consequences flowing from such a finding depending on the legal regime. It follows that a finding of dominance in one legal context does not necessarily entail the same conclusion in another legal context. The analytical approach to the assessment of dominance is not identical across sector regulation, merger control and behavioural competition law (i.e., anti-competitive agreements and abuse of dominance). The sector-regulatory and merger control frameworks adopt a teleological (forward looking) approach. In contrast, under the behavioural prohibition of abuse of dominance the inquiry is backward-looking since this informs the question of whether an abuse has actually occurred.   Given the necessity in sector-regulatory and merger control cases to identify market power before there has been observable harm in the market, there tends to be a greater risk of error. The intervention by sector regulators or competition authorities in cases where there is no violation of competition law but concerns arise from the organic growth of the company is highly controversial. These cases are inherently fact-intensive and the scope for error must not be underestimated. Too precipitate an intervention and there is a risk in implementing over-corrective measures. Conversely, the countervailing threat of new entry must be credible to displace a finding of dominance/ substantial market power *ex ante*.

6.4 EXPLOITATIVE CONDUCT

Exploitative conduct   The concept of exploitative conduct underpins the Telco Rule since it is that conduct which is prohibited by section 7Q(1) of the Telecommunications   Ordinance.   Section   7Q(4)   provides   that   the

Communications Authority may regard as prohibited by the Telco Rule exploitative behaviour in connection with the provision of interconnection. In particular, and without limiting the scope of the Telco Rule, the following examples of exploitative behaviour are prohibited: fixing and maintaining prices or charges at an excessively high level; and setting unfair trading terms and conditions.

An undertaking may possess telecommunications infrastructure that allows it to control access to a certain market or customer base. The degree of control over the infrastructure will be relevant from a competition perspective to the extent that the holder enjoys a significant degree of market power where the infrastructure is critical for a new entrant to gain market access and expand its presence. A related theme concerns potential leverage or the ability to transfer market power into related or neighbouring markets. This concern may arise where companies seek to distribute their products and services across multiple platforms. In addition, convergence in the telecommunications industry may reflect network effects, which occur when the benefit to an individual who is connected to the network increases with the addition of other individuals to the network. The concern is that the combination of network effects with market power may raise barriers to entry and result in market foreclosure of rival operators.

Interplay with Second Conduct Rule The repeal of sections 7K and 7L of the Telecommunications Ordinance (which prohibited anti-competitive practices and abuse of a dominant position) is understandable in view of the creation of specific economy-wide prohibitions of anti-competitive agreements and arrangements and abuse of substantial market power under the First and Second Conduct Rules. The repeal of section 7L and the enactment of the Telco Rule dealing with exploitative conduct may represent a potential difference in the scope of abusive practices that are prohibited in the telecommunications sector relative to other sectors of the economy. The Second Conduct Rule does not distinguish between exclusionary and exploitative abuses. The Guideline on the Second Conduct Rule, whilst accepting that the categories of abuse are not closed, has focused on practices which are exclusionary in nature in that they foreclose competitors in an anti-competitive way (i.e. predatory pricing, tying and bundling, margin squeeze, refusals to deal and exclusive dealing). This distinction between exclusionary and exploitative abuses has also featured in the debate around the scope of the EU prohibition of abuse of dominance. The European Commission's guidance on its enforcement priorities in applying Article 102 TFEU maintains a conceptual difference between exclusionary and exploitative conduct, stating that its will focus on the former, whilst accepting that exploitative behaviour, such as charging excessively high prices, is also liable to constitute an abuse of dominance which it may deal with, in particular where the protection of consumers cannot otherwise be adequately ensured.[20]

It is possible that exploitative abuses such as excessive pricing may only be sanctioned where they are in violation of the Telco Rule and that such conduct is outside the scope of the Second Conduct Rule. The reasoning is that if the Second Conduct Rule covered both exploitative and exclusionary abuses, there would no need to create a separate provision in section 7Q of the Telecommunications Ordinance to deal with such abuses in the telecommunications sector since both the Competition Commission and the Communications Authority have jurisdiction to apply the Second Conduct Rule to the very same practices. However, it is equally arguable that there is no reason to limit the scope of the Second Conduct Rule to exclusionary abuses. This raises an interesting question as to the operation of the concurrent jurisdiction of the Competition Commission and the Communications Authority in applying the Competition Ordinance, including the Second Conduct Rule, in respect of undertakings operating in the telecommunications and broadcasting sectors. One possible interpretation is that, in the case of dominant licensees falling within the scope of the Telecommunications Ordinance, such cases are more appropriately dealt with by the Communications Authority under the Telco Rule. Such an approach would, however, have a procedural significance as it would be subject to the different enforcement procedure under the Telco Rule where the Communications Authority does not need to bring a prosecution before the Competition Tribunal in order to enforce the Telco Rule.

Interplay with sector regulation   An important issue that will face the Competition Commission and the Communications Authority as they apply the Competition Ordinance is the interplay between the sector regulatory and competition regimes. This has two dimensions. First, if an agreement or practice is consistent with *ex ante* sector regulation, will it be treated as lawful under the Competition Ordinance or the Telco Rule? Second, if an agreement or practice violates *ex ante* sector regulation what implications does that have for liability under the Competition Ordinance or the Telco Rule? A possible scenario is a challenge to pricing practices under the Telco Rule where the relevant methodology or prices are compatible with sector regulation and any applicable tariff regulation.

As practice develops in this area it may be helpful to examine approaches to this question in other jurisdictions facing similar issues. In the EU, competition law plays a complementary role to sector-specific regulation, particularly in the telecommunications sector. Consistency or otherwise of a practice with sector regulation does not of itself provide insulation from the

---

[20] EU guidance on enforcement priorities in applying Article 102 TFEU to abusive exclusionary conduct by dominant undertakings, OJ 2009 C45/7.

application of EU competition law which remains applicable, including in the telecommunications sector, provided that there is scope for independent action on the part of the undertaking concerned. This is the case even where the conduct has been approved by a national regulatory authority.[21]

Fixing and maintaining excessive prices   The practice of fixing and maintaining prices or charges at an excessively high level for or in relation to the provision of interconnection may be considered exploitative under the Telco Rule. There are no cases under the previous sector-regulatory regime sanctioning excessive pricing as an abuse of dominance under the former section 7L of the Telecommunications Ordinance. The concept of excess pricing has been considered under EU competition law, which specifically provides in Article 102 TFEU that an abuse may, in particular, consist in directly or indirectly imposing unfair purchase or selling prices or other unfair trading conditions. The imposition by a dominant company of selling prices that are unfair or disproportionate to the economic value of the product or service provided can constitute an abuse.[22]   Whilst such cases have been rare in practice, allegations of excessive pricing have been upheld where a company has made use of the opportunities arising out of its position in such a way as to reap trading benefits which it would not have reaped had there been normal and sufficiently effective competition.[23]   Excessive pricing cases have been difficult to establish, not least since the European Commission does not act as a price regulator. It can, however, be easier to establish such claims where excessive pricing is coupled with a price squeeze or predation on a related market (i.e. the dominant company is charging below-cost prices in one market which it funds through excessive prices in another market where it is dominant, in order to exclude potential entry or leverage a position of dominance from one market to another). In recent EU cases, the trend has been to use the concept of proportionality to attack prices which do not bear a reasonable relationship to the cost of the relevant goods or services.[24]

Setting unfair trading terms and conditions   The practice of setting unfair trading terms and conditions for or in relation to the provision of interconnection may be considered exploitative under the Telco Rule. The repeal of section 7N of the Telecommunications Ordinance (duty of a dominant

---

[21]   Case C-280/08P, *Deutsche Telekom AG v Commission* [2010] ECR I-9555. See also, Case T-486/11, *Telekomunikacja Polska (now Orange Polska) v Commission* EU:T:2015:1002.

[22]   Case C-340-99, *TNT Traco Spa v Poste Italiane Spa* [2001] ECR I-4109.

[23]   Case C-27/76, *United Brands v Commission* [1978] ECR 207, para 249.

[24]   The English Court of Appeal has suggested that a cost plus basis of determining whether a price is excessive is not appropriate and that it is necessary to consider the full economic value on the demand side: *British Horseracing Board v Attheraces* [2007] EWCA Civ 38.

telecommunications licensee not to discriminate in its dealings with other telecommunications operators) raises a question as to whether the conduct within the scope of that provision could be subject to challenge as the imposition of unfair trading terms and conditions under new section 7Q. Without limiting the generality of the notion of unfair trading terms and conditions, it may be noted that the European Commission has applied Article 102 TFEU to unfair treatment by a dominant company, including in cases which extend beyond unfair or excessive pricing.

Discriminatory treatment of its customers by a dominant telecommunications company may infringe Article 102 TFEU as a specific category of abuse. Price discrimination consists of charging different prices to customers in the same position without justification, or charging uniform prices to customers whose circumstances are different. A challenge might be made to a dominant telecommunications company's pricing where the absence of cost differences in supplying individual customers is readily apparent.[25] Differentiated pricing structures may be more common in the telecommunications sector in future years, particularly in mobile, so that it may be more challenging to establish that discriminatory pricing is unlawful in the future. Key elements of discriminatory pricing based on EU experience include:

- prices need not be identical;
- any differences must be justified by objective and not discriminatory reasons;
- any charge must not be arbitrary;
- in the event of disparity between the prices offered to different customers it is for the allegedly dominant company to justify its reasons for the differences;
- it is irrelevant that the effects are in another market as long as the discrimination takes place in a market where the company is dominant.

Below-cost pricing or predation may be combined with cross-subsidy where a company in a dominant position on one market gains a commercial advantage on another market by exploiting its potential for leverage using revenues from that market to subsidise its entry into a competitive market. Thus, where a service in a competitive market is supplied by the beneficiary of a monopoly in another market, the price charged must cover at least the costs attributable to or incremental to the development in the competitive market. Any cost coverage below that level would be considered predatory.

---

[25] Case C-82/01, *Aeroports de Paris v Commission* [2002] ECR I-9297.

6.5 ENFORCEMENT OF THE TELCO RULE

Introduction The Office of the Communications Authority (OFCA), as the executive arm of the Communications Authority, assists the Communications Authority in processing complaints under the Telco Rule in accordance with the procedures set out in its Guide on the Telco Rule.[26] Complaints in relation to the Telco Rule can be made to OFCA. The Communications Authority may also initiate an investigation under the Telco Rule of its own volition. The Telco Rule Guide applies to both in terms of process and time-frame (insofar as applicable in respect of investigations initiated by the Communications Authority).[27] Nevertheless, the Communications Authority retains the discretion not to adhere to the time-frames or procedures set out in the Telco Rule Guide, and may make adjustments depending on the circumstances. For example, the process and time-frames may not apply to the handling of cases concerning cartels or collusive conduct.[28]

Administrative priority OFCA does not have the resources to investigate all the complaints received, and in order to ensure that its resources are used effectively, the Communications Authority has the administrative discretion under the Telecommunications Ordinance to decide whether or not to pursue, or not to pursue further, a case under the Telco Rule, having weighed the likely benefits of pursuing it against the likely resources involved and the other options available to the Communications Authority.[29] A decision by the Communications Authority not to pursue a case on the basis of administrative priority does not represent or imply any view of the Communications Authority about the merits of the case.[30] Where the Communications Authority decides not to pursue, or not to pursue further a case on the basis of administrative priority, it will, where appropriate, notify the complainant, the subject of complaint and other relevant parties of its decision in writing and the considerations that it has taken into account in reaching the decision.[31]

---

[26] A Guide on How Complaints Relating to Conduct Prohibited under Sections 7K, 7L, 7N and 7Q of the Telecommunications Ordinance are Handled by the Office of the Communications Authority, 14 December 2015.

[27] Telco Rule Guide, paras 4 and 5.

[28] Telco Rule Guide, paras 5 and 36.

[29] Telco Rule Guide, para 6. Appendix A to the Telco Rule Guide gives a non-exhaustive list of the considerations that, where it is considered appropriate, the Communications Authority will take into account in deciding whether or not to pursue, or not to pursue further a case on the basis of administrative priority.

[30] Telco Rule Guide, para 8.

[31] Telco Rule Guide, para 8.

Lodging a complaint   Complaints concerning the Telco Rule generally involve complex issues, and the processing of complaints may involve not only the factual determination of the conduct being complained of, but also the economic assessment of the impact the alleged conduct has, or might be expected to have, on the competitive process in the market. The processing of complaints therefore often results in extensive, resource-intensive enquiries which impose significant costs not only on OFCA, but also on the subject of complaint and other industry participants who may be required to supply information.   A complainant is thus generally required to articulate its complaint with sufficient details, pursuant to an Information Checklist, to enable OFCA to assess whether the complaint raises a genuine issue within the Telco Rule so as to proceed to conduct an investigation under the initial enquiry phase.   OFCA expects a complainant, especially where the complainant is an experienced and well-resourced industry participant, to make a sufficiently detailed and well-reasoned complaint submission with arguments and evidence clearly presented. The conduct complained of must be specified and there should be factual and economic evidence in support of why the complainant considers that the Telco Rule has been breached.   A general allegation that conduct is anti-competitive or exploitative is most unlikely to be considered adequate.[32]

Confidentiality   In order for OFCA to gain a more complete picture of the matter being complained of, it often needs to reveal the information it has obtained, and the source of that information, to the subject of complaint and other relevant parties for their comments on the allegations. If a complainant has any concern over the disclosure of identity, it may request that its identity be kept confidential with reasons in support.   OFCA will consider whether such request for non-disclosure of identity is justified.   However, there may be circumstances where it is not possible to pursue further action in relation to a complaint if the complainant is unwilling to disclose its identity.[33]

If a complainant has any concern over the disclosure of certain information revealed in the complaint submission or supporting documents on the basis of commercial confidentiality, it is required to submit a non-confidential version of the complaint with all the supporting documents, so that a copy of the same can be provided to the subject of complaint or other relevant parties for comments where necessary. The complainant should keep to the minimum the amount of information requested to be withheld on grounds of confidentiality

---

[32]   Telco Rule Guide, paras 9-10. The Information Checklist is set out at Appendix B to the Telco Rule Guide, though where a complainant is considered not to have the requisite knowledge or resources in preparing a complaint submission in accordance with the Information Checklist, OFCA is prepared to offer assistance as appropriate.
[33]   Telco Rule Guide, para 14.

and explain in what way the information is confidential and should not be disclosed.[34]

Only information concerning the business, commercial or financial affairs of the complainant, the disclosure of which may adversely affect the complainant's lawful business, commercial or financial affairs, may be withheld from disclosure. Generally speaking, the more historical or dated the information is, even if it concerns the business, commercial or financial affairs of the complainant, the less likely the information will lead to any adverse impact. OFCA will discuss with the complainant if it considers that any of the information which is claimed to be confidential should be disclosed. If the complainant insists on non-disclosure despite OFCA's contrary view, this may result in OFCA not being able to further process the complaint.[35]

Consideration of complaint OFCA will acknowledge receipt of a complaint in writing within 3 working days. The acknowledgement of receipt will include the contact information of the case officer handling the complaint to whom enquiries concerning the progress of the case may be made.[36] OFCA will check whether the complaint submission contains the requisite information set out in the Information Checklist. If not, it will contact the complainant requiring it to supply the information required. In this regard, OFCA will not apply the Information Checklist in a mechanical way and will consider the circumstances surrounding each case to decide whether the complainant has supplied the information required. In particular, it will take account of the size and resources available to a complainant in determining what information OFCA would expect to be included in a complaint. If, despite OFCA's request, the complainant is still not able to supply the information required, this may result in OFCA not being able to further process the complaint due to insufficiency of information.[37]

Upon receipt of all the information required, OFCA will examine the complaint in detail. If the matter being complained of is outside the scope of the Telco Rule, OFCA will not pursue the matter further and will notify the complainant in writing of the same.[38] If the matter is within the scope of the Telco Rule, OFCA will proceed to investigation and the complainant will be informed of the same in writing. An investigation may consist of two phases, the initial enquiry phase and the full investigation phase.[39]

---

[34] Telco Rule Guide, para 15.
[35] Telco Rule Guide, para 15.
[36] Telco Rule Guide, para 16.
[37] Telco Rule Guide, para 17.
[38] Telco Rule Guide, para 18.
[39] Telco Rule Guide, para 19.

Initial enquiry phase During the initial enquiry phase, OFCA will consider the complaint submission and collect further information which is considered necessary to enable the Communications Authority to decide whether to commence full investigation on the basis that there are reasonable grounds to suspect that there may be an infringement of the Telco Rule. Further information may be sought from the subject of complaint, or where necessary from other relevant parties, or by way of market enquiries, or from the complainant.[40] Upon collection of the necessary information, OFCA will conduct the initial assessment to enable the Communications Authority to determine whether there are reasonable grounds for it to suspect that there may be an infringement of the Telco Rule.[41]

The Communications Authority may consider that there is no reasonable ground for it to suspect that there may be a breach of the Telco Rule, in which case it will notify the complainant and the subject of complaint (where the subject of complaint has been informed of the complaint) in writing of its decision that a full investigation will not be commenced. It may decide not to pursue the case on administrative policy grounds without forming a view about the merits of the case.[42] Alternatively, the Communications Authority may consider that there are reasonable grounds for it to suspect that there may be a breach of the Telco Rule and may decide to commence a full investigation, in which case it will inform the complainant, the subject of complaint and other relevant parties in writing of its decision. However, the commencement of the full investigation in no way represents or implies that a view has been formed by the Communications Authority that there is a breach of the Telco Rule.[43]

OFCA will endeavour to complete the initial assessment and inform the relevant parties of the Communications Authority's decision as to whether full investigation will be commenced within twelve weeks from receipt of all the necessary information required for conducting the initial assessment.[44]

Full investigation phase If the Communications Authority decides to commence a full investigation, and depending on the complexity of the case, a roadmap setting out all the key stages of the full investigation and the proposed time-frames for completing these stages may be developed in consultation with the complainant, the subject of complaint or other relevant parties.[45] OFCA will invite the parties to make formal submissions on the complaint, which will often include submissions of facts, as well as legal and economic arguments

---

[40] Telco Rule Guide, paras 20-21.
[41] Telco Rule Guide, para 22.
[42] Telco Rule Guide, para 23.
[43] Telco Rule Guide, para 24.
[44] Telco Rule Guide, para 25.
[45] Telco Rule Guide, para 26.

with evidence in support of those arguments.[46] Parties may request non-disclosure of commercially sensitive information contained in their submissions. If such is the case, they are required to submit a non-confidential version of their submissions with the supporting documents. They should keep to the minimum the amount of information requested to be withheld on confidentiality ground and provide reasons justifying their requests.[47]

All parties who make submissions to the Communications Authority will be given the opportunity to comment on the other parties' submissions and respond to the arguments raised in those submissions. They will be provided with a copy of the others parties' submissions (or where applicable, a copy of the non-confidential version of the others parties' submissions) and be given sufficient time to respond.[48] Where necessary, the Communications Authority may exercise its formal powers under the Telecommunications Ordinance to obtain information from the relevant parties.[49]

When all the required information and submissions have been received, OFCA will conduct a full assessment to enable the Communications Authority to decide whether, on the balance of probabilities, a case of a breach of the Telco Rule is established against the subject of complaint. Even after the full investigation has been commenced, the Communications Authority may, for administrative priority reasons, decide not to pursue the case further without forming any view about the merits of the case.[50]

During the full investigation, OFCA will keep the complainant informed of progress. Currently, OFCA strives to complete 80% of full investigations, or if full investigation is still in progress, report the progress of the full investigation to the complainant, within four months from the commencement of the full investigation. Full investigation of cases may sometimes take more time, depending on, for example, the complexity of the case, the amount of information involved, and OFCA's resources.[51]

Where the conduct being complained about is still on-going and is alleged to be continually causing serious damage to consumers or other industry players, the Communications Authority may consider taking urgent action within such time-frames as the circumstances warrant to deal with the complaint. It retains the discretion not to adhere to the time-frames set out in the Telco Rule Guide and will determine a time-frame which it deems appropriate in the circumstances. Where circumstances require and if it

---

[46] Telco Rule Guide, para 27. The parties may consider it necessary to engage their own economic experts to assist them in preparing the economic evidence, and they will be given sufficient time to make the submissions accordingly.

[47] Telco Rule Guide, para 28.

[48] Telco Rule Guide, para 29.

[49] Telco Rule Guide, para 30.

[50] Telco Rule Guide, para 31.

[51] Telco Rule Guide, para 35.

considers it justifiable to do so, the Communications Authority may also depart from all or any part of the procedures set out in the Telco Rule Guide.[52]

Final decision Where a case of breach is not established, the Communications Authority will set out its provisional findings in the form of a decision (Telco Rule Decision) and invite the relevant parties to provide comments within a reasonable period of time. If, after consideration of the comments received, the Communications Authority maintains its view that a case of breach is not established, the Communications Authority will finalise the decision accordingly. The subject of complaint and other relevant parties will be informed of the Communications Authority's decision in writing. The decision will be published on the Communications Authority's website[53] for public information.

If the Communications Authority considers that a breach is established after consideration of the comments received, it will set out its provisional findings, with proposed actions or financial penalties if appropriate, in a draft Telco Rule Decision and invite the subject of complaint to make representations within a reasonable period of time depending on the complexity of the case. It will also invite other relevant parties to provide comments on the draft decision. If circumstances so require, further opportunities may be given to the subject of complaint to make representations, or to the subject of complaint or other relevant parties to provide further information or comments, for example if there is a substantive change of the Communications Authority's views after considering the parties' representations and comments. The Communications Authority will carefully consider all such further representations, information and comments received before reaching a final decision. When it is satisfied that no more representations, information or comments is required, it will make its finalised Telco Rule Decision. The subject of complaint and other relevant parties will be informed of the final decision in writing. The decision will be published on the Communications Authority's website for public information.[54]

Once the Telco Rule Decision is made but before its publication on the Communications Authority's website, the subject of complaint and other relevant parties will be given the opportunity to make representations about non-disclosure of any information contained in the decision which they consider to be commercially confidential. The Communications Authority will consider such representations in deciding the need for making any redactions in the decision before publication. It will also need to consider whether the

---

[52] Telco Rule Guide, para 36.
[53] http://www.coms-auth.hk/en/policies_regulations/competition/telecommunications/completed_abuse/index.html.
[54] Telco Rule Guide, para 33.

disclosure is necessary for the public to understand the reasoning of the Telco Rule Decision.[55]

Enforcement by the Communications Authority   The Communications Authority may issue a direction to bring contravening conduct to an end.[56]   It may also issue a warning to a licensee when, notwithstanding a finding that there is a contravention of the competition provisions, it is of the view that any other sanction is not justified by the circumstances of the case.   Where the Communications Authority considers it to be in the public interest, the licensee may be required to publish the warning.[57]

The Communications Authority may impose financial penalties on the licensee for contravening the competition provisions.   On the first occasion a penalty of up to and including HK$200,000 may be imposed, on the second occasion there may be penalty of up to and including HK$500,000, and for any subsequent occasions on which a penalty is imposed, the penalty may be up to and including HK$1,000,000.   If the Communications Authority considers that such a penalty is inadequate, it may make an application to the Court of First Instance, which may impose a financial penalty of a sum not exceeding 10% of the licensee's turnover during the period of the contravention, or HK$10,000,000, whichever is the higher.[58]

Private enforcement   Under section 39A of the Telecommunications Ordinance, a person sustaining loss or damage from a breach of the Telco Rule may bring an action for damages, an injunction or other appropriate remedy, order or relief against the person who is in breach.   No such action may be brought more than three years after: (a) the commission of the breach concerned; or (b) the imposition of a penalty in relation to the breach by the Communications Authority or, as the case may be, by the Court of First Instance, under section 36C of the Telecommunications Ordinance, whichever is the later.

---

[55]   Telco Rule Guide, para 34.

[56]   Telecommunications Ordinance, section 36B.

[57]   Guidelines to Assist Licensees to Comply with the Competition Provisions under the Telecommunications Ordinance, 11 June 2013, paras 5.12 and 5.13.   Whilst these Guidelines were prepared without specific reference to the new section 7Q of the Telecommunications Ordinance, there is no reason why the Guidelines should not apply equally to the Telco Rule.

[58]   Telecommunications Ordinance, section 36C.   For factors that the Communications Authority will take into account when imposing a penalty, see the Guidelines on the imposition of financial penalty under section 36C of the Telecommunications Ordinance, 15 April 2002, and the Guidelines to Assist Licensees to Comply with the Competition Provisions under the Telecommunications Ordinance, paras 5.17 to 5.19.

Appeals Any person aggrieved by (a) an opinion, determination, direction or decision of the Communications Authority relating to section 7Q of the Telecommunications Ordinance or any related licence condition or (b) any sanction or remedy imposed or to be imposed under the Telecommunications Ordinance by the Communications Authority in consequence of a breach of that section or any licence condition may appeal to the Telecommunications (Competition Provisions) Appeal Board[59] against such opinion, determination, direction, decision, sanction or remedy.[60] An appeal acts as a stay where the appeal subject matter concerns financial penalties as referred to in sections 36C(1A), (1B) or (1C) of the Telecommunications Ordinance, until the appeal is determined, withdrawn or abandoned.[61]

A person who wishes to make an appeal must lodge a notice of appeal with the Appeal Board not later than 14 days after he knows, or ought reasonably to have known, of the proposed appeal subject matter.[62] In the hearing of an appeal, any party shall be entitled to be heard either in person or through a counsel or solicitor, and if any party is a company, through any of its directors or other officers, or if a partnership, through any of its partners.[63]

Subject to a person's privilege against disclosure as if the proceedings were proceedings before a court of law, the Appeal Board may receive and consider any material, whether by way of oral evidence, written statements, documents or otherwise, and whether or not it would be admissible in a court of law. However, this does not entitle a person to require the Appeal Board to receive and consider any material which had not been submitted to or made available to the Communications Authority at any time before the opinion, determination, direction, decision, sanction or remedy appealed against was formed, made, imposed or to be imposed.[64]

The determination of an appeal by the Appeal Board or any order as to costs made by the Appeal Board is final, though the Appeal Board may refer any question of law arising in an appeal to the Court of Appeal for determination.[65] The Court of Appeal may determine the question stated or remit the case to the Appeal Board, in whole or in part, for reconsideration in the light of the Court's determination. The Appeal Board shall not determine the relevant appeal pending the Court of Appeal's determination of a point of law.[66]

---

[59] Established under section 32M(1) of the Telecommunications Ordinance.
[60] Telecommunications Ordinance, section 32N(1). As to who may be an aggrieved person, see sections 32N(1A), (1B) and (1C) of the Telecommunications Ordinance.
[61] Telecommunications Ordinance, section 32N(3).
[62] Telecommunications Ordinance, section 32N(4).
[63] Telecommunications Ordinance, section 32O(1)(c).
[64] Telecommunications Ordinance, sections 32O(1)(d), 32O(2) and 32P.
[65] Telecommunications Ordinance, sections 32Q and 32R(1).
[66] Telecommunications Ordinance, section 32R(2).

Chapter Seven

COMPETITION AND HONG KONG'S MAJOR ECONOMIC SECTORS

7.1 CONSTRUCTION

Introduction   The construction sector is a major part of Hong Kong's economy, contributing about 4.3% annually to its gross domestic product, , with total receipts of HK$327.4 billion in 2014.[1]   The sector has remained buoyant in recent years thanks to a number of major public rail and road infrastructure projects, together with a steady stream of smaller-scale projects. It is, however, a sector that has been prone to high levels of anti-competitive conduct.   Investigations by regulators in Europe have exposed widespread cartel conduct in the sector, particularly bid-rigging and price fixing.   In Hong Kong, the building maintenance and renovation market has been one of the first targets of the Competition Commission.   The Commission has commenced a market study into the market and indicated that bid-rigging may be common.   This section provides an outline of key features of Hong Kong's construction sector and common procurement methods.   It then discusses the sector from a competition law perspective, covering market definition, market concentration and barriers to entry.   Finally, cartel conduct in the sector is considered, including bid-rigging, price fixing, market sharing and output limitation, as well as the factors that make the sector particularly prone to cartel conduct.

The Hong Kong construction sector   The construction sector is diverse in nature.   It includes construction services providers, construction materials producers and distributors.   The Hong Kong Standard Industrial Classification divides construction works into three broad categories: (a) construction of buildings; (b) civil engineering; and (c) specialised construction activities.[2]

The construction of buildings category covers general construction of buildings of all kinds.   It includes the construction of entire dwellings, office buildings, stores, public utility buildings and farm buildings.   It covers new

---

[1]   Key Statistics on Business Performance and Operating Characteristics of the Building, Construction and Real Estate Sectors in 2014, Census and Statistics Department, 29 December 2015.

[2]   Hong Kong Standard Industrial Classification (HSIC) Version 2.0, Census and Statistics Department, 17 July 2009, pp 177-187.

work, repair, additions and alterations, and the erection of pre-fabricated and temporary building structures.

The civil engineering category covers road works, including flyovers, bridges and tunnels; railways; piers and other port works; airports; utility plants for the supply of water, gas, electricity and communication services; dock works and other industrial structures and facilities; drainage, refuse and sewerage treatment plants; gardens and parks; land formation and reclamation; landscaping and slope protection; and structures and facilities classified as site works.

The specialised construction activities category covers specialised activities carried out without responsibility for the entire project. These activities require specialised skills or equipment, such as pile-driving, foundation work, concrete work, brick laying, stone setting, scaffolding and roof covering. Specialised construction activities are mostly carried out under subcontract, but in repair construction they are usually done directly for the owner of the property. The category also includes building finishing and building completion activities, such as plumbing, heating and air-conditioning systems, antennas, alarm systems, electrical work, sprinkler systems, elevators and escalators, insulation, lighting, painting, plastering, tiling and carpentry. The rental of construction equipment with operator is also classified within this category.

7.1.1 Features of Hong Kong's construction sector

Size of companies in the sector   The construction sector is a major part of Hong Kong's economy.   There are about 25,000 companies and 190,000 people working in the sector. A small number of large main contractors form a major group in the sector. There are about 310 main contractors and together they engage about 38,000 people and have total receipts of up to HK$153 billion annually.   Many of the main contractors operate as joint ventures between major foreign development and construction companies.   The vast majority of companies in the sector are small- and medium-sized, with about 98% engaging fewer than 50 people. These companies account for about 58% of the total persons directly engaged in the sector, and about 55% of the total receipts.

There is a high degree of multi-tier subcontracting in the sector. Large and complex building contracts are usually awarded as single packages to large main contractors, who enter contracts directly with the owner of a project. The main contractors assume full responsibility for the completion of the construction work, and award subcontracts to smaller specialist subcontractors. The subcontractors may, in turn, engage other subcontractors for specific tasks. Profitability in the sector tends to be low.   Sub-contractors, in particular, typically operate on low margins and rely on high turnover. In 2014, the average gross surplus for all companies was 7%.

Government projects Public works constitute a major part of the construction sector. In recent years, the Hong Kong Government has embarked on an ambitious program of major infrastructure projects, including transport infrastructure, public housing, and medical, educational and leisure facilities. This follows the announcement in October 2007 of the Government's Ten Major Infrastructure Projects strategy. These major projects are currently being rolled out in phases, with construction on several currently underway. With a number of projects entering their construction peaks, capital works expenditure is expected to maintain relatively high levels for several years. In the 2015-16 Budget, the Government projected public expenditure on capital works to be HK$70 billion for the fiscal year ending March 2016.[3] Major public infrastructure projects that are currently in the planning or construction phase include the following:

- Central to Wanchai Bypass: a 4.5km dual three-lane trunk road with a 3.7km tunnel. Construction began in 2009 with an estimated cost of HK$36 billion.
- Guangzhou-Shenzhen-Hong Kong Express Rail Link (Hong Kong section): a 26km underground high-speed railway between Hong Kong and Shenzhen. It is targeted for completion in 2018, and the estimated construction cost is HK$85.3 billion.
- Hong Kong International Airport Third Runway: construction of a third runway and associated infrastructure, currently in the planning phase.[4]
- Hong Kong-Zhuhai-Macau Bridge: a 29.6km bridge and tunnel with dual 3-lane carriageway between Hong Kong and Zhuhai, construction of which began in December 2009. The estimated cost of the main bridge construction is RMB$38.1 billion (approximately HK$45.1 billion).[5]
- South Island Line (East): a 7km underground commuter railway connecting five MTR stations. It is targeted for completion at the end of 2016, and the estimated construction cost is HK$16.9 billion.[6]
- Sha Tin to Central Link: a 17km underground commuter railway connecting ten MTR stations. The targeted sectional opening dates are 2019 and 2021, and the approved project estimate is HK$79.8 billion.[7]

---

[3] Estimates for 2015-16, Budget Speech by the Financial Secretary, 25 February 2015, paras 162-163.

[4] http://www.threerunwaysystem.com.

[5] http://www.hzmb.hk.

[6] Progress Update of the Construction of the West Island Line, South Island Line (East) and Kwun Tong Line Extension, Transport and Housing Bureau, Highways Department, November 2015 (Legislative Council Panel Paper No. CB(4)298/15-16(02), paras 3, 13.

[7] Progress Update of the Construction of the Shatin to Central Link, Transport and Housing Bureau, Highways Department, November 2015 (Legislative Council Panel Paper No. CB(4)298/15-16(01)), para 4 and Annex 2, para 3.

- Tuen Mun-Chek Lap Kok Link: a 9km dual two-lane carriageway. As at January 2016, the northern section was targeted for completion in 2018, and the completion date of the southern section was under review. Approved funding for the construction works is HK$44.8 billion.[8]
- West Kowloon Cultural District: a large cultural district comprising performing arts, exhibition, event and open spaces, a new museum, and office and residential buildings. The district is being constructed in phases, with the majority of works due to be completed by 2020.[9]

Procurement Public procurement in Hong Kong is governed by the World Trade Organisation Agreement on Government Procurement (WTO GPA) and the Hong Kong Government's Stores and Procurement Regulations. Lower-value goods and services in the construction sector are usually procured through invitations for quotation. Procurement of higher-value goods and services must be carried out in accordance with the Government's tender procedures.[10] The Government may adopt one of the following tender procedures:

- open tendering: all interested contractors/suppliers/service providers are free to submit tenders. The Government will normally adopt this procedure, and will only invite tenders in alternative ways in special circumstances.
- selective tendering: contractors/suppliers/service providers on the relevant approved lists of providers are invited to submit tenders. Selective tendering is usually adopted for works contracts.
- single and restricted tendering: tenders are invited from only one or a limited number of contractors/suppliers/service providers. This procedure is used only when open competitive tendering would not be an effective means of obtaining the requisite stores or services or for procuring revenue contracts. The procedure may be used, for example, in cases of extreme urgency or where no conforming tenders have been received in response to an open or selective tender process.
- prequalified tendering: tenders are invited from a prequalified list of tenderers that are financially and technically capable of undertaking a particular project or supplying a particular product. These include projects that are extremely complex or technical, high value, or subject to rigid completion programmes. Invitations for prequalification are

---

[8]   http://www.hzmb.hk/eng/about_overview_04.html.

[9]   Update on the Progress of the West Kowloon Cultural District Development, West Kowloon Cultural District Authority, November 2015 (Legislative Council Panel Paper No. CB(2)302/15-16(01)), Annex B.

[10] Lower-value means less than or equal to HK$1.43 million for stores and services as well as revenue contracts, and HK$4 million for services for construction and engineering works). Higher-value means more than those amounts.

be published in the Government Gazette and advertised in newspapers or internet sites.[11]

The WTO GPA requires a degree of transparency of public procurement information. After the award of a contract, the Government must publish a public notice providing information on the tender. The notice must specify the identity of the successful tenderer, and the value of the successful tender or the highest and lowest offers taken into account in the award of the contract. In addition, on the request of an unsuccessful tenderer, the Government must provide any information necessary to determine whether the procurement was conducted fairly, impartially and in accordance with the WTO GPA. However, the Government will not provide information that might prejudice fair competition between suppliers.[12] Private companies, in contrast, can choose their purchasing strategy flexibly and are not subject to the same tender and transparency requirements as the Government. Private companies often utilise similar procurement methods as the Government, including purchasing by quotation and tendering. Many private purchasers also have a list of standard suppliers who they use regularly.

7.1.2 Competition in the construction sector

Defining the relevant market There are numerous individual markets within the construction sector from a competition law perspective, and the relevant market needs to be determined on a case-by-case basis. The construction sector may be classified as a bidding market, given that construction firms typically compete by submitting bids in response to tenders. In bidding markets, the relevant market will include all undertakings that can be viewed as credible bidders for the product at issue in the geographic area where they can place a credible bid. In determining the relevant market, the Competition Commission will consider product and geographic dimensions.

Product market The product market comprises all those products which are considered interchangeable or substitutable by buyers because of the products' characteristics, prices and intended use. Products might be regarded as being subject to competitive constraints through substitutability from the perspective of the buyer (demand-side substitutability) and substitutability from the perspective of the buyer (supply-side substitutability).

Demand-side substitutability is a central factor for the purposes of market definition. The assessment of demand-side substitutability involves an assessment of (a) the range of products viewed as substitutes by buyers and (b)

---

[11] Stores and Procurement Regulations, Chapter III.
[12] World Trade Organisation Agreement on Government Procurement, Articles XVI and XVII.

the areas where buyers would be able and willing to find substitutes for the products concerned. The process of defining the relevant product market will often start by looking at a relatively narrow potential product market definition. The potential product market is then expanded to include those substitute products to which buyers would turn in the face of a price increase above the competitive price. In the construction sector, there is limited possibility for substitutability for most construction works on the demand side. Typically when customers seek quotes from building contractors for construction work it is for a particular type of construction project. The customer (e.g. a property developer) will usually provide specifications as to the type of product or service it is seeking by way of an invitation to tender. The customer may be able to vary the specification in response to a price increase, or even not enter into a contract at all. The customer is unlikely, however, to enter into an entirely new contract in response to a small price rise.

Supply-side substitutability refers to the ability of undertakings to switch production to another product or to begin supplying the product to a different geographic area, in the event of an increase in the price of the product concerned. The Competition Commission will not generally consider supply-side substitutability when defining the relevant market. Rather, it will be considered at a later stage in the Commission's analysis where relevant. In the construction sector, the extent of supply-side substitutability is determined by the extent to which firms can commence supply of a particular type of construction work quickly and without significant extra cost in response to a small increase in price. Where this can be done within a year and without incurring substantial sunk costs, it is likely that the products fall within the same market. For construction contractors, there is a reasonable ability to switch between different types of construction works.[13]

Geographic market The geographic market comprises all those regions or areas where buyers would be able or willing to find substitutes for the products in question. The geographic market may cover a global or regional area, or be limited to Hong Kong or a part of Hong Kong. To determine the geographic market, the Competition Commission will typically begin by looking at a relatively narrow geographic area. It will then consider whether a hypothetical monopolist of the product at issue in the area could profitably sustain a price increase above the competitive level. If not, the test is repeated over wider geographic areas as appropriate until the hypothetical monopolist would find it profitable to sustain a price increase.

The geographic market in the construction sector will depend on the nature of the product or service supplied. For example, in the case of concrete, the chemical characteristics of some concrete mixtures require that the

---

[13] Competition in the Construction Industry, OECD Policy Roundtables, 1 December 2008, p. 106.

construction site is not more than 30km away from the production location.[14] This limits the geographic market to Hong Kong and potentially a limited area of mainland China. In contrast, the geographic market for railway tunnelling works services may be worldwide. This is because MTR Corporation Limited, which is responsible for the construction of all railway construction projects currently being undertaken in Hong Kong, will likely seek tenders from contractors in various countries. Many of the large construction projects carried out in Hong Kong have been awarded to international contractors.

Market concentration Market concentration refers to the number and size of undertakings in a market. A concentrated market is one with a small number of leading undertakings with a large combined market share. Market concentration can provide useful information about the market structure and can be used to assess the relative positions of the undertakings in the market as part of an assessment of market power. The Hong Kong construction sector is comprised of a variety of markets with varying levels of market concentration. There are a large number of small firms in the sector, but this does not mean the sector is unconcentrated. Many contractors carry out highly specialised work that can only be performed by a limited number of firms, and not all firms do overlapping work. For example, a plumber does not compete with a carpenter, and a company that builds stadiums does not typically compete with one that builds residential houses.

Some markets in the sector tend to be oligopolistic. For example, only a limited number of contractors are capable of managing large and complex construction projects. Many of the construction product markets are highly concentrated due to the capital requirements and economies-of-scale required to manufacture the products. For example, the asphalt industry is dominated by a small number of large asphalt manufacturers and distributors. In addition, contractors with highly specialised skills often have few competitors. Competition among smaller firms carrying out less specialised work tends to be stronger. For example, the market for contractors who do basic labour work such as bricklaying and pouring concrete tends to be closer to perfect competition [15]

Barriers to entry There are few significant barriers for many small companies to enter the construction sector. The start-up costs for entering the market tend to be low. This is because small companies usually lease, rather than purchase, equipment on an as-needed, project-by-project basis. The plentiful use of subcontracting provides opportunities for small companies to enter the market. Small companies are also able to subcontract out parts of a

[14] Market definition, OECD Policy Roundtables, 11 October 2012, page 341.
[15] Competition in the Construction Industry, OECD Policy Roundtables, 1 December 2008, pp. 9, 19, 20, 39, 40 and 78.

contract that they are not capable of performing themselves. As a result, in Hong Kong there are a large number of small construction companies carrying out work on small-scale projects and specialist subcontracting. In contrast, barriers to entry for large construction companies are higher, and as a result the market for large construction projects is more concentrated. Owners of large construction projects usually demand a track record of successfully completed relevant projects.[16] Newer firms are therefore at a disadvantage. Large construction companies also benefit from economies of scale, allowing them to lower unit costs by purchasing in bulk.

Areas of the construction sector that require high investments or specific expertise tend to be more difficult to enter. For example, barriers to entry for manufacturers of construction products tend to be high due to the need for economies of scale and capital investments such as machinery and factory capacity. Specialised markets such as underground engineering and railway construction also require investment in expensive machinery. Government laws, regulations and policies create barriers to entry into the construction sector. Under the Buildings Ordinance,[17] architects, engineers and surveyors must apply for registration and demonstrate that they are suitably qualified. Companies carrying out building works must appoint a registered structural engineer and registered geotechnical engineer. Contractors wishing to carry out general building works, specialised works and minor works must apply for registration and demonstrate that they are capable to carrying out the work. In addition, the Government maintains a list of approved contractors for public works. Contractors in the list may tender for public works contracts only in the works categories and groups for which they are approved. Companies must also acquire licenses and permits to start and finish construction work.

7.1.3 Cartels in the construction sector

Construction sector and cartel conduct The construction sector has been a major target of competition regulators around the world. The sector has been particularly prone to cartel conduct by construction contractors and construction products manufacturers. Construction cartels involving hundreds of companies have been detected. For example, in 2002, the Dutch government exposed rampant collusion in the construction sector, with 481 leniency applications and about 650 companies implicated and in 2009, 103 construction companies in England were fined for colluding with competitors in relation to 199 tenders for building projects. The Competition Commission

---

[16] Competition and Barriers to Entry the Construction Sector, Andersson N., and Malmberg, F. in 10th Symposium Construction Innovation and Global Competitiveness, Ben Obinero Uwakweh and Issam A. Minkarah CRC Press 2002, p. 465.

[17] Buildings Ordinance (Cap. 123).

has recognised the potential for anti-competitive conduct in the sector in Hong Kong. In 2015, it commenced a market study into the building maintenance and renovation market.[18] The market study followed allegations of bid rigging on tenders for building projects. The Commission investigated whether bid rigging was systematic in the market, with data indicating a prevalence of cartel conduct.[19] Commission chairperson Anna Wu said that bid rigging in the market was widespread, and she expected to receive numerous complaints.[20]

Factors contributing to cartel conduct A number of features of the construction sector make it vulnerable to collusion between competitors. There is often frequent interaction and collaboration between competitors. Construction companies generally compete against the same firms, providing opportunities for repeated interaction. Companies also regularly collaborate in joint venture and subcontracting arrangements. Companies may be competitors in some projects and partners in others. This may allow competitors to collect information from each other and provides opportunities for collusion.[21] The prevalence of subcontracting may provide an opportunity for collusion. Bidders who agree not to lower their bid or not to participate in a tender may be compensated by being awarded a subcontract by the winning bidder.[22] Active involvement in trade associations can also facilitate collusion.

Public procurement, which creates a large amount of the demand in the sector, is particularly vulnerable to cartel conduct. This is because the public procurement process is comparatively transparent and predictable. The Government usually releases information about winning tenderers, including the identity of the winner and the tender price. This transparency may allow cartel members to monitor whether other members are complying with the cartel arrangements. Frequent tenders and a predictable tender procedure also create opportunities for stable cartels to operate.

The sector is also vulnerable to cartel conduct because price is a key factor in determining which company is awarded a particular project, especially for smaller projects. This may facilitate bid rigging and price fixing between competitors. Small-scale contractors in each market tend to offer similar products and services, and buyers do not usually have a preference for which

---

[18] Hong Kong Competition Commission, Annual Report 2014/15, p. 49.
[19] MLex Global Antitrust Hong Kong competition agency asks whether bid rigging systematic in building maintenance, 3 December 2015.
[20] MLex Global Antitrust, Hong Kong antitrust chief says bid rigging "widespread" in building maintenance market, 8 December 2015.
[21] OECD Competition Committee, Competition and Procurement, 2011, p. 21.
[22] OECD Policy Roundtables, Public Procurement, 8 January 2008, p. 9.

contractor they use, so long as the contractor can carry out the work and charges a comparatively low price.[23]

7.1.4 Bid rigging

Types of bid rigging   Bid rigging occurs when bidders agree among themselves who will win a tender, and manipulate the bidding process to achieve that outcome.   After the tender is awarded, the winning bidder may compensate the co-conspirators through cash payments or by awarding them subcontracts.   Bid rigging is Serious Anti-Competitive Conduct under the Competition Ordinance and is prohibited under the First Conduct Rule.   In the construction sector, it can occur in a number of ways, including:

- cover bidding: a competitor agrees to submit a non-competitive bid that is too high to be accepted or contains terms and conditions it knows will not be acceptable to the buyer. The aim is to create a false impression that the bidding process is competitive.
- bid suppression or withdrawal: a competitor agrees not to bid or to withdraw a bid from consideration.
- bid rotation: competitors agree to take turns at winning tenders.

Bid rigging cases   Cases of bid rigging in the Hong Kong construction sector were revealed even before the Competition Ordinance took effect in December 2015.   In one case, stainless steel gate suppliers, who were the only contractors approved by the Housing Authority to supply stainless steel gates to housing projects built for the Authority, entered into a cartel agreement. The suppliers would designate one of themselves as the potential supplier and put in a tender at a pre-agreed minimum price. Other members of the cartel might also submit bids, but at higher prices. This arrangement was to enhance the chance of the designated supplier obtaining the contract.   The profit collected by the designated supplier would later be distributed to its members equally. After the dissolution of the cartel, one member sued the other members for unpaid profits from the cartel. The High Court rejected the claim on the basis that the cartel conduct was against the public interest and should be discouraged in strong terms.[24]   In October 2015, a former engineering company boss in Hong Kong admitted in the District Court to conspiring to rig the tender process for building renovation contracts and pleaded guilty to conspiracy offences under the Crimes Ordinance and Prevention of Bribery Ordinance.   The conduct involved bribes of about HK$45 million to secure tenders for the renovation of

---

[23]   Hong Kong's First Competition Law: Impact on Construction Contracting, Xiaojing Zhao; Sai On Cheung; and Yishan Guo, Journal of Legal Affairs and Dispute Resolution in Engineering and Construction, 26 September 2013, p. 4.

[24]   *Sit Kam Tai v Gammon Iron Gate Co Ltd* [2010] HKEC 1207.

two residential estates.[25] The bid rigging conduct in these cases would most likely have breached the Competition Ordinance if the conduct had taken place after the competition rules came into effect.

Construction companies and individuals have been fined for bid rigging in other jurisdictions. For example, in 2014 the South Korea Fair Trade Commission fined six construction companies that colluded in relation to tenders for the construction of an extension of the Busan subway.[26] The companies agreed on which of them would win the tenders for three sections of the rail extension. Three companies submitted sham bids that presented pre-agreed high prices and low-quality designs. The remaining three companies submitted pre-agreed lower prices and higher-quality designs. The values of each of the winning tenders were between about HK$640 and 775 million. The aim of the conduct was to give the impression that there was competition for the tenders, and also to make the tenders of the pre-arranged winners look comparatively superior. The South Korea Fair Trade Commission found that the contractors contravened South Korean competition law and imposed fines on each company of HK$8-35 million.

Detecting bid rigging Bid rigging can be difficult to detect since it is carried out covertly, but a number of factors can alert buyers to potential bid rigging. For example:

- unexplained identical prices or terms;
- unusually high or low bids;
- bid prices are higher than published price lists or engineering cost estimates;
- different bidders making the same mistakes, such as identical calculations or spelling errors;
- a bidder increasing its price compared with previous bids for the same goods or services;
- the successful bidder later subcontracting the works to other bidders;
- bidders taking turns to win in a rotating pattern;
- qualified bidders failing to bid;
- certain contractors repeatedly avoiding bidding against one another.

These factors may be indicators of collusive conduct, but they are not conclusive. There are sometimes good explanations for certain behaviour. For example, a company may decide not to bid for a project because it does not have spare capacity; or high bids may simply reflect a different assessment of the cost of a project.

Long-term bidding analysis may also be used to detect bid rigging. A regular pattern of suspicious behaviour over a period of time is often a better

---

[25] Independent Commission Against Corruption press release, *Ex-engineering firm proprietor admits $45m bribery over tender rigging exercises*, 27 October 2015.

[26] *Busan Subway Line 1 Extension*, South Korea Fair Trade Commission, 10 April 2014.

indicator of possible bid rigging than evidence from a single bid. Patterns of bid rigging behaviour may be identified if bid data is constantly monitored and analysed. The South Korea Fair Trade Commission has introduced a Bid Rigging Indicator Analysis System to detect bid rigging. A total of 322 public organisations are required to supply tender information to the Commission. It then analyses the data to identify signs of bid rigging.[27] In Switzerland, the Competition Commission analysed data from a road surfacing cartel that operated between 1999 and 2004. It compared the price volatility in the bidding during the periods when the cartel was and was not operating. The data showed significantly less price volatility when the cartel was operating.[28]

Preventing bid rigging The risk of bid rigging can be mitigated by reducing barriers to entry into the tender process and increasing bidders' participation. If a large number of bidders are able to participate, it is harder for members of a cartel to manipulate the tender process. Barriers to entry can be lowered by, for example:

- minimising the cost of preparing a bid. This may be achieved by (i) not changing bid forms unnecessarily, (ii) not requiring information that is of little use, (iii) allowing adequate time for bids to be prepared, (iv) using electronic bidding systems, and (v) paying companies for their time in preparing their bids;
- reducing the criteria for allowing companies to participate in the tender. This may be achieved by removing unnecessary restrictions on the size, composition or nature of companies that may bid;
- inviting tenders from international as well as local companies; and
- designing the tender to allow smaller companies to participate, for example by allowing bidding on a portion of a large contract.[29]

The risk of bid rigging can also be mitigated by reducing transparency in the tender process. A less transparent tender process can make it harder for cartel members to monitor other members' compliance with a bid rigging agreement.[30] Transparency can be reduced by:

- limiting the amount of information released about the tenders received, including the identity of bidders and the prices in each bid. The identity of bidders may be kept confidential by using numbers, rather than names, to identify them; and
- including multidimensional criteria in the tender, so that it is more difficult to predict how the winner will be chosen. Tender

[27] Round Table Competition Policy and Public Procurement, 12th Session of the Intergovernmental Group of Experts on Competition Law and Policy, 9 to 11 July 2012, Mr Jaeho Moon.

[28] Competition in the Construction Industry, OECD Policy Roundtables, 1 December 2008 p. 93.

[29] OECD, Designing Tenders to Reduce Bid Rigging, www.oecd.org/competition, p. 8.

[30] OECD Policy Roundtables, Competition in Bidding Markets, 4 June 2007, p. 10.

specifications may be defined in terms of functional performance rather than reference to specific products.

It may be harder to reduce transparency in public tenders as compared with private tenders. This is because the Government is obliged under the WTO GPA to publish information on the tender, including information about the winning bidder. However, the WTO GPA does allow the Government to withhold information that might prejudice fair competition between suppliers.

Bid rigging can be discouraged by reducing the frequency and consistency of tenders, and limiting communication among bidders. Companies can only sustain a bid rigging cartel if they regularly meet and interact. Reducing the number of such opportunities may make it more difficult to operate a cartel. The frequency of tenders could be reduced by, for example, holding fewer and larger tenders. Tenders can be made less predictable by varying the scope of successive contracts by aggregating or disaggregating contracts.[31] Internal procedures can also be put in place to detect signs of potential bid rigging. Procurement staff can be trained about detecting bid rigging and designing tenders to minimise the risk of bid rigging. Entities that regularly issue tenders can maintain a database of past and present bid results, and analyse the data to identify possible signs of bid rigging.

7.2 ENERGY

Introduction The Competition Ordinance makes no specific provision for either the electricity or the gas sector and, unlike many jurisdictions (for example the United Kingdom), Hong Kong lacks both a comprehensive body of regulatory law relating to the energy sector and an independent economic regulator to enforce it. Accordingly, there is no equivalent in Hong Kong to the licensing regime found in the UK and other EU Member States that governs the generation, transmission, distribution and supply of electricity and the transmission, transport, shipping and supply of gas, nor is there any equivalent in Hong Kong to the various energy packages[32] of regulations and directives adopted by the European Union since 1990 that have made provision for such matters as the compulsory unbundling of the ownership of gas and electricity transmission networks from that of energy production and supply. The third energy package also mandates third party access to transmission assets (potentially at regulated prices) and accounting separation where

---

[31] OECD Policy Brief, Fighting Cartels in Public Procurement, October 2008, p. 4.
[32] See, most recently, the EU Third Energy Package of 13 July 2009 comprising three regulations and two directives: Regulation 713/2009 (establishing the Agency for the Cooperation of Energy Regulators (ACER)); Regulations 714/2009 and 715/2009 on conditions for access to electricity and gas networks respectively; Directive 2009/72 concerning common rules for the internal market in electricity; and Directive 2009/73 concerning common rules for the internal market in gas.

undertakings carry out more than one of the activities of energy production, liquid natural gas (LNG) importation, distribution, storage or supply. As the energy sector is not excluded from the ambit of the Competition Ordinance, to the extent that any conduct by a participant in that sector might potentially breach either of the Conduct Rules, the Competition Ordinance may be engaged in the usual way.

The electricity and gas markets in Hong Kong are highly concentrated with only a small number of vertically integrated players active in each. As such, no meaningful competition is currently possible at any level of the electricity sector and there is only limited scope for competition in the gas sector. In March 2015 the Hong Kong Government launched a consultation on the future development of the electricity market in Hong Kong (Electricity Market Consultation) and, specifically, on how to introduce more competition into that market by 2023.[33] It goes without saying that the current absence of competition in the electricity sector does not automatically mean that competition law cannot be brought to bear against the conduct of participants in that sector, though the question arises whether *ex ante* regulation would be a more appropriate legal instrument to deal with any questionable conduct than *ex post* competition law.

In principle, however, there is no reason why the two Conduct Rules could not be used to sanction such conduct as exclusionary contract terms, excessive pricing or refusal of access to essential facilities. All of these potential breaches of the Competition Ordinance would be as relevant in this sector as in any other. For each of the electricity and gas sectors in Hong Kong this section will first set out the industry structure and the legal and commercial framework within which the sector operates and then discuss any proposals for reform that have been made and the potential for the future application of the Competition Ordinance.

Legal framework The closest that Hong Kong comes to a specialist energy regulator is the Environment Bureau, whose policy objectives are to:

- ensure that the energy needs of the community are met safely, reliably, efficiently and at reasonable prices; and
- minimise the environmental impact of energy production and use and promote the efficient use and conservation of energy.

The Environment Bureau recognises that these policy objectives may not entirely align and that the pursuit of one may hamper the realisation of another,[34] for example improvements to reliability of supply may require infrastructure investment that will have to be recouped from customers,

---

[33] See Environment Bureau: Public Consultation on the Future Development of the Electricity Market, March 2015 (Electricity Market Consultation), para 1.1.

[34] *Ibid*, para 1.9. The Electricity Market Consultation refers to four policy objectives, efficiency apparently having been relegated to a subsidiary role.

potentially via increased tariffs. Various legal instruments seek to give effect to these objectives.

7.2.1 Electricity

Market structure Although there are no legal impediments to market entry, the Electricity Market Consultation notes that while interested investors who meet the relevant reliability, safety and environmental performance requirements can enter Hong Kong's electricity market, given the land requirements for constructing new generating units, it may not be easy for new entrants to find suitable sites for the purpose. Also, due to the relatively small size of the electricity market, and the capital intensive nature of the industry, there have hitherto been only two power companies providing electricity to their respective service areas. [35]

The two power companies are CLP Power Hong Kong Limited (CLP) and the Hong Kong Electric Company Limited (HKE), both of which are privately owned. Although neither company has a legally defined supply region or franchise area, each has always operated in a distinct geographical territory and there is no overlap in their geographic coverage. [36] Both companies are vertically integrated in that they operate at all four of the market levels into which the electricity sector is typically segmented, namely: generation, transmission, distribution and supply.

CLP supplies electricity to Kowloon and the New Territories, including Lantau, Cheung Chau and most of the outlying islands and obtains electricity from three power stations in Hong Kong: Castle Peak, Black Point and Penny's Bay, which collectively have a total installed capacity of 6,908 MW. All three power stations are owned by Castle Peak Power Company Limited (CAPCO), 70% of whose shares are owned by CLP with the remaining 30% held by China Southern Power Grid International (HK) Company Limited, a subsidiary of China Southern Power Grid Company Limited (CSPG). [37] To supplement the output of the CAPCO stations, CLP also purchases electricity from the Daya Bay Nuclear Power Station and the Guangzhou Pumped Storage Power Station, both located in Guangdong Province in Mainland China. Power is carried to the various load centres in Hong Kong via CLP's wholly-owned

---

[35]   Electricity Market Consultation, para 1.20.
[36]   There is however limited interconnection of the HKE and CLP transmission systems via a link across Hong Kong harbour that permits each company to offer emergency support to the other, e.g. during generator failures.
[37]   CSPG supplies electricity to the five southern Mainland Chinese provinces/regions of Guangdong, Guangxi, Yunnan, Guizhou and Hainan, which have a combined population of approximately 230 million.

transmission and distribution system.[38] HKE supplies electricity to Hong Kong Island, Ap Lei Chau and Lamma Island from its Lamma Power Station whose total installed capacity is 3,757 MW.

Accordingly, CLP's market share on a Hong Kong-wide basis in 2014 was approximately 74% by electricity sales volume and approximately 80% by customer number with HKE's shares on those bases being 25% and 20% respectively.[39] Although, there is at present no competition at any level of the electricity sector in Hong Kong, the Hong Kong Government has set itself a goal to introduce competition into the electricity market "when the requisite conditions are present".[40]

Safety The Electricity Ordinance,[41] which entered into force in 1990, makes provision for the safe supply of electricity and the safety of household electrical products. It covers *inter alia* the registration of generating facilities, contractors and workers for electrical installations, wiring standards and the safe distribution and use of electricity.[42]

Environmental performance Section 13 of the Air Pollution Control Ordinance (APCO)[43] prohibits undertakings from using premises for one of a number of specified processes (including electricity works[44]) without a licence from the Environmental Protection Department (EPD) of the Hong Kong Government. By section 26G(1) of APCO, the Secretary for the Environment must impose an annual cap on each licensee's emissions of various specified atmospheric pollutants. The precise emissions limits for each pollutant are set out in technical memoranda issued by the Secretary from time to time. Under the Environmental Impact Assessment Ordinance (EIAO),[45] undertakings performing designated functions (including electricity companies) must obtain

---

[38] CLP's transmission system has also interconnected with the Guangdong transmission system since April 1979.

[39] CLP's Hong Kong electricity sales amounted to 32.9 billion kWh in 2014 and it had approximately 2.46 million customers at the year end. HKE's sales of electricity in 2014 were 11 billion kWh and at the year-end it had approximately 570,000 customers.

[40] See foreword to the Electricity Market Consultation by Mr KS Wong, Secretary for the Environment.

[41] Cap. 406.

[42] The Electrical Products (Safety) Regulation was enacted in 1997 and makes further provision for the safety of household electrical appliances. The Electricity Supply Lines (Protection) Regulation was enacted in April 2000 to deter damage to underground electricity cables and overhead electricity lines and commenced operation on 1 April 2001.

[43] Cap. 311.

[44] Defined in para 7 of Schedule 1 to APCO as works in which fossil fuel is burned either wholly or as part of the process of electricity generation where the installed capacity of such works exceeds 5MW.

[45] Cap. 499.

permits from the EPD for the construction of major infrastructure, such as generating plants and transmission lines.

Economic regulation   An attenuated form of economic regulation over CLP and HKE is achieved via Scheme of Control Agreements (SCAs) between the Government of Hong Kong and each of those companies.[46] SCAs do not grant either company an exclusive supply area but they oblige each to provide sufficient facilities to meet present and future electricity demand in the areas which they currently serve[47] pursuant to rolling five year Development Plans agreed with the Executive Council.[48]   These cover matters such as forecast demand for electricity, proposed capital expenditures, expected fuel costs, operating expenditures and proposed basic tariffs for each year.[49]   Each of the SCAs has an initial term of 10 years with an option exercisable by the Government to extend for an additional five years (i.e. until 2023).[50]

The SCAs set a permitted return of 9.99% per annum on the value of the company's average net fixed assets save for renewables net fixed assets, where the permitted return is 11%.   Once the value of the net fixed assets has been established for a company, various deductions are made to the permitted return to reflect interest paid on borrowed capital (up to prescribed levels) and excess capacity along with other incentive/penalty adjustments in respect of emissions performance, supply reliability, operational efficiency, customer services, energy efficiency and investment in the generation of electricity from renewable sources.   The net return is the result once all adjustments provided for in the SCAs have been made to the permitted return.   The basic tariffs that the companies are permitted to charge customers are set at a level designed to allow them to achieve the specified net return on assets in a given year taking into account forecast electricity demand.   As such, the SCAs operate as a form of rate of return or cost-plus price regulation on HKE and CLP.

The tariff paid by customers comprises two components: a basic tariff and a fuel charge.   The basic tariff is set in line with the methodology described above whereas the fuel charge reflects the changing price of the fuels used in

---

[46]   Agreement dated 7 January 2008 between: (i) the Government of the Hong Kong Special Administrative Region; and (ii) Hong Kong Electric Company Limited and HK Electric Investments Limited; and Agreement dated 7 January 2008 between: (i) the Government of the Hong Kong Special Administrative Region; and (ii) CLP Power Hong Kong Limited, Castle Peak Power Company Limited and ExxonMobil Energy Limited (removed with effect from 12 May 2014).

[47]   SCA recital (B) and clause 6.

[48]   SCA Schedule 3, para A(1).

[49]   SCA Schedule 1, paras A(2) and A(3).

[50]   SCA, Clause 7(4).   However by clause 7(5), if the Government elects not to extend an SCA, the provision guaranteeing the permitted rate of return on electricity-related assets will nonetheless continue in force for five years beyond the expiry of the SCA, though not on any electricity-related assets acquired after expiry unless these have been prudently purchased and the acquisition has been approved by the Government.

electricity generation and is passed directly on to customers.[51] The proposed basic tariff for a given year is reviewed by the Government in the final quarter of the previous year to verify that the assumptions underpinning the proposed basic tariff remain valid and to agree any adjustments that may be necessary with the company concerned.[52] There is no provision for review of the fuel charge. In addition, the technical, environmental and financial performances of the companies are subject to an annual auditing review conducted jointly by the Government and each of the companies.[53]

One important feature of the SCAs is that they indemnify the companies against any losses incurred as a result of changes implemented by the Government to the electricity supply market including, for example, opening the markets up to competition, that cause a material loss to a given company.[54]

Electricity Market Consultation on possible reform The Electricity Market Consultation sought views on:[55]

(a) the benefits of introducing competition to the electricity markets in Hong Kong and, in light of the experience of a number of overseas regimes, made proposals for Hong Kong;

(b) assessed the readiness of the Hong Kong market for the introduction of competition after expiry of the current SCAs in 2018, with proposals for the follow-up work to be undertaken;

(c) considered possible improvements to the regulatory framework to facilitate the introduction of competition.

The Electricity Market Consultation notes that common international practice is to divide the electricity supply chain into four vertically-related levels, each of which can be a relevant economic market for competition law purposes:

- generation: the production of electricity at power plants using primary sources of energy, e.g. coal, natural gas, renewable sources, etc.;
- transmission: the bulk transportation of electricity on higher voltage networks from power plants to local areas;
- distribution: the transportation of electricity on lower voltage networks to consumers; and
- retail: the sale of electricity to consumers, including services such as metering and billing.[56]

---

[51] As such there is arguably no incentive on the companies to economise or seek efficiencies in their consumption of fuel.

[52] SCA, Schedule 1, section B.

[53] SCA Schedule 1, section D.

[54] SCA, clause 8.

[55] Electricity Market Consultation, para 2.20. The consultation also sought views on setting the future fuel mix for electricity generation to 2020 to achieve environmental targets.

The Consultation stated that transmission and distribution businesses are generally regarded as natural monopolies, as it would not be practical or economical to have more than one transmission and distribution network in the same geographical area, so that these two segments remain largely regulated even in liberalised markets. Accordingly there was no proposal to stimulate market entry at those levels of the supply chain but competition may be introduced at the generation/wholesale level, retail level or both.[57] Again, this is consistent with international practice. The Consultation then set out various models under which competition at the generation/wholesale and retail levels could be achieved and considered whether this would be beneficial having regard to other Government policy objectives. The review of international experience of liberalised markets hints at some scepticism as to the benefits of a competitive market compared with State planning[58] and the analysis appears superficial in some respects.[59] Nevertheless, the preliminary conclusion is that the Government should continue to pursue its goal of introducing competition to the electricity market.[60]

Readiness of the electricity market for competition As regards the readiness of the Hong Kong market for the introduction of competition on expiry of the current SCAs in September 2018, given the practical constraints to new large-scale generation capacity coming on-stream within Hong Kong itself,[61] the Government considered three possible sources of increased competition:

- via enhanced interconnection capacity with mainland China;
- increased generation capacity in Hong Kong itself; and

---

[56] Note that retail markets may also be segmented into separate markets for domestic and industrial/commercial customers.

[57] Electricity Market Consultation, paras 3.4-3.5.

[58] For example, para 3.2 states "apparently market competition could also result in more suppliers and more choices for electricity customers" and, in relation to security of supply, para 3.10 observes that "the market is supposedly left to send the correct price signals" and para 3.11 states that "more choices do not necessarily lead to higher customer satisfaction."

[59] For example, para 3.7 notes that, after falling in the years immediately after market liberalisation, a fact which is attributed at least in part to the (unsupported) assertion that these assets were sold off at less than their market value, UK electricity tariffs increased between 2003 and 2011. The influence of factors such as fuel costs and Government environmental policies on this outcome, as opposed to the effects of market competition *per se*, is not discussed.

[60] Electricity Market Consultation, para 3.17.

[61] Electricity Market Consultation, para 4.10 states that "it is unlikely that there would be a new, sizable electricity supplier as land is in short supply for a new supplier to build generating plants. As an illustration, assuming that a new market player will account for 20% of the total installed capacity in Hong Kong, it will need to build six gas-generating units. An area of about 25 hectares would be required for the purpose. Even if a suitable area can be located, the concern about the potential environmental impact of the new generating units will also likely invite objection from nearby residents."

- increased competition between the two incumbents, CLP and HKE.

All three options were said to have disadvantages:

- the first because it went against the preference for local generation expressed by Hong Kong consumers in previous consultations;[62]
- the second on cost grounds[63] (at least in relation to large scale gas-fired generation, though it was recognised that small-scale distributed generation could have a part to play if access to the transmission and distribution networks could be facilitated); and
- the third also on cost grounds, though it was acknowledged that this might be a viable solution in the longer term.[64]

The Electricity Market Consultation identified the following preparatory works as prerequisites to the introduction of new market players in the longer term:

- first, the development of a legal framework to enable new suppliers to access the networks of CLP and HKE on fair and reasonable commercial terms,[65] preferably via negotiation with the incumbents rather than mandated by an independent regulator.[66] The Government proposed to conduct a joint study with the incumbents to consider possible mechanisms for determining access fees, technical standards and legal/regulatory issues (demarcation of safety responsibilities, etc.);
- second, to commission a study, involving CLP, HKE and CSPG, into possible arrangements for strengthening the interconnection links between Hong Kong and the Mainland and between the two Hong Kong networks;[67]
- third, as a possible precursor to full ownership unbundling, the Government proposed to look at imposing a requirement on CLP and HKE to publish separate accounts for their generation, transmission and distribution (but not, apparently, retail) functions, subject to the protection of commercially sensitive information.[68]

The preliminary conclusion of the Electricity Market Consultation was therefore that the conditions do not exist for the introduction of competition in 2018.[69] It then examined the changes to the current regulatory arrangements that would be required to facilitate it. The expressed preference was that the current, relatively light-touch, system of regulation via the SCAs should continue rather than a transition to a licence-based system overseen by an

---

[62] *Ibid*, para 4.9.
[63] *Ibid*, paras 4.11-4.12
[64] *Ibid*, paras 4.14-41.5.
[65] *Ibid*, paras 4.17- 4.22.
[66] *Ibid*, para 4.22.
[67] *Ibid*, para 4.23.
[68] *Ibid*, paras 4.24-4.25.
[69] *Ibid*, para 5.1.

independent regulator as exists in other jurisdictions such as the UK.[70] The Consultation considered the alternatives to the price setting mechanism (PSM) set out in the SCAs and expressed the view that the current PSM be retained[71] but with possible adjustments such as a reduction in the permitted rate of return,[72] increasing the penalty for investment in excess generating capacity,[73] making the fuel charge reviewable by the Executive Committee at tariff reviews as well as the basic tariff,[74] and various measures to incentivise fuel efficiency and performance improvements.[75] The Consultation dismissed the suggestion that the term of the SCAs should be reduced from its current ten years, extensible by a further five[76] and accordingly acknowledged that market competition would not be delivered before 2028.

Competition Commission's Response to the Consultation The Competition Commission submitted a detailed response to the Electricity Market Consultation in June 2015.[77] Whilst welcoming the Government's aspiration to introduce competition into the market, the Competition Commission rejected virtually every other preliminary finding and/or proposal set out in the Consultation. In particular, the Commission criticised the absence of any progress since 2008 towards introducing competition in the electricity sector despite this having been one of the stated objectives of the current SCAs when they were entered into in that year. It dismissed the claims made for the effectiveness of the existing system of regulation, suggesting in particular that the PSM is allowing the companies to charge excessive basic tariffs and that the fuel charge pass-through blunts their incentives to seek fuel efficiencies; and doubted that the Government's proposals would deliver any meaningful change. With regard to the rate of progress to date in introducing competition, the Commission noted that the Government had expressed the intention in 2008 to introduce competition into the market within 10 years (i.e. by 2018) when it entered into the current SCAs.[78] As the Consultation envisaged that as at 2015 competition was still at least ten years away, the Competition Commission observed that it is reasonable to conclude that limited progress has been made since 2008 to carry out the preparatory work proposed by the Government when the current SCAs were signed and that the discussions with the power companies envisaged in the SCAs had not been held. Moreover, the

---

[70]   *Ibid*, para 5.4.
[71]   *Ibid*, para 5.13.
[72]   *Ibid*, paras 5.15-5.16.
[73]   *Ibid*, para 5.17.
[74]   *Ibid*, paras 5.23-5.24.
[75]   *Ibid*, paras 5.25-5.29.
[76]   *Ibid*, para 5.14.
[77]   See submission on Public Consultation on the Future Development of the Electricity Market, Competition Commission, June 2015.
[78]   *Ibid*, paras 72-76.

key question of enhancing interconnection between the CSG grid and Hong Kong had not been addressed. [79]

With regard to tariffs, the Competition Commission was fairly scathing of the current PSM, stating that rate of return regulation is widely understood to have a strong potential to create adverse outcomes for customers. In particular, rate of return regulation is well known to create incentives for companies to over-invest in capital equipment, as the company is guaranteed a set rate of return on its investment. Because of the price-setting mechanism, the costs of any over-investment are then directly passed on to customers by way of increased prices. Rate of return regulatory mechanisms share this potentially undesirable feature with other cost-plus pricing mechanisms more generally – a provider may be incentivised to spend as much as possible (because they will be reimbursed for all spending plus a margin or rate of return), rather than spending efficiently. This suggests that the regulatory regime in place may be generating excessive investment in excess capacity and other physical capital assets, in excess of what customers would ultimately wish to fund by way of electricity charges. [80]

The Commission went on to note that such disadvantages would be exacerbated when the allowed rate of return on (potentially excessive) capital investment was in any event too high. It argued that this incentive for over-investment is significantly exacerbated where the allowed rate of return is materially higher than the entity's actual cost of capital (typically calculated as its weighted average cost of capital (WACC) taking into account the costs of both equity and debt financing). International experience suggests that regulated electricity infrastructure operators, earning safe cash flows subject to regulatory protection, tend to have costs of capital for their regulated assets of between 6% and 8% per annum. This suggests that the 9.99% rate of return currently permitted under the SCAs may be too high. In particular, the allowed rate of return may be exacerbating a tendency to excessive consumer-funded investment relative to what customers would wish to pay for – in other words, customers are paying too much for their electricity as a result of this allowed rate of return. [81]

Having considered the benefits of introducing competition at each of the generation, transmission, distribution and retail levels of the supply chain and reviewed experiences in other jurisdictions, the Commission concluded that experience from other jurisdictions suggests that potentially the most significant gains from competition can occur through the introduction of competition in generation, buttressed by the economic regulation of transmission and distribution assets. [82] It likened transmission and distribution

---

[79] *Ibid*, para 80.
[80] *Ibid*, para 52.
[81] *Ibid*, para 53.
[82] *Ibid*, para 40.

assets to essential facilities[83] and noted that their owners would have little or no incentive under the voluntary system proposed in the Consultation to offer timely access to them to third parties on fair and reasonable terms.[84] Accordingly, third party access would need to be made mandatory and on regulated tariffs. The Commission was also critical of the extent to which the Government proposed to involve CLP and HKE in the design of the new access arrangements. While acknowledging the relevance of the views of the companies, it stated that it did not believe that such discussions are the best way to achieve a policy direction that will be in the interests of Hong Kong customers and the wider Hong Kong economy.[85]

The Commission concluded that the experience since the entry into force of the existing SCAs in 2008 suggested that the Government's preparatory measures to date have not been enough to bring about the necessary access arrangement and that the measures proposed in the 2015 Consultation Paper, which take a similar approach in terms of recommending studies into the relevant issues and discussions with the power companies, are therefore unlikely to be sufficient to enable the opening of the market.[86]   It recommended that the Government should establish an appropriately resourced, independent advisory body as soon as possible with a mandate to make recommendations on:

- a regulatory and institutional framework which would include the terms and conditions of network access for potential new entrants;
- a mechanism to allow for the selling of electricity at the wholesale level to facilitate competition from new suppliers;
- the specific measures required to enhance the interconnection between the Hong Kong grids themselves, and between the power grids in mainland China and in Hong Kong; and
- the measures required to deal with the transitional issues arising from introducing competition in Hong Kong.

Such a body should be established by 2016 and be required to publish a report on the above issues within two years.[87]   This recommendation amounts, in effect, to a call for the Electricity Market Consultation to be consigned to the wastepaper basket and begun afresh. Moreover, the Government should exercise its option to extend the SCAs by five years but not enter into new SCAs.[88]   The Commission predicted that the adoption of these recommendations could allow competition to be introduced in 2023 instead of the 2028 target set out in the Consultation.

---

[83] *Ibid*, paras 34 and 37.
[84] *Ibid*, para 83.
[85] *Ibid*, para 84.
[86] *Ibid*, para 82.
[87] *Ibid*, paras 89-92.
[88] *Ibid*, para 93.

The Future Application of the Competition Ordinance The Competition Commission's dissection of the Government's proposals for introducing competition into the Hong Kong electricity market represents a vote of no confidence in the proposed system by the very agency tasked with administering it. The Government published its review of the outcome of the Consultation on 23 November 2015[89] and, perhaps not surprisingly, no specific mention is made of the Competition Commission's recommendations. There is also no indication in the review document of any substantive change to the proposals as originally formulated, though the Government noted that various stakeholders had suggested that the current voluntary third party access regime set out in the SCAs should be strengthened.[90] However the review document does not make any commitment to do so, stating instead that it will take into account the views collated in the public consultation and commence negotiation with the power companies.[91]

Accordingly, it appears that there will be a continuation, albeit in potentially modified form, of the current light touch regulatory regime in Hong Kong, to which the Competition Commission has taken such exception, rather than the imposition of sector specific *ex ante* regulation of matters such as customer tariffs and third party access conditions that the Commission recommended. However, the Commission's invocation of the essential facilities doctrine in relation to the transmission and distribution assets of HKE and CLP may signal a readiness to use competition law, in particular the Second Conduct Rule, to compel those companies to provide third party access to those assets on fair, reasonable and non-discriminatory (FRAND) terms. The requirement set out in the Competition Ordinance that, for there to be a breach of either of the Conduct Rules, the impugned agreement or conduct to have as its object or effect the harming of competition may appear on the face of it to be a potential impediment to successful enforcement action in a market context in which there is no competition. However, the Conduct Rules might be applicable to a scenario of anti-competitive foreclosure of potential market entry via, for example, a refusal to provide access to essential facilities or other exclusionary conduct such as long term exclusive dealing provisions in supply contracts, loyalty rebates, etc.

It is of course, possible, that the Government could seek to head off what it may see as the premature application of competition law to this sector either by means of a regulation made by the Chief Executive in Council under section 5 of the Competition Ordinance disapplying the Conduct Rules in respect of persons specified in that Regulation to the extent that they carry on specified activities or by means of an Order by the Chief Executive in Council under

---

[89] Legislative Council Panel on Economic Development: Future Development of the Electricity Market, LC Paper No. CB(4)217/15-16(3).

[90] *Ibid*, para 30.

[91] *Ibid*, para 40.

sections 31 or 32 exempting a specified class of agreement and/or conduct from the Conduct Rules on exceptional and compelling public policy grounds or where necessary to avoid conflict with international obligations. It would also, of course, be open to market participants in the electricity sector to apply to the Commission under sections 9 and/or 24 for an order excluding the effect of the First and/or Second Conduct Rules respectively to a given agreement or course of conduct. There is also the possibility of the Commission adopting a block exemption to a given category of agreement under section 15 which may benefit participants in the electricity sector. Such block exemptions may be adopted by the Commission on its own initiative or on the application of a party.[92] All in all, the extent to which competition law may be applicable in the electricity sector is difficult to foresee with any precision at this stage.

7.2.2 Gas

Market Structure Three types of gas are used as fuel by domestic, industrial and commercial customers in Hong Kong:

- town gas;
- liquefied petroleum gas (LPG); and
- natural gas.

Town Gas is not a naturally occurring substance but is manufactured from various components including natural gas and naphtha. In Hong Kong it is exclusively supplied by the Hong Kong and China Gas Company Limited (known as "Towngas") which manufactures it at plants at Tai Po and Ma Tau Kok.[93] Town gas is supplied to approximately 1.86 million customers in Hong Kong via a network of pipelines and is mainly used as a fuel for domestic, commercial and industrial purposes. In 2015, Towngas had a market share of approximately 87.2 per cent across those customer segments measured by the calorific value of gas supplied.

Liquid petroleum gas (LPG) is imported into Hong Kong by sea by a variety of companies and stored at five terminals on Tsing Yi Island before being distributed to approximately 430,000 domestic, commercial and industrial customers. LPG's market share across those segments was approximately 12.8% by calorific value of gas supplied in 2015. LPG is also used as a transport fuel in all taxis and many public light buses to which it is distributed via approximately 67 LPG filling stations across Hong Kong.

---

[92] The possibility also exists for an exemption under section 3 of Schedule 1 to the Competition Ordinance on the ground that application of the Conduct Rules would obstruct the performance by specified undertakings of services of general economic interest entrusted to them by the Government.

[93] See https://www.towngas.com/Eng/Corp/AbtTG/HKBus/Production.aspx.

Natural gas is used in electricity generation and in the manufacture of town gas. It is imported from mainland China by the China National Offshore Oil Corporation (CNOOC) via submarine pipelines to the Black Point, Castle Peak and Lamma Power Stations for electricity generation and to the Tai Po Plant for the production of Town Gas. On August 28, 2008, the Hong Kong Government and the Mainland Chinese National Energy Administration signed the Memorandum of Understanding under which CNOOC would continue to supply Hong Kong for a further 20 years from that date.

Safety The Gas Safety Ordinance[94] was adopted in 1990 and regulates the importation, manufacture, storage, transport, supply and use of gas and the safety of household gas appliances. In addition, the Gas Safety (Installation and Use) Regulations and the Gas Safety (Miscellaneous) Regulations were amended in 2002 to regulate the import, supply and installation of domestic gas appliances for use in Hong Kong.

Environmental performance As with the electricity sector, APCO is applicable where undertakings use premises for one of the specified purposes which includes that of a gas works which is defined to include premises both where gas is manufactured and where it is reformed, refined or odorised.[95] This definition would therefore include both the Towngas manufacturing plants and LNG import terminals. The EIAO is applicable to major infrastructure projects such as gas generation plants, undersea oil or gas pipelines and LNG and LPG storage, transfer or transhipment facilities.

Economic regulation On 6 February 2015 the Hong Kong Government entered into the latest in a series of Information and Consultation Agreements (ICAs) with Towngas. This will continue in effect until 2 April 2018. The regulatory regime under the ICA is even more light touch than that applying to the electricity companies and does not subject Towngas to any price or profit regulation. Instead, it is designed to increase the transparency of the company's tariff-setting mechanism in relation to its Core Gas Business – i.e. the production, purchase, distribution and marketing of gas in Hong Kong, together with related activities such as appliance sales, servicing and contracting.

By clause 4.1 of the ICA, Towngas must submit to the Government each year a written statement wetting out specified information on its financial, operational, environmental and safety performance during the preceding financial year. Towngas must also make such information available to the general public. Clauses 4.2 and 4.3 oblige Towngas to supply additional

---

[94] Cap. 51.
[95] See APCO, Schedule 1, para 8. See also the definition of petroleum works in para 26 of that Schedule.

information to the Government both orally and in writing in relation to respectively: (i) proposed adjustments to either the amounts or the methods for setting tariffs and fixed monthly maintenance charges; and (ii) planned capital expenditures in the following financial year. Under clause 4.4, Towngas shall also supply the Government with information on monthly sales, cost, stock levels, etc. in relation to its Core Gas Business. Clause 5 of the ICA sets out a procedure under which Towngas must consult the Government before any tariff adjustments, major system additions or changes to the fixed monthly maintenance charges paid by domestic customers. The Government may consult the Energy Advisory Committee of the Environment Bureau for advice and give recommendations to Towngas but such recommendations are not treated as the basis for any kind of rate of return regulation or mandatory price control.[96]

The Future Application of the Competition Ordinance   There is a somewhat greater diversity of supply in the Hong Kong gas sector than in the electricity sector and there are no current Government proposals to open it up to greater competition as in the case of the electricity sector (save for potentially increased supply of natural gas from mainland China). Nevertheless, as the gas sector in Hong Kong is both highly concentrated and vertically integrated, many of the concerns identified by the Competition Commission in relation to the electricity sector would potentially be applicable here as well. On that basis, intervention by the Commission in due course cannot be ruled out, subject to the possibility discussed in relation to the electricity sector of the authorities issuing one or more of the various exemptions or exclusions provided for in the Competition Ordinance.

7.3 FINANCIAL SERVICES

Introduction   Along with London, New York, Frankfurt and Singapore, the financial district of Hong Kong has always played a major role in the global financial services industry. Despite its small size, Hong Kong is well integrated into the financial networks that drive the global economy. In wholesale and investment banking the market players tend to be global businesses with diverse commercial interests. Any transaction in Hong Kong is likely to affect businesses elsewhere and vice versa. In recent years there has been a significant spotlight on the way that financial markets operate. The Libor settlement in the US as well as the more recent Forex settlement have shown the role that competition law has to play in ensuring the proper functioning of financial markets.

---

[96]   ICA, section 5.5(c) and recital F.

Competition law is not in conflict with regulatory objectives. On the contrary, it can be a useful additional tool to ensure that markets remain open and competitive. Competition law and policy need to become part of the culture of financial services markets and of the institutions that participate in those markets. As the Governor of the Bank of England has recently said, real markets are professional and open, not informal and clubby.[97] The challenge for Hong Kong will be to use its new competition law to ensure that its financial services industry remains a market leader, professional and open. There are many detailed questions on how the law applies to existing market practices. Just because something has been market standard does not mean that it is necessarily lawful. Effective compliance will mean a new approach to old problems with proper guidelines and procedures in place to ensure that problems are flagged, escalated and dealt with appropriately. This change of culture is already happening elsewhere. Hong Kong will need to keep up with the global pace for reform in order to remain a credible and global participant in this market.

Traditionally, banking markets have been split into retail and wholesale/investment banking. Retail banking raises particular issues around the regulation of personal accounts and payments, which are beyond the scope of this section. Suffice it to say that consumer protection and competition law are closely linked in retail financial services and this dimension merits particular scrutiny. In this section, the focus is on wholesale and investment banking markets due to their international nature and the fact that some conclusions can already be drawn about these markets from the international investigations that have taken place prior to the Hong Kong competition law coming into force.

7.3.1 Competition law and the financial sector

Benchmark and index manipulation The competition law risks associated with potential benchmark and index manipulation have been highlighted in the recent Libor and Euribor investigations in the US and Europe.[98] A benchmark generally provides a standard against which the performance of a security, mutual fund or investment manager can be measured. An index is an indicative portfolio of securities representing a particular market or a portion of that market. Indices and benchmarks are usually worked out by an

---

[97] Building real markets for the good of the people – speech by Mark Carney, Governor, Bank of England, 10 June 2015.

[98] See the section of LIBOR Investigation 2014 in the US Department of Justice's website: http://www.justice.gov/atr/division-update/2014/libor-investigation and the section of Euro Interest Rate Derivatives in the European Commission's website: http://ec.europa.eu/competition/elojade/isef/case_details.cfm?proc_code=1_39914.

independent organisation based on a particular methodology. Sometimes the methodology is published, but sometimes it is kept secret. There are at least three basic types of index or benchmark: (i) submissions on a particular view of the market, (ii) submissions relating to actual trade data and (iii) observations of trading at a particular point in time.

Where there is no interest on the part of traders in the level of the benchmark (for example, where it determines the price of other products which the trader does not trade), there should be no *prima facie* incentive to manipulate it. Competition law issues tend to arise where those who have an interest in the outcome of a particular index or benchmark also have a way of influencing that benchmark. In such circumstances, and where traders observe the market on a daily basis, the precise methodology underlying a benchmark matters very little as traders will have an idea of what is good and what is bad for their trading position on any particular day. They will also know that a trade in or around a certain window will have market impact, and that impact will depend on the timing of the trade, its amount and whether it is a buy or sell order. Let us assume that a trader knows that a particular trade will have a bad market impact, and decides to trade either before or after the window. In the absence of market power, that is not an antitrust problem: a trader can do his job on a unilateral basis, to the best of his ability and competition law should not intervene. A trader may also reduce bad market impact by netting his position off against the position of others in the market. For example, a direct match of +500m and -500m equals zero. Such transactions, based on unilateral but parallel incentives happen every day and should not raise an antitrust problem. This should be the case even where the object for such a netting transaction is to reduce market impact for each side. Provided the incentive is unilateral on the part of each trader, there is no object that could be caught by antitrust laws.

A more cautious approach is required where a trader's behaviour goes beyond netting and towards coordinated trading to achieve a particular outcome. However, even here a competition authority has to be very careful not to proscribe conduct that is in the unilateral interest of each trader, even if the effect (and perhaps even the object) is to reduce or increase market impact. The competition authority would need to uncover contemporaneous evidence of, for example, a trader acting in a way that either (i) is not in his/her best interest or the best interests of his/her client, (ii) demonstrates the trader being prepared to take a short term hit to favour someone else or (iii) evidences wash trades[99] which have no economic purpose. While these practices raise significant regulatory concerns, a competition authority is faced with a more challenging task than a financial services regulator, as proving a competition infringement in these circumstances requires evidence that the object of the

---

[99]   A wash trade is a form of market manipulation in which an investor simultaneously sells and buys the same financial instruments.

coordination is unlawful. Competition authorities will usually look for language suggesting a dishonest and/or fraudulent intent in the contemporaneous records. However, often no such contemporaneous evidence exists and it would therefore be inadvisable for a competition authority to proceed with a by object infringement in these cases without a careful and deliberate analysis of the trading context. Communications between traders are typically characterised by language that is replete with posturing, bravado and bluff, much of which is without consequence.

Establishing the true facts is therefore challenging, which is why competition authorities should proceed with care. Evidence of benchmark or index manipulation does not necessarily constitute a competition law infringement. In this context the US Plea Agreement of 20 May 2015 gives some indication of the factors that will be taken into account by competition regulators in these circumstances, where it states that in furtherance of the conspiracy, the defendant and its co-conspirators engaged in communications, including near daily conversations, some of which were in code, in an exclusive electronic chat room, participation in which was limited to specific traders.[100] The fact that the communications were (i) regular (ii) private and (iii) in code were indicators that these exchanges went beyond normal trading behaviour.

In May 2013, the Hong Kong Monetary Authority (HKMA) issued a statutory guideline in its Code of Conduct for Benchmark Submitters[101] to enhance the robustness of the benchmark fixing mechanism, including HIBRO. Following that guidance, the HKMA expects all benchmark-setting banks to maintain proper oversight for such activities and put in place adequate and effective systems of control.[102]

Exchange of information   The previous paragraphs shows that the exchange of information in the context of benchmarks and indices is a more delicate situation. Most competition laws draw a distinction between (i) current v forward looking information and (ii) price v non-price information. The specific issue with trading is that it involves the ongoing disclosure of current pricing information, sometimes to traders who may also be competitors. This is the very essence of trading, and such an activity should not be prescribed by competition law. Every trader will have a degree of market transparency ahead of the window, based on current market information, including a view of pricing and volumes. Sometimes traders will exchange a general view on the

---

[100] The plea agreements are available at: http://www.justice.gov/opa/pr/five-major-banks-agree-parent-level-guilty-pleas.

[101] http://www.hkma.gov.hk/media/eng/doc/key-functions/banking-stability/supervisory-policy-manual/CG-7.pdf.

[102] See HKMA press releases dated 29 April 2013 and 14 March 2014: http://www.hkma.gov.hk/eng/key-information/press-releases/2013/20130429-3.shtml; http://www.hkma.gov.hk/eng/key-information/press-releases/2014/20140314-3.shtml.

future views and intentions, ranging from "I have lots to sell" to "I will go late" to "I could do with a high/low index". However, given the lack of specificity in that information exchange it is not generally of a type that would be considered unlawful by object. Indeed, it could be argued that such exchanges are entirely ancillary to, and in the fabric of, the main trading activity and should not be considered in isolation.

What may be considered unlawful is where the information is disclosed between the parties in bilateral and/or multilateral pre-pricing discussions, and those exchanges involve information that is commercially sensitive and not generally available to other operators active in the market. These types of information exchange go beyond what is necessary in the context of trading activity, and can therefore constitute a violation of competition law. Exactly where conduct crosses the line remains a challenging question for both competition regulators and practitioners. However, the following screening questions can be applied:

- Did the information go beyond what was necessary for the legitimate negotiation of trade or market information?
- Was the information disseminated on a bilateral/multilateral basis but not available in the same detail to other market participants?
- Was there an element of pre-pricing discussion?

These questions can only be answered by reference to the context in which trading takes place, taking into account factors such as the liquidity and volatility of the market concerned in addition to the regulatory context. It is contended, however, that the vast majority of day-to-day trader communications are unaffected by this cumulative framework and should not be touched by competition law.

Exchanges and coordination around spreads   One area that is critically important to trading markets is the ability to exchange information on spreads. A spread is a two-way price given by a trader to a potential customer, in circumstances where the trader does not know whether the potential customer wants to buy or sell. The spread is effectively the price that the trader will charge the customer. Often the trader has no interest in the underlying price of the security – for him or her 50/52 is equivalent to 70/72 as in either case the spread is 2 wide. Traders, and in particular market-makers, give each other spreads the whole time because they are looking for trading opportunities. Such conduct therefore has to be presumptively lawful in the context of a trade.

Competition risks arise where there is either (i) regular information exchange between traders not in the context of a trade, or (ii) coordination on the width of a particular spread between traders. When pricing complex products, traders should also avoid reaching out to specialists in other institutions and rely entirely on the internal capabilities at their own institution. Coordinated trading raises the most obvious competition issues. Where two traders have both received the same Request for Quote (RFQ) and coordinate how they might respond, that is no different to traditional cartel behaviour. The same goes for coordinated boycotts of particular clients or trades.

Lending services Another area where competition law is potentially relevant is in lending services, in particular in the provision of syndicated loans and club deals.[103] Loan syndication and the origination of deals have a perfectly legitimate and pro-competitive purpose. They serve to provide liquidity to borrowers where no individual institution would be willing or able to carry the risk alone. The ability of banks to carry out both loan origination and loan syndication in a competition law-compliant way is essential for the effective functioning of global markets. Without syndications global financial markets could not provide the required liquidity. However, the process of underwriting and syndication is not without competition issues, as it involves banks competing with each other, but then collaborating to assess, and lay off, risk in the market. In order to understand where the competition law risks lie in loan syndication, it is therefore important to understand the distinction between loan origination and loan syndication.

Loan origination Loan origination refers to the process before a banking group is formed, and generally involves the issuing by the borrower of a Request for Proposal (RFP) and lenders replying to that RFP. The lenders will compete for the mandate under the terms of the RFP. Discussions with other banks during the origination process (and without the consent of the borrower) carry the highest competition risk, as at this stage the group has not been formed and each bank is competing individually for a role in the origination. Banks will often engage in market soundings with other banks or anchor investors to gauge the appetite for a successful syndication. However, at the point where the RFP is sent out to banks, no banking group has been formed by the borrower and such market soundings could therefore become a conduit for pricing information that may influence the banks' individual responses to the RFP. A borrower may typically authorise some market soundings around the syndication (but not the origination) in circumstances where there is a need to ascertain the level of demand for the syndication. However, as general rule, it is never appropriate to engage in discussions with other banks, unless the borrower has expressly sanctioned those discussions and/or they are specifically permitted under the Non-Disclosure Agreement (NDA).

　　The analytical framework at the pre-consortium stage can therefore be considered as follows:

- What is expressly permitted by the RFP and any associated NDA?

---

[103] For a more detailed discussion on the competition law risks associated with syndicated loans, see Competition Law and Syndicated Loans: identifying the regulatory risks, Oliver Bretz, Competition Law Journal, Issue 4/2015.

- Are market soundings required for the syndication and what borrower consents will be required for market soundings?
- In a fully-underwritten bid where there is no related syndication, each bank should take its own commercial decisions.
- In those circumstances market sounding calls without express borrower consent are inappropriate and an independent internal process should determine pricing and any proposed hold-levels.
- Any market sounding calls from other banks should be refused in such circumstances, and a proper paper trail of that refusal should be created. Any approaches should be notified to the borrower without delay – with a request to prevent further contact from rival banks.
- At no point should calls be made to 'verify' the pricing information of other banks, even if that information comes from the borrower. It is the borrower's prerogative to lie to its banks about the pricing levels of others.
- A bank's internal credit committee may apply pressure to know which other banks are considering the deal and who has received the RFP. Providing anecdotal or historic information is fine but no steps should be taken to verify that information directly with the banks concerned.

Loan syndication Loan syndication refers to the process of laying off the risk in the market, and generally takes place after the responses to the RFP have been submitted and a banking group has been formed. Once the consortium is formed, the competition analysis changes significantly. This is because the borrower has now given a mandate to (i) a group of banks (ii) to devise a single term-sheet (iii) at a given price (iv) for a certain size of loan. Syndication discussions with other banks can be permitted, provided they are specifically about the laying off of risk in the market, and they take place after the banks have been mandated and within the scope of that mandate. It is not unusual for the term-sheet to be substantially negotiated, and in such circumstances it can move against the interest of the borrower at this stage. Where a borrower is unhappy about this dynamic, it can always split up the consortium and re-commence individual negotiations with the banks. At that stage any discussions between banks should cease immediately.

The syndicated loan market is yet to be investigated by the regulatory authorities in the UK or the EU and therefore there is little guidance that can be given for the Hong Kong regime. However, the UK Financial Conduct Authority (FCA), which has concurrent powers to enforce competition law, weighed up the advantages and disadvantages of the increase in syndicated activity in its wholesale sector competition review 2014-2015.[104] On the plus

---

[104] FCA Feedback statement on the main themes arising from the responses to the call for inputs for the wholesale sector competition review: https://www.fca.org.uk/static/documents/feedback-statements/fs15-02.pdf. The FCA also referenced the OFT's

side, the FCA found that an increase in the number of banks involved in a syndicated transaction may enable the issuer (or borrower) to reach a wider range of potential investors (or banks). The FCA's review also suggested that competition could be increased by inviting more co-managers for the lead underwriting position. However, concerns were raised that larger syndicates could result in inefficient bookbuilding and allocation process, lower net fees for banks which may not motivate some banks to work in the clients' interests and some banks adding no value to the process.[105] The FCA concluded that the effect syndication has on competition depends on how the syndication process takes place, and acknowledges that the way in which syndication works for loans differs from equity and debt issuance. The FCA therefore concluded that syndication "might" be an area which would benefit from further investigation.

In May 2014 the Loan Market Association (LMA),[106] recognising the competition law risks in the syndication process, published a notice on the application of competition law to syndicated loans (the LMA Notice).[107] The LMA Notice highlighted the recent changes to the UK competition law regime, and the need for banks involved in loan arrangements to recognise the requirement for caution when competing with each other on a prospective multi-bank deal. In particular the LMA Notice recommended the need for caution in the following areas:

- general market soundings;
- conduct during the bidding phase;
- exchanging competitively sensitive information;
- interaction regarding 'flexing' of terms;
- conduct regarding refinancing/distressed arrangements.

On 29 June 2001, the HKMA published a non-statutory guidance setting out the risks associated with syndicated lending.[108] The guidance emphasises that each member should perform its own independent analysis with respect to the credit quality of the borrower and the suitability of the deal in relation to its own risk appetite,[109] that adequate policies and procedures for conducting syndicated lending should be in place, and that the policies should normally

---

2011 report on equity underwriting and associated services, which considered the syndicated loans market more generally: http://webarchive.nationalarchives.gov.uk-/20140402142426/http:/www.oft.gov.uk/shared_oft/market-studies/OFT1303.pdf.

[105] *Ibid*, paras 2.26-2.28.

[106] The key objective of the LMA is improving liquidity, efficiency and transparency in the primary and secondary syndicated loan markets in Europe, the Middle East and Africa (EMEA) and promoting the syndicated loan as one of the key debt products available to borrowers across the region.

[107] http://www.lma.eu.com/uploads/files/LMA_Notice%20on%20the%20application%20 of%20competition%20law%20to%20syndicated%20loan%20arrangements.pdf

[108] http://www.hkma.gov.hk/media/eng/doc/key-functions/banking-stability/supervisory-policy-manual/CR-S-2.pdf.

[109] Syndicated lending guidance, para 2.12.

include requirements for monitoring, reporting and independent reviews of syndicated lending activity.[110]

7.3.2 The financial sector in Hong Kong

Financial services in Hong Kong   Hong Kong is one of the world's most important financial centres, characterised by its high degree of liquidity without any restrictions on capital flows or exchange controls. The regulatory framework in Hong Kong adheres to international standards and is recognised as effective and transparent. Hong Kong has repeatedly been ranked first in terms of economic freedom and its government abides by the principle of minimum market intervention. There is a wide array of products and services available to both local and international customers and investors.[111]

The Hong Kong banking sector maintains a three-tier system of deposit taking. There is a high degree of concentration of banks in Hong Kong, with more than 70 out of 100 of the largest banks in the world operating in the city. The money market in Hong Kong consists primarily of the interbank market and it has an average daily turnover of HK$239 billion as of February 2015. The stock market in Hong Kong is the eighth largest in the world in terms of market capitalisation[112] and there are 1,866 companies listed on the Stock Exchange of Hong Kong.[113]   In 2014, the Hong Kong dollar debt market achieved a record high for the sixth consecutive year and the total issue volume climbed to HK$2.43 trillion.[114]   The insurance market in Hong Kong recorded total gross premiums of HK$329.7 billion in 2014. The compulsory pension scheme of the Mandatory Provident Fund (MPF) System was introduced in 2000 and the accrued net assets of MPF schemes reached HK$594.8 billion as at the end of March 2015.

Financial services regulation in Hong Kong   The main regulators of the financial services sector in Hong Kong are the Hong Kong Monetary Authority (HKMA) (banking), the Securities and Futures Commission (SFC) (securities and futures), the Office of the Commissioner of Insurance (OCI) (to be replaced by the newly established Independent Insurance Authority (IIA) by

---

[110] Syndicated lending guidance, para 3.12.

[111] See Hong Kong government fact sheet on the financial services sector in Hong Kong, June 2015: http://www.gov.hk/en/about/abouthk/factsheets/docs/financial_services.pdf.

[112] As at end of September 2015, per SFC:
http://www.sfc.hk/web/EN/files/SOM/MarketStatistics/a01.pdf.

[113] As at end of December 2015, per SFC. Available at:
http://www.sfc.hk/web/EN/files/SOM/MarketStatistics/b01.pdf.

[114] The Hong Kong Debt Market in 2014, Monetary Management Department, HKMA:
http://www.hkma.gov.hk/media/eng/publication-and-research/quarterly-bulletin/qb201503/fa1.pdf

the end of 2016[115]) (insurance) and the Mandatory Provident Fund Schemes Authority (MPFA) (pension schemes).   HKMA and SFC have been predominantly responsible for investigating allegations of competition law infringements.

The investigative powers of the HKMA and SFC over competition law issues in the financial sector are derived from their wide statutory mandates as the sectoral regulators under the Banking Ordinance[116] and the Securities and Futures Ordinance (SFO).[117]   There is no specific provision in the Banking Ordinance or the SFO empowering the HKMA and SFC to investigate competition law infringements.   However, it is noteworthy that reference is made to both competitiveness[118] and the principle of competition[119] in the SFO. In light of the statutory functions of the HKMA and SFC, the power of investigation given to them under the respective ordinances have been considered wide enough to cover investigations on competition law issues.

Functions and powers of investigation of the HKMA   The principal function of the HKMA is to promote the general stability and effective working of the banking system.[120] This includes ensuring that authorised institutions (banks, restricted licence banks and deposit taking companies)[121] are operated in a responsible, honest and business-like manner,[122] promoting and encouraging proper standards of conduct and sound and prudent business practices,[123] preventing or aiding the prevention of illegal, dishonourable or improper

---

[115] See Hong Kong government press release dated 29 January 2016:
       http://www.info.gov.hk/gia/general/201601/29/P201601290412.htm
[116] The Banking Ordinance (Cap. 155) is an ordinance to "regulate banking business and the business of taking deposits; to make provision for the supervision of authorized institutions so as to provide a measure of protection to depositors; to promote the general stability and effective working of the banking system; to make provision for the supervision of money brokers; and to provide for matters incidental thereto or connected therewith".
[117] The Securities and Futures Ordinance (Cap. 571) (SFO) came into being on 1 April, 2003.   It is an ordinance to "consolidate and amend the law relating to financial products, the securities and futures market and the securities and futures industry, the regulation of activities and other matters connected with financial products, the securities and futures market and the securities and futures industry, the protection of investors, and other matters incidental thereto or connected therewith, and for connected purposes."   The SFO was the result of the consolidation and modernisation of ten existing ordinances into one composite piece of legislation governing the securities and futures markets.
[118] SFO, sections 4(a) and 5(1)(a).
[119] SFO, section 6(2)(c).
[120] Banking Ordinance, section 7(1).
[121] Banking Ordinance, section 2.
[122] Banking Ordinance, section 7(2)(b).
[123] Banking Ordinance, section 7(2)(c).

practices in relation to the business practices[124] and ensuring any business carried out by an authorised institution is carried on with integrity, prudence and the appropriate degree of professional competence.[125] Although these provisions do not specifically refer to competition law infringements, the language is sufficiently wide enough to cover them.

The HKMA has powers under the Banking Ordinance to conduct investigations on behalf of the Financial Secretary if it is of the view that it is in the interests of depositors of an authorized institution or a former authorized institution or in the public interest that an inquiry should be made into the affairs, business or property of that institution.[126] The HKMA also has general powers to enter the premises of authorised institutions and their branches, subsidiaries etc. in order to examine and investigate books, accounts and transactions etc.[127] Under the SFO, the HKMA also has the power to authorise a person to conduct an investigation in relation to the securities business of authorised institutions.[128]

Functions and powers of investigation of the SFC The main functions of the SFC are maintaining and promoting the fairness, efficiency, competitiveness, transparency and orderliness of the securities and futures industry[129] and suppressing illegal, dishonourable and improper practices in the securities and futures industry.[130] In pursuing its regulatory objectives and performing its functions, the SFC is to have regard to the principle that competition among persons carrying on activities regulated by the SFC under any of the relevant provisions should not be impeded unnecessarily.[131]

The SFC has the power to conduct investigations under a wide range of circumstances,[132] including, *inter alia*, when the SFC has reasonable cause to believe that an offence under the relevant provisions of the SFO has been committed[133] or that market misconduct may have taken place.[134]

The role of COMPAG in assessing competition law complaints The Competition Policy Advisory Group (COMPAG), chaired by the Financial Secretary, was established in December 1997 to provide a high-level and dedicated forum to review competition-related issues which have substantial

---

[124] Banking Ordinance, section 7(2)(d).
[125] Banking Ordinance, section 7(2)(g).
[126] Banking Ordinance, section 117.
[127] Banking Ordinance, section 55.
[128] SFO, section 180.
[129] SFO, section 5(1)(a).
[130] SFO, section 5(1)(n).
[131] SFO, section 6(2)(c).
[132] SFO, sections 179-181 set out the SFC's general powers to investigate.
[133] SFO, section 182(1)(a).
[134] SFO, section 182(1)(d).

policy or systemic implications, and examine the extent to which more competition should be introduced in the public and private sectors. In addition to publishing a Statement on Competition Policy in 1998 and issuing a set of guidelines in 2003 to provide objectives, benchmarks and principles to assess Hong Kong's overall competitive environment, COMPAG receives and takes follow up actions on competition-related complaints.[135]   COMPAG refers competition-related complaints in the financial services sector to the HKMA and SFC for investigation and reports the findings by the authorities to the complainants and the public accordingly.

7.3.3 Competition law investigations in the
financial sector in Hong Kong

Benchmark fixing: Foreign exchange (2014)   On 19 December 2014, the HKMA announced the outcome of its investigations into the foreign exchange (FX) trading operations of ten banks in Hong Kong.[136]   The investigation commenced in October 2013, following information received from banks and overseas regulators. The HKMA opened an investigation into ten banks[137] to assess whether the banks concerned had engaged in any rigging of FX benchmark fixing, collusion, and/or other inappropriate activities. The HKMA applied the same methodology adopted by overseas regulators for similar investigations and the banks were required to appoint external legal firms to examine relevant communication records for the period from 2008 to 2013.

The HKMA did not find any collusion among the banks in relation to benchmark rates, nor was there any clear evidence of rigging of the benchmark fixing of Treasury Market Association (TMA) FX rates in Hong Kong. The HKMA did uncover one example of a Hong Kong based trader of Standard Chartered Bank attempting to rig an Asian currency benchmark fixing in another jurisdiction, but there was insufficient evidence to demonstrate that the trades had been affected. In relation to spot rates, HKMA found evidence of an attempt by a Hong Kong-based trader of Deutsche Bank to influence the USD/HKD spot rate in order to make a gain in an over-the-counter currency option booked in an overseas jurisdiction. However, the HKMA again found that the effect on trades had not been what the traders had intended. The investigation also revealed certain internal control deficiencies in all ten of the banks, which resulted in cases of communication indiscretions by traders in

---

[135] See http://www.compag.gov.hk/about/.
[136] See   HKMA   press   release   dated   19   December   2014,   available   at:
　　　 http://www.hkma.gov.hk/eng/key-information/press-releases/2014/20141219-5.shtml.
[137] The 10 banks were Bank of America, Barclays Bank, BNP Paribas, Citibank, Deutsche
　　　 Bank, HSBC, JPMorgan Chase Bank, Royal Bank of Scotland, Standard Chartered
　　　 Bank, and UBS.

which possible competitors' or clients' information was inappropriately disclosed to other banks.

Based on the HKMA's findings, both Standard Chartered and Deutsche Bank were required to take appropriate actions against the relevant traders, and to refer the cases to the overseas authorities. The HKMA also required the two banks to engage an independent external reviewer to conduct an assessment of the incidents and make recommendations, which the banks would need to implement.   All banks under investigation were required to review their internal control mechanisms and to implement any appropriate measures in a manner agreed with the HKMA.

Benchmark fixing: HIBOR (2014)   On 14 March 2014, the HKMA announced the outcome of its investigations into the Hong Kong Interbank Offered Rate (HIBOR) fixing.[138] The HKMA had been initially alerted to the possibility of misconduct by UBS in relation to HIBOR fixing via overseas authorities. On 19 December 2012, the HKMA announced that it was opening an investigation into UBS. The HKMA later extended the investigation to cover eight other HIBOR reference banks.[139] All nine banks were required to appoint external firms, approved by the HKMA, to examine the relevant communication records (including internal and external chat messages) for periods between 2005 and 2012. In February 2014, the HKMA required another bank to conduct an external review of its communication records, which is in progress. The investigation of UBS found around 100 internal chat messages between September 2006 and June 2009 by several UBS traders to the UBS HIBOR submitter, which contained change requests with a view to rigging the bank's submissions for HIBOR fixing. The HKMA found evidence that about one-third of these change requests affected the HIBOR fixing rates submitted by UBS. However, there was no evidence to suggest that the outcome of the HIBOR fixing was affected by the remaining two-thirds. In October 2010, UBS ceased to be a HIBOR reference bank and no longer makes submissions for the HIBOR fixing. All of the individuals concerned have left UBS. Although misconduct in the submission of HIBOR rates by UBS was identified, the HKMA concluded that the UBS change requests had a negligible impact on the actual outcome of the HIBOR fixing. The HKMA therefore concluded that there was no evidence of collusion between the banks to rig the HIBOR fixing.

Refusal to supply: financing during IPOs (2007) In January 2007, the Hong Kong Association of Online Brokers (HKAOB) submitted a complaint to the

---

[138] http://www.hkma.gov.hk/eng/key-information/press-releases/2014/20140314-3.shtml.
[139] Bank of Tokyo Mitsubishi UFJ, Citibank, Crédit Agricole Corporate and Investment Bank, Deutsche Bank, Hongkong & Shanghai Banking Corporation, JPMorgan Chase Bank, Royal Bank of Scotland and Société Générale.

SFC regarding alleged unfair practices by banks in the provision of financing during Initial Public Offerings (IPO).[140] The HKAOB alleged that certain banks had discriminated against brokers by (i) refusing to quote interest rates to brokers on the first day of an IPO, (ii) quoting rates that were higher than those offered to the banks' own retail clients and (iii) refusing to provide IPO financing to brokers. The HKAOB argued that the practices were anti-competitive as they drove retail clients away from brokers and distorted the market by driving up interest rates, particularly when there was a significant demand for an IPO. This resulted in fewer applications for shares. The HKAOB also alleged that some brokers had seen clients abandon their IPO subscriptions as a direct result of the banks' practices. The SFC, in consultation with the HKMA, concluded that the banks' behaviour did not raise any anti-competitive concerns. Just one month later, in February 2007, the SFC responded to the HKAOB accordingly.

Predatory pricing: Securities (2005) In October 2005 the Hong Kong Stockbrokers Association (HKSA), now known as the Hong Kong Securities Association,[141] raised concerns with the Financial Services Branch (FSB) of the Financial Services and the Treasury Bureau (FSTB)[142] that banks were engaging in anti-competitive behaviour when conducting securities related business. The alleged behaviour included charging zero commission and low interest rates for IPO related activities to new securities clients. In November 2005, the complainants (which included around 100 broker firms and a number of associations of brokers) went one step further and placed a full-page advert in three local Chinese newspapers calling on the Chief Executive to enact the "fair competition law" and setting out the allegations and expressing concerns at the unfair competition from banks, the charging of zero commission by the banks, and the dual regulatory standards applied to banks and brokers. The FSB sought the views of the SFC and the HKMA on the allegations made by the brokers. However, both regulators were of the view that the SFO provides a level-playing field and does not allow banks any unfair advantage over brokers in conducting securities related business. Specifically, the SFC did not consider it unfair competition for banks to launch promotional offers as it held that competition on commission fees exists not only between banks and brokers, but also among brokers themselves, so that such competition can provide investors with more choice and benefits.[143]

---

140 COMPAG Annual Report 2006-2007, paras 30-33.
141 http://www.hksa.com.hk/eng/index.php.
142 The concerns were raised at a meeting with the Financial Services Branch of the Financial Services and the Treasury Bureau on 27 October 2005. See COMPAG Annual Report 2005-2006, paras 61-64.
143 COMPAG Annual Report 2005-2006, para 63.

Price fixing/market allocation: Life Insurance (2003)   In May 2003, a consumer submitted an individual complaint to the COMPAG Secretariat explaining that under the existing regulatory arrangements in the insurance industry, he was forced to take out life insurance through insurance brokers in Hong Kong and could not buy directly from overseas insurance companies. The consumer alleged that such an arrangement was anti-competitive, and had the same effect as a cartel and a price fixing arrangement. The FSTB did not agree, considering that the distribution channel for insurance products in Hong Kong was a commercial decision for the relevant insurers. The FSTB therefore deemed the existing regulatory arrangements for the insurance industry to be appropriate.[144]

Exclusivity arrangements: Mortgage Insurance Program (2002)   On 12 December 2002 a complaint was sent to the Secretary of the FSTB regarding a clause in an Incentive Scheme Agreement (ISA) for the Hong Kong Mortgage Corporation's (HKMC) Mortgage Insurance Program (MIP).   The clause required every bank joining the ISA to use the HKMC as their exclusive provider of mortgage insurance. The complainant alleged that (i) the clause amounted to an anti-competitive exclusivity arrangement which restricted the ability of banks to use competing mortgage insurance providers in the private sector and (ii) the HKMC was taking advantage of its status to monopolise the market for mortgage insurance.   However, the FSTB did not consider the clause to be anti-competitive, concluding instead that the clause was intended to be a risk mitigation measure. This was based on the following findings by the FSTB: (i) it was entirely optional for banks to opt-in or opt-out of the incentive scheme and they were not prohibited from entering mortgage insurance arrangements with other service providers; (ii) the purpose of the exclusivity clause was to guard against the risk of adverse selection i.e. banks assigning the riskier mortgages to the HKMC and the less risky loans to insurance providers associated with the bank; (iii) it was legitimate for the HKMC to take appropriate risk management measures to control its risk of business and (iv) the HKMC had recently provided a let-out to the exclusivity requirement.[145]

7.3.4 Financial sector focus for the future

Future application of competition law to financial services   As the investigations set out above indicate, the financial sector in Hong Kong has not entirely evaded competition law regulatory scrutiny.   However, the overwhelming consensus in the majority of cases has been to find the

---

[144] COMPAG Annual Report 2003-2004, p. 19.
[145] COMPAG Annual Report, pp. 35-36.

competition law complaints unsubstantiated. The question is whether this was
due to the absence of the Competition Ordinance or the result of a more
ingrained reticence to interfere with the functioning of the financial markets in
Hong Kong.

The Competition Ordinance is not applicable to recognised exchange
companies, clearing houses and exchange controllers, which are regulated
under the SFO.[146]   The Hong Kong Government is of the view that the
securities, futures and derivatives market is sufficiently regulated under the
SFO, and does not therefore warrant further regulation under the Competition
Ordinance. The Government has also emphasised that the SFC is establishing
a regular dialogue with the Competition Commission to discuss competition
matters relating to the excluded entities.[147]   However, this dialogue is
dependent on an effective and efficient working relationship between the two
regulators, something which remains to be seen and is discussed further below.

Co-operation with financial regulators   The existing financial regulators in
Hong Kong work very closely together, and have agreed various memoranda
of understanding (MOU) in order to set out the legal framework underpinning
their relationship and to enhance co-operation.[148]   However, there is not (as
yet) any MOU or similar arrangement between the existing financial regulators
and the Competition Commission.   Contrary to the position regarding the
Communications Authority, which allows for mechanisms for the disclosure of
confidential information between the competition authorities;[149] the transfer of
competition matters;[150] and the creation of a formal MOU,[151]   there are no
provisions in the Competition Ordinance setting out concurrent powers for the
enforcement of competition law by both the Competition Commission and the
existing financial regulators in Hong Kong.   The Commission has also
published Guidelines on its Enforcement Policy in which it states that it will
maintain close liaison with other domestic authorities as permitted by the
Competition   Ordinance   and   subject   to   the   Commission's   operational

---

[146] The full list of excluded entities is contained in the Schedule of the Competition
(Disapplication   of   Provisions)   Regulation   (Cap.   619B),   available   at:
http://www.hklii.hk/eng/hk/legis/reg/619B/sch.html.

[147] See paras 7-11 of the Discussion Paper prepared by the Commerce and Economic
Development Bureau in November 2014 for discussion in the Legislative Council Panel
on   Economic   Development: http://www.legco.gov.hk/yr14-15/english/panels/edev/
papers/edev20141124cb4-166-3-e.pdf.

[148] See for example details on supervisory co-operation on the HKMA and SFC websites:
http://www.hkma.gov.hk/eng/key-functions/banking-stability/banking-policy-and-
supervision/supervisory-co-operation.shtml;
http://www.sfc.hk/web/EN/about-the-sfc/collaboration/local.html.

[149] Competition Ordinance, section 126(1)(h).

[150] Competition Ordinance, section 160.

[151] Competition Ordinance, section 161 and Schedule 6.

requirements to achieve an appropriate outcome in cases where multiple authorities are working on the same broader conduct.[152]

These provisions, although not specifically relevant to the financial sector, provide a useful indication of how the Competition Commission may be expected to work alongside other domestic regulators. However, the financial regulators in Hong Kong have traditionally taken a light touch approach to regulation, with the general consensus being that the financial sector should regulate itself. There was consequently some expectation amongst the financial community in Hong Kong that the Commission would also be a light touch regulator. However, this would appear not to be the case. Consequently, the publication of the Commission's Procedural Guidelines caused some consternation. During the consultation period on the draft Procedural Guidelines, the Hong Kong Association of Banks (HKAB) lobbied the Commission to acknowledge a form of deference to the existing financial regulators. The HKAB emphasised that agencies such as the HKMA and the SFC have a significant oversight of the banking industry, and urged the Commission to expressly include the existence of other regulatory regimes and the views of any concurrent regulators as an additional factor to be considered in handling complaints and investigations.[153] The HKAB also requested the Commission to reassure the banking industry that it would not take any enforcement action before having commenced a dialogue with the relevant regulators and allow banks a sufficient period of time to implement resulting regulatory changes.[154] In a later submission, the HKAB recommended that the Commission should take into account regulatory requirements (including those set out in circulars, guidance and directives) when deciding on which cases to investigate and to consider the views of the existing financial regulators when coming to a decision in any competition investigation.[155]

In the revised Procedural Guidelines, the Commission stated that investigations would include gathering information from third parties, and that this could include both public and regulatory authorities. However, the Commission emphasised that it could not, in the abstract, bind itself to the views of public or regulatory authorities, who may pursue different policy objectives.[156] The HKAB made a further submission on the revised Guidelines, acknowledging that the Commission did not wish to bind itself, but commenting that there is no reason why the Commission should not provide the necessary comfort for regulated industries and commit to speaking to other

---

[152] Enforcement Policy, November 2015, para 4.7, available at http://www.compcomm.hk/en/pdf/policy_documents/Enforcement_Policy_Eng.pdf.

[153] HKAB Submission on Draft Procedural Guidelines, 10 November 2014, paras 1.7 -1.10.

[154] Ibid, para 2.6.

[155] HKAB Submission on Draft Procedural Guidelines, 19 December 2014, paras 1.6 and 3.1-3.3.

[156] Guide to the Revised Draft Guidelines issued under the Competition Ordinance, 30 March 2015, para 60.

regulators and taking their views and the existing regulatory regimes into account, in considering whether to pursue a matter.[157]

It is important to recognise that the Commission is an independent statutory body, independent of both government and other regulators. The HKMA and SFC, on the other hand, are both governmental bodies and consequently have different mandates and incentives. It therefore remains to be seen how the Commission and the financial regulators will co-operate in practice, but it is clear that the Commission intends to operate relatively independently. This is fundamental for the Commission to effectively carry out its intended purpose.

Challenges for the Competition Commission The Competition Ordinance has been under consideration for a number of years and there are some who had questioned whether it would ever become law. Much of the reticence and opposition emanated from the financial sector, with a significant number of the largest financial institutions in Hong Kong lobbying against the introduction of the Competition Ordinance, viewing their competitors as business partners. The Hong Kong General Chamber of Commerce (HKGCC)'s submission on the Competition Commission's proposed leniency policy is indicative of the endemic resistance to a culture of competition. The HKGCC considered it premature to introduce a leniency policy at this stage, commenting that this new law and cultural shift should be allowed to sink in first before introducing the leniency policy, which effectively it viewed as encouraging undertakings to betray their business partners.[158]

On 19 November 2015 the Competition Commission published its Enforcement Policy,[159] stating that the first years of enforcement would be focused on encouraging compliance with the Competition Ordinance across the Hong Kong economy as a whole, rather than focusing on specific sectors. The Commission will target cartel conduct, agreements breaching the First Conduct Rule that will cause significant harm to competition and abuse of substantial market power involving exclusionary behaviour. The extent to which the financial sector will come under the spotlight is not as yet clear. However, there is a strong feeling in Hong Kong that banks and other financial institutions will come under significant scrutiny, with at risk areas including exchange rates, syndicated lending, credit cards and involvement in trade associations.[160]

The challenge for the Hong Kong authorities will be to apply competition law in a way that will keep its markets professional and open and not informal and clubby. In doing so the Competition Commission will need to keep an eye

---

[157] HKAB Comments on Revised Guidelines, 20 April 2015, para 1.3.
[158] HKGCC Submission on Leniency Policy, 23 October 2015, para 10.
[159] *Ibid*, para 57.
[160] See for example, Competition Commission set to produce fresh banking targets for investigation, South China Morning Post, 22 November 2015.

not to chill normal competitive interactions between banks and to foster an environment of appropriate escalation and compliance. Careful and targeted interventions, in cooperation with the existing financial regulatory authorities, will be a step in the right direction, in particular if they are coordinated internationally.

7.4 RETAIL

Introduction   Local, regional and global retailers have favoured Hong Kong as a place to do business as a result of its stable economy, highly developed infrastructure, free port and free market conditions. Sales of consumer goods make up a very significant proportion of Hong Kong's economy. According to the Hong Kong Census and Statistics Department the value of total retail sales in Hong Kong in 2014 was HK$475.2 billion.[161] Retailers have historically benefited from comparatively low levels of regulation, making Hong Kong an attractive market in which to invest. Hong Kong has also been used as a test-bed for global brands wishing to enter the wider Asian market. While retail tourism from mainland China may have weakened more recently, Hong Kong's retail sector continues to benefit from this phenomenon, particularly where luxury brands are concerned. The introduction of competition law in Hong Kong marks a sea-change for a market hitherto largely unfettered by economic regulation. Competition in some parts of the sector is said to be limited, with a small number of powerful firms benefiting from large market shares.   Hong Kong's liberal economic policy has, in part, encouraged aggressive competition, particularly in more fragmented markets, but it has also meant that practices that are unlawful in other jurisdictions, including cartel arrangements, the sharing of strategic information with competitors, resale price maintenance (RPM) and predatory pricing, have largely gone unchecked in the Hong Kong retail sector.

7.4.1 Horizontal cooperation

Mergers, joint ventures and other forms of horizontal cooperation   As the Merger Rule is, at least for the time being, not applicable where neither party involved holds a carrier licence[162] or, directly or indirectly, controls an

---

[161]   http://www.censtatd.gov.hk/press_release/pressReleaseDetail.jsp?charsetID=1&press-RID=3605;http://www.censtatd.gov.hk/press_release/pressReleaseDetail.jsp?charsetID=1&pressRID=3807

[162]   As defined in the Telecommunications Ordinance, section 2(1).

undertaking that holds a carrier licence, the Merger Rule is likely to be of limited application to mergers in the retail sector.

Joint ventures are common in Hong Kong, particularly as a means for getting western brands to market. Such arrangements are, generally speaking, likely to be pro-competitive, as they facilitate market entry of new brands. In the retail context, arrangements such as where competing firms cooperate to jointly sell, distribute or market their products, which do not qualify as a merger under the Competition Ordinance, will need to be assessed against the First Conduct Rule. Where joint selling, distribution or marketing is used to facilitate market entry for a new product, which the collaborating firms could not otherwise have launched and could not have achieved with a smaller number of firms than those involved, the arrangement is unlikely to give rise to competition concerns. However, where such an arrangement is not objectively justifiable, for example, because the parties and products in question are well-established in the relevant market and the arrangement simply enables the joint venture partners to agree pricing, restrict output, share markets or share commercially sensitive information, it is likely to be considered as having the object of restricting competition and could be regarded as Serious Anti-Competitive Conduct.

In addition, other restrictions (for example commitments from co-operating parties not to be involved in businesses which compete with the joint venture) need to be assessed to establish if they may have the effect of harming competition in contravention of the First Conduct Rule or if they amount to an abuse of a substantial degree of market power in breach of the Second Conduct Rule. More generally, companies now need to exercise caution before entering into any arrangements or agreements with their competitors.

Cartels Cartel behaviour tends to be more likely to be sustainable in highly transparent, concentrated markets and where there is a high degree of product homogeneity. Conversely cartels are more difficult to sustain in less transparent, fragmented sectors where the goods and services in question are highly differentiated. As a result, retail markets have not commonly been particularly susceptible to cartelisation. However, in some sectors of the Hong Kong retail market, the number of competitors is limited. For this reason, it cannot be ruled out that the Competition Commission may take cartel cases in the sector.

Anecdotal evidence suggests that cartel activity in Hong Kong may have been prevalent historically particularly among smaller businesses and enterprises. It has not been unknown for industry-wide cartel agreements to be announced publicly. For example, in April 2005 eleven driving schools, covering 80% of the 900 driving instructors in Hong Kong, announced standardisation of their fees at the 1997 level to counter social and economic conditions and saturation in the market. In November 2004, the Hong Kong Laundry Association called for all laundries to raise prices by 10%. The petrol retail[163] and the travel industry[164] have both been noted as markets in which cartel activity may exist or may have existed in Hong Kong. The Competition Ordinance does not have retroactive effect. However, to the extent that conduct commences or continues beyond the 14 December 2015 implementation date, tackling this type of infringement will be a high priority for the Commission.[165]

Generally, cartel cases will involve competitors agreeing to fix prices to a particular level (or to fix some other measure of price, for example, margins or discount levels), to limit supply, to allocate/share sales, markets, territories or customers or to rig bids or a combination of these. Cartel decisions in other jurisdictions in consumer markets provide illustrations of the kinds of agreement that may be prohibited under the Competition Ordinance. In the Airline Passenger Fuel Surcharge case, the United Kingdom's Office of Fair Trading found that British Airways (BA) and Virgin Atlantic had participated in a cartel in relation to the pricing of fuel surcharges on long-haul passenger flights to and from the United Kingdom. BA agreed to pay a fine of £58.5 million in 2012.[166] The Malaysian Competition Commission found that 150 members of the Cameron Highlands Floriculturist Association, who are involved in the planting, distribution and export of flowers, had entered into an agreement to implement a 10% increase in the price of cut flowers sold in Malaysia and abroad (except Japan).[167]

Information exchange Information exchanges can be pro-competitive, for example, allowing companies to bench-mark their own customer service or website user ratings against those of competitors. Information transparency is beneficial to consumers allowing them to assess different products and services, and make comparisons between them, reducing search costs. Information exchange can, therefore, enhance competition in a market. However, information exchange has increasingly become a focus for competition law authorities in other jurisdictions, with some taking a particularly hard line. The European Commission, for example, has said that

---

[163] South China Morning Post, Petrol prices in Hong Kong will be first big test for new competition law, 7 August 2015: http://www.scmp.com/comment/insight-opinion/article/ 1847142/petrol-prices-hong-kong-will-be-first-big-test-new.

[164] TTG Asia, Hong Kong's travel consultants question new competition law, 16 June 2015: http://ttgasia.com/article.php?article_id=25306.

[165] According to the Competition Commission's Enforcement Policy, para 3.5, it will prioritise cartel conduct, as well as other agreements causing significant harm to competition in Hong Kong and abuses of substantial market power involving exclusionary behaviour.

[166] OFT Decision of 19 April 2012 in Case CE/7691-06. Virgin, being the whistleblower, benefited from full immunity.

[167] Malaysian Competition Commission, Decision of 6 December 2012 in Case MyCC/0003/2012(ACA).

the communication of information among competitors with the object, in particular, of fixing prices or quantities, will normally be considered a cartel and fined as such.[168] A similar approach has been taken by the Competition Commission in its Guideline on the First Conduct Rule, which states that the Commission regards information relating to price, elements of price, or price strategies, customers, production costs, quantities, turnover, sales, capacity, product quality, marketing plans, risk investments, technologies and innovations as competitively sensitive information.[169] Indirect exchanges of commercially or competition-sensitive information may also be caught by the First Conduct Rule. Hub and spoke cases have been brought in North America and the United Kingdom. Such cases have generally involved exchange of information relating to current or future pricing. In February 2003, in a case involving one of the largest toy and games suppliers in the United Kingdom at the time, Hasbro UK Limited (Hasbro) and two major retailers, Argos and Littlewoods, the OFT levied fines totalling £22.5 million where the arrangements between Hasbro and the retailers involved the exchange of information relating to each of the retailers' future pricing intentions to the other retailer. This had the effect of restricting the retailers' ability to sell Hasbro toys and games at prices other than Hasbro's recommended list price with the object of maintaining prices at higher levels and preventing the retailers from discounting.[170]

Hub and spoke cases do not always, however, concern pricing practices. For example in the US in 2002, Toys "R" Us was found to have orchestrated a horizontal boycott arrangement, in which its suppliers agreed to refuse to supply one of its competitors.[171] More recently, in June 2015, the Belgian Competition Authority (BCA) settled a hub and spoke case, fining 18 retailers and suppliers of branded drugstore, perfumery and hygiene products €174 million for implementing the arrangement across the whole of the Belgian territory from 2002 to 2007. The BCA was alerted to the case through an application for immunity by major conglomerate, Colgate-Palmolive. The case involved indirect contact between the largest Belgian retail chains via the

---

[168] EU Guidelines on the applicability of Article 101 TFEU to horizontal co-operation agreements, para 59.

[169] Guideline on the First Conduct Rule, para 6.39.

[170] Decision of the Office of Fair Trading, No. CA98/8/2003 – Agreements between Hasbro U.K, Argos Ltd and Littlewoods Ltd fixing the price of Hasbro toys and games, 21 November 2003 (Case CP/0480-01) http://webarchive.nationalarchives.gov.uk/20140402142426/http://www.oft.gov.uk/shared_oft/ca98_public_register/decisions/hasbro3.pdf;jsessionid=F761D36B35390ED5771697F48219A5F7; See also Decision of the Office of Fair Trading No. CA98/06/2003, Price-fixing of Replica Football Kit, 1 August 2003 (Case CP/0871/01) and Decision of the Office of Fair Trading, CA98/03/2011, Dairy retail price initiatives, 26 July 2011 (Case CE/3094-03) and *Argos Limited and Littlewoods Limited v Office of Fair Trading and JJB Sports plc v Office of Fair Trading* [2006] EWCA Civ 1318.

[171] *Toys "R" Us, Inc. v. Fed. Trade Comm'n*, 221 F.3d 928 (7th Cir. 2000).

suppliers for different products with the object of stabilising retail prices for the products in question. It resulted in coordinated increases in the prices paid by consumers for the relevant products. The BCA did not find any evidence of direct contacts between the suppliers or the retailers involved. It was able to demonstrate that both the retailer providing information to the supplier and the retailer receiving the information from the supplier were aware of the context and the objective of providing the information – to stabilise and/or increase retail prices. This state of mind is likely to be critical to the finding of a hub and spoke cartel by the Competition Commission, as without it there is unlikely to be an agreement or concerted practice capable of falling within the scope of the First Conduct Rule.

Questions around information exchange in Hong Kong are particularly likely to arise in the context of trade associations and similar trade bodies. Market intelligence data gathering is particularly common in the retail sector and highly granular information is available via electronic point of sale systems. Where firms are considering sharing competitively sensitive data via a third party such as a trade association or a market intelligence firm, they must be careful that the information is not individualised data for other participants in the exchange. If exchanging information could have the effect of harming competition, steps can be taken to reduce the risk of the exchange. The parties should try to ensure that the information cannot be reverse-engineered so that the participants in the exchange can learn competition-sensitive information from it. This means that the data should be aggregated, anonymised and suitably historic, which the Competition Commission has said means that it is old enough not to pose any risk of harm to competition.[172]

Participating in trade associations and other trade bodies The competition rules relate to any kind of trade organisations, including cooperatives, professional associations or bodies, societies, associations without legal personality and associations of associations. There are multiple benefits for firms participating in trade associations. Membership can provide a means of keeping up-to-date with news, policy, legal developments and risks in the sector, sharing best practice, bench-marking, statistical analysis, developing sector-wide standards, educating consumers and influencing public policy while creating time and cost efficiencies, as well as making it possible for retailers to speak with one voice in relation to matters of legal and economic policy. They also offer training and advice and other services for members. The activities of trade associations are therefore generally speaking pro-competitive and beneficial to consumers. However, as the Malaysian cut flowers case demonstrates, trade associations can also provide a forum for facilitating anti-competitive conduct. For this reason, businesses must ensure

---

[172] Guideline on the First Conduct Rule, para 6.47.

they have safeguards in place to minimise the risks that trade associations can represent.[173]

Trade associations in Hong Kong will need to consider whether their practices are compliant with the Competition Ordinance. The fact that a practice is well-established and has been operating for many years will not be a defence under the Competition Ordinance. Trade associations will either need to cease practices that have the potential to breach competition law, make an application to the Competition Commission for exemption under the Competition Ordinance or accept the risk of enforcement action by the Commission. It has been suggested that the activities of the Kowloon Pearls, Precious Stones, Jade, Gold and Silver Ornament Merchants Association, which for the past 50 years has set a daily gold price recommendations for jewellery retailers, are potentially problematic under the Competition Ordinance. The association has suggested that the daily rate is merely a recommendation provided as a reference point for its 600 members, which are not required to follow the recommendations. The association has applied to the Commission for an exemption.[174]

The Competition Commission indicated in advance of the Ordinance coming into force that it considered that guidance issued by the Hong Kong Travel Industry Council (TIC) on ticketing charges would be likely to contravene the Ordinance. The Council subsequently agreed to withdraw the guidance prior to the entry into force of the Ordinance. TIC rescinded the directive setting a price ceiling for service charges on outbound package tours (Directive number 215) on 1 June 2015. This price included a service fee for tour guides at the end of the tour, which was not part of published package prices.[175] Moreover, in the lead up to the Competition Ordinance coming into effect some associations announced that they had released members from previous controls on pricing and in particular, discounting. Fierce competition in several parts of the retail sector, including between electronics retailers, has broken out. The Hong Kong government has pointed to an immediate impact on the market with the effect of consumer prices dropping, attributing this to the Ordinance coming into force. It clearly sees such developments as an early achievement of the new regime.

---

[173] Malaysian Competition Commission, Decision of 6 December 2012 in Case MyCC/0003/2012(ACA).

[174] South China Morning Post, Hong Kong gold pricing continues despite legal misgivings, 15 December 2015, http://www.scmp.com/news/hong-kong/economy/article/1891228/hong-kong-gold-pricing-continues-despite-legal-misgivings.

[175] TTG Asia, Hong Kong's travel consultants question new competition law, 16 June 2015: http://ttgasia.com/article.php?article_id=25306.

7.4.2 Distribution routes to market

Different routes to market A key consideration for suppliers of consumer goods and services in Hong Kong is the strategy they should adopt to get those products and services to market. Vertical agreements (namely agreements between businesses at different levels of the supply chain, for example a supplier and a retailer) are within scope of the First Conduct Rule in the same way as horizontal agreements between competitors at the same level of the supply chain.

Open distribution Some suppliers, particularly where low-cost, commodity products are concerned, choose to make sales both directly to consumers and through an open distribution system, supplying to multiple retailers who then sell on to consumers, with few restrictions placed on them by the supplier. Suppliers need to be mindful in these circumstances that the retailers are both customers (i.e. they are in a vertical relationship with the supplier) and competitors (i.e. they compete horizontally, as both the supplier and the retailer sell on to customers). Accordingly, it is imperative that, as independent undertakings, the retailers and supplier formulate their commercial retail strategies independently of each other. Suppliers also need to be careful in open distribution systems that they are not imposing burdensome resale restrictions, for example restricting the other brands that retailers may sell, which might only be appropriate in a selective or exclusive distribution system. Where more complex goods and services are involved, firms may choose to appoint only those distributors that meet specified criteria, under selective distribution systems, or to exclusively appoint one dealer to a territory or customer group. In general, there will be a clearer justification for imposing more extensive restrictions on such distributors than in an open distribution system.

Selective distribution The basis of selective distribution is that distributors have to meet certain criteria to distribute the supplier's products. These criteria may be qualitative (i.e. they impose minimum standards of service on the retailer), or quantitative (in that they limit the number of retailers or impose minimum purchase or sales volumes on the retailer). Authorised resellers are also generally restricted from selling the suppliers' products to unauthorised resellers. Accordingly, selective distribution is a means of strengthening the reputation and preserving the identity of a brand and ensuring a standardised, quality customer experience with trained staff. Unsurprisingly, given the strength of the luxury and electronic goods markets in particular, this mode of distribution is commonly employed in Hong Kong and in many cases can be pro-competitive, as it increases inter-brand competition.

   The Guideline on the First Conduct Rule distinguishes between qualitative and quantitative selective distribution systems. Quantitative systems, for example, where the supplier limits the number of retailers in a particular geographic area, or where it sets the retailers minimum or maximum sales targets, are generally considered to be more restrictive of competition than qualitative systems, where retailers are selected purely on the basis of the qualities and capabilities of the reseller. The Competition Commission has specifically identified the following as potentially amounting to qualitative criteria: training or qualifications for staff, criteria relating to the appearance of a retail outlet, or the type of equipment to be available there, requirements for the products to be sold in a specialist shop, and having specialist displays, particular opening hours or providing after sales services. In applying such criteria, suppliers should ensure that the criteria do not inadvertently become quantitative. For example, while requiring retailers to have sufficient stock to meet the needs of customers in store would be consistent with qualitative selective distribution, requiring retailers to maintain stock significantly in excess of customers' needs could lead to the criteria being considered quantitative.

   Where the criteria used to select distributors are purely qualitative and specific conditions set out in the Guideline on the First Conduct Rule are met, the selective distribution system will not come within scope of the First Conduct Rule. These conditions are that: (a) the nature of the product is such as to require a selective distribution network in order to preserve its quality and ensure its proper use; (b) the members of the network (the authorised retailers) are selected on the basis of non-discriminatory qualitative criteria relating to their technical ability to handle the product or the suitability of their premises to protect the brand image of the product; and (c) the relevant criteria do not go beyond what is necessary for the particular product concerned.[176] Where those specific conditions are not met, the Commission has signalled that it is unlikely that the arrangement would have the object of restricting competition but that its effects would need to be examined and in particular whether it gives rise to anti-competitive foreclosure at the distributor or retailer level or facilitates collusion between suppliers or distributors/retailers.

   The Commission specifically states that restrictions in any selective distribution system on sales between members of the system (known as cross supplies) or outside of a particular class of customers could adversely affect competition. Where a supplier has market power, the number of authorised distributors or retailers is small, inter-brand competition[177] is limited or if

---

[176] Guideline on the First Conduct Rule, para 6.123.
[177] Inter-brand competition is competition between suppliers or dealers selling rival brands of the same or equivalent goods.

selective distribution systems are prevalent in a particular market, the system is more likely to give rise concerns under the First Conduct Rule.[178]

Exclusive distribution Alternatively, firms may choose to appoint distributors or retailers exclusively to serve a given territory or customer group. As with selective distribution, the guidance given by the Competition Commission relating to exclusive distribution is limited. The Commission states in its Guideline on the First Conduct Rule that exclusive distribution and exclusive customer allocation agreements will not generally be considered to have the object of harming competition and will generally require an analysis of their effects or likely effects on competition in the relevant market. In particular, the Commission will assess the effect on intra-brand[179] and inter-brand competition, the extent of the territorial or customer sales limitations, and whether exclusive distributorships are common generally in the relevant markets. Exclusive distribution or customer allocation might meet the cumulative conditions of the economic efficiency exclusion where investments by distributors are required to protect or build up brand image, or where specific equipment/skills/experience is required for a particular group of customers.[180]

Franchising An alternative distribution model, often employed in Hong Kong, is franchising. Franchising effectively enables franchisees to operate as independent businesses whilst using the name and knowhow of the franchisor. Accordingly, franchising enables the supplier/franchisor to quickly establish a consistent distribution network whilst maintaining and protecting the supplier/franchisor's brand. The main distinguishing feature between franchising and other forms of distribution is the transfer of IP rights from the franchisor to the franchisee. This feature means that franchising agreements usually contain a series of restrictions on how those IP rights can be used. The Guideline on the First Conduct Rule recognises that restrictions designed to legitimately protect the franchisor's know-how and expertise are unlikely to raise concerns under the First Conduct Rule.[181] Franchising agreements also commonly include restrictions on how premises are presented, where premises are located (so as to avoid being located in the same area as another franchisee) and the business method to be used. Whilst these kind of restrictions limit franchisees' commercial freedom, it is recognised that, where these restrictions

---

[178] Guideline on the First Conduct Rule, para 6.125.
[179] Intra-brand competition is competition between suppliers or dealers of the same brand of goods.
[180] Guideline on the First Conduct Rule, para 6.87.
[181] Guideline on the First Conduct Rule, para 6.120.

relate directly to, and are necessary for, the implementation of the franchise agreement, they are unlikely to infringe the First Conduct Rule.[182]

7.4.3 Vertical restraints

Vertical price-fixing The Competition Commission considers that vertical agreements are less likely to harm competition, and therefore infringe the First Conduct Rule, than horizontal agreements.[183] However, whilst most vertical restrictions will need to be analysed as to whether they have anti-competitive effects, vertical agreements may amount to Serious Anti-Competitive Conduct in certain cases.[184] Competition concerns are most likely where either or both of the supplier or buyer parties have market power, since vertical arrangements between small and medium-sized undertakings are unlikely to be capable of harming competition.[185]

One potentially high risk area for companies in the retail sector is vertical price restrictions, and in particular RPM. RPM involves a supplier of goods or services fixing or setting a minimum price, at which the buyer must resell the goods or services. Anecdotal evidence suggests that RPM is a common feature of vertical arrangements in Hong Kong. In the build up to the Competition Ordinance coming into force, one of the main cosmetic trade associations announced that it was working to abolish industry-wide RPM practices. Meanwhile, on the sportswear market prices were cut heavily in the days leading up to the Competition Ordinance coming into force. Local media reported that one major American footwear manufacturer had informed its retailers that its resale pricing had been put on hold and that they should disregard the brand's recommended retail prices and fixed prices.[186] Such developments are perhaps unsurprising, given the position adopted by the Competition Commission in the Guideline on the First Conduct Rule on RPM, and the fact that price competition is central to its regime.

In Europe and Asia an increased focus on vertical agreements in recent years has resulted in significant enforcement activity and investigations. This is particularly evident in China, where, for example, the National Development and Reform Commission (NDRC) issued a record fine against two distillers of premium liquor for engaging in RPM.[187] Nestlé was investigated by the

---

[182] Guideline on the First Conduct Rule, para 6.119.
[183] Guideline on the First Conduct Rule, para 6.6.
[184] Guideline on the First Conduct Rule, para 5.6.
[185] Guideline on the First Conduct Rule, para 6.9.
[186] mLex market insight, Hong Kong chief executive says antitrust law to bring down consumer prices, 15 December 2015.
[187] China Law Vision, *Rumors Come True: NDRC Imposes Record High Penalties on Luxury Chinese Liquors*: http://www.chinalawvision.com/2013/02/articles/competition

Malaysian Competition Commission pursuant to allegations that its brand equity protection policy, which Nestlé argued was implemented to prevent its products being used by retailers as loss leaders,[188] prevented resellers from setting their prices independently. Following the investigation, Nestlé agreed to amend the provisions that were considered likely to infringe the prohibition on anti-competitive agreements under the Malaysian Competition Act.[189]

The position on RPM in the China is somewhat less clear. On the one hand, the NDRC considered RPM to be an object infringement in its investigation into a number of eyewear manufacturers, including Johnson & Johnson and Carl Zeiss. The eyewear manufacturers were found to have engaged in anti-competitive conduct by imposing contractual provisions on resellers to control resale prices and promotional activity. The manufacturers were also found to have taken action to enforce recommended retail prices (RRPs) by, *inter alia*, refusing to pay commission to resellers for non-compliance. The NDRC imposed fines of more than RMB 19 million.[190] However, this approach was at odds with that taken by the Shanghai Intermediate People's Court when considering a complaint about alleged RPM by Johnson & Johnson's subsidiaries in relation to medical equipment and related products sold to hospitals in China. The Shanghai Intermediate People's Court did not consider RPM to be a *per se* infringement and instead, held it should be determined whether the agreement has the effect of eliminating or restricting competition.[191] This approach was confirmed by the Shanghai People's High Court. The position on RPM in the PRC is therefore somewhat unclear. Given the conflicting approaches to RPM, it is difficult to determine how such cases will be considered in the future and whether the

---

antitrust-law-of-th/rumors-come-truendrc-imposes-record-high-penalties-on-luxury-chinese-liquors.

[188] Loss-leaders are goods or services that are sold at below cost price with a view to bringing customers into the retail outlet on the assumption that customers are likely to buy full price items as well when they are in store.

[189] Malaysian Competition Commission Press Release, 25 February 2013: http://www.mycc.gov.my/sites/default/files/media-releases/News-Release-Nestle-withdraws-exemption-application.pdf.

[190] South China Morning Post, Multinational Lens Makers Fined For Price Fixing, 30 May 2014, re-published by The Cosmetic & Perfumery Association of Hong Kong: http://www.scmp.com/business/companies/article/1521551/multinational-lens-makers-fined-price-fixing.

[191] *Ruibang Yonghe Technology & Trade Co. Ltd (v Rainbow Medical Equipment & Supplies Co.) v Johnson & Johnson Medical Medical (China) Ltd.* (filed 2010, dismissed 2012); Legal Daily, The Johnson & Johnson Resale Price Maintenance Case Trial Begins, 4 February 2012, 17 China Competition Bulletin 3 (January/February 2012). http://www.anzsog.edu.au/magma/media/upload/ckeditor/files/Research/Public-ations/ The%20china%20Bulletin%20Competition/82_China-Competition-Bulletin_Jan-uary_ February-2012.pdf.

approach adopted on the mainland will inform that taken by the Hong Kong Competition Commission, if at all.

Whether agreements enhance overall economic efficiency will be assessed on a case-by-case basis. However, in its Guideline on the First Conduct Rule, the Competition Commission notes that using RPM to tackle free-rider problems might qualify under the efficiency exclusion.[192]   In this situation, RPM could be used to encourage distributors to provide certain sales services for the benefit of consumers, particularly for experience or complex products. Whilst other jurisdictions have stated that they too would consider efficiency arguments for RPM,[193] in practice there are very few cases where this justification has been successful. However, in December 2014, the Australian Competition and Consumer Council (ACCC) granted conditional authorisation to Tooltechnic Systems, to encourage its distributors to offer the full range of services for its premium, complex Festool power tools. Tooltechnic Systems had a small market share in a highly competitive market. Under the Australian Trade Practices Act 1974, companies are able to seek authorisation from ACCC for RPM. In this case the ACCC was satisfied that the conduct was likely to result in public benefits that outweighed the likely public detriments in that, although price competition had been restricted, given the nature of the complex and highly differentiated attributes and quality of the product, it was important for customers to get pre-sale services, explanations and demonstrations as well as after-sale services such as training and repairs.

Minimum advertised pricing (MAP) Minimum advertised pricing programs are where a supplier seeks to set a minimum price at which a product may be advertised, without restricting the actual sales price. This means that discounts can be applied to the advertised price when the product is actually sold. Anecdotal evidence suggests that MAP has commonly been used in Hong Kong. Although some would argue that MAP is distinct from RPM, since retailers remain free to set their sales prices, there is a risk that MAP may act as a form of indirect RPM where it discourages retailers from using prices or discounts other than those set under the MAP (i.e. where the MAP effectively acts as a minimum or fixed resale price). The United Kingdom's competition authority has previously concluded that MAP may constitute an object-based infringement in circumstances where the supplier seeks to have in place an enforcement mechanism (e.g. where the supplier ensures that the MAP is complied with by way of threat of less favourable pricing structures or the risk of having supply terminated).[194] Where a MAP is recommended only, it is

---

[192] Guideline on the First Conduct Rule, para 6.84.
[193] See, for example, EU Guidelines on Vertical Restraints 2010, para 225.
[194] Mobility scooters supplied by Pride Mobility Products Limited: prohibition on online advertising of prices below Pride's RRP, CE/9578-12, 27 March 2014.

likely that an authority would evaluate the MAP in terms of its effect on the market.

Maximum and recommended prices   Suppliers may stipulate maximum prices, or inform retailers of a recommended retail price (RRP), providing that it is clear to the retailer that it retains complete freedom to set its price, and every other part of its commercial strategy, independently of the supplier. Unless they are combined with other practices, and treated as fixed or minimum prices, maximum prices and RRPs will not be considered by the Competition Commission to have the object of restricting competition. They will therefore be examined for potential anti-competitive effects. Where maximum prices or RRPs are used by distributors as a focal point for pricing, or to dampen competition between suppliers, this will give rise to concerns, particularly where the supplier has market power. The Commission has not given any assurances that maximum resale prices or RRPs will be treated as a generally accepted commercial practice. Where companies suggest RRPs or impose maximum prices on distributors, this could be scrutinised for anti-competitive effects. The Commission has indicated that maximum resale prices could help to ensure that a brand competes more effectively with other brands, for example by avoiding double marginalisation.[195]

Price parity agreements   Price parity agreements involve a retailer agreeing to set its resale price for one supplier's product by reference to its retail price for the equivalent product of another supplier.[196] The Guideline on the First Conduct Rule is silent on this type of arrangement, suggesting that they should be assessed subject to an effects-based analysis.

Other types of vertical restraint   RPM is the only type of restraint that is identified as being an infringement by object. The Guideline on the First Conduct Rule is silent on most other forms of vertical restraint, save where they are considered in the context of a specific form of distribution. Other

---

[195] Guideline on the First Conduct Rule, para 6.84(b). Double marginalisation is where both the supplier and the buyer have market power and both apply a higher margin when selling the product than would be the case if the supplier and buyer were a vertically integrated monopolist, meaning that a maximum price serves to reduce the end price and increase output.

[196] The United Kingdom's competition authority brought a case on price parity concerning retail supply and sale of tobacco, although with mixed success since some of the parties appealed the decision, which was overturned in respect of those parties on procedural grounds. The decision stands in relation to parties that had settled their case with the authority. See: Competition Act 1998, Decision of the Office of Fair Trading, Case CE/2596-03 - http://webarchive.nationalarchives.gov.uk/20140402142426/http://www-.oft.gov.uk/shared_oft/ca98_public_register/decisions/tobacco.pdf: Tobacco, 15 April 2010 and (1) *Imperial Tobacco Group plc* (2) *Imperial Tobacco Limited v Office of Fair Trading* [2011] CAT 41.

restrictions such as most favoured customer clauses,[197] exclusive purchase commitments, restrictions on the retailer's ability to purchase and sell the products of competing suppliers,[198] or imposition of minimum purchase requirements on the buyer would be likely (at least in the absence of substantial market power on the part of one or other of the parties) to require assessment as to anti-competitive effects.

Online sales While bricks and mortar shopping retains its popularity in Hong Kong, online retail is growing. Many electronic goods are purchased online and online sales of clothing and health and beauty products are increasing.[199] The Guideline on the First Conduct Rule does not specifically address restrictions relating to online sales. However, this should not necessarily be understood as a permissive attitude on the part of the Competition Commission to restrictions on online sales. It is reasonable to assume that any restrictions on online sales included in vertical agreements would be likely to be assessed as to whether those restrictions may have anti-competitive effects.

This approach contrasts with that of the European Commission, which considers that in principle every distributor must be allowed to use the internet to sell products[200] and that, in the context of selective distribution for example, criteria for online sales should be overall equivalent to the criteria imposed for bricks and mortar sales. European competition authorities in particular are increasingly focused on removing online sales restrictions. By way of example, the European Commission has conducted a sector inquiry into e-commerce[201] and the German Competition Authority has issued a series of proceedings against suppliers for imposing terms which have an adverse effect on online trade. These cases have considered terms such as: bans on sales over

---

[197] Where the supplier agrees with the buyer that it will supply contract goods on the same terms as its most-favoured customer, or it will not supply the goods on better terms to other buyers.

[198] Note this is considered in the Guideline on the First Conduct Rule in the context of Franchise Agreements at para 6.118(d). In the context of franchise arrangements, such a restriction is permissible in certain circumstances to protect the identity and reputation of the franchise network.

[199] 2015-2016 Outlook for the Retail and Consumer Products Sector in Asia – PWC, February 2015, available at http://www.pwchk.com/webmedia/doc/635593-364676310538_rc_outlook_201516.pdf?bcsi_scan_571fca99b36dc46b=0&bcsi_scan_fil ename=635593364676310538_rc_outlook_201516.pdf.

[200] EU Guidelines on Vertical Restraints, para 54. In the context of selective distribution, see Case C-439/09 *Pierre Fabre Dermo-Cosmétique SAS v Président de l'Autorité de la Concurrence* [2001] ECR I-9419; Decision no. 12-D-23, 12 December 2012, *Bang & Olufsen.*

[201] European Commission inquiry into e-commerce: http://ec.europa.eu/com-petition/ antitrust/sector_inquiries_e_commerce.html.

online markets[202] (e.g. Amazon and eBay); performance rebates which encourage bricks and mortar sales over online platforms;[203] and bans of the use of price comparison websites.[204]

7.4.4 Undertakings with substantial market power

Market structure in the retail sector   Parts of Hong Kong's retail sector are characterised by a high degree of concentration.[205] The groceries market is an oft-cited example with ParknShop and Wellcome as well-established market leaders and there are many more markets which are characterised by a small number of companies with substantial combined market shares. While the Second Conduct Rule is not expressed to be applicable to more than one firm, the Competition Commission has clearly noted in its Guideline on the Second Conduct Rule that it would be possible for more than one undertaking to have a substantial degree of market power in a relevant market.[206] Where there is one, or only a small number of strong players on a market, firms will need to consider whether they could be regarded as having substantial market power within the meaning of the Second Conduct Rule.

In the context of retail markets, practices such as predatory pricing, as well as supplier-enforced exclusivity, loyalty-inducing rebates and tying and bundling are prohibited under the Second Conduct Rule if employed by firms with a substantial degree of market power. Some have speculated that the failed attempt of online retail outlet, Admart, to establish itself in the retail market could have been caused, at least in part, by predatory pricing by established bricks and mortar rivals, ParknShop and Wellcome.[207] However, the Consumer Council did not find any strong evidence that demonstrated that supermarket chains have used market power to affect prices, quality, or the

---

[202] See, for example, the German Competition Authority's decision B3-137/12 dated 27 June 2014, available at   http://www.bundeskartellamt.de/SharedDocs/Entscheidung /DE/Fallberichte/Kartellverbot/2014/B3-137-12.html.

[203] See, for example, German Competition Authority, Bundeskartellamt concludes mattress case with another fine, 22 October 2015:
http://www.bundeskartellamt.de/SharedDocs/Meldung/EN/Pressemitteilungen/2015/22_ 10_2015_Tempur.html.

[204] See for example, German Competition Authority, Unlawful restriction of online sales of ASICS running shoes, 27 August 2015:   http://www.bundeskartellamt.de/ SharedDocs/Meldung/EN/Pressemitteilungen/2015/27_08_2015_ASICS.html.

[205] Guideline on the Second Conduct Rule, para 3.13.

[206] Guideline on the Second Conduct Rule, para 3.3.

[207] The Emergence of Competition Law in the Asia-Pacific Region: A Contrarian Perspective, Hans Mahncke, Asia Pacific Law Review /2006/Volume 14/Number 1/ (2006) 14-1 APLR 1.

product range of goods and services at the local market level during its Grocery Market Study.[208]

In March 2012, the Competition Commission of Singapore investigated the local soft drinks market, having received a complaint about Coca Cola Singapore Beverages Ltd (CCSB). The complaint concerned CCSB's supply agreements with its on-premise retailers, which contained restrictive provisions, including exclusivity conditions and conditional rebates. In light of the investigation, CCSB volunteered to amend its supply agreements to remove these provisions and gave undertakings as follows: (i) not to impose exclusivity restrictions on its on-premise retailers except in limited circumstances; (ii) not to require its on-premise retailers who wish to sell other brands to negotiate with CCSB in the first instance; (iii) not to grant loyalty-inducing rebates that have an effect of inducing on-premise retailers to purchase exclusively or almost exclusively from CCSB; and (iv) to allow its on-premise retailers to use up to 20% of the space in coolers provided by CCSB to store other brands beverages, where these retailers have no access to alternative cooling equipment on their premises.[209]

Enforcement priorities The Competition Commission's Enforcement Policy prioritises cartel conduct, other anti-competitive agreements that cause significant harm to competition in Hong Kong and abuses of substantial market power.[210] However, there are certain features of retail markets that make them less conducive to cartel conduct. In the absence of a clear candidate cartel case, the Competition Commission may be minded to enforce against other forms of anti-competitive activity in the retail sector, for example hub and spoke information exchanges, RPM or abuses of market power. The Commission has committed itself to fostering a culture of competition in Hong Kong to the benefit of consumers.[211] To date, the Hong Kong Consumer Council has played a significant role in shining a light on potential competition issues in various markets. It has led regular public campaigns and undertook the Grocery Market Study in the period prior to the Competition Commission getting its market study powers, urging the Commission to look into the sector

---

[208] Grocery Market Study, Market Power of Supermarket Chains Under Scrutiny, Hong Kong Consumer Council, 19 December 2013, para 21.

[209] Competition Commission of Singapore Press Release, Coca-Cola Singapore Beverages changes business practices in local soft drinks market following enquiry by CCS, 10 January 2013: https://www.ccs.gov.sg/media-and-publications/media-releases/cocacola-singapore-beverages-changes-business-practices-in-local-soft-drinks-market-following-enquiry-by-ccs.

[210] Competition Commission Enforcement Policy, November 2015, para 3.5.

[211] Annual Report 2014 / 2015, Competition Commission, page 2, see here: https://www.compcomm.hk/en/media/reports_publications/files/2014_15_CC_Annual_Report.pdf.

once the Competition Ordinance was fully implemented.[212] Greater awareness of, and emphasis on, consumer rights has developed over time and therefore consumer protection has risen up the agenda.[213] Against this backdrop, it is reasonable to assume that the Commission will want to take enforcement cases where the greatest, most widespread consumer benefit will be felt. An examination of petrol prices might be an obvious place to start, not least due to the scrutiny this market has already been subjected to in the media, as would the groceries market.

7.5 TELECOMMUNICATIONS AND BROADCASTING

7.5.1 Development of telecommunications and broadcasting competition and regulatory framework

The first generation of sector specific competition law Unlike other economic sectors in Hong Kong, the Competition Ordinance is the third competition law regime to apply to the telecommunications and broadcasting sectors. The first generation of competition law for the telecommunications sector comprised General Conditions (GC) attached to operating licences from the mid-1990s until 2000. In June 2000, the GCs for the telecommunications industry were replaced with prohibitions set out in the Telecommunications Ordinance (TO)[214] and, for the first time, television programme services licensees were subject to competition law prohibitions under the Broadcasting Ordinance (BO).[215] In almost the same terms, the TO, BO and the earlier GCs prohibited anti-competitive conduct and abuse of dominance.[216] The TO, although not the GCs or the BO, also prohibited discriminatory conduct by a dominant firm and anti-competitive mergers (from 2003 onwards). These competition prohibitions were supplemented in both the TO and BO by consumer protection prohibitions (that were often invoked in the same cases that applied the competition provisions) and, in the telecommunications sector only, by regulatory provisions concerning inter-operator interconnection.

A negotiate-arbitrate form of regulation applied, empowering (but not requiring) the relevant authority to settle telecommunications interconnection disputes if the operators could not reach agreement on the price or non-price

---

[212] Grocery Market Study, Market Power of Supermarket Chains Under Scrutiny, Hong Kong Consumer Council, 19 December 2013, para 27.

[213] Report on the Review of Hong Kong's Competition Policy, Competition Policy Review Committee, June 2006.

[214] Cap. 106.

[215] Cap. 562.

[216] The GCs also required a telecommunications operator with a dominant position to seek approval from the regulator to the tariffs that it proposed to charge, to publish them and only to give discounts from those tariffs with the approval of the regulator.

terms of interconnection on application by either party to the dispute. Initially the GCs, TO and BO were enforced by the Telecommunications Authority and the Broadcasting Authority respectively. From 2012 the two agencies were dissolved and replaced with the Communications Authority (although the TO and BO that the Communications Authority enforced remained distinct legal instruments). Under the former competition law regimes applying to these sectors, there were a multitude of competition law investigations and decisions by the Telecommunications Authority, the Broadcasting Authority and the Communications Authority. Due to the differences in structure between the telecommunications industry and the broadcasting industry, most of the conduct cases have arisen in relation to telecommunications and most of the abuse of dominance cases have arisen in the broadcasting sector.

Evolution of the telecommunications sector in Hong Kong Reasonably quickly after being opened up to competition in 1995, Hong Kong's telecommunications industry evolved to become one of the most competitive in the world. This evolution can be attributed to high levels of market penetration, given the high geographic concentration of the population, and a regulatory environment that has been conducive to market entry. The incumbent fixed line operator (now PCCW) has been subject to higher levels of competition than its equivalents in many other countries because there is a very high proportion of high-rise residential and commercial developments with strong property developers who enjoy a gate-keeper position. This enabled a significant number of subscribers to be aggregated into packages of business that warranted substantial new investments and facilitated competitive entry. Indeed, one of Hong Kong's largest property developers, the CKI group also owns the global mobile telecommunications operator, Hutchison, which is also a substantial fixed line telecommunications operator with domestic subscribers in Hong Kong and an owner of international trunk lines.

PCCW did not enter mobile telephony until its acquisition of SUNDAY Communications in 2005. By that time, the mobile telephone market was already well established and vibrant competition existed between a multitude of physical and virtual mobile operators. Again, Hong Kong's concentrated population facilitated entry by mobile operators more quickly and in greater numbers than in other countries because, through relatively smaller investments, a high proportion of effective network coverage can be achieved. Although in 2002 PCCW and the Telecommunications Authority agreed in submissions to the Appeals Board that PCCW held a dominant position in relation to fixed line services, by 2007 the Authority had decided that the market was sufficiently competitive to deregulate interconnection charges. In appeals related to that deregulation, the Appeals Board and then the High Court of the Hong Kong SAR accepted evidence that there were at that time 11 fixed line operators with a total of 3.8 million lines equating to 95 lines per 100 households covering 55.8% of the population. There were 14 mobile operators with 9.3 million subscriptions amounting to one of the highest penetration rates in the world at 135%. In the last twenty years there have been a multitude of physical and virtual mobile operators in Hong Kong with various international proprietors of these businesses either entering by acquisition (e.g. China Mobile) or exiting (e.g. Telstra). Most acquisitions have been cleared by the Authority unconditionally but some have been cleared on the basis of behavioural (or at most quasi-structural conditions such as the sale or relinquishment of spectrum).

Mobile telephony was initially introduced as a premium/luxury service and interconnection with the fixed line operator was charged on a mobile party pays basis. In other words, unlike the predominant charging model that applies in the rest of the world by which only the party initiating the call pays for it, or the bill and keep approach that applies in North America by which each of the initiating and receiving parties pay for a proportion of the cost of the call, for many years in Hong Kong, calls from a fixed line to a mobile number were charged to the mobile subscriber and calls from a mobile number to a fixed line were also paid for wholly by the mobile party. However, upon deregulation of pricing, the mobile party pays basis was progressively wound back.

Evolution of the broadcasting sector in Hong Kong   By contrast to the highly competitive telecommunications industry, the broadcasting sector has been more concentrated than in many other jurisdictions. For almost all of the period since competition law was introduced for the sector, there have been two free to air broadcasters with multiple channels (Television Broadcasts Limited (TVB), which has consistently been the stronger of the two, and Asia Television Limited (ATV). TVB is a substantial producer of domestic television programming and also operates the smallest of the three licensed pay TV businesses. The other two pay television operators are HKCTV (owned and operated by i-Cable) and the pay television arm of telecommunications fixed line incumbent, PCCW. HKBN also provides pay TV but given that its channel to market is via the internet, it is not required to be licensed and therefore it was not subject to the competition provisions of the BO.

Over-all, broadcasting industry competition law cases have been related to the strong position of TVB which has accounted for the majority of viewing share on either an all-TV viewing or free-to-air TV viewing basis for the whole period that competition law has applied to the sector as well as being the largest employer of talent through its extensive television production interests. On 1 April 2016, after prolonged financial difficulties, ATV's licence expired without renewal. HKTVE (a PCCW/IPTV joint venture) has been granted a free-to-air licence and there is the potential for a further free-to-air licence to be granted to i-Cable.

Pre-Competition Ordinance cases   Given that Hong Kong is a common law jurisdiction with a reasonably litigious business community, a significant number of enforcement actions have been taken by the Communications Authority or its predecessors both on its own motion and at the behest of competitors and customers. A number of administrative appeals and judicial review cases were also brought. Since the Competition Ordinance came into force, the former TO and BO continue to have transitional operation where the conduct or investigation pre-dated the Competition Ordinance or where there is an appeal to be heard on a decision that pre-dated its introduction. Because the GCs, TO and BO only applied to licensees, an important issue in these pre-Competition Ordinance cases was sometimes the issue of whether or not the conduct was undertaken by an entity that was subject to the relevant Ordinance or not. Although this kind of case may not occur in the future for conduct cases, it may still be relevant when applying the Merger Rule because this rule will apply only to the direct and indirect proprietors of licensed telecommunications businesses.

Since the Communications Authority is the most experienced competition regulator in Hong Kong, with specialist knowledge of the sector, the Competition Ordinance will be concurrently enforced by the Communications Authority and Competition Commission pursuant to a Memorandum of Understanding. With respect to the conduct rules such as the prohibition against anti-competitive conduct or abuse of substantial market power, the Competition Ordinance provisions are similar to the sector-specific forerunners although there are some important changes to the competition law standards that now apply to the telecommunications and broadcasting sectors under the Competition Ordinance compared with the former GCs, TO and BO.

7.5.2 Change from sector specific competition law regulation to the new general competition law regime

Application to licensee v undertaking   The first difference between the former sector-specific regime and the Competition Ordinance regime concerns the difference between applying prohibitions to a licensee (as the TO and BO did) compared with applying the prohibition to an undertaking. Under the TO and BO, if the relevant conduct was engaged in by a non-licensee there was no breach even if the non-licensee was in the same corporate group as a licensee. For example, in the *Apple Asia* decision, the Communications Authority decided that conduct engaged in by Apple Inc could not be imputed to the only relevant Hong Kong licensed entity within the corporate group, its subsidiary, Apple Asia. By contrast, the question under the Competition Ordinance is whether the conduct is undertaken by an undertaking – i.e. an entity, regardless of its legal status, carrying on economic activity. This concept imports EU case law by which an undertaking may include several legal entities within a corporate group, partnership or only a division of a larger legal entity such as a

Government Department that operates a stand-alone function in supplying goods or services on the market.

Substantive standard of prohibited conduct   The second important difference concerns the substantive standard in the prohibitions. The language of the former prohibitions contained elements drawn from different legal systems, reflecting the unique character of Hong Kong as a dynamic domestic jurisdiction with diverse international influences. The TO and BO prohibitions concerning conduct by non-dominant licensees provided that a licensee must not engage in conduct which, in the opinion of the Authority, has the purpose or effect of preventing, distorting or substantially restricting competition.[217] Certain kinds of conduct (e.g. price fixing, action to prevent or restrict the supply of services or geographic market sharing) were listed that the Authority could explicitly consider in applying the above prohibition. As can be seen from this prohibition, the TO/BO prohibition applied to a broad range of conduct rather than the three forms of conduct that are explicitly proscribed under the Competition Ordinance. Consistent with EU law, the Competition Ordinance proscribes only agreements, concerted practices and decisions of an association of undertakings.

The TO and BO proscribed certain conduct with an anti-competitive purpose or effect whereas the Competition Ordinance proscribes conduct with an anti-competitive object or effect. There is an important distinction between these two phrases, the first of which is imported from Australia and New Zealand competition law, while the latter is imported from jurisdictions that follow the EU standard. Under both systems, an effects based analysis is the same. It involves a full economic analysis of whether the conduct in question actually does prevent, distort or substantially restrict competition. A by object analysis proceeds by recognising that certain kinds of conduct are inherently damaging to competition such that conduct (e.g. naked price fixing) is found to be a by object breach without conducting a full economic analysis of whether, in that particular case, the conduct in question actually did substantially lessened competition. By contrast, a purpose case concerns an analysis of what was the purpose of the parties to the conduct even if, for example, the parties wrongly believed that they would succeed in achieving an anti-competitive outcome.

Similarly, the Competition Ordinance contains a prohibition concerning unilateral conduct that is differently worded from its equivalent in the TO and BO. The former prohibition provided that a licensee in a dominant position in a telecommunications/television programme service market must not abuse its position.[218] A licensee in a dominant position was deemed to have abused its position if, in the opinion of the Authority, the licensee had engaged in conduct

---

[217] GC 15, section 7K of the TO and section 13 of the BO.
[218] GC 16(1), section 7L(1) of the TO and section 14(1) of the BO.

which had the purpose or effect of preventing or substantially restricting competition in a telecommunications/television programme service market.[219] A licensee in a dominant position in a telecommunications market was obliged not to discriminate between persons who acquire the services in the market on charges or the conditions of supply.[220]

The core abuse of dominance provision was imported from EU competition law and can be contrasted with the substantial degree of market power concept that is drawn from the U.S. and those jurisdictions that have applied that standard such as Australia and New Zealand. The European Commission has previously asserted that dominance connotes the same degree of market power as a substantial degree of market power and from an economic viewpoint it may be that the two standards are the same. However, from a legal viewpoint, it can be argued that the jurisdictions that apply the dominance standard require a degree of coordination (albeit falling short of a cartel) to be proved whereas under the substantial degree of market power standard the courts examine directly the question of whether each party accused of having a substantial degree of market power can raise price above the competitive level for an enduring period.

The deeming provision of the GC, TO and BO concerning conduct with the purpose or effect of preventing or substantially restricting competition was substantially drawn from Australian and New Zealand competition law and, in a looser way, the non-discrimination provision echoes US competition law. An important implication of the above structure is that the Authority was empowered to take action on the basis of distinctively EU case theories or in some respects to take action on distinctively Australian/New Zealand case theories. For example, the abuse of dominance standard could be used to take action against exploitative abuses such as excessive pricing drawn from EU competition law heritage that are not known to the Australasian/American competition law systems. Alternatively, a wholly purpose based case theory could be applied by the Authority to find a contravention on the basis of the licensee's business documents without needing to prove that the conduct had any effect whatsoever. Wholly purpose based prosecutions against unilateral conduct are a feature of Australian and New Zealand competition law systems.

Enforcement model   The third significant difference is that the Hong Kong Government decided to introduce penalties for natural persons as principals to illegal conduct, and to natural persons who are accessories to breaches by corporate entities, as part of the new Competition Ordinance. For example, the definition of an undertaking explicitly refers to natural persons as being a potential undertaking to which the principal liability attaches and additionally

---

[219]   GC 16(3), section 7L(4) of the TO and section 14(4) of the BO.
[220]   Section 7N of the TO. This prohibition only applied if the Authority was of the opinion that the conduct had the purpose of substantially restrict competition.

the Competition Ordinance prohibits a person (such as a staff member of a company) from aiding and abetting or being knowingly concerned in a breach of the law. Under the TO and BO there were no natural persons who were licensees and those instruments did not contain accessorial liability provisions. Although this difference is of marginal direct relevance to the telecommunications and broadcasting sectors, it necessitates a further difference of considerable importance concerning how the Competition Ordinance is enforced compared with the TO and BO.

Under the TO and BO regimes, the Authority investigated, determined liability and imposed any remedies only on licensees. Further, many of the former prohibitions explicitly stated that what was illegal was to engage in conduct that was relevantly anti-competitive in the opinion of the Authority rather than being anti-competitive in an objective sense. Because the TO and BO applied the prohibitions only to corporate entities as part of a licensing system, it was acceptable under Hong Kong's Basic Law to have a single Authority that investigated, decided liability and imposed a penalty. This enforcement model could not be retained when the Competition Ordinance was adopted. Where a general law applies prohibitions to both corporate entities and natural persons, and significant penalties potentially apply, Hong Kong's Basic Law entitles the accused to a fair trial. The most straightforward way to ensure that the Basic Law's requirement for a fair trial is satisfied is to adopt a court based enforcement model. Even if the single agency model were to remain, at the very least the subjective elements of the prohibition would need to have been removed and a greater level of court oversight provided by which the full merits of the initial decision could be reconsidered.

Under the Competition Ordinance, the Government elected to take the more straightforward, court enforcement approach. The Authority investigates but it cannot determine liability or itself impose a penalty or other punitive order. Rather, following an investigation (and potentially a failed attempt to resolve the matter administratively by issuing an infringement notice), the Authority must litigate the matter before the Competition Tribunal that applies the provisions of the Competition Ordinance according to the evidence presented to it and applying an objective test as opposed to adopting the opinion of the Authority. The change in enforcement approach has substantially increased the burden upon the Authority in competition law cases and, in other words, enhanced the accountability of the enforcement system. It is doubtful that some of the former cases could have been concluded without further investigation had they been taken under the Competition Ordinance as opposed to the TO or BO.

Mergers With respect to mergers, the economic standard is similar under the former TO and the current Competition Ordinance in that the prohibitions are against any merger that has, or is likely to have, the effect of substantially lessening competition in a telecommunications market (TO) and has or is likely to have the effect of substantially lessening competition in Hong Kong (Competition Ordinance). Superficially, the Competition Ordinance covers only the same scope as the TO prohibition because it only applies to undertakings that directly or indirectly control a telecommunications licensee. However, the legal drafting of the Competition Ordinance already has the potential for much broader application of the merger prohibition since it is not expressed to be limited to applying to effects on telecommunications markets. For example, there would appear to be no explicit constraint against the Authority taking action against a merger in which the owner of a dominant telecommunications licensee purchased a business in another industry – say the broadcasting industry – and the Authority reached the view that the merged firm would act anti-competitively by leveraging from the dominant position in the telecommunications industry into the other industry. Indeed, the explicit drafting of the Competition Ordinance potentially brings within the jurisdiction of the Merger Rule any corporate transactions of a merger type in industries wholly unrelated to telecommunications markets simply on the basis that the acquirer owns a telecommunications licensee.

Notwithstanding the breadth of the explicit drafting, there are two ways that the effect of the Competition Ordinance provisions could be confined to the telecommunications industry. First, the Authority may choose to restrict any intervention to effects upon telecommunications markets as a matter of administrative discretion. The other possibility is that the Competition Tribunal or the courts may accept arguments that there is an implied constraint upon the Merger Rule applying beyond cases that affect telecommunications markets.

7.5.3 Horizontal and vertical multi-party conduct cases

Advance notifications of price rises In 2000 the Telecommunications Authority investigated press reports that six mobile operators had raised prices simultaneously. The Authority did indeed find that extensive communications and advanced notifications of price rises between the operators had occurred. The Authority was concerned that this raised issues under the anti-competitive conduct conditions of the operator licenses. However, when the carriers agreed to reverse their price rises, the Authority closed the file with a mere warning.

Anti-competitive conduct by affiliates In 2003 the Telecommunications Authority investigated a complaint from residents at the Banyan Garden estate that Hutchison's fixed line business had benefited from the anti-competitive conduct of its affiliates, the property developers of the estate. The developers of the estate with 2,500 residential dwellings had undertaken a survey of competing telecommunications providers and selected Hutchison after considering the responses. The Authority found that Hutchison had been given preferential treatment when it was chosen to be the only party to roll out infrastructure for the estate. Whilst this excluded all other competitors from effectively supplying services on the estate, the Authority found that Hutchison was unaware that it would be given a preference and it had acted competitively in the offers it made to supply services to the estate. Consequently, the Authority held there had not been a breach of the TO.

Bundling In 2003 the Telecommunications Authority investigated a complaint that the largest pay TV operator, HKCTV, had engaged in anti-competitive bundling involving pay TV and internet services. The Authority considered two theories of harm: (i) whether there would be a foreclosure of the internet services market on the basis that households might require pay TV services and only find it economically viable to take internet services from HKCTV or (ii) that the incremental costs of the internet services within the bundle might amount to predatory behaviour. However, the Authority found that neither case theory was made out. Pay TV was not a must have service and foreclosure was therefore unlikely. The short duration of the promotion suggested that it could not have a predatory effect with only a limited time for uptake, following which the 15 competing internet service providers would certainly be able to defeat any attempt to recoup. Consequently, there was no breach of the GCs of the licence or the TO.

Service interruptions In 2008 a commercial telephone subscriber with a substantial number of fixed line connections throughout Hong Kong lodged a complaint in connection with service interruptions arising from its decision to switch provider from Pacnet to Hutchison. The incumbent fixed line operator, PCCW, was also involved because before Hutchison could take over the lease on the relevant lines from Pacnet, they needed to be reassigned by PCCW as the wholesaler to Pacnet and Hutchison. The complainant substantiated a series of factual allegations to the effect that none of the three operators concerned had processed the transfer efficiently or in accordance with the correct procedure. Nevertheless, the Authority found that none of the operators had engaged in conduct with the purpose or effect of lessening competition.

SIM locking In 2012 HKT lodged a complaint urgently seeking a prohibition order from the Authority against Apple Asia (a Hong Kong subsidiary of Apple Inc) and three other mobile network operators alleging that a number of new iPhones and iPads were SIM locked. Important background to the complaint was that in 1997, very early after the inception of competition provisions in telecommunications licences, the Telecommunications Authority had concluded a detailed inquiry into the practice of SIM locking and issued a statement setting out its views on the practice. Amongst other things, it stated that, if SIM Lock is solely used for the purpose of tying customers to networks rather than for the purpose of recovering handset subsidies or preventing theft, it may adversely affect competition in the mobile industry. Therefore this practice was forbidden. The complaint was initially filed as both a conduct complaint and an abuse of dominance complaint but the latter allegation was not pursued. The conduct complaint had two limbs, firstly an allegation of *per se* illegality on the basis that Apple had supplied a product on condition that the customer purchased services from one of the three mobile operators and secondly, as conduct that had an illegal anti-competitive purpose and effect.

A series of disputes ensued between HKT and the Authority as to whether HKT had provided sufficient information for the Authority to investigate and whether the Authority had acted properly in suspending its inquiries. HKT took the matter to the Appeal Board. Although the Appeal Board rejected Apple's contention that there was a genuine concern about the performance of the products on HKT's network, it dismissed a *per se* allegation and remitted the substantive question as to whether there had been conduct that substantially lessened competition to the Authority. By the time the investigation finally proceeded in earnest, the three mobile network operators had satisfied the Authority that they had not been involved in any agreement to block access of the products to HKT's network. Apple Asia's defence before the Authority was two-fold: first, Apple Asia denied that any SIM lock had been implemented (but it impliedly accepted that there was another reason the equipment would not function on HKT's network); secondly, to the extent any Apple group entity had engaged in relevant conduct, the conduct was engaged in by Apple Inc (a non-licensee over which the Communications Authority had no jurisdiction) rather than Apple Asia (a licensee over which the Communications Authority had jurisdiction). The Communications Authority accepted that Apple Inc was the only entity to have engaged in the relevant conduct and since it was not a licensee, the Authority had no jurisdiction over that conduct.

7.5.4 Abuse of dominance (Telecommunications)

Predatory pricing In 2000 the Telecommunications Authority investigated a complaint by the association of internet service providers that the incumbent fixed line operator (now known as PCCW) had engaged in predatory pricing when it launched an internet service as an adjunct to its i-TV service at a price that competitors alleged was both below the wholesale charge and loss-making. The Authority dismissed the complaint after having undertaken a costing analysis that suggested that the retail charge was not loss making and may not have been below the wholesale access charge (depending on how duration based charging is compared with volume based charging). The Authority also noted that a company launching a new service is likely to price it inexpensively to attract initial uptake of customers, suggesting that the Authority may not have found a breach even if it had found the price to be loss making.

In 2003 the Telecommunications Authority considered whether PCCW had engaged in predatory pricing when it offered fixed fee international calling plans to business customers. Similarly, a complaint was made that its pre-paid calling card to the Philippines (that was popular with the high number of guest workers from that country) amounted to predatory pricing. Although the Authority decided that its cost/price analysis was inconclusive in each case, it could nevertheless reach the view that there was no breach on two bases: PCCW lacked market power in the international call market due to there being lower barriers to entry and low barriers to entry would prevent PCCW from recouping any losses even if it were able to drive out other competitors in the short term.

Excessive pricing Until 2007 telecommunications operators were required to provide any-to-any connectivity and the Telecommunications Authority had issued guidance concerning interconnection rates between fixed and mobile operators to address PCCW's fixed line dominance. Reflecting the initial introduction of mobile telephony as a premium or luxury service, the guidance provided that fixed line operators should be able to charge for mobile telephone calls both to and from their fixed line networks. After an inquiry, and with the assistance of expert telecommunications economists, Ovum, the Authority proposed to remove the guidance on interconnection with the assumption that bi-directional mobile party pays charging would end. The Authority retained, however, the requirement for any-to-any connectivity.

However, this reform sparked a series of controversies. First, PCCW appealed on the basis that since the Authority had formed the view that the industry was sufficiently competitive for the interconnection charges to be deregulated, it was not rationally possible to concurrently apprehend a market failure requiring the retention of the regulatory requirement for any-to-any interconnectivity. There was also a bias allegation on the basis that the Authority had commenced the process with a preconceived view that market failure would result if it removed the any-to-any interconnection requirement. This resulted in a series of procedural disputes before the Appeal Board and the High Court which ultimately ordered that the Authority's decision should not be quashed.

Second, the mobile operators complained when PCCW filed with the Telecommunications Authority a substantial increase in the mobile to fixed bi-directional charges in the 11 month transitional period before deregulation. Initially, PCCW had sought to increase the charge from 4.36 cents per minute to 9.5 cents per minute but then reduced it to 5.45 cents per minute and at that point all but one mobile operator settled the dispute. Smartone, however, maintained its appeal alleging that PCCW had engaged in anti-competitive conduct, engaged in excessive pricing which amounted to an abuse of its dominant position and discriminated in favour of its own mobile affiliate. The anti-competitive conduct complaint was difficult to sustain on the basis that no enduring effects were likely beyond the 11 month transitionary period and the discrimination complaint was difficult to sustain given that PCCW's mobile affiliate was in fact charged equivalent interconnection fees. The excessive pricing complaint, however, required a detailed analysis. A series of interlocutory disputes were taken particularly concerning the access by Smartone to the data to enable it to undertake its own excessive pricing analysis (which were dismissed) and ultimately the Appeal Board and the High Court declined to overturn the decision by the Telecommunications Authority that PCCW had not breached any of the above provisions.

Discriminatory treatment In 2001 the Telecommunications Authority investigated whether PCCW as a provider of wholesale services had engaged in discriminatory action between its own affiliated downstream retail internet service provider vis a vis other ISPs. The allegation was that it had discriminated when making retail service connections. Also in 2001 the Chinese language daily newspaper the Oriental Daily alleged that when six internet service providers ceased trading, PCCW's wholesale business gave preferential treatment to its retail operations by making preferential, smoother churn arrangements than it provided to the remaining competing operators who might seek to win over the customers of the failed ISPs. Upon investigation, the Telecommunications Authority found that there were no anti-competitive agreements between the failed ISPs and PCCW and nor had PCCW actually given preferential treatment so no abuse or discrimination arose.

Margin squeeze In 2003 the Telecommunications Authority investigated an allegation that PCCW had engaged in a margin squeeze amounting to an abuse of dominance in relation to internet access such that PCCW's downstream internet service competitors would be disadvantaged. Although the Authority recognised that a margin squeeze could amount to an abuse of dominance, it took the view that this could only occur if PCCW had been making excessive profits at the wholesale level that were then used to fund losses in the downstream business as an implicit predatory subsidy to the benefit of its downstream affiliated business. In this case, the Authority accepted evidence that PCCW had dropped its wholesale charges by 12% and its retail charges by 50%. However, the Authority concluded on the basis of a limited analysis that PCCW's wholesale operations (which did face a range of competitors) were not earning excessive profits and that PCCW's retail operations were only making an insignificant loss. Ultimately, the Authority decided that the evidence before it was not sufficiently robust to base a conclusion that there had been a breach of the TO and, in any event, the limited analysis that was possible, suggested there may not be an anti-competitive margin squeeze.

Other anti-competitive terms and conditions In 2001 the Telecommunications Authority investigated a complaint referred to it by the Consumer

Council that requiring a seven day cancellation period for its retail internet service before the customer could churn to a competitor was anti-competitive. The Authority found that this was not an anti-competitive practice given the formalities required to give effect to the churn. Also in 2001 the Telecommunications Authority closed an investigation into whether PCCW's creditworthiness requirements for customers who did not have the PCCW fixed line service but who wanted to have an international direct dial service were anti-competitive. PCCW required such IDD-only customers to provide a copy of their last three phone bills and either an auto-pay arrangement or a HK$2,000 deposit. Although the Authority found these to be the highest creditworthiness requirements in the industry, competitors (Hutchison, New T&T, New World, City Telecom and One.Tel) all imposed some form of like requirement. Consequently, the Authority found there was no anti-competitive case to answer.

There were also a number of investigations into whether PCCW had offered unauthorised discounts in contravention of the specific prohibition against a dominant operator from charging below the tariffs that were filed with, and approved by, the Authority. These investigations occurred throughout the period until 2003. These complaints generally failed for lack of evidence that there had in fact been any such discount.

7.5.5 Abuse of dominance (Broadcasting)

Acquisition of exclusive rights In the broadcasting sector in 2004 the Broadcasting Authority investigated a complaint by PCCW's pay TV subsidiary that HKCTV's acquisition of exclusive football rights, together with a 30 month subscriber offer amounted to either conduct that prevented, distorted or substantially restricted competition or amounted to an abuse of dominance. The Broadcasting Authority concluded that HKCTV was dominant (through a combination of substantive analysis of the barriers to entry and by applying a market share presumption) but that the conduct in question was unlikely to breach either the prohibition against anti-competitive conduct or abuse of dominance. The Broadcasting Authority concluded that the scope of the rights acquired was insufficient to result in an anti-competitive effect and that subscribers had sufficient flexibility in the choices available to them that the anti-competitive effect would not arise.

Exclusive provision of content In 2005 the Broadcasting Authority considered whether the exclusive provision of content by Hong Kong's leading free-to-air broadcaster and substantial content producer, TBV, to pay operator, Galaxy, would have an anti-competitive effect of foreclosing the pay TV market. The investigation was in response to a complaint by the leading pay TV operator, HKCTV. TVB had offered the exclusive pay TV rights to the very popular Korean drama, Jewel in the Palace, and five channels through a bidding process and Galaxy was successful in acquiring Jewel in the Palace and four of the five channels. The controversy primarily arose because Galaxy was in substantial part owned by TVB. The authority accepted that the case theory in the complaint was relevant to test under the dominance provisions of the BO but decided that HKCTV had failed to provide evidence that the drama programme or the four channels in question were must have content for operating a pay TV business.

Predatory and discriminatory conduct In 2005 a cable television subscriber made an allegation of predatory and discriminatory pricing amounting to an abuse of dominance by HKCTV. Specifically, the allegation concerned Channel A that the operator offered for sale to individual subscribers at a stand alone price of HK$24 to $30 per month or HK$70 per month as part of a package. By contrast, the discounts for collective subscriptions for building complexes were offered with the effect that the per connection price paid by residents of such complexes could be as little as one tenth the individual subscriber rate. Although the Broadcasting Authority affirmed the applicability of a presumption set out in its guidelines, and that HKCTV should be regarded as dominant on account of having a 55% share of pay television subscribers, the Authority rejected the notion that the discounts amounted to an abuse of a dominant position, holding that discounts and price reductions are essential components of the competitive process and do not normally cause regulatory concerns.

Restriction on termination of services In 2008 the cable TV business that is associated with fixed line telecommunications incumbent, PCCW, lodged a complaint with the Broadcasting Authority that its main cable television rival, HKCTV was engaged in anti-competitive conduct by hindering or preventing its customers from terminating their service when shifting to PCCW. The Authority concurred that certain factual allegations made in the complaint were made out. For example, customer hotlines did not answer calls, fax lines were busy, termination requests were lost and terminations were processed slowly such that additional fees were incurred by the customer before terminations took effect. However, the Authority found that HKCTV did not hold a dominant market position, an anti-competitive purpose had not been established and the effects appeared not to be enduring. Therefore, the Authority declined to make a finding of breach.

Exclusive contracts In 2009 the Authority received a complaint from Asia Television Limited (ATV) alleging that Television Broadcasts Limited (TVB) had abused a dominant position by entering into exclusive contracts with artists, or instituting policies directed towards artists, that constrained the artists' freedom to appear on other TV networks in particular types of programming or speaking Cantonese. One-show and serial contracts with artists required that they obtain TVB's permission before working for a competing station and not to use their original voices on competing networks. They were also prevented from attending promotional events put on by competing networks. More than 90% of singers were also restrained from appearing on competing networks. A non-contractual policy was enforced that prevented singers from singing in Cantonese on competing networks. There were also restraints on these artists using their original voice in promotions.

After an extensive process, in 2012 the Authority found that TVB had a dominant position in the all-TV viewing market and the TV advertising market and, applying EU law principles, as a dominant firm TVB had a special responsibility not to distort competition. The Authority found that the restrictions were for the purpose, and had the effect, of illegally foreclosing access to the relevant markets for the purpose and effect of preventing, distorting or substantially restricting competition. For this breach of the BO, the Authority imposed a fine of HK$900,000. The Authority decided, however, that certain other allegations made in the 2009 complaint were not substantiated. These concerned unwritten rules of retaliation, unfair restrictions that prevented advertisers from advertising on competing networks and requiring film companies who hire TVB contracted artists to ensure that the film was not shown on a competing network.

Interference with intellectual property rights With respect to the interaction between competition and intellectual property law, in 2014 an aspiring television programme service provider, HKTVN, lodged a complaint with the Communications Authority alleging that the incumbent television programme service provider TVB had abused a dominant position in relation to trade marks. The allegations were that TVB made both blocking registrations of trade marks that HKTVN claimed were similar to marks it was intending to use and that TVB took action to object to trade mark registrations that HKTVN had lodged. The conduct complained of was alleged to have been part of a broader series of initiatives by TVB to prevent entry and foreclose the market but none of the other allegations (apart from the trade mark allegations) were pursued in detail in HKTVN's complaint.

The Communications Authority reaffirmed its previous decision that TVB had a dominant position in either the all-TV viewing market or the narrower free-to-air only TV market. The Authority took the view that the purpose of the conduct was a genuine commercial dispute about which company had previously used the relevant brands and that there was no evidence that the purpose was to foreclose the market. The Authority also declined to find that the conduct had the effect of foreclosing the market because neither party had provided any evidence concerning the effect of the trade mark actions on market entry/foreclosure. On this basis, the Authority distinguished this case from the European precedents in *AstraZeneca*[221] and *Osram/Airam*.[222]

7.5.6 Merger cases (Telecommunications only)

Sector-specific merger control The Hong Kong telecommunications industry has been subject to merger control since 2000. The authorities have been empowered to take action against mergers that have the effect or likely effect of substantially lessening competition in a telecommunications market. They have operated a voluntary informal clearance system under which the operators may choose whether to notify the Authority and how much data and analysis to provide. The incentive to notify is that once the Authority has become aware of a transaction, it has only a limited window within which it must take action. Under the TO the period was 14 days and under the Competition Ordinance the period is 30 days. The parties to mergers have generally chosen to notify the authorities.

Pre-Competition Ordinance enforcement The Communications Authority or the Telecommunications Authority have approved the following non-contentious transactions under the merger provision of the Telecommunications Ordinance:[223]

- in January 2009, the privatisation of PCCW Limited through the buyout of its public shareholding by its two major shareholders, PCDR Limited and Netcom Group (a mainland China state-owned enterprise), and subsequent cancellation of the listed status of the company;
- in May 2007, the acquisition of an interest in Asia Satellite Telecommunications Holdings Limited, a privately owned Asia-wide regional satellite operator and holder of 7 Hong Kong telecommunications licences, by General Electric Capital Corporation;
- in February 2007, the acquisition of an interest in Pacific Internet Limited by Connect Holdings Limited, in circumstances where both companies wholly owned a cable-based external fixed carrier licensee in Hong Kong, respectively, Pacific Internet (Hong Kong) Limited and Asia Netcom Hong Kong Limited;
- in September 2006, the purchase of Asia Netcom Hong Kong Limited, a licensee providing overland and submarine facilities to/from Hong Kong, in circumstances where the investor group owned another fixed carrier licensee company;

---

[221] C-457/10 P, *AstraZeneca v Commission* EU:C:2012:770.
[222] *Osram/Airam, Eleventh Report on Competition Policy* 1981, 97 (1982).
[223] Telecommunications Ordinance, section 7P.

- in March 2006, an agreement for the New World PCS Limited and CSL Limited mobile telecommunications operations in Hong Kong to be combined and integrated into a joint-owned mobile telephony network business;
- in December 2005, the acquisition of China Resources Peoples Telephony Company Limited, one of six mobile network operators in Hong Kong at the time, by China Mobile (Hong Kong) Limited, a company indirectly owned by one of the two licensed mobile telephony services providers on the mainland (China Mobile Communications Corporation);
- in July 2005, the acquisition of shares in SUNDAY Communications Limited, a provider of mobile and data services in Hong Kong, by the incumbent fixed line operator PCCW Limited; and
- in April 2005, the acquisition of 20% of PCCW Limited's share capital by China Netcom, a state-owned mainland China operator.

Of these transactions, several warrant a brief comment. In the Authority's consideration of the acquisition of SUNDAY by PCCW, the Authority considered whether, absent the transaction, PCCW was a likely entrant into the mobile telephony market and decided that it was not. The Authority also considered the potential for anti-competitive bundling by PCCW of fixed and mobile services and decided that there was no indication that this would occur and, even if it did, the general competition provisions of the TO could address that issue. The New World PCS and CSL Limited transaction in 2006 involved two substantial mobile operators but there remained four significant independent operators. The two transactions involving mainland China operators (i.e. China Netcom/PCCW and China Mobile/China Resources Peoples) involved an analysis of whether there was a likelihood of entry by the mainland carrier to Hong Kong and whether a substantial anti-competitive effect would arise from the potential for discriminatory terms for roaming or international interconnection charges between the Hong Kong and mainland operators. In each case the authorities decided that this was unlikely.

Finally, there was there was one merger in which the Communications Authority apprehended a substantial lessening of competition that required the imposition of remedies to resolve the competition concerns when the owners of the combined New World and CSL mobile business sold their business to PCCW. It decided that the proposed acquisition would have, or would be likely to have, an effect of substantially lessening competition in two relevant telecommunications markets: the downstream retail mobile telecommunications services market, and the upstream market for wholesale mobile network access which enabled a number of virtual mobile operators to compete with operators with infrastructure. The combined entity would have a 45.9% share of supply in the significant 3G/4G market which, in accordance with its merger guidelines, the Authority considered was highly concentrated. The Authority found that HKT Limited had not made out a case that the proposed acquisition would result in a benefit to the public and therefore HKT and CSL were required:

- to divest 29.6 MHz of the 3G Spectrum (namely the paired spectrum in the 1.9-2.2 GHz band);
- not to participate in any 3G Spectrum auction in Hong Kong for a period of five years;
- to notify the Communications Authority and all other mobile network operators of any plan for the closure of any base transceiver station sites for a period of five years;
- to continue to provide wholesale network access to mobile virtual network operators based on the existing agreements for a period of three years; and
- to continue to give effect to its existing 3G network capacity sharing agreement with China Mobile Hong Kong Company Limited (CMHK).

Conclusion There has been a wealth of competition law cases under the telecommunications and broadcasting competition law requirements predating the Competition Ordinance. Consistent with Hong Kong's highly litigious common law tradition, the Authorities, appeals board and courts have handled almost every conceivable kind of case in response to complaints from customers, competitors and consumer advocates as well as on their own initiative. Although a high proportion of these complaints were dismissed when the Authority collected sufficient factual information to show that the allegations were unfounded, there have been a number of detailed competition assessments.

7.6 TRANSPORT

Introduction Hong Kong was founded as a trade outpost with a focus on facilitating trade with China. Despite Hong Kong covering a small territorial area of just 1,104 square kilometres, with a population of 7.24 million in 2014 it punches far above its weight in international sea and air transport. Hong Kong is home to the world's fifth-busiest container port. Hong Kong International Airport (HKIA) is second only to Beijing as Asia's busiest passenger airport[224] and is the world's busiest airport for international air cargo, a title it has held since 1996.[225] The domestic transport sector, although smaller, is no less significant. In total, public transport enables 12.5 million

---

[224] Airports Council International, OAG Schedules (December 2015).
[225] http://www.hongkongairport.com/eng/business/about-the-airport/air-cargo/air-cargo-intro.html

passengers to complete their journeys on average each day.[226] The success of some Hong Kong operators has seen them go on to become leading transport operators in Southeast Asia and beyond. Hong Kong was also the second country to oversee the development and implementation of contactless smart card technology with its Octopus card allowing consumers to travel on multiple public transport modes using a single payment card - an innovation now exported and replicated worldwide.

This section describes the Hong Kong transport sector, subdivided into shipping, passenger aviation, cargo aviation and public transport namely trains, buses, and taxis/Uber, and how it might be impacted by the Competition Ordinance.

Transport sector under the Competition Ordinance   The Competition Ordinance does not treat the transport sector differently from any other sector. This is largely because the Competition Ordinance is entirely new, it has not evolved over time and does not form part of a greater system of planning and cooperation. By contrast, for example, EU competition law initially generally excluded the transport sector and Articles 90-100 TFEU contain special provisions relating to transport. Over time, the EU rules on competition became applicable to all modes of transport so that now the sector is subject to the same procedural and substantive competition rules as the rest of the EU economy. There remains, however, one bespoke block exemption, Regulation 906/2009[227] which is the block exemption for liner shipping consortia agreements. Another key point to note is that the Merger Rule does not apply to Hong Kong's transport sector at all. This distinguishes Hong Kong competition law as it applies to transport from, for example, EU and Chinese competition law, which do subject transport sector mergers to competition law scrutiny.

7.6.1 Shipping

Hong Kong is a key maritime centre   Hong Kong is currently the fourth-busiest container port in the world behind Shenzhen, Singapore and Shanghai, although it has slipped from the number one position it occupied during the early 2000s. In 2014, over 189,000 ocean-going and river-trade vessels for cargo and passenger traffic visited the port of Hong Kong and the port handled an estimated 22.3 million twenty-foot equivalent units. As of October 2015, there were over 2,465 vessels[228] on the Hong Kong Shipping Register, totalling over 100 million GT making it the fourth-largest register after Panama, Liberia

---

[226] http://www.td.gov.hk/en/transport_in_hong_kong/public_transport/index.html.
[227] OJ 2009 L256/31.
[228] http://www.mardep.gov.hk/en/pub_services/pdf/mon_stat.pdf.

and the Marshall Islands.[229]   In addition, Hong Kong has become a major centre for ship management, finance and insurance.

Several factors make Hong Kong attractive.[230]   Since January 2000, Hong Kong-registered ships have received preferential rates for port charges when calling at Chinese ports.[231]   Another key consideration is that Chinese cabotage rules (which prohibit foreign-flagged vessels from moving cargoes from one mainland coastal port to another) are waived for Hong Kong as it is considered a foreign port for these purposes.[232]   Further, Hong Kong's profit tax rate of 16.5% is modest and the tax regime is territorial, which means that income derived from the international operation of Hong Kong registered ships is exempted from profits tax.

Hong Kong is a freeport, with only tobacco, liquor, hydrocarbon oil and methyl alcohol incurring any excise duties.[233]   This freeport regime facilitates the movement of cargo into and through Hong Kong.   Customs procedures are simple and efficient, not least as, unlike many other jurisdictions, Hong Kong customs play little role in revenue collection.   Another consideration is that in recent years Hong Kong has significantly increased the number of its double taxation agreements from just four to over forty,[234] with more under negotiation.   One focus of these agreements has been shipping income.

In terms of direct economic contribution, in late 2015 there were over 700 companies in Hong Kong offering a wide range of quality and high-value added maritime services, such as ship agency and management, chartering and broking, finance, insurance, maritime law and arbitration and maritime and port industries directly contributed 1.2% ($24 billion) to Hong Kong's GDP and 2.5% (92,000 jobs) of total employment.[235]   In the past, there was also some shipbuilding in Hong Kong; however, higher labour costs, as well as the high prices of Hong Kong real estate, have led to Hong Kong's shipbuilders moving across the border into mainland China.

Competitiveness of the port industry in Hong Kong   In October 2014, the Executive Summary to a government-commissioned Study on the Strategic Development Plan for Hong Kong Port 2030[236] by BMT Asia Pacific was

[229]   http://hong-kong-economy-research.hktdc.com/business-news/article/Hong-Kong-Industry-Profiles/Maritime-Services-Industry-in-HongKong/hkip/en/1/1X000000/1X09WBHM.htm.

[230]   http://www.mardep.gov.hk/en/pub_services/reg_gen.html.

[231]   http://www.info.gov.hk/gia/general/200001/24/0121161.htm.

[232]   http://www.seatrade-maritime.com/news/asia/china-cabotage-rules-benefit-hong-kong-hit.html.

[233]   http://www.customs.gov.hk/en/trade_facilitation/dutiable/types/.

[234]   http://www.mic.gov.hk/eng/agreement/taxation.htm.

[235]   http://www.legco.gov.hk/yr1516/english/panels/edev/papers/edev20151123cb4-217-6-e.pdf.

[236]   http://www.mic.gov.hk/docs/ES%20Eng%20(28.11.2014).pdf.

released. The Study's main focuses were to review the dynamic containerised cargo market in Hong Kong, recommend a development plan to enhance the competitiveness of Hong Kong Port (HKP) and to facilitate its continued growth. The Study described HKP as both a gateway port for South China cargo and as a transhipment hub, with the following competitive strengths:

- a geographic location that is attractive for transhipment;
- high frequency of sailings and good connectivity;
- quality of service: reliability, security and low likelihood of damage to cargo;
- shorter lead time;
- freeport status; and
- status as the only port along the China coast where foreign owned carriers can tranship China-related cargo.

However, it found that HKP is not competitive in terms of cost and there is diminishing distinction between HKP and competitors in terms of quality or capacity. The Study anticipated that HKP will retain a certain level of market share of the South China cargo base due to increasing labour costs and the possible RMB appreciation impacting other South China ports and thus enhancing the cost competitiveness of HKP. HKP has a captive market for foreign carriers wishing to tranship China related cargo, and may also compete as an international transhipment hub over the wider Asia region. A forecast of HKP's containerised throughput related to South China and international transhipment shows that demand for facilities will continue to grow at HKP up to 2030, but at a slow rate, averaging 1.5% per annum over this period. These challenges are not new. The earlier Hong Kong Port 2020 Master Plan and 2005-07 Port Cargo Forecasts[237] by the consultancy GHK identified similar threats to HKP and projected stagnating growth unless remedial action was taken.

Ports are in international competition, and HKP, more than most, operates in an intensely competitive market. Whereas 15 years ago, HKP enjoyed several service advantages, and hence price premium, versus the emerging neighbouring port in Shenzhen, its competitors have rapidly developed their capacity and services to the extent they largely match Hong Kong's. Meanwhile, these competitor ports benefit from lower costs and better surface access to the South China import/export cargo hinterlands. Hong Kong's land constrained terminals have increasingly struggled to compete in this market, switching to the lower revenue international ocean transhipment markets, where Hong Kong maintains an advantage due to the cabotage restrictions faced by mainland China's ports.

---

[237] http://www.pdc.gov.hk/eng/plan2020/index.htm,
        http://www.logisticshk.gov.hk/board-/PCF05-06ES.pdf

In the second quarter of 2015, total port cargo throughput decreased by 11% compared with a year earlier to 68.4 million tonnes.[238] This trend may continue unless measures are taken to safeguard and indeed promote the international competitiveness of HKP, although in many respects it may be too late to reverse the loss of cargo to competitor ports. It is also important to note that the key consideration in terms of competition has been competition inter-port rather than intra-port. Whilst the two main terminal operators at Hong Kong, MTL and Hong Kong International Terminals (a subsidiary of Hutchison International Port Holdings), do compete with each other and customers (i.e. lines) have switched between the terminals, greater attention has focused on the competitiveness of HKP as a whole versus the neighbouring South China ports and other international transhipment hubs.

Hong Kong Shipping Register The Hong Kong Shipping Register was set up on 3 December 1990 under the Hong Kong Merchant Shipping (Registration) Ordinance. The Register is operated by the Hong Kong Government through the Marine Department and registers ships which comply with international standards for safety and protection of the marine environment that are able to meet the requirements for registration in Hong Kong, provided that a majority interest in the ship is owned by one or more qualified persons, or operated under a demise charter by a corporation that is a qualified person, the ship is not registered elsewhere, and a representative person is appointed in relation to the ship.

Marine Department Unusually, Hong Kong does not have a port authority or similar regulatory body. The Marine Department is currently the main body most responsible for administering HKP, the responsibility vesting in the Director of Marine. The Director of Marine is supported by various Government bodies: the Port Operations Committee, the Pilotage Advisory Committee, the Local Vessels Advisory Committee and, until their merger, the Hong Kong Port Development Council and Hong Kong Maritime Industry Council. The Marine Department ensures that ships are able to enter HKP, load or discharge cargo and then leave HKP as quickly and as safely as possible. It also regulates aspects of safety and pollution and carries out port state control inspections on ships visiting HKP in accordance with IMO Resolution A1052(27) and the Tokyo MoU Port State Control Manual. However, the Marine Department has no responsibility for strategic planning, development, landside management or economic regulation.

Reforms of and proposals to replace the Marine Department On 19 April 2013, the Lamma Island Accident Investigation Board submitted a report to the

---

[238] http://www.censtatd.gov.hk/press_release/pressReleaseDetail.jsp?charsetID=1&press-RID=3671.

Hong Kong Government[239] which *inter alia* made certain suggestions to the Marine Department. A Steering Committee on Systemic Reform of the Marine Department was set up in May 2013 to steer and supervise the Marine Department in undertaking a comprehensive systemic review and reform.[240] The Steering Committee has focused its work on three areas, namely reviewing and improving the business processes and operational procedures of the Marine Department, the manpower strategy and training matters of the Department, and enhancing marine safety by means of improvement measures. A Task Force on Reform has also been formed within the Marine Department to support the work of the Steering Committee and to co-ordinate implementation of the various improvement measures.

The creation of an independent Marine and/or Port Authority has been advocated by a number of industry stakeholders and consultancy studies, including the Final Report issued by BMT Asia Pacific in April 2014 and the Consultancy Study on Enhancing Hong Kong's Position as an International Maritime Centre.[241] The Government therefore looked at the creation of a new body. However, if created, it was feared that such new body might still have drastically curtailed powers and would primarily engage in only promotion and research rather than being the sort of entity or Port Authority seen in other jurisdictions.

In his 2016 Policy Address, the Hong Kong Chief Executive announced the merger of the existing Maritime Industry Council and Port Development Council to form a new Hong Kong Maritime & Port Board. The Government decided to set up the Board having taken on board the findings and recommendations of the business case study commissioned in mid-2014 to look into the feasibility of setting up a new maritime body, as well as views and suggestions received from stakeholders during the study period. The Board, officially established in April 2016, will be a high-level steering body to assist the Government in formulating strategies and policies to drive the growth of high value-added and professional maritime services in Hong Kong, foster talent development (including overseeing the implementation of the Maritime and Aviation Training Fund), and promote Hong Kong as an international maritime hub. Three functional committees will be formed under the Board, respectively focusing on manpower development, promotion and external relations, and industry development. Each of these committees will be chaired by an industry representative. The new Board will cooperate with

---

[239] http://www.gov.hk/en/theme/coi-lamma/pdf/COI_Report.pdf.
[240] http://www.legco.gov.hk/yr14-15/english/panels/edev/papers/edev20150527cb4-1034-4-e.pdf;
http://www.thb.gov.hk/eng/psp/pressreleases/transport/maritime/2013/20131016.htm.
[241] http://www.mic.gov.hk/docs/8870%20IMC%20Final%20Report%20-%20ENG%20(16.04.2014).pdf.

Hong Kong Trade Development Council and Invest Hong Kong to expand efforts to raise Hong Kong's profile in the international maritime landscape.

Regulatory scrutiny The shipping sector has not as yet been scrutinised by a Hong Kong sector regulator in respect of competition law matters. Nevertheless, Hong Kong Liner Shipping Association (HKLSA), which represents approximately 90% of the containerised liner industry in Hong Kong,[242] has applied for a block exemption order from the prohibition against anti-competitive agreements.

Competition law enforcement trends in Hong Kong shipping Broadly, the maritime sector can be divided between liner shipping and tramp vessel services. Liner shipping involves the transport of cargo, chiefly by container, on a regular basis to ports on a particular geographic route, generally known as trades. Other general characteristics of liner shipping are that shipping schedules or timetables with sailing and dates are advertised in advance and are made available to any transport use, either directly or on-line. Tramp vessel services involve the transport of goods in bulk or in break bulk in a vessel chartered wholly or partly to one or more shippers on the basis of a voyage or time charter or any other form of contract for non-regularly chartered or non-advertised sailings, where the freight rates are freely negotiated case by case in accordance with the conditions of supply and demand. It is mostly the unscheduled transport of one single commodity which fills the vessel.

The market organisation of liner shipping has traditionally featured a variety of cooperative elements:

- conferences (no longer prevalent in the industry): which recommend freight rates (non-binding) and set surcharges (Bunker Adjustment Factor (BAF), Currency Adjustment Factor (CAF), Terminal Handling Charge (THC), and regulate capacity etc.;
- looser Voluntary Discussion Agreements (VDAs): which have no common tariff but provide a forum for members to discuss the trade and may provide recommendations for General Rate Increases (GRI);
- alliances: agreements between carriers to cooperate on space and capacity on a global or regional basis; and
- consortia and Vessel Sharing Agreements (VSAs): agreements which focus on a particular route.

These cooperative elements are usually forbidden for other industry sectors by competition laws, but the liner industry has enjoyed special status with a number of exemptions from antitrust regulations, although in recent years, the regulatory balance has shifted in some jurisdictions.

---

[242] http://www.compcomm.hk/en/enforcement/consultations/past_consultations/-files/S21_Hong_Kong_Liner_Shipping_Association.pdf

Block exemption application by HKLSA   Two activities of liner shipping companies which might be impacted by competition law and, in particular, might fall foul of the First Conduct Rule are:

- vessel sharing agreements (VSAs) and alliances - these are operational arrangements allowing carriers to join into an alliance which then allows them to coordinate vessel space and operations either on a specific route or on a global or regional basis. They do not cover the commercial aspects of pricing. New alliances have recently been formed in response to the introduction of mega-vessels which carriers cannot fill on their own – hence the need for alliances; and
- information sharing including voluntary discussion agreements (VDAs) - which allow members to study trade information and discuss rate levels, supply and demand trends, charges and other commercial issues. These do not allow members to fix or coordinate prices, but only to recommend increases which are voluntarily applied.

Shipping lines, in theory, can self-assess whether they can rely upon the efficiency exclusion to the First Conduct Rule. However, the HKLSA has made it clear, from at least 2012 onwards, that liner shipping companies crave the legal certainty of a block exemption.[243]   In its submission, HKLSA argued that both types of discussion are necessary to achieve efficiencies. While it is widely agreed that the liner shipping industry is characterised by unusually high fixed and operating costs, the nature of liner shipping requires a vessel to sail a particular route whether or not it is full. As such, VDAs and VSAs are crucial in enabling carriers to provide regular, fixed day sailing schedules at rates that are not subject to severe fluctuation. They are therefore necessary for the proper functioning of the industry. Initially it seemed that the Competition Commission considered that its hands were tied until the block exemption sections of the Competition Ordinance came into operation on 14 December 2015. On 28 October 2015, however, it announced that it may, in specific cases, indicate to applicants that it would be unlikely to initiate enforcement action in respect of conduct or arrangements already existing at the date of full commencement of the Competition Ordinance while it is considering an application in respect of that conduct or the relevant arrangements. Such indications will be publicised and reconsidered by the Competition Commission after six months.[244]

Experience in other jurisdictions   As part of a modernisation package, in October 2006, the EU lifted exclusions for tramp shipping and cabotage. Most importantly, in October 2008 the EU removed a block exemption in favour of

---

[243]   http://www.compcomm.hk/en/enforcement/consultations/past_consultations/files-/S21_Hong_Kong_Liner_Shipping_Association.pdf.
[244]   http://www.compcomm.hk/en/media/press/files/20151028_PressRel_further_arrange-ments_Applications_Eng.pdf.

liner conferences (which previously allowed them to set prices and regulate capacity). The rationale behind the removal of the block exemption was that it was felt by some that traditional liner shipping conferences imposing fixed tariffs were becoming unappealing and failed to provide consumers with efficient and reliable services. In 2008, to provide guidance to companies impacted by the removal of the conference block exemption, the EU issued (non-binding) guidelines on the application of Article 101 TFEU to maritime transport services (Marine Transport Guidelines),[245] including liner shipping (e.g. information sharing), tramp shipping (e.g. pools) and cabotage, to assist in understanding market share and when efficiency-based exclusions might be available. The guidelines also discussed how technical agreements may not constitute cartel activities if their sole object and effect is to implement technical improvements, technical cooperation or implementation of environmental standards. However, in 2013, the European Commission decided that there was no longer any need for sector-specific guidelines, so that horizontal cooperation agreements in the maritime transport sector are now subject to the European Commission's Guidelines on Horizontal Cooperation Agreements. That said, since there are no EU guidelines which replace or contradict the Marine Transport Guidelines, they may still be helpful in that it may be that the European Commission will take a similar approach to that outlined in those guidelines.

Regulation 906/2009, which is the EU's Liner Shipping Consortia Block Exemption, came into force on 26 April 2010 and was extended unchanged for another 5 years in 2015. The Regulation extends to all liner shipping services which provide services from one or more EU ports, whether containerised or not and makes it clear that a consortium may be comprised of not just a single agreement but also a set of interrelated agreements between many carriers. While the Regulation prohibits hard core restrictions, such as price-fixing to third parties, it exempts agreements between consortia members to operate joint services, make joint capacity adjustments in response to fluctuations of demand and supply, jointly operate and use port terminals, pursue pooling arrangements and co-ordinate timetables and ports of call and cross-charter slots. The exemptions are subject to the consortium's market share not exceeding 30% (by volume). Above this threshold, a consortium will not benefit from the block exemption. Even where consortia do not fulfil the requirements of Regulation 906/2009, they may still meet the criteria for the application of Article 101(3) TFEU.

On the other hand, consortia are not to be confused with conferences which, amongst other things, co-ordinate prices. Indeed there have been several EU cases in which members of liner conferences were found to have dominated their market position collectively under Article 102 TFEU with the conference

---

[245] OJ 2008 C245/2. These guidelines expired on 26 September 2013.

having been considered a single entity.[246] Singapore permits co-operation on price, remuneration and technical operations, and commercial arrangements, subject to aggregate market share not exceeding 50%.[247] The Ministry for Trade and Industry extended the block exemption order for liner shipping agreements for five more years until December 31, 2020.[248] South Korea and Taiwan have longstanding competition law exemptions for all types of cooperative carrier agreements.[249] Japan also has an antitrust exemption for ocean carriers. Since 7 July 2014 Malaysia has granted a block exemption for VSAs and VDAs which is valid for three years [250.]

Proposal for a block exemption order for VSAs In September 2016, a block exemption has been proposed by the Commission covering VSAs, but not VDAs. In recent years, the further enhancing of Hong Kong's status as an international shipping centre was listed as one of the Government's priorities.[251] Further, the Board has been set up *inter alia* to promote Hong Kong as an international maritime centre and a major port in overseas and mainland China markets.[252] In the EU, Regulation 906/2009 exempts liner consortia agreements, subject to various conditions, such as a market share of no more than 30%. The Competition Commission may also have been swayed by the fact that the Singapore Minister for Trade and Industry has recently extended the Competition (Block Exemption for Liner Shipping Agreements) Order, in its current form, for another five years until 31 December 2020.[253] Singapore is the second busiest container port in the world and, like Hong Kong, is dependent on transhipment services. These services can be provided in a number of competitor ports. Both Hong Kong and Singapore offer shipping lines a relatively modest hinterland of import/export cargo, as compared with mainland China, Europe or the US. Hence there is no

---

[246] Case T-191/98, *Atlantic Container Line v Commission ('TACA')* [2003] ECR II-3275.

[247] https://www.ccs.gov.sg/legislation/block-exemption-order.

[248] https://www.ccs.gov.sg/~/media/custom/ccs/files/public%20register%20and-%20consultation/public%20consultation%20items/2015%20public%20consultation%20on%20proposed%20recommendation%20to%20extend%20beo%20for%20liner%20shipping%20agreements/beo%20agreement%20order%202015.ashx.

[249] http://www.oecd.org/officialdocuments/publicdisplaydocumentpdf/?cote=DAF/-COMP/WP2(2015)3&docLanguage=En.

[250] http://mycc.gov.my/sites/default/files/P.U.%28A%29%20195-Competition%20Block-%20Exemption%20for%20Vessel%20Sharing%20Agreements.pdf.

[251] http://www.budget.gov.hk/2013/eng/budget14.html.

[252] http://www.hkmpb.gov.hk/en/reference.html.

[253] Media Release, CCS Recommends Extending the Block Exemption Order for Liner Shipping Agreements for another five years https://www.ccs.gov.sg/~/media/custom/ccs/files/media%20and%20publications/media%20releases/ccs%20recommends%20extending%20beo%20for%20liner%20shipping%20agreements%20for%20another%205%20yrs/ccs%20media%20release%20on%20beo%20for%20liner%20shipping%20agreements.ashx.

compelling reason for the main shipping lines and largest vessels to call at Hong Kong, save for the additional transhipment business that lines can undertake. However, if VSAs were not to be exempted, there is a concern that this may dissuade carriers from calling at Hong Kong to avoid the risk of legal action. Shipping lines are unlikely to break-up their global VSAs, purely for the sake of Hong Kong's small import/ export market, rather they may switch their transhipment services to other ports.

Competition authorities across the world broadly apply the same rules on cartels. Thus, it would be very surprising for the Competition Commission or any other competition authority to strike down an agreement with which the European Commission, the American Federal Maritime Commission (FMC) and Chinese authorities were comfortable. For example, the major alliances such as G6, 2M, CKYHE and OCEAN3 are all currently allowed by the European Commission, the FMC and the Chinese MOFCOM and Ministry of Transport. These alliances operate internationally so it would be unusual for Hong Kong, a major transhipment hub competing in global markets, to take a different approach. China is slightly different with its evolving merger control law – it was this law that was used to veto the proposed P3 VSA– not control of anti-competitive agreements. The market share of these alliances is significant and further consolidation in the sector may warrant further investigation. The case for VDAs is not as clear cut, and were thus excluded from the scope of the proposed block exemption. That said, in the context of extreme international competition, the approach taken by other competition regulators in Asia – many of whom even allow conferences – is even more relevant than the approach taken by the EU.

In February 2016 the European Commission announced that it is market-testing commitments offered by major container carriers which, if implemented, will mean the end of public General Rate Increases (GRIs) announcements on routes to and from Europe, at least for three years. The European Commission was concerned that public GRIs are pricing signals to carrier competitors intended to raise freight rates. Instead of public GRIs, according to the European Commission, the price figures that the carriers announce will benefit from further transparency and include at least the five main elements of the total price (base rate, bunker charges, security charges, terminal handling charges and peak season charges if applicable). In addition, price announcements will not be made more than 31 days before they enter into force.[254] Fifteen of the largest global carriers have committed to be bound by these maximum prices for the announced period of validity, but carriers will remain free to offer prices below these ceilings. It appears that these changes will affect only spot rates and will not affect contract rates. They will also not enable carriers to set minimum prices. Shippers will still be able to negotiate

---

[254] European Commission press release IP-16-317 dated 16 February 2016.

lower rates than the maximum rates. The European Commission is currently consulting the industry about the proposed commitments.

Finally, it might be noted that the Competition Commission has already signalled in its Guideline on the First Conduct Rule, that it will not allow conferences (which involve price recommendations). Hypothetical Example 10 envisages a trade association for junk owners collecting from and circulating to its members information on their respective proposed future prices, including information as to the proposed prices for specific journeys. The information is not made available to the public and is circulated to members in advance of a seasonal price review by the association members. Absent a decision of the association giving rise to the information exchange or evidence of an agreement between members to engage in the information exchange, the Commission would infer that this arrangement is implemented as part of a concerted practice with the object of harming competition. The conduct allows the junk owners to adjust their future pricing to reflect the proposed pricing of competitors and thus reduces price competition in the market. The information exchange arrangement is an indirect form of price fixing. The Commission would also regard the conduct to be Serious Anti-Competitive Conduct under the Ordinance.

7.6.2 Aviation

Hong Kong is a key aviation centre   Hong Kong International Airport (HKIA), Chek Lap Kok, opened in July 1998. It is now second only to Beijing Capital International Airport in terms of passenger traffic in China and is the world's busiest airport for international air cargo, a title it has held since 1996. In 2014, 64.7 million passengers passed through HKIA along with 4.38 million tonnes of freight.[255] In part, Hong Kong's success is the result of its strategic location, excellent connectivity with mainland China and overseas jurisdictions, efficient modern logistics operations, Hong Kong's free port policy and competitive labour force. However, HKIA faces increasing competition from airports in China including Shanghai and Guangzhou for China's passenger market share and other airport hubs such as Singapore and Kuala Lumpur for international and regional passengers and cargo. Similar to its port, Hong Kong's airport is largely a transit destination which connects passengers to a wider range of holiday and business destinations, accounting for a third of passenger numbers.[256]

---

[255] http://www.hongkongairport.com/eng/business/about-the-airport/air-cargo/air-cargo-intro.html.

[256] http://skift.com/2015/10/08/asias-busiest-international-airport-has-to-wait-10-years-for-a-new-runway.

Airports can be considered a two-sided market. On the one hand, an airport must attract airlines that pay landing charges and demand ground handling services. In addition, the airport must attract passengers who pay fares and surcharges, parking charges and demand retail and food and beverage services. At the same time, many jurisdictions tightly control access to their airports by airlines, with preference given to home base or national carriers. To be competitive, airports must be efficient, offer a high number of destinations and access to a large number of airlines with a high frequency of flights to key destinations. The success of HKIA is borne out by the fact that it currently attracts over 100 airlines, flying to over 190 destinations, including 50 in China,[257] and has been consistently voted one of the best airports in the world by passengers.[258]

Hong Kong is planning to open a third runway in 2023 after a near 10-year delay in winning planning approval for the extension. The new runway will enable Hong Kong to handle 58% more passengers, raising its capacity to 100 million a year by 2023 at a cost of HK$141.5 billion ($18 billion). Other regional airports, including those in Singapore and Kuala Lumpur, are planning to expand to a similar capacity.[259] From a competition perspective, the increased capacity would allow space for new entrants and in particular low cost carriers to operate in Hong Kong.[260]

Aviation and competition issues　Unlike the UK where there are multiple airports to compete with each other for airlines and passengers, Hong Kong's competitors are located in other jurisdictions. Thus, much like the discussion of the port sector above, conduct which attracts more passengers, cargo and airlines to HKIA is a benefit to the Hong Kong economy and is therefore unlikely to be a focus of the Competition Commission. As with the port and maritime industry, the economic importance of the sector to Hong Kong is an important consideration as is the risk that antitrust action may simply drive airlines and the related economic activity away from Hong Kong to competitor airports. However, as airport-airline vertical relationships are increasingly important to the competitiveness of airports, there has been a renewed focus on their impact on competition in airline markets. While there are benefits to strong airport-airline relationships, such as preferential flight scheduling and services for airlines that designate an airport as a hub, co-investment in infrastructure by airlines and greater certainty for airports are also considered

---

[257] http://www.hongkongairport.com/eng/business/about-the-airport/facts-figures/facts-sheets.html.

[258] http://www.worldairportawards.com.

[259] http://skift.com/2015/10/08/asias-busiest-international-airport-has-to-wait-10-years-for-a-new-runway/.

[260] http://www.hongkongairport.com/eng/pdf/future/project-profile.pdf.

to have positive impacts on efficiency,[261] which in turn enables more effective competition with rival airport-airline hubs. The concern is that these relationships are also a source of entry barriers for airlines[262] and that the hub premium can also harm consumers.[263]

Hong Kong airline passenger market Major airlines based in Hong Kong include Cathay Pacific, Dragon Air, Hong Kong Airlines and Hong Kong Express Airways. Other regional and international carriers operating from HKIA include Air China, China Eastern Airlines, Singapore Airlines, Japan Airlines, American Airlines, and Emirates among many others. Operating a hub and spoke model, these airlines largely use HKIA to transit arriving passengers from hub-to-hub to regional flights, and vice versa. Competitiveness is dependent upon hubs like Hong Kong offering a high number of destinations and frequency of flights to efficiently connect passengers to their final destination. The level of competition between airlines can differ on both hub and spoke components of the journey. To offer flights at the lowest cost and to an increasing number of destinations, airlines must fill as many seats as possible to make efficient use of the capacity available. Where a passenger journey involves more than one flight and possibly different airlines, efficient outcomes are only possible by cooperating on schedules, sharing passenger information and coordinating ground handling operations and ticketing. For these reasons, alliances between airlines are a common feature of the airline market. The depth of cooperation and coordination can differ from code sharing through to joint ventures.

The concern is that while these alliances generate efficiency savings and enable an expanded schedule to be offered by airlines, they lead to increased market power and can facilitate price fixing behaviour to the detriment of consumers. For those airlines considering entry to a market, alliances can also be regarded as a barrier to entry. A recent study evaluating joint ventures in the Singapore airline market for the Singapore Competition Commission found them to be broadly beneficial for passengers as the overall market increased by 10% (mostly on joint venture flights) and most fares did not change.[264] Recent literature looking at airlines operating in the Pacific region, in contrast, found that fares increased with joint ventures.[265] As both studies only looked at a

---

[261] Oum, T, H. and Fu, X. (2008):Impacts of Airports on Airline Competition, available at: http://www.internationaltransportforum.org/jtrc/RoundTables/RToct08Oum.pdf.

[262] Alfonso,, Tiziana. and Nastasi, A. (2012): Vertical relations in the air transport industry: A facility-rivalry game. Transportation Research Part E: Logistics and Transportation Review Vol.48, Issue 5, September 2012, pages 993-1008.

[263] DOT (2001) EU decision to disallow Charleroi airport's subsidy to Ryanair http://www.justice.gov/atr/case-document/file/485581/download.

[264] https://www.ccs.gov.sg/~/media/custom/ccs/files/media%20and%20publications/.

[265] Zou et al (2011): Assessing the price effects of airline alliances on complementary routes , Transport research Part E: Logistics and Transportation Review.

sample of mainly direct flights, more research is needed to understand better the efficiency arguments and price changes on indirect flights, which is difficult as fares and costs are not immediately separable between two or more parts of the same journey.

A final competition concern relates to capacity at HKIA, which limits the potential for new entry. For example, compared to other major airports in Asia, low-cost carriers represent only a small share of the business in Hong Kong. Low cost carriers control about 45% of the business in South Asia, whereas the share of low cost carriers is closer to 5-6 % in Hong Kong. Part of the reason for limited low cost carrier penetration in the market may be the lack of capacity at HKIA, which operates at near full capacity and the reliance of the airport on transit (hub and spoke) passengers.

Air cargo   Air cargo has been the subject of competition investigations in many jurisdictions including Australia,[266] Canada, the EU[267] and Singapore where freight forwarders in the air cargo industry were sanctioned for fixing and exchange of information regarding fees and surcharges in December 2014.[268]   The investigations related, *inter alia*, to the fuel surcharge and the security surcharge (the latter having been introduced to address the costs of certain security measures imposed following the terrorist attacks of 11 September 2001). Recently the Competition Commission of India (CCI) imposed penalties on three Indian airlines for concerted action in fixing and revising fuel surcharges for transporting cargo.[269]   With Hong Kong ranked the world's busiest airport in terms of international cargo throughput, the impact of the Competition Ordinance on the air cargo market could be significant. One important factor that carriers should consider is having a documented independent price strategy, with the common practice of follow the leader on pricing being a risky strategy from a competition law position. Similarly the timing and format of price/cost announcements must not be designed to influence other carriers. Another lesson to be learned from these cases is that once one competition regulator has launched an investigation into certain agreements/ practices, others often follow suit in their jurisdictions.

Like passenger airlines and liner shipping, alliances are common in the cargo sector to share freight capacity on passenger aircraft and on cargo

---

[266]   http://www.australiancompetitionlaw.org/readingroom/2014clarke-aircargo.html.

[267]   http://europa.eu/rapid/press-release_IP-10-1487_en.htm?locale=en.

[268]   CCS (2014): CCS Fines 10 Freight Forwarders for Price Fixing – Case Ref: 700/003/11, decision reached 11 December 2014:
https://www.ccs.gov.sg/~/media/custom/ccs/files/public%20register%20and%20consult ation/public%20consultation%20items/ccs%20fines%202010%20freight%20fowarders/air %20freight%20forwarding%20%20infringement%20decision%20nonconfidentialpublic %20register.ashx.

[269]   http://www.cci.gov.in/sites/default/files/press_release/Press%20release- %20Air%20Cargo.pdf.

aircraft, increase efficiency and expand the range of destinations which can be reached by air.   For the customer (freight forwarders), this may improve service quality, reduce delivery times and reduce costs.   Airlines face much greater restrictions on access to routes and markets than their shipping line counterparts, and hence airline alliances are also often formed in part as workarounds to these restrictions on market access.   The market is, however, complicated by a high degree of vertical integration within the logistics sector. The same company can provide a door-to-door delivery service using its own assets, including any required storage.   Alternatively, the company can use partners such as passenger airlines to transport the cargo and shippers located in other parts of the world to carry out other aspects of the supply chain.   This requires a high level of cooperation and coordination between rivals for efficiency.   These conditions are, however, conducive to price fixing and similar anti-competitive conduct.   For Hong Kong as a transit destination, the potential adverse competition effects may not be a concern as many customers and suppliers paying for the service are located in other jurisdictions.

Civil Aviation Department   The Civil Aviation Department (CAD) is the industry regulator.   In addition, the CAD acts as an air navigation service provider and provides air traffic control services to all aircraft operating in and out of HKIA and within the Hong Kong Flight Information Region.[270] Before the coming into effect of the Competition Ordinance, there was no operative competition law applicable to the sector and the aviation sector has not as yet been scrutinised by a Hong Kong sector regulator in respect of competition law matters.   The CAD will not have any jurisdiction under the Competition Ordinance to regulate competition.   This is to be contrasted for example with the UK Civil Aviation Authority which enjoys concurrent powers to enforce UK competition law on airport operations and air traffic services.

Block exemption application   The Competition Ordinance provides the opportunity for undertakings (including airlines) to apply for a block exemption where they consider a cooperation agreement (including an alliance) to have efficiency effects in excess of any anti-competitive impacts on price or quality of service. In a joint consultation submission dated 6 November 2014, Cathay Pacific Airways Limited and Hong Kong Dragon Airlines Limited submitted that the Guideline on Applications for exclusions and exemptions ought to give formal recognition to the legitimacy of conduct or agreements that have already been granted exclusions or exemptions by other competition authorities and that joint operating services which raise novel issues should be considered for approval by the Competition Commission.[271] They argued that

---

[270] http://www.cad.gov.hk/english/welcome.html.
[271] http://www.compcomm.hk/en/enforcement/consultations/past_consultations/files/S2_-Cathay_Pacific.pdf.

absent clear guidance for a self-assessed compliance with the conditions enabling an exclusion, undertakings are subject to an unduly onerous burden of ensuring that their activities fall strictly within the boundaries of the law. For example, the weight to be attributed to cost and qualitative efficiencies, how they will be measured and the extent to which they are capable of counteracting potential restrictive effects, are questions that currently only the Commission is in a position to answer.

International obligations exemption   Under section 32 of the Competition Ordinance, an international obligation which may give rise to an exemption from the First and Second Conduct Rules includes an obligation under:[272]

    (a) an air service agreement or a provisional arrangement referred to in Article 133 of the Basic Law; and

    (b) an international arrangement relating to civil aviation.

Experience in other jurisdictions   Traditionally, airlines were state sponsored national champions (British Airways, Alitalia, Air France, Lufthansa etc.) and as a result exempt at least to some degree from competition law. This is less and less the case partly because of privatisation, the growth of non-scheduled charter flights and the growth of the aviation industry. Now block exemptions no longer exist for airlines in overseas jurisdictions, and indeed alliances are coming under increased scrutiny. In this day and age, one-time national champions that could previously count on a captive domestic market are finding their market share under attack from other airlines offering services in their "home skies" and low cost carriers.

Agreements relating to aviation transport are now covered by in EU law by Regulation 1/2003, the general implementing regulation. Further, although the European Commission still has the power to grant block exemptions under Regulation 487/2009, those previously applicable to various types of commercial agreements in aviation (e.g. for consultations between carriers on passengers tariffs on routes within the EU and for arrangements on slot allocation and scheduling) have all been allowed to expire, the application of competition law to the aviation sector accelerating with a first liberalisation package in 1987. However, companies are able to self-assess whether their agreements are exempt (from Article 101 TFEU) on efficiency grounds. Furthermore, mergers and full function joint ventures above the relevant thresholds require notification and prior clearance under the EUMR.

Exchange of information   Caution needs to be exercised where information is exchanged and preventative steps are generally taken by airlines to avoid such exchanges falling foul of competition laws. In particular, discussions regarding pricing are not allowed but interline discussions may be acceptable –

---

[272] Competition Ordinance, section 32(7).

in fact the last (expired) block exemption granted by the EU for air transport, under Regulation 1459/2006, related to passenger tariffs on scheduled air services and slot allocation at airports. Since 2007, the International Air Transport Association (IATA) (which was set up in 1945 to promote cooperation between airlines) no longer benefits from a block exemption.

Tariff fixing/alliances/code sharing joint ventures EU case law suggests that competition issues arise from alliances' code shares if the airlines are particularly strong on certain routes or hold a large number of slots at busy airports. Thus approval by the Commission for alliances is often contingent on the surrender of slots or interlining[273] agreements with new entrants being entered into. This is often done by way of commitments. For example, commitments were given in respect of the world-wide alliance announced in 2008 (and cleared in 2010) between British Airways, American Airlines and Iberia and in May 2013 from Air Canada, United Airlines and Lufthansa in relation to the New York-Frankfurt route.

Normally under a code sharing agreement two airlines come to an agreement for the joint operation of services on specified routes – the operating carrier operates the flights whereas the marketing carrier purchases seats or gains access to inventory on the flight operated by the operating carriers and is allowed to apply its own IATA designator code and flight number on tickets issued to passengers. To the extent that code sharing agreements allow carriers to provide services that they would have not otherwise been able to provide they tend to be seen as falling outside the Article 101(1)TFEU prohibition. However to the extent that the carriers both already operate flights on the route, the agreements must satisfy the exemption tests under Article 101(3)TFEU. Furthermore, ancillary to the code share, carriers can be tempted into sharing confidential information (e.g. when synchronising schedules) which may in itself be a breach of EU competition law. While there is little case law on code sharing - two examples are SAS/Maersk (where a fine of €52.5 million in total was imposed for market sharing but the code sharing agreement itself was not condemned) and the 2011 investigations (by way of dawn raid) into TAP and Brussels Airlines – the question is whether this is a new trend. The lesson to be learned is that carriers considering code shares must self-assess (and document) whether their routes overlap and if so whether there are efficiency gains and consumer benefits to be gained through the contemplated agreement.

The Guideline on the First Conduct Rule contains a sector specific example which relates to a code share agreement. The scenario examined is where airlines A and B together have more than 70% of the passenger traffic on the route between destination X and Hong Kong. A and B agree to coordinate

---

[273] Interlining occurs when a passenger is carried for part of all of his journey by an airline different to the one he booked his ticket with.

their schedules and certain of their tariffs on the route in the context of a code share arrangement. Following the agreement, prices rise by between 30% and 50% for the various fares on the route. There are three other airlines operating on the same route; the largest, a low cost carrier, has about 15% of the passenger traffic on the route. The other two carriers are niche operators. There has been no new entry in recent years and the parties to the agreement did not lose significant sales following the price increases. The existing competitors brought no significant new capacity to the route and no new entry occurred. According to the example, the Competition Commission would consider that, in light of the market positions of the parties and the absence of a competitive response to their joint conduct, it might reasonably be concluded that the parties to the agreement are not subject to any significant competitive pressures. It is more likely that in such a market where competition is already weak, the agreement on the coordination of tariffs and schedules may afford the undertakings concerned the possibility of eliminating competition in respect of a substantial part of the services in question and therefore reliance on the efficiency exclusion would be misplaced.[274]

Computer reservation systems   Computer reservation systems (CRS) are services provided by computerised systems containing information about carriers' schedules, availability, fares and fare rules. Generally they are accessible to travel agents who are able to obtain up to date information on them and sometimes also issue tickets. CRS are often owned by groups of airlines. The competition issue that might be seen to arise is that the parent airlines obtain faster access to commercially valuable information on competitors' prices and capacity. Also, computer reservation systems might be used to discriminate against non-parent company airlines. In the EU, Regulation 2299/89 established a Code of Conduct for Computer Reservation Systems (CRS) under which, for example, a fine of €10,000 was imposed on Lufthansa in 1999.[275] Regulation 2299/89 was replaced by other regulations, most recently Regulation 80/2009, which prohibits the imposition of unfair and/or unjustified conditions by CRS vendors on participating carriers and also prohibits discrimination (by refusal to provide data).[276]

Ground handling services   Traditionally only airports themselves or national champion airlines were allowed to supply ground handling services, which led to many complaints that this was anti-competitive. In 1996, the EU adopted Directive 96/67 on access to the ground handling market at EU airports, which liberalised the ground handling sector to allow greater access to the market.

---

[274] Guideline on the First Conduct Rule, Hypothetical Example 25.
[275] Commission Press Release IP/99/542, 20 July 1999.
[276] A block exemption for CRS in Regulation 3652/93 expired in 1998 and was never renewed.

Ground handling services are defined as including all technical and operational services generally provided on the ground at airports, such as loading/ unloading, refuelling, aircraft maintenance and servicing, passenger, mail and freight handling and services for in-flight catering. Denying access to companies seeking to provide a competing service and refusal to permit self-handling by airlines may amount to the abuse of a dominant position.

7.6.3 Public rail and road transport

MTR/rail Hong Kong is served by two railways, the Mass Transit Railway (MTR), an urban railway of 177.4 kilometres and 85 stations which connects the vast population of Hong Kong, and a light railway which connects outlying regions in the New Territories. The MTR has increased its share of public transport in Hong Kong from 33% to 37% over the period 2010-2014, taking some passengers from franchised buses and minibuses which can be considered substitutable on most transport routes. In part, this shift in demand is driven by the expansion of the MTR network.

Since 2006, Kowloon-Canton Railway Corporation (KCRC) and MTRC have been a merged single railway company, MTR Corporation Limited (MTRCL). The merger was intended to create value and efficiency, while also benefiting society. MTRCL is a private company which is monitored by KCRC as the asset holder and functionary of the Hong Kong Government. Several conditions were attached to the merger to ensure passengers benefited:

- no fare increase for 24 months from the date of the announcement of the merger was permitted;
- the second boarding charge of $1-$7 was abolished and a global fare reduction of $0.2 for Octopus card users paying full fares was introduced. An additional reduction of $1 was also implemented for journey fares at or above $12. This brought simplicity to fares and cost reductions for passengers;
- guaranteed minimum fare reductions for all rail passengers of 10% and 5% at fare intervals above $8.50;
- senior citizens to enjoy a concessionary fare of $2 on Sundays and public holidays during the first year of the merger; and
- a requirement that the fare reductions would be applicable to MTR (except Airport Express Line), West Rail, East Rail (excluding Lo Wu trips) and Ma On Shan Rail.

Along with a series of concessionary benefits to passengers of the MTRCL, a Fare Adjustment Mechanism (FAM) was built into the Operating Agreement, signed and agreed by the Government and the MTRCL. The FAM allows adjustment of the fare annually, based on a formula which factors in the composite Consumer Price Index (CPI) as a measure of inflation, the nominal wage index in the transport sector and a productivity factor. The productivity factor takes into account the efficiency saving the merged firm should generate and ensure that these savings are passed on to passengers. Fare adjustments which are equal to or less than 1.5% are carried over to the following year to avoid repeated menu costs and confusion for passengers. The implication is that MTRCL has limited ability to determine price as this is regulated by the FAM. Where train routes overlap with the routes served by other modes of transport, they are considered to be in competition, adding a further constraint on price. In most cases, the closest substitutes are registered bus services. The FAM is scheduled to be reviewed in 2017, one year ahead of schedule, in view of the profits made by MTRCL.[277]

The KCRC is listed as a statutory body exempt from the competition rules.[278] The KCRC today is effectively a railway asset holder, with responsibility for monitoring that the MTR Corporation Limited complies with the terms of the service concession agreement.[279] This is largely because, in December 2007, as part of the merger, the KCRC granted a 50-year service concession to the MTRCL to operate its railway lines, the latter having to pay to KCRC a fixed annual concession payment of HK$750 million, plus a variable annual payment based on gross revenue generated from the operation of KCRC's rail network and related business on a scale of increasing revenue-sharing percentages. KCRC properties, including the development and management rights, were also sold to MTRCL.[280]

The MTR was built in the 1970s and is operated by MTRCL. MTRCL was established as a statutory corporation but was subsequently partially privatised and listed on HKSE.[281] The MTRCL operates abroad (e.g. Crossrail in the UK) as well as in Hong Kong. The Mass Transit Railway Ordinance[282] describes the MTRCL as a company incorporated under the Companies Ordinance. It is, therefore, not a statutory body, which means that it is not excluded from the application of the Competition Ordinance.

A feature of all public transport modes in Hong Kong is the use of the transport ticketing scheme Octopus which is operated by MTRCL. Transport ticketing schemes are written agreements between operators allowing for passengers to purchase tickets that can be used on the services of the participating operators. Without such schemes, passengers would have to buy from each operator individual tickets valid for use only on that operator's services. In the UK, such schemes are the subject of a block exemption under competition laws, which UK competition authorities have just recommended

---

[277] http://www.scmp.com/news/hong-kong/economy/article/1929317/cheaper-mtr-tickets-horizon-after-hong-kong-officials-ask.

[278] http://www.legco.gov.hk/yr09-10/english/bc/bc12/papers/bc120214cb1-1031-2-e.pdf.

[279] http://www.kcrc.com/en/about-kcrc/overview.html.

[280] http://www.kcrc.com/en/about-kcrc/overview.html.

[281] http://www.legco.gov.hk/yr99-00/english/bc/bc01/general/bc01_brf.htm.   ;
http://www.mtr.com.hk/en/corporate/investor/investor_faq.html.

[282] Cap 556.

should be renewed for a further 10 years.[283] There may be reason to seek a similar exemption in Hong Kong.

Buses Hong Kong operates a system of franchised and non-franchised buses. There are six bus franchises awarded by the Hong Kong Government to private companies through a bidding process. In 2014, the largest licensed bus operator was the Kowloon Motor Bus Company, which had a 67% market share with 3850 buses, followed by Citybus with a 17% share and 957 buses and New World First Bus, with a 12% market share and 711 buses. Each franchise requires the winning company to provide a frequency of service along predefined routes for the length of the franchise, currently 2007-2017. On some routes there may be only one provider, on others where routes overlap there is some competition. Any rationalisation of services or change of route requires the agreement of Government. In total, franchised buses account for a declining share of passenger journeys, decreasing from 40% of total passenger journeys in 2002 to 31% in 2014. In part, this is due to the expansion of rail services which offer a fast and frequent mode of mass transit. This approach is different to overseas jurisdictions such as Japan where bus services are provided by the public sector and are subsidised by taxpayers.

Bus operators' services are monitored by the Transport Department of government under the Public Bus Services Ordinance. The Public Bus Services Ordinance stipulates that the fares to be charged are determined and approved by the Chief Executive in Council. Consistent with the practice for trains, any fare adjustment is based on a supportable fare adjustment formula. In practice, bus operators have limited scope to increase fares or reduce the service offered. There is an argument that if there were no licences, operators would be free to offer competing or at least an increased frequency of bus services on busy routes. Operators would also be free to offer new routes and rationalise unprofitable routes. However, there is no evidence to indicate what the impact on fares and service quality would be. This is something the Competition Commission may wish to consider, but the Competition Ordinance is likely to have limited implications for the franchised bus sector as it currently operates.

Registered private bus services account for less than 3% of all passenger journeys, but nevertheless play an important role in relieving heavy demand on the franchised bus and other transport modes during peak hours and filling gaps in passenger demand on routes which are not served by other transport means. As a consequence, services do not typically operate as frequently as franchised buses, operating a tailor-made service for specific groups of passengers. Rather than substitutes for franchised buses, private buses are considered supplementary. As at 30 November 2015, there were 606

---

[283] CMA(2015): Public transport ticketing schemes block exemption review: final report and recommendations to the Secretary of State 10 December 2015.

registered private buses[284] in respect of which a cap on passenger service licences has been in place since 2005. As demand for transport has increased, a function of population growth and increased inbound tourism, but supply remains fixed, so the value of licences has increased to around HK$1.9 million per bus.[285] This may indicate that the market is not functioning as well as it might, leading to less than optimal services and higher fares. However, this is considered a policy failure of the regulating framework rather than a market failure which might suggest the Competition Ordinance would not have any impact.

A similar situation exists for minibus services, coloured green and red, which also operate in Hong Kong. Minibuses have no more than 16 seats and the number operating in Hong Kong is fixed to 4,350. Green minibuses operate on fixed routes at fixed fares set by their licence conditions. Red minibuses are free to operate anywhere without controls on routes or fares. Minibuses play an important role in meeting passenger demand for those areas not served by train or franchised bus services. They are also important for holiday groups, schools and associations to transport persons to specific locations at arranged times. Accounting for 15% of passenger journeys on average, the sector has also experienced a decline in demand as trains replace buses. In a declining market, the fixed supply may be less of a concern, but nevertheless the market may not necessarily function optimally for passengers in the absence of new entrants and greater competition. Again this is a product of the cap on licences, which the Competition Ordinance is unlikely to affect. The creation of the Competition Commission does however provide the opportunity for a market investigation which could see recommendations for a better functioning market to be made to Government.[286]

Taxis Common to many jurisdictions, taxi services are licensed to ensure the quality of service (i.e. the knowledge of the driver), safety (vetting of drivers, maintenance of the vehicle and insurance) and to regulate the number of taxis on the road. Taxis are installed with a taximeter to calculate the fare based on the distance travelled together with any waiting time incurred while the taxi is hired. Taxi drivers are also allowed to charge supplementary fees to recover fixed costs for additional charges and for the costs of tolls. Recommended fares exist on certain routes in Hong Kong, such as from Honk Kong International Airport to Hong Kong Island.

In Hong Kong, different taxis have designated operating areas. Urban taxis operate in most areas in Hong Kong. New Territories taxis mainly operate in

---

[284] http://www.td.gov.hk/en/transport_in_hong_kong/public_transport/buses/non_fran-chised/index.html.

[285] Webb-site Reports (2015): Busting HK's road transport cartels, 14 December 2015 http://webb-site.com/articles/roadcartels.asp.

[286] http://hub.hku.hk/bitstream/10722/28399/1/FullText.pdf?accept=1.

the north-eastern part and north-western part of the New Territories. Lantau taxis operate only on Lantau Island and Chek Lap Kok. All taxis are allowed to provide services at the passenger terminals of Hong Kong International Airport and Hong Kong Disneyland. Different colours designate the area in which the taxi is licensed to operate. The number of licences has been fixed since 1997. There are currently 18,138 taxis licensed in Hong Kong, which compares to 28,000 in Singapore,[287] a jurisdiction of similar size and population. These characteristics of the market ensure that taxi operators are protected from unlicensed competitors entering the market and face limited competition in each designated area. Each taxi licence is at present valued on the open market at about HK$7 million. The car itself, the standard Toyota Crown Comfort taxi, costs only about HK$230,000. It is unclear what the insurance and licensing costs for the taxi operator are, but anecdotally, the evidence suggests the protected nature of the market may be generating excess returns and that passengers are paying more for taxi journeys than they would do in an open market.

In some other jurisdictions, reforms to increase the number of taxi licences have opened up the sector to increased competition in recent years. In the UK and US, Uber has applied the sharing economy model to the taxi sector through technology, thus intensifying competition. However, there is concern that unlicensed operators lack adequate insurance, reduce service quality and compete unfairly as they do not incur any licensing costs. In August 2015, Hong Kong police raided Uber's office and arrested staff and five driver-partners for allegedly operating unlicensed transport and failing to carry adequate insurance.[288] The response to Uber differs by jurisdiction, with both France and Germany outlawing some parts of its business model, which are now under review by the European Commission.[289] In Hong Kong the issue is mainly one of licensing – and thus of competition policy (set by Government) rather than of competition law (under the Competition Ordinance). Whilst the Government and statutory bodies are outside of the ambit of the Competition Ordinance, the Competition Commission might choose to engage in advocacy on this issue.

---

[287] Webb-site Reports (2015): Busting HK's road transport cartels, 14 December 2015 http://webb-site.com/articles/roadcartels.asp.

[288] South China Morning Post Article "Can Hong Kong's new competition law help break the current taxi monopoly?", 2 November 2015: http://www.scmp.com/comment/insight-opinion/article/1874968/can-hong-kongs-new-competition-law-help-break-current-taxi.

[289] The Parliament Magazine (2015) EU Commission launches study on Uber https://www.theparliamentmagazine.eu/articles-/news/eu-commission-launches-study-uber.

Chapter Eight

COMPARATIVE COMPETITION LAW: CHINA, JAPAN AND SOUTH KOREA

8.1 COMPETITION LAW IN CHINA AND HONG KONG

Introduction Although Hong Kong's Competition Ordinance was signed into law on 22 June 2012, its full implementation had to wait until the end of 2015. Across the Sham Chun River, mainland China has been governed by a different competition law since 2008. The fundamental principle of one country, two systems formulated by Deng Xiaoping allows mainland China and Hong Kong to preserve their differences in political, economic, financial and legal institutions and yet come together under the same sovereignty - the People's Republic of China. This creative and pragmatic political design makes it possible for both mainland China and Hong Kong to develop competition policies in response to divergent social and economic needs. A comparison of the evolution of China's Anti-Monopoly Law (AML) and Hong Kong's Competition Ordinance in light of the disparities in their social and economic drivers highlights major differences between two sets of rules and sheds light on the practical implications of Hong Kong's Competition Ordinance for Chinese companies.

Origins of competition law Modern competition law is not a homegrown project for China and Hong Kong. Its origin can be traced back to the United States where it was initially designed to address social concerns about industrial concentration during the mid- to late-nineteenth century.[1] A century or more later, prevailing social and economic factors motivated China and Hong Kong's decisions to transplant competition law into quite different soil. Despite the dynamics and complexity of competition law rule making, the main elements involved in this process might be grouped into three categories: the changing economic landscape, the transition of regulatory pattern and external influences. These factors played different roles in shaping competition laws in Hong Kong and China. For Hong Kong, the determinant

---

[1] Lawrence A. Sullivan & Wolfgang Fikentscher, On the Growth of the Antitrust Idea, 16 Berkeley Journal of International Law, 197, 199-208 (1998); Wentong Zheng, Transplanting Antitrust In China: Economic Transition, Market Structure, and State Control, 32 University of Pennsylvania Journal of International Law, 643, 647 (2010-2011).

factor was the transition of economic structure that ultimately made competition law a necessary step to address increasingly visible market failures and to maintain its competitiveness in a global market. Adjustments in regulatory patterns to embrace competition policies were made to respond to such economic changes, even if the process was hesitant and slow. By contrast, the AML resulted from an active reform on the part of the Chinese government which established the market as the controlling mechanism in the economy when China decided to proceed further in its globalization plans by joining the World Trade Organisation (WTO). Economic transition and free trade commitments under international treaties in turn pushed the Chinese government to finally adopt the AML to secure fair competition in the domestic market.

8.1.1. Social and economic drivers in Hong Kong

Changing economic landscape The past two decades have witnessed Hong Kong's transition into a service economy. This period has also been marked by the surging costs of doing business in Hong Kong and increasing levels of concentration in many business sectors, both of which led to growing doubts over the long-held belief that Hong Kong's domestic market was still as competitive as before. As early as 1999, manufacturing accounted for only 5.7% of GDP in Hong Kong, which was three quarters less than the share in 1984.[2] Nowadays, services in trade, banking, tourism and other areas account for around 90% of Hong Kong's GDP.[3] The competition implications of such economic transition are significant. These developments challenged the long-held belief that an open and export-oriented market like Hong Kong does not need competition law because competition from abroad will discourage any anti-competitive attempts by Hong Kong's producers.[4] Such beliefs, however, suit a manufacturing-based economy rather than a service-driven economy. Unlike manufactured goods, most services are locally produced and consumed. Consumers of most services are confined to the local market in Hong Kong. Service suppliers, hence, are exposed to limited international competition

---

[2]   Mark Williams, Competition Policy and Law in China, Hong Kong and Taiwan, (Cambridge University 2005), 237.

[3]   Hong Kong Trade and Development Council, Economic and Trade Information on Hong Kong (September 2015), http://hong-kong-economy-research.hktdc.com/business-news/article/Market-Environment/Economic-and-Trade-Information-on HongKong/etihk/en/1/1X48LWJT/1X09OVUL.htm.

[4]   Y.C. Richard Wong, Understanding Competition in Hong Kong, 20 Hong Center for Economic Research Letters (1993), http://www.hkcer.hku.hk/Letters/v20/rwong.htm.

compared to manufacturers who usually compete head to head with foreign producers while Hong Kong has few trade barriers.[5]

Meanwhile, levels of concentration in some key industries have been climbing and the extensive interconnection and cross-ownership among corporations in Hong Kong is striking, further raising competition concerns. Some attributed these to the small economy in Hong Kong. With a population of only 7.24 million and 1,104 square kilometers of land, Hong Kong can only support a few players in some industries.[6] Others blamed government policies for artificially distorting the market on the one hand, and failing to intervene with competition policies on the other. For instance, it has been argued that the government monopoly in land artificially raised real estate prices which facilitated the creation of an interlocking web of conglomerate companies that, through network effects, have had a substantial foreclosing effect on competitors attempting to enter many market sectors.[7] Small developers usually could not match big property companies backed with huge cash reserves in financial resources. Dominant property companies further leveraged into other sectors, such as the telecommunications, gas or electricity industries by signing contracts only with gas, electricity, and telecommunications companies affiliated to them.[8] It was also alleged that certain conglomerates restricted competition in the supermarket sector by preventing competitors of their affiliated supermarket chains from operating in the vicinities of their property.[9] A small market like Hong Kong formed an easier context for competitors to communicate and reach anti-competitive agreements.[10]

Regulation in transition Hong Kong has long taken pride in its laissez-faire economy which has minimal intervention from the government[11] and has been recognised as the freest economy for almost 20 years in a roll by the Heritage Institute Economic Freedom Index. Throughout Tong Chee-Hwa's initial term of office, it was generally believed that an open and free economy would

---

[5]   Suk-Ching Ho and Chi-Fai Chan, In Search of a Competition Policy in a competitive Economy: The Case of Hong Kong, 37(1) The Journal of Consumer Affairs, 68, 73 (2003).

[6]   Ho and Chan, 80; for latest demographics of Hong Kong, see:
http://www.censtatd.gov.hk/hkstat/sub/so20.jsp.
http://www.gov.hk/en/about/abouthk/facts.htm.

[7]   Williams, 241.

[8]   Lam Pun Lee, Competition in Energy, The Hong Kong Economic Policy Series, (City University of Hong Kong Press 1997) 83.

[9]   Ho and Chan, 80; Williams, 247; for a comprehensive investigation on alleged anticompetitive conducts in supermarket business, see Hong Kong Consumer Council, Report on the Supermarket Industry in Hong Kong (1994).

[10] Ho and Chan, 74.

[11] Competition Policy Review Committee, Report on The Review of Hong Kong's Competition Policy, 8 (2006) (Review Report).

guarantee fair competition in Hong Kong. The administration led by Tong Chee Hwa after the handover in 1997 concluded that sector specific competition policy would suffice to maintain a sound competition order,[12] while, for the rest of the economy, a minimum intervention approach was adopted. Such complacency, however, was later found to be based on the shaky judgment of the relative steadiness of the market in Hong Kong.

The constant efforts of the Consumer Council since the early 1990s have revealed the existence and consequences of anti-competitive conduct and monopolistic or oligopolistic market structures in Hong Kong.[13] Furthermore, as Hong Kong transitioned into a service economy, there was a growing recognition that an open and free economy is not a guarantee of fair competition. It was recognised that in a market with high entry barriers, price-inelastic demand, limited product differentiation, predictable demand and market shares and vertical integration, anti-competitive behaviours would be possible, regardless of the size of the economy. Moreover, efforts of the Consumer Council had enhanced consumer awareness of anti-competitive behaviours. An increasing number of consumer complaints had been received by the Consumer Council related to sectors such as transport and utilities, sale of auto-fuel, supermarkets, port related fees and charges, exhibition services and supply of fresh pork. Hence, there were realistic demands for a cross-sector competition law to counter the risk that a sector-specific approach may further distort the market by treating different sectors of economy discriminatively.[14]

Those efforts laid the foundation for the 2006 report of the Competition Policy Review Committee (Review Report), led by the then chief executive Donald Tsang under the Competition Policy Advisory Group (COMPAG). The Review Report recommended the adoption of a general competition law applicable to all sectors of the economy. It also recommended that a Competition Commission should be set up to carry out thorough investigations into allegations of anti-competitive conduct. It has to be noted that although the Donald Tsang administration recognised that government had an important role in maintaining fair competition in market, its approach was not a sharp

---

[12]   In the Statement on Competition Policy, the government introduced a sector specific approach in competition policy and statutory competition rules were adopted in 2000 for the telecommunications and broadcasting sectors. Ho and Chan, 81; John Hickin and Gerry O'Brien, Hong Kong's Competition Law Landscape—Present and Future, Asia Law, 1, 3 (March 2008).

[13]   Ping Lin and Edward K. Y. Chen, Fair Competition under Laissez-Faireism: Policy Options for Hong Kong, Lingnan University of Hong Kong, Research Paper, 5 (2008); Hong Kong Consumer Council, Are Hong Kong Depositors Fairly treated? (1994), Report on the Supermarket Industry in Hong Kong (1994), Assessing Competition in the Water Heating and Cooking Fuel Market (1995), Report on Competition in the Foodstuffs and Household Necessities Retail Sector, (2003).

[14]   Review Report, 9, 38.

turnaround from the previous administration and it remained cautious as to
how much intervention was needed to correct anti-competitive conduct. The
Competition Policy Review Committee accepted that given the small size of
Hong Kong's economy, competition law should not target market structure and
the government should refrain from regulating natural monopolies or mergers
and acquisitions. Furthermore, during the fierce debate within and outside the
Legislative Council, strong business sectors voiced their concerns and doubts
about the Competition Bill, pushing the government to make concessions.[15]

External pressure A changing economic structure has made Hong Kong a
costly place for business, gradually eroding Hong Kong's competitiveness as a
destination for investment and trading partners.[16] Hong Kong has felt
increasing peer pressure from its neighbouring regions such as Singapore,
Taiwan, South Korea, Japan and mainland China. Meanwhile, competition law
has taken on increasing prominence in countries such as South Korea, India,
and mainland China for the past decade. Singapore also adopted competition
law in 2004, even though it used to believe, like Hong Kong, that competition
law is not necessary for small economies.[17] Other than competitive pressure,
Hong Kong has also faced pressure from international organisations whose
policy review and suggestions may also affect Hong Kong's image as the freest
economy in the world.[18] In its Trade Policy Review on Hong Kong in 2002,
the WTO, in particular, voiced its concern that Hong Kong's lack of coherent
measures to address anti-competitive practices in all but a few sectors
constituted an obstacle to greater competition.[19]

Hong Kong, as the second largest destination and the source for foreign
direct investment and as the world's eighth largest trading economy and
fifteenth largest exporter of commercial services,[20] relies heavily on its
dynamic export-oriented and foreign investment friendly economy. Hence, an
aggressive merger control policy was not considered as proper for Hong Kong.
Besides, the Competition Policy Review Committee did not believe there
would be many mergers and acquisitions in the domestic market, and hence,

---

[15] Thomas K. Cheng, Ready for Action: Looking Ahead to the Implementation of Hong
Kong's Competition Ordinance, 5 (2)Journal of European Competition Law and
Practice, 90 (2014);

[16] Ho and Chan, 75; Williams, 288.

[17] Thomas K. Cheng, A Tale of Two Competition Law Regimes—The Telecom-Sector
Competition Regulation in Hong Kong and Singapore, 30 (3) World Competition, 501,
502, (2007).

[18] Economic and Trade Information on Hong Kong, http://hong-kong-economy-research.-
hktdc.com/business-news/article/Market-Environment/Economic-and-Trade-
Information-on-Hong-Kong/etihk/en/1/1X48LWJT/1X09OVUL.htm

[19] Review Report, 10.

[20] Economic and Trade Information on Hong Kong, supra note 22.

recommended to limit the application of merger control in the Competition Ordinance.[21]

8.1.2 Social and economic drivers in China

Regulatory transition In the case of China, the regulatory transition came earlier and was more pressing than the changing economic context since, without political determination to further the transition from a centrally planned economy, or command economy, to a market economy, there were few economic changes that required the introduction of competition law. In 1978, economic construction was established as the central work of the Chinese Communist Party (CCP) and the government in the Third Plenary Session of the Eleventh Central Committee of the CCP. Despite fierce debate as to the role of government in economic construction and the relationship between public and private ownership, in 1992 the pace of economic reform was accelerated when the Fourteenth Congress of the CCP declared the socialist market economy as the central goal of China's economic reform. This landmark event indicated that the market is to be the controlling mechanism of the economy in China while the government is to retreat substantially from economic sectors that it used to dominate.

It should be noted that the market economy in China is qualified with socialist characteristics, under which public ownership is supposed to retain a key position in the economy. Along with the transition of the role of government, more specific questions were raised such as where, when and what government intervention in the market is needed. The Chinese government responded by adopting a pragmatic approach, using different strategies for different industries. For years, government and state capital have gradually and cautiously exited from industries which government believed should be opened up to market competition. By contrast, for industries such as electricity, banking, insurance, telecommunications, petroleum, civil aviation, and railroads, believed to be critical to the national economy and security, state capital retains a key position and the reforms in these sectors have been focused on separating government's role as the owner from its role as regulator.[22] As a result of such reform, Chinese State Owned Enterprises (SOEs) have undergone a massive process of privatisation and corporatisation since the early 1990s. Meanwhile private and foreign enterprises have gradually been allowed into the market as administrative restraints on market access have been reduced year by year.

---

[21] Review Report, 38; Cheng, 89.
[22] Wentong Zheng, Transplanting Antitrust in China: Economic Transition, Market Structure, and State Control, 667-668.

Concomitantly, price control has been reduced substantially. In the centrally planned economy, price was determined within government cabinets, not by the interaction between supply and demand in the market.[23] With the objective of establishing a market economy, the government, step by step, adopted a hands-off strategy by limiting its control to only an exclusive list of commodities and let the market play a major role in determining prices. By the end of 2005 (prior to the enactment of the AML), official statistics show that the percentage of market-determined prices in China accounted for over 90%.[24] Given that price is one of the major areas of competition in the market, this reform substantially facilitated and stimulated competition among goods and service suppliers.

Another important reform involved the fiscal relations between central and local governments. Fiscal reform, starting in 1980, transformed the previous centralised fiscal regime into a decentralised regime, granting local government greater shares of revenue generated by local enterprises and greater autonomy over taxation, budgets and expenditure.[25] This reform however incentivised local governments to encourage the creation of new local enterprises.[26] Local protectionism hence also increased and resulted in many administrative restrictions that prevented competition from out-of-province competitors.[27] These restrictions led to a serious balkanisation of the domestic market, which threatened to keep economic development in China at a fraction of its capability by preventing the free flow of resources according to market demand.[28]

Changing economic landscape The changing economic landscape in China is essentially conditioned by this regulatory transition. Since the early 1990s, Chinese SOEs have undergone massive privatisation and only large SOEs in key sectors remain under the control of the government. The remaining SOEs have been gradually converted into corporations where the state plays the role of shareholder rather than manager. Meanwhile, they were given substantial autonomy in business management and allowed to retain a substantial part of

---

[23] Zheng, 652.

[24] National Development and Reform Commission, 2005 Percentage of Market-determined Price increase in 2005. This further increased to ninety-seven percent in 2015; see State Council Information Office regarding promotion of price mechanism reform:
http://www.sdpc.gov.cn/fzgggz/jggl/zhdt/200611/t20061117_94026.html.
http://www.scio.gov.cn/xwfbh/xwbfbh/wqfbh/2015/33640/index.htm.

[25] Vivek B. Arora and John Norregaard, Interngovernmental Fiscal Relations: The Chinese System in perspective, IMF Working Paper, 10-11(1997).

[26] Zheng, 657.

[27] Bruce M. Owen, Su Sun, Wentong Zheng, China's Competition Policy Reforms: The Anti-Monopoly Law and Beyond, 75 (1) Antitrust Law Journal, 231, 254-255 (2008).

[28] Eleanor M. Fox, An Anti-Monopoly Law for China—Scaling the Walls of Government Restrictions, 75 (1) Antitrust Law Journal, 173, 174 (2008).

their revenues.[29]   Besides, not all SOEs are monopolies in their respective sectors as the Chinese government has increasingly removed or reduced market access restrictions and allowed private and foreign competitors to compete head to head with SOEs in business sectors considered not key to the national economy or security.[30]   Nevertheless, when the drafting of the AML was underway, economic reform in China was far from complete given that government intervention has remained prevalent and excessive.

The market in China has been divided into three categories to which access by private or foreign companies is prohibited, restricted or permitted, manifesting a market landscape with different degrees of competition. In some key sectors, previously segmented industries were consolidated into conglomerates, raising concerns of state sponsored monopolies or oligopolies. Local governments are still heavily involved in economic sectors that are generally considered not essential for national security and economy. It is common for local government to retain substantial control over large SOEs within their jurisdiction and restrain outside competition even if they operate in highly competitive sectors. Those SOEs, although they are not monopolies, may still undermine fair competition by means of cartels facilitated by local protectionism and the segmented domestic market.[31]   After all, it has to be recognized that SOEs are different from profit-maximising firms in significant respects. Usually, profit maximisation gives way to other goals such as providing employment and social services.[32]

Foreign direct investment and WTO membership   Another feature that has marked China's changing economic landscape is the flooding of foreign direct investment (FDI) into China. Since economic reform, China has remained one of the most popular destinations in the world for FDI.[33]   An increasing number of transnational corporations (TNC) invested in China by virtue of acquiring or merging with Chinese companies. It was cautioned that some TNCs may leverage their power, based on experience, international market penetration, advanced technology and economies of scale, and grow into monopolies or oligopolies in technology and capital intensive industries before Chinese enterprises are able to compete with them.[34]   Perhaps partly because of such

---

[29]   Angela Huyue Zhang, Taming the Chinese Leviathan: Is Antitrust Regulation a False Hope? 51 Stanford Journal of International Law, 195, 201 (2015).

[30]   Zheng, 660; Zhang, 204.

[31]   Zhang, 206.

[32]   Zheng, 666.

[33]   Trading Economics, China Foreign Direct Investment:
http://www.trading-economics.com/china/foreign-direct-investment.

[34]   For theories explaining monopoly power of TNCs in developing countries, see Abera Gelan, The Monopoly Power of Multinational Enterprises in the Service Sector of a Developing Country, 42 The Journal of Developing Areas 1 (2009); Asta Zilinske, Negative and Positive Effects of Foreign Direct Investment, 15 Economics and

concerns, before enacting the AML, the Chinese government has made several attempts, either through issuing *ad hoc* limitations on mergers and acquisitions or by the promulgation of merger control rules to limit foreign investment in certain sectors.[35]

External influence cannot be neglected in the promulgation of the AML. Joining the WTO was the main external influence that impelled the drafting process of the AML. When China joined in WTO in 2001, competition policy topics were debated intensively, thereby exerting influence on the policy aspect.[36] Moreover, since joining the WTO, China has been further integrated into the global economy. To fulfil its free trade commitments, China is obliged to remove all quantitative trade barriers for imported goods and exercise no discrimination against foreign products. All these obligations propelled China to strengthen its reform towards market economy and resort to competition law to provide a level playing field for foreign companies and Chinese enterprises alike.[37]

8.1.3 Development of competition law in Hong Kong and China

The long road to promulgating domestic competition laws   It was a marathon race for both Hong Kong and China to finally promulgate domestic competition laws. For Hong Kong, it took almost two decades to finish this race and around thirteen years for China.[38] Even though the AML was passed into law in 2007, that does not mean that China had no competition policy to address anti-competitive conduct before that. Previous experiences laid important foundation for the final promulgation of the AML. The evolution process was gradual, pragmatic and deliberate but also, inevitably, it turned out

---

Management 332 (2010); Yong-jun Chen, Zhen Yang, FDI and Manufacturing Industry Markup Dynamics: Competitive or Monopolistic, 10 China Industrial Economics 52 (2012).

[35] See the Provisional Regulations Regarding Mergers and Acquisitions of Domestic Enterprises by Foreign Investors (2003); The Regulations on Merger and Acquisition by Foreign Investors (2006).

[36] Yong Huang, The Juristic Foundation of China's Anti-Monopoly Law – Response and Support to the Reform on the Market Economy, China Price Supervision and Anti-Monopoly, 2 (2014).

[37] Pierrette B. Gaasbeek and Peter A.G. van Bergeijk, Chinese Competition: Do We Need A New Competition Policy Regime? Working Paper for International Institute of Social Studies (2011), 14.

[38] Calculated from the date when competition policies were first put on the official agenda in Hong Kong and China.

to be inconsistent given that China's economy is still in transition from a centrally planned to a market economy.[39]

Stages in the adoption of competition law in Hong Kong   In Hong Kong, competition policies were officially addressed for the first time in 1992, when the then Hong Kong Governor Chris Patten, in his policy speech to the Legislative Council, responded to public concerns about possible monopolisation in some important commodity markets and promised to ask his Business Council to put competition policy on the top of its agenda.[40] To this end, the Consumer Council was granted HK$2.7 million to conduct research on the competitive environment of the domestic economy. Under this mandate, in 1996 the Consumer Council issued its comprehensive report, Competition Policy: The Key to Hong Kong's Future Economic Success, in which it advised the government to adopt a comprehensive competition law to safeguard fair competition in Hong Kong in recognition that a laissez-faire regime alone was not enough. It was also suggested that an independent enforcement authority and an appeal body should be established to enforce competition law.[41]

In 1997, Tong Chee-Hwa took office in the first Special Administrative Region administration. Having a close relationship with the business sector, the Tong Chee-Hwa administration did not embrace the suggestion of adopting a general competition law. Instead, it rejected most of the proposals of the Consumer Council and reiterated that Hong Kong's open and export-oriented economy was very competitive.[42] Although the government denied the necessity of adopting a cross-sector competition law, it decided to adopt a sector-specific approach in its *Statement on Competition* and a competition regime was introduced only for the telecommunications and broadcasting industries in 2001. The government set up the COMPAG to review Hong Kong's competition-related issues and to handle complaints without entrusting it the power to carry out investigations. Although the COMPAG addressed the complaints related to the supermarket, oil electricity supply and residential property development sectors, it could only deal with them in a general manner due to the lack of access to the information needed to carry out in-depth analysis.

---

[39] Pierrette B. Gaasbeek and Peter A.G. van Bergeijk, Chinese Competition: Do We Need A New Competition Policy Regime? Working Paper for International Institute of Social Studies (2011), 11.

[40] Hong Kong Government, Our Next Five Years: The Agenda for Hong Kong. (Hong Kong Government Printer 1992), 3-4.

[41] Consumer Council, Competition Policy: The Key to Hong Kong's Future Economic Success (1996).

[42] HKSAR Government Trade and Industry Bureau, Government Response to Consumer Council's Report - Competition Policy: The Key to Hong Kong's Future Economic Success (1997) 13-14.

Donald Tsang took office in 2005 after Tong Chee Hwa's resignation. In an effort to distance himself from the previous pro-business administration and appeal to the populist instincts of constituencies, he appointed the Competition Policy Review Committee to examine the need to introduce a comprehensive and cross-sector Competition Bill. After two stages of public consultations, the Tsang administration finally presented a draft Competition Bill to the Legislative Council in 2010 and it was later passed into law as the Competition Ordinance in 2012. During the legislative debate, SMEs were concerned that the vague and broad wording in the Bill, especially concepts such as anti-competitive agreements, concerted practices and market power, would result in uncertainty in implementation. They were also concerned about the standalone private right of action, fearing that it would be used by large competitors to file frivolous cases against them in the attempt to drag them into costly competition litigation. As a compromise, the government agreed to remove the standalone private right of action from the Bill. Moreover, the government made further concessions by dividing anti-competitive conducts into hard core activities (including price-fixing, bid-rigging, market allocation and output control) and non-hard core activities. Other than these four identified hard core activities, all other activities that may raise competition concerns would fall under non-hard core activities, for which the government should issue a warning notice to the concerned undertaking before any further action is taken.[43] Moreover, the CO takes a leap forward in institutional design. A two-tiered adjudicative enforcement model is adopted. The Competition Commission acts as investigator and prosecutor at the first tier and the Competition Tribunal is established at the second tier to make decisions and adjudicate disputes.

Stages in the adoption of competition law in China Before economic reform, there was no market as such in China and there was no need to compete since there was only one supplier, the government. From 1978 to 1992, the government implemented the so-called planned market economy, meaning only limited competition was allowed and the government still played a major role in allocating resources and in organising production. Still, rampant local protectionism caught the attention of the central government. In 1987, with the purpose of breaking up regional blockades and sectoral compartmentalisation, the State Council promulgated the Provisional Regulation on the Development and Protection of Socialist Competition.[44]

As the socialist market economy was established as one of the goals of the CCP in 1992, drafting a competition law was soon listed on the legislative agenda of the Standing Committee of the Eighth National People's Congress in

---

[43] HKSAR Government Commerce and Economic Development Bureau, Bills Committee on Competition Bill-Responses to Concerns on the Competition Bill (2011), 3-4.

[44] Shang Ming, Antitrust in China—A Constantly Evolving Subject, 5 Competition Law International 4 (2009).

1994. The drafting of the AML went through three phases. In the first phase, the Anti-Monopoly Law Drafting Group was jointly established by the State Economic and Trade Commission and the State Administration for Industry and Commerce. This body developed a draft to be reviewed by the Legislative Affairs Office of the State Council at the second phase. In the third phase, the Standing Committee of the National People's Congress did the final review and eventually passed it into law in 2007.[45] During this period, the economic landscape was substantially diversified as private and foreign investors were permitted to enter into the market, which was playing an increasingly important role in setting prices. There was an urgent need for government to change its role from the supplier and price setter to regulator in order to ensure fair competition in the market. While the AML was in deliberation, anti-competitive issues were addressed by various laws, regulations, administrative rules and regulatory documents. Early efforts were made in the Anti-Unfair Competition Law and the Consumer Protection Law of the People's Republic of China, both enacted in 1993, which attached priority to consumer protection. In the Anti-Unfair Competition Law, in particular, five types of anti-competitive conduct were covered, including bid-rigging, predatory pricing, abuses of dominant market positions by public enterprises and tying.[46] Later in 1997 and 1999, respectively, predatory pricing was again regulated under the Price Law of the People's Republic of China, and bid-rigging under the Bidding Law of the People's Republic of China. In addition, in 1993 the State Administration for Industry and Commerce (SAIC) enacted Certain Regulations on Prohibiting Competition Restricting Practices of Public Enterprises and in 1998 regulated bid-rigging under the Provisional Regulation on the Prohibition of Bid-Rigging.

Against the background of soaring acquisitions of domestic enterprises by foreign companies, the Provisional Regulations Regarding Mergers and Acquisitions of Domestic Enterprises by Foreign Investors were promulgated in 2003 and the Regulations on Mergers and Acquisitions by Foreign Investors were adopted in 2006. Merger review requirements since then have been imposed on foreign companies for deals satisfying certain criteria. Nevertheless, the government's attitudes to SOE mergers were different. Since the 1980s, along with economic reform, the Chinese government privatised large numbers of small SOEs while retaining its hold over large SOEs in key economic sectors. The remaining large SOEs have been strategically consolidated into even larger groups partly in response to a segmented market resulting from local protectionism and partly due to the need to promote national champions.[47] Against this background, the treatment of SOE mergers

---

[45]   Xiaoye Wang, The Evolution of China's Anti-Monopoly Law, (Edward Elgar 2014) xv.
[46]   Shang, 5.
[47]   Zheng, 713-714.

in the AML remained ambivalent. Particularly, Article 7 has continuously invited suspicions of a protectionist intent behind the AML.[48]

With regard to enforcement agency, unlike the situation of Hong Kong where government, for a long time, had been hesitant to take measures to tackle anti-competitive conduct, in China government agencies were very active, which even resulted in some inconsistencies.[49] Streamlining the competition enforcement institutions in China is not an easy task and the AML did not solve this puzzle. In China, business owners still face three agencies: the National Development and Reform Commission (NDRC), the Ministry of Commerce (MOFCOM) and SAIC, and the allocation of tasks among them is not clear-cut in certain respects. According to the *San Ding* notices issued by the State Council, MOFCOM is in charge of merger control. NDRC is responsible for investigating all price-related monopoly agreements, abuses of dominance, and anti-competitive abuses of administrative powers. Those anti-competitive conducts unrelated to price are governed by SAIC. Nevertheless, concurrent or parallel jurisdiction among these three authorities is still highly possible.[50]

8.1.4 Implications for Chinese companies of Hong Kong competition law

Trading relationship   Economic interaction between Hong Kong and mainland China has been substantially intensified and strengthened, with trade and investment steadily growing since 1997. The latest records suggest that Hong Kong is the most important entrepôt, foreign investment source, and key offshore capital-raising centre for Chinese enterprises. Meanwhile, mainland China has become Hong Kong's largest source of external investment.[51] Considering the intensity of economic transactions occurring everyday between enterprises in mainland China and Hong Kong, it is crucial for Chinese companies to be aware of the implications of the Competition

---

[48]   US Chamber of Commerce, Competing Interests in China's Competition Law Enforcement: China's Anti-Monopoly Law Application and the Role of Industrial Policy, 15 (2014).

[49]   Mao Xiaofei, An Overview of the Anti-Monopoly Practice in the People's Republic of China, in H. Qaqaya and G. Lipimile (eds), The Effects of Anticompetitive Business Practices on Developing Countries and their Development Prospects, (UNCTAD 2008), 497.

[50]   Adrian Emch, Chinese Antitrust Instituions—Many Cooks in the Kitchen, 10 (1) Competition Policy International 217, 230-232 (2014); Hannah Ha and Gerry O'Brien, China's Anti-Monopoly Law – A great leap forward? Asia Law, at 30, 31 (2008).

[51]   Economic and Trade Information on Hong Kong, http://hong-kong-economy-research.hktdc.com/business-news/article/Market-Environment/Economic-and-Trade% 20 Information-on-Hong-Kong/etihk/en/1/1X48LWJT/1X09OVUL.htm

Ordinance on their everyday activities related to Hong Kong, not least in relation to the scope and extraterritorial application of the Competition Ordinance.

Scope of subjects The Competition Ordinance applies to undertakings. This is broadly defined as to include any entity, even natural persons, who engages in economic activity, regardless of its legal status or the way in which it is financed. This approach gives priority to the nature of the activity performed instead of the entity or the person conducting it. In other words, the major consideration is whether an entity is engaged in economic activities. Economic activity generally consists of offering goods or services on a market and such activity could be carried on to make profits. Although the Competition Ordinance provides an exception for statutory bodies, this exception does not extend to SOEs in China. A statutory body is a body of persons, corporate or unincorporated, established or constituted by or under an Ordinance or appointed under an Ordinance. SOEs in China are not established according to Ordinance in Hong Kong. For the Chief Executive in Council to provide special exemption, specific criteria need to be satisfied according to the Competition Ordinance. In the legislative process, the government identified 575 statutory bodies, and exempted all but six of them, yet little references have been made to Chinese SOEs.[52]

Scope of behavioural rules In general, the AML and the Competition Ordinance target similar practices, but there are some divergences worth noting.[53] In the Competition Ordinance, the First Conduct Rule differentiates Serious Anti-Competitive Conduct from other conduct. Serious Anti-Competitive Conduct encapsulates price fixing, market sharing, output limitation and bid rigging. For such conduct, the Competition Commission does not need to issue a warning notice before bringing proceedings. Such differentiation is made in part in response to SMEs' demands for more predictability in the enforcement of the Competition Ordinance.

The Second Conduct Rule prohibits undertakings with a substantial degree of market power from abusing that power. The AML provides presumptions of market share in determining market dominance, while there is no such presumption under the Competition Ordinance. This difference, which was also a concession made in response to the demands of the business sector, also takes account of the small size of the domestic market in Hong Kong and the Competition Ordinance attempts to focus more on the conduct and its effect than the market structure.[54]

---

[52] Thomas Cheng, 94.
[53] Suzanne Rab and Jet Deng, Competition Law Across the River, China Business Law Journal 56- 61 (October 2015).
[54] Hickin and O'Brien, 3 (2008).

Extraterritorial application   One of the major concerns for Chinese companies is the extraterritorial application of the Competition Ordinance. Both the First Conduct Rule and the Second Conduct Rule govern activities that have the object or effect of preventing, restricting or distorting competition in Hong Kong. These provisions do not require the contravening entity to have a presence in Hong Kong. In this sense, even if a mainland company carries on most of its business in mainland China, it may be subject to competition scrutiny as long as its operation has an anti-competitive object or effect in Hong Kong.

Major differences from Chinese competition law   Perhaps the most intriguing difference between the AML and the Competition Ordinance is that the latter does not embrace a fully-fledged sector wide merger control rule. Instead, the Merger Rule is limited to licensed undertakings in the telecommunications sector. It is also explicitly provided that the First and Second Conduct Rules do not apply to mergers.[55] Given that an increasing number of Chinese companies are investing in Hong Kong by way of mergers and acquisitions, it is highly likely that most of these operations would not be caught under the Competition Ordinance as long as they do not involve licensees under the Telecommunications Ordinance.

There are other less prominent differences in the substantive rules between the AML and the Competition Ordinance. The Competition Ordinance imposes a penalty of up to 10% of annual local, instead of global, turnover based on the gross turnover for each year of the infringement (up to three years). In addition, the Competition Ordinance makes provision for the Tribunal to disqualify a person from serving as a company director for up to five years if he/she is a director in a company contravening the Competition Ordinance and he/she was responsible for such contravention. On the generous side, the Competition Ordinance provides different exemptions for SMEs. The conduct of entities (not including Serious Anti-Competitive Conduct) that do not satisfy certain turnover levels specified in the Competition Ordinance may not be subject to competition scrutiny for violation of the Conduct Rules.[56]

Future challenges Although both Hong Kong and China faced the same question as to how much government intervention is appropriate to ensure competition in the domestic market, they faced different predicaments determined by their divergent social and economic contexts.   Rule-makers in Hong Kong, facing strong suspicion from the business sector, were concerned

---

[55]   Peter Waters and Melanie Tan, Hong Kong's First Cross-Sector Competition Law: "A Modern Competition Law with Hong Kong Characteristics" 7:
http://www.gtlaw.com.au/wp-content/uploads/CIIAI-Symposium.pdf.
[56]   For the First Conduct Rule, the threshold is HK$200 million and for the Second Conduct Rule is HK$400 million.

about curing market failures without losing Hong Kong's competitiveness as a free, open and export-oriented economy. As a result, the Competition Ordinance opted for a relatively conservative approach, in line with the Hong Kong government's minimum intervention tradition, limiting the application of merger control and providing less stringent rules on non-hard core anti-competitive conduct. Chinese legislators, by comparison, were perplexed by a thorny balance among socialist goals, consumer welfare and efficiency and the ongoing economic reform brought even more unresolved challenges. This explains why the AML reflects an ambivalent attitude towards SOEs, and provides a long list of exception clauses to deal with issues beyond competition concerns. It also helps to understand why China employs competition law to address administrative monopolies, which is largely unheard of in other jurisdictions. Nevertheless, it is worth noting that both China and Hong Kong are moving towards, although slowly, international mainstream practice, recognising that the market should be the controlling mechanism in the economy and that government intervention is a useful supplement when the market fails to deliver fair competition.

For Chinese companies doing business or having commercial interests in Hong Kong, it is advisable to have some knowledge of the legislative background and development of the competition laws in these two jurisdictions, which will assist them in a better understanding of the big picture of the changing market climate, as well as in adjusting their past risky practices and implementing a compliance programme on a timely basis. Although the anti-competitive conducts targeted by the AML and the Competition Ordinance are similar, there are still some prominent differences in such substantive areas as merger control, the subjects and scope of legal liability and exemptions (not to mention many huge differences in procedure). Additionally, in practice, enforcement priorities in mainland China and in Hong Kong will probably be different. Hence, with the concept of one country, two competition laws in mind, Chinese companies need to have two sets of practice guidelines in place to protect them from inadvertent breach of the somewhat different red lines.

8.2 COMPETITION LAW IN JAPAN

Introduction   Japan is Hong Kong's third-largest trading partner after mainland China and the United States, and Hong Kong is Japan's eighth-largest trading partner. Bilateral trade, in 2010, totalled 3.83 trillion yen (€29 billion), with Japan's exports accounting for 3.70 trillion yen (€28 billion) and its imports accounting for 133 billion yen (€1 billion) of that figure. Hong Kong has been the largest importer of Japanese food since 2007; other major imports include telecommunications as well as sound recording equipment. Major exports from Hong Kong to Japan include electrical machinery, appliances and parts. Of approximately 7,000 overseas companies with bases in Hong Kong, more than 220 regional headquarters and 900 regional or local offices are affiliates of Japanese companies, making up the second-largest group of overseas companies after those from the United States.[57] It should also be noted that over 21,000 Japanese citizens resided in Hong Kong in 2011, and over 1.3 million Japanese visitors travelled to Hong Kong in 2010, while over 500,000 people visited Japan from Hong Kong.[58]

Japan's competition law Competition law was originally introduced in Japan based on the political goal of the US occupation authorities to cultivate economic democratisation through dissolution of the Zaibatsu, large family-owned conglomerates that had oligopolised various industries during World War II. The key competition legislation in Japan is the Act on Prohibition of Private Monopolisation and Maintenance of Fair Trade 1947 (AMA). The AMA provides that its goals are to promote fair and free competition, and thereby the democratic and sound development of the national economy, and to ensure the interest of general consumers. It aims to achieve these goals by prohibiting (a) unreasonable restraint of trade, (b) private monopolisation, (c) unfair trade practices; and (d) business combinations the effect of which may be substantially to restrain competition. The Japan Fair Trade Commission (JFTC) is the main agency responsible for implementing the AMA.

Enforcement of the AMA in the 1950s and 1960s conflicted with Japan's industrial policy, which favoured cartels as a means to rationalize production. At the end of the 1980s, however, Japan came under pressure from foreign governments such as that of the US to enforce its competition laws more strictly. Because of this change in circumstances, JFTC established and promoted extensive guidelines to demonstrate its determination to enforce the AMA more vigorously.[59] Since then, the competition law's enforcement mechanisms have been significantly strengthened.[60]

Horizontal restraints: Lack of a *per se* rule Under the AMA, cartels (including bid rigging) and other anti-competitive practices are prohibited as unreasonable restraints of trade, which requires substantial restraint of competition in demonstrating the agreement to be a breach of the prohibition. Due to this requirement, the AMA contains no *per se* rule against price-fixing, and the JFTC must define relevant markets and establish the existence of a substantial restraint of competition there. This is clearly different from Hong Kong's First Conduct Rule, in which agreements and concerted practices can

---

[57] Website of the Government of the Hong Kong Special Administrative Region: http://www.hketotyo.gov.hk/japan/en/business-hongkong.

[58] Website of the Consulate-General of Japan in Hong Kong: http://www.hk.emb-japan.go.jp/eng/news.html.

[59] Guidelines Concerning Distribution Systems and Business Practices (1991).

[60] Simon Van de Walle & Tadashi Shiraishi, Competition Law in Japan: http://ssrn.com/abstract=2636263.

be regulated based on their object or effect, and the JFTC has sometimes encountered difficulty demonstrating substantial restraint of competition, even in obvious cartel cases.

Private monopolisation Although there is no prohibition of monopolisation or abuse of a dominant position, the prohibition on private monopoly[61] can be viewed as comparable to the prohibition on abuse of a dominant position in the EU and monopolisation in the US. However, it has an important difference from the EU and US rules: it has no requirement for monopoly power or a dominant position to be established. Instead, proof of private monopolisation requires a substantial restraint of competition, which can generally be demonstrated by the existence of a dominant position or market power.[62]

Unfair trade practices The AMA prohibits companies from engaging in unfair trade practices.[63] It defines sixteen types of unfair trade practices, which cover almost all types of unfair vertical restraints and activity such as predatory pricing, tying and abuse of superior bargaining position. The prohibition of unfair trade practices requires neither any substantive restraint of trade nor evidence of a dominant position or market power. Rather, it precludes a tendency to impede competition. The JFTC's established practice has been to favour the unfair trade practices prohibition over private monopolisation and thereby reduce its burden of proof for anti-competitive effects.

One of the most actively investigated forms of conduct is abuse of superior bargaining position, which prohibits unfair and abusive conduct by more powerful companies, such as inappropriate requests for rebates from inferior parties. This prohibition can be seen as similar or almost equivalent to a prohibition of exploitative abuse, which is regulated by Article 102 TFEU. Although the Hong Kong Competition Commission's Guideline on the Second Conduct Rule might focus only on exclusionary abuse, exploitative abuse may also be covered and prohibited by the Second Conduct Rule.

Industry-specific exemptions In Hong Kong, there are no industry-specific defences or exemptions to date, although some industries such as marine transportation may want their operational arrangements with competitors to be exempted from the application of Hong Kong's competition law. In contrast, Japanese regulation has industry-specific exemptions, which were originally

---

[61] AMA, Article 3.
[62] The JFTC's enforcement policy is to prioritise investigations against companies with a market share in excess of 50% when opening investigations against private monopolisation. Japan Fair Trade Commission, Guidelines for Exclusionary Private Monopolisation under the Japanese AMA (28 October 2009).
[63] AMA, Article 19.

introduced to address conflicts with Japan's industrial policies in the 1950s and 1960s, favouring cartels as a means of strengthening Japanese industries.

For example, the Marine Transportation Act provides an exemption from applications of the AMA for some categories of agreements and other concerted activities among ship carriers in relation to space charter agreements and similar co-operation agreements.[64] Parties to such agreements are required to submit a prior report to the Minister of Land, Infrastructure and Transportation (MLIT), and the MLIT may order its contents altered or prohibit any acts it considers unreasonably prejudicial or discriminatory. In practice, the MLIT typically consults with the JFTC to discuss whether such contemplated agreements would be unreasonably prejudicial or discriminatory before deciding whether or not to order changes or block such agreements.

In the JFTC's recent investigation of international ocean shipping companies, it issued an administrative prohibition decision against Japanese and non-Japanese shipping companies.[65] This case is noteworthy in that the JFTC also requested the MLIT to take necessary measures including withdrawal of previously granted exemptions, based on the finding that the freight rates were determined through bilateral negotiation between consignors and shipping companies on the North American route and other routes. Hence, the tariffs (freight rate tables uniformly applied to all consignors) stipulated in the exempted agreements were rarely if ever applied to actual transactions.

Leniency Leniency regimes became effective in Japan in January 2008, with 61 leniency filings being made in the 2014 fiscal year. This can be understood as an indicator that the regime is accepted by the Japanese business community and is properly functioning. Leniency applications must be made by facsimile to the JFTC's leniency officer so that the order of reports can be precisely recorded. This differs from the leniency policy in Hong Kong, which stipulates that leniency applications under the Cartel Leniency Policy can only be made by calls to the Leniency Hotline.

While Hong Kong's leniency policy makes leniency available only to the first cartel member who reports the cartel's conduct to the Competition Commission and meets all the requirements for receiving leniency, under the leniency programme in Japan, not only the first-in applicant, but a maximum of five companies will be granted reductions in applicable administrative fines. The first applicant to come forward before the start of a JFTC investigation is granted full immunity, while the second applicant is granted a 50% reduction and the third, the fourth and the fifth are granted 30% reductions. The JFTC has no discretion in determining the order of leniency applicants nor the percentage of reduction granted for cooperation. Once these five slots have

---

[64]   Marine Transportation Act, Article 28.

[65]   JFTC press release of 18 March, 2014:
       http://www.jftc.go.jp/en/press-releases/yearly-2014/March/140318.html.

been filled, the JFTC cannot offer any further leniency to other companies regardless of whether they make a useful contribution to the JFTC's investigation, which would mean that the timing of such applications (rather than the contents of facts and relevant evidence produced to the JFTC) is of crucial importance.

Right to counsel and legal professional privilege In 2013, after a bill amending the AMA was enacted to require the Japanese government to review the JFTC's investigative procedures and take appropriate measures to ensure that sufficient rights to defence are protected, an advisory panel was established to address investigative practices such as attorney-client privilege, which are not currently granted to companies under investigation by the JFTC. While arguments were made in support of adopting attorney-client privilege based on the understanding that introducing such privilege would enable a company to freely consult with its attorney and therefore encourage better compliance with the law, the majority of members of the advisory panel took the view that it should not be introduced for the following reasons: attorney-client privilege could be abusively exercised and thereby impede the JFTC's ability to effectively uncover anti-competitive conduct; and there is no cultural evidence supporting the belief that a societal interest exists in respecting attorney-client privilege. The advisory panel published a report in December 2014.[66] In December 2015, the JFTC issued guidelines based on the advisory panel's conclusions for its investigative measures and companies' rights of defence.

International cooperation The JFTC has been one of the most active competition authorities in the Asian region in addressing cartel regulation, increasing its international profile through recent vigorous prosecution of international cartels resulting from parallel investigations and cooperation with foreign authorities, including the US Department of Justice and the European Commission. The JFTC continues to play an active role in international efforts toward strengthening links and cooperation among competition authorities. As the most recent example, the JFTC completed a Memorandum on Cooperation with the National Development and Reform Commission (NDRC) of China on 13 October 2015,[67] providing that where companies in the jurisdiction of one competition authority are involved in a case being investigated by other competition authorities, the competition authority conducting the investigation may notify the others of the case.

---

[66] Report Issued by the Advisory Panel on Administrative Investigation Procedures under the Anti-Monopoly Act 18 (2014):
http://www.cao.go.jp/chosei/dok-kin/finalreport.html.

[67] http://www.jftc.go.jp/en/pressreleases/yearly-2015/October/151013.files-/151013_2.pdf.

Extra-territoriality Extra-territoriality has been a controversial issue, but the JFTC's recent administrative hearing decision has made clear that cartel agreements affecting sales of products for Japanese consumers should be subject to cartel regulations under the AMA, regardless of whether or not the cartel members are Japanese companies or whether or not the cartel agreement was reached in Japan. Hong Kong competition law adopted substantially similar regulations, in which the Conduct Rules apply if the agreement or conduct has the object or effect of harming competition in Hong Kong, even if put into effect outside Hong Kong or the conduct concerned takes place outside Hong Kong. This stance, sometimes referred to as the effects doctrine, has been widely shared among competition authorities. Thus, companies in Hong Kong should be mindful to observe Japanese and other foreign competition law in the sales of products to customers outside of Hong Kong. In addition, such convergence will likely enhance international cooperation between the JFTC and the Hong Kong Competition Commission in international cases, especially those whose major manufacturers or suppliers have bases in both Hong Kong and Japan, which will strengthen these authorities' capacities to effectively collect evidence and secure cooperation from companies.

Abolition of the administrative hearing system The AMA is primarily enforced by the JFTC through administrative proceedings, and the JFTC can issue an administrative order independently. For cartels, the JFTC can issue a prohibition decision as well as an order to pay an administrative fine, without consulting with other government agencies. The JFTC was established as an independent administrative office with broad enforcement powers and is composed of a chairman and four commissioners, a structure comparable to that of the Hong Kong Competition Commission. The JFTC has primary jurisdiction over the enforcement of merger control under the AMA. In cases of price-fixing and bid-rigging, criminal proceedings have also been brought, although these have been quite rare to date.

For appeal procedures, the Cabinet Office published a bill to amend the AMA to abolish the current administrative hearing procedure in favour of a more detailed judicial appeal procedure. This bill was passed in December 2013 and took effect in April 2015. The outline of the bill included the following proposed changes: (1) repeal of the JFTC's administrative hearing procedure for appeals of JFTC orders and implementation of an enhanced hearing procedure prior to the issuance of orders; and (2) the introduction of a system in which addressees of JFTC orders can appeal to the Tokyo District Court, then to the Tokyo High Court, and finally to the Supreme Court, thereby giving addressees three different levels of judicial appeal. Accordingly, appeals against the JFTC's cease-and-desist orders will be addressed by the Tokyo District Court instead of through the JFTC's administrative hearing procedure. Practitioners generally expect this to introduce more transparent and fair appeal procedures.

In Hong Kong, the Competition Tribunal comprises judges of the Hong Kong Court of First Instance. The Japanese system does not have a specially designated tribunal for competition law cases, but we can expect uniform and consistent interpretation of the AMA as all appeals against the JFTC's orders will be handled by a designated chamber of the Tokyo District court with two judges with experience as JFTC hearing officers.

Impact of Hong Kong's competition law on Japanese companies   A survey by the Hong Kong Japanese Chamber of Commerce and Industry in 2003 found approximately 2,100 Japanese companies and businesses operating in Hong Kong. A more recent survey found that 1,085 Japanese companies had offices in Hong Kong as of the end of 2011. In addition, Japanese banks are also well represented in Hong Kong, with 15 licensed banks maintaining branches or offices in Hong Kong.[68] Due to the close economic relationship between Hong Kong and Japan, Japanese companies must be careful not to breach Hong Kong's competition law and will want to pay close attention to the Competition Commission's enforcement guidelines. In particular, Japanese companies that have established joint ventures with local companies as a way to enter into the Hong Kong market and are operating businesses for Hong Kong consumers should immediately introduce appropriate compliance programmes for their local executives and employees, who may not sufficiently understand fair competition concepts and the authorities' rigorous scrutiny against unfair competition practices.

8.3 COMPETITION LAW IN SOUTH KOREA

Introduction   South Korea and Hong Kong have many things in common. Traditionally, both have been included in the Chinese-character civilisation. Thus, people in both regions, even if they cannot speak each other's language, can communicate with each other by expressing their minds in written Chinese characters. They also share a similar social culture in which people in the same industry tend to maintain close relationships rather than fiercely competing against each other. They are also both small economic regions open to the world by sea. Hong Kong is a small island, while South Korea is a small peninsula, both in the Pacific Ocean. With scarce natural resources and very dense population, both regions wisely pursued export-driven economic development making the best use of their geographic circumstances. As for South Korea, it began rapid economic growth in the 1960s by exporting various products in the world markets. In this process, large companies in South Korea grew by being exposed to fierce competition with foreign

---

[68]   See website of Consulate-General of Japan in Hong Kong: http://www.hk.emb-japan.go.jp/eng/news.html.

companies on a global scale. Similarly, Hong Kong achieved rapid economic growth by playing the role of an intermediary trade and financial hub. As a result, in the 1980s, South Korea and Hong Kong became one of four Asian dragons along with Taiwan and Singapore, which means very rapidly growing small economies in the Asian region.

Now, with the official launch of the competition rules in Hong Kong, South Korea and Hong Kong come to have one more aspect in common. South Korea has had active enforcement of competition law for about 35 years since April 1981 when the Monopoly Regulation and Fair Trade Act (MRFTA), South Korea's main competition law, took effect and when the Korea Fair Trade Commission (KFTC) was established to enforce the MRFTA. Hong Kong may take some inspiration from South Korea as it begins to embed its competition rules in its markets and social culture. This section focuses on the following four major implications to enhance understanding of competition law enforcement drawing from the experience of South Korea: (i) sophisticated procedural rules to ensure transparency and effective quasi-judicial system, (ii) detailed substantive guidelines to determine illegality based on economic principles, (iii) active international enforcement especially against cartels, and (iv) active competition advocacy.

Trade and investment flows   Hong Kong is one of the most important trade partners of South Korea. To South Korea, Hong Kong is one of the four largest trade markets and is the market where South Korea records the largest trade surplus without any trade conflict. Hong Kong also plays the role of the regional headquarters for Korean companies which intend to expand their businesses into mainland China. To Hong Kong, South Korea is the seventh largest export market and sixth largest import origin. Recently, many Hong Kong financial institutions entered financial markets in South Korea by investing in Korean financial institutions. Annual exports from South Korea to Hong Kong exceed US$20 billion and annual imports from Hong Kong into South Korea exceed US$8 billion.

Competition procedural rules   The KFTC's investigation procedure is composed of the following two stages: (i) investigation by a case handler and (ii) deliberation by the Commission. To ensure the quasi-judicial system within the KFTC, the KFTC's operations are divided into largely two parts, one concentrating on investigation depending on the type of violation (merger review, cartel, unilateral unfair trade practices and consumer protection) and the other concentrating on determination of illegality and the level of sanction which is ultimately decided by the consensus of nine Commissioners (Chairman, Vice Chairman, three Standing Commissioners and four Non-Standing Commissioners from outside of the KFTC).

Typically, the KFTC's investigation begins with a leniency application (only available in cartel cases), report by the victim of the potential violation and detection by the KFTC's own methods through various sources including news articles.   The case handler conducts dawn raids, requests relevant information and material, and conducts interviews with relevant employees to confirm the facts of the case. After a lengthy investigation, if the case handler finds that there is a violation, an Examiner's Report is prepared, summarising the result of his investigation and suggesting the grounds of illegality and the level of sanctions.

After the Examiner's Report is served on the investigated company, the deliberation stage begins.   One of the three Standing Commissioners is assigned to the case as a main deliberation Commissioner, and a deliberation assistant team is also assigned to assist him in issue-spotting, research on relevant domestic and international precedents and any other relevant factors to be considered in making a determination of illegality and the level of sanctions. The investigated company is given the opportunity to present its Rebuttal Opinion to the allegations raised in the Examiner's Report.   After the main deliberation Commissioner and his deliberation assistant team complete a full review of both the Examiner's Report and Rebuttal Opinion, a hearing date is fixed.   In the hearing, typically held only once even though in rare cases it can be held multiple times, both the case handler and the investigated company present their arguments in front of the Commissioners who, in turn, check relevant facts and raise questions to the case handler and/or the investigated company. After the hearing is over, the Commissioners reach a consensus on whether the case violates the competition law and, if so, what should be the sanction.   If the case is determined as a violation of competition law, the official written ruling is served on the investigated company and publicised through the KFTC's website.

Participation by investigated companies and interested third parties   The KFTC's enforcement began to attract public attention from the late 1990s when, in the face of the economic crisis, it imposed large surcharges (fines) against affiliates of Chaebols (large business groups) for inter-affiliate support. During the first half of the 2000s, the KFTC announced that cartels were the biggest enemy to the market economy and began active enforcement against them, gradually increasing the surcharge amount to be imposed on cartels.[69] The annual total surcharge imposed by the KFTC has been increasing at a

---

[69]   Previously, the penalty on cartels was not very high. On 1 April, 2004, the Guidelines on Imposition of Surcharge were significantly revised and the maximum surcharge in a cartel case was increased to 5% of the relevant turnover (which is defined as the sales turnover of all products which may have been directly or indirectly affected by the collusive agreement during the period of the violation). In addition, on 1 April, 2005, the Guidelines on Imposition of Surcharge were further revised and the maximum surcharge in a cartel case was again increased to 10% of the relevant turnover. After this revision, because of the increase in the maximum surcharge, the average surcharge rate to be applied to most cartel cases was sharply increased.

remarkable rate. In 2014, it handled over 80 cases involving a combined value of KRW785 billion.

As the sanctions imposed by the KFTC increased dramatically, investigated companies increased their demand for better acknowledgement of their rights of defence. Investigated companies are entitled to retain copies of the documents and materials taken by the KFTC during a dawn raid. Legal counsel can attend the interview by the KFTC with relevant employees of the investigated company and instruct the interviewee to raise any objection to the draft written summary of the interview prepared by the case handler before signing it. When the Examiner's Report is served, a list of evidentiary documents is also provided so that the investigated company can request any evidentiary documents for its own review. During the hearing, the investigated company can defend itself and present its arguments in an adversary system.

The need to expand the scope for any interested third parties to participate in the entire process of the KFTC's investigation and deliberation procedures has also been increasing. In most merger reviews where the underlying transaction is potentially likely to have anti-competitive effect in the relevant markets, it is the usual practice of case handlers to collect third party opinions from customers, competitors, industry experts and academia. The KFTC tries to ensure third party participation also in the investigation of unilateral unfair trade practice cases, as many of those cases are initiated by the report of the sufferers from the alleged illegal conduct. By these means, the KFTC can obtain active cooperation from the third parties in collecting evidence of violations, and can at the same time try to resolve the underlying dispute between the investigated company and the third party in an efficient way. While a third party cannot see the Examiner's Report on confidentiality grounds, it is entitled to participate in the hearing as an observer and can present its position after getting approval by or at the request of the Commissioners.

Judicial review Under the MRFTA, the ruling by the KFTC has the same effect as a decision by the First Instance Court, and the investigated company opposing the KFTC's ruling can file an administrative lawsuit with the Seoul High Court of Appeals.[70] The decision by the Seoul High Court of Appeals can further be appealed to the Supreme Court of Korea. Judicial review is frequently brought by the investigated companies with the courts tending to neutrally review the KFTC's ruling *de novo*, resulting in the KFTC's ruling often being overruled.[71] In addition, because the level of sanctions imposed by

---

[70] MRFTA, Article 55.

[71] According to the KFTC, of 88 cases decided by the Supreme Court in 2015 (until the end of October), the KFTC won entirely 61 cases (69.3%), won partly and lost partly 13 cases (14.7%) and lost entirely 14 cases (15.9%). During the past five years, the KFTC lost entirely in 5.6% to 18.1% of Supreme Court cases annually.

the KFTC is remarkably increasing, companies tend to file an administrative lawsuit in most cases.

Future improvements On 21 October 2015, the KFTC announced the Case Handling Procedure 3.0 plan, which pursues reform in its investigation practice in order to strengthen the procedural rights of investigated companies. For this, the KFTC promised (i) to enact the Guidelines on Investigation Procedure which will ensure the right to refuse an investigation which is beyond the proper scope and the participation of legal counsel in the entire investigation procedure, (ii) to revise the Guidelines on Case Handling to strengthen internal control to expedite the investigation and to ensure transparency and fairness and (iii) to enact the Rules on Keeping Case Records to oblige the KFTC to keep all records related to a case.

While this shows the KFTC's commitment to enhance procedural rights of the investigated companies, there are still outstanding issues to be discussed and ultimately reflected in the KFTC's procedures. For example, attorney-client privilege is not yet recognised by the KFTC. Rather, there was even a case where the KFTC obtained during a dawn raid a legal memorandum analysing the legal risk of the company's particular conduct and used it as evidence to show the company's prior awareness of the antitrust violation. Because of the KFTC's heavy case load compared to limited resources and the necessity to be more careful substantively and procedurally, it takes a very long time for an investigation to be completed with, typically, cartel investigations tending to take two to three years and unilateral unfair trade practice cases taking more than a year. The KFTC promised when announcing the Case Handling Procedure 3.0 plan that it will complete its investigation within six months in unilateral unfair trade practice cases and nine months in cartel cases.

Detailed substantive guidelines Conduct cannot be easily assessed from the perspective of competition law without balancing the anti-competitive effect and countervailing efficiency-enhancing effect caused by the conduct, especially in the context of merger review and unilateral unfair trade practice. This is the main reason why economic evidence is so important. In South Korea, just like in most other jurisdictions, cartels among competitors are treated as nearly *per se* illegal. However, since it is becoming more and more difficult for the KFTC to prove the existence of a cartel agreement with direct evidence, circumstantial evidence of various kinds is also used in the cartel context in order to show collusive conduct indirectly. Given this, unless there are clear standards to objectively determine the illegality of a certain conduct, companies will be at a loss because it is difficult for them to predict whether their conduct constitutes an antitrust violation.

The KFTC has enacted guidelines dealing with specific issues in competition law, such as cartels, unfair trade practices and merger control. It continues to update the guidelines as often as possible to keep its enforcement activity up to date with developments in theory and in practice both domestically and internationally. By this, the KFTC seeks to maintain transparency and consistency in its interpretation and enforcement of the MRFTA. Companies can assess whether their conduct may potentially be regarded as a violation in advance, and take the necessary measures to minimise the risk of being exposed to the KFTC's investigation and sanction.

Active international enforcement   In its Rating Enforcement 2015, the Global Competition Review rated the KFTC in the Very Good category by giving it four and a half stars along with the European Commission, Japan, Australia, Brazil, Spain and the UK. The KFTC was behind only four agencies (France, Germany, U.S. Department of Justice (DOJ) and Federal Trade Commission (FTC)) which were rated in the Elite category with five stars.[72] Such a successful result for the KFTC may partly be attributed to the fact that the KFTC is actively engaged in enforcing the MRFTA against many global companies doing business in international markets. Ten years of extensive international enforcement has led the KFTC to keep abreast of other advanced competition authorities in terms of the level of enforcement. Thanks to the KFTC's active enforcement effort in international competition discussion forums such as OECD and ICN, the KFTC is a frequently-invited speaker to share its enforcement experience with other participants. In turn, this also contributes to sharpening the KFTC's enforcement in the future.

The first case where the issue of whether the KFTC can extra-territorially exercise its jurisdiction was heavily disputed was the graphite electrode cartel case back in 2002.[73] After observing the DOJ's enforcement of the international cartel by six graphite electrode manufacturers in the United States, Germany and Japan, the KFTC launched an investigation into whether the conduct may have affected the Korean market by inflicting harm on Korean customers. When the foreign investigated companies filed appeals with the courts mainly challenging the appropriateness of the KFTC's extra-territorial application of the MRFTA, both the Seoul High Court of Appeals and the Supreme Court of Korea affirmed the KFTC's decision holding that the KFTC has proper jurisdiction over international companies as long as their conduct adversely affected Korean markets. To incorporate this decision, on 31 December 2004 the MRFTA was revised to contain a new clause which clarifies the possibility of the extra-territorial application of the MRFTA. This new clause provides that the MRFTA applies even to conduct which took place outside of Korea, if such conduct affects Korean markets.[74]

---

[72] http://www.globalcompetitionreview.com/surveys/article/38900/star-ratings.
[73] The KFTC imposed KRW11,242 million fines in total on six graphite electrode manufacturers for price fixing and market allocation (KFTC's Ruling 2002-077).
[74] MRFTA, Article 2-2.

Since then, the KFTC has actively enforced the MRFTA against foreign companies. On 1 July 2003, the KFTC revised the Merger Notification Guidelines to make it clear that foreign-to-foreign transactions which meet a certain local nexus threshold should be notified to the KFTC. On 24 February 2006, after more than four years of investigation, the KFTC imposed a heavy sanction on Microsoft for abusing its market dominant position by tying various products.[75] In 2008, the KFTC made an organisational change to create the International Cartel Division which concentrates only on enforcement against international cartel cases. The accumulation of international enforcement cases has given the KFTC confidence to pursue its own investigations, although, since foreign companies are sensitive in securing their right of defence, the KFTC has to be careful not to allow for procedural challenges be raised during the investigation and deliberation process.

By investigating international cases simultaneously with other competition authorities in foreign jurisdictions, the KFTC can frequently discuss various substantive issues with other authorities. For example, in February 2006, the KFTC joined the global simultaneous dawn raid on airline companies to investigate an international cartel on air cargo along with the US and EU authorities. In cartel cases, the KFTC frequently requests waiver from leniency applicants to allow it to discuss procedural and substantive issues with other foreign competition authorities. In merger review, the KFTC frequently coordinates with other foreign competition authorities the remedies to be imposed on the merging parties to address anti-competitive harm on each other's domestic markets.

Active competition advocacy Besides active enforcement of competition law in particular cases, it is also an important task for a competition authority to actively engage in competition advocacy to promote a competitive environment that is deeply rooted in the entire market and social culture. While law enforcement role is an *ex post* measure to sanction past violations, the competition advocacy role is an *ex ante* measure to seek to prevent future violation. One of the important competition advocacy activities by the KFTC is to review laws and regulations which contain anti-competitive aspects and recommend that they be revised in a more competition-friendly way. For this, all national and local government agencies should consult with the KFTC before enacting or revising any laws and regulations to check whether they contain any anti-competitive aspects. Even without such prior consultation, the KFTC conducts comprehensive research on its own initiative on a regular basis to seek to detect anti-competitive rules and regulations. The KFTC has identified regulations that contain procedures which facilitate collusive activity among competitors or entail discriminatory treatment of local companies and their external competitors, favouring the former. While the relevant

---

[75] KFTC's Ruling 2006-042.

government agencies may have their own policy goals in mind when introducing such provisions, the KFTC persistently consults with those agencies to seek to reach a compromise which ensures more competition-friendly regulation to achieve the same policy goals.

Another important aspect of the KFTC's competition advocacy role is its relationship with other government bodies. The MRFTA contains a provision which allows exemption from the application of the MRFTA to anti-competitive conduct which justifiably takes place pursuant to other laws or orders enforced by other government bodies.[76] While this is a provision to avoid confusion arising from the conflicting contents of different laws, the KFTC tries to enhance the role of competition advocacy wherever possible by interpreting this provision very narrowly. That is, while many investigated companies argue that their conduct originated from governmental guidance or pressure, the KFTC does not easily recognise that such conduct is justifiable unless the relevant laws enforced by such government agencies directly require the companies to engage in particular conduct. The inter-government agency relationship is more important when it comes to the relationship between the KFTC and various industry regulators such as Financial Supervisory Commission (FCS), Korea Communications Commission (KCC), Ministry of Land, Infrastructure and Transport (MOLIT) and Ministry of Agriculture, Food and Rural Affairs. These industry regulators tend to protect the interest of companies under their supervision in the name of facilitating and promoting business. The role of the KFTC is to enhance the competitive culture not only among the companies in regulated industries but also among the regulatory bodies with whom the KFTC enters into cooperative memoranda to coordinate enforcement activities and promote harmony between regulation and competition.

The law enforcement activity by the KFTC may not be sufficient to promote a competitive environment in markets and social culture. These days, there are increasing numbers of cases where alternative enforcement effort is effectively pursued. For example, private damages lawsuits are increasingly filed to recover compensation for harms caused by antitrust violations. Such private damages lawsuits originally began with the Korean government suing four oil refinery companies for damages arising from their cartel in the supply of oil for military use in 2000.[77] Recently, private damages lawsuits are filed in most cartel cases and in an increasing number of unfair trade practice cases.

Enforcement by other government authorities   Other government authorities also actively participate in indirect enforcement of competition law.

---

[76]   MRFTA, Article 58.

[77]   After more than 10 years of lengthy litigation, the government and the defendants finally agreed to settle the litigation at the compensation amount of KRW135.5 billion in August 2013.

The prosecutor's office is very active in criminal enforcement. While in the past their criminal sanctions involved relatively small criminal fines imposed on companies, the prosecutor's office now actively pursues sanctions not only against the companies but also against the individuals who directly participated in the antitrust violation. The Small and Medium Business Administration, the Public Procurement Service (PPS) and the Board of Audit and Inspection (BAI) actively exercise their recently-acquired authority to request the KFTC to report certain antitrust violation to the prosecutor's office for criminal investigation with which the KFTC must comply. The BAI urges public entities who suffered harm from bid rigging in their construction or procurement projects to actively file a private damages action to recover taxpayers' money from the construction companies. The PPS actively sanctions companies who were involved in cartel activity in the bidding process managed by the PPS, by restricting them from participating in future bids for a certain period (usually from six months to two years).

International cooperation The KFTC actively pursues competition advocacy in the international dimension as well. Since South Korea is unique in that it achieved rapid economic development in a short period of time and successfully strengthened competitive discipline in less than a generation. In addition to active participation in the international competition discussions in the OECD and ICN, the KFTC initiates technical support for developing countries by inviting government officials in charge of competition in those countries to the annual seminar held by the KFTC in conjunction with the Korea International Cooperation Agency. The KFTC operates a short-term dispatch programme where it sends competition experts to selected countries to share their expertise with the competition authorities in those countries.

APPENDIX

THE COMPETITION ORDINANCE (Cap. 619)

An Ordinance to prohibit conduct that prevents, restricts or distorts competition in Hong Kong; to prohibit mergers that substantially lessen competition in Hong Kong; to establish a Competition Commission and a Competition Tribunal; and to provide for incidental and connected matters.

SUMMARY OF CONTENTS

Part 4
Enforcement Powers of Commission

Division 1
Commitments

Division 2
Infringement Notices

Division 3
Leniency

Division 4
Warning Notices

Part 5
Review by Tribunal

PART 1

Preliminary

1. Short title and commencement

(1) This Ordinance may be cited as the Competition Ordinance.

(2) This Ordinance comes into operation on a day to be appointed by the Secretary for Commerce and Economic Development by notice published in the Gazette.

2. Interpretation

(1) In this Ordinance-

"agreement" includes any agreement, arrangement, understanding, promise or undertaking, whether express or implied, written or oral, and whether or not enforceable or intended to be enforceable by legal proceedings;

"Commission" means the Competition Commission established by section 129;

"Communications Authority" means the Communications Authority established by section 3 of the Communications Authority Ordinance (Cap 616);

"company", in addition to the meaning given by section 2(1) of the Companies Ordinance (Cap 622), includes a "non-Hong Kong company" within the meaning of that Ordinance and a company registered under Part IX of the Companies Ordinance (Cap 32) as in force from time to time before the commencement date* of section 2 of Schedule 9 to the Companies Ordinance (Cap 622) or under Part 17 of the Companies Ordinance (Cap 622); (Amended 28 of 2012 ss. 912 & 920 and L.N. 162 of 2013);

"company secretary" includes any person occupying the position of company secretary, by whatever name called;

"competition authority" means—

(a) the Commission; or

(b) the Communications Authority;

"competition matter" means any matter involving or having a connection with—

(a) a contravention or alleged contravention of a competition rule; or

(b) any decision relating to a competition rule, that has been made or is to be made under this Ordinance;

"competition matter" means any matter involving or having a connection with—

(a) a contravention or alleged contravention of a competition rule; or

(b) any decision relating to a competition rule, that has been made or is to be made under this Ordinance;

(c) the merger rule;

"conduct" means any conduct, whether by act or omission;

"conduct rule" means—

(a) the first conduct rule; or

(b) the second conduct rule;

"confidential information" has the meaning given by section 123;

"contract of employment" means any agreement, whether in writing or oral, express or implied, under which one person (an "employer") agrees to employ another and that other agrees to serve the employer as an employee, and also includes a contract of apprenticeship;

"director" includes any person occupying the position of director or involved in the management of a company, by whatever name called, and includes a shadow director;

"document" includes information recorded in any form;

"first conduct rule" has the meaning given by section 6;

"funds of the Commission" means the funds of the Commission, as specified in section 21 of Schedule 5;

"Government " does not include a company that is wholly or partly owned by the Government;

"information" includes information contained in a document;

"infringement notice" means an infringement notice issued under section 67(2);

"investigation" means an investigation conducted under Part 3;

"leniency agreement" means a leniency agreement made under section 80;

"member", in relation to the Commission, means a member of the Commission appointed under section 2 of Schedule 5;

"merger" has the meaning given by section 3 of Schedule 7 read together with section 5 of that Schedule;

"merger rule" has the meaning given by section 3 of Schedule 7;

"person", in addition to the meaning given by section 3 of the Interpretation and General Clauses Ordinance (Cap 1), includes an undertaking;

"President" means the President of the Tribunal appointed under section 136;

"reviewable determination" has the meaning given by section 83;

"second conduct rule" has the meaning given by section 21;

"serious anti-competitive conduct" means any conduct that consists of any of the following or any combination of the following—

(a) fixing, maintaining, increasing or controlling the price for the supply of goods or services;

(b) allocating sales, territories, customers or markets for the production or supply of goods or services;

(c) fixing, maintaining, controlling, preventing, limiting or eliminating the production or supply of goods or services;

(d) bid-rigging;

(Note: see also subsection 2)

"shadow director", in relation to a company, means a person in accordance with whose directions or instructions all the directors or a majority of the directors of the company are accustomed to act, but a person is not to be regarded as a shadow director by reason only that all the directors or a majority of the directors act on advice given by that person in a professional capacity;

"statutory body" means a body of persons, corporate or unincorporate, established or constituted by or under an Ordinance or appointed under an Ordinance, but does not include—

(a) a company;

(b) a corporation of trustees incorporated under the Registered Trustees Incorporation Ordinance

(c) (Cap 306);

(d) a society registered under the Societies Ordinance (Cap 151);

(e) a co-operative society registered under the Co-operative Societies Ordinance (Cap 33); or

(f) a trade union registered under the Trade Unions Ordinance (Cap 332);

"Tribunal" means the Competition Tribunal established by section 134;

"undertaking" means any entity, regardless of its legal status or the way in which it is financed, engaged in economic activity, and includes a natural person engaged in economic activity.

(2)   For the purposes of the definition of "serious anti-competitive conduct"—

"bid-rigging" means—

(a) an agreement—

(i)   that is made between or among 2 or more undertakings whereby one or more of those undertakings agrees or undertakes not to submit a bid or tender in response to a call or request for bids or tenders, or agrees or undertakes to withdraw a bid or tender submitted in response to such a call or request; and

(ii) that is not made known to the person calling for or requesting bids or tenders at or before the time when a bid or tender is submitted or withdrawn by a party to the agreement or by an entity controlled by any one or more of the parties to the agreement; or

(b) a submission, in response to a call or request for bids or tenders, of bids or tenders that are arrived at by an agreement—

(i)   that is made between or among 2 or more undertakings; and

(ii) that is not made known to the person calling for or requesting bids or tenders at or before the time when a bid or tender is submitted or withdrawn by a party to the agreement or by an entity controlled by any one or more of the parties to the agreement;

"goods" includes real property;

"price" includes any discount, rebate, allowance, price concession or other advantage in relation to the supply of goods or services;

"supply"—

(a) in relation to goods, means sell, rent, lease or otherwise dispose of the goods, an interest in the goods or a right to the goods, or offer so to dispose of the goods or of such an interest or right; and

(b) in relation to services, means sell, rent or otherwise provide the services or offer so to provide the services.

(3)   A note located in the text of this Ordinance is provided for information only and has no legislative effect.

3.   Application to statutory bodies

(1)   The following provisions do not apply to a statutory body—

    (a)   Part 2 (The conduct rules);

    (b)   Part 4 (Enforcement powers of Commission);

    (c)   Part 6 (Enforcement before Tribunal); and

    (d)   Schedule 7 (Mergers).

(2)   Despite subsection (1), the provisions referred to in that subsection apply to—

    (a)   a specified statutory body; and

    (b)   a statutory body, to the extent that it is engaged in a specified activity.

(3)   In this section—

    (a)   "specified" means specified in a regulation made for the purpose of this section by the Chief Executive in Council under section 5; and

    (b)   a reference to a statutory body includes an employee or agent of the statutory body, acting in that capacity.

4.   Application to specified persons and persons engaged in specified activities

(1)   The provisions referred to in section 3(1) do not apply to—

    (a)   a specified person; or

    (b)   a person, to the extent that the person is engaged in a specified activity.

(2)   In this section—

    (a)   "specified" means specified in a regulation made for the purpose of this section by the Chief Executive in Council under section 5; and

    (b)   a reference to a person includes an employee or agent of the person, acting in that capacity.

5.   Regulations

(1)   The Chief Executive in Council may, by regulation—

    (a)   apply the provisions referred to in section 3(1) to—

        (i) any statutory body; or

        (ii) any statutory body, to the extent that it is engaged in an activity specified in the regulation; and

    (b)   disapply the provisions referred to in section 3(1) to—

        (i) any person; or

        (ii) any person, to the extent that the person is engaged in an activity specified in the regulation.

(2)   The Chief Executive in Council may only make a regulation under subsection (1)(a)(i) or (ii) with respect to a statutory body if he or she is satisfied that—

    (a) the statutory body is engaging in an economic activity in direct competition with another undertaking;

    (b) the economic activity of the statutory body is affecting the economic efficiency of a specific market;

    (c) the economic activity of the statutory body is not directly related to the provision of an essential public service or the implementation of public policy; and

(d) there are no other exceptional and compelling reasons of public policy against making such a regulation.

(3)   In subsection (1), a reference to a statutory body or a person includes an employee or agent of the statutory body or person, acting in that capacity.

PART 2

The Conduct Rules

Division 1

Agreements etc, Preventing, Restricting or Distorting Competition

Subdivision 1

First Conduct Rule

6.   Prohibition of anti-competitive agreements, concerted practices and decisions
(1)   An undertaking must not—
   (a) make or give effect to an agreement;
   (b) engage in a concerted practice; or
   (c) as a member of an association of undertakings, make or give effect to a decision of the association,
   if the object or effect of the agreement, concerted practice or decision is to prevent, restrict or distort competition in Hong Kong.
(2)   Unless the context otherwise requires, a provision of this Ordinance which is expressed to apply to, or in relation to, an agreement is to be read as applying equally to, or in relation to, a concerted practice and a decision by an association of undertakings (but with any necessary modifications).
(3)   The prohibition imposed by subsection (1) is referred to in this Ordinance as the "first conduct rule".

7.   "Object" and "effect" of agreement
(1)   If an agreement, concerted practice or decision has more than one object, it has the object of preventing, restricting or distorting competition under this Ordinance if one of its objects is to prevent, restrict or distort competition.
(2)   An undertaking may be taken to have made or given effect to an agreement or decision or to have engaged in a concerted practice that has as its object the prevention, restriction or distortion of competition even if that object can be ascertained only by inference.
(3)   If an agreement, concerted practice or decision has more than one effect, it has the effect of preventing, restricting or distorting competition under this Ordinance if one of its effects is to prevent, restrict or distort competition.

8. Territorial application of first conduct rule

The first conduct rule applies to an agreement, concerted practice or decision that has the object or effect of preventing, restricting or distorting competition in Hong Kong even if—

(a) the agreement or decision is made or given effect to outside Hong Kong;

(b) the concerted practice is engaged in outside Hong Kong;

(c) any party to the agreement or concerted practice is outside Hong Kong; or

(d) any undertaking or association of undertakings giving effect to a decision is outside Hong Kong.

Subdivision 2

Decisions

9.   Application for decision

(1)   An undertaking that has made or given effect to, is giving effect to or is proposing to make or give effect to an agreement may apply to the Commission for a decision as to whether or not the agreement is—

(a) excluded from the application of the first conduct rule by or as a result of Schedule 1;

(b) exempt from the application of the first conduct rule by virtue of a block exemption order issued under section 15;

(c) exempt from the application of the first conduct rule by virtue of an order of the Chief Executive in Council made under section 31 (Exemptions on public policy grounds) or section 32 (Exemption to avoid conflict with international obligations); or

(d) excluded from the application of this Part by virtue of section 3 (Application to statutory bodies) or section 4 (Application to specified persons and persons engaged in specified activities).

(2)   The Commission is only required to consider an application under this section if—

(a) the application poses novel or unresolved questions of wider importance or public interest in relation to the application of exclusions or exemptions under this Ordinance;

(b) the application raises a question of an exclusion or exemption under this Ordinance for which there is no clarification in existing case law or decisions of the Commission; and

(c) it is possible to make a decision on the basis of the information provided.

(3)   The Commission is not required to consider an application under this section if the application concerns hypothetical questions or agreements.

10.   Consideration of application

(1)   Before making a decision on an application made under section 9, the Commission must—

(a) in order to bring the application to the attention of those the Commission considers likely to be affected by the decision, publish notice of the application—

    (i) through the Internet or a similar electronic network; and

    (ii) in any other manner the Commission considers appropriate; and

(b) consider any representations about the application that are made to the Commission.

(2)   A notice under subsection (1) must specify the period within which representations may be made to the Commission about the application.

(3)   The period specified for the purpose of subsection (2) must be a period of at least 30 days beginning after the day on which the notice is first published.

11. Decision by Commission

(1)   After considering the representations, if any, made within the period referred to in section 10, the Commission may make a decision as to whether or not the agreement in question is excluded or exempt from the application of the first conduct rule or this Part.

(2)   A decision by the Commission may include conditions or limitations subject to which it is to have effect.

(3)   After the Commission has made its decision, it must inform the applicant in writing of the decision, the date of its decision and the reasons for it.

12. Effect of decision

(1)   Subject to subsection (2), if the Commission makes a decision that an agreement is excluded or exempt from the application of the first conduct rule or this Part then each undertaking specified in the decision is immune from any action under this Ordinance with regard to that agreement.

(2)   The immunity provided by subsection (1) applies to an undertaking only to the extent of the first conduct rule or this Part, and in so far as that undertaking complies with every condition and limitation subject to which the decision is to have effect.

13. Non-compliance with condition or limitation

(1)   If an undertaking fails or ceases to comply with a condition or limitation subject to which a decision has effect, the immunity provided by section 12 ceases to apply with respect to that undertaking with effect from the date on which the non-compliance begins.

(2)   If an undertaking starts to comply or resumes compliance with the condition or limitation, the immunity provided by section 12 applies to that undertaking with effect from the date on which the compliance begins or resumes.

(3)   Action may be taken under this Ordinance against any undertaking relating to a contravention of the first conduct rule by that undertaking, that occurs during any period in which the immunity provided by section 12 does not apply to it.

14. Rescission of decision

(1)   The Commission may rescind a decision made under section 11 if it has reason to believe—

      (a) that there has been a material change of circumstances since the decision was made; or

      (b) that the information on which it based its decision was incomplete, false or misleading in a material particular.

(2)   Before rescinding a decision under this section the Commission must—

      (a) in order to bring the proposed rescission to the attention of those undertakings the Commission considers likely to be affected by it, publish notice of the proposed rescission—

          (i) stating that the Commission is considering rescinding the decision and the reasons why it is considering the rescission; and

          (ii) inviting the undertakings to make representations about the proposed rescission within the period specified in the notice; and

      (b) consider any representations received within the period specified in the notice.

(3)   The notice referred to in subsection (2) must be published—

      (a) through the Internet or a similar electronic network; and

      (b) in any other manner the Commission considers appropriate.

(4)   The period specified in the notice published under subsection (2) must be a period of at least 30 days beginning after the day on which the notice is published.

(5)   If, after—

      (a) the expiry of the period specified in the notice published under subsection (2); and

      (b) considering any representations received within that period, the Commission is of the view that the decision should be rescinded, it may, by notice in writing given to each undertaking for which the decision provides immunity, rescind that decision.

(6)   A notice of rescission given under subsection (5) must inform the undertakings of—

      (a) the rescission and the reasons for the rescission;

      (b) the date on which the determination to rescind the decision was made; and

      (c) the date from which the rescission takes effect.

(7)   If the Commission is satisfied that any information—

      (a) on which it based its decision; and

      (b) which was provided to it by a party to the agreement,

was incomplete, false or misleading in a material particular, the date specified in a notice under subsection (6)(c) may be earlier than the date on which the notice is given.

(8)   If a decision is rescinded under this section, each undertaking specified in the notice of rescission loses its immunity from action under this Ordinance, as from the date the rescission takes effect, with regard to anything done after that date.

(9)   A rescission of a decision under this section may be made with regard to all of the undertakings for which the decision provides immunity or with regard to only one or more of them.

Subdivision 3

Block Exemptions

15.   Block exemption orders

(1)   If the Commission is satisfied that a particular category of agreement is an excluded agreement, it may issue a block exemption order in respect of that category of agreement.

(2)   The Commission may, either of its own volition or on application by an undertaking or an association of undertakings, issue a block exemption order.

(3)   The Commission may, in a block exemption order—

  (a) impose conditions or limitations subject to which the block exemption order is to have effect; and

  (b) specify a date from which the order is to cease to have effect.

(4)   The Commission must, in a block exemption order, specify a date, being a date not more than 5 years after the date of the order, upon which it will commence a review of the block exemption order.

(5)   In this section—

  "excluded agreement" means an agreement that is excluded from the application of the first conduct rule by or as a result of section 1 (Agreements enhancing overall economic efficiency) of Schedule 1.

16.   Procedures regarding block exemption orders

(1)   Before issuing a block exemption order, the Commission must—

  (a) in order to bring the proposed block exemption order to the attention of those the Commission considers likely to be affected by it, publish notice of the proposed block exemption order—

    (i) through the Internet or a similar electronic network; and

    (ii) in any other manner the Commission considers appropriate; and

  (b) consider any representations about the proposed block exemption order that are made to the Commission.

(2)   A notice under subsection (1) must specify the period within which representations may be made to the Commission about the proposed block exemption order.

(3)   The period specified for the purpose of subsection (2) must be a period of at least 30 days beginning after the day on which the notice is first published.

17.   Effect of block exemption order

(1)   Subject to subsection (2), an agreement that falls within a category of agreement specified in a block exemption order is exempt from the application of the first conduct rule.

(2)   The immunity provided by subsection (1) to undertakings making or giving effect to an agreement applies to an undertaking only if it complies with every condition and limitation subject to which the block exemption order has effect.

18. Non-compliance with condition or limitation

(1) If an undertaking fails or ceases to comply with a condition or limitation subject to which a block exemption order has effect, the block exemption order ceases to apply with respect to that undertaking with effect from the date on which the non-compliance begins.

(2) If an undertaking starts to comply or resumes compliance with the condition or limitation, the block exemption order applies to that undertaking with effect from the date on which the compliance begins or resumes.

(3) Action may be taken under this Ordinance against any undertaking relating to a contravention of the first conduct rule by that undertaking, that occurs during any period in which the block exemption order does not apply to it.

19. Review of block exemption order

(1) The Commission must commence a review of a block exemption order on the date specified in the order for the commencement of the review.

(2) Despite subsection (1), the Commission may review a block exemption order at any time if it considers it appropriate to do so.

(3) Without limiting the matters that may be considered in deciding, under subsection (2), whether or not to review a block exemption order, the Commission must consider the following—

    (a) the desirability of maintaining a stable and predictable regulatory environment in relation to competition;

    (b) any developments that have taken place in the economy of Hong Kong or in the economy of any place outside Hong Kong that affect the category of agreement that is the subject of the block exemption order; and

    (c) whether any significant new information relating to the particular category of agreement has come to the knowledge of the Commission since the block exemption order was first issued.

20. Variation or revocation of block exemption order

(1) If the Commission considers that it is appropriate to do so, after reviewing a block exemption order, it may issue an order varying or revoking the block exemption order with effect from a date specified in the order.

(2) Before varying or revoking a block exemption order, the Commission must—

    (a) in order to bring the proposed variation or revocation to the attention of those the Commission considers likely to be affected by it, publish notice of the proposed variation or revocation—

        (i) through the Internet or a similar electronic network; and

        (ii) in any other manner the Commission considers appropriate; and

    (b) consider any representations about the proposed variation or revocation that are made to the Commission.

(3) A notice under subsection (2) must specify the period within which representations may be made to the Commission about the proposed variation or revocation.

(4) The period specified for the purpose of subsection (3) must be a period of at least 30 days beginning after the day on which the notice is first published.

(5)   An order made under this section—

     (a) must specify the date on which it is to have effect; and

     (b) may contain any transitional and savings provisions the Commission considers necessary or expedient.

Division 2

Abuse of Market Power

Subdivision 1

Second Conduct Rule

21.   Abuse of market power

(1)   An undertaking that has a substantial degree of market power in a market must not abuse that power by engaging in conduct that has as its object or effect the prevention, restriction or distortion of competition in Hong Kong.

(2)   For the purpose of subsection (1), conduct may, in particular, constitute such an abuse if it involves—

     (a) predatory behaviour towards competitors; or

     (b) limiting production, markets or technical development to the prejudice of consumers.

(3)   Without limiting the matters that may be taken into account in determining whether an undertaking has a substantial degree of market power in a market, the following matters may be taken into consideration in any such determination—

     (a) the market share of the undertaking;

     (b) the undertaking's power to make pricing and other decisions;

     (c) any barriers to entry to competitors into the relevant market; and

     (d) any other relevant matters specified in the guidelines issued under section 35 for the purposes of this paragraph.

(4)   The prohibition imposed by subsection (1) is referred to in this Ordinance as the "second conduct rule".

22.   "Object" and "effect" of conduct

(1)   If conduct has more than one object, it has the object of preventing, restricting or distorting competition under this Ordinance if one of its objects is to prevent, restrict or distort competition.

(2)   An undertaking may be taken to have engaged in conduct that has as its object the prevention, restriction or distortion of competition even if that object can be ascertained only by inference.

(3)   If conduct has more than one effect, it has the effect of preventing, restricting or distorting competition under this Ordinance if one of its effects is to prevent, restrict or distort competition.

23. Territorial application of second conduct rule

The second conduct rule applies to conduct that has as its object or effect the prevention, restriction or distortion of competition in Hong Kong even if—

(a) the undertaking engaging in the conduct is outside Hong Kong; or

(b) the conduct is engaged in outside Hong Kong.

Subdivision 2

Decisions

24. Application for decision

(1) An undertaking that has engaged in, is engaging in or is proposing to engage in certain conduct may apply to the Commission for a decision as to whether or not the conduct is—

(a) excluded from the application of the second conduct rule by or as a result of Schedule 1;

(b) exempt from the application of the second conduct rule by virtue of an order of the Chief Executive in Council made under section 31 (Exemptions on public policy grounds) or section 32 (Exemption to avoid conflict with international obligations); or

(c) excluded from the application of this Part by virtue of section 3 (Application to statutory bodies) or section 4 (Application to specified persons and persons engaged in specified activities).

(2) The Commission is only required to consider an application under this section if—

(a) the application poses novel or unresolved questions of wider importance or public interest in relation to the application of exclusions or exemptions under this Ordinance;

(b) the application raises a question of an exclusion or exemption under this Ordinance for which there is no clarification in existing case law or decisions of the Commission; and

(c) it is possible to make a decision on the basis of the information provided.

(3) The Commission is not required to consider an application under this section if the application concerns hypothetical questions or conduct.

25. Consideration of application

(1) Before making a decision on an application made under section 24, the Commission must—

(a) in order to bring the application to the attention of those the Commission considers likely to be affected by the decision, publish notice of the application—

(i) through the Internet or a similar electronic network; and

(ii) in any other manner the Commission considers appropriate; and

(b) consider any representations about the application that are made to the Commission.

(2)   A notice under subsection (1) must specify the period within which representations may be made to the Commission about the application.

(3)   The period specified for the purpose of subsection (2) must be a period of at least 30 days beginning after the day on which the notice is first published.

26.   Decision by Commission

(1)   After considering the representations, if any, made within the period referred to in section 25, the Commission may make a decision as to whether or not the conduct in question is excluded or exempt from the application of the second conduct rule or this Part.

(2)   A decision by the Commission may include conditions or limitations subject to which it is to have effect.

(3)   After the Commission has made its decision, it must inform the applicant in writing of the decision, the date of its decision and the reasons for it.

27.   Effect of decision

(1)   Subject to subsection (2), if the Commission makes a decision that conduct is excluded or exempt from the application of the second conduct rule or this Part then each undertaking specified in the decision is immune from any action under this Ordinance with regard to that conduct.

(2)   The immunity provided by subsection (1) applies to an undertaking only to the extent of the second conduct rule or this Part, and in so far as that undertaking complies with every condition and limitation subject to which the decision is to have effect.

28.   Non-compliance with condition or limitation

(1)   If an undertaking fails or ceases to comply with a condition or limitation subject to which a decision has effect, the immunity provided by section 27 ceases to apply with respect to that undertaking with effect from the date on which the non-compliance begins.

(2)   If an undertaking starts to comply or resumes compliance with the condition or limitation, the immunity provided by section 27 applies to that undertaking with effect from the date on which the compliance begins or resumes.

(3)   Action may be taken under this Ordinance against any undertaking relating to a contravention of the second conduct rule by that undertaking, that occurs during any period in which the immunity provided by section 27 does not apply to it.

29.   Rescission of decision

(1)   The Commission may rescind a decision made under section 26 if it has reason to believe—

    (a) that there has been a material change of circumstances since the decision was made; or

    (b) that the information on which it based its decision was incomplete, false or misleading in a material particular.

(2)   Before rescinding a decision under this section the Commission must—

(a) in order to bring the proposed rescission to the attention of those undertakings the Commission considers likely to be affected by it, publish notice of the proposed rescission—
  (i) stating that the Commission is considering rescinding the decision and the reasons why it is considering the rescission; and
  (ii) inviting the undertakings to make representations about the proposed rescission within the period specified in the notice; and
(b) consider any representations received within the period specified in the notice.

(3)   The notice referred to in subsection (2) must be published—
(a) through the Internet or a similar electronic network; and
(b) in any other manner the Commission considers appropriate.

(4)   The period specified in the notice published under subsection (2) must be a period of at least 30 days beginning after the day on which the notice is published.

(5)   If, after—
(a) the expiry of the period specified in the notice published under subsection (2); and
(b) considering any representations received within that period,
the Commission is of the view that the decision should be rescinded, it may, by notice in writing given to each undertaking for which the decision provides immunity, rescind that decision.

(6)   A notice of rescission given under subsection (5) must inform the undertakings of—
(a) the rescission and the reasons for the rescission;
(b) the date on which the determination to rescind the decision was made; and
(c) the date from which the rescission takes effect.

(7)   If the Commission is satisfied that any information—
(a) on which it based its decision; and
(b) which was provided to it by an undertaking engaging in the conduct,
was incomplete, false or misleading in a material particular, the date specified in a notice under subsection (6)(c) may be earlier than the date on which the notice is given.

(8)   If a decision is rescinded under this section, each undertaking specified in the notice of rescission loses its immunity from action under this Ordinance, as from the date the rescission takes effect, with regard to anything done after that date.

(9)   A rescission of a decision under this section may be made with regard to all of the undertakings for which the decision provides immunity or with regard to only one or more of them.

Division 3

Exclusions and Exemptions

Subdivision 1

Exclusions from Conduct Rules

30. Exclusions
The conduct rules do not apply in any of the cases in which they are excluded by or as a result of Schedule 1.

Subdivision 2

Exemptions from Conduct Rules

31. Exemptions on public policy grounds
(1) The Chief Executive in Council may, by order published in the Gazette, exempt—
   (a) a specified agreement or a specified class of agreement from the application of the first conduct rule; or
   (b) specified conduct or a specified class of conduct from the application of the second conduct rule,
   if he or she is satisfied that there are exceptional and compelling reasons of public policy for doing so.
(2) An order under subsection (1) may be made subject to any conditions or limitations that the Chief Executive in Council considers appropriate.
(3) An order made under this section remains in force for the period that is specified in the order.
(4) Before the expiry of an order, the Chief Executive in Council may, by order published in the Gazette, extend the period of its validity.
(5) An order made under subsection (1) may provide that the conduct rule in question has never applied to any agreement or conduct specified in the order.

32. Exemption to avoid conflict with international obligations
(1) The Chief Executive in Council may, by order published in the Gazette, exempt—
   (a) a specified agreement or a specified class of agreement from the application of the first conduct rule; or
   (b) specified conduct or a specified class of conduct from the application of the second conduct rule,
   if he or she is satisfied that it is appropriate to do so, in order to avoid a conflict between this Ordinance and an international obligation that directly or indirectly relates to Hong Kong.

(2)   An order under subsection (1) may be made subject to any conditions or limitations that the Chief Executive in Council considers appropriate.

(3)   An order made under this section remains in force for the period that is specified in the order.

(4)   Before the expiry of an order, the Chief Executive in Council may, by order published in the Gazette, extend the period of its validity.

(5)   If an international obligation has ceased to have effect or has been varied, the Chief Executive in Council may, by order published in the Gazette, revoke an order made under this section, or (as the case requires) amend it to the extent warranted by the variation.

(6)   An order made under subsection (1) may provide that the conduct rule in question has never applied to any agreement or conduct specified in the order.

(7)   In this section—

"international obligation" includes an obligation under—

(a) an air service agreement or a provisional arrangement referred to in Article 133 of the Basic Law;

(b) an international arrangement relating to civil aviation; and

(c) any agreement, provisional arrangement or international arrangement designated as an international agreement, international provisional arrangement or international arrangement by the Chief Executive in Council by order published in the Gazette.

33.   Orders to be published and placed before Legislative Council

(1)   The Chief Executive is to arrange for every order made under section 31 or 32 to be—

(a) published in the Gazette; and

(b) laid on the table of the Legislative Council at the next sitting of the Council after its publication in the Gazette.

(2)   The Legislative Council may, by resolution passed at a sitting of the Legislative Council held not later than 28 days after the sitting at which an order is laid on the table of the Council (the "relevant period"), amend the order in any manner consistent with the power of the Chief Executive in Council to make the order in question.

(3)   If the relevant period would but for this section expire after the end of a session or a dissolution of the Legislative Council, but on or before the day of its second sitting in the next session, the period for amending the order is deemed to be extended and to expire on the day after that second sitting.

(4)   The Legislative Council may, before the expiry of the relevant period, by resolution extend the period for amending the order to the first sitting of the Council held not earlier than the twenty-first day after the day of that expiry.

(5)   If the relevant period is extended under subsection (3), the Legislative Council may, before the expiry of the extended period, by resolution extend that extended period to the first sitting of the Council held not earlier than the twenty-first day after the day of the second sitting in the next session referred to in that subsection.

(6)   A resolution passed by the Legislative Council in accordance with this
        section must be published in the Gazette not later than 14 days after the
        passing of the resolution or within such further period as the Chief
        Executive may allow in any particular case.

(7)   An order made by the Chief Executive in Council under section 31 or 32
        comes into operation—
        (a) if on the expiry of the relevant period or that period as extended under
            subsection (3), (4) or (5), the Legislative Council has not passed a
            resolution amending the order, on the expiry of the relevant period or
            that period as so extended (as the case may be); and
        (b) if the Legislative Council passes a resolution amending the order, at
            the beginning of the day on which the resolution is published in the
            Gazette.

(8)   If an order is not laid on the table of the Legislative Council in accordance
        with this section, it is of no effect.

(9)   In this section—
        "sitting", when used to calculate time, means the day on which the sitting
        commences and only includes a sitting at which subsidiary legislation is
        included on the order paper.

Division 4

Miscellaneous

34.   Register of decisions and block exemption orders
(1)   The Commission must establish and maintain a register of—
        (a) all decisions made in respect of applications made under section 9 or
            24;
        (b) all notices of rescissions of such decisions, made under section 14 or
            29;
        (c) all block exemption orders issued under section 15; and
        (d) all orders varying or revoking block exemption orders, issued under
            section 20.

(2)   The Commission may omit confidential information from any entry made
        in the register under this section; and where confidential information has
        been omitted, that fact must be disclosed on the register.

(3)   The Commission must make the register available for inspection by any
        person—
        (a) at the offices of the Commission during ordinary business hours;
        (b) through the Internet or a similar electronic network; and
        (c) in any other manner the Commission considers appropriate.

35.   Guidelines
(1)   The Commission must issue guidelines—
        (a) indicating the manner in which it expects to interpret and give effect to
            the conduct rules;
        (b) regarding the manner and form in which it will receive applications
            for a decision or block exemption order; and

    (c) indicating how it expects to exercise its power to make a decision or grant block exemptions.

(2)   The Commission may amend any guidelines it issues under this section.

(3)   Guidelines issued under this section, and any amendments made to them, may be published in any manner the Commission considers appropriate.

(4)   Before issuing any guidelines or amendments to them under this section, the Commission must consult the Legislative Council and any persons it considers appropriate.

(5)   The Commission must make available copies of all guidelines issued under this section and of all amendments made to them—

    (a) at the offices of the Commission during ordinary business hours;

    (b) through the Internet or a similar electronic network; and

    (c) in any other manner the Commission considers appropriate.

(6)   A person does not incur any civil or criminal liability only because the person has contravened any guidelines issued under this section or any amendments made to them.

(7)   If, in any legal proceedings, the Tribunal or any other court is satisfied that a guideline is relevant to determining a matter that is in issue—

    (a) the guideline is admissible in evidence in the proceedings; and

    (b) proof that a person contravened or did not contravene the guideline may be relied on by any party to the proceedings as tending to establish or negate the matter.

36.   Amendment of Schedule 1

(1)   The Chief Executive in Council may by order amend Schedule 1.

(2)   An order made under subsection (1) is subject to the approval of the Legislative Council.

PART 3

Complaints and Investigations

Division 1

Complaints

37.   Complaints

(1)   Any person may, in accordance with guidelines issued under section 38, lodge a complaint with the Commission alleging that an undertaking has contravened, is contravening or is about to contravene a competition rule.

(2)   The Commission is not required to investigate a complaint if it does not consider it reasonable to do so and may, in particular, refuse to investigate a complaint if it is satisfied that—

    (a) the complaint is trivial, frivolous or vexatious; or

    (b) the complaint is misconceived or lacking in substance.

38. Guidelines regarding complaints

The Commission must issue guidelines indicating the manner and form in which complaints are to be made.

Division 2

Investigations

39. Power to conduct investigations

(1) The Commission may conduct an investigation into any conduct that constitutes or may constitute a contravention of a competition rule—

(a) of its own volition;

(b) where it has received a complaint under this Part;

(c) where the Court of First Instance or the Tribunal has referred any conduct to it for investigation under section 118; or

(d) where the Government has referred any conduct to it for investigation.

(2) Despite subsection (1), the Commission may only conduct an investigation under this Part if it has reasonable cause to suspect that a contravention of a competition rule has taken place, is taking place or is about to take place.

40. Guidelines regarding investigations

The Commission must issue guidelines indicating—

(a) the procedures it will follow in deciding whether or not to conduct an investigation under this Part; and

(b) the procedures it will follow in conducting any investigation under this Part.

41. Powers to obtain documents and information

(1) This section applies where the Commission has reasonable cause to suspect that a person has or may have possession or control of documents or information or may otherwise be able to assist it in relation to a matter that constitutes or may constitute a contravention of a competition rule.

(2) For the purpose of conducting an investigation, the Commission may by notice in writing require any person—

(a) to produce to it any document or a copy of any document; or

(b) to provide it with any specified information,

relating to any matter it reasonably believes to be relevant to the investigation.

(3) A notice under subsection (2) must indicate—

(a) the subject matter and purpose of the investigation; and

(b) the nature of the offences created by section 52 (Failure to comply with requirement or prohibition), section 53 (Destroying or falsifying documents) and section 55 (Providing false or misleading documents or information).

(4) The Commission may also specify in the notice—

(a) the time and place at which any document is to be produced or any information is to be provided; and

(b) the manner and form in which any document is to be produced or any information is to be provided.

(5) The power under this section to require a person to produce a document includes power—

(a) if the document is produced—

(i) to make copies of it or to take extracts from it; or

(ii) to require that person or any other person who is a present or past employee or partner of that person, or was at any time employed by that person, to give an explanation of or further particulars about the document;

(b) if the document is not produced, to require that person to state, to the best of the person's knowledge and belief, where it is.

(6) The power under this section to require a person to provide specified information includes power—

(a) in relation to information recorded otherwise than in legible form, to require the production of a copy of the information in a visible and legible form or in a form from which it can readily be produced in a visible and legible form; and

(b) to require the provision of instruction on the operation of equipment containing information stored electronically.

(7) In this section—

"specified" means—

(a) specified, or described, in the notice; or

(b) falling within a category that is specified, or described, in the notice.

42. Persons may be required to attend before Commission

(1) For the purpose of conducting an investigation, the Commission may, by notice in writing, require any person to attend before the Commission, at a time and place specified in the notice, to answer questions relating to any matter it reasonably believes to be relevant to the investigation.

(2) A notice under subsection (1) must indicate—

(a) the subject matter and purpose of the investigation; and

(b) the nature of the offences created by section 52 (Failure to comply with requirement or prohibition), section 53 (Destroying or falsifying documents) and section 55 (Providing false or misleading documents or information).

43. Statutory declaration regarding evidence

(1) The Commission may require a person giving any explanation, further particulars, answer or statement to the Commission under this Part to verify the truth of the explanation, particulars, answer or statement, by statutory declaration.

(2) For the purpose of subsection (1) any member of the Commission may administer an oath or affirmation.

(3) If a person fails to comply with a requirement made under this Part to give any explanation, further particulars, answer or statement to the Commission, the Commission may require that person to state, by statutory declaration, the reasons for the failure.

44. **Immunity**

(1) A person who gives evidence to the Commission under this Part and any counsel, solicitor, or other person who appears before the Commission under this Part has the same privileges and immunities as the person would have if the investigation were civil proceedings in the Court of First Instance.

(2) In subsection (1), the reference to the giving of evidence includes a reference to producing any document, making any statement, giving any information, explanation or further particulars and answering any question.

45. **Self-incrimination**

(1) A person is not excused—

(a) from giving any explanation or further particulars about a document; or

(b) from answering any question, under this Division on the grounds that to do so might expose the person to proceedings referred to in subsection (3).

(2) No statement made by a person—

(a) in giving any explanation or further particulars about a document; or

(b) in answering any question,

under this Division is admissible against that person in proceedings referred to in subsection (3) unless, in the proceedings, evidence relating to the statement is adduced, or a question relating to it is asked, by that person or on that person's behalf.

(3) The proceedings referred to in subsections (1) and (2) are—

(a) proceedings in which the Commission applies for an order for—

(i) a pecuniary penalty under section 93; or

(ii) a financial penalty under section 169; and

(b) any criminal proceedings other than proceedings for—

(i) an offence under section 55 (Providing false or misleading documents or information);

(ii) an offence under Part V (Perjury) of the Crimes Ordinance (Cap 200); or

(iii) an offence of perjury.

46. **Obligation of confidence**

(1) A person is not excused from providing to the Commission any information or producing any document to the Commission under this Part in respect of which an obligation of confidence is owed to any other person.

(2) A person who, when required to do so under this Ordinance, produces any document or provides any information to the Commission, in respect of which an obligation of confidence is owed to any other person, is not personally liable for that act.

Division 3

Search and Seizure

47. Appointment of authorized officers

The Commission may, in writing, appoint any employee of the Commission as an authorized officer of the Commission (an "authorized officer") for the purposes of this Part.

48. Warrant to enter and search premises

(1) A judge of the Court of First Instance may issue a warrant authorizing a person specified in the warrant, and any other persons who may be necessary to assist in the execution of the warrant, to enter and search any premises if the judge is satisfied, on application made on oath by an authorized officer, that there are reasonable grounds to suspect that there are or are likely to be, on the premises, documents that may be relevant to an investigation by the Commission.

(2) A warrant under subsection (1) may be issued subject to any conditions specified in it that apply to the warrant itself or to any further authorization under it (whether granted under its terms or any provision of this Ordinance).

49. Duty to produce evidence of authority

An authorized officer executing a warrant must, if requested, produce for inspection—

(a) documentary evidence of his or her identity;

(b) documentary evidence of his or her authorization under section 47; and

(c) the warrant.

50. Powers conferred by warrant

(1) A warrant issued under section 48 authorizes the persons specified in it—

(a) to enter and search the premises specified in the warrant;

(b) to use such force for gaining entry to the premises and for breaking open any article or thin found on the premises as is reasonable in the circumstances;

(c) to make use of such equipment as is reasonable in the circumstances;

(d) to remove by force any person or thing obstructing the execution of the warrant;

(e) to require any person on the premises to produce any document that appears to be a relevant document, in the possession or under the control of that person;

(f) to make copies of or take extracts from any document that appears to be a relevant document found on the premises or produced to a person executing the warrant;

(g) to prohibit any person found on the premises from—

(i) altering or otherwise interfering with any document that appears to be a relevant document; or

(ii) removing any such document from the premises or causing or permitting any other person to remove such document from the premises;

(h) to take possession of any documents found on the premises that appear to be relevant documents if—

(i) such action appears to be necessary for preserving the documents or preventing interference with them; or

(ii) it is not reasonably practicable to take copies of the documents on the premises;

(i) to take any other steps that appear to be necessary for the purpose mentioned in paragraph (h)(i);

(j) to take possession of any computer or other thing found on the premises that the person executing the warrant has reasonable grounds for believing will, on examination, afford evidence of a contravention of a competition rule;

(k) to require any person on the premises to give an explanation of any document appearing to be a relevant document or to state, to the best of his or her knowledge and belief, where such an explanation may be found or obtained;

(l) to require any information which is stored in electronic form and is accessible from the premises and which the person executing the warrant considers relates to any matter relevant to the investigation, to be produced in a form—

(i) in which it is visible and legible or from which it can readily be produced in a visible and legible form; and

(ii) in which it can be taken away.

(2) In this section—

"relevant document" means a document of a kind that could be required to be produced to the Commission under this Part.

Division 4

Offences in Relation to Investigations

51. Interpretation

In this Division—

"Commission" includes any member, employee or authorized officer of the Commission;

"information" includes information provided in answer to a question.

52. Failure to comply with requirement or prohibition

(1) A person who, without reasonable excuse, fails to comply with a requirement or prohibition imposed on that person under—

(a) section 41 (Powers to obtain documents and information);

(b) section 42 (Persons may be required to attend before Commission);

(c) section 43 (Statutory declaration regarding evidence); or

(d) section 50 (Powers conferred by warrant),

commits an offence.

(2)   A person who commits an offence under subsection (1) is liable—

      (a) on conviction on indictment, to a fine of $200000 and to imprisonment for 1 year; or

      (b) on summary conviction, to a fine at level 5 and to imprisonment for 6 months.

53.   Destroying or falsifying documents

(1)   A person commits an offence if, having been required to produce a document under section 41 (Powers to obtain documents and information) or section 50 (Powers conferred by warrant), the person—

      (a) intentionally or recklessly destroys or otherwise disposes of it, falsifies it or conceals it; or

      (b) causes or permits its destruction, disposal, falsification or concealment.

(2)   A person who commits an offence under subsection (1) is liable—

      (a) on conviction on indictment, to a fine of $1000000 and to imprisonment for 2 years; or

      (b) on summary conviction, to a fine at level 6 and to imprisonment for 6 months.

54.   Obstruction of search

(1)   It is an offence for a person to obstruct any person exercising a power under a warrant issued under section 48.

(2)   A person who commits an offence under subsection (1) is liable—

      (a) on conviction on indictment, to a fine of $1000000 and to imprisonment for 2 years; or

      (b) on summary conviction, to a fine at level 6 and to imprisonment for 6 months.

55.   Providing false or misleading documents or information

(1)   If any person produces or provides any document or information to the Commission under this Part, that person commits an offence if—

      (a) the document or information is false or misleading in a material particular; and

      (b) the person knows or is reckless as to whether the document or information is false or misleading in a material particular.

(2)   A person who—

      (a) provides any document or information to another person, knowing the document or information to be false or misleading in a material particular; or

      (b) recklessly provides any document or information to another person that is false or misleading in a material particular,

knowing that the document or information is to be used for the purpose of providing information to the Commission in connection with any of its functions under this Part, commits an offence.

(3)   A person who commits an offence under this section is liable—

      (a) on conviction on indictment, to a fine of $1000000 and to imprisonment for 2 years; or

(b) on summary conviction, to a fine at level 6 and to imprisonment for 6 months.

Division 5

Miscellaneous

56. Retention of property

(1)   If property is produced to the Commission in response to a requirement under this Part or is obtained under a warrant issued under section 48, the Commission may retain that property—

(a) for as long as may be necessary for the purpose of its investigation; or

(b) where it may be required for legal proceedings, for as long as may be necessary for the purpose of those proceedings.

(2)   If a document obtained under this Part is in the possession of the Commission, the Commission must, if requested by a person otherwise entitled to possession of the document, supply that person with a copy of the document certified by a member of the Commission to be a true copy of the original.

(3)   Until such a certified copy is issued, the Commission must, at any time and place it considers appropriate, allow a person otherwise entitled to possession of the document, or a person authorized by that person, to inspect and make copies of or take extracts from the document.

(4)   A certified copy of a document issued under this section is admissible in evidence in all courts as if it were the original.

57. Disposal of property

(1)   If any property has come into possession of the Commission under this Ordinance, the Tribunal may order the disposal of the property in the manner provided in this section.

(2)   The Tribunal may, either of its own motion or on application—

(a) make an order for the delivery of the property to the person who appears to the Tribunal to be entitled to the property;

(b) if the person entitled to the property is unknown or cannot be found, make an order that the property be sold or retained in the possession of the Tribunal or the Commission; or

(c) if the property is of no value, order that the property be destroyed.

(3)   An order for the delivery, sale or destruction of property must not, except where the property is perishable, be made under subsection (2) unless the Tribunal is satisfied that the property will not be required for the purpose of any proceedings before the Tribunal or any other court.

(4)   If—

(a) the Tribunal orders the sale or retention of any property under subsection (2); and

(b) no person establishes a claim to the property or the proceeds of sale of the property within 6 months after the day on which the order is made, the Tribunal may, either of its own motion or on application by the Commission, order that the property or the proceeds of sale become the property of the Government.

(5) An order made under subsection (2), other than an order for the retention of property, must not, except where the property is perishable, be carried out until the period allowed for making an appeal againstmthe order has expired or, where such an appeal is made, until the appeal is finally disposed of.

(6) An appeal is finally disposed of, for the purpose of subsection (5)—

(a) if it is determined and the period for bringing any further appeal has ended; or

(b) if it is abandoned or otherwise ceases to have effect.

58. Legal professional privilege

(1) Subject to subsection (2), this Part does not affect any claims, rights or entitlements that would, but for this Part, arise on the ground of legal professional privilege.

(2) Subsection (1) does not affect any requirement under this Ordinance to disclose the name and address of a client of a counsel or solicitor.

59. Guidelines

(1) The Commission may amend any guidelines it issues under this Part.

(2) Guidelines issued under this Part, and any amendments made to them, may be published in any manner the Commission considers appropriate.

(3) Before issuing any guidelines or amendments to them under this Part, the Commission must consult the Legislative Council and any persons it considers appropriate.

(4) The Commission must make available copies of all guidelines issued under this Part and of all amendments made to them—

(a) at the offices of the Commission during ordinary business hours;

(b) through the Internet or a similar electronic network; and

(c) in any other manner the Commission considers appropriate.

(5) A person does not incur any civil or criminal liability only because the person has contravened any guidelines issued under this Part or any amendments made to them.

(6) If, in any legal proceedings, the Tribunal or any other court is satisfied that a guideline is relevant to determining a matter that is in issue—

(a) the guideline is admissible in evidence in the proceedings; and

(b) proof that a person contravened or did not contravene the guideline may be relied on by any party to the proceedings as tending to establish or negate the matter.

(7) Guidelines issued under this Part and all amendments made to them are not subsidiary legislation.

Part 4

Enforcement Powers of Commission

Division 1

Commitments

60. Commitments

(1) The Commission may accept from a person a commitment to—
    (a) take any action; or
    (b) refrain from taking any action,
that the Commission considers appropriate to address its concerns about a possible contravention of a competition rule.

(2) The action referred to in subsection (1)(a) does not include making a payment to the Government.

(3) If the Commission accepts a commitment under this section, it may agree—
    (a) not to commence an investigation or, if it has commenced an investigation, to terminate it; and
    (b) not to bring proceedings in the Tribunal or, if it has brought proceedings, to terminate them.

(4) If the Commission accepts a commitment under this section, it may not—
    (a) commence or continue an investigation; or
    (b) bring or continue proceedings in the Tribunal,
in relation to any alleged contravention of a competition rule in so far as that investigation or those proceedings relate to matters that are addressed by the commitment.

(5) To avoid doubt, the Commission may still commence or continue an investigation or bring or continue proceedings in the Tribunal, after accepting a commitment under this section—
    (a) in relation to matters that are not addressed by the commitment; or
    (b) in relation to persons who are not subject to the commitment.

(6) If the Commission decides to accept a commitment under this section, it must, as soon as practicable after accepting it—
    (a) give notice in writing of that decision to the person who made the commitment, together with a copy of the commitment; and
    (b) register the commitment on the register of commitments maintained under section 64 (Register of commitments).

61. Withdrawal of acceptance of commitment

(1) The Commission may, by notice in writing given to the person who made the commitment, withdraw its acceptance of a commitment, with effect from the date specified in the notice, if—
    (a) it has reasonable grounds for believing that there has been a material change of circumstances since the commitment was accepted;
    (b) it has reasonable grounds for suspecting that the person who made the commitment has failed to comply with the commitment; or

(c) it has reasonable grounds for suspecting that the information on which it based its decision to accept the commitment was incomplete, false or misleading in a material particular.

(2) If the Commission is satisfied that any information—

(a) on which it based its decision to accept the commitment; and

(b) which was provided to it by the person who made the commitment,

was incomplete, false or misleading in a material particular, the date specified in the notice given under subsection (1) may be earlier than the date on which the notice is given.

(3) If an acceptance is withdrawn under this section—

(a) the commitment is no longer binding on the person who made it; and

(b) subject to subsection (4), the Commission may—

(i) commence an investigation; or

(ii) bring proceedings in the Tribunal,

with respect to any alleged contravention of the relevant competition rule that has occurred after the date specified in the notice given under subsection (1).

(4) The Commission may not bring proceedings authorized by subsection (3) more than 2 years after the date specified in the notice given under subsection (1).

62. Variation, substitution and release of commitment

(1) At any time after the Commission has accepted a commitment, it may accept from the person who has made it—

(a) a variation of the commitment; or

(b) a new commitment in substitution for it,

if it is satisfied that the variation or new commitment will address its concerns about a possible contravention of a competition rule.

(2) The Commission may release any person from a commitment that the person has made under this Part if—

(a) it is requested to do so by that person; or

(b) it has reasonable grounds for believing that its concerns about the alleged contravention of the competition rule no longer arise.

63. Enforcement of commitment

(1) If the Commission considers that a person has failed to comply with any commitment that the person has made under this Part (including a commitment to comply with the requirements of an infringement notice) and which has been accepted by the Commission, it may apply to the Tribunal for an order under subsection (2).

(2) If the Tribunal is satisfied that a person has failed to comply with a commitment that the person has made under this Part and which has been accepted by the Commission, the Tribunal may make all or any of the following orders—

(a) an order directing the person to take such action or refrain from taking such action, as is specified in the commitment;

(b) an order directing the person to pay to the Government an amount not exceeding the amount of any profit gained or loss avoided by that person as a result of the person's failure to comply with the commitment;

(c) an order directing the person to compensate any person for any loss or damage caused by the person's failure to comply with the commitment; and

(d) any other order that the Tribunal considers appropriate.

64.   Register of commitments

(1)   The Commission must establish and maintain a register of commitments made under this Part (including commitments to comply with the requirements of an infringement notice) containing—

(a) a copy of all commitments accepted under this Part (including any commitment accepted in substitution for another);

(b) a copy of all variations of commitments accepted under this Part;

(c) where any acceptance of a commitment has been withdrawn, notice of that withdrawal; and

(d) where any commitment has been released, notice of that release.

(2)   The Commission may omit confidential information from any entry made in the register under this section; and where confidential information has been omitted, that fact must be disclosed on the register.

(3)   The Commission must make the register available for inspection by any person—

(a) at the offices of the Commission during ordinary business hours;

(b) through the Internet or a similar electronic network; and

(c) in any other manner the Commission considers appropriate.

65.   Procedural requirements regarding commitments

Schedule 2 has effect regarding the procedural requirements for—

(a) the acceptance of commitments;

(b) the withdrawal of acceptance of commitments; and

(c) the variation and release of commitments,

under this Division.

Division 2

Infringement Notices

66.   Interpretation

In this Division—

"compliance period" means the period within which a person who has notified the Commission that the person proposes to comply with the requirements of an infringement notice must make a commitment to comply with the requirements of the notice;

"notification period" means the period (being a period of not more than 28 days) within which a person to whom an infringement notice has been issued must notify the Commission whether or not the person proposes to comply with the requirements of the notice.

67. **Commission may issue infringement notice**

(1)   Subsection (2) applies where—
  (a) the Commission has reasonable cause to believe that—
    (i) a contravention of the first conduct rule has occurred and the contravention involves serious anti-competitive conduct; or
    (ii) a contravention of the second conduct rule has occurred; and
  (b) the Commission has not yet brought proceedings in the Tribunal in respect of the contravention.

(2)   The Commission may, instead of bringing proceedings in the Tribunal in the first instance, issue a notice (an "infringement notice") to the person against whom it proposes to bring proceedings, offering not to bring those proceedings on condition that the person makes a commitment to comply with requirements of the notice.

(3)   The requirements of an infringement notice may include, but are not limited to, the following requirements—
  (a) to refrain from any specified conduct, or to take any specified action, that the Commission considers appropriate; and
  (b) to admit to a contravention of the relevant conduct rule.

(4)   The action that may be specified by the Commission under subsection (3)(a) does not include making a payment to the Government.

68. **Person not obliged to make commitment**

A person is not obliged to make a commitment to comply with the requirements of an infringement notice, but if a person does not make the commitment within the compliance period, the Commission may bring proceedings against that person in the Tribunal in relation to the alleged contravention of the conduct rule.

69. **Contents of infringement notice**

An infringement notice must—
  (a) identify the conduct rule alleged to have been contravened;
  (b) describe the conduct that is alleged to contravene that conduct rule;
  (c) identify the person whose conduct is alleged to constitute the contravention;
  (d) identify the evidence or other materials that the Commission relies on in support of its allegations;
  (e) specify the requirements to be complied with by the person to whom the notice is addressed;
  (f) specify both the notification period and the compliance period; and
  (g) be accompanied by a copy of section 68 (Person not obliged to make commitment).

70. **Notice of proposal to issue infringement notice**

(1)   Before issuing an infringement notice to any person under section 67, the Commission must—
  (a) give that person a notice under this section; and
  (b) consider any representations made in accordance with the notice.

(2)   A notice under this section must—
  (a) state that an infringement notice is proposed to be issued;

(b) contain a draft of the proposed infringement notice; and

(c) specify a period, being a period of not less than 15 days, within which representations may be made as to why the infringement notice should not be issued.

(3) If a person makes a representation in response to a notice issued under this section—

(a) evidence or information provided to the Commission in that representation may not be used against that person; and

(b) no person may obtain discovery of that information or evidence against the Commission,

in any proceedings, other than proceedings against that person for an offence under section 172 (Provision of false information).

71. Decision not to issue infringement notice

If after considering any representations made in response to a notice given under section 70, the Commission decides not to issue an infringement notice, it must give notice of that decision to the person to whom the notice under section 70 was given.

72. Effect of issue of infringement notice

(1) If an infringement notice has been issued to any person, no proceedings may be brought by the Commission against that person in respect of the contravention referred to in the notice if—

(a) the compliance period has not expired; and

(b) the infringement notice has not been withdrawn.

(2) The Commission may not publish an infringement notice (or disclose the whole or any part of its contents)—

(a) before the expiry of its compliance period;

(b) if a commitment to comply with the requirements of the notice is not made within the compliance period; or

(c) if the Commission has withdrawn the notice.

73. Withdrawal of infringement notice

The Commission may at any time before the expiry of the compliance period, by notice in writing given to a person to whom an infringement notice has been issued, withdraw the infringement notice with effect from a date specified in the notice.

74. Extension of compliance period

(1) The Commission may, either of its own volition or on application made to it in writing, extend the compliance period specified in an infringement notice if it considers that there is a good reason for doing so.

(2) An application for an extension under subsection (1) must be made before the expiry of the period sought to be extended.

75. Effect of commitment to comply with requirements of infringement notice

If a person makes a commitment to comply with the requirements of an infringement notice within the compliance period, the Commission may not bring proceedings in the Tribunal against that person in respect of the alleged contravention specified in the notice.

76. Failure to comply with requirements of infringement notice

(1) This section applies where a person has made a commitment to the Commission to comply with the requirements of an infringement notice.

(2) Nothing in section 75 prevents the Commission from bringing proceedings in the Tribunal, where it has reasonable grounds for suspecting that the person who has made the commitment has failed to comply with one or more of the requirements of the infringement notice.

77. Registration of commitments

The Commission must register commitments made under this Division in the register maintained by the Commission under section 64 (Register of commitments) and the provisions of that section also apply, with any necessary modifications that the circumstances require, to commitments made under this Division.

78. Publication of infringement notices

If a person has made a commitment under this Division to comply with the requirements of an infringement notice, the Commission may publish the infringement notice—

(a) through the Internet or a similar electronic network; and

(b) in any other manner the Commission considers appropriate.

Division 3

Leniency

79. Interpretation

In this Division—

"officer" means—

(a) in relation to a corporation, a director, manager or company secretary of the corporation, and any other person involved in the management of the corporation; and

(b) in relation to an undertaking (other than a corporation or partnership), any member of the governing body of that undertaking.

80. Commission may make leniency agreements

(1) The Commission may, in exchange for a person ' s co-operation in an investigation or in proceedings under this Ordinance, make an agreement (a "leniency agreement") with the person, on any terms it considers appropriate, that it will not bring or continue proceedings under Part 6 for a pecuniary penalty in respect of an alleged contravention of a conduct rule against—

(a) if the person is a natural person, that person or any employee or agent of that person;

(b) if the person is a corporation, that corporation or any officer, employee or agent of the corporation;

(c) if the person is a partner in a partnership, that partnership or any partner in the partnership, or any employee or agent of the partnership; or

(d) if the person is an undertaking other than one referred to in paragraph (a), (b) or (c), that undertaking or any officer, employee or agent of the undertaking,

in so far as the contravention consists of the conduct specified in the agreement.

(2)   The Commission must not, while a leniency agreement is in force, bring or continue proceedings under Part 6 for a pecuniary penalty in breach of that leniency agreement.

81.   Termination of leniency agreement

(1)   The Commission may terminate a leniency agreement if—

(a) the other party to the agreement agrees to the termination;

(b) it has reasonable grounds to suspect that the information on which it based its decision to make the agreement was incomplete, false or misleading in a material particular;

(c) the other party to the agreement, or if the agreement was made by a person as an officer, employee or agent of an undertaking, that undertaking has been convicted of an offence under Part 3; or

(d) it is satisfied that the other party to the agreement, or if the agreement was made by a person as an officer, employee or agent of an undertaking, that undertaking has failed to comply with the terms of the agreement.

(2) The Commission may terminate a leniency agreement by giving notice in writing to the other party to the agreement and to any other person who appears to the Commission to be likely to benefit from the agreement, stating—

(a) the date of the termination; and

(b) the reasons for the termination.

(3)   A notice under subsection (2) must specify the period within which representations may be made to the Commission about the proposed termination.

(4)   The period specified for the purpose of subsection (3) must be a period of at least 30 days beginning after the day on which the notice is given.

(5)   Before terminating a leniency agreement, the Commission must consider any representations about the proposed termination that are made to it.

Division 4

Warning Notices

82.   Warning notices

(1)   If the Commission has reasonable cause to believe that—

(a) a contravention of the first conduct rule has occurred; and

(b) the contravention does not involve serious anti-competitive conduct,

the Commission must, before bringing proceedings in the Tribunal against the undertaking whose conduct is alleged to constitute the contravention, issue a notice (a "warning notice") to the undertaking.

(2)   A warning notice must—

(a) describe the conduct (the " contravening conduct ") that is alleged to constitute the contravention;

(b) identify the undertaking (the " contravening undertaking ") that has engaged in the contravening conduct;

(c) identify the evidence or other materials that the Commission relies on in support of its allegations;

(d) state—

(i) that the Commission requires the contravening undertaking to cease the contravening conduct within the period (the "warning period") specified in the notice, and not to repeat that conduct after the warning period;

(ii) that, if the contravening conduct continues after the expiry of the warning period, the Commission may bring proceedings in the Tribunal against the contravening undertaking in respect of the contravening conduct; and

(iii) that, if the contravening undertaking repeats the contravening conduct after the expiry of the warning period, the Commission may bring proceedings in the Tribunal against the contravening undertaking in respect of the contravening conduct and the repeated conduct; and

(e) indicate the manner in which the contravening undertaking may cease the contravening conduct.

(3)   In determining the warning period, the Commission must have regard to the amount of time which the contravening undertaking is likely to require to cease the contravening conduct.

(4)   After the expiry of the warning period—

(a) if the Commission has reasonable cause to believe that the contravening conduct continues after the expiry, the Commission may bring proceedings in the Tribunal against the contravening undertaking in respect of the contravening conduct; and

(b) if the Commission has reasonable cause to believe that the contravening undertaking repeats the contravening conduct after the expiry, the Commission may bring proceedings in the Tribunal against the contravening undertaking in respect of the contravening conduct and the repeated conduct.

(5)   To avoid doubt, proceedings under subsection (4) may not be brought in respect of any period that precedes the warning period.

(6)   The Commission may, either of its own volition or on application made to it in writing, extend the warning period specified in a warning notice if it considers that there is a good reason for doing so.

(7)   An application for an extension under subsection (6) must be made before the expiry of the period sought to be extended.

Part 5

Review by Tribunal

83. Interpretation

In this Part—

"reviewable determination" means—

(a) a decision regarding an agreement, made by the Commission under section 11;

(b) a rescission of a decision regarding an agreement, made by the Commission under section 14;

(c) a decision relating to the issue of a block exemption order, made by the Commission under section 15;

(d) a decision relating to the variation or revocation of a block exemption order, made by the Commission under section 20;

(e) a decision regarding specific conduct, made by the Commission under section 26;

(f) a rescission of a decision regarding specific conduct, made by the Commission under section 29;

(g) a decision relating to the variation of a commitment, made by the Commission under section 62;

(h) a decision relating to the release of a person from a commitment, made by the Commission under section 62;

(i) a decision relating to the termination of a leniency agreement, made by the Commission under section 81;

(j) a decision regarding a merger or proposed merger, made by the Commission under section 13 of Schedule 7; or

(k) a rescission of a decision regarding a merger or proposed merger, made by the Commission under section 15 of Schedule 7.

84. Review of reviewable determination

(1) An application may be made to the Tribunal by any person or undertaking specified or referred to in section 85 for a review of a reviewable determination.

(2) An application under subsection (1) may only be made with the leave of the Tribunal.

(3) Leave may not be granted under subsection (2) unless the Tribunal is satisfied that—

(a) the review has a reasonable prospect of success; or

(b) there is some other reason in the interests of justice why the review should be heard.

85. Who may apply for review

(1) An application for a review under this Part may be made—

(a) in the case of a decision or a rescission of a decision, by the undertaking that applied for the decision;

(b) in the case of a decision relating to the variation of a commitment or the release of a person from a commitment, by the person who made the commitment; or

(c) in the case of a decision relating to the termination of a leniency agreement, by a party to the agreement.

(2) A person who does not fall under subsection (1) may also apply to the Tribunal for a review of a reviewable determination, other than a decision regarding a merger or proposed merger, if the Tribunal is satisfied that the person has a sufficient interest in the reviewable determination.

86. Tribunal may state case for Court of Appeal

(1) Before or after the determination of an application for review made under section 84, the Tribunal may, either of its own motion or on application, refer any question of law arising in, or that has arisen in, the review to the Court of Appeal for determination by way of case stated.

(2) The Tribunal may only refer a question of law to the Court of Appeal under subsection (1) if it is satisfied—

(a) that the party who has applied for the question of law to be referred has a reasonable prospect of success; or

(b) that there is some other reason in the interests of justice why the question of law should be referred.

(3) On the hearing of the case, the Court of Appeal may—

(a) determine the question stated;

(b) amend the case or require the Tribunal to amend the case in any manner the Court specifies; or

(c) remit the case to the Tribunal for reconsideration in the light of the decision of the Court.

87. Decision of Tribunal on application for review

In determining an application for a review, the Tribunal may—

(a) confirm or set aside the whole or part of the determination to which it relates; and

(b) where it sets aside the whole or part of a determination, refer the matter back to the Commission with a direction to reconsider and make a new determination in accordance with the decision of the Tribunal.

88. Time limit for applying for review

(1) An application for the review of a reviewable determination must be made within 30 days after the day on which the determination was made.

(2) Despite subsection (1), the Tribunal may extend the time referred to in that subsection if it is satisfied that—

(a) there is a good reason for doing so; and

(b) no injustice would be caused as a result of the extension.

(3) Despite subsection (2), an application for a review of a reviewable determination may not be made more than 3 years after the day on which the determination was made.

89.   Stay of execution of reviewable determination

(1)   The making of an application for review does not by itself operate as a stay of execution of the determination to which the application relates.

(2)   A person or undertaking that has made an application for review may, at any time before the application is determined by the Tribunal, apply to the Tribunal for a stay of execution of the determination to which the application relates.

(3)   When an application is made under subsection (2), the Tribunal must, as soon as reasonably practicable, conduct a hearing to determine the application, and may, where it considers it appropriate, order a stay of execution of the determination to which the application relates.

(4)   An order for a stay of execution under this section may be made subject to such conditions as to costs, payment of money into the Tribunal or otherwise as the Tribunal considers appropriate.

Part 6

Enforcement before Tribunal

Division 1

Introductory

90.   Interpretation

In this Part—

"disqualification order" means an order made by the Tribunal under section 101 disqualifying a person from being a director of a company or from otherwise being concerned in the affairs of a company;

"pecuniary penalty" means a pecuniary penalty ordered to be paid, under section 93.

91.   Persons involved in contravention of competition rule

A reference in this Part to a person being involved in a contravention of a competition rule means a person who—

(a) attempts to contravene the rule;

(b) aids, abets, counsels or procures any other person to contravene the rule;

(c) induces or attempts to induce any other person, whether by threats or promises or otherwise, to contravene the rule;

(d) is in any way, directly or indirectly, knowingly concerned in or a party to the contravention of the rule; or

(e) conspires with any other person to contravene the rule.

Division 2

Pecuniary Penalty

92. Commission may apply for pecuniary penalty

(1)   If, after carrying out such investigation as it considers appropriate, the Commission considers it appropriate to do so, it may apply to the Tribunal for a pecuniary penalty to be imposed on any person it has reasonable cause to believe—

(a) has contravened a competition rule; or

(b) has been involved in a contravention of a competition rule.

(2)   An application under subsection (1) may not be made—

(a) in the case of an application with respect to a contravention of the merger rule, more than 6 months after the day on which the merger was completed or the Commission became aware of the merger, whichever is the later; or

(b) in the case of an application with respect to a contravention of a conduct rule, more than 5 years after the day on which the contravention ceased or the Commission became aware of the contravention, whichever is the later.

93. Tribunal may impose pecuniary penalty

(1)   If the Tribunal is satisfied, on application by the Commission under section 92, that a person has contravened or been involved in a contravention of a competition rule, it may order that person to pay to the Government a pecuniary penalty of any amount it considers appropriate.

(2)   Without limiting the matters that the Tribunal may have regard to, in determining the amount of the pecuniary penalty, the Tribunal must have regard to the following matters—

(a) the nature and extent of the conduct that constitutes the contravention;

(b) the loss or damage, if any, caused by the conduct;

(c) the circumstance in which the conduct took place; and

(d) whether the person has previously been found by the Tribunal to have contravened this Ordinance.

(3)   The amount of a pecuniary penalty imposed under subsection (1) in relation to conduct that constitutes a single contravention may not exceed in total—

(a) subject to paragraph (b), 10% of the turnover of the undertaking concerned for each year in which the contravention occurred; or

(b) if the contravention occurred in more than 3 years, 10% of the turnover of the undertaking concerned for the 3 years in which the contravention occurred that saw the highest, second highest and third highest turnover.

(4)   In this section—

"turnover" means the total gross revenues of an undertaking obtained in Hong Kong;

"year" means the financial year of an undertaking or, if the undertaking does not have a financial year, a calendar year.

Division 3

Other Orders

94. Other orders of Tribunal

(1) If the Tribunal is satisfied that a person has contravened, or been involved in a contravention of a competition rule, it may (whether or not it makes an order under section 93 imposing a pecuniary penalty), either of its own motion or on application made for this purpose, make any order it considers appropriate against that person, including all or any of the orders specified in Schedule 3.

(2) An application for an order under subsection (1) may not be made—

    (a) in the case of an application with respect to a contravention of the merger rule, more than 6 months after the day on which the merger was completed or the Commission became aware of the merger, whichever is the later; or

    (b) in the case of an application with respect to a contravention of a conduct rule, more than 5 years after the day on which the contravention ceased or the Commission became aware of the contravention, whichever is the later.

(3) Despite subsection (2)(a), the Tribunal may, on application made before the expiry of the period referred to in that subsection, extend the period within which an application under subsection (1) may be made with respect to a contravention of the merger rule if the Tribunal considers it reasonable to do so.

95. Interim orders

(1) Subject to subsection (2), if the Tribunal is satisfied that a person is engaged in or is proposing to engage in conduct that constitutes or would constitute a contravention of the competition rules, it may, either of its own motion or on application made for this purpose, make an interim order pending its determination of an application for an order under section 94.

(2) A person other than the Commission is not entitled to make an application under subsection (1) by reason that any other person is engaged in or is proposing to engage in conduct that contravenes or would contravene the merger rule.

(3) An interim order remains in force for the period, being a period of not more than 180 days, specified in the order, but this period may be extended by the Tribunal for a further period of not more than 180 days on any one occasion.

(4) An interim order may be made whether or not an application for a pecuniary penalty under section 92 or an order under section 94 has been made.

(5) The Tribunal may make an order under this section whether or not—

    (a) the person against whom the order is to be made intends to engage again in or intends to continue to engage in the conduct that is to be the subject of the order;

(b) the person against whom the order is to be made has previously engaged in the conduct that is to be the subject of the order; or

(c) there is an imminent danger of damage or loss being incurred by any person if the order is not made.

96. Order to pay costs of Commission investigation

(1) The Tribunal may order any person who has contravened a competition rule to pay to the Government an amount equal to the amount of the costs of and incidental to any investigation into the conduct or affairs of that person, reasonably incurred by the Commission in connection with proceedings for the contravention.

(2) In this section—

"costs" include fees, charges, disbursements, expenses and remuneration.

Division 4

Contraventions of the Merger Rule

Subdivision 1

Anticipated Mergers

97. Proceedings in relation to anticipated mergers

(1) If the Commission, after conducting an investigation, has reasonable cause to believe that arrangements are in progress or in contemplation which, if carried into effect, will result in a merger that is likely to contravene the merger rule, it may apply to the Tribunal for an order under this section.

(2) If the Tribunal is satisfied, on application made under this section, that arrangements are in progress or in contemplation which, if carried into effect, will result in a merger that is likely to contravene the merger rule, it may make an order directed against a party to the arrangements or any other person—

(a) ordering the person against whom the order is directed not to proceed with the merger;

(b) ordering the person against whom the order is directed not to proceed with a part of the merger;

(c) in addition to or instead of an order referred to in paragraph (b), prohibiting the person against whom the order is directed from doing anything that will result in a merger.

(3) If the Tribunal is not satisfied that an arrangement, if carried into effect, will result in a merger that is likely to contravene the merger rule, it may make a declaration to that effect.

(4) An order under this section may contain anything permitted by Schedule 4.

98. Interim orders

(1) If an application has been made to the Tribunal under section 97 but has not yet been finally determined, the Tribunal may, either of its own motion or

on application by the Commission, make interim orders for the purpose of preventing pre-emptive action, including orders—

(a) prohibiting or restricting the doing of things that the Tribunal considers would constitute preemptive action;

(b) imposing on any person concerned obligations as to the carrying on of any activities or the safeguarding of any assets;

(c) providing for the carrying on of any activities or the safeguarding of any assets either by the appointment of a person to conduct or supervise the conduct of any activities (on any terms and with any powers that may be specified or described in the order) or in any other manner.

(2) In this section—

"pre-emptive action" means any action that might prejudice the hearing of the application under section 97 or any final order that the Tribunal might make on the hearing of the   application.

Subdivision 2

Mergers

99.   Application to Tribunal for order

(1)   If the Commission, after carrying out such investigation as it considers appropriate, has reasonable cause to believe that a merger contravenes the merger rule, it may apply to the Tribunal for an order under section 100.

(2)   An application for an order under subsection (1) must be made within the period of 6 months after the day on which the merger was completed or the Commission became aware of the merger, whichever is the later.

(3) Despite subsection (2), the Tribunal may, on application by the Commission made before the expiry of the period referred to in that subsection, extend the period within which an application under subsection (1) may be made if the Tribunal considers it reasonable to do so.

100.   Proceedings in relation to mergers

(1)   If the Tribunal is satisfied, on application by the Commission under section 99, that a merger contravenes the merger rule, it may make any order it considers appropriate for the purpose of bringing the contravention to an end.

(2)   An order made under subsection (1) may contain anything permitted by Schedule 4.

Division 5

Disqualification Orders

101.   Disqualification order

(1)   In the circumstances specified in section 102, the Tribunal may, on application by the Commission, make a disqualification order against a person.

(2)   A disqualification order is an order that a person may not, without the leave of the Tribunal—

(a) be, or continue to be, a director of a company;

(b) be a liquidator or provisional liquidator of a company;

(c) be a receiver or manager of a company's property; or

(d) in any way, whether directly or indirectly, be concerned or take part in the promotion, formation or management of a company,

for a specified period, not exceeding 5 years, beginning with the date of the order.

(3)   In this section—

"specified" means specified in the disqualification order.

102.   Circumstances in which disqualification order may be made

The Tribunal may only make a disqualification order against a person if both of the following conditions are satisfied in relation to that person—

(a) it has determined that a company of which the person is a director has contravened a competition rule; and

(b) it considers that the person's conduct as a director makes the person unfit to be concerned in the management of a company.

103.   Unfitness to be concerned in management of company

(1)   For the purpose of deciding under section 102(b) whether a person is unfit to be concerned in the management of a company, the Tribunal—

(a) must have regard to whether subsection (2) applies to the person; and

(b) may have regard to the conduct of the person as the director of a company, in connection with any other contravention of a competition rule.

(2) This subsection applies to a person if as a director of the company—

(a) the person's conduct contributed to the contravention of the competition rule;

(b) the conduct of the person did not contribute to the contravention, but the person had reasonable grounds to suspect that the conduct of the company constituted the contravention and took no steps to prevent it; or

(c) the person did not know but ought to have known that the conduct of the company constituted the contravention.

104.   Applications for disqualification order and for leave under an order

(1)   An application for a disqualification order may be made only by the Commission.

(2)   An application for leave of the Tribunal to participate in the affairs of a
        company in one of the ways prohibited under section 101(2) (Disqualification
        order) may be made only by or on behalf of the person against whom the
        order was made.

105.   Contravention of disqualification order
        A person who contravenes a disqualification order commits an offence and is
        liable—
        (a) on conviction on indictment, to a fine of $1000000 and to imprisonment
            for 2 years; or
        (b) on summary conviction, to a fine at level 6 and to imprisonment for 6
            months.

Part 7

Private Actions

Division 1

General

106.   Interpretation
        In this Part—
            "follow-on action" means an action brought by a person who has a right to
            bring the action under section 110(1).

107.   Persons involved in contravention of conduct rule
        A reference in this Part to a person being involved in a contravention of a
        conduct rule means a person who—
        (a) attempts to contravene the rule;
        (b) aids, abets, counsels or procures any other person to contravene the rule;
        (c) induces or attempts to induce any other person, whether by threats or
            promises or otherwise, to contravene the rule;
        (d) is in any way, directly or indirectly, knowingly concerned in or a party to
            the contravention of the rule; or
        (e) conspires with any person to contravene the rule.

108.   No proceedings independent of this Ordinance
        No person may bring any proceedings independently of this Ordinance,
        whether under any rule of law or any enactment, in any court in Hong Kong,
        if—
        (a) the cause of action is the defendant's contravention, or involvement in a
            contravention, of a conduct rule; or
        (b) the proceedings are founded on more than one cause of action and any of
            the causes of action is the defendant's contravention, or involvement in a
            contravention, of a conduct rule.

109. Pure competition proceedings not to be brought in Court of First Instance

No person may bring any proceedings in the Court of First Instance under this Part if the cause of action is only the defendant's contravention, or involvement in a contravention, of a conduct rule.

Division 2

Follow-on Action

110. Follow-on right of action

(1)   A person who has suffered loss or damage as a result of any act that has been determined to be a contravention of a conduct rule has a right of action under this section against—

(a) any person who has contravened or is contravening the rule; and

(b) any person who is, or has been, involved in that contravention.

(2)   Subject to section 113, a claim to which this section applies may only be made in proceedings brought in the Tribunal, whether or not the cause of action is solely the defendant's contravention, or involvement in a contravention, of a conduct rule.

(3) For the purpose of subsection (1), an act is taken to have been determined to be a contravention of a conduct rule if—

(a) the Tribunal has made a decision that the act is a contravention of a conduct rule;

(b) the Court of First Instance has decided, in any proceedings transferred to it by the Tribunal under section 114(3), that the act is a contravention of a conduct rule;

(c) the Court of Appeal has decided, on an appeal from a decision of the Tribunal or the Court of First Instance, that the act is a contravention of a conduct rule;

(d) the Court of Final Appeal has decided, on an appeal from a decision of the Court of Appeal, that the act is a contravention of a conduct rule; or

(e) a person has made an admission, in a commitment that has been accepted by the Commission, that the person has contravened a conduct rule.

111. Commencement of follow-on actions

(1)   The periods during which proceedings for a follow-on action may not be brought are—

(a) in the case of a decision of the Tribunal, the period during which an appeal may be made to the Court of Appeal under section 154;

(b) in the case of a decision of the Court of First Instance, the period during which an appeal may be made to the Court of Appeal; and

(c) in the case of a decision of the Court of Appeal, the period during which a further appeal may be made to the Court of Final Appeal,

and, where any such appeal or further appeal is made, the period specified in paragraph (a), (b) or (c) includes the period before the appeal is determined.

(2)   Despite subsection (1), the Court of First Instance or the Tribunal may, on the application of the party seeking to bring the proceedings, permit proceedings for a follow-on action to be brought   within any period specified in subsection (1).

(3)   Proceedings for a follow-on action may not be brought more than 3 years after the earliest date on which the action could have been commenced following the expiry of a relevant period specified in subsection (1).

112.   Tribunal orders in follow-on actions

The Tribunal in a follow-on action may make any one or more of the orders specified in Schedule 3.

Division 3

Procedure

113.   Transfer of proceedings from Court of First Instance to Tribunal

(1)   Subject to subsection (2), the Court of First Instance must transfer to the Tribunal so much of the proceedings before the Court that are within the jurisdiction of the Tribunal.

(2)   Subsection (1) does not apply to any proceedings that—
    (a) are within the jurisdiction of the Tribunal under section 142(1)(g); and
    (b) the Court of First Instance considers should not, in the interests of justice, be transferred to the Tribunal.

(3)   Without limiting subsection (1) but subject to section 115(2), if, in any proceedings before the Court of First Instance, a contravention, or involvement in a contravention, of a conduct rule is alleged as a defence, the Court must, in respect of the allegation, transfer to the Tribunal so much of those proceedings that are within the jurisdiction of the Tribunal.

(4)   The practice and procedure of the Tribunal apply to the proceedings transferred by the Court of First Instance under subsection (1) or (3).

114.   Transfer of proceedings from Tribunal to Court of First Instance

(1)   The Tribunal must transfer to the Court of First Instance so much of the proceedings brought in the Tribunal that are within the jurisdiction of the Court but are not within the jurisdiction of the Tribunal.

(2)   Subject to subsection (1), the Tribunal may transfer to the Court of First Instance any proceedings brought in the Tribunal but only if—
    (a) those proceedings are within the jurisdiction of the Tribunal under section 142(1)(g); and
    (b) the Tribunal considers that those proceedings should, in the interests of justice, be transferred to the Court.

(3)   If the Court of First Instance transfers any proceedings to the Tribunal under section 113(3), the Tribunal may transfer back to the Court so much of those proceedings that the Tribunal considers should, in the interests of justice, be transferred back to the Court.

(4)   The practice and procedure of the Court of First Instance apply to the proceedings transferred by the Tribunal under subsection (1), (2) or (3).

115. **No further transfer of proceedings from Court of First Instance to Tribunal**

(1)   If the Tribunal transfers any proceedings to the Court of First Instance under section 114(2), the Court must not transfer back those proceedings to the Tribunal.

(2)   If the Tribunal transfers any proceedings to the Court of First Instance under section 114(3)—

(a) section 113(3) does not apply to those proceedings; and

(b) the Court must not transfer back those proceedings to the Tribunal.

116. **No further transfer of proceedings from Tribunal to Court of First Instance**

If the Court of First Instance transfers any proceedings to the Tribunal under section 113(1), the Tribunal must not transfer back those proceedings to the Court.

117. **Costs in transferred proceedings**

(1)   If the Court of First Instance makes an order transferring proceedings to the Tribunal under section 113, it may make an order for costs prior to the transfer and of the transfer.

(2)   If the Tribunal makes an order transferring proceedings to the Court of First Instance under section 114, it may make an order for costs prior to the transfer and of the transfer.

118. **Reference by Court of First Instance or Tribunal to Commission for investigation**

(1)   In any proceedings before the Court of First Instance or the Tribunal in which a contravention, or involvement in a contravention, of a conduct rule is alleged, the Court or the Tribunal may, either of its own motion or on application by a party to the proceedings, refer the alleged contravention or alleged involvement to the Commission for investigation under this Ordinance.

(2)   Where the Court of First Instance or the Tribunal has referred an alleged contravention, or alleged involvement in a contravention, of a conduct rule to the Commission for investigation, it may stay the proceedings before it pending—

(a) in the case of a referral by the Tribunal, the completion of the Commission's investigation; or

(b) in the case of a referral by the Court, the completion of the Commission's investigation and any subsequent proceedings in the Tribunal brought as a result of the investigation.

119. **Findings of contravention of conduct rules**

(1)   This section applies to proceedings under this Part before the Court of First Instance or the Tribunal in which a contravention, or involvement in a contravention, of a conduct rule is alleged in relation to a particular act.

(2)   Subject to subsection (3), in such proceedings the Court of First Instance or the Tribunal (as the case requires) is bound by an earlier decision of the Court

or Tribunal that the act in question is a contravention, or involvement in a contravention, of the conduct rule.

(3)   Subsection (2) does not apply in relation to a decision of the Court of First Instance or the Tribunal until the period specified in subsection (4) has expired.

(4)   The period mentioned in subsection (3) is—

(a) the period during which an appeal may be made to the Court of Appeal under section 154; and

(b) where an appeal has been made to the Court of Appeal, the period during which a further appeal may be made to the Court of Final Appeal,

and, where such an appeal or further appeal is made, the period specified in paragraph (a) or (b) includes the period before the appeal is determined.

120. Intervention by Commission

(1)   This section applies to proceedings involving an alleged contravention, or alleged involvement in a contravention, of a conduct rule, before the specified Court or the Tribunal, that are brought by a person other than the Commission.

(2)   The Commission may, with the leave of the specified Court or the Tribunal, and subject to any conditions imposed by the specified Court or the Tribunal, intervene in any such proceedings.

(3)   An application for leave under this section must be made in the prescribed form and must be served by the Commission on each party to the proceedings.

(4)   If the Commission intervenes in proceedings under this section, the Commission becomes, as from the date of the grant of leave, a party to the proceedings and has all the rights, duties and liabilities of a party to the proceedings.

(5)   In this section—

"specified Court" means—

(a) the Court of Final Appeal;

(b) the Court of Appeal; or

(c) the Court of First Instance.

121. Commission may participate in proceedings

(1)   The Commission may, with the leave of or at the invitation of the specified Court or the Tribunal (as the case requires), participate in proceedings before the specified Court or the Tribunal involving an alleged contravention, or alleged involvement in a contravention, of a conduct rule that have been brought by another person and, in particular may—

(a) make written submissions to the specified Court or the Tribunal; or

(b) apply for, or join an application for, the adjournment of the proceedings pending the completion of the Commission's investigation into the alleged contravention or involvement that is in issue in the proceedings.

(2)   In this section—

"specified Court" means—

(a) the Court of Final Appeal;

(b) the Court of Appeal; or

(c) the Court of First Instance.

Part 8

Disclosure of Information

122. Interpretation

In this Part—

"employee" means a person engaged for the provision of services, whether under a contract of employment or otherwise;

"specified person" means—

(a) the Commission;

(b) any person who is or was a member, employee or agent of the Commission;

(c) any person who is or was a member of a committee of the Commission, established under section 28 of Schedule 5;

(d) the Communications Authority;

(e) any person who is or was a member of the Communications Authority;

(f) any person who is or was a member of a committee of the Communications Authority, appointed under section 17 of the Communications Authority Ordinance (Cap 616);

(g) any person who is or was a public officer serving in the Office of the Communications Authority;

(h) any person who is or was an employee or agent of the Office of the Communications Authority; or

(i) any person appointed to assist any person referred to in paragraphs (a), (b), (c), (d), (e), (f), (g) and (h) in the exercise of the powers of the Commission under Part 3.

123. Confidential information

(1)   In this Part—

"confidential information" means—

(a) information that has been provided to or obtained by the Commission in the course of, or in connection with, the performance of its functions under this Ordinance, that relates to—

(i) the private affairs of a natural person;

(ii) the commercial activities of any person that are of a confidential nature; or

(iii) the identity of any person who has given information to the Commission;

(b) information that has been given to the Commission on terms that or in circumstances that require it to be held in confidence; or

(c) information given to the Commission that has been identified as confidential information in accordance with subsection (2).

(2)   If a person—

(a) identifies information that the person has given to the Commission as confidential; and

(b) provides a statement in writing setting out the reasons why, in that person's opinion, the information is confidential, the information is also to be regarded as confidential information under this Part.

124. Duty to establish and maintain safeguards

(1)   The Commission and the Communications Authority must establish and maintain adequate procedural safeguards to prevent the unauthorized disclosure of confidential information.

(2)   In this section—

"unauthorized disclosure" means disclosure that is either prohibited or not authorized by or under this Ordinance.

125. Preservation of confidentiality

(1)   A specified person—

(a) must preserve and aid in preserving the confidentiality of any confidential information;

(b) must not disclose confidential information to any other person; and

(c) must not suffer or permit any other person to have access to confidential information.

(2)   Subsection (1) does not apply to the disclosure of confidential information with lawful authority within the meaning of section 126.

(3)   A specified person who contravenes subsection (1) commits an offence and is liable—

(a) on conviction on indictment, to a fine of $1000000 and to imprisonment for 2 years; or

(b) on summary conviction, to a fine at level 6 and to imprisonment for 6 months.

(4)   It is a defence for a person charged with an offence under this section to show that at the time of the alleged offence the defendant—

(a) believed that there was lawful authority for the disclosure of the information concerned and the defendant had no reasonable cause to believe otherwise; or

(b) did not know and had no reasonable cause to believe that the information disclosed was confidential information.

126. Disclosure with lawful authority

(1)   Disclosure of confidential information is to be regarded as made with lawful authority if the disclosure is made—

(a) subject to section 127, with the required consent, as specified in subsection (2);

(b) subject to subsection (3), in the performance of any function of the Commission or in carrying into effect or doing anything authorized by this Ordinance;

(c) in accordance with an order of the Tribunal or any other court or in accordance with a law or a requirement made by or under a law;

(d) in connection with judicial proceedings arising under this Ordinance;

(e) for the purpose of obtaining advice from counsel, a solicitor or other professional adviser acting or proposing to act in a professional capacity in connection with any matter arising under this Ordinance;

(f) with a view to the bringing of, or otherwise for the purposes of, any criminal proceedings, or any investigation carried out under the laws of Hong Kong, in Hong Kong;

(g) with respect to information that has already been lawfully disclosed to the public on an earlier occasion; or

(h) by one competition authority to another.

(2) The consent required for the purposes of subsection (1)(a) is—

(a) if the information was obtained from a person who had the information lawfully and the Commission knows the identity of that person, the consent of that person;

(b) if the information relates to the affairs of a natural person, the consent of that person;

(c) if the information relates to the activities of an undertaking, the consent of that undertaking,

and that consent may be given—

(i) if the undertaking is a company, by a director or company secretary of the company;

(ii) if the undertaking is a partnership, by a partner; or

(iii) if the undertaking is an unincorporated body (other than a partnership), by a person concerned in the management or control of the body.

(3) In deciding whether or not to disclose confidential information, where disclosure is lawful under subsection (1)(b), the specified person must consider and have regard to—

(a) the need to exclude as far as is practical, from such disclosure—

(i) information the disclosure of which would, in the opinion of the specified person, be contrary to public interest;

(ii) commercial information the disclosure of which would or might be likely to, in the opinion of the specified person, significantly harm the legitimate business interests of the person to whom it relates; and

(iii) information relating to the private affairs of a natural person, the disclosure of which might (in the opinion of the specified person) significantly harm the interest of that person; and

(b) the extent to which the disclosure is necessary for the purpose sought to be achieved by the disclosure.

127. Notice of proposed disclosure

(1) If the disclosure of confidential information is lawful by virtue of section 126(1)(a), a specified person must, before disclosing any such information—

(a) give notice of the proposed disclosure to—

(i) the person who provided the information to the Commission; and

(ii) any person who is, in the opinion of the specified person, likely to be affected by the disclosure; and

(b) consider any representations that are made about the proposed disclosure.

(2) A notice under subsection (1) must—

(a) give a description of the information (having due regard to the requirements of confidentiality) that the specified person proposes to disclose;

(b) state the reasons why the disclosure is proposed;

(c) identify the person to whom it is proposed to disclose the information; and

(d) state any other facts that the specified person considers relevant to the question of the proposed disclosure.

(3) A notice under this section must specify the period within which representations may be made about the proposed disclosure.

(4) The period specified for the purpose of subsection (3) must be a period of at least 30 days beginning after the day on which the notice is given.

128. Obligation of third party not to disclose confidential information

(1) A person, other than a specified person, who—

(a) has received confidential information from the Commission; or

(b) has otherwise, directly or indirectly, received such information from a specified person, must not disclose that information to any other person or suffer or permit any other person to have access to that information.

(2) Subsection (1) does not apply to the disclosure of information where—

(a) the Commission has consented to the disclosure;

(b) the information has already been lawfully disclosed to the public on an earlier occasion;

(c) the disclosure is for the purpose of obtaining advice from counsel, a solicitor or other professional adviser, acting or proposing to act in a professional capacity in connection with any matter arising under this Ordinance;

(d) the disclosure is made in connection with any judicial proceedings arising under this Ordinance; or

(e) the disclosure is made in accordance with an order of the Tribunal or any other court or in accordance with a law or a requirement made by or under a law.

(3) A person who contravenes subsection (1) commits an offence and is liable—

(a) on conviction on indictment, to a fine of $1000000 and to imprisonment for 2 years; or

(b) on summary conviction, to a fine at level 6 and to imprisonment for 6 months.

Part 9

Competition Commission

Division 1

Establishment, Functions and Powers

129. Establishment of Commission
(1)   There is established, by virtue of this section, a body to be known as the Competition Commission.
(2)   The Commission is a body corporate and may—
         (a) acquire, hold and dispose of movable and immovable property;
         (b) sue and be sued in its own name; and
         (c) so far as is possible for a body corporate, exercise all the rights and powers, enjoy all the privileges and incur all the liabilities of a natural person of full age and capacity.
(3) Schedule 5 (which contains constitutional, administrative and financial provisions) has effect with respect to the Commission.

130. Functions of Commission
         The Commission has the following functions—
         (a) to investigate conduct that may contravene the competition rules and enforce the provisions of this Ordinance;
         (b) to promote public understanding of the value of competition and how this Ordinance promotes competition;
         (c) to promote the adoption by undertakings carrying on business in Hong Kong of appropriate internal controls and risk management systems, to ensure their compliance with this Ordinance;
         (d) to advise the Government on competition matters in Hong Kong and outside Hong Kong;
         (e) to conduct market studies into matters affecting competition in markets in Hong Kong; and
         (f) to promote research into and the development of skills in relation to the legal, economic and policy aspects of competition law in Hong Kong.

131. Powers of Commission
(1)   The Commission may do all such things as appear to it to be necessary, advantageous or expedient for it to do for, or in connection with, the performance of its functions.
(2)   Without limiting the scope of subsection (1), the Commission may—
         (a) make, give effect to, assign or accept the assignment of, vary or rescind any agreement;
         (b) receive and spend money;
         (c) with the approval of the Financial Secretary, borrow money;
         (d) invest funds of the Commission that are not immediately required, in a manner approved by the Financial Secretary;

(e) with the approval of the Chief Executive, become a member or affiliate of any international body, whose functions or objects include the promotion of competition or competition law.

Division 2

Relationship to Government

132. Commission not servant or agent of Government

The Commission is not a servant or agent of the Government and does not enjoy any status, immunity or privilege of the Government.

133. Personal immunity of members of Commission etc.

(1) A person to whom this subsection applies is not personally liable for anything done or omitted to be done by the person in good faith in the performance or purported performance of any function of the Commission under this Ordinance.

(2) The persons to whom subsection (1) applies are—

(a) members of the Commission;

(b) any person who is an officer or employee of the Commission;

(c) any person who is a member of any committee of the Commission; and

(d) any person who is performing any service for the Commission under a contract of services.

(3) The protection conferred by subsection (1) does not affect any liability of the Commission for the act or omission.

Part 10

Competition Tribunal

Division 1

Constitution

134. Establishment of Tribunal

(1) There is established, by virtue of this section, a tribunal to be known as the Competition Tribunal.

(2) The Tribunal is a superior court of record.

135. Constitution of Tribunal

(1) The Tribunal consists of the judges of the Court of First Instance appointed in accordance with section 6 of the High Court Ordinance (Cap 4), by virtue of their appointments as such judges.

(2) A Justice of Appeal who sits in the Court of First Instance is not a member of the Tribunal.

Subdivision 1

President and Deputy President

136. President

(1) The Chief Executive, acting in accordance with the recommendation of the Judicial Officers Recommendation Commission, is to appoint one of the members of the Tribunal to be the President of the Tribunal.

(2) The President is to hold office for a term of at least 3 years, but not more than 5 years, as is stated in his or her letter of appointment, but is eligible for re-appointment.

(3) The President may give directions as to the arrangement of the business of the Tribunal, and is to perform such other functions as are assigned to the President under this Ordinance.

137. Deputy President

(1) The Chief Executive, acting in accordance with the recommendation of the Judicial Officers Recommendation Commission, is to appoint one of the members of the Tribunal to be the Deputy President of the Tribunal.

(2) The Deputy President is to hold office for a term of at least 3 years, but not more than 5 years, as is stated in his or her letter of appointment, but is eligible for re-appointment.

(3) The Deputy President may, subject to any directions given by the President, perform all the functions of the President.

(4) Every decision or other act or omission of the Deputy President while acting under subsection (3) is to be regarded as a decision, act or omission of the President.

138. Acting President

(1) If for any reason the President is unable, whether temporarily or otherwise, to perform the functions of the President, the Deputy President may act as President.

(2) If for any reason the Deputy President is unable, whether temporarily or otherwise, to perform the functions of the President when the President is unable to perform them himself or herself, the Chief Justice may appoint another member of the Tribunal to act as President.

(3) A person acting as President under this section may perform all the functions of the President.

(4) Every decision or other act or omission of a person acting as President under this section is to be regarded as the decision, act or omission of the President.

(5) The Chief Justice may at any time revoke an appointment made under subsection (2).

139. Resignation as President or Deputy President

(1) The President and Deputy President may, at any time, resign from their office by giving written notice of resignation to the Chief Executive.

(2) If the President or Deputy President resigns from office under this section, he or she continues to be a member of the Tribunal.

140. Vacancy in office of President or Deputy President

(1) The office of President or Deputy President becomes vacant if the President or Deputy President (as the case may be)—

    (a) dies;

    (b) ceases to be a judge of the Court of First Instance;

    (c) is appointed to be a Justice of Appeal, or to a higher judicial office; or

    (d) resigns his or her office under section 139.

(2) If the office of President or Deputy President has become vacant, the Chief Executive, acting in accordance with the recommendation of the Judicial Officers Recommendation Commission, is to appoint one of the members of the Tribunal to be the President or Deputy President (as the case requires).

(3) The President or Deputy President appointed under this section is to hold office for a term of at least 3 years, but not more than 5 years, as is stated in his or her letter of appointment, but is eligible for re-appointment.

Subdivision 2

Assessors

141. Assessors

(1) In any proceedings under this Ordinance, the Tribunal may appoint one or more specially qualified assessors and may dispose of the proceedings, wholly or in part, with the assistance of such assessor or assessors, but the decision of the Tribunal is that of the members of Tribunal only.

(2) The Tribunal may determine the remuneration, if any, to be paid to an assessor appointed under this section, but no remuneration may be paid to an assessor who is a public officer.

(3) An assessor is not personally liable for anything done or omitted to be done by the assessor in good faith in the performance of his or her functions or purported performance of his or her functions under this Ordinance.

Division 2

Jurisdiction and Powers

142. Jurisdiction of Tribunal

(1) The Tribunal has jurisdiction to hear and determine—

    (a) applications made by the Commission with regard to alleged contraventions, or alleged involvements I contraventions, of the competition rules;

    (b) applications for the review of reviewable determinations;

    (c) private actions in respect of contraventions, or involvements in contraventions, of the conduct rules;

    (d) allegations of contraventions, or involvements in contraventions, of the conduct rules raised as a defence;

(e) applications for the disposal of property;

(f) applications for the enforcement of commitments; and

(g) any matter related to a matter referred to in paragraph (a), (b), (c), (d), (e) or (f) if the matters arise out o the same or substantially the same facts.

(2) In the exercise of its jurisdiction, the Tribunal has the same jurisdiction to grant remedies and reliefs, equitable or legal, as the Court of First Instance.

143. Powers of Tribunal

(1) The Tribunal has, with respect to—

(a) the attendance, swearing and examination of witnesses;

(b) the production and inspection of documents;

(c) the enforcement of its orders; and

(d) all other matters necessary for the exercise of its jurisdiction,

all the powers, rights and privileges of the Court of First Instance. (Amended 15 of 2014 s. 3)

(2) Without limiting the scope of subsection (1), in proceedings before the Tribunal, the Tribunal may—

(a) receive and consider any evidence, whether by way of oral evidence, written statements, documents or otherwise, and whether or not it would otherwise be admissible in a court of law;

(b) determine the manner in which it will receive evidence referred to in paragraph (a);

(c) by notice in writing, signed by the presiding member of the Tribunal, summon any person—

(i) to produce any article or document that is relevant to the proceedings and is in that person's possession or under that person's control;

(ii) to appear before it and to give any evidence relevant to the proceedings; and

(c) exercise such other powers as may be necessary or ancillary to the conduct of any proceedings.

Division 3

Practice and Procedure

144. Procedures

(1) The Tribunal may decide its own procedures and may, in so far as it thinks fit, follow the practice and procedure of the Court of First Instance in the exercise of its civil jurisdiction, and for this purpose, has the same jurisdiction, powers and duties of the Court in respect of such practice and procedure, including the jurisdiction, powers and duties of the Court in respect of costs.

(2) Without limiting subsection (1), the Tribunal has the same jurisdiction, powers and duties of the Court of First Instance in respect of the punishment of a person guilty of contempt.

(3) The Tribunal is to conduct its proceedings with as much informality as is consistent with attaining justice.

145. Hearing and determination of applications

(1)   An application to the Tribunal may be heard and determined by a Tribunal constituted by any of the following—

(a) the President;

(b) the President and one or more other members appointed by the President; or

(c) one or more other members appointed by the President.

(2)   If the President is sitting with one or more other members, the President is to preside over the hearing; if the President is not sitting and there is more than one other member sitting, the President is to appoint one of those other members to preside over the sitting.

(3)   Any difference between the members exercising the jurisdiction of the Tribunal is to be decided by majority vote and, in the event of an equality of votes, the member presiding is to have a second or casting vote.

146. Absence of member during course of proceedings

(1)   If, after the commencement of any proceedings, a member of the Tribunal, other than the presiding member, is absent for any reason, the presiding member may, with the consent of the parties—

(a) direct that the proceedings be continued in the absence of that member; or

(b) direct that another specified member take the place of the absent member in the proceedings.

(2)   If, after the commencement of proceedings, the presiding member of the Tribunal is absent for any reason, then—

(a) if there is only one member of the Tribunal remaining, and the parties agree, the proceedings may be continued in the absence of the presiding member; or

(b) if there is more than one member of the Tribunal remaining, and the parties agree—

(i) the proceedings may be continued in the absence of the presiding member; and

(ii) the most senior of the remaining members is to preside, with seniority determined according to the priority of their appointments as judges of the Court of First Instance.

(3)   If—

(a) the presiding member has given a direction under subsection (1); or

(b) the members and parties have agreed to proceed under subsection (2),

the Tribunal as so constituted is to be regarded as properly constituted.

147. Rules of evidence

In proceedings under this Ordinance, other than proceedings in which the Commission applies for an order for—

(a) a pecuniary penalty under section 93; or

(b) a financial penalty under section 169,

the Tribunal is not bound by the rules of evidence and may receive and take into account any relevant evidence or information, whether or not it would be otherwise admissible in a court of law.

148. Evidence that might tend to incriminate

(1) A person appearing before the Tribunal to give evidence, other than in proceedings in which the Commission applies for an order for—

(a) a pecuniary penalty under section 93; or

(b) a financial penalty under section 169,

is not excused from answering any question on the grounds that to do so might expose the person to proceedings referred to in subsection (3).

(2) No statement or admission made by a person answering any question put to the person, in any proceedings to which subsection (1) applies, is admissible in evidence against that person in proceedings referred to in subsection (3).

(3) The proceedings referred to in subsections (1) and (2) are—

(a) proceedings in which the Commission applies for an order for—

(i) a pecuniary penalty under section 93; or

(ii) a financial penalty under section 169; and

(b) any criminal proceedings, other than proceedings for—

(i) an offence under section 55 (Providing false or misleading documents or information);

(ii) an offence under Part V (Perjury) of the Crimes Ordinance (Cap 200); or

(iii) an offence of perjury.

149. Findings of fact by Tribunal

(1) A finding of fact by the Tribunal, which is relevant to an issue arising in any other proceedings, either in the Tribunal or in the Court of First Instance, relating to a contravention of a conduct rule, is evidence of that fact in those proceedings if—

(a) the time for bringing an appeal in respect of the finding has expired and the relevant party has not brought such an appeal; or

(b) the final decision of a court on such appeal has confirmed the finding.

(2) In this section—

"relevant party" means—

(a) in relation to the first conduct rule, a party to the agreement which is the subject of the alleged contravention; and

(b) in relation to the second conduct rule, the undertaking whose conduct is alleged to have contravened the conduct rule or any other person involved in the contravention.

150. Findings of fact by Court of First Instance

(1) A finding of any fact by the Court of First Instance in any proceedings transferred to it by the Tribunal under section 114(3), which is relevant to an issue arising in any other proceedings, either in the Court or in the Tribunal, relating to a contravention, or involvement in a contravention, of a conduct rule, is evidence of that fact in those other proceedings if—

(a) the time for bringing an appeal in respect of the finding has expired and the relevant party has not brought such an appeal; or

(b) the final decision of a court on such appeal has confirmed the finding.

(2) In this section—

"relevant party" has the meaning given by section 149(2).

151A Order prohibiting departure from Hong Kong

(1)   The Tribunal may make an order prohibiting a person from leaving Hong Kong (prohibition order)—

   (a) to facilitate the enforcement or to secure the compliance of—

   (i) a judgment or order against the person for the payment of a specified sum of money;

   (ii) a judgment or order against the person for the payment of an amount to be assessed; or

   (iii) a judgment or order against the person requiring the person to deliver any property or perform any other act; or

   (b) to facilitate the pursuance of a civil claim (other than a judgment)—

   (i) for the payment of money or damages; or

   (ii) for the delivery of any property or the performance of any other act.

(2)   The Tribunal must not make a prohibition order against a person under subsection (1)(a)(ii) or (iii) unless it is satisfied that there is probable cause for believing that—

   (a) the person is about to leave Hong Kong; and

   (b) because of the circumstance mentioned in paragraph (a), satisfaction of the judgment or order concerned is likely to be obstructed or delayed.

(3)   The Tribunal must not make a prohibition order against a person under subsection (1)(b) unless it is satisfied that there is probable cause for believing that—

   (a) there is a good cause of action;

   (b) the person—

   (i) incurred the alleged liability, being the subject of the claim, in Hong Kong while the person was present in Hong Kong;

   (ii) carries on business in Hong Kong; or

   (iii) is ordinarily resident in Hong Kong;

   (c) the person is about to leave Hong Kong; and

   (d) because of the circumstance mentioned in paragraph (c), any judgment or order that may be given against the person is likely to be obstructed or delayed.

(4)   The Tribunal may make a prohibition order against a person subject to any conditions that it thinks fit, including the condition that the prohibition order is to have no effect if the person—

   (a) satisfies the judgment, order or claim concerned; or

   (b) provides the security that the Tribunal orders.

(5)   A person on whose application a prohibition order is made must serve a copy of the prohibition order and a copy of any other order ancillary to the prohibition order on—

   (a) the Director of Immigration;

   (b) the Commissioner of Police; and

   (c) the person against whom the prohibition order is made, if the person can be found.

(6)   In this section—

   "Tribunal" includes the Registrar of the Tribunal.

151B Duration and discharge of prohibition order

(1) A prohibition order is valid for 1 month beginning on the date of the prohibition order unless extended or renewed under this section.

(2) The Tribunal may, on application by a person on whose application a prohibition order is made, extend the prohibition order for a period that, in combination with the initial period and any other period of extension, does not exceed 3 months.

(3) The Tribunal may, on application by a person on whose application a prohibition order is made, renew the prohibition order.

(4) A renewed prohibition order is valid for 1 month beginning on the date of renewal and may be extended under subsection (2).

(5) A reference to the initial period in subsection (2) is a reference to the period of 1 month mentioned in subsection (1) or (4).

(6) A person on whose application a prohibition order is made must, as soon as reasonably possible after the prohibition order is no longer required—
    (a) serve on the Director of Immigration a notice stating that fact; and
    (b) file with the Registrar of the Tribunal a copy of the notice mentioned in paragraph (a).

(7) If the notice under subsection (6) is served and the copy of the notice under that subsection is filed on the same date, the prohibition order ceases to have effect on that date, but if the notice is served and the copy of the notice is filed on different dates, the prohibition order ceases to have effect on the later of those dates.

(8) The Tribunal may, on application, discharge a prohibition order, either absolutely or subject to any conditions that it thinks fit.

(9) In this section—
    "prohibition order" means an order made under section 151A;
    "Tribunal" includes the Registrar of the Tribunal.

151C Contravention of prohibition order

(1) If—
    (a) the Tribunal makes a prohibition order against a person; and
    (b) the person, having been served with a copy of the prohibition order or otherwise informed of its existence and effect, attempts to leave Hong Kong in contravention of the prohibition order,
    the person may be arrested by an immigration officer, a police officer or a bailiff of the Tribunal.

(2) A person arrested under subsection (1) must be brought before the Tribunal before the expiry of the day after the day of arrest, and the Tribunal may—
    (a) make an order discharging the person from arrest, either absolutely or subject to any conditions that it thinks fit; or
    (b) either—
        (i) if the prohibition order is made under section 151A(1)(a)(i), make an order for the examination or imprisonment of the person, under the rules of the Tribunal made under section 158, that the Tribunal considers appropriate; or
        (ii) if the prohibition order is made under section 151A(1)(a)(ii) or (iii) or (b), make an order for the imprisonment of the person until the prohibition order ceases to have effect or is discharged.

(3)   Section 71 of the Interpretation and General Clauses Ordinance (Cap 1) does not apply to subsection (2).

(4)   The Director of Immigration is not liable for any failure to prevent a person against whom a prohibition order is made from leaving Hong Kong.

(5)   In this section—

"prohibition order" means an order made under section 151A;

"Tribunal" includes the Registrar of the Tribunal.

152.   Decisions of Tribunal

(1)   A decision of the Tribunal must be recorded in writing.

(2)   Where it is appropriate to give reasons for a decision, the decision may be made initially without giving reasons but, if this is done, the reasons must be recorded in writing.

153.   Orders of Tribunal

An order made by the Tribunal must be recorded in writing.

153A. Interest on debts and damages

(1)   In proceedings (whenever instituted) before the Tribunal for the recovery of a debt or damages, the Tribunal may include in a sum for which judgment is given simple interest on—

(a) all or a part of the sum for which judgment is given; or

(b) all or a part of a sum in respect of which payment is made before judgment.

(2)   Interest under subsection (1) may be awarded—

(a) for the sum for which judgment is given, for all or a part of the period beginning on the date when the cause of action arose and ending on the date of the judgment; and

(b) for a sum in respect of which payment is made before judgment, for all or a part of the period beginning on the date when the cause of action arose and ending on the date of the payment.

(3)   In proceedings (whenever instituted) before the Tribunal for the recovery of a debt, if the person from whom the debt is sought (defendant) pays the whole debt to the person seeking the debt (plaintiff) otherwise than in compliance with a judgment in the proceedings, the defendant is liable to pay the plaintiff simple interest on all or a part of the debt for all or a part of the period beginning on the date when the cause of action arose and ending on the date of the payment.

(4)   Interest under this section is to be calculated at a rate that the Tribunal thinks fit.

(5)   Interest in respect of a debt may not be awarded under this section for a period during which, for whatever reason, interest on the debt already runs.

(6)   Interest under this section may be calculated at different rates for different periods.

(7)   Subsections (1), (2) and (3) are subject to the rules of the Tribunal made under section 158.

153B. Interest on judgment debts

(1)   A judgment debt is to carry simple interest—

(a) at the rate that the Tribunal specifies by order; or

(b) in the absence of such an order, at the rate that the Chief Justice from time to time determines by order, on the total amount of the judgment debt, or on the part of the judgment debt that for the time being remains unpaid, from the date of the judgment until payment.

(2) Interest under this section may be calculated at different rates for different periods.

154. Appeal to Court of Appeal

(1) Subject to subsection (2) and section 155, an appeal lies as of right to the Court of Appeal against any decision (including a decision as to the amount of any compensatory sanction or pecuniary penalty), determination or order of the Tribunal made under this Ordinance.

(2) An appeal does not lie—

(a) against an order of the Tribunal allowing an extension of time for appealing against a decision, determination or order of the Tribunal;

(b) against a decision, determination or order of the Tribunal if it is provided by any Ordinance or by the rules of the Tribunal made under section 158 that the decision, determination or order is final; or

(c) without the leave of the Court of Appeal or the Tribunal, against an order of the Tribunal made with the consent of the parties or relating only to costs that are left to the discretion of the Tribunal.

(3) Rules of the Tribunal made under section 158 may provide for decisions, determinations or orders of any prescribed description to be treated for any prescribed purpose connected with appeals to the Court of Appeal as final or interlocutory.

(4) An appeal does not lie against a decision of the Court of Appeal as to whether a decision, determination or order of the Tribunal is, for any purpose connected with an appeal to the Court, final or interlocutory.

(5) The Court of Appeal has jurisdiction to hear and determine an appeal under subsection (1) and may—

(a) confirm, set aside or vary the decision, determination or order of the Tribunal;

(b) where the decision, determination or order of the Tribunal is set aside, substitute any other decision, determination or order it considers appropriate; or

(c) remit the matter in question to the Tribunal for reconsideration in the light of the decision of the Court.

(6) Except in the case of an appeal against the imposition, or the amount, of a pecuniary penalty, the making of an appeal under this section does not suspend the effect of the decision, determination or order to which the appeal relates.

155. Leave to appeal required for interlocutory appeals

(1) Except as provided by the rules of the Tribunal made under section 158, an appeal does not lie to the Court of Appeal against any interlocutory decision, determination or order of the Tribunal unless leave to appeal has been granted by the Court of Appeal or the Tribunal.

(2)   Rules of the Tribunal made under section 158 may specify an interlocutory decision, determination or order of any prescribed description as being an interlocutory decision, determination or order to which subsection (1) does not apply and accordingly an appeal lies as of right against the decision, determination or order.

(3)   Leave to appeal for the purpose of subsection (1) may be granted—

> (a) in respect of a particular issue arising out of the interlocutory decision, determination or order; and
>
> (b) subject to any conditions that the Court of Appeal or the Tribunal considers necessary in order to secure the just, expeditious and economical disposal of the appeal.

(4)   Leave to appeal may only be granted under subsection (1) if the Court of Appeal or the Tribunal is satisfied that—

> (a) the appeal has a reasonable prospect of success; or
>
> (b) there is some other reason in the interests of justice why the appeal should be heard.

155A. Enforcement by Tribunal of payment of penalties and fines

(1)   The Tribunal may enforce payment of—

> (a) a pecuniary penalty imposed under section 93;
>
> (b) a financial penalty imposed under section 169; or
>
> (c) a fine imposed by the Tribunal,

in the same manner in which a judgment of the Court of First Instance for the payment of money may be enforced.

(2)   If a penalty or fine described in subsection (1) is not paid in full when it is due—

> (a) the Tribunal may certify in writing to the Registrar of the Tribunal the sum payable; and
>
> (b) the Registrar is to enforce payment of the sum certified as a judgment debt due to the Registrar.

Division 4

Miscellaneous

156. Registrar and other staff of Tribunal

Every Registrar, temporary registrar, senior deputy registrar, temporary senior deputy registrar, deputy registrar, temporary deputy registrar and any other officer such as a Bailiff of the High Court, by virtue of that appointment, holds the corresponding office or position in the Tribunal.

156A. Jurisdiction and powers of Registrar of Tribunal

(1)   The Registrar of the Tribunal—

> (a) has the same jurisdiction and privileges, in so far as they are applicable to the business and proceedings of the Tribunal, as the Registrar of the High Court; and

> (b) may exercise the same powers and perform the same duties, in so far as they are applicable to the business and proceedings of the Tribunal, as the Registrar of the High Court.

(2)   The Registrar of the Tribunal has any other jurisdiction, privileges, powers and duties that may be conferred or imposed on him or her by or under the rules of the Tribunal made under section 158 or any other law.

156B. Jurisdiction and powers of deputy registrars of Tribunal

(1)   A senior deputy registrar of the Tribunal—

> (a) has the same jurisdiction and privileges, in so far as they are applicable to the business and proceedings of the Tribunal, as a senior deputy registrar of the High Court; and
>
> (b) may exercise the same powers and perform the same duties, in so far as they are applicable to the business and proceedings of the Tribunal, as a senior deputy registrar of the High Court.

(2)   Subject to the rules of the Tribunal made under section 158, a senior deputy registrar of the Tribunal—

> (a) has all the jurisdiction and privileges conferred on the Registrar of the Tribunal; and
>
> (b) may exercise all the powers conferred, and perform all the duties imposed, on the Registrar of the Tribunal.

(3)   A deputy registrar of the Tribunal—

> (a) has the same jurisdiction and privileges, in so far as they are applicable to the business and proceedings of the Tribunal, as a deputy registrar of the High Court; and
>
> (b) may exercise the same powers and perform the same duties, in so far as they are applicable to the business and proceedings of the Tribunal, as a deputy registrar of the High Court.

(4)   Subject to the rules of the Tribunal made under section 158, a deputy registrar of the Tribunal—

> (a) has all the jurisdiction and privileges conferred on the Registrar of the Tribunal; and
>
> (b) may exercise all the powers conferred, and perform all the duties imposed, on the Registrar of the Tribunal.

156C. Jurisdiction and powers of temporary registrars of Tribunal

(1)   A temporary registrar of the Tribunal has, during the period for which he or she is appointed, all the jurisdiction, privileges, powers and duties of the Registrar of the Tribunal.

(2)   A temporary senior deputy registrar of the Tribunal has, during the period for which he or she is appointed, all the jurisdiction, privileges, powers and duties of a senior deputy registrar of the Tribunal.

(3)   A temporary deputy registrar of the Tribunal has, during the period for which he or she is appointed, all the jurisdiction, privileges, powers and duties of a deputy registrar of the Tribunal.

(4)   If a temporary registrar of the Tribunal adjourns the hearing of any proceedings or reserves judgment in any proceedings, the temporary registrar has power to resume the hearing and determine the proceedings or deliver judgment, even though before the hearing is resumed or judgment is

delivered, his or her appointment as a temporary registrar has expired or has been terminated.

(5) Subsection (4) applies to a temporary senior deputy registrar and a temporary deputy registrar of the Tribunal as it applies to a temporary registrar of the Tribunal.

156D. Protection of Registrar of Tribunal

(1) A person may not bring an action against the Registrar of the Tribunal for an act done or omitted to be done by a bailiff of the Tribunal without directions from the Registrar.

(2) A person may not bring an action against the Registrar of the Tribunal for a direction given to a bailiff of the Tribunal with regard to the execution or non-execution of process if—

    (a) the direction is given in accordance with an order made by the Tribunal under section 156E; and

    (b) the Registrar has not wilfully misrepresented or suppressed any material fact.

156E. Registrar of Tribunal may apply to Tribunal for order

(1) In relation to a matter regarding the execution or non-execution of process, the Registrar of the Tribunal may, in case of doubt or difficulty, apply summarily to the Tribunal for an order for the direction and guidance of a bailiff of the Tribunal.

(2) The Tribunal may make any order in the matter that it considers just and reasonable.

157. Seal of Tribunal

(1) The Tribunal is to have a seal approved by the Chief Justice.

(2) All writs, judgments, orders and other documents, and any exemplification or copies of writs, judgments, orders and other documents, are to be sealed with the seal.

(3) All writs, judgments, orders and other documents, and any exemplification or copies of writs, judgments, orders and other documents, when purporting to be so sealed, are admissible in evidence before any court on production without further proof.

157A. Reimbursement of witness expenses

In any proceedings before the Tribunal, a member of the Tribunal may order the reimbursement of a witness for any expenses reasonably and properly incurred by the witness by reason of his or her attendance at the proceedings.

158. Tribunal rules.

(1) The Chief Judge may, after consulting the President, make rules regulating and prescribing—

    (a) the practice and procedure to be followed in the Tribunal in all matters with respect to which the Tribunal has jurisdiction; and

    (b) any matters incidental to or relating to that practice or procedure.

(2) Without limiting subsection (1), rules may be made for the following purposes—

(aa) prescribing the jurisdiction of the Tribunal that the Registrar, a senior deputy registrar or a deputy registrar of the Tribunal may exercise (including provision for appeal against decisions made in the exercise of the jurisdiction);

(a) prescribing fees and regulating matters relating to the fees payable in connection with applications to the Tribunal and proceedings in the Tribunal;

(b) prescribing the manner and form in which documents are to be issued or served in relation to proceedings in the Tribunal;

(c) prescribing the manner in which and the terms on which proceedings are conducted with the assistance of an assessor;

(d) prescribing the manner and form in which documents may be filed in the Tribunal and the manner in which evidence may be given in proceedings;

(e) prescribing the allowances to be paid to witnesses appearing before the Tribunal; and

(f) prescribing the form of any order that the Tribunal may make under this Ordinance.

158A. Suitors' Funds Rules

(1) The Chief Judge may, after consulting the President, make rules for regulating the following matters—

(a) the deposit, payment, delivery, and transfer in, into, and out of the Tribunal of money, securities and movable property of suitors;

(b) the evidence of such deposit, payment, delivery, or transfer, and the investment of and other dealings with money, securities and movable property in the Tribunal;

(c) the execution of the orders of the Tribunal; and

(d) the powers and duties of the Registrar of the Tribunal with reference to such money, securities and movable property.

(2) Without limiting subsection (1), rules made under that subsection may provide for—

(a) regulating the placing on and withdrawal from deposit of money in the Tribunal, and the payment or crediting of interest on money placed on deposit;

(b) determining the smallest amount of money on deposit on which interest is to be credited to an account to which money placed on deposit belongs;

(c) determining the time at which money placed on deposit is to begin and to cease to bear interest and the mode of computing such interest;

(d) determining the cases in which money placed on deposit is to begin and to cease to bear interest and the mode of computing such interest;

(e) determining the cases in which interest on money placed on deposit is, and the dividends on any securities standing in the name of the Registrar of the Tribunal are, to be placed on deposit; and

(f) disposing of money remaining unclaimed in the Tribunal.

(3) In this section—

"securities" *i*ncludes shares.

Part 11

Concurrent Jurisdiction Relating to
Telecommunications and Broadcasting

159.   Concurrent jurisdiction with Communications Authority
(1)   The Communications Authority may perform the functions of the Commission under this Ordinance, in so far as they relate to the conduct of undertakings that are—
   (a) licensees under the Telecommunications Ordinance (Cap 106) or the Broadcasting Ordinance (Cap 562);
   (b) persons who, although not such licensees, are persons whose activities require them to be licensed under the Telecommunications Ordinance (Cap 106) or the Broadcasting Ordinance (Cap 562); or
   (c) persons who have been exempted from the Telecommunications Ordinance (Cap 106) or from specified provisions of that Ordinance under section 39 of that Ordinance.
(2)   So far as is necessary for the purpose of subsection (1), references in this Ordinance to the Commission are to be read as including the Communications Authority.

160.   Transfer of competition matter between competition authorities
(1) Where one competition authority is performing a function in relation to a competition matter and another competition authority also has jurisdiction to perform functions in relation to that matter, the competition authorities may agree that the matter be transferred to and be dealt with by one of them.
(2)   Where more than one competition authority has jurisdiction to perform functions in relation to a competition matter, if one of them is performing or has performed a function in relation to that matter, then, unless there is an agreement of a kind mentioned in subsection (1), the other competition authority must not perform any function in relation to that matter.

161.   Memorandum of Understanding
(1)   As soon as is reasonably practicable after the coming into operation of this section, the Commission and the Communications Authority must prepare and sign a Memorandum of Understanding, for the purpose of co-ordinating the performance of their functions under this Ordinance.
(2)   Without limiting subsection (1), the Memorandum of Understanding must provide for any or all of the matters set out in Schedule 6.
(3)   The Commission and the Communications Authority may amend or replace any Memorandum of Understanding prepared and signed under this section.
(4)   Before signing any Memorandum of Understanding, or any amendment to it, under this section, the Commission and the Communications Authority must consult the Legislative Council.
(5)   The Commission and the Communications Authority must, within 6 weeks after the Memorandum of Understanding, or any amendment to it, is signed by them, publish it in any manner they consider appropriate.

(6) The Commission and the Communications Authority must make available copies of any Memorandum of Understanding prepared and signed under this section and of all amendments made to it—

(a) at their offices during ordinary business hours;

(b) through the Internet or a similar electronic network; and

(c) in any other manner they consider appropriate.

(7) A Memorandum of Understanding prepared and signed under this section and all amendments made to it are not subsidiary legislation.

Part 12

Miscellaneous

Division 1

General

162. Mergers

Schedule 7 (Mergers) has effect.

163. Determination of turnover of undertaking

(1) For the purposes of this Ordinance, the turnover of an undertaking is to be determined in accordance with the regulations made by the Secretary for Commerce and Economic Development under subsection (2).

(2) The Secretary for Commerce and Economic Development may, by regulations published in the Gazette, provide for the determination of the turnover of an undertaking.

(3) Without limiting subsection (2), the regulations made under that subsection may—

(a) specify a period as the turnover period of an undertaking for the purpose of section 5(4) or 6(3) of Schedule 1;

(b) provide for different ways for the determination of the turnover of an undertaking obtained in Hong Kong or outside Hong Kong; and

(c) provide for different ways for the determination of the turnover of an undertaking in respect of different periods, including—

(i) a calendar year;

(ii) a financial year; and

(iii) a period specified as the turnover period of the undertaking under paragraph (a).

164. Fees

(1) The Commission may charge a fee for—

(a) the making of an application to the Commission under this Ordinance; and

(b) the provision of any service.

(2) The Chief Executive may make regulations prescribing the amount of the fees chargeable under this section.

(3) The amount of any fee that may be prescribed in a regulation made under subsection (2) is not limited by reference to the amount of administrative or other costs incurred or likely to be incurred in relation to the application or service to which the fee relates.

(4) A regulation made under this section may provide for—

(a) the amount of any fee to be charged by reference to a scale set out in the regulation;

(b) the payment of different fees by different persons or different classes or descriptions of person;

(c) fees that are to be paid annually or at other intervals; and

(d) the reduction, waiver or refund, in whole or in part, of any fee, either upon the happening of a certain event or in the discretion of the Commission.

(5) The Commission may recover any fee payable under this section as a civil debt due to the Commission.

165. Personal immunity of public officers

(1) A public officer is not personally liable for anything done or omitted to be done by the public officer in good faith in the performance of a function or purported performance of a function under this Ordinance.

(2) The protection conferred by subsection (1) does not affect any liability of the Government for the act or omission

Division 2

Service of Documents

166. Service of documents on Commission

(1) A notice or other document required to be served on the Commission under this Ordinance may be served—

(a) by sending it by post to the offices of the Commission;

(b) by leaving it at the offices of the Commission;

(c) by sending it by facsimile transmission to the facsimile number of the Commission;

(d) by sending it by electronic mail transmission to the electronic mail address of the Commission; or

(e) by sending it by any other method specified in rules made by the Commission for this purpose under section 34 of Schedule 5.

(2) A notice or other document served in accordance with subsection (1) is to be taken, in the absence of evidence to the contrary, to have been served—

(a) if served by post, on the second day after the day on which it was posted;

(b) if left at the offices of the Commission, on the day after the day on which it was so left;

(c) if sent by facsimile transmission, on the day after the day on which it was transmitted; or

(d) if sent by electronic mail transmission, on the day after the day on which it was transmitted.

167. Service of documents other than on Commission
(1) A notice, direction or other document required to be served by the Commission for the purposes of this Ordinance may be served—
 (a) in the case of service on a natural person—
  (i) by delivering it to the person personally;
  (ii) by sending it by post in a letter addressed to the person at the person's usual place of residence or business or, if the person's address is unknown, addressed to the person's last known place of residence or business;
  (iii) by sending it by facsimile transmission to the facsimile number of the person or, if that number is unknown, to the last known facsimile number of the person; or
  (iv) by sending it by electronic mail transmission to the electronic mail address of the person or, if that address is unknown, to the last known electronic mail address of the person;
 (b) in the case of service on a body corporate—
  (i) by delivering it to any place in Hong Kong at which the body corporate carries on business and giving it to any person in the place who appears to be concerned in the management of, or employed by, the body corporate;
  (ii) by sending it by post in a letter addressed to the body corporate at its registered office in Hong Kong or at any place in Hong Kong at which the body corporate carries on business or, if the body corporate ' s address is unknown, addressed to the body corporate's last known place of business;
  (iii) by sending it by facsimile transmission to the facsimile number of the body corporate or, if that number is unknown, to the last known facsimile number of the body corporate; or
  (iv) by sending it by electronic mail transmission to the electronic mail address of the body corporate or, if that address is unknown, to the last known electronic mail address of the body corporate;
 (c) in the case of service on a partnership—
  (i) by delivering it to any place in Hong Kong at which the partnership carries on business and giving it to any person in the place who appears to be concerned in the management of, or employed by, the partnership;
  (ii) by sending it by post in a letter addressed to the partnership at any place in Hong Kong at which the partnership carries on business or, if the partnership's address is unknown, addressed to the partnership's last known place of business;
  (iii) by sending it by facsimile transmission to the facsimile number of the partnership or, if that number is unknown, to the last known facsimile number of the partnership; or
  (iv) by sending it by electronic mail transmission to the electronic mail address of the partnership or, if that address is unknown, to the last known electronic mail address of the partnership; or
 (d) in the case of service on an undertaking other than a natural person, a body corporate or a partnership—

(i) by delivering it personally to an officer of the undertaking or a member of its governing body;

(ii) by sending it by post in a letter addressed to the undertaking at any place in Hong Kong at which the undertaking carries on business or, if the undertaking ' s address is unknown, addressed to the undertaking's last known place of business;

(iii) by sending it by facsimile transmission to the facsimile number of the undertaking or, if that number is unknown, to the last known facsimile number of the undertaking; or

(iv) by sending it by electronic mail transmission to the electronic mail address of the undertaking or, if that address is unknown, to the last known electronic mail address of the undertaking.

(2) A notice, direction or other document served in accordance with subsection (1) is to be taken to have been served—

(a) if served by post, on the second day after the day on which it was posted;

(b) if sent by facsimile transaction, on the day after the day on which it was transmitted; or

(c) if sent by electronic mail transmission, on the day after the day on which it was transmitted.

Division 3

Indemnities

168. Certain indemnities of officers, employees or agents void

(1) Subject to section 170, no person may indemnify another person who is or was an officer, employee or agent of an undertaking against liability for paying—

(a) a pecuniary penalty under Part 6; or

(b) costs incurred in defending an action in which that other person is—

(i) convicted of contempt of the Tribunal;

(ii) convicted of an offence under this Part or Part 3; or

(iii) ordered to pay a pecuniary penalty under Part 6.

(2) An indemnity given in contravention of subsection (1) is void.

(3) In this section—

"employee" in relation to an undertaking, means a person engaged by the undertaking for the provision of services, whether under a contract of employment or otherwise;

"officer" means—

(a) in relation to an undertaking being a corporation, a director, manager or company secretary of the undertaking, and any other person involved in the management of the undertaking; and

(b) in relation to an undertaking not being a corporation, any member of the governing body of that undertaking.

169. Financial penalty for contravention of section 168

(1) If it appears to the Commission that a person has indemnified any other person in contravention of section 168, the Commission may apply to the Tribunal for an order imposing a financial penalty on that person.

(2) If the Tribunal is satisfied that a person has contravened section 168, it may make an order imposing a financial penalty on that person.

(3) The amount of a financial penalty imposed under this section may not exceed twice the value of the indemnity given in contravention of section 168.

170. Provision of funds for indemnity for defending proceedings

(1) Section 168 does not prohibit any person from providing funds to another person who is or was an officer, employee or agent of an undertaking to meet expenditure incurred or to be incurred by that other person in defending any proceedings under Part 6 for a pecuniary penalty, if it is done on the following terms—

(a) that the funds are to be repaid in the event of the other person being required by the Tribunal to pay the pecuniary penalty; and

(b) that they are to be repaid not later than the date when the decision of the Tribunal becomes final.

(2) For the purpose of this section a decision of the Tribunal becomes final—

(a) if not appealed against, at the end of the period for bringing an appeal; or

(b) if appealed against, when the appeal or further appeal is finally disposed of.

(3) An appeal is finally disposed of, for the purpose of subsection (2)—

(a) if it is determined and the period for bringing any further appeal has ended; or

(b) if it is abandoned or otherwise ceases to have effect.

(4) In this section—

"employee" has the meaning given by section 168(3);

"officer" has the meaning given by section 168(3).

Division 4

Offences

171. Criminal proceedings not to be brought in Tribunal

(1) Criminal proceedings for an offence under this Ordinance may not be brought in the Tribunal.

(2) To avoid doubt, subsection (1) does not affect the jurisdiction, powers and duties of the Tribunal in respect of the punishment of a person guilty of contempt, granted by section 144(2).

172. Provision of false information

(1) A person commits an offence if the person, in any representation made to the Commission under this Ordinance—

(a) provides any information that is false or misleading in a material particular; and

(b) knows or is reckless as to whether the information is false or misleading in a material particular.

(2)   A person who commits an offence under this section is liable to a fine at level 6 and to imprisonment for 6 months.

173. Employees not to suffer termination etc. for assisting Commission

(1)   A person who employs another person under a contract of employment (an "employee") must not—

(a) terminate or threaten to terminate the employment of that employee;

(b) discriminate in any way against that employee;

(c) intimidate or harass that employee; or

(d) cause that employee any injury, loss or damage, because the employee has taken any action referred to in subsection (2).

(2)   The actions referred to in subsection (1) are—

(a) providing any material to the Commission in connection with the Commission's functions; or

(b) giving evidence or agreeing to give evidence in any proceedings brought by the Commission for the enforcement of this Ordinance.

(3) A person who contravenes subsection (1) commits an offence and is liable to a fine at level 4 and to imprisonment for 3 months.

174. Obstruction of specified persons

(1)   A person who, without reasonable excuse, obstructs a specified person in the performance of any function under this Ordinance commits an offence and is liable—

(a) on conviction on indictment, to a fine of $1000000; or

(b) on summary conviction, to a fine at level 6.

(2) In this section—

"specified person" has the meaning given by section 122.

175. Offences by bodies corporate and partners

(1)   If a person by whom an offence under this Ordinance is committed is a body corporate, and it is proved that the offence—

(a) was committed with the consent or connivance of a director, manager, company secretary or other person concerned in the management of the body corporate; or

(b) was attributable to any neglect or omission on the part of a director, manager, company secretary or other person concerned in the management of the body corporate,

the director, manager, company secretary or other person also commits the offence.

(2)   If a person by whom an offence under this Ordinance is committed is a partner in a partnership, and it is proved that the offence—

(a) was committed with the consent or connivance of any other partner or any person concerned in the management of the partnership; or

(b) was attributable to any neglect or omission on the part of any other partner or any person concerned in the management of the partnership,

the partner or the person concerned in the management of the partnership also commits the offence.

Division 5

Consequential, Related, Transitional and Savings Provisions

176. Consequential and related amendments

Schedule 8 contains consequential and related amendments to other enactments.

177. Transitional and savings provisions in relation to amendments made by this Ordinance

(1) Schedule 9 contains transitional and savings provisions in relation to amendments made by this Ordinance to the Telecommunications Ordinance (Cap 106), the Broadcasting (Miscellaneous Provisions) Ordinance (Cap 391) and the Broadcasting Ordinance (Cap 562).

(2) The Chief Executive may make regulations containing transitional provisions and savings that are necessary or convenient for the transition to the provisions of this Ordinance from the provisions of the Telecommunications Ordinance (Cap 106), the Broadcasting (Miscellaneous Provisions) Ordinance (Cap 391) or the Broadcasting Ordinance (Cap 562) as amended by this Ordinance.

(3) Without limiting subsection (2), regulations made under this section may, in particular, provide for—

(a) the application of provisions of this Ordinance to telecommunications services or broadcasting services; or

(b) the continued application of provisions of the Telecommunications Ordinance (Cap 106), the Broadcasting (Miscellaneous Provisions) Ordinance (Cap 391) or the Broadcasting Ordinance (Cap 562) in force immediately before the commencement of any provision of this Ordinance to telecommunications services or broadcasting services.

(4) Regulations made under this section may, if they so provide, be deemed to have come into operation on a date earlier than the date on which they are published in the Gazette but not earlier than the date on which this Ordinance is published in the Gazette.

(5) To the extent that any regulations made under this section come into operation on a date earlier than the date on which they are published in the Gazette, those regulations are to be construed so as not to—

(a) affect, in a manner prejudicial to any person, the rights of that person existing before the date on which the regulations are published in the Gazette; or

(b) impose liabilities on any person in respect of anything done, or omitted to be done, before the date on which the regulations are published in the Gazette.

(6) If there is any inconsistency between any regulations made under this section and the provisions of Schedule 9, Schedule 9 prevails to the extent of the inconsistency.

Schedule 1

GENERAL EXCLUSIONS FROM CONDUCT RULES

[Sections 9, 15, 24,
30, 36 & 163]

1.   Agreements enhancing overall economic efficiency

The first conduct rule does not apply to any agreement that—

    (a) contributes to—

        (i) improving production or distribution; or

        (ii) promoting technical or economic progress,

        while allowing consumers a fair share of the resulting benefit;

    (b) does not impose on the undertakings concerned restrictions that are not indispensable to the attainment of the objectives stated in paragraph (a); and

    (c) does not afford the undertakings concerned the possibility of eliminating competition in respect of a substantial part of the goods or services in question.

2.   Compliance with legal requirements

(1)   The first conduct rule does not apply to an agreement to the extent that it is made for the purpose of complying with a legal requirement.

(2)   The second conduct rule does not apply to conduct to the extent that it is engaged in for the purpose of complying with a legal requirement.

(3)   In this section—

    "legal requirement" means a requirement—

        (a) imposed by or under any enactment in force in Hong Kong; or

        (b) imposed by any national law applying in Hong Kong.

3.   Services of general economic interest etc.

Neither the first conduct rule nor the second conduct rule applies to an undertaking entrusted by the Government with the operation of services of general economic interest in so far as the conduct rule would obstruct the performance, in law or in fact, of the particular tasks assigned to it.

4.   Mergers

(1)   To the extent to which an agreement (either on its own or when taken together with another agreement) results in, or if carried out would result in, a merger, the first conduct rule does not apply to the agreement.

(2)   To the extent to which conduct (either on its own or when taken together with other conduct) results in, or if engaged in would result in, a merger, the second conduct rule does not apply to the conduct.

5.   Agreements of lesser significance

(1)   The first conduct rule does not apply to—

    (a) an agreement between undertakings in any calendar year if the combined turnover of the undertakings for the turnover period does not exceed $200000000;

      (b) a concerted practice engaged in by undertakings in any calendar year if the combined turnover of the undertakings for the turnover period does not exceed $200000000; or

      (c) a decision of an association of undertakings in any calendar year if the turnover of the association for the turnover period does not exceed $200000000.

(2)   Subsection (1) does not apply to an agreement, a concerted practice, or a decision of an association of undertakings, that involves serious anti-competitive conduct.

(3)   Subject to subsection (4), the turnover period of an undertaking is—

      (a) if the undertaking has a financial year, the financial year of the undertaking that ends in the preceding calendar year; or

      (b) if the undertaking does not have a financial year, the preceding calendar year.

(4)   The turnover period of an undertaking is the period specified as such for the purpose of this subsection in the regulations made under section 163(2) if—

      (a) for an undertaking that has a financial year—

          (i) the undertaking does not have a financial year that ends in the preceding calendar year; or

          (ii) the financial year of the undertaking that ends in the preceding calendar year is less than 12 months; or

      (b) for an undertaking that does not have a financial year—

          (i) the undertaking is not engaged in economic activity in the preceding calendar year; or

          (ii) the period in which the undertaking is engaged in economic activity in the preceding calendar year is less than 12 months.

(5)   In this section—

"preceding calendar year" means the calendar year preceding the calendar year mentioned in subsection (1)(a), (b) or (c);

"turnover" —

      (a) in relation to an undertaking that is not an association of undertakings, means the total gross revenues of the undertaking whether obtained in Hong Kong or outside Hong Kong; and

      (b) in relation to an association of undertakings, means the total gross revenues of all the members of the association whether obtained in Hong Kong or outside Hong Kong.

6.   Conduct of lesser significance

(1)   The second conduct rule does not apply to conduct engaged in by an undertaking the turnover of which does not exceed $40000000 for the turnover period.

(2)   Subject to subsection (3), the turnover period of an undertaking is—

      (a) if the undertaking has a financial year, the financial year of the undertaking that ends in the preceding calendar year; or

      (b) if the undertaking does not have a financial year, the preceding calendar year.

(3)   The turnover period of an undertaking is the period specified as such for the purpose of this subsection in the regulations made under section 163(2) if—

      (a) for an undertaking that has a financial year—

(i) the undertaking does not have a financial year that ends in the preceding calendar year; or

(ii) the financial year of the undertaking that ends in the preceding calendar year is less than 12 months; or

(b) for an undertaking that does not have a financial year—

(i) the undertaking is not engaged in economic activity in the preceding calendar year; or

(ii) the period in which the undertaking is engaged in economic activity in the preceding calendar year is less than 12 months.

(4)   In this section—

"preceding calendar year" means the calendar year preceding the calendar year in which the conduct mentioned in subsection (1) is engaged in;

"turnover" means the total gross revenues of an undertaking whether obtained in Hong Kong or outside Hong Kong.

Schedule 2

COMMITMENTS

[Section 65]

Part 1

Procedural Requirements for Acceptance and Variation of Commitments

1.   Application

Section 2 of this Schedule applies where the Commission proposes to—

(a) accept a commitment under section 60;

(b) accept a variation of such a commitment under section 62; or

(c) accept a new commitment in substitution for such a commitment under section 62.

2.   Notice

(1)   Before accepting a commitment or variation, the Commission must—

(a) give notice of the proposed commitment or variation in any manner it considers appropriate for bringing it to the attention of those it considers likely to be affected by it; and

(b) consider any representations made (and not withdrawn) in response to the notice.

(2)   A notice under subsection (1) must state—

(a) that the Commission proposes to accept the commitment or variation;

(b) the intended object and effect of the commitment or variation;

(c) whether the commitment or variation constitutes an admission of contravention of a competition rule;

(d) the situation that the commitment or variation is seeking to deal with;

(e) any other facts that the Commission considers to be relevant to the acceptance or variation of the commitment;

(f) a means of gaining access, at all reasonable times, to an accurate version of the proposed commitment or variation; and

(g) the period within which representations may be made in relation to the proposed commitment or variation.

(3)   The period stated for the purpose of subsection (2)(g) must be at least 15 days beginning on the day on which the notice is given.

3.   Notice of decision not to accept

If, after giving notice under section 2 of this Schedule, the Commission decides not to accept the commitment or variation concerned, the Commission must give notice that it has so decided.

4.   Notice of acceptance

As soon as practicable after accepting a commitment or a variation of a commitment, the Commission must publish the commitment or variation—

(a) through the Internet or a similar electronic network; and

(b) in any other manner the Commission considers appropriate.

5.   Manner of giving notice

A notice under section 2 or 3 of this Schedule must be given by—

(a) sending a copy of the notice to any person or persons the Commission considers are likely to be affected by the matter to which the notice relates; or

(b) publishing the notice—

    (i) through the Internet or a similar electronic network; and

    (ii) in any other manner the Commission considers appropriate,

for the purpose of bringing the matter to which the notice relates to the attention of those the Commission considers likely to be affected by it.

Part 2

Procedural Requirements for Withdrawal of Acceptance of Commitments

6.   Application

Section 7 of this Schedule applies where the Commission proposes to withdraw its acceptance of a commitment under section 61.

7.   Notice

(1)   Before withdrawing its acceptance of a commitment, the Commission must—

(a) give notice of the proposed withdrawal in any manner it considers appropriate for bringing it to the attention of those it considers likely to be affected by it; and

(b) consider any representations made (and not withdrawn) in response to the notice.

(2)   A notice under subsection (1) must state—

(a) that the Commission proposes to withdraw its acceptance of the commitment;

(b) the reasons for the proposed withdrawal;

(c) any other facts that the Commission considers to be relevant to the proposed withdrawal; and

(d) the period within which representations may be made in relation to the proposed withdrawal.

(3)   The period stated for the purpose of subsection (2)(d) must be at least 15 days beginning on the day on which the notice is given.

8.   Notice of decision not to withdraw

If, after giving notice under section 7 of this Schedule, the Commission decides not to withdraw its acceptance of the commitment concerned, the Commission must give notice that it has so decided.

9.   Notice of withdrawal

As soon as practicable after withdrawing its acceptance of a commitment, the Commission must publish the withdrawal—

(a) through the Internet or a similar electronic network; and

(b) in any other manner the Commission considers appropriate.

10.   Manner of giving notice

A notice under section 7 or 8 of this Schedule must be given by—

(a) sending a copy of the notice to any person or persons the Commission considers are likely to be affected by the matter to which the notice relates; or

(b) publishing the notice—

(i) through the Internet or a similar electronic network; and

(ii) in any other manner the Commission considers appropriate,

for the purpose of bringing the matter to which the notice relates to the attention of those the Commission considers likely to be affected by it.

Part 3

Procedural Requirements for Release of Commitments

11.   Application

Section 12 of this Schedule applies where the Commission proposes to release a person from a commitment, under section 62.

12.   Notice

(1)   Before releasing the person from the commitment, the Commission must—

(a) give notice of the proposed release in any manner it considers appropriate for bringing it to the attention of that person; and

(b) consider any representations made (and not withdrawn) in response to the notice.

(2)   A notice under subsection (1) must state—

(a) that the Commission proposes to release the person from the commitment;

(b) the reasons for the proposed release;

(c) any other facts that the Commission considers to be relevant to the proposed release; and

(d) the period within which representations may be made in relation to the proposed release.

(3) The period stated for the purpose of subsection (2)(d) must be at least 15 days beginning on the day on which the notice is given.

13. Notice of decision not to proceed

If, after giving notice under section 12 of this Schedule, the Commission decides not to proceed with the release, it must—

(a) give notice that it has so decided; and

(b) send a copy of the notice to the person who made the commitment.

14. Notice of decision to release

As soon as practicable after releasing a person from a commitment, the Commission must—

(a) publish the release—

(i) through the Internet or a similar electronic network; and

(ii) in any other manner the Commission considers appropriate; and

(b) send a copy of the release to that person.

15. Manner of giving notice

A notice under section 12 or 13 of this Schedule must be given by—

(a) sending a copy of the notice to any person or persons the Commission considers are likely to be affected by the matter to which the notice relates; or

(b) publishing the notice—

(i) through the Internet or a similar electronic network; and

(ii) in any other manner the Commission considers appropriate,

for the purpose of bringing the matter to which the notice relates to the attention of those the Commission considers likely to be affected by it.

Schedule 3

ORDERS THAT MAY BE MADE
BY TRIBUNAL IN RELATION TO
CONTRAVENTION OF COMPETITION RULES

[Sections 94 & 112]

1. Orders

The Tribunal may make the following orders with respect to a contravention of the competition rules—

(a) a declaration that a person has contravened a competition rule;

(b) an order restraining or prohibiting a person from engaging in any conduct that constitutes the contravention or the person's involvement in the contravention;

(c) an order requiring a person who has contravened a competition rule or been involved in the contravention to do any act or thing, including the taking of steps for the purpose of restoring the parties to any transaction to the position in which they were before the transaction was entered into;

(d) an order restraining or prohibiting a person from acquiring, disposing of or otherwise dealing with any property specified in the order;

(e) an order requiring a person to dispose of such operations, assets or shares of any undertaking specified in the order, in the manner specified in the order;

(f) an order appointing a person to administer the property of another person;

(g) an order prohibiting a person from making or giving effect to an agreement;

(h) an order requiring the parties to an agreement (the making or giving effect to which constitutes the contravention of the competition rules) to modify or terminate that agreement;

(i) an order declaring any agreement (the making or giving effect to which constitutes the contravention of the competition rules) to be void or voidable to the extent specified in the order;

(j) an order prohibiting the withholding from any person of—
  (i) any goods or services; or
  (ii) any orders for any such goods or services;

(k) an order requiring a person to pay damages to any person who has suffered loss or damage as a result of the contravention;

(l) an order prohibiting requiring as a condition of the supply of goods or services to any person—
  (i) the buying of any goods or services;
  (ii) the making of any payment in respect of goods or services other than the goods or services supplied; or
  (iii) the doing of any other similar thing or the refraining from doing of anything mentioned in subparagraph (i) or (ii) or any other similar thing;

(m) an order prohibiting a person from exercising any right to vote that is exercisable by virtue of the holding of any shares, stock or securities;

(n) an order requiring that any person or class of person be given access to goods, facilities or services specified in the order on the terms specified in the order;

(o) an order requiring that any person or class of person be given the right to use goods, facilities or services specified in the order on the terms specified in the order;

(p) an order requiring any person to pay to the Government or to any other specified person, as the Tribunal considers appropriate, an amount not exceeding the amount of any profit gained or loss avoided by that person as a result of the contravention; or

(q) for the purpose of securing compliance with any other order made under this section, an order requiring any person who has contravened or been involved in the contravention to do or refrain from doing anything specified in the order.

2. Registration of orders relating to immovable property

If any property specified in an order made under section 1(d) of this Schedule is immovable property, the order is, for the purpose of the Land Registration Ordinance (Cap 128)—

(a) to be regarded as an instrument affecting land; and

(b) registrable, as an instrument affecting land, in the Land Registry under that Ordinance in any manner the Land Registrar considers appropriate.

3. Interpretation

In section 1(j) of this Schedule, a reference to "withholding" includes—

(a) agreeing or threatening to withhold; and

(b) procuring others to withhold or to agree or threaten to withhold.

Schedule 4

PROVISIONS THAT MAY BE CONTAINED IN ORDERS
MADE BY TRIBUNAL IN RELATION TO
ANTICIAPATED MERGERS AND MERGERS

[Sections 97 & 100]

1. An order may provide for—

(a) the division of any business (whether by the sale of any part of its assets or otherwise); or

(b) the division of any undertaking or association of undertakings.

2. An order made under section 1 of this Schedule may contain any provisions that the Tribunal considers appropriate to effect or take account of the division including, in particular, provision as to—

(a) the transfer or creation of property, rights, liabilities or obligations;

(b) the number of persons to whom the property, rights, liabilities or obligations are to be transferred or in whom they are to be vested;

(c) the time within which the property, rights, liabilities or obligations are to be transferred or vested;

(d) the adjustment of contracts (whether by discharge or reduction of any liability or obligation or otherwise);

(e) the creation, allotment, surrender or cancellation of any shares, stock or securities;

(f) the formation or winding up of any company or other body of persons corporate or unincorporate;

(g) the amendment of the memorandum and articles or other instruments regulating any such company or other body of persons;

(h) the extent to which, and the circumstances in which, provisions of the order affecting a company or other body of persons corporate or unincorporate in its share capital, constitution or other matters may be altered by the company or other body of persons concerned;

(i) the registration of the order under any enactment by a company or other body of persons corporate or unincorporate which is affected by it as mentioned in paragraph (h);

(j) the continuation, with any necessary change of parties, of any legal proceedings;

(k) the approval by any person of anything required by virtue of the order to be done or of any person to whom anything is to be transferred, or in whom anything is to be vested, by virtue of the order; or

(l) the appointment of trustees or other persons to do anything on behalf of another person which is required of that person by virtue of the order or to monitor the doing by that person of any such thing.

3. An order may prohibit or restrict—

(a) the acquisition by any person of the whole or part of another person's business; or

(b) the doing of anything that will or may result in a merger.

4. An order may provide that if—

(a) an acquisition of the kind mentioned in section 3(a) of this Schedule is made; or

(b) anything is done that results in a merger,

the persons concerned or any of them must observe any prohibitions or restrictions imposed by or under the order.

Schedule 5

COMPETITION COMMISSION

[Sections 2, 122, 129 & 166]

Part 1

Interpretation

1. Interpretation

In this Schedule—

"auditor" means the auditor appointed under section 24 of this Schedule;

"Chairperson" means the Chairperson of the Commission appointed under section 8 of this Schedule;

"Chief Executive Officer" means the Chief Executive Officer of the Commission appointed under section 10 of this Schedule;

"financial year" means the financial year of the Commission as defined in section 20 of this Schedule;

"statement of accounts" means the statement of the accounts of the Commission required to be prepared by section 23 of this Schedule.

Part 2

Members of Commission

2.   Composition of Commission

(1)   The Commission is to consist of not less than 5 and not more than 16 members appointed by the Chief Executive.

(2)   In considering the appointment of a person as a member of the Commission, the Chief Executive may have regard to that person's expertise or experience in industry, commerce, economics, law, small and medium enterprises or public policy.

(3)   Subject to this Schedule, a member holds office for the period, not exceeding 3 years, that is specified in the member's letter of appointment, but is eligible for re-appointment.

(4)   The Chief Executive must publish a notice in the Gazette of all appointments made under this section.

3.   Terms of appointment

(1)   A member is entitled to such terms (including remuneration and allowances) as the Chief Executive may determine.

(2)   The remuneration and allowances of a member are to be paid out of the funds of the Commission.

4.   Resignation of member

(1)   A member may, at any time, resign from office by giving written notice of resignation to the Chief Executive.

(2)   A notice of resignation is not effective unless it is signed by the member concerned.

(3)   A notice of resignation takes effect—
        (a) on the date on which the notice is received by the Chief Executive; or
        (b) if a later date is specified in the notice, on that later date.

5.   Removal from office

(1)   The Chief Executive may remove a member from office if the member—
        (a) fails to attend 3 consecutive meetings of the Commission without (in the opinion of the Chief Executive) sufficient cause;
        (b) fails to comply with a conflict of interest disclosure obligation set out in any rules made by the Commission under section 34 of this Schedule;
        (c) becomes bankrupt or is for the time being bound by a voluntary arrangement with his or her creditors;
        (d) is, under the Mental Health Ordinance (Cap 136), found by the Court of First Instance (or any judge of the Court of First Instance) to be incapable, by reason of mental incapacity, of managing and administering his or her property and affairs;
        (e) has been found by the Tribunal or another court to have contravened a competition rule;
        (f) is an officer of an undertaking that has been found by the Tribunal or another court to have contravened a competition rule;

(g) has made a commitment with the Commission under this Ordinance, or is an officer of an undertaking that has made such a commitment;

(h) becomes a member of the Tribunal or a judge of another court;

(i) is appointed by the Tribunal as an assessor under section 141; or

(j) is otherwise, in the opinion of the Chief Executive, unable or unfit to perform the functions of a member.

(2) If a member is removed from office under this section, the Chief Executive must give that member notice in writing informing the member of his or her removal from office.

(3) In this section—

"officer" means—

(a) in relation to a corporation, a director, manager or company secretary of the corporation, and any other person involved in the management of the corporation; and

(b) in relation to an undertaking (other than a corporation or partnership), any member of the governing body of that undertaking.

6.   Vacancy in office

The office of a member becomes vacant if the member—

(a) dies;

(b) completes a term of office and is not reappointed;

(c) resigns from office by written notice of resignation given to the Chief Executive; or

(d) is removed from office by the Chief Executive under section 5 of this Schedule.

7.   Filling of vacancy

(1) If the office of a member becomes vacant, the Chief Executive may appoint a suitable person to fill the vacancy.

(2) A person appointed to fill a vacancy under this section holds office for the term that is specified in the member's letter of appointment and that term may extend beyond the remainder of the term of the member whose office became vacant.

8.   Chairperson

(1) The Chief Executive is to appoint one of the members of the Commission (other than a member who is a public officer) to be the Chairperson of the Commission.

(2) The Chairperson may, at any time, resign from that office by giving written notice of resignation to the Chief Executive.

(3) A notice of resignation is not effective unless it is signed by the Chairperson.

(4) A notice of resignation takes effect—

(a) on the date on which the notice is received by the Chief Executive; or

(b) if a later date is specified in the notice, on that later date.

(5) The resignation of a person from the office of Chairperson does not affect that person's term of office as a member.

(6) If the Chairperson ceases to be a member, he or she also ceases to be the Chairperson.

9.   Acting chairperson

If the Chairperson is temporarily unable to perform the functions of the office of Chairperson because of illness or absence from Hong Kong or for any other cause or if the office of Chairperson becomes vacant, the Chief Executive may appoint another member to act in place of the Chairperson and perform the functions of the office of Chairperson.

Part 3

Chief Executive Officer, Staff, etc

10.   Chief Executive Officer

(1)   The Commission is, with the approval of the Chief Executive, to appoint a Chief Executive Officer of the Commission on such terms as, subject to subsection (3), the Commission may determine.

(2)   The Chief Executive Officer is responsible for—

(a) managing the administrative affairs of the Commission; and

(b) performing any other functions that may be assigned or delegated to the Chief Executive Officer by the Commission.

(3)   The Chief Executive Officer is to be paid out of the funds of the Commission such remuneration, benefits and expenses as the Commission, with the approval of the Chief Executive, may determine.

11.   Power to employ staff, etc.

(1)   The Commission may employ such staff and engage on contract for services such other persons as it considers necessary to perform its functions.

(2)   The Commission may determine the remuneration and other conditions of employment of its staff and persons engaged on contracts for services.

(3)   The Commission may provide and maintain schemes (whether contributory or not) for the payment of retirement benefits, gratuities or other allowances to its employees or former employees and their dependants.

Part 4

Meetings

12.   General procedure for meetings of Commission

(1)   Meetings of the Commission are to be held as often as necessary to enable the Commission to perform its functions.

(2)   A meeting of the Commission may be convened by the Chairperson.

(3)   The Chairperson must convene a meeting of the Commission on being given a notice for that purpose by 2 or more other members.

(4)   The procedure for convening meetings of the Commission and for the conduct of business at those meetings is, subject to this Schedule and to any rules made under section 34 of this Schedule, to be determined by the Commission.

13. Quorum for meetings of Commission

(1) The quorum for a meeting of the Commission is a majority of its members.

(2) A member who participates in the meeting by telephone, video conferencing or other electronic means is to be regarded as being present at the meeting if—

(a) that member is able to hear the other members who are actually present at the meeting; and

(b) the members who are actually present at the meeting are able to hear that member.

14. Presiding member at meetings of Commission

A meeting of the Commission is to be presided over by—

(a) the Chairperson; or

(b) in the absence of the Chairperson, the acting chairperson.

15. Voting at meetings of Commission

(1) Subject to subsection (2), each member who is present at a meeting of the Commission has one vote at the meeting.

(2) The member presiding at a meeting of the Commission has a deliberative vote and also has a casting vote if the number of votes for and against a motion is equal.

(3) Voting must not be carried out by secret ballot. The member presiding at a meeting of the Commission must ask each member to indicate how he or she has voted, and the result of the vote, showing which way each member has voted, must be recorded in the minutes.

(4) A decision supported by a majority of the votes cast at the meeting of the Commission at which a quorum is present is the decision of the Commission.

16. Minutes

The Commission must cause minutes of the proceedings, including a record of all decisions made, at each meeting of the Commission to be recorded and preserved.

17. Written resolutions

(1) A resolution is a valid resolution of the Commission, even if it is not passed at a meeting of the Commission, if—

(a) it is in writing;

(b) proper notice of it is given to all members; and

(c) it is signed, or assented to, by a majority of the members by letter, fax or other electronic transmission.

(2) Subject to subsection (3), the date of a resolution referred to in this section is the date on which the last of the members constituting a majority of the members signs or assents to the resolution.

(3) If any member requests, by notice in writing addressed to the Chairperson, that a resolution proposed to be made under subsection (1) be referred to a meeting of the Commission for consideration, the proposed resolution must be referred to a meeting of the Commission.

(4) A request under subsection (3) must be made within 14 days after the day on which the notice referred to in subsection (1)(b) is given.

18. Decisions not invalidated by defects in appointment etc.

Decisions of the Commission are not invalidated solely by—

(a) any defect in the appointment of a member;

(b) a vacancy amongst its members;

(c) the absence of a member from the meeting at which the decision was taken; or

(d) any irregularity in the procedures adopted by the Commission that does not affect the decision taken.

Part 5

Financial Provisions

19. Commission to submit estimates

The Commission must, not later than 31 December in each financial year, submit to the Chief Executive estimates of its income and expenditure for the next financial year.

20. Financial year

The financial year of the Commission is—

(a) the period beginning on the day on which this Schedule comes into operation and ending on the next 31 March; and

(b) the period of 12 months ending on 31 March in each subsequent year.

21. Funds of Commission

The funds of the Commission consist of—

(a) all money paid by the Government to the Commission and appropriated for that purpose by the Legislative Council; and (Amended 18 of 2014 s. 174)

(b) all other money and property, including fees, interest and accumulations of income, received by the Commission.

22. Commission is exempt from taxation

(1) The Commission is exempt from taxation under the Inland Revenue Ordinance (Cap 112).

(2) To avoid doubt, subsection (1) does not apply to or in relation to any remuneration, benefits or expenses paid out of the funds of the Commission to a member of the Commission.

Part 6

Accounts, Audit and Account Report

23. Accounts

(1) The Commission must—

(a) keep accounts and other records that accurately record and explain its financial transactions and its financial position; and

(b) ensure that a statement of accounts is prepared as soon as practicable after the end of each financial year.

(2)   The statement of accounts must give a true and fair view of—

(a) the state of affairs of the Commission as at the end of that financial year; and

(b) the results of the operations and cash flows of the Commission in that financial year.

24.   Commission to appoint auditor

(1)   As soon as practicable after the commencement of this section, the Commission must appoint an auditor to audit its statement of accounts.

(2)   The auditor must, as soon as practicable after the end of each financial year—

(a) audit the accounts and statement of accounts required under section 23 of this Schedule; and

(b) submit a report on the statement of accounts to the Commission.

25.   Annual report

(1)   As soon as practicable, and in any case within 6 months after the end of each financial year, the Commission must prepare a report dealing with its activities in the preceding financial year.

(2)   The report must contain the following information in relation to the financial year—

(a) an outline of the investigations carried out by the Commission;

(b) a summary of complaints received; and

(c) an outline of all proceedings brought before the Tribunal.

26.   Annual report and audited accounts to be laid on table of Legislative Council

As soon as practicable, and in any case within 6 months after the end of a financial year, the Commission must give a copy of—

(a) its annual report, prepared under section 25 of this Schedule;

(b) its statement of accounts; and

(c) the auditor's report on the statement of accounts,

to the Chief Executive who must arrange for them to be laid on the table of the Legislative Council.

27.   Director of Audit's examination

(1)   The Director of Audit may, in respect of any financial year of the Commission, conduct an examination into the economy, efficiency and effectiveness with which the Commission has used its resources in performing its functions.

(2)   For the purpose of conducting an examination under this section, the Director of Audit is entitled, at all reasonable times—

(a) to have full and free access to all accounts, records and documents in the custody or under the control of the Commission;

(b) to make a copy of the whole or any part of those accounts, records and documents; and

             (c) to require any person who holds or is accountable for the accounts, records or documents to give any information or explanation that the Director of Audit considers necessary.

(3)   The Director of Audit may report to the President of the Legislative Council the results of an examination conducted under this section.

(4)   Subsection (1) does not operate to entitle the Director of Audit to question the merits of the policy objectives of the Commission.

Part 8

Register and Disclosure of Interests

29.   Register of interest

(1)   A member of the Commission, or a member of a committee established by the Commission, must disclose to the Commission any interest that the member has which is of a class or description determined by the Commission under subsection (2)—

        (a) in the case of a member of the Commission, on the member's first appointment to the Commission;

        (b) in the case of a member of the committee who is not also a member of the Commission, on the member's first appointment to the committee;

        (c) at the beginning of each calendar year after the member's appointment;

        (d) on becoming aware of the existence of an interest not previously disclosed under this subsection; and

        (e) after the occurrence of any change to an interest previously disclosed under this subsection.

(2)   The Commission may, for the purposes of this section—

        (a) determine the class or description of the interest required to be disclosed;

        (b) determine the details of the interest required to be disclosed and the manner in which such interest is to be disclosed; and

        (c) from time to time change any matter determined under paragraph (a) or (b).

(3)   The Commission is to establish and maintain a register relating to any disclosure required to be made under subsection (1) (the "register").

(4)   If a person makes a disclosure as required by subsection (1), the Commission must cause the person's name and the particulars of the disclosure to be recorded in the register, and if a further disclosure is made, the Commission must cause the particulars of the further disclosure to be recorded in the register.

(5)   The Commission must make the register available for inspection by any person—

        (a) at the offices of the Commission during ordinary business hours;

        (b) through the Internet or a similar electronic network; and

        (c) in any other manner the Commission considers appropriate.

30.   Disclosure of interests

(1)   If a member of the Commission has—

        (a) a pecuniary interest, whether direct or indirect; or

(b) a personal interest greater than that which the member has as a member of the general public,

in any matter under discussion at a meeting of the Commission, the member must disclose the nature of the interest at the meeting.

(2) The following provisions apply for the purposes of a disclosure under subsection (1)—

(a) the disclosure must be recorded in the minutes;

(b) if the disclosure is made by the member presiding, the member must vacate the chair during the discussion;

(c) the member (including one who has vacated the chair under paragraph (b)) must, if so required by the majority of the other members present, withdraw from the meeting during the discussion and must not in any case, except as otherwise determined by the majority of the other members present, vote on any resolution concerning the matter under the discussion or be counted for the purpose of establishing the existence of a quorum.

(3) When a matter is being dealt with by way of the circulation of written resolutions under section 17 of this Schedule, and a member of the Commission has—

(a) a pecuniary interest in the matter, whether direct or indirect; or

(b) a personal interest in the matter greater than that which the member has as a member of the general public,

the member must disclose the nature of the interest by attaching to the resolutions being circulated a note recording the disclosure.

(4) If a member has made a disclosure under subsection (3), the member's signature (if any) is not to be counted for the purpose of section 17(1) of this Schedule unless the Chairperson directs otherwise.

(5) If the member making a disclosure in respect of a matter under subsection (3) is the Chairperson, section 17 of this Schedule ceases to apply to the matter.

(6) The validity of any proceeding of the Commission is not affected by the failure by a member of the Commission to comply with this section.

(7) Subsections (1), (2) and (6) apply to a member of a committee established by the Commission, as if any reference to the Commission in subsections (1) and (6) were a reference to the committee.

Part 9

Delegation

31. Delegation by Commission

(1) Subject to subsection (2), the Commission may delegate any of the functions of the Commission to—

(a) a person who is a member of the Commission;

(b) a committee established by the Commission;

(c) the Chief Executive Officer;

(d) an employee of the Commission by name; or

(e) the holder of any office in the Commission, designated by the Commission.

(2) Despite subsection (1), the Commission may not delegate any of the following functions—

    (a) subject to sections 32 and 33 of this Schedule, its power to delegate the Commission's functions under subsection (1);

    (b) the power to issue a block exemption order under section 15;

    (c) the power to vary or revoke a block exemption order under section 20;

    (d) the power to issue an infringement notice under section 67;

    (e) the power to appoint the Chief Executive Officer and to determine that officer's terms of employment, under section 10 of this Schedule;

    (f) the duty to give a copy of its annual report, its statement of accounts, and the auditor's report on the statement of accounts, to the Chief Executive under section 26 of this Schedule;

    (g) the power to establish any committee under section 28 of this Schedule;

    (h) the power to refer any matter to a committee;

    (i) the power to appoint any person to be the chairperson or a member of a committee (or to revoke any such appointment) under section 28 of this Schedule;

    (j) the power to amend the terms of reference of a committee under section 28 of this Schedule;

    (k) the power to discharge or reconstitute a committee under section 28 of this Schedule;

    (l) the duty to submit the Commission's estimates of income and expenditure to the Chief Executive under section 19 of this Schedule;

    (m) the duty to ensure that an annual statement of accounts is prepared, under section 23 of this Schedule;

    (n) the duty to prepare and issue guidelines under this Ordinance;

    (o) the power to make any application to the Tribunal, under this Ordinance other than an application for an interim order under section 95 or 98;

    (p) the power to appeal to the courts;

    (q) the power to borrow money under section 131 with the approval of the Financial Secretary;

    (r) the power to invest funds of the Commission, in a manner approved by the Financial Secretary, under section 131; or

    (s) the power to authorize a person to authenticate the application of the seal of the Commission under section 35 of this Schedule.

(3) A person purporting to act under an authorization granted under subsection (1) is to be regarded, unless the contrary is proved, to have been lawfully authorized under this section.

32. Subdelegation

(1) When the Commission delegates a function under section 31 of this Schedule, it may, subject to any condition it considers appropriate, authorize the delegate to subdelegate the performance of that function, in whole or in part, to any person.

(2) A person purporting to act under an authorization granted under subsection (1) is to be regarded, unless the contrary is proved, to have been lawfully authorized under this section.

33.   Delegation of power to obtain documents and information

Despite section 31 (Delegation by Commission) of this Schedule and section 32 (Subdelegation) of this Schedule, the Commission may delegate its power under section 41 (Powers to obtain documents and information) only to a member of the Commission, and that member may not subdelegate that power.

Part 10

Miscellaneous

34.   Rules

The Commission may make rules—

(a) regulating the procedure to be followed at meetings of the Commission and at meetings of its committees;

(b) regulating the administration of the Commission; and

(c) regarding conflict of interest.

35.   Seal of Commission

(1)   The Commission must provide itself with a seal.

(2)   The application of the seal must be authenticated by the Chairperson, or by some other member of the Commission authorized by the Commission for this purpose.

(3)   Judicial notice is to be taken of the seal of the Commission and any document sealed with the seal is—

(a) admissible in evidence; and

(b) presumed to have been properly sealed unless the contrary is proved.

Schedule 6

MATTERS THAT MUST BE PROVIDED FOR IN
MEMORANDUM OF UNDERSTANDING

[Section 161]

1.   The manner in which the parties to a Memorandum of Understanding will perform the functions that they have jurisdiction to perform concurrently under this Ordinance.

2.   The manner in which the parties will resolve any dispute between themselves.

3.   The provision of assistance by one party to another.

4.   The allocation between the parties of responsibility for particular matters or classes of matters.

5.   Arrangements for the supply of information relating to a competition matter by one party to another.

6.   Arrangements for the keeping of the other party informed about progress when one party is performing functions that may be performed concurrently under this Ordinance.

7. The joint authorship of educational material or guidelines on competition matters.

Schedule 7

MERGERS

[Sections 2, 3, 83 & 162]

Part 1

Preliminary

1. **Interpretation**
    In this Schedule—
    "carrier licence" means a carrier licence within the meaning of the Telecommunications Ordinance (Cap 106).

2. **Territorial application**
    This Schedule applies to a merger even if—
    (a) the arrangements for the creation of the merger take place outside Hong Kong;
    (b) the merger takes place outside Hong Kong; or
    (c) any party to the arrangements for the creation of the merger, or any party involved in the merger is outside Hong Kong.

Part 2

The Merger Rule

3. **Mergers substantially lessening competition prohibited**
(1) An undertaking must not, directly or indirectly, carry out a merger that has, or is likely to have, the effect of substantially lessening competition in Hong Kong.
(2) For the purpose of this section, a merger takes place if—
    (a) 2 or more undertakings previously independent of each other cease to be independent of each other;
    (b) one or more persons or other undertakings acquire direct or indirect control of the whole or part of one or more other undertakings; or
    (c) an acquisition by one undertaking (the "acquiring undertaking") of the whole or part of the assets (including goodwill) of another undertaking (the "acquired undertaking") has the result set out in subsection (3).
(3) The result referred to in subsection (2)(c) is that the acquiring undertaking is in a position to replace the acquired undertaking, or to substantially replace the acquired undertaking, in the business or in part of the business concerned (as the case requires) in which the acquired undertaking was engaged immediately before the acquisition.

(4) The creation of a joint venture to perform, on a lasting basis, all the functions of an autonomous economic entity also constitutes a merger within the meaning of subsection (2)(b).

(5) The prohibition imposed by subsection (1) is referred to in this Ordinance as the "merger rule".

4. Application of merger rule
The merger rule applies only in the following cases—
(a) in the case referred to in section 3(2)(a) of this Schedule, one or more of the undertakings participating in the merger holds a carrier licence or, directly or indirectly, controls an undertaking that holds a carrier licence;
(b) in the case referred to in section 3(2)(b) of this Schedule, the undertaking or the person or persons acquiring control or the undertaking in which control is acquired holds a carrier licence or, directly or indirectly, controls an undertaking that holds a carrier licence; and
(c) in the case referred to in section 3(2)(c) of this Schedule—
(i) the acquiring undertaking or the acquired undertaking holds a carrier licence or, directly or indirectly, controls an undertaking that holds a carrier licence; and
(ii) the relevant business conducted by the acquired undertaking immediately before the acquisition was conducted under a carrier licence.

5. Control
(1) For the purposes of this Schedule, control, in relation to an undertaking, is to be regarded as existing if, by reason of rights, contracts or any other means, or any combination of rights, contracts or other means, decisive influence is capable of being exercised with regard to the activities of the undertaking and, in particular, by—
(a) ownership of, or the right to use all or part of, the assets of an undertaking; or
(b) rights or contracts which enable decisive influence to be exercised with regard to the composition, voting or decisions of any governing body of an undertaking.

(2) For the purposes of this Schedule, control is acquired by any person or other undertaking if the person or undertaking—
(a) becomes a holder of the rights or contracts, or entitled to use the other means, referred to in subsection (1); or
(b) although not becoming such a holder or entitled to use those other means, acquires the power to exercise the rights derived from them.

(3) In determining whether influence of the kind referred to in subsection (1) is capable of being exercised, regard must be had to all the circumstances of the matter and not solely to the legal effect of any instrument, deed, transfer, assignment or other act done or made.

6. Matters that may be considered in determining whether competition substantially lessened
Without limiting the matters that may be taken into account in determining whether a merger has, or is likely to have, the effect of substantially lessening

competition in Hong Kong, the following matters may be taken into consideration in any such determination—

(a) the extent of competition from competitors outside Hong Kong;

(b) whether the acquired undertaking, or part of the acquired undertaking, has failed or is likely to fail in the near future;

(c) the extent to which substitutes are available or are likely to be available in the market;

(d) the existence and height of any barriers to entry into the market;

(e) whether the merger would result in the removal of an effective and vigorous competitor;

(f) the degree of countervailing power in the market; and

(g) the nature and extent of change and innovation in the market.

Part 3

Investigations

7.   Time limit for commencement of investigation of merger

(1)   Despite section 39 (Power to conduct investigations), the Commission may only commence an investigation of a merger within 30 days after the day on which the Commission first became aware, or ought to have become aware, that the merger has taken place.

(2)   The Commission is to be taken to have become aware that a merger has taken place if it has been notified, in accordance with guidelines issued under this Schedule, of that fact by one of the parties to the merger.

(3)   If the Commission—

(a) has made a decision under section 13 of this Schedule that a merger or proposed merger is or would be excluded from the application of the merger rule or this Schedule; and

(b) has rescinded that decision, the date on which the Commission became aware that the merger has taken place is to be taken to be the date of the rescission of its decision.

Part 4

Exclusions and Exemptions

Division 1

Exclusions from Merger Rule

8.   Exclusions

(1)   The merger rule does not apply to a merger if the economic efficiencies that arise or may arise from the merger outweigh the adverse effects caused by any lessening of competition in Hong Kong.

(2)   In any proceedings in which it is alleged that the merger rule has been contravened by a merger, any undertaking claiming the benefit of subsection (1) has the burden of proving that the conditions of that subsection are satisfied.

Division 2

Exemption from Merger Rule

9.   Exemption of merger on public policy grounds
(1)   The Chief Executive in Council may, by order published in the Gazette, exempt a specified merger or proposed merger from the application of the merger rule if he or she is satisfied that there are exceptional and compelling reasons of public policy for doing so.
(2)   An order under subsection (1) may be made subject to any conditions or limitations that the Chief Executive in Council considers appropriate.

10.   Orders to be published and placed before Legislative Council
(1)   The Chief Executive is to arrange for every order made under section 9 of this Schedule to be—
        (a) published in the Gazette; and
        (b) laid on the table of the Legislative Council at the next sitting of the Council after its publication in the Gazette.
(2)   The Legislative Council may, by resolution passed at a sitting of the Legislative Council held not later than 28 days after the sitting at which an order is laid on the table of the Council (the "relevant period"), amend the order in any manner consistent with the power of the Chief Executive in Council to make the order in question.
(3)   If the relevant period would but for this section expire after the end of a session or a dissolution of the Legislative Council, but on or before the day of its second sitting in the next session, the period for amending the order is deemed to be extended and to expire on the day after that second sitting.
(4)   The Legislative Council may, before the expiry of the relevant period, by resolution extend the period for amending the order to the first sitting of the Council held not earlier than the twenty-first day after the day of that expiry.
(5)   If the relevant period is extended under subsection (3), the Legislative Council may, before the expiry of the extended period, by resolution extend that extended period to the first sitting of the Council held not earlier than the twenty-first day after the day of the second sitting in the next session referred to in that subsection.
(6)   A resolution passed by the Legislative Council in accordance with this section must be published in the Gazette not later than 14 days after the passing of the resolution or within such further period as the Chief Executive may allow in any particular case.
(7)   An order made by the Chief Executive in Council under section 9 of this Schedule comes into operation—
        (a) if on the expiry of the relevant period or that period as extended under subsection (3), (4) or (5), the Legislative Council has not passed a

resolution amending the order, on the expiry of the relevant period or that period as so extended (as the case may be); and

(b) if the Legislative Council passes a resolution amending the order, at the beginning of the day on which the resolution is published in the Gazette.

(8) If an order is not laid on the table of the Legislative Council in accordance with this section, it is of no effect.

(9) In this section—

"sitting", when used to calculate time, means the day on which the sitting commences and only includes a sitting at which subsidiary legislation is included on the order paper.

Part 5

Decisions

11. Application for decision

(1) If an undertaking—

(a) has carried out a merger; or

(b) is carrying out, or is proposing to carry out a merger,

it may apply to the Commission for a decision under subsection (2).

(2) The decision referred to in subsection (1) is a decision as to whether or not the merger is, or the proposed merger would if completed be—

(a) excluded from the application of the merger rule by or as a result of section 8 (Exclusions) of this Schedule; or

(b) excluded from the application of this Schedule by virtue of—

(i) section 3 (Application to statutory bodies); or

(ii) section 4 (Application to specified persons and persons engaged in specified activities).

(3) The Commission is only required to consider an application under this section if—

(a) the application poses novel or unresolved questions of wider importance or public interest in relation to the application of exclusions under this Ordinance;

(b) the application raises a question of an exclusion under this Ordinance for which there is no clarification in existing case law or decisions of the Commission; and

(c) it is possible to make a decision on the basis of the information provided.

(4) The Commission is not required to consider an application for a decision if the application concerns hypothetical questions or conduct.

12. Consideration of application

(1) Before making a decision on an application made under section 11 of this Schedule, the Commission must—

(a) in order to bring the application to the attention of those the Commission considers likely to be affected by the decision, publish notice of the application—

(i) through the Internet or a similar electronic network; and

(ii) in any other manner the Commission considers appropriate; and

(b) consider any representations about the application that are made to the Commission.

(2) A notice under subsection (1) must specify the period within which representations may be made to the Commission about the application.

(3) The period specified for the purpose of subsection (2) must be a period of at least 30 days beginning after the day on which the notice is first published.

13. Decision by Commission

(1) After considering the representations, if any, made within the period referred to in section 12 of this Schedule, the Commission may make a decision as to whether or not the merger is, or the proposed merger would if completed be, excluded from the application of the merger rule or this Schedule.

(2) A decision by the Commission may include conditions or limitations subject to which it is to have effect including, in the case of a proposed merger, specifying a date by which the proposed merger must be completed.

(3) After the Commission has made its decision, it must inform the applicant in writing of the decision, the date of the decision and the reasons for it.

14. Effect of decision

If the Commission makes a decision that—

(a) a merger is excluded from the application of the merger rule or this Schedule; or

(b) a proposed merger would if completed be excluded from the application of the merger rule or this Schedule,

then the Commission may not take any action under this Ordinance with respect to the merger or proposed merger unless it rescinds its decision under section 15 of this Schedule or the merger as implemented is materially different from the proposed merger to which the decision relates.

15. Rescission of decision

(1) The Commission may rescind a decision made under section 13 of this Schedule if it has reason to believe—

(a) if the merger has not been carried into effect, that there has been a material change of circumstances since the decision was made; or

(b) whether or not the merger has been carried into effect—

(i) that the information provided by a person involved in the merger, on which it based its decision was incomplete, false or misleading in a material particular; or

(ii) that an undertaking has failed to observe any condition or limitation subject to which the decision has effect.

(2) Before rescinding a decision under this section, the Commission must—

(a) in order to bring the proposed rescission to the attention of those persons the Commission considers likely to be affected by it, publish notice of the proposed rescission—

(i) stating that the Commission is considering rescinding the decision and the reasons why it is considering the rescission; and

(ii) inviting the persons to make representations about the proposed rescission within the period specified in the notice; and

(b) consider any representations received within the period specified in the notice.

(3) The notice referred to in subsection (2) must be published—

(a) through the Internet or a similar electronic network; and

(b) in any other manner the Commission considers appropriate.

(4) The period specified in a notice under subsection (2) must be a period of at least 30 days beginning after the day on which the notice is given.

(5) If, after—

(a) the expiry of the period specified in the notice given under subsection (2); and

(b) considering any representations received within that period,

the Commission is of the view that the decision should be rescinded, it may, by notice in writing given to each undertaking specified in the decision, rescind that decision.

(6) A notice of rescission given under subsection (5) must inform the undertakings of—

(a) the rescission and the reasons for the rescission;

(b) the date on which the determination to rescind the decision was made; and

(c) the date from which the rescission takes effect.

(7) If a decision is rescinded under this section, each undertaking specified in the notice of rescission loses its immunity from action under this Ordinance, as from the date the rescission takes effect, with regard to anything done after that date.

16.   Register of merger decisions

(1) The Commission must establish and maintain a register of—

(a) all decisions made in respect of applications made under section 11 of this Schedule; and

(b) all notices of rescissions of such decisions, made under section 15 of this Schedule.

(2) The Commission may omit confidential information from any entry made in the register under this section; and where confidential information has been omitted, that fact must be disclosed on the register.

(3) The Commission must make the register available for inspection by any person—

(a) at the offices of the Commission during ordinary business hours;

(b) through the Internet or a similar electronic network; and

(c) in any other manner the Commission considers appropriate.

Part 6

Guidelines

17.   Guidelines

(1)   The Commission must issue guidelines indicating the manner in which it expects to interpret and give effect to the provisions of this Schedule including, in particular—

(a) the manner in which it will determine whether or not a merger has, or would be likely to have, the effect of substantially lessening competition in Hong Kong;

(b) the manner in which it will determine whether or not a merger would fall within the exclusion referred to in section 8(1) of this Schedule; and

(c) the manner and form in which it should be notified of any merger.

(2)   The Commission may amend any guidelines it issues under this section.

(3)   Guidelines issued under this section, and any amendments made to them, may be published in any manner the Commission considers appropriate.

(4)   Before issuing any guidelines or amendments to them under this section, the Commission must consult the Legislative Council and any persons it considers appropriate.

(5)   The Commission must make available copies of all guidelines issued under this section and of all amendments made to them—

(a) at the offices of the Commission during ordinary business hours;

(b) through the Internet or a similar electronic network; and

(c) in any other manner the Commission considers appropriate.

(6)   A person does not incur any civil or criminal liability only because the person has contravened any guidelines issued under this section or any amendments made to them.

(7)   If, in any legal proceedings, the Tribunal or any other court is satisfied that a guideline is relevant to determining a matter that is in issue—

(a) the guideline is admissible in evidence in the proceedings; and

(b) proof that a person contravened or did not contravene the guideline may be relied on by any party to the proceedings as tending to establish or negate the matter.

(8)   Guidelines issued under this section and all amendments made to them are not subsidiary legislation.

Schedule 8

CONSEQUENTIAL AND RELATED AMNDMENTS

[Section 176]

(Sections 1-12 omitted)

13. Section 7Q added [to the Telecommunications Ordinance (Cap 106)]

"7Q. Exploitative conduct

(1)   A licensee in a dominant position in a telecommunications market must not engage in conduct that in the opinion of the Authority is exploitative.

(2)   A licensee is in a dominant position if, in the opinion of the Authority, it is able to act without significant competitive restraint from its competitors and customers.

(3)   In considering whether a licensee is dominant, the Authority must take into account relevant matters including, but not limited to—

(a) the market share of the licensee;

(b) the licensee's power to make pricing and other decisions;

(c) any barriers to entry to competitors into the relevant telecommunications market;

(d) the degree of product differentiation and sales promotion;

(e) any other relevant matters specified in guidelines issued under section 6D for the purposes of this section.

(4)   Without limiting subsection (1), the Authority may consider the following conduct to be exploitative—

(a) fixing and maintaining prices or charges at an excessively high level; and

(b) setting unfair trading terms and conditions,

for or in relation to the provision of interconnection of the type referred to in section 36A(3D)."

(Sections 14-37 omitted.)

Schedule 9

TRANSITIONAL AND SAVINGS PROVISIONS

(Sections 1-4 omitted.)

INDEX